*Praise for Ian Urbina's*
# THE OUTLAW OCEAN

"These chapters are vibrant as individual stories, but as a collection they're transcendent, rendering a complex portrait of an unseen and disturbing world. Urbina pursues a depth of reportage that's rare because of the guts and diligence it requires. . . . The result is not just a fascinating read, but a truly important document."
—Blair Braverman, *The New York Times Book Review*

"[A] tour de force of intrepid global inquiry. . . . His biggest fear is that his risky quest may do harm to people rather than good, but there is no doubt that the bravely gleaned and galvanizing facts about maritime savagery and brewing catastrophes, which he so vividly and cogently presents, coalesce into an exposé of immense magnitude and consequence."                        —*Booklist* (starred review)

"The most valuable contribution of *The Outlaw Ocean* may be to the literature, unfortunately quite extensive by now, of pessimism about human nature. . . . In aggregate his stories reveal that something like a Hobbesian state of nature still exists and is available to anyone willing to float a few dozen miles offshore."        —*The Wall Street Journal*

"What we learn from Urbina's journeys is nothing less than the deepest aspects of humanity itself. Dropped into a world without terra firma's systems and foibles, our darkest impulses emerge. But our most noble intentions—to save, to protect, to establish fair rule of law—appear as well."                                    —*Paste*

"In *The Outlaw Ocean*, Urbina focuses that eye on understanding his characters and their context to show why these crimes get committed and why the culprits rarely get prosecuted. Urbina goes further than most to do this. He shows you a problem from the front lines, by talking to the people there."                        —*VICE*

## IAN URBINA
# THE OUTLAW OCEAN

Ian Urbina is an investigative reporter who writes regularly for *The New York Times*, *The Atlantic*, *National Geographic*, and other venues. He has won a Pulitzer Prize for Breaking News and a George Polk Award for Foreign Reporting. Several of his stories have been developed into major feature films and one was nominated for an Emmy Award. He has degrees in history and cultural anthropology from Georgetown University and the University of Chicago. Before being on staff at the *Times* for nearly two decades, he wrote about the Middle East and Africa for various outlets, including the *Los Angeles Times*, *Vanity Fair*, and *Harper's Magazine*. He lives in Washington D.C., with his family.

www.theoutlawocean.com

# THE OUTLAW OCEAN

Journeys Across the Last Untamed Frontier

## IAN URBINA

VINTAGE BOOKS
*A Division of Penguin Random House LLC*
*New York*

FIRST VINTAGE BOOKS EDITION, SEPTEMBER 2020

Portions of this work were originally published in *The New York Times* on July 25, 2015.

The Library of Congress has cataloged the Knopf edition as follows:
Name: Urbina, Ian, author.
Title: The outlaw ocean : journeys across the last untamed frontier / Ian Urbina.
Description: First edition. | New York : Alfred A. Knopf, 2019.
Identifiers: LCCN 2019001735
Subjects: LCSH: Fisheries—Corrupt practices. | Law of the sea. | Oceania. | Ocean. |
Urbina, Ian—Travel. | BISAC: TRAVEL / Special Interest / Adventure. | TRAVEL /
Asia / General. | TRUE CRIME / General.
Classification: LCC SH319.A2 U73 2019 | DDC 639.2—dc23
LC record available at https://lccn.loc.gov/2019001735

Vintage Books Trade Paperback ISBN: 978-1-101-97237-3
eBook ISBN: 978-0-451-49295-1

*Author photograph © Jabin Botsford*
*Book design by Betty Lew*

www.vintagebooks.com

Printed in the United States of America
10  9  8  7  6  5  4  3  2  1

## TO AIDAN

For all its mayhem and exhaustion,
there has been no greater adventure and no
prouder project than being a part of your pit crew

# CONTENTS

# INTRODUCTION

About a hundred miles off the coast of Thailand, three dozen Cambodian boys and men worked barefoot all day and into the night on the deck of a purse seiner fishing ship. Fifteen-foot swells climbed the sides of the ship, clipping the crew below the knees. Ocean spray and fish innards made the floor skating-rink slippery. Seesawing erratically from the rough seas and gale winds, the deck was an obstacle course of jagged tackle, spinning winches, and tall stacks of five-hundred-pound nets.

Rain or shine, shifts ran eighteen to twenty hours. At night, the crew cast their nets when the small silver fish they target—mostly jack mackerel and herring—were more reflective and easier to spot in darker waters. During the day, when the sun was high, temperatures topped a hundred degrees Fahrenheit, but they worked nonstop. Drinking water was tightly rationed. Most countertops were crawling with roaches. The toilet was a removable wooden floorboard on deck. At night, vermin cleaned the boys' unwashed plates. The ship's mangy dog barely lifted her head when the rats, which roamed on board like carefree city squirrels, ate from her bowl.

If they were not fishing, the crew sorted their catch and fixed their nets, which were prone to ripping. One boy, his shirt smudged with fish guts, proudly showed off his two missing fingers, severed by a net that had coiled around a spinning crank. Their hands, which virtually never fully dried, had open wounds, slit from fish scales and torn from the nets' friction. The boys stitched closed the deeper cuts themselves. Infections were constant. Captains never lacked for amphetamines to help the crews work longer, but they rarely stocked antibiotics for infected wounds.

On boats like these, deckhands were often beaten for small transgressions, like fixing a torn net too slowly or mistakenly placing a mackerel into a bucket for sablefish or herring. Disobedience on these ships was less a misdemeanor than a capital offense. In 2009, the UN conducted a survey of about fifty Cambodian men and boys sold to Thai fishing boats. Of those interviewed by UN personnel, twenty-nine said they witnessed their captain or other officers kill a worker.

The boys and men who typically worked on these ships were invisible to the authorities because most were undocumented immigrants. Dispatched into the unknown, they were beyond where society could help them, usually on so-called ghost ships—unregistered vessels that the Thai government had no ability to track. They usually did not speak the language of their Thai captains, did not know how to swim, and, being from inland villages, had never seen the sea before this encounter with it.

Virtually all of the crew had a debt to clear, part of their indentured servitude, a "travel now, pay later" labor system that requires working to pay off money they often had to borrow to sneak illegally into a new country. One of the Cambodian boys approached me, and deeper into our conversation he tried to explain in broken English how elusive this debt became once they left land. Pointing to his own shadow and moving around as if he were trying to grab it, he said, "Can't catch."

This was a brutal place, one that I spent five weeks in the winter of 2014 trying to visit. Fishing boats on the South China Sea, especially in the Thai fleet, had for years been notorious for using so-called sea slaves, mostly migrants forced offshore by debt or duress. The worst among these ships were the long haulers, many of which fished hundreds of miles from shore, staying at sea sometimes for over a year as mother ships provided supplies and shuttled their catch back to shore. No captain had been willing to carry me and a photographer the full distance, more than a hundred miles, out to these long-haul boats. So, we instead hopscotched from boat to boat—forty miles on one, forty on the next, and so on—to get out far enough.

As I watched the Cambodians, who, like some water-bound chain gang, chanted to ensure synchronicity in pulling their nets, I was reminded of an incongruity that confronted me time and again over several years of reporting offshore. For all its breathtaking beauty, the ocean is also a dystopian place, home to dark inhumanities. The rule of law—often so solid on land, bolstered and clarified by centuries of careful wordsmithing, hard-fought jurisdictional lines, and robust enforcement regimes—is fluid at sea, if it's to be found at all.

There were other contradictions. At a time when we know exponentially more about the world around us, with so much at our fingertips and but a swipe or a tap away, we know shockingly little about the sea. Fully half of the world's peoples now live within a hundred miles of the ocean, and merchant ships haul about 90 percent of the world's goods. Over 56 million people globally work at sea on fishing boats and another 1.6 million on freighters, tankers, and other types of merchant vessels. And yet journalism about this realm is a rarity, save for the occasional story about Somali pirates or massive oil spills. For most of us, the sea is simply a place we fly over, a broad canvas of darker and lighter blues. Though it can seem vast and all-powerful, it is vulnerable and fragile in part because environmental threats travel far, transcending the arbitrary borders that mapmakers have applied to the oceans over the centuries.

Like a dissonant chorus in the background, these paradoxes captivated me throughout my journeys spanning forty months, 251,000 miles, eighty-five planes, forty cities, every continent, over 12,000 nautical miles across all five oceans and twenty other seas. Those travels provided the stories for this book, a compendium of narratives about this unruly frontier. My goal was not only to report on the plight of sea slaves but also to bring to life the full cast of characters who roam the high seas. They included vigilante conservationists, wreck thieves, maritime mercenaries, defiant whalers, offshore repo men, sea-bound abortion providers, clandestine oil dumpers, elusive poachers, abandoned seafarers, and cast-adrift stowaways.

Since I was young, I've been enchanted by the sea, but it was not until one brutally cold Chicago winter that I acted on my fascination. Five years into a doctoral program in history and anthropology at the

University of Chicago, I decided to procrastinate on completing my dissertation by fleeing to Singapore for a temporary job as a deckhand and resident anthropologist on a marine research ship called the RV *Heraclitus*. For three months, the whole time I was there, the ship never left port due to paperwork problems, and I spent the time getting to know the crews from other ships docked nearby.

This stranded stint port side in Singapore offered my first real exposure to merchant seafarers and long-haul fishermen, and the experience left me riveted by what seemed like a transient tribe of people. These workers are largely invisible to anyone leading a landlocked lifestyle. They have their own lingo, etiquette, superstitions, social hierarchy, codes of discipline, and, based on the stories they told me, catalog of crimes and tradition of impunity. Theirs is also a world where lore holds as much sway as law.

What became especially clear in these conversations is that moving freight by sea is much cheaper than by air partly because international waters are so uncluttered by national bureaucracies and unconstrained by rules. This fact has given rise to all manner of unregulated activity, from tax sheltering to weapons stockpiling. There is, after all, a reason that the American government, for instance, chose international waters as the location for disassembling Syria's chemical weapons arsenal, for conducting some of its terrorism-related detention and interrogation, and for disposing of Osama bin Laden's body. Meanwhile, the fishing and shipping industries are as much victims of offshore lawlessness as they are beneficiaries and perpetrators of it.

I never finished my dissertation. Instead, I took a job in 2003 at *The New York Times,* and over the next decade, as I learned how to be a reporter, I occasionally and unsuccessfully pitched the notion of doing a series about this offshore world. I leveraged every persuasive comparison I could muster. An all-you-can-eat allegory buffet, the seas offer inestimable opportunity, I argued. From a storytelling perspective, this two-thirds of the planet is virgin snow, I contended, because few, if any, other reporters are comprehensively exploring it.

In 2014, Rebecca Corbett, my editor at the time, agreed and in embracing the proposal, wisely nudged me toward focusing more on the people than on the fish, delving primarily into the human rights and labor concerns, because the environmental issues would arise as well through that lens. The first story from *The New York Times*'s Outlaw Ocean series ran in the paper in July 2015, with another dozen or so pieces published in the subsequent year. I took a fifteen-month leave from the paper, starting in January 2017, to continue reporting for this book.

.   .   .

During my travels, I had a lot of downtime, which I spent immersing myself in books about the ocean. Experientially and philosophically, the sea is and has always been many different things to different people. It is a metaphor for infinity and a place of the purest form of freedom, distinctly divorced from government meddling. An escape for some, the sea is also a prison for others. Full of devouring storms, doomed expeditions, shipwrecked sailors, and maniacal hunters, the canon of sea literature offered a vibrant picture of a watery wilderness and its untamed rogues. Like birds on the Galápagos, these men, over centuries, had done mostly as they pleased, evolving largely without predators. The surprising fact is that they still do. My hope with this book is to offer a sketch that brings into the present our awareness of these people and this place.

To make the book more of a first-person travelogue ("Tell stories, don't write articles," my editors used to remind me), I tried to rely less on shoreside interviews or archival testimonials than on reporting from the ships themselves. Mostly these were fishing ships, but also cargo vessels, cruise liners, medical boats, floating armories, and research and advocacy ships, as well as navy, port police, and Coast Guard cutters.

As a writing project, there was real risk in tackling such an ambitious topic—or, as the expression goes, trying to "boil the ocean." At times, the reporting process was so zigzagging that it felt less like journalism than an attention deficit disorder. But the more I traveled, the more one story led to another—none of them neat or tidy, none of them split clearly between right and wrong, villain and hero, predator and prey. Like the oceans themselves, the stories that emerged were too sprawling to force into a single, straight-line narrative. So, instead, I organized the chapters as a series of essays, confident that readers would connect the dots in their own ways, beyond the patterns I spotted.

In the end, the goal of this project is to bear witness to a world rarely seen. It recounts a maritime repo man spiriting a tanker from a Greek port into international waters, and a doctor clandestinely shuttling pregnant women from Mexican shores to the high seas to administer otherwise illegal abortions. It chronicles the work of vigilante conservationists, who in the South Atlantic Ocean chased Interpol's most wanted poacher ship and then in the Antarctic hunted and harassed Japan's last factory whaling ship. In the South China Sea, I landed in the middle of an armed standoff between two countries, each of which had taken hostages from the other. Off the coast of Somalia, I found myself temporarily stranded on a small wooden fishing boat in pirate-infested waters. I saw a ship sink, rode out violent storms, and watched a near mutiny. Reporting these stories took me from a submarine in the Antarctic and South Atlantic Oceans to offshore weapons depots in the Gulf of Oman, and to oil platforms in the Arctic and the Celebes Sea.

For all that adventure, though, the most important thing I saw from ships all around the world, and have tried in this book to capture, was an ocean woefully under-protected and the mayhem and misery often faced by those who work these waters.

# THE OUTLAW OCEAN

# STORMING THE *THUNDER*

The strongest of all warriors are these two—Time and Patience.

—Leo Tolstoy, *War and Peace*

The hunt had been under way for three days when Captain Peter Hammarstedt peered closely at his radar screen. Ever since he had piloted his ship, the *Bob Barker,* out of port in Hobart, Australia, Hammarstedt had scanned this desolate patch of Antarctic waters, searching among the icebergs that peppered the horizon of the Southern Ocean. As he stood on the bridge on the evening of December 17, 2014, three red blips drifted across the radar. He studied them carefully. Two moved slowly with the current, and it was clear they were icebergs. But the third was different, moving steadily in the opposite direction.

Hammarstedt slid the *Bob Barker* closer. In the perpetual daylight of the Antarctic summer, the spotter in the crow's nest overhead saw a flock of seabirds wheeling and diving behind a distant fishing trawler. Hammarstedt grabbed for a binder. Inside was Interpol's Purple Notice list of the world's worst maritime fishing scofflaws and the telltale silhouettes of the vessels. Hammarstedt leafed through until he found the profile for the world's most notorious fishing scofflaw, a Nigerian-flagged 202-foot ship called the *Thunder.* Peering at the fishing trawler, now about three miles in the distance, he confirmed that the ship had the same outline as the *Thunder.* He smiled, paused for a moment, then punched the alarm—five short blasts—alerting the crew to man their stations. Hammarstedt had found his prey.

Born in Stockholm, Hammarstedt joined Sea Shepherd at eighteen,

Captain Peter Hammarstedt on the bridge of the *Bob Barker*

shortly after high school. Lanky and baby-faced, he looked more like Howdy Doody than Blackbeard. He was stiffer and more formal than one might expect from a thirty-year-old who'd spent over a decade at sea. Even his one-paragraph emails had proper punctuation and indentation. Prone to meticulously arranging his pencils and pens before starting work at his desk, he was an orderly man in a disorderly line of work. Hammarstedt had been on almost all of Sea Shepherd's major campaigns since 2003, including ten missions chasing Japanese whalers in Antarctica. In his stern countenance, his crew saw a young man who took his job seriously and was always calm under fire.

For Sea Shepherd, the pursuit of the *Thunder* was about more than exacting justice or protecting a disappearing species of fish. It was about adding teeth to the halfhearted policing of laws on the high seas. But even calling these laws halfhearted would be giving them more credit than they were due. For bad actors like the *Thunder,* the seas were a vast free-for-all. Largely hidden in the sheer expanse of the world's ocean, poachers had little reason to look over their shoulders. Offshore, laws were as murky as the watery boundaries are blurry, and most governments had neither the resources nor the interest to go chasing after them. At the time, Interpol's Purple Notice list comprised just six rogue ships that had evaded capture for decades and come to be nicknamed the Bandit 6—the only vessels in the world to earn this distinction. And for years, they'd operated with impunity.

Hundreds of miles from the safety of shore, Hammarstedt and his crew were doing the perilous police work that governments would not.

Even though the *Thunder*'s officers were considered the world's worst fishing outlaws, no country was willing or able to chase them. But Hammarstedt's organization, the nonprofit maritime environmental group Sea Shepherd, took up the challenge. Deputizing themselves as pro bono bounty hunters, the group was hunting for the rogue vessel in this desolate patch of ocean at the bottom of the earth, deep in Antarctic waters. It was a battle of bold vigilantism against persistent criminality.

On his radio, Hammarstedt raised Siddharth Chakravarty, the captain of a second Sea Shepherd ship, the *Sam Simon,* which had left port late because of engine problems. Maritime camouflage striped both Sea Shepherd ships, with gaping shark jaws on the forward hull and a Jolly Roger knockoff flying over the prow: a skull with a trident crossed with a shepherd's hook. "I think we've found the *Thunder,*" Hammarstedt said. "There are several buoys in the water and we have a visual ID on the vessel."

The *Bob Barker*

As Hammarstedt crept closer at three knots, a crew member said he could read "Thunder, Lagos" on the back of the trawler. Over the radio, Hammarstedt announced himself to his adversary.

*Bob Barker:* Thunder, Thunder, Thunder. This is the *Bob Barker.*
 You are fishing illegally.
*Thunder:* Sorry, sorry. No English. Only Spanish.
*Bob Barker:* That is very lucky because *hablo español también.*

Hammarstedt summoned a Spanish-speaking photographer to the bridge. She began translating.

*Bob Barker:* You are fishing illegally. Do you have a license to fish?
*Thunder:* We have a license; we have a license. The ship has a Nigerian flag, and we are sailing in international waters. Over.
*Bob Barker:* You are fishing in CCAMLR-region 58.4.2, and we have an Interpol wanted notice on you.
*Thunder:* We are on our way and are not fishing. Besides, what kind of ship is that? I see that you have a pirate flag. What is that?

Sea Shepherd is an international conservation police force, Hammarstedt said through the interpreter. We intend to detain—"arrest," in maritime parlance—the *Thunder,* he added.

*Thunder:* No, no, no. Negative, negative. You have no authority to arrest this vessel. You have no authority to arrest this vessel. We are going to continue sailing, we are going to continue sailing, but you have no authority to arrest this ship, over.
*Bob Barker:* We have authority. We have reported your position to Interpol and Australian police.
*Thunder:* Okay, okay, you can send our position, but you cannot board this vessel. You cannot arrest it. We are sailing in international waters and we will continue.
*Bob Barker:* We are going to follow you, and you are under arrest. Change course to Fremantle, Australia.

I would later learn that though the *Thunder* had broken the law, its captain was correct: Sea Shepherd did not have the authority to arrest anyone. Still, the bluff had its desired effect. The *Thunder*'s crew, which had been working on the aft deck tossing fish scraps over the side, disappeared inside. Abruptly, the rogue vessel, over a thousand tons of reinforced steel, turned, gunned its engines, and began trying to outrun the smaller, faster Sea Shepherd ship. Hammarstedt made a notation in the ship's log on December 17, 2014, at 9:18 p.m.: "Bob Barker will maintain hot pursuit and report on the F/V Thunder's position to Interpol."

. . .

That was how the longest pursuit of an illegal fishing vessel in nautical history began. Over the next 110 days, across more than 11,550 nautical miles, three oceans, and two seas, the cat-and-mouse pursuit of the *Thunder* would take Sea Shepherd's crew through an unforgiving obstacle course of stadium-sized ice sheets, a ferocious storm, violent clashes, and a near collision.

The *Bob Barker* and the *Sam Simon* chase Interpol's most wanted poacher ship, the *Thunder,* in the longest pursuit of an illegal fishing vessel in nautical history.

Most of the *Thunder*'s forty-man crew were Indonesian, according to documents that were later seized from the ship, but the officer ranks included seven Spanish, two Chileans, and one Portuguese. The ship was under the command of a Chilean captain named Luis Alfonso R. Cataldo. Five of the ship's Spaniards came from La Coruña, Galicia. One of Spain's poorest regions, Galicia is often described as the "Sicily of Spain" because it is home to the country's most famous crime syndicates known for smuggling drugs, black-market tobacco, but most often illegal fish.

There's little mystery as to why unscrupulous shipowners poach at sea: the illicit seafood trade is a thriving global business that generates an estimated $160 billion in annual sales. The trade in illegal fish has grown over the past decade as improved technology—stronger radar, bigger nets, faster ships—has enabled fishing vessels to plunder the oceans with remarkable efficiency.

The *Thunder* was among the best at this trade and, in the eyes of conservationists, the worst of the Bandit 6, a reputation earned over decades of poaching the ghastly-looking toothfish, a species found only in the earth's coldest waters. Also known as icefish, the toothfish can grow to over six feet long and gets its name from a sharklike double row of steel-sharp teeth. Among Antarctica's largest predators, the grisly gray-black creature can prowl at depths of more than two miles, and its heart beats unusually slowly—once per six seconds—to preserve energy in the frigid depths. Its eyes are the size of billiard balls that grotesquely bulge from their sockets when fishermen pull them up to shallower depths with lower pressures.

The fish is also a favorite entrée in upscale restaurants in the United States and Europe, costing about $30 a fillet. But diners won't find "toothfish" on menus. There, it is sold under a more palatable name: Chilean sea bass. Demand soared in the 1980s and 1990s after a Los Angeles fish wholesaler with a flair for marketing renamed the fish. The rebranding worked a little too well. The oily fish, rich in omega 3, soon came to be known on docks worldwide as white gold. Most scientists now agree that the toothfish population is dwindling at an unsustainable rate.

Typically, the *Thunder* set out on two fishing expeditions to the Antarctic for six months each. A catch of a hundred tons per trip was enough to break even. Some years it caught more than seven times that amount, according to port records where it off-loaded its ill-gotten gains. For most of the 1990s, the *Thunder*'s seafood piracy put the ship on several blacklists run by marine conservation groups and various governments, and it was banned from fishing in Antarctica in 2006. And yet surveillance planes, satellite firms, and fishing boats often reported spotting it toothfishing in the Southern Ocean. Among the Bandit 6, the *Thunder* stood out because of the size of its illicit profits: Interpol estimated that its owners had earned more than the others—over $76 million in illicit fish sales in the prior decade.

In December 2013, Interpol issued an all points bulletin for police worldwide to arrest the *Thunder*. This Purple Notice hardly mattered, though, if the *Thunder* was able to avoid notice. Finding a single ship in the millions of square miles of open sea was hard enough. Scofflaw ships like the *Thunder* deftly used the tangled skein of confusing, conflicting maritime laws, difficult-to-enforce treaties, and deliberately lax national regulations to evade the law and shed their identities. With a couple of phone calls, payoffs of a few thousand dollars, and a can of paint, the ship could, as it had in the past, take a new name and register with a new flag as it steamed to its next fishing grounds.

The 2,200-horsepower trawler changed names more than a dozen times in its forty-five-year career. During that time, it flew nearly as many flags, including the colors of the U.K., Mongolia, the Seychelles, Belize, and Togo. After it was added to the EU's blacklist for pirate vessels, Togo revoked the right to fly its flag in 2010. Like an international criminal with multiple passports, the ship's owner responded by adding the *Thunder* to two new registries at once. Sometimes the ship flew the Mongolian flag, other times the Nigerian. For a ship of this size, it would likely have cost about $12,000 for a new flag and an additional $20,000 for the safety and equipment certifications needed to qualify for the registry. The *Thunder*'s name and port registry were not painted on its hull. Instead, they were painted on a metal sign hung from its stern, to be swapped out quickly if needed. Sailors called these signs "James Bond license plates."

By keeping its locational transponder, or AIS, turned off, the *Thunder* could avoid being tracked. It was a simple drill. Time and again, it slipped into port, off-loaded its catch to complicit or unwitting buyers, refueled, and was on its way before anyone noticed. Unless, of course, there was someone like Hammarstedt tailing it, watching its every move, and calling ahead to alert local officials and Interpol.

In 2014, Sea Shepherd launched Operation Icefish to prove that these kinds of bandits could be found and arrested. The mission took months of preparation. Before embarking on this mission, Chakravarty flew to Mumbai to comb its junkyards and ship-breaking fields in search of parts to build a more powerful winch on the *Sam Simon* that could haul up the gill nets they hoped to confiscate. Sea Shepherd had also outfitted its ships with $10,000 frequency scanners to pick up buoy transmitters that fishing boats attach to their nets.

To narrow their search of the more than five million square miles of Antarctic waters prowled by toothfish boats, Chakravarty overlaid three types of maps. Ice charts demarcated the ever-shifting melting line where the frozen, impenetrable Antarctic shelf ended and the thawed, navigable fishing waters began. Maritime maps indicated the patches of ocean that were beyond national jurisdiction. Nautical charts located the tallest and broadest of underwater plateaus where toothfish liked to congregate.

Hammarstedt had assumed it would take at least two weeks to patrol the whole area. The radar on Sea Shepherd's ships provided a visual circumference of about twelve nautical miles, but floating icebergs were a deceptive presence that often looked like ships on the screen. (A nautical mile is 15 percent longer than a regular mile.) Crew members with binoculars took turns in the crow's nest, a steel perch more than twenty-five feet above the upper deck. It was a loathsome job because the height exaggerated the swaying of the ship, causing bouts of intense seasickness. Later, when I was aboard the *Bob Barker,* I would spend hours in the crow's nest, taking in the view and seeing how long I could last. The scariest of carnival rides, it felt as though I were perched atop a swinging metronome.

When the *Bob Barker* spotted the *Thunder,* it was fishing in a remote stretch of the Antarctic Sea called Banzare Bank. Also known as the Shadowlands, these rarely traversed swaths of the Southern Ocean were among the planet's most remote and inhospitable waters, a roughly two-week journey to the nearest port. This region, which I crossed on a later voyage, is known to experience winds over 130 miles per hour and temperatures cold enough to freeze the fluid in your eyes.

To avoid frostbite while working on deck, the Sea Shepherd crews often wore survival suits. Weighing nearly ten pounds, the suits were made of neoprene, a type of rubber that is completely waterproof and designed to withstand extreme cold. Awkwardly puffy and usually bright orange to attract the attention of passing ships if a person fell overboard, the suits were nicknamed Gumbies, after the famous clay animation character. The suits also caused severe chafing and stank of dried sweat. "Bleed or freeze," one deckhand said to me as he helped me put mine on at one point. "Those are your options."

. . .

After the *Thunder* bolted north, the *Bob Barker* stayed in dogged pursuit. But Chakravarty and the *Sam Simon* hung back. For several weeks, he had remained in Antarctica to reel in the illegal gill net that the *Thunder* had left behind—essential evidence for prosecution. Though the net was valuable, likely worth more than $25,000, the prospect of getting caught must have seemed worse to the captain of the *Thunder,* so they'd fled without it.

Gill nets are banned because they are particularly blunt instruments. The bottom of the nets are weighted to drop to the seafloor. Buoys hold up the tops, creating an imperceptible mesh wall that can stretch seven miles across and twenty feet high. Forming an inescapable maze, the *Thunder* set up dozens of these walls to zigzag the underwater plateaus where toothfish congregate. The buoys at the tops of the nets helped the fishing boats find them later when they returned to pull the mesh back on board, usually loaded with catch.

Hauling in the net from the frigid water was a dangerous and brutally arduous task. The net was forty-five miles long, triple the length of Manhattan, and Antarctica is among the coldest and windiest places on earth. The deck of the *Sam Simon* was partially frozen and cluttered. The crew's spit froze before landing. The ship's railings were low. Tripping was easy. Marbled with slush, the polar water below dipped in some places to ninety degrees Fahrenheit below freezing. Falling overboard would have meant almost certain death within a couple of minutes, most likely from cardiac arrest, unless quickly rescued. When the sway was severe, deckhands wore harnesses and latched themselves to the ship to avoid getting swept away.

Clipboards in hand, several of the *Sam Simon*'s crew tallied the *Thunder*'s catch. The resulting logs, which the group eventually handed over to Interpol, detailed the gill nets' catch. For every four sea creatures netted, one was a toothfish; the rest were bycatch that nobody would want even if they were alive. Virtually all of Sea Shepherd's crew were vegetarian or vegan, many of them motivated by a concern for animal rights. Untangling the dead and dying wildlife from those nets, including rays, giant octopuses, dragonfish, and large crabs, was difficult work, emotionally and physically. Some cried, others vomited, but all of them kept working, typically twelve hours a day. By the second week of hauling, nearly a third of the crew was taking pain pills for strained backs.

The exhausting work often took a grisly turn. Toothfish can weigh more than 250 pounds each, and the ones that the *Sam Simon*'s crew pulled on board in the nets had started to rot. The decomposition caused gas to build up inside the carcasses, and with the pressure of the nets some of the bulging fish exploded as they slammed onto the deck.

After nearly a week of twenty-hour days, Chakravarty dropped anchor and parked the *Sam Simon* before heading to bed just before 6:00 a.m. on December 25, 2015. A phone call awoke him twenty minutes later: "We need you on the bridge. It's urgent." He arrived to find his first mate, Wyanda Lublink, at the helm. The no-nonsense former Dutch navy commanding officer pointed out the window at an iceberg—about seven stories tall, roughly a mile across—rapidly approaching the *Sam Simon*'s rear deck.

"What are you waiting for?" Chakravarty asked.

"We have time," one of the officers replied.

"No, we don't," Chakravarty said, reminding the officer that their ship's engine was fully off, and it would need at least fifteen minutes to warm up before they could move. The iceberg might reach them before that.

Captain Siddharth Chakravarty on the bridge of the *Sam Simon*

"Clear the aft deck, now!" Chakravarty ordered, worried about the safety of the crew working there. "Start the engine immediately." Eighteen minutes later, with the iceberg just fifty feet away and moments from hitting the ship, the *Sam Simon* shoved through the pack ice and slipped out of harm's way.

By late January, the *Sam Simon* had finished collecting the *Thunder*'s nets. "My primary motive at this point is to help all concerned parties link this gillnet set to the F/V/ Thunder," Chakravarty wrote in an email to Interpol, "and use it as evidence that could help prosecute her." The *Sam Simon* delivered the net to Mauritius, a small island nation in the Indian Ocean, east of Madagascar. They were met dockside by a group of seven local fishery agents and officers from Interpol, who were gathering information related to the *Thunder* and the other purple-listed vessels.

As the crowd of uniformed officers huddled around him, snapping photographs and scribbling notes, Chakravarty walked them through his seventy-two-point list that itemized the unique characteristics of *Thunder's* netting. Fishing is as much art as science, he explained. The best captains had to be able to navigate the fiercest storms, endure the longest journeys. They also had their faithful superstitions, secretive sweet spots for fishing, and, in gillnetting, their trademark style for handling their mesh. Chakravarty treated his dockside lecture with the meticulousness of an evidentiary hearing. A toothfish captain's signature was his knot tie, net gridding, and rope splicing, and Chakravarty showed the officers what was unique about the *Thunder's* nets, a kind of fingerprint to remove doubt about the identity of its original owner.

For an entire day, Chakravarty explained the evidence to police officers gathered at the pier. Then he ordered his crew to hand over to Interpol only a small amount of the *Thunder's* illegal gill net. The remainder—forty-four miles' worth of net stacked in a shimmering aqua-green mound taller and longer than a semitrailer truck—would stay on board the *Sam Simon*. Banned gill net of this type was worth tens of thousands of dollars on the black market. Local authorities had warned that it would likely disappear if left in storage in Mauritius. That stage of his mission accomplished, Chakravarty returned to join the *Bob Barker* in its pursuit of the *Thunder*.

. . .

I heard about the chase several weeks after it had started. An old source of mine—a former navy intelligence officer—called my cell phone one afternoon and asked if I'd heard about "this thing down in Antarctica." He told me, "It's shaping up to be the longest law enforcement chase in nautical history, even though it doesn't involve law enforcement." I was immediately intrigued, even if his statement didn't initially make sense to me. As he explained to me what was going on, it struck me as an ideal opportunity to witness firsthand how Sea Shepherd's vigilantism worked in practice.

I quickly contacted the CEO of Sea Shepherd, Alex Cornelissen, to ask if I could cover the mission and come aboard one of the ships. As often happens in stories like this, the first answer was no.

Him: They're moving too fast.
Me: I can commission a boat that will catch up. [I had no clue yet how I would do this.]
Him: They're too far offshore.
Me: I've traveled for weeks at sea and have no problem doing it again. [This was true.]
Him: It's too dangerous.
Me: I've reported from war zones in the Middle East, embedded with militias in Africa, and in a former life worked at sea. This is not too dangerous.
Him: Fine!

Cornelissen finally acquiesced after half a dozen calls from me. But you will have to be in Accra, Ghana, within seventy-two hours, he told me.

For more than a year, I had been reporting on the seamiest, most dangerous aspects of the fishing industry, chronicling the illegal machinations of an industry that operated in the dark, where slavery and sadism thrived, where people were treated like the commodities that they pulled from the oceans. The idea of embarking on a mission to bring justice to even a single arrested ship was appealing to me. Even still, joining Sea Shepherd gave me pause.

I had known Sea Shepherd's founder, Paul Watson, for a couple of years. We first met when I shared the stage with him at a speaking engagement about ocean plastic. Blunt and confident, he was a man surrounded by great folklore that I hoped to penetrate. I began to make a point of asking people who knew him for their candid opinions. Responses were often contradictory. They described him as exaggerated or authentic, megalomaniacal or selfless, complicated or simplistic. And yet, the one characteristic everyone agreed on was "committed."

In the early 1970s, Watson and two dozen other environmental activists founded Greenpeace. In 1977, the organization's board of directors expelled Watson over an incident in Newfoundland. After he led a team of Greenpeace activists to protest seal hunting, Watson furiously confronted a sealer, throwing the man's pelts and club in the water. Greenpeace viewed Watson's behavior in the incident as too aggressive and kicked him out of the organization. He promptly founded Sea Shepherd, branding it as a more radical and more aggressive group than Greenpeace.

What fascinated me about the history of these two advocacy groups was that despite their differences they shared a singular role in the outlaw ocean. No other organization—government or otherwise—routinely patrolled the high seas, policing against legal violations. To differing degrees, both Greenpeace and Sea Shepherd believed that the ends justified the means. They were willing to operate outside the law themselves to stop criminals; the only question was how far they would be willing to stray.

Sea Shepherd had its own creative narrative that justified its behavior and relationship to written laws. When I finally arrived on board the *Bob Barker,* I asked Hammarstedt whether Sea Shepherd had legal rights to chase and harass illegal fishing ships like the *Thunder.* He said his crew drew authority from a provision in the UN World Charter for Nature that called on nongovernmental groups to assist in safeguarding nature in areas beyond national jurisdiction.

Several maritime lawyers and international policy experts have disagreed with this interpretation. Obstructing fishing vessels (even poachers) and confiscating their gear is illegal, they said. "But no one would prosecute this because it pales in comparison to what the *Thunder* was doing," said Kristina Gjerde, an expert on high-seas policy at the International Union for Conservation of Nature, a coalition of environmental groups. "Sea Shepherd knows this."

Nicknamed Neptune's Navy, Sea Shepherd has a fleet of five large ships, half a dozen fast inflatables, two drones, and a ready crew on standby of up to 120 persons representing twenty-four nationalities. Much of the group's money comes from celebrity donors like Mick Jagger, Pierce Brosnan, Sean Penn, Uma Thurman, Ed Norton, and Martin Sheen. The *Bob Barker* was named after the former host of *The Price*

*Is Right,* who contributed $5 million to buy the ship in 2010. The *Sam Simon* was bought in 2012 for more than $2 million, largely funded by the co-creator of *The Simpsons.* With an annual budget of more than $4 million, Sea Shepherd's offices in Australia and Amsterdam ran the $1.5 million operation to track the *Thunder.*

Widely known for its antiwhaling work captured in the Animal Planet series *Whale Wars,* Sea Shepherd was at a pivotal moment when it launched Operation Icefish. Watson had been arrested in 2012 in Germany on a decade-old criminal charge from Costa Rica over a collision between Sea Shepherd and a shark-finning vessel. After spending eight days in a high-security German prison, Watson was released on bail. Placed under house arrest in Frankfurt, he fled to the sea shortly thereafter. Extradition had been a real possibility because the Japanese had pursued the issue for years and behind the scenes were applying considerable political pressure on foreign leaders.

Watson had formally stepped down as president of Sea Shepherd U.S.A. and as captain of the *Steve Irwin,* the organization's flagship. But his fugitive status still complicated matters. Japan, which announced plans to extradite him as soon as he was recaptured, had also launched an expensive legal fight that was draining Sea Shepherd's coffers. As of October 2017, Watson remained the target of two international arrest warrants, or Interpol Red Notices, because of ramming incidents and charges filed by police in Japan and Costa Rica. In Watson's pursuit of the *Thunder,* the irony was rich: an Interpol red lister was chasing a maritime purple lister.

As an organization, Sea Shepherd cared less about legal nuances than it did about using what it called "direct action" to protect global marine life. Dozens of times over the past several decades, the group had rammed Japanese whaling ships and other vessels that it said were fishing illegally. The modified Jolly Roger, the maritime camouflage, and the shark maw on the prow, like a World War II bomber, put the organization's zeal on display for all to see. The organization's mantra captured its vigilante spirit: "Takes a pirate to catch a pirate."

For Captains Hammarstedt and Chakravarty, Operation Icefish was a chance for Sea Shepherd to remake itself with new targets and tactics. The group had decided, for example, that rather than ramming any of the Bandit 6, they would instead try to stay within the bounds of the law, shadowing while harassing them to the point of stopping. "Loud hailers" is how Hammarstedt described his group's role. Unlike other missions, Sea Shepherd was also collaborating with Interpol this time rather than defying it.

Chakravarty's presence in Mauritius, working with Interpol, was also part of Sea Shepherd's effort to rebrand itself. I called several sources in the maritime division at Interpol to get their insights. None would go on the record, but all of them said they were quietly helping Sea Shepherd. "They're getting results," one of them said.

By the time I joined the pursuit in early April 2015, the hunt for the *Thunder* had far surpassed the previous record for a chase of this scale. In 2003, Australian authorities pursued a ship called the *Viarsa 1* for twenty-one days and nearly four thousand nautical miles. Like the *Thunder,* the *Viarsa* was a toothfishing ship. It was finally seized near South Africa, and its operators were eventually tried and acquitted in 2005 for lack of evidence. Little had changed since then: a similar cast of characters was stealing the same type of fish from the same locations. But this time around, the chase was far longer, more dangerous, and led not by law enforcement officers but by a group of eco-vigilantes. As I joined the Sea Shepherd crew, the pursuit of the *Thunder* felt like an old story that in repeating itself had morphed into something new and more erratic.

. . .

By April 2015, I had already been at sea for six months reporting for *The New York Times* on other trips, off the coast of Thailand, the U.A.E., the Philippines, and elsewhere. Many of these reporting trips had been launched with extreme haste because such opportunities rarely emerged with much warning and I was often trying to get to a moving target. This one was no different. By now, the scramble was well rehearsed. I called my brother-in-law and my mother, both of whom lived near me in Washington, D.C., to ask them to help my wife with school pickups and drop-offs of my teenage son while I was gone.

At home, I kept a backpack always ready. In it, I kept $5,000 in cash, dispersed between hiding places (under the soles of my running shoes, in a secret pouch sewn into the inseam of the backpack, and under a false bottom of my tin of pills). All gadgets (extra batteries, GoPro cameras, headphones, satellite phone, laptop computer, backup cell phone with international SIM card) were fully charged. Antibiotic and antifungal ointments had been resupplied, having learned the hard way on a filthy fishing boat in the South China Sea where I'd given my supply to a deckhand in severe need, only to watch a week later as a gash on my own arm became dangerously infected for lack of medicine.

The hardest conversation before these trips was always the one with my wife, and this time was even tougher because it wasn't clear when I'd be back. "Might be three weeks or could be three months," Chakravarty had said, explaining that it all depended on how long the *Thunder* ran and whether they were ever near shore. "Go. We'll be fine," my wife, Sherry, said, as she always did. "Just make sure you come back."

As I headed to Accra, I reached out to two persons for help. First was Koby Koomson, a former Ghanaian ambassador to the United States, whom I knew because my wife, who is a Spanish teacher, taught at his son's high school. Ambassador Koomson quickly put me in touch with several important figures in the Ghanaian government to help me get my visa approval accelerated.

The second person was Anas Aremeyaw Anas, a Ghanaian reporter I'd known for several years. Though Anas is possibly the most famous investigative journalist in Africa, virtually no one knows his face because he does most of his work undercover. Photographs of him on the internet are either masked or digitally doctored. His investigations, which led to high-profile arrests in half a dozen countries, have taken on arms dealers, warlords, drug smugglers, and corrupt government officials. So feared is Anas among government functionaries in some parts of Africa that his name is invoked by African rappers as a boogey-man of sorts in songs about hustlers and corrupt cops, warning the wayward in the Twi language to watch out because "Anas is coming!"

Anas lent me his personal assistant, a young man named Selase Kove-Seyram, so I could move safely in Accra and efficiently through the Ghanaian bureaucracy. Within hours, Kove-Seyram had lined us up a ride with the Ghanaian port police, who had a relatively new cutter that they were eager to test-drive. That plus $1,500, which more than covered expenses, was enough to persuade them to taxi me to my offshore meeting.

Shortly after I arrived in Accra, I learned that the *Times* staff photographer who had been assigned to join me wasn't able to board his flight from Brazil because his visa approval had hit a snag. I asked

Kove-Seyram, who also happened to be a talented photographer, if he had any interest in heading to sea with me for an uncertain amount of time. Without hesitating, he agreed. Before heading to the harbor, we dashed to the store to buy supplies.

When I had the option, I almost always carried the same staples: My low-weight, high-calorie sustenance was peanut butter and dried fruit. I usually brought lots of chewing gum, mixed nuts, and sometimes cigarettes to hand out and break the ice with the crew. Powdered lemonade helped mask the rusty taste of the water on most ships. M&M's were durable treats, relatively safe from the heat, that I could dole out to myself slowly, a few each day. Within twelve hours after having arrived in the country, I boarded a forty-foot police cutter and sped out to sea feeling amazed that all was falling into place. Our plan was to arrive early at our rendezvous coordinates more than a hundred miles off the coast, drop anchor, and wait (likely for about twenty hours) to get picked up.

As I had prepared to leave, Chakravarty had called me on his satellite phone from the *Sam Simon* to explain that his AIS would be switched off because he did not want the *Thunder* to know that one of its two pursuers had peeled off. He warned me that whoever transported me out to sea should not worry if they were unable to see Sea Shepherd coming. "We'll be there," Chakravarty said before adding that they could not wait for me for very long without risking losing the *Thunder*. "Don't be late."

This is when things started falling apart. Only one of the ten members of the crew on the Ghanaian port police boat we'd arranged a ride on had ever been in waters more than a dozen miles from shore. These were macho guys, eager to impress their visitor, so when several of them started to get seasick, they were embarrassed. Seventy miles off the coast, the waves swelled to fifteen feet high, and I sensed that the men, not without reason, were getting scared. The mood on board grew tense. Because we were burning extra fuel to fight the current, several of them predicted that we were going to either capsize or run out of diesel. Worry among the lower-ranking crew members erupted into a heated argument with the officers.

The thing about danger is you become desensitized to it the more you experience it and emerge unscathed. I don't experience danger as a drug, nor do I seek it out simply for the thrill, but you become somewhat inured to fear. By the time I found myself surrounded by these Ghanaians, in a moment when a normal person's internal danger meter would begin flashing yellow, I could see the possible risks, but I didn't feel the potential peril. I'd been in far more dangerous binds at sea on far less equipped ships, and I felt confident that the Ghanaian cutter was plenty strong to handle the conditions. If only its officers stayed calm.

Soon, however, the odds turned against us. The officers had underestimated not only the amount of fuel we needed for the trip but also the depth of the waters we were crossing. The anchor on their cutter was not long enough to reach the seafloor more than a thousand feet below us, which meant that during our long wait for the *Sam Simon* the Ghanaians would not be able to turn off our engine, lest we drift too far and pitch too wildly. I called Chakravarty by satellite phone, using up most of my battery, and explained our predicament. Surely, Sea Shepherd would not want to turn us back, I figured, and lose the publicity and potential funding in getting their story covered. Chakravarty asked me to tell the Ghanaians that when he arrived he would siphon excess fuel from his ship's backup tanks and provide it to them so they could safely return to shore.

His offer did not reassure the Ghanaians. The arguments on our ship began escalating from shouting to shoving. It was just the moment that I'd normally resort to doling out my "icebreakers"—not just gum, nuts, and cigarettes, but also canned tuna and hard candy—in hopes of easing the mood, but four hours into the trip I'd already depleted my stash. In my head, I had initially dismissed this hollering as a short-lived flare-up from exhaustion and bravado. I started taking the tension more seriously, though, when two of the bigger deckhands stood up and began yelling in the faces of the officers while gesturing at me. It seemed mutiny might be nearing, and I was on the wrong side.

Kove-Seyram, who had been translating for me from various Ghanaian languages, was by now intensely seasick and vomiting over the side of the boat. I no longer knew what the crew members were yelling, but the standoff was clear: the crew wanted to return to port right away, and the senior officers were determined to complete the mission. After twenty minutes of screaming, the lower crewmen, who were bigger and outnumbered the officers, won the argument. We turned back to land, and for the next couple of hours an awkward and angry silence filled our boat.

Our luck soon worsened. As we returned toward shore, we inexplicably lost all power to our dashboard—an electrical short, likely—disabling the ship's navigational equipment. No other boats were in sight or radio proximity. Without knowing our exact location, charting a course home became impossible. With limited fuel, there was no margin for error; otherwise, we would end up in foreign and unfriendly waters. With one bar of battery life left on my satellite phone, I called a marine researcher who had become a source, waking her in the middle of the night. "Can you get onto the AIS website and look for the ship I'm on?" I apologetically asked her. We were still transmitting our position with a battery-powered transponder, which is why I figured she might be able to see us. My phone died before she could get me the answer.

For the next four hours, we drifted in the dark of night, each of us lost in our thoughts and fears. I was terrified that I might not talk to my wife and son again. I also was incredulous that this was how my reporting project might end. This bizarre scenario was not one I had ever imagined when I was thinking through all the potential dangers. I kicked myself for not having backup batteries for my phone.

As we bobbed in the darkness, a flicker of light on the horizon interrupted my worry. "Ay!" yelled one of the crew on our aft deck, pointing at the light, as the others began clapping with excitement. It was a rickety trawler, and after we made contact with our handheld radio, the fishermen came alongside. Boarding us to help with the electrical short on our dash panel, they gave us our coordinates. Bottom trawling was prohibited in the area where we stalled. Still, I thought it probably best not to point out that our law enforcement ship was being rescued by a boat that quite likely had been fishing illegally. It was a little piece of irony I'd have to enjoy by myself.

We resumed our journey back to port, the mood still tense but no longer explosive. As I climbed off the ship in Accra, the cutter's commanding officer apologized for not carrying me to our intended destination. He then put me in an unmarked car with a soldier named Abu, instructing him to take us back to our hotel.

It was daylight by then, and Accra was coming to life. I was exhausted—drained from sleep deprivation and the anxiety of being temporarily lost at sea. Still, we had just enough time to make the rendezvous if we could quickly line up another boat. I asked Abu if he might be interested in earning good money by taking us instead to the nearby fishing port and helping us hire a ride out to sea. "No problem," Abu said. I was determined—perhaps too determined—to witness the chase of the *Thunder*.

About six feet four and 250 pounds, Abu was a mountain of a man, and his military uniform added to his formidable presence. Prone to long loaded stares, he communicated as much through his silence as his words. As we drove to the port in the unmarked car, checkpoints that had previously required fifteen minutes of haggling to pass through now waved us along without our driver even rolling down his window. Within an hour, Abu had us on a bigger cargo ship, piloted by a more experienced captain, for $800. Seeming genuinely concerned that we arrive on time and curious to see whom we were meeting, Abu decided to join us in the boat. After a six-hour trip, we arrived at our designated coordinates with barely twenty minutes to spare. The captain idled the engine to wait. Surreal and stressful, it felt like a fever dream.

"I can't believe we pulled it off," Kove-Seyram whispered to me. I replied with an inconspicuous low five. The celebration didn't last long. As we scanned the horizon for the *Sam Simon*'s skiff, our cargo ship's captain had been growing increasingly agitated. He finally broke the silence and said to me that he did not like the idea of meeting up with a ship he could not see on AIS and whose crew and captain he did not know personally. "How do I know you aren't setting me up to get hit by pirates?" he asked. I explained that the *Sam Simon* had turned off its locational transponder because it was trying to follow another ship, undetected. My earnest response only seemed to make him more nervous.

The *Sam Simon*'s skiff soon appeared. Rather than reassuring the captain, the sight of the tattooed, stocky Sea Shepherd guys dressed all in black and driving a fast-moving military-style boat sent our captain into a panic. Assuming they were mercenaries, he whipped our cargo boat around and pressed full throttle toward shore. I pleaded with him to stop, but he refused. I shot Abu a do-something-now look. Standing up, Abu took a deep breath through his nose that seemed to increase his height by several inches and in a booming voice ordered the captain to turn the boat around. The captain did so immediately.

As we climbed off the cargo ship and into the Sea Shepherd skiff, I handed the Ghanaian boat captain the second half of the $800 I owed him. Though he had insisted that he was not looking to be paid to help us, I forced $200 into Abu's hand as we shook to say good-bye. Looking relieved to be rid of us, the two men wished Kove-Seyram and me good luck. The Ghanaian cargo ship sped back to shore. The Sea Shepherd crew on the skiff revved its engine and turned the craft farther in to the Gulf of Guinea to bring us to the *Sam Simon*.

. . .

In February, two months after the chase had begun, but two months before I climbed on board the Sea Shepherd ship, the captain on the *Bob Barker,* Hammarstedt, and his adversary on the *Thunder* had come to a shared realization that neither intended to give up the chase. At the time, the two men were crossing some of the world's most perilous waters. According to an old sailing proverb, below latitude 40° south there is no law, and below 50° south, no God. So furious and dangerous are the winds and weather in this part of the planet, situated just under the southernmost tip of Argentina, that they have fed centuries' worth of fear and sunk untold numbers of ships. During this chase, these two ship captains had already careened across thousands of miles through the "Godless Sixties" as they headed north into what sailors call the "Roaring Forties" and "Furious Fifties."

In this famously rough stretch of the Southern Ocean, storms gather force for tens of thousands of miles as they travel east across open water, technically called the fetch, unimpeded by land except for South America's lower tip. Winds can top two hundred miles per hour. Waves reach ninety feet tall. Polar fronts and trade winds generate an average of one angry storm per week. To pass through this region, ships typically wait on the periphery to slip between these storms. The *Thunder* did not.

Following the *Thunder* into this treacherous region, Hammarstedt hunched over his laptop studying weather maps. Yellow splotches indicated winds over forty-five miles per hour. Red patches showed those blowing more than fifty-five miles per hour. Peering over his shoulder, Adam Meyerson, the ship's chief mate and a stocky former auto mechanic from California, chimed in. "It's okay to be in the mustard,"

The *Thunder* tries to escape by charging through a perilous patch of ice fields in Antarctica's Southern Ocean.

he said. "We just need to stay out of the ketchup." For the next two days, it was pure ketchup.

As the wider, heavier *Thunder* held steady over the next two days in the storm, the *Bob Barker* swayed back and forth, listing forty degrees and battered by fifty-foot waves. Below deck, fuel sloshed in the *Barker*'s tanks, splashing through ceiling crevices and filling the ship with diesel fumes. In the galley, a plastic drum tethered to the wall broke free, coating the floor in vegetable oil that bled into the cabins below. Half the crew was seasick. "It was like working on an elevator that suddenly dropped and climbed six stories every ten seconds," Captain Hammarstedt recalled.

When I interviewed them later, the crew compared the experience of crossing the storms to being "a coin inside a washing machine," "a Ping-Pong ball in a bathtub," and a "driver in a demolition derby." Though I was not on board the *Barker* for this leg of the trip, I knew what the crew meant. I traversed these same waters on a later voyage and listened as walls of water packed such powerful punches that they made my ship groan, wail, and screech for relief from the relentless pounding.

During such storms, you tend to stay lying down inside your cabin in hopes of lessening the seasickness. Even the halls inside the ship can be dangerous because things invariably fly around if they aren't properly tied down. Because you can't see much outside, you never quite know when the next wave is going to hit and how bad it will rattle the ship. So your imagination fills in the blanks. Hours of lying around your cabin can drift into days, at which point the boredom becomes a danger in itself.

For the Sea Shepherd crew, lying around was not an option. When ships dock, they often dangle bulky rubbery "Yokohama fenders" over the side—they look like mini-submarines covered in tires—to prevent the ship from scraping or slamming into port walls or pier pilings. During one of the storms, a fender that had been tied down under the wheelhouse of the *Bob Barker* broke from its tethers. Nearly ten feet long and weighing more than a ton, the fender was swinging wildly less than three feet from destroying the ship's speedboat. "You simply don't go on deck in storms this big," Hammarstedt said. "Except when you have no choice." Two of the crewmen—a bosun named Alistair Allan and the engineer, Pablo Watson, both Australians—volunteered for the job. Climbing into emergency suits, they latched themselves to the side railing and shinnied their way to the forward deck to refasten the fender in the driving wind and rain.

As much as it was a test of wills and daring, the chase of the *Thunder* was a game of endurance. In prior weeks, the *Thunder* had done everything in its power to prevent its adversaries from replenishing themselves. The *Bob Barker* and the *Sam Simon* typically sailed parallel to each other, spread apart by about half a mile. When they moved near each other, the *Thunder*'s captain assumed they were trying to exchange supplies or top up the other's fuel tank so he swung his ship around and wedged it between his adversaries. The Sea Shepherd captains laughed at the move because they were stocked well enough not to need resupplying for at least a couple months more. I never got a straight answer from the Sea Shepherd captains as to why they kept moving their ships near each other. I suspected it was simply to play head games with their opponent.

If riding through angry storms at sea is a rough form of claustrophobia, like being locked inside a tumbling box, then making it to the other side brings a rare and powerful euphoria. A weight lifts. You feel as if you can finally breathe again. You emerge from days spent stuck in your closet-sized cabin. You step on deck to see that ominously low cloud ceiling lifting. Maybe there's even sun. Doors are latched open. Fresh air pours in. For Sea Shepherd, this euphoria was even sweeter. They had the added pride of having foiled the *Thunder*'s efforts to shake them.

Over the next several days, as the ships passed through stiller waters, Sea Shepherd tried to assess how much fuel the *Thunder* had left. Photographers on the *Bob Barker* and the *Sam Simon* took video and photographs of the *Thunder* to calculate how high it sat in the water, a clue to its petrol levels.

Before Sea Shepherd let me on board, I had to agree to several conditions, including promising to never reveal anything about the ships' fuel capacities. "Our adversaries don't need to know how long they're going to have to run from us," Chakravarty explained. Also verboten was publishing ship blueprints, which could be seen on display on the walls of the bridge. If there was a confrontation with the *Thunder*, a water cannon aimed at the right ventilation portal could flood essential areas of one of the Sea Shepherd vessels.

Nearly two months into the chase, Sea Shepherd and the *Thunder* were in an area called Melville Bank, located several hundred miles south of Madagascar in the Indian Ocean. Thick clouds muted the afternoon sun. After abruptly slowing down, the *Thunder* began making circles. Hammarstedt called over the radio to Cataldo, the *Thunder* captain, to ask if everything was okay. There was no reply, which was unusual. Though bitter adversaries, the two captains talked frequently, usually with Cataldo yelling, cursing, and taunting ("You piece of shit," "You're an imbecile," and "You don't deserve to be a captain") while Hammarstedt maintained his cool, adding the occasional touch of sarcasm ("Thank you for saying that," "The feelings are mutual").

Soon, the *Thunder*'s rear spotlights turned on, the trawl door at the back opened, and the ship's crew threw out about half a mile of buoyed fishing nets. The officers on the *Bob Barker* watched from their bridge in stunned silence. Hammarstedt ordered his pilot to move the *Bob Barker* quickly out of the path of the nets to avoid them getting caught in its propellers. No toothfish were to be found in this patch of ocean because it was too shallow, less than four hundred feet deep. Were they fishing to eat? Hammarstedt wondered. Or maybe they were just spoiling for a fight.

Half an hour later, the *Thunder* looped back to retrieve its nets, and Hammarstedt tried blocking its path. Cataldo responded by gunning his engine and charging full bore toward the *Bob Barker*. Hammarstedt immediately pulled his throttle into reverse, avoiding a collision by about ten feet. Ships ramming each other—something I'd experience later in Palau, Thailand, and Indonesia—sounds and feels more violent and panic inducing than a car crash. The stakes are higher because such collisions typically result in one or both vessels sinking. The noise also lasts longer, almost as if in slow motion, metal-on-metal screaming, fiberglass shattering, wood buckling, then snapping like a bent tree. Luckily, that did not happen this day, because these were far bigger ships. Cataldo's men retrieved their catch on deck, and the ship went dark again.

The *Bob Barker* nearly collides with the *Thunder.*

The next night, the *Thunder* again opened its trawl door and shot its nets. When Cataldo radioed him, Hammarstedt took a more confrontational tack.

*Thunder: Bob Barker, Thunder.*
*Bob Barker:* What do you want?
*Thunder:* Good afternoon, to communicate to you that by order of the Government of Nigeria, and of our contracting agency, we are going to perform another fishing labor, so that you are careful with your stern not to get entangled in our gear.

*Bob Barker:* If you fish, we are going to cut your nets.

*Thunder:* If you cut our nets, we are going to inform the Government of Nigeria. You are taking private property from this ship. We are going to work and we have authorization from Nigeria, as I told you before, with our license up to date, with all our things up to date. What you are going to do would be illegal.

*Bob Barker:* You do not have a permit. There's no point in putting a net out now. If you do, we will cut the net. Nigeria has told us that you do not have permission to fish. If you drop the net, we will cut it.

It was unclear whether one of the captains was bluffing or if Nigeria had been speaking out of both sides of its mouth. But by this time, the nets were in the water. As the *Thunder* dragged them, Hammarstedt moved the *Bob Barker* into the wake but stayed back far enough to avoid becoming entangled. Hammarstedt then moved alongside the nets and instructed his crew to grab the line that connected them to the *Thunder.* They cut their buoys, causing sections of the net to fall to the ocean floor, while the *Bob Barker*'s crew tugged the rest out of the water. Cataldo made a sharp U-turn. "Hurry up," Hammarstedt ordered. "The *Thunder* is coming back around toward us."

The danger to the crew on the *Bob Barker* was real. It was one of many such moments in my reporting about the outlaw ocean that raised a basic question: Why would these young people take such risks with their lives? Over the next several years, as I'd spend months at sea with such ocean conservation advocates, I developed a list of factors that I thought answered that question. Yes, they cared about fish or, more generally, marine life. To ask them about their purpose was to hear a narrative about resisting broader forces like greed, climate change, and the needless killing of living creatures. But there were visceral motivations, too: adventure, the chance to travel, the thrill of a good fight, seeing places few others knew existed, acquiring practical seafaring skills, the camaraderie of shared purpose. One thing, though, was clear: as in most professions, mine included, the longer they did the work, the more they bought into the central narrative that the higher calling at its core is what fortified them at scary moments like this.

Cataldo called over the radio, fuming with rage and accusing Hammarstedt of theft. Hammarstedt fired back that Cataldo was the one breaking the law. "You started this war," Cataldo said, adding that he would chase Sea Shepherd until they gave him back his net. The *Bob Barker* gunned its engine. The *Thunder* followed at full throttle, five hundred yards behind.

Confident he could outpace the *Thunder* and delighted that Cataldo was wasting precious fuel chasing him, Hammarstedt deadpanned that he was more than willing to give the confiscated nets back. The *Thunder* would simply need to follow him to the nearest port and turn itself in to the police, he added. Cataldo was not amused. "Whatever it takes, whatever happens," Cataldo said, "we have instructions, we have our orders, and they are to recover our buoy."

For the next several hours, the chaser was the chased. Hammarstedt began referring to his Spanish adversary as "Pamplona's bull." Finally, Cataldo stopped. Turning his ship around, he returned to his original course. To where, no one knew.

．　．　．

More than three thousand miles away from Operation Icefish, a different drama was unfolding in the northwest corner of Spain. In Galicia, police raided several offices of suspected illegal fishing companies, including the former headquarters of Vidal Armadores, the infamous fish-poaching company. When officers arrived at the company offices, the staff were furiously shredding documents. Police stopped them and within half an hour left with the remaining tens of thousands of pages.

The raid was part of Operation Sparrow, which took its tongue-in-cheek name from Jack Sparrow, Johnny Depp's character in the Pirates of the Caribbean movies. The sting was the first time Spanish authorities tried to enforce a new fisheries law, introduced in 2015, that allowed them to prosecute Spanish nationals involved in illegal fishing anywhere in the world.

Spanish police and other authorities suspected that Vidal Armadores had ties to the *Thunder*. But the *Thunder*'s ownership remained a mystery, shrouded by shell companies in the Seychelles, Nigeria, and Panama. Most of all, these companies were protected by distance and transience as their ships stayed in motion and far away from easy inspection. Still, the poachers had an Achilles' heel. Try as they might to stay at sea, the operators of these ships knew as well that their lives were inextricably tied to land. Their financial resources were always moored to land-based institutions and transactions. Their crews had families to see and debts to pay off. These were inescapable facts of life, and the Spanish investigators knew how to leverage them toward prosecution. For cash-strapped governments, sometimes the best use of their resources was to sit back and wait for these ships to return to shore.

As the Spanish government's investigation into these companies gathered steam, sources began providing me with a wealth of documents related to the case. Some of the documents suggested that the *Thunder*'s owner was a Panamanian company called Estelares, which Interpol officials said was run by a man from Galicia named Florindo González Corral. Other maritime records cited the *Thunder*'s owners as a different Panama-registered company called Trancoeiro Fishing. Several of the directors of this company were Spaniards who had been convicted before of fishing crimes and who Interpol officials said were tied to Vidal Armadores. Trancoeiro Fishing officials failed to reply to repeated requests from me for comment. An email from Carlos Pérez-Bouzada, a Spanish lawyer who in the past had represented Vidal Armadores, said his client "had no connection whatsoever" to the *Thunder*.

Sifting through these documents, which were almost always cryptic, partial, and misleading, was tedious but educational. For all the adrenaline involved in kicking down doors to seize such documents and all the exciting press coverage that comes from chasing ships across the world's oceans in hopes of capturing their officers, the toughest and arguably the most important part of enforcing the law was the unglamorous process of building a prosecution.

After all, the real value in chasing the *Thunder* at sea was to capture the evidence needed for prosecuting its operators on land. Investigating crimes like money laundering, document fraud, and tax evasion—the ones that can land real jail time and hefty fines—takes painstaking diligence and resources. It's tough enough to make the public care about fish, much less fish laundering, which involves faking the fish's origin. It's harder still to get tax dollars dedicated to multinational investigations into ostensibly "bloodless" crimes that seem to matter only on paper.

Some of this forensic work was being done by two tireless Norwegian journalists, Eskil Engdal and Kjetil Sæter, who traveled repeatedly to Spain and half a dozen other countries in an impressive effort to map the corporate labyrinth surrounding the *Thunder*. They struggled, however, as did I, to establish with certainty who owned the ship.

And that was precisely the goal of this system. In good times, vessel owners, insurers, bankers, ship operators, fish buyers, flag registries, and even governments profit from rampant fish piracy on the high seas. In bad times, these actors were insulated from the liability and prying eyes of Interpol, union organizers, human rights advocates, and reporters.

. . .

By mid-February, the chase had stretched into its seventh week. More than four hundred miles directly below South Africa, the *Thunder* sat high in the water and low on fuel in heavy seas of the Indian Ocean. Then, on February 16, officers on the bridge of the *Bob Barker* noticed tall flames on the back of the *Thunder* throwing off thick black smoke. An oil slick trailed their ship.

Responding to a radio inquiry from Sea Shepherd, the *Thunder*'s officers claimed, unconvincingly, that it was just their kitchen and bathroom waste—boxes, wrappers, toilet paper, cigarette cartons, and the like. Burning such waste was legal. The flames burned continuously for two days, longer than usual for such fires on a ship of this size. Around the same time, the pile of nets stacked on the back of the *Thunder* began to shrink. Chakravarty speculated that the *Thunder* was disposing of evidence. He had good reason for this suspicion. When fishery agents from Indonesia and Australia boarded the *Thunder* in 2012, they were at first puzzled by the absence of fishing gear. They later discovered the captain had cut his nets into pieces and burned them inside a rusty oven on the stern deck.

Six days after Chakravarty saw the smoke on the *Thunder*, he put several of his crew in a skiff to make a delivery. The men carried a black trash bag with ten sixteen-ounce plastic bottles, their caps sealed shut with yellow tape and weighted with a handful of rice to make the bottles easier to throw. The bottles also contained copies of a note typed in Indonesian and English. Hammarstedt wanted to tell the

*Thunder*'s Indonesian crew that Sea Shepherd was on their side. The notes pointed out that because the crew were just following officers' orders, they would not be charged with any crimes themselves. "We have no intentions of putting you in trouble," the 450-word note said. "We should work together."

The goal was to make sure the *Thunder*'s officers were prosecuted for illegal fishing, Hammarstedt added in the note. If the Indonesians wanted to get word back to their families or ask for anything, they should just indicate that in their reply message and put it in the bottle to throw back when the Sea Shepherd skiff came near next time, Hammarstedt's note said. Information about the officers would be helpful if they could share that as well. "We have more fuel and food than the *Thunder* and will pursue the ship until harbor."

A *Thunder* officer, concealing his face, throws a chain at a small Sea Shepherd boat.

Pulling within range, Sea Shepherd's crew threw the bottles on board. Moments later, a man appeared on the *Thunder*'s upper deck wearing a black ski mask. He hurled a short length of chain that splashed into the water a couple inches from the skiff's twin outboard motors. Then a round metal tube, roughly the size of a roll of duct tape, came hurtling through the air, hitting one of Sea Shepherd's crew on his shoulder;

he was bruised but otherwise unharmed. Bottles delivered, mission accomplished, Hammarstedt ordered his crew to pull back.

. . .

Since its founding in 1977, Sea Shepherd had been viewed by the global fishing industry as unpredictable and prone to extremism. For almost as long, the organization's own leadership had described its mission as "coercive conservation" and referred to its members as "eco-warriors" in the fight to save the oceans.

And so it came as a surprise to many people when the *Atlas Cove,* a 223-foot fishing ship, showed up in the South Atlantic Ocean to support Sea Shepherd's campaign pursuing the *Thunder.* Appearing roughly a thousand miles west of Gabon on March 25, the *Atlas Cove's* captain, a New Zealander named Steve Paku, radioed the *Sam Simon* to ask if he might be allowed to fall into position alongside Sea Shepherd's ships as a gesture of solidarity. Hammarstedt replied that he was more than welcome.

The plans for this meeting, though, had been worked out quietly beforehand. In launching Operation Icefish, Sea Shepherd emphasized to the press that it was not opposed to fishing, just illegal fishing. This was not a distinction I had heard Sea Shepherd make before, and it struck me as part of the organization's newly emergent pragmatism. Motivated partly by the success of the Japanese legal pursuit to prosecute Paul Watson, board members within Sea Shepherd had come to believe that their organization needed to cultivate allies if it was to have true impact.

For months, Sea Shepherd had been in communication with an Australian company called Austral Fisheries that owned the *Atlas Cove* and a fleet of other toothfishing ships. Having tracked illegal toothfishing boats in the Antarctic for years, Austral Fisheries was delighted to see Sea Shepherd go after the poachers. As irked by the competition from these illegal ships as by the burden of having to follow the law when others didn't, Austral Fisheries began arming the eco-warriors with vital intelligence about who was doing what and where in the Antarctic waters.

After pulling alongside the *Sam Simon,* an engineer on the *Atlas Cove* began reading a message to the *Thunder* over the radio.

*Atlas Cove:* Your ship is one of those that continues to fish illegally

the engineer said, speaking in Spanish on behalf of his captain. He went on to explain that as part of the Coalition of Legal Toothfish Operators, the *Atlas Cove* had set a course to meet the *Bob Barker* and the *Sam Simon* and support their fight against illegal fishing activities, the engineer explained.

> *Atlas Cove:* The people behind you won't let you go passively . . . Their reputation speaks for itself.

> *Atlas Cove:* If you want to keep fishing in the Southern Ocean, do it through the right channels like everybody else does and become a responsible person . . . We have to take care of the little that is left in the seas because if we don't, there will be nothing left for our children, grandchildren, and great-grandchildren. Over.

As the engineer finished his speech, the *Thunder* made a sharp turn and aimed itself at the starboard side of the *Atlas Cove*. Hammarstedt warned Paku over the radio that he was about to be rammed, but Paku was already angling out of the way. The *Sam Simon* was on one side, the *Bob Barker* on the other, and the *Atlas Cove* directly in front. Cataldo then announced himself on the radio.

> *Thunder:* The *Thunder* is sailing in international waters under the Nigerian flag. And now you are three ships. What's the problem?
> *Sam Simon:* The problem is that you are fishing illegally, like our colleague has said, and we are trying to stop you.

The two men bickered further. Each side accused the other of intimidation and unsafe behavior. Both sides chest-thumped that they would not be cowed. The *Thunder* eventually went on its way, the radio falling silent. The *Atlas Cove* joined the Sea Shepherd ships in shadowing the *Thunder* for a couple more hours before bidding farewell and splitting off. Sea Shepherd quickly posted online a press release about the visit from the *Atlas Cove,* shaming countries for failing to help bring the *Thunder* to justice and leaving it to advocacy groups and fishing companies to enforce the laws of the ocean.

I couldn't help but wonder whether anyone in these governments actually read the press release. If they had, I figured, they likely either shrugged or merely concluded that because this was happening on the high seas, it was not their problem to fix.

. . .

By early April, over a hundred days since the chase began, and roughly around the time I joined Sea Shepherd, the *Thunder* seemed headed for Nigerian waters. Interpol officials and Sea Shepherd's crew believed that the *Thunder*'s owners had ordered its officers to stop fleeing. In March, Nigerian authorities had stripped the *Thunder* of its flag, but the Sea Shepherd crew speculated that perhaps the rogue ship hoped for leniency from maritime officials in Lagos if it docked there, because the ship previously flew Nigeria's flag.

There was, however, the outside chance that the *Thunder* was bound for Nigerian waters for other reasons. The country was home to a booming black market in stolen bunker fuel, which is the heavy residual oil burned by most seagoing ships. Nigeria also had an abundance of marine officials willing, for the right price, to help the *Thunder* escape by blocking Sea Shepherd's entry into national waters.

The U.S. State Department had sent a letter to the Nigerian government threatening sanctions for continuing to allow the *Thunder* to fly its flag, despite years of well-documented violations. I couldn't help but see this threat as empty. The United States has historically been reluctant to pursue other countries for labor or environmental violations for fear of impinging on trade opportunities or drawing attention to some of the United States' own questionable practices.

Interpol had also informed the Nigerian government that there was a simple way to end this chase: it should submit a formal request for the arrest of the ship. The South African Navy was ready, eager even, to board and detain the *Thunder* if only the Nigerians would give it the green light. But making such a request was risky for Nigeria because doing so would obligate it to investigate and prosecute the case, not something the government had the desire or resources to do.

As so often happens in such cases, Nigeria took the easier route. It simply off-loaded the problem to someone else, stripping the *Thunder* of its flag and turning the ship into a stateless vessel. Technically, this move authorized marine authorities from any country to board the *Thunder,* but on a practical level it also made that less likely to happen. "Why would they take on this headache and cost when no one even requested their help?" the South Africans asked.

In failing to force the *Thunder* to return to port for inspection, and declining to request help from the Australian military, Nigeria released what loose grip it might have had on the scofflaw ship. It was the clearest example I could find of the so-called tragedy of the commons, or the idea that something owned by everyone is more likely to be neglected than it is to be protected. That Nigeria so readily relinquished its duty as a flag registry is an example of all that is flawed with the modern way that ships are flagged.

For centuries, the world's merchant and fishing fleets flew the flag of the country of their home port. That country was responsible for ensuring the proper treatment of the crew and safety of the vessel. This began to change in the early twentieth century with the emergence of "open registries," also called "flags of convenience." After World War I, the United States had a glut of ships, and it sold many of them to Panama. Often, American businessmen still intended to operate the ships but wanted to do so remotely and with the advantage of fewer burdensome regulations.

Prohibition also drove the shift toward flags of convenience as passenger ships sought to circumvent a U.S. court ruling that American ships could not serve alcohol, even in international waters. In the run-up to World War II, the United States re-flagged more of its merchant ships to Panama in hopes of providing Britain with goods and materials without dragging America into the war or violating the Neutrality Act.

Today, many countries, including landlocked ones such as Mongolia and Bolivia, sell the right to fly their flag. Some of the biggest registries are run by overseas businesses, like the Liberian registry that is overseen by a firm based in Virginia. The company collecting fees for the right to fly a certain flag is also responsible for policing its customers, ensuring they abide by safety, labor, and environmental rules, and conducting investigations when things go wrong. But in practice, flags of convenience double as cloaks of misconduct, creating a perverse incentive for ship operators to shop around for the most lax registries with the lowest prices and fewest regulations. This regulatory regime was quite decidedly designed not to provide true oversight but to provide the illusion of oversight. And the way it functions is akin to being allowed to slap a license plate from any country on your car, regardless of where you live or intend to drive, and the police in charge of inspecting the vehicles and investigating accidents are paid by the drivers themselves.

After more than three months in pursuit of the *Thunder,* the mood on both Sea Shepherd ships was a mix of boredom, fear, and anticipation. The news that Nigeria had de-flagged the *Thunder* served as further proof that the ship was viewed as a pariah, but it also showed how broken the rules were, and it highlighted that Sea Shepherd was on its own in this fight.

The Gulf of Guinea near Nigeria was famously treacherous, prowled by hundreds of well-armed pirates. The *Bob Barker* and the *Sam Simon* were running round-the-clock watches in case of an attack. Both crews had readied their water cannons, butyric acid (stink bombs), and "prop-foulers"—thick dragging ropes thrown into the sea and meant to tangle outboard propellers.

Every couple of days, Sea Shepherd's crew had shuttled Kove-Seyram and me in a skiff between their two vessels so that we could see what was happening in both places. Moving across ships at sea, which typically took fifteen minutes, was risky, especially between large, high-sided ships like the *Bob Barker* and the *Sam Simon.*

Getting into the skiff involved climbing down several stories on a rope ladder. But then the real challenge started. Because the skiff was so much smaller than the ship and bobbed on the heavy waves, we had to time our jump into the skiff as if we were trying to leap into a fast-moving elevator. Plus the ships were usually not stationary, but in five-knots forward motion because the *Sam Simon* and the *Bob Barker* could not afford to stop while making these transfers, lest they risk losing sight of the *Thunder.* Neither of us was tethered because a rope tied to us was even more dangerous. We were warned that if we fell overboard during one of these transfers, our top concern should be to avoid getting crushed between or trapped under the two boats. How to do that was utterly unclear.

During the first of these transfers, Kove-Seyram stood at the railing, put on a helmet, then, pausing, put his hand on my shoulder. "Ian," he said, "I just want to thank you for bringing me. This is an incredible experience." We'd been up a full thirty hours, and both of us were deeply exhausted, so I was especially touched. Then he climbed over the railing, hanging on with one hand to the first plank of the fraying wooden ladder that swung over a wild sea. "Also, Ian," he added, before beginning his long, treacherous descent, "I don't know how to swim." Over our ten days offshore, we would make this transfer half a dozen times, and though my skills improved, it never felt anything less than deadly perilous.

I had worked hard to prove to the Sea Shepherd crew, most of whom were ten to twenty years younger than me, that I was fluent in maritime norms, decently fit, and generally able to keep up with their grueling fifteen-hour workdays. The ladder climbing scared me not just because I was usually carrying lots of expensive equipment (a drone, my GoPro camera kit, some of Kove-Seyram's high-end zoom lenses), and not just because the fall could well be fatal, but also because I desperately did not want to embarrass myself in front of these young people who seemed always to view me skeptically as an outsider.

Days on the Sea Shepherd ships were regimented: mandatory 7:00 a.m. meetings, chores for everyone (Kove-Seyram and I cleaned bathrooms), one shower per day limited to under three minutes to conserve water. To avoid disclosures like our location or direction that might make our ships more susceptible to pirate attacks, an onboard officer inspected all outgoing emails sent by the crew by reviewing them from the ships' central server. (My communications were exempt from scrutiny because I used my own satellite phone.)

We were a bit like castaways stuck on a lonely island, creating our own rituals and rules. Alcohol and cigarettes were prohibited. Voluntary group exercise started daily at 4:00 p.m. on the middle deck, where there was a training area stocked with a stationary bike, rowing machine, treadmill, free weights, and pull-up and dip bars. A weekly calisthenics-heavy workout routine was posted on the bulletin board each Sunday night. Painfully sore in my core on my second day on board, I learned quickly not to underestimate how much more grueling burpees are when done on a seesawing ship.

At night, there was a book club. They read *In Patagonia* by Bruce Chatwin and *The Happy Isles of Oceania* by Paul Theroux. They also watched movies—*The Secret Life of Walter Mitty, Mad Max: Beyond Thunderdome,* and *The Perfect Storm,* the third of which felt to me like a busman's holiday, hardly the distraction I would have chosen given our setting. The lounge was stocked with a wide variety of musical instruments—acoustic and electric guitars, traditional drums, a clarinet, a keyboard—and many of the crew were talented musicians. So jam sessions were a treat.

Some of the crew of the *Sam Simon* hold a staff meeting in the mess hall.

Though the Sea Shepherd crew was a diverse bunch—nine nationalities, and two dozen languages were spoken—virtually all of them were college educated and between the ages of twenty and thirty-five. Meetings and other work were conducted in English. About half the staff were women, a rare ratio in maritime work, which is overwhelmingly male. From what I could tell, the ships upheld a fairly egalitarian ethic, with females doing all the same jobs and holding the same ranks as males. Romantic relationships among crew were not forbidden, but they were expected to remain unobtrusive, especially if they involved pairing across ranks.

I spent most of my time on the *Sam Simon*'s bridge with Chakravarty. Behind him hung a laminated poster, with red letters across the top that said, WANTED—ROGUE TOOTHFISH POACHING VESSELS—THE "BANDIT 6." Underneath were photographs of the six vessels: *Thunder, Viking, Kunlun, Yongding, Songhua,* and *Perlon.* Chakravarty told me about growing up in Bhopal, India, and about the decade he spent working on chemical tankers, climbing his way up the ranks to captaincy before joining Sea Shepherd in 2011.

Thirty-two years old, he was a small man with a commanding presence and an unflappably gentle demeanor. At one point, I clumsily knocked a full mug of hot coffee onto his open laptop, soaking its motherboard. Most of Chakravarty's notes about the *Thunder* were stored on the computer. He quietly stood up, scalding brew running off his lap, and turned the laptop over, hoping to drain the liquid. "It's okay," he said. "I've got a good memory of my notes." I sensed that his calm, generous reaction was partly instinctual but also concentrated and decided, like an extension of a personal agenda. As is true of many adventurers, and many of the direct-action conservationists I met, Chakravarty seemed to be on an inward quest as much as an outward one.

This pointed to a commonly held misconception about these advocates. They were often dismissed as dreadlocked, pierced, and tattooed kids and portrayed as undisciplined and naïve escapists fleeing personal responsibility, the "real world," and nine-to-five jobs. Mostly, that was false, especially the nine-to-five part because, in fact, they worked even longer days at sea. Both the crews on the Sea Shepherd ships and those on the Greenpeace vessels I'd cover later were driven people, type A even, just that their goals were not traditional résumé fodder. Aside from their ocean campaigns, many of them were on self-improvement missions. Complain less, focus better, actually listen, be more present. "It's a daily reminder to be thankful that I have this job," one deckhand told me when I asked why he always signed up for bathroom-cleaning duty. "If I'm going to have these politics, I need to think through the unintended consequences," another told me when I asked her why she was reading what looked like a deeply boring book about global food policy.

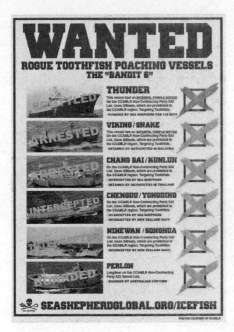

The *Thunder* was just one of the vessels that Sea Shepherd pursued during its Operation Icefish.

. . .

Around 7:00 p.m. on April 5, officers on the *Bob Barker* noticed strange behavior on the back deck of the *Thunder.* Men, some wearing orange vests, were hustling around the ship in the darkness. "Flashlights in motion and uncommon deck lights on" is what the *Bob Barker*'s logbook said of the scene. Early the next morning, one of the *Thunder*'s crewmen threw a rope ladder over the side as if preparing to leave, which indeed they were. Then came a distress call.

"Assistance required, assistance required," Cataldo said over the radio. "We're sinking." The *Thunder* had collided with something, he said, possibly a cargo ship. "We need help," he added, estimating that his ship would sink in fifteen minutes.

It was an implausible claim. Aside from the Sea Shepherd vessels, no other ships had been anywhere near the *Thunder* for days. Hammarstedt alerted Chakravarty, who was roughly three hours away, having made a detour to drop off a crew member in port. Chakravarty turned around and raced the *Sam Simon* toward the scene. The *Thunder*'s crew lowered several lifeboats into the water and climbed into them. One man slipped and fell into the water, then heaved himself back into the boat.

I had left the *Sam Simon* only a couple days earlier. Still making my way back home, I'd gotten as far as Accra's airport when I received a phone call from one of the Sea Shepherd crew. "You're not going to believe this," the deckhand said. "The *Thunder* is sinking right in front of me." Aside from the shock at the news, I was overwhelmed with a searing annoyance to be missing the event. Completely irrationally, I remember looking up for a couple of moments at the airport's flight board to see if there was any way I could fly to a nearer port and get back out to the Sea Shepherd ship.

Hammarstedt and Chakravarty decided that the more spacious *Sam Simon,* once it arrived at the scene, would take the *Thunder's* crew on board. Chakravarty called a meeting on his bridge. "We're outnumbered two to one," he warned. "This is very dangerous for us." He instructed everyone to change out of shorts and T-shirts and into "proper attire," which meant black work pants and black shirts with the Sea Shepherd logo. No horseplay and no chitchat, Chakravarty emphasized. The guests were only allowed to visit the bathroom if escorted. There would be two-man watches from the upper deck at all times. Apologizing to his female staff, Chakravarty explained that for safety reasons in case things turned physically violent, only men would guard the *Thunder's* crew. No one was to ask any questions related to fishing. "This is strictly a rescue operation now," he said.

By late morning on April 6, roughly seven hours after making its distress call, the *Thunder* still had not sunk, though it was listing perilously to the starboard side and steadily taking on water. The *Thunder's* crew had been floating in lifeboats under the hot sun for over three hours. Several had thrown up from the swaying because the swells were more than eight feet tall. Cataldo was refusing to leave his ship. Hammarstedt told him that he would not remove anyone from the lifeboats until the entire crew had exited the *Thunder.* Hammarstedt was suspicious that Cataldo might have called for a ride from a smaller, faster local boat and could still try to make a run for it while the *Bob Barker* was pulling the other men from the lifeboats.

Several Sea Shepherd crew members were standing by in skiffs alongside the tilting *Thunder,* hoping to get on board before it went down so they could collect evidence. At 12:46, Cataldo finally climbed down the rope ladder into a lifeboat on one side of the *Thunder,* and a Sea Shepherd engineer and a photographer scrambled up another on the far end of the ship.

"I'm giving you ten minutes," Hammarstedt told the two Sea Shepherd crew climbing onto the half-submerged *Thunder.* They took thirty-seven. As the ship listed starboard at a twenty-degree angle, the men wended their way into its bowels, hustling from cabin to cabin, engine room to bridge, checking for any additional crew. In the galley, a chicken sat defrosting on the counter. In a hall, there were socks and shirts that someone had dropped on his way out. On the bridge, papers were strewn across the floor.

Several minutes later, the photographer appeared on the deck with a garbage bag carrying a camera, a cell phone, and papers from the *Thunder*'s wheelhouse. He tossed it down to his colleagues waiting in the skiff below. In a drawer on the bridge, the photographer had also found pictures of the crew of the *Bob Barker* pulled from the Sea Shepherd website. He threw them to the skiff along with several maps and charts. One of the charts fluttered into the water.

The *Thunder* was sinking faster, and Hammarstedt, pacing back and forth on the bridge, worried that if his men lingered too long below deck, the inward rush of water and downward suction of the ship would trap them inside. The Sea Shepherd photographer running around the *Thunder* had a GoPro strapped to his helmet. The bumpy, dark footage that we watched later showed the ship's engine room almost completely filled with murky water. Its fishing hold was about a quarter full with toothfish.

Certain clues hinted that the *Thunder* was scuttled intentionally. The ship's airtight doors were tied ajar. Valves were opened to flood the engine room. There were no telltale signs—like upended shelves or burst pipes—that suggested the *Thunder* had collided with another ship. With only a day or so more fuel left in it, the *Thunder*'s fuel tank offered the most likely explanation for why Cataldo had finally stopped running.

Boarding the *Thunder* while it sank was an incredibly dangerous move. When I later interviewed one of Sea Shepherd's deckhands about the decision, I must have had a tone of disapproval until he turned the tables on me. "Ian, are you telling me that had you still been on the ship with us, you wouldn't have climbed onto the *Thunder*? You would pass up the chance to see what we chased for so long?" He had a point.

As the *Thunder*'s crew climbed onto the *Sam Simon,* the Sea Shepherd staff patted them down for weapons, took their cigarette lighters, gave them water and fruits, and sat them down together on the back deck. The *Thunder*'s officers were surly and untalkative. Cataldo balked at handing over the crew's passports, but they were soon discovered stashed in one of the men's belongings. Chakravarty alerted the nearest port officials in São Tomé, a small island nation about 160 miles west of Gabon. Police and Interpol officials in São Tomé responded that they would be standing by for their arrival. *"¡Estúpido!"* yelled one of the *Thunder*'s officers as he lunged at the Sea Shepherd photographer taking pictures of the men.

Wearing dark sunglasses, a blue baseball cap with gold-embroidered dragons, and a green Heineken T-shirt, Cataldo was a short man with a closely cropped black beard and a pinched look on his face. He complained to Chakravarty that he did not want to be photographed. Chakravarty, who was wearing a microphone under his shirt to document everything, ignored his complaints. Instead, Chakravarty continued instructing Cataldo of the ground rules on board the Sea Shepherd ship. "Why are you speaking to me this way?" Cataldo said with annoyance. "We are both captains, and we should be speaking to each other as equals." Adding that he should not have to wait on the outside deck during their trip along with his men, Cataldo said that he planned to file a formal complaint with international maritime authorities about his treatment. "Be my guest," Chakravarty replied.

When the *Thunder* finally went down, Cataldo cheered. It was an odd reaction that reinforced the suspicion that he had sabotaged the ship. In all likelihood, the owners of the *Thunder* would be content for the ship to go down too, because it was out of fuel and likely to have

On April 6, 2015, the *Thunder* suddenly sank near the coast of São Tomé and Príncipe in what was widely believed to be an effort by its captain to scuttle the ship on purpose to dispose of evidence of his crimes.

soon been confiscated with incriminating evidence on board. Half an hour later, Cataldo climbed onto a five-foot-high stack of his confiscated nets at the back of the *Sam Simon*. He stretched out and went to sleep. A couple of hours later, Cataldo and the rest of his crew were awoken and taken into custody, two miles from shore, by police and navy officers wearing combat fatigues.

. . .

Over the next six months, the Indonesian crew was flown home. Cataldo and the ship's chief engineer and second mechanic were tried and convicted of forgery, pollution, damage to the environment, and recklessness. They were collectively fined over $17 million but mysteriously released, even though their appeal failed in court.

Meanwhile, in Spain, the prosecution of Vidal Armadores, the company that many suspected was tied to the *Thunder*, fell flat. The Supreme Court ruled that because the illegal fishing had occurred in international waters, the Spanish government did not have jurisdiction to prosecute. But a separate civil case brought by the Spanish government against Florindo González Corral for his ties to the *Thunder* and its illegal fishing proved successful, and the courts levied a $10 million fine.

On one matter there can be no argument: the campaign was a victory for Sea Shepherd. "This is what we fight for," Hammarstedt said, when I asked him later about the $10 million fine. Sea Shepherd had put the *Thunder* out of business. The organization was the main reason the culprits faced jail time. Would the impact last? Would the case send a message to other poachers? I had my doubts. Such messages rarely traveled far across oceans. The economic draw for poachers was as powerful as the laws and regulators were muddled. Still, there was no denying that the case of the *Thunder* had drawn global attention to a widely overlooked problem.

After some time off, Chakravarty left Sea Shepherd to start his own conservation organization called Enforceable Oceans. Hammarstedt went to Gabon to help that country patrol its waters against illegal fishing. Many of the officers from the *Sam Simon* and the *Bob Barker* soon returned to the Southern Ocean. This time, they would chase the world's last industrial-scale whaling ship. The international court had recently banned the Japanese ship from whaling in the Antarctic, but no one was enforcing the ruling. It seemed like a perfect opportunity for Sea Shepherd to get involved. So, after restocking and recreating, Neptune's Navy set back out for the Southern Ocean.

# THE LONE PATROL

Boundless and imperishable, the cosmic waters are at once the immaculate source of all things and the dreadful grave.

——Heinrich Zimmer, *Myths and Symbols in Indian Art and Civilization*

There's no shortage of laws governing the seas. The real problem is lax enforcement. After all, there is a cold calculus about pursuing ocean-bound territorial battles that is markedly different from land. While some countries will fight over inches of dirt on either side of a border, ocean boundaries are less clear, which makes chasing poachers seemingly futile.

This is why one of every five fish on dinner plates is caught illegally and the global black market for seafood is worth more than $20 billion. Most of the world's fish stocks are in crisis from overfishing. By 2050, some studies predict, there will be more plastic waste in the sea than fish, measured in weight. The oceans are despoiled and depleted because most governments have neither the inclination nor the resources to protect them. It is hard enough to get the public's attention about the dangers of global warming, even as the effects of it become clear, including hotter temperatures, rising seas, and more severe storms. But dwindling fish stocks? They hardly register.

Starting in 2006, however, Palau began charting a different course, vowing to chase and arrest the flotilla of illegal Chinese, Vietnamese, and other foreign ships raiding its waters. This promised to be a difficult fight. A relatively poor country with no military of its own, Palau had eighteen police officers assigned to patrol its waters. They were

Palauan marine police board and arrest a Vietnamese boat engaged in illegal fishing in 2015.

equipped with just one patrol boat, the *Remeliik,* responsible for guarding an offshore area the size of France.

Did they stand a chance? A glimpse of an answer was offered around 2:00 a.m. on January 21, 2015, in a one-story office building in West Virginia. As he pounded out another email, Bjorn Bergman, a researcher from an environmental group called SkyTruth, was washing down what was left of his salmon and swiss on an onion bagel with his sixth coffee of the day.

"Try and cut them off rather than making for the last known position," Bergman wrote. Nearly nine thousand miles away, the *Remeliik* was chasing a ten-man Taiwanese pirate fishing ship, the *Shin Jyi Chyuu 33.* Bergman's job was to advise the Palauan skipper on the fastest course to pursue the ship. "It may be advisable for the Remeliik to turn southeast," he wrote.

The *Shin Jyi Chyuu 33* crew had raided several local fisheries and was fleeing to Indonesian waters, beyond Palau's jurisdiction. If the poachers made it to the Celebes or Banda Seas, they could easily unload their catch and disappear amid the thousands of small Filipino or Indonesian islands on that side of the western Pacific Ocean. To intercept them, the *Remeliik*'s skipper was pushing twenty knots, the ship's maximum speed, a pace that worried its engineer. In the previous six months, Palauan police had spotted but failed to catch nearly a dozen other pirate fishing ships. As Bergman watched his computer screen, the *Remeliik*'s officers knew that if they miscalculated their heading by even a small fraction, they would miss their target and likely run out of fuel.

Bergman had tipped off the Palauans about the suspected poachers two days earlier. Before moving to Shepherdstown, West Virginia, to become a data analyst for SkyTruth in 2014, Bergman, who was thirty-four at the time, worked in Alaska for three years as a marine observer on pot boats, long-liners, and trawlers that were catching king crab, cod, and pollack. His job was to maintain ship logs, detailing catch size, location, and gear—enforcement data required of fishing companies by federal and state fishery authorities. At SkyTruth, Bergman's policing work moved to a much higher altitude, monitoring boats around the world from space. Though sitting behind a desk was certainly less adventurous, Bergman told me he was ready to have a bigger impact on the problems he witnessed firsthand.

For months, Bergman had been studying the satellite feed from above Palau. He knew the squiggles and slashes of traffic patterns by memory: A passenger boat out of Pitcairn Island appeared every few weeks; a U.S. Navy ship from Diego Garcia conducted regular maneuvers nearby; a Chinese research vessel was doing a survey of some sort in a grid pattern; a Taiwanese ship that never seemed to stop to fish made repeated trips out to meet other long-liners. I couldn't keep up with his analysis, but he knew the movement grids and recognized when something was askew. And something was askew with the *Shin Jyi Chyuu 33*. Though it had no license to fish in Palau's waters, its zigzag suggested it was doing just that.

After Bergman made the call advising the men on the *Remeliik* where to go, an unlikely international team gathered in the cramped police command center at the Malakal Harbor in Koror, Palau's most populous island. The group included three local police officers, an American-educated political consultant, and two Australian naval officers on loan to Palau to advise on everything from running the *Remeliik* (which the Australians also donated) to using new fishery and satellite software. An officer from the U.S. Coast Guard base in Guam was also on the line with an offer to help with air support. Working through the night, the team radioed the information they received from West Virginia to Allison Baiei, a Palauan marine police officer who was on board the *Remeliik,* named after Haruo Ignacio Remeliik, Palau's first president.

The bustle of Palau's dockside command center that day offered a window on the ad hoc collaboration between countries, companies, and nongovernmental organizations that will probably be necessary to save the world's oceans. Palau had also emerged as a testing ground for some of the technology—including drones, satellite monitoring, and military-grade radars and cameras used in Iraq and Afghanistan—that might finally empower countries to spot and arrest the pirates, poachers, polluters, traffickers, and other scofflaws who prowl the seas with impunity.

After a fifty-one-hour push, much of it through heavy seas, the *Remeliik*'s unrelenting pace paid off; its crew caught up with the Taiwanese ship less than a dozen miles before it would have escaped into Indonesian waters. The poacher ship surrendered without a struggle, and the Palauan officers escorted it back to port, before opening the hold. Baiei could hardly believe his eyes. Inside, among the stacks of tuna, were hundreds of shark fins—so many, in fact, that when the Palauan officers ran out of space stacking them on the *Shin Jyi*'s deck, they piled them in a bloody heap on the dock. "Disgusting" was all Baiei would say about seeing so much carnage of an animal that is legally protected and culturally revered in Palau. After counting, measuring, and photographing the shark fins for prosecutors, the officers dumped them into the sea.

For Baiei and the other officers, the capture of the *Shin Jyi* was proof that they could win their David-and-Goliath fight. After confiscating the rest of its catch, the police sent the poacher ship and its crew back to Taiwan several months later. They banned the ship's owners from returning to Palau's territorial waters and fined them $100,000. The amount, which was determined by a Palauan judge, was high compared with typical penalties but minuscule relative to what larger fishing companies earn in annual profits. Still, in principle, for the Palauan marine officers who'd put their lives on the line, the fine was a victory.

"It was a good day," Baiei said. "We just need more of those."

· · ·

There was something invigorating to me about Palau's determination, and I went there hoping to see what it looked like in practice. But, truth be told, I also expected to witness an exercise in futility. In prior reporting, I had seen how difficult it was for a powerful country like Indonesia, with a veritable armada of marine police ships, to effectively police its waters. How could a tiny nation like Palau, with just one boat, possibly manage?

As my twenty-two-hour flight from Washington, D.C., descended over the turquoise waters before touching down in the capital, Ngerulmud, I marveled at the isolation of this place. It was a tiny speck of a nation insulated by ocean like few other locations on the planet. This remoteness, it seemed to me, was both its attraction and its Achilles' heel.

Situated in the western Pacific Ocean about six hundred miles east of the Philippines and five hundred miles north of New Guinea, Palau's twenty-one thousand residents are scattered across this archipelago nation's more than 250 islands. By landmass and population, it is one of the world's smallest countries. But Palau's islands are spread out, and under international law a country's exclusive economic zone, or the waters where it maintains authority, extend 200 nautical miles from its coasts. This means that while Palau consists of only about 177 square miles of land (roughly the size of New York City), its sovereignty extends across 230,000 square miles of wide-open seas (nearly the size of Texas). These are rich fishing grounds, attractive to poachers. It is also home to various types of tuna, including the Pacific bluefin, just one of which can sell for over $1 million, and Chinese delicacies like sea cucumbers, which sell in restaurants for over $150 a plate.

Though remote, Palau is still cursed by its location, bordered by some of the world's largest fishing fleets and most insatiable fish markets—Japan, China, and Taiwan to its northwest, Indonesia to the southwest. And despite its stunning natural beauty, Palau is enmeshed in the larger dystopian seascape of the western Pacific Ocean. The region is teeming with super trawlers, state-subsidized poacher fleets, mile-long drift nets, and predator buoys and is being battered by mega cyclones, ocean acidification, rising sea levels, warming marine temperatures, and a Texas-sized gyre of floating trash. By any measure, the nation of Palau was dealt as tough a hand as anyone could imagine.

Palau's president, Tommy Remengesau Jr., is a sturdy man with an intense stare who clasps your shoulder while shaking your hand firmly. We met in his cluttered, wood-paneled office in Palau's capital. He explained that Palau's economic survival depended on marine conservation. More than half of its gross domestic product comes from tourism—mostly people visiting to dive on Palau's reefs, home to more coral fish and other invertebrates per square mile than almost anywhere else on earth.

One of Palau's biggest draws for tourist divers is its shark population. When I asked for Remengesau's reaction to the hundreds of shark fins found in the hold of the *Shin Jyi,* he immediately launched into an explanation of the economic impact of killing sharks. Alive, an individual shark is worth over $170,000 annually in tourism dollars, or nearly $2 million over its lifetime, he said. Dead, each sells for $100, and usually that money goes to a foreign poacher. Even if his numbers seemed a bit overstated, there was no doubting the financial consequences of killing the sharks.

More than a dozen countries, including Palau and Taiwan, had banned shark finning. But demand for the fins, especially in Asia, remained high. Served at Chinese weddings and other official banquets, shark-fin soup, which can sell for over $100 per bowl, has for centuries signified wealth. The delicacy became especially popular in the late 1980s as a status symbol for the rapidly growing middle and upper classes in China. To make the soup, the fins, which are cartilage, are ground into translucent noodles. Adding more texture than nutrition or flavor, they are believed to have aphrodisiac and anti-aging effects.

Catching sharks is not easy, nor is it usually inadvertent. In longline fishing, the ship uses a longline made of thick microfilament, with baited hooks attached at intervals. Many tuna long-liners, like the *Shin Jyi Chyuu 33,* directly target sharks, using special steel leads, designed not to break as the bigger, stronger sharks try to yank themselves free.

To offset poverty wages, ship captains typically allow their crews to supplement their income by keeping the fins to sell at port. The bodies of the sharks take up valuable space in the hold of smaller ships. When they decompose, the carcasses produce ammonia that contaminates the other catch. I'd encountered this pungent odor before on a fishing ship in the Philippines that had a stack of the carcasses in its hold, and it smelled like cat urine.

To avoid wasting space and contaminating more valuable catch, deckhands usually throw the rest of the shark back into the water after they cut off the fins, which can sell for a hundred times the cost of the rest of the meat. It is a slow death: the sharks, alive but unable to swim without their fins, sink to the seafloor, where they starve, drown, or are slowly eaten by other fish. Scientists estimate that more than ninety million sharks are killed every year for their fins. By 2017, roughly a third of all shark species were nearing extinction.

Sharks are keystone species: a reduction in their population can collapse an entire food web all the way down to reef habitats. Without the apex predator, too many smaller fish survive and eat too many of the microorganisms that sustain the reefs. Enforcing rules against shark poaching doesn't just protect the sharks; it gives the reefs a fighting chance at survival.

A stern man not prone to sentimentality, Remengesau said he was motivated less by the desire to protect animals than by a commitment to defend his nation's economic sovereignty. He was also sober about his odds. Holding up a regional map, he pointed to where most of the poaching occurred. "Small land, big ocean," he said about the vast area surrounding the thin necklace of islands that made up his country.

No nation has been more aggressive in marine conservation than Palau. In 2006, it was among the first countries to ban the destructive practice of bottom trawling, which involves dragging large weighted nets across the ocean floor to catch the fish at those depths. The nets indiscriminately kill virtually everything in their path. In 2009, Palau created the world's first shark sanctuary, prohibiting commercial shark fishing in its waters. In 2015, Palau announced plans to put observers on board all tuna long-liner ships licensed to fish in its waters. Most other countries in the world require observers on less than 10 percent of licensed vessels. Palau's most aggressive move, though, was creating a "no-take" reserve in 2015, banning export fishing, drilling, and mining over an area of 193,000 square miles.

In 2012, Palau partnered with Greenpeace, which sent a large ship to help patrol nearby waters for several months. Palau claims to be the first nation to launch a campaign on Indiegogo, a crowdfunding platform, that by 2014 raised more than $50,000 (enough to cover the *Remeliik*'s fuel expenses for roughly a year) in small, private donations to help the country police its waters. Palau had even started talking to the private security company formerly called Blackwater, which had offered its policing services, though the talks eventually broke down.

As we sat in his office, Remengesau listed what he needed to gain control over his waters. There would have to be more thorough port inspections, he said. Fishing ships would need to pay for better locational transponders that ping more often and cannot be turned off so that they can be monitored continually and in real time. After a long pause, Remengesau added that the most important factor would be more police and more arrests. Without those, he said, Palau's reserve would be just lines drawn on the water. I wondered if even his entire wish list would be enough.

I needed Remengesau's permission to go to sea with the *Remeliik*. I explained to him that I wanted to understand what exactly makes this policing work so difficult and who are the foreign fishermen that travel so far to work in Palau's waters. One of Remengesau's aides had warned me that these marine patrols were not fun. "Boredom and misery," he said, describing what the Palauan officers typically encounter at sea. "And sometimes violence." I knew boredom at sea already from prior reporting. But I wanted to understand the misery and violence.

"Of course you can go with them," Remengesau said without hesitation, likely seeing publicity as a possible path to increased foreign funding of his efforts. As I left his office, I heard him mutter something about being merely glad that anyone cared about "a place so far away."

. . .

Baiei was assigned to be my liaison on board the *Remeliik*. Barrel-chested and short, he was Eagle Scout earnest and deeply knowledgeable about crimes at sea, after working as a marine police officer for nearly a decade. On my drive back to my hotel, I called my photographer, Ben Lowy, on his cell to tell him that we'd be leaving soon. We embarked the next morning at 4:30.

As a general rule, I knew it best to keep quiet when first arriving as a visitor at a place where visitors rarely get invited. So, for the first several hours on board the *Remeliik,* I did not ask any questions, move around much, or do anything else to draw notice. I simply tried to sit as still and wordless as the Palauans.

Cutting through ten-foot swells, the *Remeliik* headed first from the harbor in Koror to an area popular among poachers near Kayangel, an atoll in the country's far north. The trip took over nine hours, during most of which the Palauan officers on the *Remeliik*'s bridge stared silently through the front windshield. As is customary for many Palauans, the men were chewing what they call betel nut, which is actually a mix of areca nut wrapped in betel leaf with lime, piper leaf, and tobacco. Each man had his own empty soda bottle. And every couple minutes he spat the chalky red saliva that had accumulated in his mouth. Stuck between the lip and the gum, the betel nut served as a mild stimulant, causing a warming sensation in the body and slightly heightened alertness.

At one point, I gestured with a curious look at an officer as he pre-pared his chew, and he extended his hand offering me to try some. The other officers looked on. Everyone understood that the offering was as much a playful dare as a polite gesture. Of course, I took the bait, mimicked what I'd seen the others do, and stuck a small clump into my mouth.

The men grinned widely in surprise. The taste was peppery, and I immediately got light-headed. After ten minutes of toughing it out, I slipped off the bridge to the bathroom, where I promptly vomited. I thought I'd been quiet in so doing, but when I returned pale and sweaty to the bridge, the officers burst into laughter as several patted me on the back. It was theorized later that I'd taken too much or had possibly swallowed some, which you're not supposed to do. Either way,

Sleeping quarters aboard the Palauan patrol ship, the *Remeliik*

my self-imposed initiation was complete, and the officers seemed to loosen up with me after that.

We arrived at Kayangel late in the day. A tiny, rugged fleck of land, roughly half a square mile around, the island was truly a world apart: a frontier outpost on the outermost edge of this archipelago nation. It had no airstrip, no boats that could make it to the capital, and, most of the time, no power or cell service.

When we arrived, we met Bob Johnson, a Palauan who works as a Fish & Wildlife Protection ranger, based on the island there full-time. A burly man who clearly preferred keeping his own company rather than meeting strangers, Johnson explained that policing the area had become tougher as the atoll's population dwindled, which meant fewer people to spot and report poachers. The reason people were leaving? "The storms," said Johnson. He estimated there were fewer than two dozen residents left. As abruptly as he had appeared, Johnson disappeared. I had hoped to ask him more questions, but once he saw we had no supplies to offer, he was gone.

Typhoon Bopha had leveled Kayangel in December 2012, driving away its several hundred residents and ravaging its nearby coral reefs. Eleven months later, Typhoon Haiyan hit. With winds over 170 miles per hour, these Category 5 storms were among the strongest tropical cyclones ever recorded.

Most scientists agree that climate change is the reason for increasingly intense storms. A 2014 study that modeled the economic consequences of climate change on fisheries in the territorial waters of sixty-seven countries predicted that Palau would be hit harder than any other nation. Another study from 2014 estimated that Palau would lose a quarter of its potential fisheries catch by 2050 from climate change alone.

"I guess we can't arrest the climate," Baiei said as we circled Kayangel in the *Remeliik*. "We can just arrest people, the illegals, who come here to take our fish." After a long silence, another officer muttered something in Palauan that was later translated for me: "Easier said than done."

Baiei agreed and explained that the turning point for Palau—the moment when much of the country realized it needed more and better policing—came in March 2012. The mere mention of the date prompted groans from other officers on the bridge.

Baiei explained. Over a stretch of several days, two Chinese poacher boats had been spotted near Kayangel, but they kept escaping because they were equipped with three 60-horsepower outboard motors. The local Palauan Fish & Wildlife rangers, with only one outboard motor on their inflatable boat, knew that chasing them was futile.

The third time that the Palauan rangers saw one of the Chinese speedboats, around 7:00 a.m. on March 31, they managed to get close enough to try to shoot out its engines. But several of their bullets hit a Chinese deckhand, Lu Yong, in the right shoulder, abdomen, and right thigh. (Palauan police say they were not aiming for him and that the bullets ricocheted off an outboard motor.) Several of the officers took a smaller speedboat and rushed Yong to an island twenty-five minutes away where a nurse lived. Yong, who was thirty-five, bled to death, leaving behind a nine-year-old son and a three-year-old daughter in mainland China.

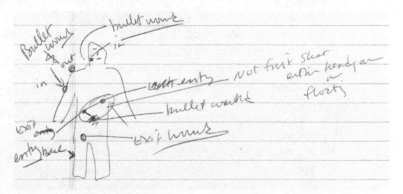

With entrance and exit wounds labeled, a police sketch of Lu Yong, a Chinese deckhand who was killed by Palauan police during a chase

The officers who remained on the *Remeliik* boarded the poachers' speedboat and interrogated the rest of the crew. The Palauan rangers soon learned that there was a larger "mother ship" parked farther out at sea, orchestrating the poaching raids. Two Palauan policemen and an American pilot were dispatched in a rented single-engine Cessna to help search. As night fell, though, the pilot got lost, and the plane vanished from radar.

Others searched by boat for the mother ship. About thirty-five nautical miles from shore, the Palauans finally discovered the eighty-foot vessel, which immediately bolted, ignoring warning shots fired across its bow. After several hours of running, the ship suddenly stopped, engulfed in flames. Its crew scrambled into a lifeboat just before the ship sank, taking evidence of its crimes down with it.

While the Cessna was still lost and wandering somewhere above the watery expanse surrounding Palau, authorities on land tried a Hail Mary. They figured that if they could illuminate the islands brightly enough, the Cessna might just see them and find its way back home. The public safety director ordered all emergency vehicles to drive to the highest points in Koror, the country's most populous island, and turn on their flashing lights. An official in Angaur, an island on the nation's southern tip, even suggested setting some of the outer-atoll wooded areas on fire—an idea that was quickly dismissed. "Aim spotlights upward," yachters were instructed. The stadium lights at Palau's Asahi baseball field were switched on. Residents were asked to turn on all household lights. Some stood in the streets waving flashlights. Paul Allen, the billionaire co-founder of Microsoft, who happened to be in Palau at the time, offered up the two helicopters on his 414-foot mega-yacht, the *Octopus,* for search and rescue. One of Allen's crew was instructed to fire forty-nine flares, one per minute, into the air.

Losing track of the Cessna was especially agonizing for the Palauan police because they could hear the pilot, Frank Ohlinger, and the two officers who were his passengers, Earlee Decherong and Willie Mays Towai, on the radio. Ohlinger, on the other hand, could not hear anyone on land, perhaps because of some frayed cable or short in the speakers in his plane. Between Ohlinger's 3:30 p.m. takeoff through his 8:16 p.m. Mayday call, they listened to his voice's growing panic, his frustration with the plane's broken GPS and compass, and, ultimately, his request that someone alert his next of kin. "On a good glide slope, heading north," Ohlinger said in the end. He explained that he hoped to ease the plane, as best he could, into the waves. "We are at six thousand feet, doing sixty-five knots, out of fuel." The wreckage was never found. "It swallowed them," Baiei said of the abyss where the Cessna disappeared.

Newspapers around the world wrote about the debacle for weeks. The Chinese government sent a diplomatic envoy to Palau to discuss the shooting. Palau's president and attorney general opened an investigation. At that moment, it became painfully clear that the Palauan government was outmatched in the battle to safeguard its waters. "Palauans are a very proud people," Baiei said. "The whole thing was a tragedy and a really embarrassing one."

As the Palauan officers finished telling their story, our attention suddenly shifted to a threat that was larger than Chinese poachers. As the *Remeliik* reached the southern end of the country, one of the Palauan officers pointed in the direction of Helen Reef, about 360 miles southwest of the main island chain, near Palau's sea border with Indonesia. Mostly uninhabited except for four to six Palauan rangers, Helen Reef was a low-lying, sandy island, about 600,000 square feet (roughly twice the size of the U.S. Capitol Reflecting Pool).

In coming decades, the sea will likely swallow small remote island nations everywhere. Portions of Kiribati, the Maldives, Fiji, Nauru, and Tuvalu are already sliding under rising tides. The disappearance of Helen Reef is distinctly important for Palau because its reefs set the country's southernmost boundary. When this outpost slips under the waterline, Indonesia's claim to Palau's waters would expand by about fifty-four thousand square miles. In the same way that the Industrial Revolution started causing irreversible damage to the climate, it transformed the very nature of fishing with deep and lasting consequences for the oceans.

. . .

Understanding the present plight of the oceans requires reviewing their past—what has changed and what has not. Through many months of reporting on fishing, I was struck by the age-old consistency of the vocation: the typical workday for a fisherman hadn't changed since the days of Galilee. It was backbreaking labor punctuated by crushing boredom. You shot your net, cast your line, waited, waited more, then hopefully hoisted or reeled in a catch. Over the past century, however, technology has transformed fishing from a type of hunting into something more akin to farming. With highly mechanized ships that operate more like floating factories, the industry became brutally efficient at stripping the seas of virtually everything in them.

By 2015, about ninety-four million tons of fish were caught each year, more than the weight of the entire human population. Much of the credit and blame goes to the building boom in the 1930s of purse seiners. These ships surround an entire school of fish with a deep curtain of netting, sometimes nearly a mile around, with a thick wire that runs through rings along the bottom of the mesh. After setting the net, the ship hauls in the bottom wire, and the net is pursed, or cinched, like a laundry bag. A crane lifts the net out of the water, the fish are dumped into a gaping funnel, sorted (often by conveyor belt), and swallowed into the ship hold.

World War II spurred engineers to develop lighter, faster, more durable ships that could travel farther on less fuel. Submarine combat propelled innovation in sonar, helping illuminate the dark fathoms. Finding fish became more a science of spreadsheets than an art of dead reckoning. Subzero onboard freezers freed fishermen from their race against melting refrigerator ice. Innovations in plastics and monofilaments lengthened fishing lines from feet to miles. Lightweight polymer-based nets enabled super-trawlers to rake the ocean with the ruthlessness of two tanks rolling through a rain forest, a mesh of steel cables strung between them.

As the size and strength of nets increased, so too did the amount of bycatch that was inadvertently killed and thrown back. More than half the global catch is now tossed overboard dead, or it is ground up and pelletized to feed pigs, poultry, and farmed fish. For instance, feeding a single "ranched" tuna can require catching and pelletizing over thirty times the weight of that tuna in fish pulled from the sea. These technological advances, as well as the industrialization of fishing, are a big reason why catches from the high seas rose 700 percent in the last half a century. They also partly explain why many of the world's fish stocks are at the brink of collapse.

Two stubborn misconceptions have also played a big role. The first is that aquatic creatures represent a lower order of life. "Think of the word 'seafood' itself," said Paul Greenberg, a fishing historian. In German, French, Spanish, and most other western European languages, seafood is "sea fruit." An entire ecosystem that encompasses millions of species of creatures is lumped together in popular consciousness, consisting not of distinct animals but of things we consume. So-called pescetarians, indignant over the suffering of farm cows and chickens, frequently include wild fish in their diets, he said. While kosher laws mandate the merciful slaughter of mammals and birds, they have no such requirements for fish. Indeed, a large portion of these animals are killed not for our consumption but to fatten up the other animals we eat. Fish are cold-blooded and not cuddly. People have always viewed them differently from other animals.

The second and more important misconception is that the ocean is a place of sui generis abundance. The nineteenth-century British political commentator Henry Schultes captured this notion in 1813, when he wrote, "In addition to a highly productive soil, the seas which surround us afford an inexhaustible mine of wealth—a harvest, ripe for gathering at every time of the year—without the labour of tillage, without the expense of seed or manure, without the payment of rent or taxes."

This belief carried into the twentieth century, in writings from the likes of Hawthorne Daniel, from the American Museum of Natural History in New York, and Francis Minot, from the oceanographic institute at Woods Hole, Massachusetts, who co-published a book in 1954 called *The Inexhaustible Sea*. "As yet we do not know the ocean well enough," they wrote. "Nevertheless, we are already beginning to understand that what it has to offer extends beyond the limits of our imagination—that someday men will learn that in its bounty the sea is inexhaustible."

The pace of overfishing has certainly been accelerated by the image of tireless plenty and the notion that these creatures are more edible than worthy of protection. On the other hand, many conservationists saw hope in technology's ability to slow this process down and to tame and police this vastness. Since the 1990s, ships had been able to deploy the automatic identification system, or AIS, a collision-avoidance system that used onboard VHF transmitters to transmit their position, identity, and speed continuously to other ships and to satellites. In 2002, the UN's maritime organization started phasing in AIS for all passenger ships regardless of size and all commercial vessels, fishing boats included, with a gross tonnage of more than three hundred (typically a 130-foot-long vessel).

Alas, AIS has its shortcomings: Captains could and were allowed to turn the transponders off when they feared being tracked by pirates or competitors. The system could be hacked to give false locations. Many of the boats involved in the worst crimes, like the *Shin Jyi*, were smaller than three hundred tons.

As a condition for being licensed to fish in their waters, many countries also required that boats carry an additional device, called a vessel monitoring system, or VMS, which transmitted their location and other data to local fishery authorities. For policing, VMS was better than AIS because it was far tougher to tamper with or turn off. The logic was that the more visible legal boats became, the harder it would be for poachers to unload their illicit catch in ports if they lacked the necessary tracking equipment.

More sea-traffic data would become available as countries deployed sonar and camera buoys as well as low-cost floating hydrophones to catch boats approaching restricted areas. Satellites, mostly used by governments and armed with synthetic-aperture radar, could also detect a vessel's position regardless of weather conditions.

As the 2015 capture of the *Shin Jyi* proved, all this information became especially powerful when coupled with sophisticated monitoring software that triggered alerts if, for instance, a vessel went "dark" by turning off its transponder or if a poacher entered a no-fishing area. Now, instead of blindly patrolling broad swaths of ocean, police had, in effect, eyes in the sky.

Still, this new technology was not a panacea. Popular television shows like *Homeland* and *Person of Interest* make aerial surveillance seem as reliable as Google Maps, but capturing this detailed imagery from the sky depends largely on military-grade drones. Taking high-resolution photographs from space is extremely costly (often over $3,500 per picture), and requests for images have to be made a week in advance so that the companies or governments operating the satellites know to aim their lens at the precise spot as they hurtle around the earth.

The vastness of the ocean also complicates surveillance efforts, even by sophisticated satellite tracking used by the likes of SkyTruth's Bergman in West Virginia. Seen from above, the world's largest fishing trawler, the Dutch-flagged *Annelies Ilena,* has a surface area of about thirty-five hundred square meters—equivalent to eight NBA courts. Even if a satellite were scanning just 1 percent of the Atlantic Ocean, the *Annelies Ilena* would take up only three-billionths of that swath. If a ship turns off its transmitter, any knowledge of its whereabouts can quickly evaporate.

. . .

For centuries, local fishermen have taken advantage of fish's instinct to huddle near floating objects for protection and mating. By building special buoys with plastic and bamboo flotsam strung together with old nets, these fishermen attract fish to one spot, making them easier to catch and greatly cutting the time required to keep their boats at sea. The buoys, which modern researchers began calling "fish aggregating devices," or FADs, have had a particularly powerful impact on the seas near Palau.

To attract species like tuna and blue marlin, fishing companies are increasingly using "smart" FADs equipped with sonar and GPS, which let boat captains sit back and wait on land to be alerted when it's time to gather up their haul. They're so effective, in fact, that in some places in the world fishermen hire armed guards to sit on or near the FADs to ensure that competitors don't destroy them or steal the fish around them.

In Indonesia, fishermen told me about villagers hired to stand guard on floating tarp-covered platforms alongside FADs, dozens of miles from shore. Usually these guards were supplied with several jugs of water, salted fish, a gun, and promises that someone would visit them in a week or so to provide new supplies or to take them back to shore. Sometimes, those promises were not kept or a storm killed the men, washing their bodies ashore. I heard similar stories in the Philippines, where FAD guards had been killed in firefights with other fishermen.

Over the past three decades, FADs became especially popular in commercial fishing fleets, partly as an unintended consequence of the movement to save dolphins. These fleets used to find tuna by looking first for dolphins, which often followed and swam near the surface above tuna schools because it helps them ward off predators. This approach led to hundreds of thousands of dolphins being inadvertently killed as bycatch when they were netted with tuna. In the 1980s and 1990s, the demand for "dolphin-free" tuna pushed many fleets to relocate. They moved out of the tropical eastern Pacific, near Baja, and into the central and western Pacific, near Palau, where the dolphins typically do not follow tuna as closely. Due to temperature fluctuations in the western Pacific waters, tuna swim much deeper than dolphins usually do, so spotting them shadowing each other is less common.

As a result, many of these ships turned to FADs as their new tool for finding tuna, which would feed on the fish gathered there. But this new approach had its problems. Fish other than tuna were drawn to the FADs, which meant fishermen indiscriminately killed large numbers of sharks and sea turtles as well as juvenile tuna before they could breed. The impact of removing so many baby tuna soon became apparent. A 2014 study found that the population of yellowfin tuna in the waters around Palau and other Pacific islands had fallen to 38 percent of the size it had been before the FADs were deployed.

As the *Remeliik* sliced its way through battering waves, there were subtle but ominous signs that Palau was losing the fight to protect its fish. About ten miles off the country's eastern coast, the officers stopped at a FAD so I could dive into the warm, translucent blue water to get a closer look. The marine officers looked at me as if I were crazy. In years past, this FAD was crowded with large fish, which also meant it was frequented by the sharks that preyed on them, they cautioned.

My photographer, Lowy, did not hesitate to put on his scuba tank and fall backward into the water. Having lots of experience photographing sharks, he didn't seem scared. I followed his lead, though secretly I was nervous. My job was to warn him if any came from behind, but I didn't actually understand what that meant. How do you warn someone fast enough when you are both underwater? I wondered.

Low-tech and anchored, the FAD was little more than a plastic buoy attached to a thick, mollusk-coated rope tethered to cinder blocks more than five hundred feet below. Large bamboo leaves ran down the first fifty feet of the rope, flapping like fuzzy moth wings. Hundreds of tiny inch-long silver fish darted under the shade of the leaves. Not one fish was more than a foot long.

I held on to the line anchoring the FAD and went as deep as I could, roughly twenty feet, but almost immediately I lost sight of Lowy, who disappeared quickly, much deeper. When I returned to the surface, I splashed on my back like an otter, and turning around, I discovered that one of the marine officers was pointing a shotgun at me. Confused but out of breath, I could muster only a "Hey?" The officer replied that he was watching for sharks and intended to shoot them if he spotted any. "Maybe just yell at us instead," I suggested. "Don't shoot." We visited three more FADs during the patrol that day, traversing over a hundred nautical miles. None had the large fish that they were supposed to attract.

With the sun setting as we were about five miles off Palau's nearest northern shore, one of the marine officers said they wanted to check a final FAD near an islet called Orak. Their interest this time was more parochial; they wanted to fish for dinner. After dragging their fishing line in circles around it for an hour, they gave up, empty-handed. Docking instead at a nearby island, the officers bought some chicken stew from the local market. I asked at the tiny grocery hut near port if the chicken had been grown on the island. The man at the counter said no. "Imported from China." Ironic, I thought. The same country poaching Palau's fish was supplying its chicken.

The absence of fish near the FADs served as a reminder that the seas, though vast, were inextricably linked and by no means inexhaustible. The success of Palau's reserve depended in part on other countries creating their own. "They're getting taken before they get here," Baiei said about the missing fish.

Tuna, like many large ocean fish, are migratory. Near Palau, populations of yellowfin, bigeye, and skipjack are in sharp decline, partly because they never make it to Palau's reserve. They are being picked off beforehand in a number of ways, including being netted at one of the more than fifty thousand floating FADs in the western and central Pacific Ocean, most of which are perfectly legal.

In its grand fight to safeguard its waters, Palau was doing many of the right things, including having created a marine reserve that protected nearly 80 percent of its territorial waters from industrial fishing. But for the country's conservation efforts to succeed, Palau needed other governments and industries to follow suit. Palau could not succeed on its own.

.   .   .

As we passed time on the bridge of the *Remeliik,* Baiei complicated the picture for me even further. He said he worried about more than just tuna and sharks. Near-shore tropical fish populations have also been decimated. I pointed out that this was partly the fault of Palau's unfettered tourism. More than half of the country's gross domestic product was based on ecotourism, mostly because of people drawn to the world-class snorkeling and scuba diving. In 2015, the average number of tourists per month coming from China soared to nearly eleven thousand from about two thousand the year prior.

It turned out, though, that many of these tourists were as eager to eat the fish as they were to see them. Not coincidentally, the variety of exotic seafood appearing on local restaurant menus in Palau grew as well, including banned fish like Napoleon wrasse, hump-head parrot fish, and hawksbill turtles that were mostly caught by local fishermen. Even as the Palauans tried to keep foreign poachers from entering their waters, they struggled to stop local fishermen from supplying protected fish to their own restaurants.

Before boarding the *Remeliik,* I visited Jellyfish Lake, a roughly twelve-acre body of salt water on an uninhabited islet in Palau's Rock Islands. I went there because, as one of Palau's proudest attractions, it seemed like a perfect place to witness the distinct burden that tourism was putting on the country's marine environment. Fluorescent green, the lake is home to millions of jellyfish that do not sting. They were pulsating orange blobs, and they ranged in size from Ping-Pong balls to bowling balls.

In the prior five years, several Chinese tourists had been arrested for netting fish on the resort's reef-rimmed beachfront and for taking jellyfish from the lake, allegedly planning to cook and eat them in their hotel rooms using hot plates that they had brought in their luggage. As a Palauan guide explained in English to the boisterous crowd climbing into the lake that they should not touch the jellyfish, two dozen of the wet-suit-wearing Chinese tourists ignored him and were already lifting the creatures out of the water to inspect them.

· · ·

That looming feeling of futility traveled with me on the *Remeliik* as the Palauan officers stopped a Taiwanese tuna long-liner, the *Sheng Chi Huei 12,* about seventy nautical miles from shore. Boarding it for inspection, the officers corralled the six-man Indonesian crew at the front of the boat. As I started to climb onto an upper deck, one of the six deckhands lunged forward and grabbed my wrist. Startled, I realized

Palauans inspect the catch aboard the *Sheng Chi Huei 12,* a Taiwanese tuna long-liner in Palauan waters.

my hand was inches from touching an electrified steel cable that they used to stun the bigger fish that flop wildly when first pulled on deck. The deckhand pointed to a six-inch black burn mark on another man's arm, warning me of what the cable could do. As much as I thought I knew about the dangers on these ships, I was still learning.

For Palau's marine officers, catching poachers was just the first step. After they brought them to shore, there was no guarantee that Palau would have the translators to communicate with the foreign crews, jail space to hold them, or even the laws to effectively prosecute them. Most of the poachers they arrested were from small boats owned by family businesses. These operators typically had nowhere near the $500,000 to pay some of the tougher fines, much less the expense of repatriating their crews. When these boats were seized, Palau was stuck with the cost of feeding, housing, and flying the crews home.

As the *Remeliik's* officers inspected the *Sheng Chi Huei 12,* I headed toward the back of the ship to look at the crew's quarters below deck. A ladder led down a hatch to a four-foot-high tunnel. Running the length of the vessel, it was lined by a dozen six-foot-long cubbies, each with a small bundle of clothes to serve as a pillow.

Fishing ships, particularly in the developing world, are not especially hygienic places. Cram dozens of men into a dank, confined space for months, where they are handling thousands of dead and decaying creatures day in and day out, and you can expect infections. By the time I arrived in Palau, I had already spent time on dozens of fishing boats, and I had learned that for my own safety I needed to adjust certain habits. No more nail biting; you don't want your hands anywhere near your mouth. Even small cuts get infected quickly and severely. I stopped wearing contact lenses because putting them in and taking them out was a wobbly, germ-laden process that kept resulting in styes. Ear infections were a constant battle from the persistent moisture. Daily drops of a concoction of 50 percent vinegar, 50 percent rubbing alcohol helped manage the problem but often it stung like hell.

The *Sheng Chi Huei 12* was an especially dirty ship, and to travel from Taiwan, it had crossed about fourteen hundred nautical miles, which took a little over a week. In high seas and heavy weather, staying on deck for the crew was out of the question.

Crawling deeper into the belly of this ship seemed like a patently bad idea, but my curiosity was overwhelming. I wanted to see where these men slept and passed the time when storms hit. Farther down the tunnel, it grew darker and muggier, with a heavier flow of fumes, heat, and noise. A rat scurried ahead. Rancid brown goop dripped from above in some spots: runoff from the upper-deck cutting tables.

The sleeping cubbies ran virtually the full length of the crawl space. At the deepest end of the tunnel was the ship's huge diesel engine, churning furiously. The fumes were backed up around the engine because the opening through which they should have risen and exited was partially obstructed. I sat in that tight space for a couple minutes to take in the scene. I tried to breathe only through my mouth because the air was so hot that it felt as if it were singeing my nostrils. It then dawned on me that the passageway that I had just crawled down was not just the men's sleeping quarters. It was also the engine's main exhaust pipe.

The more I explored the outlaw ocean, the tougher it became to distinguish the predators from the prey. I had traveled to Palau to focus on the fragile and bleak state of the fish and other marine life here and to understand the foreign poachers who were the tip of the spear of this global oceanic pillage. But it was quickly becoming apparent that this contrast was neither as stark nor as simple as I figured. The men chasing these fish were no less to blame for the depletion of Palau's waters, but they seemed equally, if not more, vulnerable themselves.

Later that afternoon, back on the *Remeliik,* I passed the time reading the Palauan government's investigation report about the 2012 disappearance of the Cessna and the killing of the Chinese deckhand. The document included transcripts of interviews with the twenty-five fishermen from the illegal Chinese boats, who had been arrested and held in the Koror jail for seventeen days.

Most of the men in the report had never been to sea and did not know the name of their ship, the fishing company they worked for, or even the full name of their captain. Most had handed their identity cards over to the bosun when they stepped on board. Most said that on the day the marine officers chased their boat, they were fleeing because they thought the Palauans, who were not in uniform, were planning to rob them. They were also unaware they were fishing illegally, the documents said. "He said he knew nothing of permits," a police interview recounted one of the Chinese deckhands saying. "Just did what the captain told him."

In a plea deal, the crew members later agreed to each pay a $1,000 fine, which their families and the government wired to Palau on their behalf. Their small fast boat was destroyed, and their gear was confiscated. They were then flown home, with their slain colleague, Lu Yong, in a casket, on a charter flight sent by the Chinese government. "He should not have received the death penalty," Lu Chuanan, who later visited Palau, said about Yong, his dead cousin.

One line in the report stood out and lent a chilling coda to the story. After the Chinese poachers traveled hundreds of miles to steal fish from the Palauan waters, leaving behind families and risking life and limb, the crew caught fewer than a dozen fish, over several days of poaching, primarily Lapu Lapu, and several large clams. It seemed like a pathetically small yield and more proof of the area's thinning fish stocks.

In the wheelhouse of the *Remeliik* that night, the officers conducted a postmortem of the day's boarding. The sea around us was still and dark, with the lights of far-flung islets far in the distance. The conversation turned to the crews that work on these poacher ships. "Aren't they the enemy?" I asked. Several of the officers shook their heads to say no. "You do the work you can find," one of them said.

Baiei explained that after they seize a fishing boat and arrest the crew, his fellow officers typically help find clothes for the deckhands, who tend to have little to their name. Many of the T-shirts that the officers donate are from former Palauan political campaigns because these T-shirts are abundant and handed out publicly for free. Baiei said that in an odd but recurring spectacle, at least once a year a deckhand on an illegal fishing ship from Taiwan, China, or Vietnam reappears in Palauan waters wearing a shirt touting a particular Palauan candidate. Another officer added that he arrested a pirate captain in 2016, and then six months later the same man showed up on a different boat. This time, the man was working as a deckhand. The frequency of these "repeat fliers" spoke to their persistence and desperation. It also left me wondering if Baiei's mission was more myth of Sisyphus than David and Goliath.

"Have you ever seen someone bend?" Baiei asked me at one point on our trip back to port. He explained that many of the poachers his patrol team chased are Vietnamese "blue boats," so named because of their brightly painted hulls. Most of these vessels targeted sea cucumbers that live on the ocean floor and look like giant, leather-skinned slugs. When they stop to fish for them, the Vietnamese crews hold rubber hoses in their mouths attached to an onboard air compressor. They strap lead weights around their waists to help them dive, often dangerously deeper than a hundred feet, to collect the cucumbers, which can fetch over $300 per pound in China. During an arrest in 2016, Baiei said, one of these divers shot to the surface too quickly, causing excruciating bubbles to form in his joints, getting what is called the bends.

"He just kept moaning for days," Baiei said, adding that those cries still haunted him. One of the other officers, who had been listening to the conversation, looked up from his inspection logs. He said of the deckhands on these fishing ships, "They're the real bycatch."

In Baiei's story about the moaning worker, I saw a sobering lesson. It was, in fact, the same lesson I took from the disappeared Cessna, the empty FADs, the leveled atoll, and the jellyfish tourists. I had come to Palau looking for inspiration and to learn about the global prospects for ocean conservation. If the world's fish stocks were to have any chance to survive, this archipelago nation might offer some guidance. But I left Palau less with hope than with a painful sense of the barriers to marine preservation. The threats facing the oceans were far bigger and more complex than criminality. Palau's true adversaries were not best understood as legal or illegal. They were bigger: climate change, unchecked tourism, a vastly untamed geography, and a level of poverty that filled boats with men who cared more about survival than about laws. In this colossal battle, Palau was leading by example; the only question was whether anyone would follow.

# A RUSTY KINGDOM

Men go out into the void spaces of the world for various reasons. Some are actuated simply by a love of adventure, some
have the keen thirst for scientific knowledge, and others again
are drawn away from the trodden paths by the "lure of little
voices," the mysterious fascination of the unknown.

—Ernest Shackleton, *The Heart of the Antarctic*

On Christmas Eve 1966, while the rest of his country sat home cel-
ebrating, the retired British army major Paddy Roy Bates drove a
small boat with an outboard motor seven miles off the coast of England
into the North Sea. He had snuck out of his house in the middle of the
night, inspired with a nutty idea for a perfect gift for his wife, Joan.

Sealand in 2002

Using a grappling hook and rope, he clambered onto an abandoned anti-aircraft platform and declared it conquered. He would name it Sealand and make it hers.

His gift was no romantic maritime palace. Built in the early 1940s as one of five forts for defending the Thames, the HMF (His Majesty's Fort) Roughs Tower was a sparse and windswept hulk. "Roughs," as the abandoned platform was popularly called, was little more than a wide deck about the size of two tennis courts set atop two hollow, concrete towers, sixty feet above the ocean. Roy took his Brutalist outpost with the utmost gravity, as seriously as Cortés or Vasco da Gama.

In its wartime heyday, Roughs had been manned by more than a hundred British seamen and armed with two 40 mm Bofors light anti-aircraft guns and two 94 mm Vickers heavy anti-aircraft guns, whose barrels stretched longer than fifteen feet to take better aim at Nazi bombers. Suddenly obsolete with Germany's defeat, the station was abandoned by the Royal Navy. Unused and neglected, it fell into disrepair, a forlorn monument to British vigilance. As the owner of a large shipping fleet, Roy was familiar with the platform. He sailed by it often, importing meat, rubber, and fish into Britain after the war.

British authorities, not surprisingly, frowned on Roy's seizure of their platform and ordered him to abandon it. But Roy was as daring as he was stubborn—just the lad to tell them to bugger off. The London native had joined the International Brigade at age fifteen to fight on the Republican side in the Spanish Civil War. When he returned, he signed up with the British army, rising quickly through the ranks to become the youngest major in the force at the time. During World War II, he served in North Africa, the Middle East, and Italy. He once suffered serious wounds after a grenade exploded near his face. In a later incident, he was taken prisoner by Greek fascists after his fighter plane crashed, but managed to escape. He consumed life with two hands.

Initially, Roy used Roughs for a "pirate" radio station. The BBC, which had a monopoly over the airwaves at the time, played the Beatles, Kinks, Rolling Stones, and other pop bands only in the middle of the night, much to the frustration of young audiences. Defiant entrepreneurs like Roy answered the call by setting up unlicensed stations on ships and other platforms to play the music twenty-four hours a day from just beyond Britain's borders. After taking over his platform in 1966, Roy stocked it with tins of corned beef, rice pudding, flour, and scotch and lived on it, not returning to land sometimes for several months at a time. He had previously launched a pirate radio station on another offshore platform. Authorities quickly shut that one down because it was inside Britain's territorial waters, which at the time extended three nautical miles from the coast. Roughs, on the other hand, was well outside those territorial boundaries.

Several months after establishing his new radio station on the gunnery platform and formally gifting it to his wife for her birthday, Roy was out for drinks at a bar with her and friends. "Now you have your very own island," Roy said to his wife. As was often the case with Roy, no one could tell whether the gift was sincere or tongue-in-cheek. She replied, "It's just a shame it doesn't have a few palm trees, a bit of sunshine, and its own flag." One of the friends took the banter a step further: Why not make the platform its own country? Everyone laughed and moved on to the next round of pints. Everyone except Roy, that is. A few weeks later, he announced to the world the establishment of the new nation of Sealand. The motto of the country over which he reigned was *E Mare, Libertas,* or "From the Sea, Freedom."

. . .

The ocean can be a cold and predatory environment, a watery incubator for the worst instincts of man and a habitat for the brutal exercise of evolutionary fitness among marine creatures. It's also a place of discovery, of limitless aspiration and reinvention. The improbable creation story of the world's tiniest maritime nation was an emblem of offshore eccentricity and a thumb in the eye of international law. But it also represented something more—a rich legacy of adventurism on the seas, a stubbornly insistent claim of right, and a flamboyant declaration of sovereignty.

Constituted as a principality, Sealand had its own passport, coat of arms, and flag—red and black with a white diagonal stripe. Its currency was the Sealand dollar, bearing Roy's wife's image. In more recent years, it launched a Facebook page, a Twitter account, and a YouTube channel.

Though no country formally recognized Sealand, its sovereignty was hard to deny. Half a dozen times, the British government and assorted other groups backed by mercenaries tried and failed to take over the platform by force. In virtually every instance, the Bates family scared them off by firing rifles in their direction, tossing petrol bombs, dropping cinder blocks onto their boats, or pushing their ladders into the sea. Britain had once controlled a vast empire over which the sun never set. Now it found itself unable to touch a rogue micronation barely bigger than the main ballroom in Buckingham Palace.

The reason goes back to first principles of sovereignty: a country's ability to enforce its laws extends only as far as its borders. The British government learned this lesson in May 1968, after Roy's son, Michael, fired a .22-caliber pistol from Sealand at workers servicing a buoy nearby. Michael claimed that they were mere warning shots to remind these workers of Sealand's territorial sovereignty. No one was hurt in the incident, but the consequences for Britain's legal system—and Sealand's geopolitical status—were far-reaching.

The British government soon brought firearms charges against Michael, for illegal possession and discharge. But the court subsequently ruled that his actions happened outside British territory and jurisdiction, making them unpunishable under British law. Emboldened by the ruling, Roy later said to a British official that he could order a murder on Sealand if he so chose, because "I am the person responsible for the law in Sealand."

In the annals of swashbuckling sea stories, few are as bizarre. And though the story of Sealand can feel like a Monty Python sketch at times, it seemed to me to offer an opportunity to explore a serious point about the gaping loopholes in governance of the oceans. Especially striking was the fact that for all his brazenness, Roy appeared to be operating legally or at least opportunistically within a legal void.

In its five decades of existence, no more than half a dozen people, guests of the Bates family, ever lived on this desolate outpost. On the platform's flattop, the big guns and helicopters from World War II were replaced by a wind-powered generator, which provided flickering electricity to the space heaters in Sealand's ten chilly rooms. Each month, a boat ferried supplies—tea, whiskey, chocolate, and old newspapers—to its residents. In recent years, its permanent citizenry has dwindled to one person: a full-time guard named Michael Barrington.

As absurdist and fanciful as Sealand seemed, the British took it seriously. Recently declassified U.K. documents from the late 1960s reveal that Sealand prompted considerable fretting among officers,

SUN
23·10·68

INDEPENDENT

BRITISH KEEP OUT

INDEPENDENT

SEALAND

INDEPENDENT

" SAYS HIS NAME IS SMITH — WANTS
TO KNOW HOW WE GOT AWAY WITH IT."

A cartoon that ran on October 23, 1968, in the London-based newspaper *The Sun* offers some context on Sealand's status as a nascent postcolonial breakaway nation with a reference to Rhodesia, which had declared independence from Britain in an attempt to preserve white minority rule.

who feared that another Cuba was being created, this time on England's doorstep. These officers debated and ultimately rejected naval plans to bomb the installation. In the 1970s, a German businessman named Alexander Gottfried Achenbach hired a team of Dutch mercenaries to stage a coup at Sealand, resulting in a hostage crisis and a tense diplomatic row between Germany and England. In the early 1980s, during the Falklands War, a group of Argentinians tried to buy the platform for a training camp. More recently, WikiLeaks explored moving its servers there, and Sealand appeared in the Panama Papers as a haven for organized crime.

The sea had summoned me in a dozen ways since I had begun reporting, but Sealand was a different frontier in the outlaw ocean. The sheer audacity of the place was stunning, as were its philosophical underpinnings—an exercise in pure libertarianism, yet awkwardly cinched into the arcane manners of maritime law and diplomacy.

I would travel in October 2016 to the platform with Roy Bates's son, Michael, who was then sixty-four, and his son James, who was twenty-nine. It had taken me several months and half a dozen phone calls to persuade the family to give me permission to visit their principality. I never fully understood their hesitation. Perhaps they did not want to risk jeopardizing the folklore surrounding the place.

When I finally arrived in England, I was surprised to learn that the two men operated not from Sealand, but out of Essex, England, where they ran a fleet of cockle-fishing boats. Michael looked like a retired hockey player. Short and square in build, he had a shaved head and was missing a front tooth. He had a quick and throaty laugh and a raucous air. James, on the other hand, was thin and demure, with a college-educated poise to him. Where James chose his words carefully, always calibrating nuance and measure, his father favored verbal stun grenades: "You can write about us whatever you bloody please!" Michael said soon after we met. "What do we care?" I suspected he actually cared a lot.

The father-son duo picked me up in a skiff in the port town of Harwich shortly before dawn on a frigid windy day in October 2016. The Bates men sat in the middle of the skiff while I sat in the rear as the small craft pounded up and down through the surf. In the biting wind, conversation was impossible, so I hung on in silence.

When waves are high, as they were that day, traveling in a ten-foot skiff can feel like riding a galloping horse. There is a rhythm, but unlike in galloping, the beat shifts often and unpredictably. The hour-long zigzag to Sealand was pure rodeo. My internal organs felt concussed; my legs shook with exhaustion from gripping the oblong seat.

The skiff rocketed across the surf toward a speck on the horizon that grew larger as we approached until I could see the mottled concrete stilts, the wide expanse of the platform above, and the web address painted in bold letters below the helipad in the middle. The famed micronation looked more rugged than regal. As we approached the platform, it became clear that the principality's best defense was its height. Nearly impregnable from below, it had no mooring post, landing porch, or ladder. We idled our boat near one of the barnacle-coated columns as a crane swung out over the edge, six stories above.

Clad in bright blue overalls, Barrington lowered a cable with a small wooden seat that looked as if it belonged on a backyard tree swing. He was a graying man in his sixties, round-bellied and given to smiling. I climbed on and was hoisted up—a harrowing ascent in the howling wind. "Welcome," Barrington yelled above the wind. Swiveling the crane around, he then plopped me on deck. The place had a junkyard feel: piles of industrial drums, stacks of plastic crates, balls of tangled wires, mounds of rusty bric-a-brac—all surrounding a whirring wind turbine that seemed ready to pull loose at any minute. As the waves picked up, the whole structure groaned like an old suspension bridge.

Barrington lifted James and Michael one at a time. Finally, he hoisted the boat itself and left it suspended in the air. "Precaution-

Visiting in 2016, Michael Bates is lifted onto Sealand using a swing attached to a crane.

ary," Barrington said, explaining why he hadn't left it below in the water. Michael escorted me inside from the chaotic deck into the kitchen that served as the Sealandic seat of government. He put on a kettle of tea so we could talk. "Let's get you through customs," he deadpanned as he inspected and stamped my passport. I watched his face closely for any sign that it was safe for me to laugh. None came.

. . .

I hadn't quite known what to expect from my visit to Sealand before I arrived. I had done some reading about the rich and fanciful history of aquatic micronations. At least since Jules Verne's *Twenty Thousand Leagues Under the Sea* was first published in 1870, people have dreamed of creating permanent colonies on or under the ocean.

Typically, these projects were inspired by the view that government was a kind of kryptonite that weakened entrepreneurialism. Many of the founders were bullish on technology and its potential, when unencumbered by government, to solve human problems. The backers of these micronations—they included quite a few dot-com tycoons in the first decade of the twenty-first century—were usually men of means, steeped in Ayn Rand and Thomas Hobbes. Conceived as self-sufficient, self-governing, sea-bound communities, these cities were envisioned as part libertarian utopia, part billionaire's playground. They were often called seasteads, after the homesteads of the American West.

In the early 1970s, a Las Vegas real estate magnate named Michael Oliver sent barges loaded with sand from Australia to a set of shallow reefs near the island of Tonga in the Pacific Ocean, declaring his creation the Republic of Minerva. Planting a flag and some guards there, Oliver declared his micronation free from "taxation, welfare, subsidies, or any form of economic interventionism." Within months, Tonga sent troops to the site to enforce its twelve-mile offshore territorial claim, expelling the Minervan occupants and removing their flag—a single torch on a blue background. In 1982, a group of Americans led by Morris C. "Bud" Davis, a military engineer who designed missiles, again attempted to occupy the reefs. Within weeks, they too were forced off by Tongan troops.

Elsewhere, many others tried and failed. In 1968, a wealthy American libertarian named Werner Stiefel attempted to create a floating micronation called Operation Atlantis in international waters near the Bahamas. He bought a large boat and sent it to his would-be territory. It soon sank in a hurricane. Another wealthy libertarian, Norman Nixon, raised about $400,000 as a down payment in 1999 to create a floating city called the Freedom Ship, a forty-five-hundred-foot vessel about four times the length of the *Queen Mary 2*. The ship was never built.

Many of these projects might have made sense in theory, but they never accounted for the harsh reality of ocean life. At sea, there is plenty of wind, wave, and solar energy to provide power, but building renewable-energy systems that could survive the weather and the corrosive seawater was difficult and costly. Communication options remain limited: satellite-based connections were prohibitively expensive, as was laying a fiber-optic cable or relying on point-to-point lasers or microwaves that tethered the offshore installation to land. Traveling to and from seasteads was challenging. Waves and storms could be especially disruptive. "Rogue" waves occur when smaller waves, sometimes traveling in different directions, meet and combine. They can be taller than 110 feet—almost twice the height of Sealand.

Running a country—even a pint-sized one—isn't free. Who, for example, would subsidize basic services (the ones usually provided by the tax-funded government that seasteading libertarians sought to escape)? Keeping the lights on and protecting against piracy would be expensive.

In 2008, these visionaries united around a nonprofit organization called the Seasteading Institute. Based in San Francisco, the organization was founded by Patri Friedman, a Google software engineer and grandson of Milton Friedman, the Nobel Prize–winning economist best known for his ideas about the limitations of government. The institute's primary benefactor was Peter Thiel, a billionaire venture capitalist and the co-founder of PayPal who donated more than $1.25 million to the organization and related projects.

Thiel also invested in a start-up venture called Blueseed. Its purpose was to solve a thorny problem affecting many Silicon Valley companies: how to attract engineers and entrepreneurs who lacked American work permits or visas. Blueseed planned to anchor a floating residential barge in international waters off the coast of Northern California. Never getting beyond the drawing-board phase, Blueseed failed to raise the money necessary to sustain itself.

. . .

As we sipped our tea, I asked Michael Bates whether the seasteaders or Thiel had ever approached him, and he said they never seemed interested. "Maybe just as well," he added. Michael had reason to be skeptical about whom his family chose as partners or allies. Over the years, the biggest threats to Sealand were not just from governments but also from people his family thought were friends.

In Sealand's early years, these attacks came from fellow pirate radio DJs. For example, Ronan O'Rahilly, who ran a pirate radio station called Radio Caroline from a nearby ship, tried to storm Sealand in 1967. Bates used petrol bombs to repel him and several of his men. Later, the coup attempts on Sealand came from turncoat investors. Michael recounted two examples. In 1977, Roy was approached by a consortium of German and Dutch lawyers, and diamond merchants, who said they wanted to build a casino on the platform. Invited to Austria in 1978 to discuss the proposition, Roy left Sealand under the watch of Michael, then a young man in his twenties. Arriving in Salzburg, Roy was greeted warmly by five men who arranged for them to meet again later that week to discuss business ideas. When no one showed, Roy grew suspicious and began phoning fishing captains who worked near Sealand, which had no telephone or radio capabilities of its own. When one of these skippers told Roy that he had seen a large helicopter landing at Sealand, the nervous father scrambled back to England.

Around 11:00 a.m. on August 10, 1978, Michael had heard the thwump-thwump of approaching rotors. Grabbing a World War II–

vintage pistol from Sealand's weapons locker, he darted upstairs to find a helicopter hovering overhead, unable to land because of a thirty-five-foot mast intended to deter just such uninvited guests. The helicopter's bay doors were open, and a cameraman was leaning out while gesturing that he wanted to set down. Michael aggressively waved him off. But within moments, several men had rappelled down a rope dangling from the helicopter and were standing on the platform.

Armed and standing guard in 1978, Michael Bates waits on Sealand with several others as a helicopter approaches.

After the helicopter flew away, Michael soon recognized the thick accent and deep voice of one of the men standing before him. Michael had previously overheard the man on the phone with his father as they made plans to meet in Austria. Showing him a forged telegram, the men told Michael that his father had given them permission to come to Sealand as part of their business negotiations. Skeptical, Michael figured he had no choice but to host the men. So, the group headed inside to talk. When Michael turned his back to pour one of them a whiskey, the men slipped out the door, locking him in the room, tying a cord around the external handle.

Orchestrating the putsch was a German named Alexander Gottfried Achenbach. A former diamond dealer and entrepreneur, Achenbach had approached the Bates family in the early 1970s with the idea of greatly expanding the principality. His plan involved building adjacent but attached to the platform a casino, a square lined with trees, a duty-free shop, a bank, a post office, a hotel, a restaurant, and apartments. The Bates family embraced the idea, though they were slow to act on it.

But Achenbach was a man on a mission, and by 1975 he had been deputized as Sealand's "foreign minister," at which point he moved to the platform to help write its constitution. Achenbach filed a petition to renounce his German citizenship, demanding he instead be recognized as a citizen of Sealand. Local authorities in Aachen, Germany, where he made the petition, refused his request.

In his effort to win Sealand official recognition, Achenbach then sent the constitution to 150 states around the world, as well as to the United Nations, with the request that it be ratified. But foreign leaders remained skeptical. Sealand was missing three fundamental character- istics that it needed to be considered a nation under international law: national territory, state authority, and people. A court in Cologne ruled that the platform was not part of the earth's surface, that it was lacking in community life, and that its minuscule territory did not constitute a living space that was viable over the long term.

Achenbach grew increasingly impatient about his stalled plans for Sealand, and he blamed the Bates family for a lack of commitment. He soon hatched an idea for speeding things along. He hired the helicop- ter and sent his lawyer, Gernot Pütz, and two other Dutchmen to take control of the platform. The men held Michael hostage for several days before putting him on a fishing boat headed to Holland, where he was released back to his parents. Though Achenbach was not present at the scene of the coup, declassified British records and other documents that came to light after release of the Panama Papers made it clear that he was the likely puppeteer behind the curtain.

Roy was furious about the coup. "He got really silent when you knew he was mad, and at this point all words just stopped," Michael said about his father. Not to be outdone, Roy soon decided to take his micronation back by force. After returning to England, he enlisted John Crewdson, a friend and helicopter pilot who had worked on some of the early James Bond movies, to fly an armed team to the platform. They arrived just before dawn, approaching from downwind to lessen the noise from their rotors. Sliding down a rope from the helicopter,

Michael hit the deck hard, jarring and firing the shotgun strapped to his chest, nearly hitting his father. Startled that the intruders were already opening fire, the German guard on deck immediately surrendered. Sealand's founders were back in charge.

Roy quickly released all the men except Pütz, who was charged with treason and locked in Sealand's brig for two months. "The imprisonment of Pütz is in a way an act of piracy, committed on the high sea but still in front of British territory by British citizens," officials from the German embassy wrote in a plea for help to the British government. In a separate correspondence, a Dutch foreign affairs officer offered a suggestion for solving their problem: "Is there any chance of a British patrol vessel 'passing by' the Fort and somehow knocking it into the sea?" The British government responded that it lacked jurisdiction to take any action.

West Germany eventually sent a diplomat to Sealand from London to negotiate Pütz's release, a move that Michael later described as de facto recognition of Sealand's sovereignty. Made to wash the toilets and prepare coffee while he awaited his fate, Pütz was released from Sealand after paying a fine of 75,000 deutsche marks, or about $37,500, to the Bates family.

The whole incident took an even more confusing turn several years later. In 1980, when Roy went to the Netherlands to file charges against one of the Dutchmen, he was represented by Pütz, his former prisoner. This led some observers to question whether the coup was merely an elaborate charade by Roy and Pütz to gain publicity for Sealand and legal recognition of it as a sovereignty. When I asked about the allegation, Michael rejected it. "There's photographic proof," he said about their taking back the fortress. "It was entirely real." I waited before asking more questions, letting his reply air out a bit, because I fully expected, hoped even, that he would add some qualifying relativism about there being no myths, only truths viewed by skeptics. He didn't give me the satisfaction. He offered no explanation for how Pütz went so quickly from foe to friend.

Michael also dismissed my suggestion that the coup was karmic. "No honor among thieves, right?" I asked. Sealand was born not of thievery but of conquest, he rebutted, which felt to me like a distinction without a difference. "We govern Sealand. It's not a lawless place." Michael was emphatic on this point, repeating it often.

If linguists say that the difference between a dialect and a language is an army, and theologians contend that a cult is a church with no political clout, then the Bates family's view seemed to be that a platform becomes a country based on its ability to control its narrative. Granted, the narrative seemed so bizarre at times, spinning off into tangents and conspiracy theories, that it would be a challenge for anyone to control. But the Bates family remained the unofficial historians, and years of practice have honed their ability to tell a good tale.

Sealand's second coup posed the bigger threat. Michael explained that he thought they were done with Achenbach. But then the FBI called in 1997. They wanted to talk about the murder of the fashion designer Gianni Versace on the front steps of his Miami home. "By this point, we were pretty accustomed to getting bizarre phone calls related to Sealand," Michael said. The killer, Andrew Cunanan, committed suicide on a houseboat he had broken into several days after murdering Versace. But during the investigation the owner of the boat, a man named Torsten Reineck had presented forged Sealand passports to authorities. Reineck also allegedly drove around Los Angeles in a Mercedes sedan with Sealand "diplomatic plates."

Michael told the FBI that Sealand had issued only about three hundred "official" passports to people he vetted personally. The FBI, in turn, pointed Michael to a website claiming to be run by Sealand's "government in exile" that sold passports and boasted of a "diaspora" population of

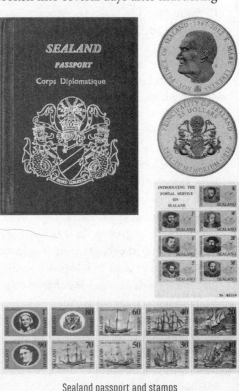

Sealand passport and stamps

160,000 persons, with embassies around the world. Investigators traced the passports and the website to Spain, where they found evidence that Achenbach had waited patiently to stage another coup, though this time from afar. Michael unpersuasively claimed to know nothing about the numerous fraudulent schemes that peddled Sealand's name and diplomatic credentials online and in the real world.

There were stranger turns to come. Later that same year, the Civil Guard, Spain's paramilitary police, arrested a flamenco nightclub owner named Francisco Trujillo for selling diluted gasoline at his Madrid filling station. Identifying himself as Sealand's "consul," Trujillo produced a diplomatic passport and claimed immunity from prosecution. Contacted by police, Spain's Foreign Ministry said no such country existed. The police then raided three Sealand offices in Madrid and a shop that made Sealand license plates. They found that Trujillo had been describing himself as a colonel of Sealand, having even designed military uniforms for himself and other officers.

Spanish police also discovered that Sealand's "government in exile" had sold thousands of Sealand passports embossed with the Bates seal—two crowned sea creatures. These passports had reportedly appeared all over the globe, from eastern Europe to Africa. Nearly four thousand were sold in Hong Kong when many residents scrambled to obtain foreign documents before Britain handed the colony over to China in 1997. Among the people whom Spanish police tied to the passports were Moroccan hashish smugglers and Russian arms dealers. Several of these underworld characters had also tried to broker a $50 million deal to send fifty tanks, ten MiG-23 fighter jets, and other combat aircraft, artillery, and armored vehicles from Russia to Sudan, according to Spanish police. About eighty people were accused of committing fraud, falsifying documents, and pretending to be foreign dignitaries, the *Los Angeles Times* reported.

I asked Michael if he thought these transactions were part of a larger scheme to take over Sealand, physically or in name. He said maybe. "Most likely, though," he added, "they just wanted to make money off it as an idea." Whatever their motivations, these negotiations were orchestrated by a business called Sealand Trade Development Authority Limited. The Panama Papers included evidence that this company, set up by the Panama City law firm Mossack Fonseca, was tied to a vast global network of money launderers and other criminals.

The story line was loopy, even absurd, and hard at times to keep track of what was real. Sealand's German and Spanish "governments in exile" were a fictitious duplicate of a questionable original. It all reminded me of a quotation from the Jorge Luis Borges short story "Circular Ruins": "In the dream of the man who was dreaming, the dreamt man awoke."

. . .

I sat across from Michael at the table in Sealand's cluttered, dirty kitchen for several hours. Our tea grew cold as he unspooled the long and tangled yarns of Sealand's Byzantine history. After he finished, Michael watched me expressionless, as if waiting for my reaction. I stared back, waiting for him to continue. Instead, he got up and prepared another cup of tea. I noticed my notebook on the table and realized that I'd been so fascinated that I had stopped taking notes.

Before visiting this strange place, I'd read thousands of pages of old newspaper and magazine articles and declassified British documents. I'd even found some old radio and television reports. Though most of what Michael told me corresponded to what I already knew from my research, hearing it directly from the source made the stories more credible. Or, I wondered, was he just selling me the same malarkey he'd used to get the British government off his back?

I needed some air and asked Michael if he could give me a tour. We headed out of the kitchen and down the hall and squeezed down a steep spiral staircase. Each of Sealand's two legs was a tower, stacked with circular rooms. Each room was twenty-two feet in diameter. Made of concrete, they were cold and clammy and smelled of diesel and mold. Like inverse lighthouses that extended beneath the waves rather than above, most of the floors were under the waterline, which filled them with a faint gurgling sound. Some of the rooms were lit by a single dangling bulb, providing the mood lighting of a survivalist's bunker. Barrington, Sealand's guard, joined us on the tour and said that at night you could hear the pulsing throb of passing ships.

The north tower housed guest rooms, a brig, and a conference room, which was where Barrington stayed. "I like the cold, actually," he said when I asked whether the space heater was enough to keep him warm in the winter. As we descended, he paused at one room that had been outfitted as a minimalist and ecumenical chapel. An open Bible sat on a table decorated with an ornate cloth. A Koran sat on a shelf alongside works of Socrates and Shakespeare. It was a surreal and claustrophobic nook, like a library on a submarine.

We exited the top of the north tower and crossed the platform to the south tower. Michael began telling me about Sealand's most recent—and in many ways most audacious—plan: to host a server farm with sensitive data beyond the reach of snooping governments. The informational equivalent of a tax haven—and called HavenCo—the company, founded in 2000, offered web hosting for gambling, pyramid schemes, porn, subpoena-proof emails, and untraceable bank accounts. It turned away clients tied to spam, child porn, and corporate cyber sabotage. "We have our limits," Michael said. (I refrained from asking him the question on my mind, which was why pyramid schemes were okay if spam was not.) He added that in 2010 he had declined a request from representatives of WikiLeaks for a Sealand passport and safe haven for the group's founder, Julian Assange. "They were releasing more than made me comfortable," he added.

The idea of moving online services offshore was not new. Science-fiction writers had dreamed of data havens for years. Perhaps the most famous was in Neal Stephenson's *Cryptonomicon,* published in 1999, in which the sultan of Kinakuta, a fictional, small, oil-rich island between the Philippines and Borneo, invites the novel's protagonists to convert an island into a communications hub free from copyright law and other restrictions.

Not all of those efforts are fiction or fantasy. Since 2008, Google has been working to build offshore data centers that would use seawater to cool the servers—a green answer to cutting enormous air-conditioning costs on land. In 2010, a team of researchers from Harvard and MIT published a paper suggesting that if high-speed stock-trading firms hoped to get an edge, they should consider shortening the distance that the information has to travel by relocating their servers at sea. Though these plans have yet to come to fruition, the scholars presented some of their proposals at a conference hosted by the Seasteading Institute.

HavenCo was the brainchild of two tech entrepreneurs. Sean Hastings was a programmer who had moved to the British territory of Anguilla in the eastern Caribbean to work on online gambling projects. Ryan Lackey was a coder and an independent-minded MIT dropout.

Both young men were deeply committed cyber libertarians opposed to government limits on free speech or digital privacy. After persuading the Bates family to create the company at Sealand, Hastings and Lackey recruited investors, including two successful internet businessmen.

The founders of HavenCo had big plans. To deter intruders, they would protect the servers with at least four heavily armed guards. The rooms housing the machines would be filled with a pure nitrogen atmosphere. The nitrogen was unbreathable, which meant anyone entering the room would have to wear scuba gear. An elite team of coders and online security specialists would police against hackers. To avoid network connections being disrupted by Britain or other governments that wanted to crack down on HavenCo because of the content it hosted, Sealand would have redundant internet connections to multiple countries and, as a further backup, a satellite tie. Customers' data would be encrypted at all times so that even HavenCo employees would not know what clients were doing.

Most of the plans failed. "It was a disaster," Michael said mournfully, pausing in a room to stare at a wall of ten-foot-tall empty shelves where HavenCo's servers were once stacked. Cooling the server rooms became virtually impossible. Most rooms lacked outlets. Fuel for generators was always in short supply. One of the companies that HavenCo was supposed to partner with to get internet services went bankrupt. The satellite link it relied on in its place had only 128 Kbps of bandwidth, the speed of a slow home connection from the early years of the twenty-first century. The south tower of Sealand was never full of servers. The bit about nitrogen being piped into the server rooms for added security was a marketing ploy and never happened. Cyber attacks on HavenCo's website had crippled its connectivity for days. HavenCo attracted about a dozen clients, mostly online gambling sites, but these clients grew increasingly frustrated by HavenCo's outages and ineptitude, and soon they took their business elsewhere.

By 2003, Lackey had left HavenCo and grown disgruntled with his former partners. That same year, he appeared at DEF CON, the annual conference of hackers and coders, where he revealed that much of what his company had originally promised was fake or had proven unworkable. "Almost all time was spent dealing with press," Lackey told the DEF CON audience. "No one took responsibility for sales, and there was no ticketing system, so basically all initial inquiries were lost or mishandled."

Michael cited other problems. "Let's just say that we also didn't see eye to eye with the computer guys about what sort of clients we were willing to host," he said. In particular, the royal family nixed Lackey's plan to host a site that would illegally rebroadcast DVDs to its users. In Lackey's view, this type of service was exactly the sort that HavenCo had been built to provide. For all their daring, the Bates family was wary of antagonizing the British and upsetting their delicately balanced claim to sovereignty. I couldn't tell if the Bates's self-preservationist caution toward the British government was the result of maturation or had been there all along, hidden beneath so much bluster. I did have the sense, though, that their falling-out with Lackey had more to do with personality than with principle ("He was just weird," Michael kept saying) and their drawing of the line at knockoff DVDs was pure pretext. After Lackey quit HavenCo, he moved to Iraq, where he founded an internet service provider in 2004 called Blue Iraq, providing web access for the U.S. military and private contractors.

As we finished one last cup of tea in the kitchen, where we had started the day, Michael grinned unexpectedly. He seemed as proud of the convoluted story behind his family's bizarre creation as he was of Sealand's resilience. Taking advantage of a gap in international law, Sealand had grown old while other attempts at seasteads never made it far beyond what-if imaginings. The Bates family was certainly daring, but the secret to Sealand's survival was its limited ambitions. Irreverent but inconsequential, Sealand was not Al-Qaeda or ISIS seeking to create a grand caliphate. In the view of its powerful neighbors, Sealand was merely a rusty kingdom, easier to ignore than to eradicate.

The Bates family members are also masterful mythologizers, and they eagerly cultivated and protected Sealand's narrative, which in turn reinforced its sovereignty. Sealand was never a utopian safe haven; it was always more of an island notion than an island nation, or as one observer once put it, "somewhere between an unincorporated family business and a marionette show." A Hollywood movie about their project was in the works (it was unclear to me how far along it was, and the Bates family kept hush-hush about details). In the meantime, Sealand is largely financed through the principality's online "shopping mall,"

Michael and Roy Bates in 1973 at Sealand

which is run by the Bates family. The mall's merchandise is priced not in Sealand dollars but in British pounds sterling. Mugs go for £9.99, about $14.00; titles of nobility, £29.99, or $40.00, and up.

When it was time for me to return to shore, the crane lowered me down in the silly wooden seat to the bobbing skiff below in the North Sea. The goofiness of that childish swing, situated as it was at the entrance and exit of this bizarre place, seemed perfectly surreal. Back on the boat alongside Sealand's concrete legs, I looked up at the rusting platform and waved good-bye to Barrington. He stood above, like some lonely Sancho Panza, keeper of the quixotic vision. The wind raking over us, Michael and James started the engine and turned the boat toward the coast. Sealand slowly receded in the distance as father and son retreated to dry land and their warm homes in Essex, where they proudly reigned over their principality from afar.

# THE SCOFFLAW FLEET

This was in truth not living; it was scarcely even existing, and
they felt that it was too little for the price they paid. They were
willing to work all the time; and when people did their best,
ought they not to be able to keep alive?

—Upton Sinclair, *The Jungle*

On the night of August 14, 2010, the captain of a South Korean trawler,
the *Oyang 70*, left Port Chalmers, New Zealand, for what would be
his final journey. The ship was bound for fishing grounds about four
hundred miles east in the South Pacific Ocean. When the ship arrived
three days later, the captain, a forty-two-year-old man named Hyonki
Shin, ordered his crew to cast the net over the vessel's rusty stern. As
the men worked furiously on the illuminated deck, the ship soon began
hoisting in thousands of pounds of a lithe, slender fish called southern
blue whiting, which writhed and flapped across the deck. With each
haul, the silvery mound of fish grew.

A type of cod, blue whiting was sometimes ground up into fish
sticks or imitation lobster. More often it was pelletized and sold as
protein-rich food for farmed carnivorous fish like salmon. At about
nine cents per pound, blue whiting was a low-price catch, which meant
the *Oyang 70* had to catch a lot to make a profit. As the crew pulled in
the net, ton after ton of the fish slid to the deck—eighty-six thousand
pounds in all, a decent haul.

The battered 242-foot ship was long past its prime. The average age
for distant-water fishing boats in the South Korean fleet was twenty-
nine, and the *Oyang 70* was thirty-eight years old. Port captains called
the *Oyang 70* "tender," a euphemism for unstable. A month before it set
sail, a New Zealand inspector ranked the ship as "high risk," citing over

a dozen safety violations, including one of the ship's main doors below deck that was not watertight. The inspector later cleared the ship to sail after its operator claimed that all problems had been fixed.

One of the *Oyang*'s unsolved problems was the man at the helm. Shin had replaced the previous captain, who fell overboard in a drunken stupor and drowned. When the ship cast its first net that day, Shin had been at the helm for nine months. Former crew members referred to him as an "angry man"—sullen, prone to screaming, and almost always carrying a bottle of clear liquid that he swigged. Deckhands debated whether it was water or grain alcohol. None was reckless enough to ask.

Shin drove his men hard. As the first net was pulled that night, they sorted the squirming, oily mound on the aft deck, quickly heaving the fish down a chute to the ship's interior to make space for the next haul. One floor down, in the ship's factory, over a dozen men stood cramped before the "slime line," a conveyor belt, wielding knives and operating circular saws. Their job was to remove heads, guts, and bycatch, while the valuable part of the fish continued down the line for packing and freezing. The men needed roughly half a day to fully process the first catch. But before they made it through the load, Shin ordered the men on deck to put the net back in the water. Work continued virtually nonstop over the next twenty-four hours.

Around 3:00 a.m. on August 18, 2010, the ship's first mate, Minsu

The fish-sorting counter on a South Korean ship

Park, frantically roused Shin from his sleep. The net was too full, Park told him. It was pulling the boat under. Water in the engine room was already several feet deep. The crew on deck was begging to cut the net. The captain jumped from his bunk and raced to the bridge. But instead of ordering the net cut, he demanded that the bosun, the man in charge of the deckhands, command them to keep hoisting. That order would be Shin's last.

. . .

For the Sajo Oyang Corporation, which operated the vessel, the poor treatment of workers and the dismal condition of its ship was nothing unusual. Time and again, Sajo Oyang abused its crew members, often treating them with the same disregard as it treated the bycatch in its nets—as a distraction and annoyance. Sometimes, that disregard cost men their lives. The infamy of the Sajo Oyang fleet, as well as the fate that befell its captain and crew, was well-known in maritime circles.

In many of the outlaw ocean stories I covered, one consistent theme was how the vastness of the seas made it difficult to chase down bad actors—finding the criminals in the first place was often impossible. What stood out about the story of the Oyang ships was that safety risks and violations, and the persistent mistreatment of workers, were hiding in plain sight. But at every turn, inspectors and regulators largely shrugged off their responsibilities, often with a crass disdain for the lives at stake.

As with some plane crashes that are caused by mechanical failures, there is often a narrative that is pieced together after the fact that makes it seem almost inevitable, a series of tiny mistakes playing out in slow motion, each one building on the one before, in which everyone knows the fate of the victims before they do. In the case of the Oyang fleet, such forensics was almost laughably redundant; anyone familiar with the ships would know that catastrophe was virtually a foregone conclusion.

In the spring of 2017, I flew to New Zealand and Indonesia to investigate this scofflaw fleet and the disasters that befell half a dozen Oyang ships. What I learned as I pored over the case files was a sobering lesson not just in the abject cruelties inflicted upon fishing crews but also in the fate of the men who survive and speak up.

Aside from the eight Korean officers, the crew of the *Oyang 70* consisted of thirty-six Indonesians, six Filipinos, and one Chinese. On average, the Indonesians earned $180 per month. The officers derided the Muslims on board as "dogs" or "monkeys." The drinking water was often brown and tasted of metal, workers would later tell investigators and lawyers. After a certain point, the only food on board for the crew was rice and the fish they caught. Men were docked pay if they ate too slowly. The crew described the ship as "a floating freezer"; the heater on board barely worked. The shared toilet lacked running water. There were so many roaches that a crew member later said he could smell roaches cooking as they fell onto the hot engine block.

The *Oyang 70* was known as a stern trawler, towing a long, cylindrical net from behind. The ship's most intense work happened in the dark because blue whiting is a schooling fish that lives near the seabed, more easily caught at night when it feeds on plankton, small shrimp, and krill closer to the surface.

As the crew struggled with the net on August 18, everyone on board knew it was more fish than the boat could handle. No one knew by how much, though, because there were no batteries in the net's weight sensors. The cost of replacing the ship's trawl net was more than $150,000. The price of losing a net full of fish would be the captain's job.

As the net was winched up the stern ramp in the early morning darkness, it looked like a monstrous whale. At the chute, the net mouth opened and the whale regurgitated a flood of fish, so much that the hold soon clogged. The closed end, or "cod" end, of the net stretched down into the sea behind them. Trailing the ship, this mesh cylinder stretched nearly a hundred feet. A fishing captain would later describe it as likely having looked like "a big silver sausage." At the far end underwater, the net bulged to cover an area the size of six tennis courts. About six tons of fish were on the ship's slipway, while another hundred tons remained underwater—easily more than $20,000 worth.

Other captains would later testify that this catch was more than double the size of a "bag" that they would have been willing to pull onto a ship of its size. Behind the ship, the bloated net began dragging the *Oyang 70*'s rudder deep underwater, jutting its bow awkwardly toward the inky sky.

A typical captain would have immediately identified how dangerous the situation aboard the *Oyang 70* had become. Like fighter pilots, deep-sea fishing captains are as much born as made. It takes a rare, almost instinctual calm and spatial acuity to steady a 1,870-ton ship while reading the tides, countering gusts, and directing a dozen men scrambling on deck. This is especially true when hoisting a hundred-ton net, which has to be carefully centered behind the ship.

Shin lacked this instinct. He was not calm, nor was his ship stable in the best of circumstances, and certainly not when his net suddenly slipped to the port side, abruptly tipping the *Oyang 70* to a fifteen-degree list. In the factory below deck, the men on the slime line continued working, even as the ship tilted and even as the water rose to their knees. In a desperate attempt to right the ship, Shin ordered some of the men to move any heavy equipment they could budge to starboard and tether it there.

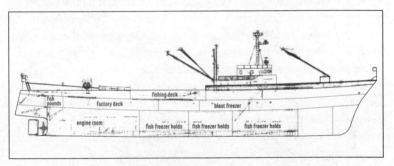

Schematic of the *Oyang 70*

But the list remained, and water began rushing in through the open "offal chute," a port-side door for expelling fish guts and heads into the ocean. At the same time, dead fish and debris clogged the ship's scuppers, trapping on board the water that should have drained off. The door to the engine room below, which also should have been sealed, was open. So, too, was the fish hold.

Everything began flowing in the wrong direction. Water bubbled up through floor drains and sprayed in through portholes, and walls became waterfalls. The ability of a boat to flush its decks is as essential as humans' ability to breathe. Water always needs to be leaving the vessel faster than it's entering. When it's not, problems multiply quickly.

The crew had stacked flattened cardboard boxes over the generator in a futile effort to protect it from the water coming in from above. Soon, the sump pumps, designed to drain water, shut off. Even before the *Oyang 70* began taking on water, the ship was off-kilter because the captain had ordered most of the boxed fish to be stacked in one hold rather than spreading them across two. The ship's fuel tanks had not been "pressed up," or filled to maximum, adding to the *Oyang*'s instability because of internal sloshing, also known as a "free-surface effect."

Around 4:00 a.m., a heated argument erupted on the bridge. The chief engineer was in tears and screaming in Korean at the captain, pleading with him to cut the net. The captain finally gave in. The bosun put on a harness and shinnied onto a section of the mesh, knife in hand. Other crewmen followed him, and they all slashed frantically at the net. Too little, too late, as the ship continued to roll over.

What had been obvious before was now unavoidable: the *Oyang 70* was going down. Chaos overtook the ship. On the bridge, Shin made a distress call on the VHF radio. Men began leaping into the sea. Only the Korean officers wore life jackets. The *Oyang*'s rescue boat was in the water. But it, too, had been overturned by the waves.

The water temperature before dawn that morning was about forty-four degrees Fahrenheit. The ship had sixty-eight survival suits, designed to insulate against the cold—more than enough for the fifty-one men on board. None of the crew put one on. It's unclear whether any of them knew how.

Greed, not water, sank the *Oyang 70*. The ship had tried to swallow too much fish; the ocean swallowed the ship instead. The last men off the drowning ship said that they saw Shin in the wheelhouse, refusing to abandon his post or put on a life jacket. Hugging a pole and clutching his clear bottle, he was muttering in Korean and crying. The *Amaltal Atlantis*, a New Zealand–flagged fishing boat, heard the VHF call and headed to the scene, arriving an hour later. Much later and the forty-five men it rescued would likely have frozen or drowned.

The final moments of a sinking ship are a frightening and gut-wrenching sight—something I'd witnessed up close once before in Indonesia. It looks as if a monster were dragging down the vessel from below. The final moments of suction can be so strong that it pulls down nearby men in the water with it. "Within 10 minutes, the boat was gone," said Greg Lyall, captain of *Amaltal Atlantis,* during the coroner's investigation. "No alarms, no lighting, nothing."

Several of the survivors suffered acute hypothermia. Rescuers never recovered the captain's body. Among the five other crew members who died, three were found frozen, floating in a lifeboat. On land, a preventable disaster like this might have spelled the end of a company. Not so on the open ocean.

The *Oyang 70* in June 2006

.  .  .

In the world of deep-sea fishing, the Sajo Group is a leviathan. Founded in 1971, the group oversees a huge fleet of more than seventy fishing ships. The company's slogan is "Nature is delicious." By 2010, the group had made over $1 billion in annual revenue, millions of dollars of which came from fish pulled from New Zealand waters.

The Sajo Oyang's corporate presence in New Zealand was structured like a family of Russian nesting dolls: larger companies enveloping subsidiaries and subsidiaries of subsidiaries. In New Zealand, the Sajo Oyang company partnered with a smaller firm called Southern Storm Fishing, which helped manage the fleet's operations. Southern Storm contracted with another company called Fisheries Consultancy to oversee many of the ships' other needs. The men who worked on the boats were recruited and contracted not by the Sajo Oyang company directly but by manning agencies based in Indonesia, Myanmar, South Korea, and elsewhere. Such was the norm for international fishing companies. By outsourcing the recruitment, logistics, and payroll of foreign crews, the company centralized profits and decentralized liability.

The sinking of the *Oyang 70* made headline news in New Zealand. To handle damage control, the company tapped a pugnacious lobbyist and spokesman named Glenn Inwood. Famous for representing several other controversial and difficult industries, most notably whaling and tobacco, Inwood knew just what to do, and he sprang into action, arguing that the tragedy was an isolated accident.

Fishing was difficult and dangerous work, Inwood argued. Accidents happen. Other companies had lost ships, too. Human rights and ocean advocates were fabricating the criticisms of the Sajo Oyang fleet, he said. Competitors also raised red flags because they wanted the foreign fleet expelled from New Zealand's waters, he contended.

About eight months after the *Oyang 70* sank, its replacement, the *Oyang 75,* arrived at Lyttelton Port in New Zealand after two months of fishing in New Zealand's waters, he said. Shortly before it departed again for the fishing grounds, Inwood gave reporters a tour of the new vessel, which he hailed as a model of the highest labor and fishing standards.

But even Sajo Oyang's deft fixer couldn't control the publicity surrounding what happened next. Early on the cold morning of June 20, 2011, a parishioner went to her church in Lyttelton, where she discovered thirty-two Indonesian men hiding in the nave. Hemmed in by mountains that form a natural amphitheater on the eastern edge of New Zealand's southern island, Lyttelton is a quiet port town of about twenty-two hundred residents just outside Christchurch. Shivering and distraught, the Indonesian men had fled the "model" *Oyang 75* while the ship was being unloaded.

Waking up around 4:00 a.m., the Indonesians had snuck off the ship while the captain was still asleep. Because they were Muslim, the men had wandered the streets looking for a mosque; finding none, they took refuge in the church instead.

One by one, the men described to church officials and later to government investigators their captivity on a ship of horrors. A chief engineer broke a deckhand's nose for inadvertently bumping into him. Another officer punched a crew member in the head so often that he lost part of his vision. Insubordinate crew were sometimes locked in the refrigerator. Others were forced to eat rotten fish bait. On good days, shifts lasted twenty hours. Sometimes they worked for forty-eight hours straight. "I often thought about asking for help," Andi Sukendar, one of the Indonesian deckhands, said in court papers. "But I didn't know who to ask."

The worst part, the men said, was the sexual assaults, mostly at the hands of a sadistic bosun named Wongeun Kang. The forty-two-year-old Korean stole their clothing as they bathed so that he could chase them as they ran naked back to their bunks. In the galley, he approached the men from behind and jabbed them with his exposed erection. When they passed him in the halls, he grabbed their genitals. Other Korean officers made advances, the crewmen said, but none were as aggressive as the bosun. He assaulted deckhands while they showered. He climbed into their bunks at night when they were sleeping. "The bosun tried to teach me how to have sex with him but I refused," one crew member recounted. Others were not able to stave him off.

I wish I could say I was surprised by these reports. But what I read was sickeningly familiar. The expanse of the sea and the dictatorial power of officers over crews allow cruel and abusive behavior that is often only uncovered when a ship sinks.

As police interviewed the *Oyang 75*'s crew in Lyttelton, the ship's owner refused to pay for their accommodation or food, claiming that they no longer worked for him. The bosun was fired and quickly sent back to Korea, avoiding prosecution in New Zealand. The manning agents in Indonesia who had recruited the men to the ships repeatedly called the crew members' families, pressuring them to be quiet and not talk to reporters or lawyers.

Over the next year, a New Zealand journalist, Michael Field, and two University of Auckland researchers, Christina Stringer and Glenn Simmons, investigated further. Interviewing dozens of crewmen from several Sajo Oyang company vessels and hundreds of men from other foreign ships fishing in New Zealand waters, they revealed a broad pattern of abuse.

Beyond the abhorrent working conditions on its ships, the Oyang fleet was putting entire ecosystems at risk with its fishing practices. One ship was impounded in Russia for illegal fishing and later fined in New Zealand for discharging thousands of gallons of used engine oil into the sea. Two other Sajo Oyang ships had been caught in New

Zealand's waters dumping hundreds of thousands of dollars' worth of fish overboard, a practice known as high-grading, used to circumvent catch quotas and make room for fresher or more valuable fish.

The worst part, though, were the labor abuses. Workers on Sajo Oyang ships described meals speckled with dead bugs and mattresses riddled with biting mites, men hiding in closets from violent officers, and rapes that occurred in nearby bunks that they felt powerless to stop. Crewmen recounted being issued torn hand-me-downs and ill-fitting boots, tattered jackets and gloves. Captains kept the sailors' passports and certification papers to ensure they could not leave.

On one of the company's other ships in New Zealand's waters, a deckhand named Santoso accidentally crushed his finger under a heavy roll of rope. When it was later amputated, he was sent immediately back to work below deck, reopening his wound. He woke up at night to find roaches crawling on it, drawn by the dried blood. Another deckhand named Abduladis said that when the ship was loaded with fish, the heater that the men relied on to keep warm was turned off to divert power to the freezer. Unwanulloh, an engineer, told investigators that the crew was only allowed to wash garments with seawater in bags used for fish processing, leaving him little choice but to wear rancid-smelling work clothes every day. Warsila, who worked in the ship's storage area, described food flecked with bugs; he ate it anyway, because he was so hungry.

· · · ·

Among the most illustrative parts of piecing together the story of the Oyang fleet was what it taught about entrapment. Why did men take these jobs? Once they saw how bad the conditions were, why didn't they flee immediately? The obvious answer was desperation, but I wanted to know what else had been at play.

Most of the crew members on the Sajo Oyang ships were from Tegal in central Java, Indonesia, recruited by labor agents and manning agencies through an intricate system of debt bondage. They had signed contracts in English, a language they did not speak. Typically, their salary was about $235 per month—a fraction of the minimum wage required under law, at least while they worked in New Zealand's waters.

Indonesian and Filipino sailors from the sunken *Oyang 70* wait in line to leave New Zealand in August 2010.

From this wage, labor agents deducted expenses like "currency variations," "transfer fees," and medical checkups, which, in some instances, amounted to 30 percent of their earnings.

To get the jobs, the men often had paid over $175 in fees—more than a month's salary for some. And as collateral, they often handed over their most prized possessions to ensure the completion of their two-year contracts: home deeds, car registrations, and in one case the land grant certificate for a community mosque. I knew that fleet owners exploited their crews, but the stories of these deckhands offered an unusually clear distillation of how they exert control, including blacklisting threats, cultural shame, and leveraging through property liens.

Breaching the contracts would bring economic ruin to their families. Susanto, a deckhand on the *Oyang 77*, put up his elementary and junior high school graduation certificates. In his small village, such records are irreplaceable. If he failed to get the papers back, he would be unemployable. The documents were "the only things of value he had," one affidavit said.

· · ·

News of the scams and abuse in this work rarely made it back to the small villages where new crew members were recruited because those who had been tricked were too ashamed to talk about it and to warn others. Even those who knew the risks were willing to try their luck because they were desperate for work.

As the conditions on these ships came to light in New Zealand, the public was horrified, and lawmakers began cracking down. The fishing industry went on the offensive. Inwood, the industry's all-purpose fixer, led the charge, arguing that working long hours was a standard practice on all fishing ships. The failure to pay wages was the fault not of the Sajo Oyang company but of manning agents in Indonesia who were responsible for handling such matters. Koreans tend to be more physical and vocal than Indonesians. Some of the abuse allegations on the ships were misunderstandings stemming from these cultural differences, he argued.

"During its entire period of operating in New Zealand, Sajo Oyang, its officers, crew, and representatives have never been the subject of a prosecution," Inwood wrote in a letter to the editor of a New Zealand newspaper in July 2012. "That is a rare accomplishment in an industry as highly regulated as the New Zealand fishing industry."

Other fishing companies argued that the problems in the Sajo Oyang fleet were isolated and should not be used to justify new regulations. "The New Zealand fishing industry is already a bureaucrat's paradise," argued Aurora Fisheries Limited. Sealord, another large seafood company based in New Zealand, said that the foreign ships only harvested low-value species that are "unprofitable and/or not practicable for New Zealand vessels to harvest." Because many of these foreign ships brought the fish they caught to shore for processing in New Zealand, Sealord argued that the loss of these vessels would result in $196 million in lost exports and job losses for Kiwis.

Meanwhile, the Sajo Oyang company worked to protect its brand. To try to figure out who was funneling information to Michael Field, the New Zealand reporter who continued to dominate coverage of the industry, Inwood submitted open-records requests to government agencies and the University of Auckland, seeking emails and other documents. When the U.S. ambassador on human trafficking, Luis CdeBaca, traveled to New Zealand to discuss the claims of abuse in the fishing industry, Michael Field reported that the Sajo Oyang company hired a private investigator to trail him.

While reporting in Auckland in the spring of 2017, I met with Christina Stringer, one of the two University of Auckland researchers who had brought to light many of the abuses in New Zealand's waters. She recounted how, at one point during her investigation into foreign fishing fleets, she and her research partner, Glenn Simmons, were dining at a local Chinese restaurant with several Indonesian crew members from one of the Oyang ships. The men were living in safe houses at the time and, having no income, were dependent on the kindness of strangers to eat. The former boss of the crew happened to be dining at the same restaurant, and after he took pictures of the crew with his cell phone and made some calls, a group of men appeared outside the restaurant, glaring at the crew as they waited for them to leave. Simmons hustled the crew to a car out the back and managed to lose the group, though not without a chase.

The company had good reason to fight the bad publicity. The New Zealand government had begun issuing fines: the equivalent of $340,200 for the *Oyang 75*'s dumping of low-value catches to replace them with more valuable fish, $8,500 for illegally dumping oil at sea, and $97,600 for when the *Oyang 77* tossed more than seventy-three tons of fish overboard.

Pressure was also mounting from abroad. The U.S. State Department released its annual "Trafficking in Persons Report" in June 2012, which explicitly faulted New Zealand for poor treatment of foreign fishing workers. In response, New Zealand took a drastic step. In August 2014, the parliament passed a law expelling all foreign fishing vessels from its national waters. Fishing companies had two years to comply and were given the option of changing the nationality—their ships' "flag"—to New Zealand.

The law was meant to better protect the roughly fifteen hundred foreign nationals working on foreign-chartered vessels in its waters by forcing these ships to comply with New Zealand's labor standards. It was a bold move because it would cost New Zealand hundreds of millions of dollars in foreign investment as fishing companies moved elsewhere rather than shoulder the added burden and cost of the new regulations. To fish in New Zealand's waters, all crew had to be provided with access to personalized bank accounts to deposit wages, observers would be required on virtually all foreign-owned fishing vessels, and there would be independent audits of wages.

The existence of forced labor on fishing ships was not a revelation. Stories of sea slavery had been reported for over a decade on boats from Thailand, Ireland, Taiwan, and elsewhere. But no country had ever acted as aggressively as New Zealand did in response.

Still, seafarer unions and lawyers for the fishing boat workers questioned whether the government had gone far enough. They argued that the effect of New Zealand's law would be to push bad behavior elsewhere as the worst scofflaws simply opted to leave New Zealand's waters and set up shop in jurisdictions that exert even less control over foreign fishing fleets. I'd seen how a crackdown in one country just makes other countries with more lax enforcement more appealing.

Had New Zealand wanted to take an even more aggressive stand, it had the right, for example, to confiscate the *Oyang 75* and the *Oyang 77* for fishery crimes. The government could have seized and sold these ships to send a stronger message to the Sajo Oyang company, and to repay the foreign workers their back wages. Instead, the government released both ships back to the company once the fines were paid. The *Oyang 75* subsequently traveled to East Africa near Mauritius, while the *Oyang 70* sailed to an area near the Falkland Islands. Both were spotted by satellite in banned areas.

The regulatory response to the Oyang tragedies was a textbook case of dissipated outrage. Amid the revelations of horrifying mistreatment of ship workers, the public's shock forced lawmakers and regulators to act. But over time, the shipping industry shifted and muddied the narrative. And the response never fully addressed the core problem.

For rogue ship operators, there were other waters. And the inspectors whose job it was to ensure the safety of the ships and crews ignored violations that were staring them in the face.

·  ·  ·

It didn't take long for another disaster to strike the Sajo Oyang fleet—this time in the Bering Sea between Alaska and Russia. About four months after the parliament in Wellington passed its watershed law, another ship owned by the Sajo Oyang company was fighting for its life. Built in Tokyo in 1964, the 1,753-ton *Oryong 501* was a stern trawler, like the *Oyang 70*. The sixty-man crew included eleven South Koreans, thirty-five Indonesians, thirteen Filipinos, and one Russian fisheries inspector, whose job it was to keep tabs on how many and what types of fish were caught. The captain was a forty-six-year-old Korean man named Kim Kye-hwan. These men would meet a terrible fate almost identical to the one that killed a half dozen of the crew on their sister ship the *Oyang 70,* which sank near New Zealand four years earlier in 2010.

The *501* had embarked from Busan, South Korea's southernmost port. Under a fisheries deal with Russia, it was one of six South Korean trawlers allowed to catch pollack, best known as the main ingredient of the McDonald's Filet-O-Fish sandwich. Pollack is also a popular dish in South Korea, which has at least twenty-eight names for the fish depending on its age, size, and location. South Korea began trawling for pollack in the Bering Sea in the late 1970s and early 1980s after depleting the stocks in its own waters.

On December 1, 2014, a fierce snowstorm battered the fishing grounds off the coast of Russia's far eastern Chukotka region. Winds topping sixty miles per hour sent forty-foot waves across the *Oryong*'s deck. A dozen men struggled to stay on their feet while trying to pull in a net filled with twenty tons of pollack. The rain was so intense that one man later said it seemed more like fog because visibility was so limited. The men could hear but not see the waves coming at them.

Storm waves in the Bering Sea have been known to grow to more than ninety feet, the stuff of apocalyptic movies. Walls of water that big can roll a ship in seconds. But the size of a wave isn't its only deadly threat. Timing is critical. A medium-sized wave can topple an already-listing ship. Placement matters, too: Is it a broadside blow or a top-down slam? The upkeep of a vessel, especially its drainage capacity, also can determine whether it survives a good drubbing. The wave that sank the *Oryong* was not especially large by oceangoing standards—about twenty-five feet tall—but the blow had deadly timing and was aimed squarely at a soft target.

Kye-hwan made two stupendously bad calls. First, he ordered his men to keep working through the foul weather. "Forced overfishing" was the expression that investigators later used in faulting him for not standing down that day. Second, Kye-hwan overruled his bosun, who pleaded with him not to open the fish hold where the nets dump their load. The bosun was worried about downflooding, the technical term for a catastrophic rush of water into the body of a ship. The captain opened the hold anyway.

The wave landed on the *501* from above the hold, delivering a roaring crush of water directly inside the ship. The wave punched a hole the size of a car tire in the wooden wall of the storage area. It was among the half a dozen factors that contributed to the sinking of the ship that day. Men on and below deck were knocked off their feet. "The boat has begun to tilt because the seawater is not draining properly," Kye-hwan said in a radio call. "It is blocked by the fish." He had turned off the engine so the crew could focus on draining, he added. "It is impossible to steer because of the leaked seawater."

Much like its sister ship the *Oyang 70*, the *Oryong 501* was poorly maintained. In South Korea, the mechanics who had worked on the *501* would later tell government investigators that its drainage system was not working properly when it left port. The vessel was also manned by a relatively inexperienced crew. Four of the eleven Koreans, including the captain, were under-qualified and didn't have the required licenses for their positions. The skipper and the chief engineer had Class 3 marine technician licenses instead of Class 2. The second mate and the first engineer also lacked proper certification. The vessel was without a second engineer, third mate, or communications operator. It was an airplane without a pilot, a classroom without a teacher. A disaster in waiting, sent out to sea.

An hour after his initial radio call, the *Oryong*'s captain radioed again. The ship was still filling with water, he said. "I tried to turn the boat, but it began to tilt," he said, sounding more panicked. "I am trying to steer it again."

As I read the description of this final panicked scene captured in news reports and government documents, I couldn't help feeling as if I were watching an exact replay of the horrific closing sequence of the fatal *Oyang 70* voyage. In a desperate attempt to right the list, Kye-hwan ordered the men to move whatever they could to the other side of the ship and secure it into place. Below deck in the factory, six men were up to their waists in frigid water. They were instructed to use manual pumps to drain the flood. Three hours later, they were still pumping as the water was up to their chests. By the time the captain ordered the crew to evacuate to lifeboats, half of the *Oryong*'s stern was submerged.

"We will have to abandon the ship soon," Kye-hwan said over the radio shortly after 4:00 p.m. "Please prepare for rescue."

Sajo Oyang claimed that there were seventy-four survival suits for the ship's crew of sixty, though, once again and for unknown reasons, few of the men wore the suits when tragedy struck. Only the Russian inspector on the ship and a Korean crewman put them on. All but seven men on board the ship died that night.

"I think I have to give you my parting words," Kye-hwan said in his final radio transmission to his longtime friend, a captain named Lee Yang-woo who was on another Oyang ship nearby. "Don't say that," Yang-woo urged. "Calmly evacuate the crewmen. You have to come out, quickly." All the lights had now gone off, Kye-hwan said. "I am staying with the boat till the very end," he added. The boat sank less than an hour later, at 5:15 p.m.

On the *Oryong 501*, much like the *Oyang 70*, neither the ships themselves nor their captains were ready to go to sea, and their crews paid the ultimate price.

. . .

The horrors that repeatedly befell the hapless crews of Sajo Oyang ships were infuriating and tragic. More important, though, they illustrated the chaotic, desultory nature of maritime regulation. A company in any other industry that tolerated repeated disasters, saw withering public scrutiny, and yet was still able to continue its business largely uninterrupted would be an international scandal. In the fishing industry, it was par for the course. Trying to prosecute a fishing industry scofflaw was like trying to catch a fish with only your hands.

I went to Indonesia in May 2017 to learn why. By talking to some of the former crew members from various Sajo Oyang ships, I hoped to tell their stories more accurately, building on what I couldn't learn from the court records and investigator reports. I had found their names using government documents and with help from lawyers and labor rights advocates. Many of the men declined to talk. Prosecutions of shipboard malfeasance often hinged on evidence collected from crews, and the Sajo Oyang company was adept at silencing potential witnesses. The Sajo Oyang company had pressured the men I found into signing nondisclosure contracts, or "peace agreements," as it called them. In exchange for partial financial settlements, these workers agreed to keep quiet and withdraw all claims—criminal and civil.

But it was not just the company that had an interest in keeping abused crew out of the public eye. After I arrived in Indonesia, I discovered that the New Zealand academic Glenn Simmons had called ahead and advised other former crew members not to talk to me. I had previously met with Simmons for coffee in Auckland, where he explained that he would not introduce me to any of the Sajo Oyang workers he knew, nor would he encourage them to talk to me if they asked him for advice. He did not trust reporters, he said, adding that he had his own research about worker safety and those workers were essential for that purpose. A lack of collegiality was one thing. Blocking journalists from talking to workers was something else entirely.

Still, with help from other academics and lawyers, I was able to meet with a dozen former Sajo Oyang crew in Jakarta. In grim progression, they filed in and sat with me in a small conference room that I rented for a day at the JW Marriott hotel in downtown Jakarta. One by one, they described how their lives took distressing turns after they tried to get unpaid wages from the Sajo Oyang company.

A man named Madrais wept as he explained that his wife had moved a month earlier to Dubai to work in another man's house as a live-in maid. She took the job to help pay back the loan shark who had fronted the money that Madrais paid to get a job on the *Oyang 77*. A second worker named Jarwadi, a former deckhand on the *Oyang 77*, described how manning agencies blacklisted him when he got back to Indonesia because he previously spoke to a lawyer about his treatment at sea. Another man named Wayhudi, who worked on the *Oyang 70*, said that he too was blacklisted. "We stood up," he said about his fight against the company. "Now the rest are benefiting and we can't work again."

An Auckland-based attorney named Karen Harding represented many of the former Sajo Oyang workers. She had spent the previous two years trying to force the New Zealand government to seize and resell the *Oyang 75*, worth $1.5 million, and the *Oyang 77*, worth $7.5 million. Her goal was to use the proceeds to pay the wages that the crew never received.

When I met Harding in Jakarta, she was in a foul mood. She had just heard that day from an appellate court in New Zealand that back wages for workers rescued from the *Oyang 70* could not come from seizing and selling other ships belonging to the company. "They expect us to force the company to get wages by selling a ship that's sitting on the seafloor," she said. Personally in debt more than $50,000 from the case, Harding planned to appeal the matter to New Zealand's Supreme Court.

A lawyer and human rights advocate in South Korea named Jong Chul Kim said that in the case of the *Oyang 70*, the company had submitted documents, including bank records, to the New Zealand government, showing that it paid its crew. Advocates reviewed the documents and determined they were fake. Kim's organization, called APIL, had tried and failed to get the government to indict the Sajo Oyang company. The perpetrators of physical and sexual abuse had returned to sea, the victims were unwilling to testify, and Korean prosecutors refused to pursue the matter, he explained.

Another lawyer in Jakarta named David Surya represented the families of six men who died on the *Oryong 501*. At the scene of the sinking, rescuers recovered four bodies that were in the lifeboats or floating in the water. Surya said that because these families were Muslim, they had hoped to get the bodies of their loved ones back faster so that, for religious reasons, they could bury them sooner. The company took advantage of this rush, he said, and called the families incessantly, visited their homes, and offered them money to sign papers promising not to sue. Each family was still owed more than $60,000 in unpaid wages, and Surya said he had reached an impasse in the Korean courts in trying to get their nondisclosure or "peace agreements" thrown out.

Meanwhile, Sajo Oyang ignored half a dozen emails and calls I made to the company. After several days of interviews with crew members, I sat in a café in Jakarta one evening and sifted through what I had heard during my conversations with these workers and their advocates, trying to make sense of it all.

The presumption at the heart of this type of reporting is that by casting light on malfeasance, you help deter it from continuing. But in cases like this, it's hard not to question the journalistic mission. Was I chasing some grand theory of lawlessness at sea? Was the goal to bring to justice the people who abused these men? Perhaps the more I pursued the culprits in crimes like those on the Oyang ships, the more these culprits ran, and the less likely their victims would be to get what little was owed them.

New Zealand's bold decision to expel the Sajo Oyang fleet and other foreign ships from its waters had undoubtedly raised global awareness of the abhorrent conditions in the industry. That ruling was due in part to the tireless work of lawyers, advocates, journalists, and academics. In March 2018, the Supreme Court in New Zealand ruled favorably on Harding's petition requiring the company to pay more than $7 million in back wages. Still, the victims of these abuses paid a heavy price even once they were on land, and meanwhile the Sajo Oyang company remained relatively recalcitrant.

Even though I had reported on quite a few grim industries over the years (coal mining, long-haul trucking, sex work, garment and glue factories), I was still stunned by the conditions on fishing boats. There were some obvious explanations—the lack of unions, the confining and transient nature of the job, and the vast distance from shore and from government oversight.

Culture certainly plays a role as well. Ships are masculine and military-like arenas. There is honor in hardship and the ability to endure it without complaint. Governance on board is rigidly hierarchical and decidedly undemocratic. Feedback from the rank and file is generally unwelcome.

Silence is core to the way of life on ships, and breaking it can be a dangerous crime. Perhaps the best advice I heard early during my reporting came from a British first mate. "You want to fit in?" he said as we left port. "Take up as little space as possible." His counsel was less about the cramped living quarters than about the social risk of idle chatter. A respect for this silence, a comfort with it, the ability to use it at the right moments, was possibly the single most valuable tool I picked up during my reporting, because it was the key that allowed me to access people and places.

I came to admire mariners' quiet self-possession and their comfort with these long silences, some of which seemed to last for days. Over time, I also came to respect the silence itself, particularly in contrast to the world back home, where so much of my life was online, a place prone to oversharing and immediate gratification. Life on these ships, on the other hand, was so utterly off-line and defined by privacy, quiet, and waiting.

And yet I also wondered if this silence was what made mariners so famously gruff and frequently ill-suited for life back onshore. If nothing else, this silence was the backdrop for an almost theological resignation that many seafarers had about their fate. Many deckhands, especially in Indonesia, knew about what happened to the *Oyang* crew, and it seemed almost to bolster the grim inevitability that many of them perceived in this profession. The *Oyang* case reminded workers that when they stood up to the industry, they often lost. They were not wrong to assume that sometimes it was safest to keep silent.

. . .

For months after my frustrating trip to New Zealand, I continued to monitor the *Oyang 75* from afar. Satellite technology made it easier to identify illegal behavior. More than eight thousand miles from Jakarta, a crew of forty-seven men was working the waters near the Falkland Islands off the coast of Argentina, hauling tons of squid onto the *Oyang 75*. It had been about six years since a crew from this same ship had fled in 2011 to the church in Lyttelton, New Zealand, to escape the rapes and beatings on board.

The location where I found the *Oyang 75* was a strange, almost mystical stretch of water known as the City of Lights. Home to hundreds of illegal fishing boats, by some estimates the highest concentration in the world, the area earned its name because at night several hundred jiggers used industrial-strength lamps to attract squid. These lights were so bright that the night sky glowed in satellite photographs of this patch of ocean.

The City of Lights was attractive to ships hoping to fish illegally, or those with checkered pasts, like the *Oyang 75,* because a territorial dispute between Argentina and England created a jurisdictional vacuum. The Argentinian government had tried to police the City of Lights, most of which overlaps with its territorial waters, but its navy never recovered from its failed fight with the British over the islands. Argentina's Coast Guard had but eight ships to patrol more than one million square miles of ocean. The fishing ships that worked these waters were virtually never checked for labor, environmental, or fishing violations.

The *Oyang 75* lacked a license to trawl for squid in the City of Lights, and as I tracked the ship by satellite, I watched it routinely enter Argentinian waters to fish illegally, according to Argentinian navy officials. When the ship headed to port in Montevideo, the capital of Uruguay, I saw an opportunity to visit with its crew. I quickly hired an Argentinian investigator to fly to Uruguay. After the *Oyang 75* docked, the investigator boarded the ship with help from the ITF, the international seafarers' union, when the captain was gone and began to question the crew about working conditions. My goal was to see whether anything had changed since the Sajo Oyang fleet was expelled from New Zealand's waters.

The *Oyang 75* was now a tidy ship—far more so than the doomed *Oyang 70*. Its crew, which consisted of twenty-seven Indonesians, twelve Filipinos, seven Koreans, and one Chinese, knew little about which nation's waters they were in at any given moment. A dozen of the men sat in the mess hall and explained that while the captain drove them hard, physical and sexual abuse did not occur anymore. Bycatch was no longer thrown overboard. Shark finning and high-grading (tossing old catch for newer) also had stopped, they said.

What the crew described was certainly an improvement from what conditions had once been. Still, the men on the ship said they worked twenty-hour days, six to seven days a week, earning roughly $400 per month. Most of them had paid $150 to a manning agency for access to the job, and their first three months' salary was withheld until the completion of the two-year contract. They complained that when their salary was wired home, the exchange rate used by the company to convert their wages into Indonesian currency was artificially low.

Because the ship was flagged to South Korea, it was supposed to comply with its labor laws. After contacting two law firms in Seoul—Moon & Song and Cho & Lee—that specialized in maritime and labor law, I described to them what the workers had said, and asked whether these constituted violations of Korean law. The lawyers from both firms responded that the up-front fees, exchange-rate downgrades, withheld wages, and working hours were illegal.

Forcing scofflaws to follow labor laws, to observe fishing regulations, and to abide by national boundaries requires robust enforcement regimens, constant vigilance, and a dogged dedication to a higher legal—if not moral—code. But usually it requires something else, too, an ingredient that is often missing: participation and cooperation of the men on the receiving end of abuse.

In the calamities that befell the Oyang fleet, there was plenty of blame to share. Governments were at fault for having turned a blind eye to glaring problems beforehand, followed by half steps and a lack of follow-through after tragedies struck. The fishing industry was to blame for assiduously denying the problem, spinning facts to distort the truth, entrapping workers in predictably abusive conditions, and then entrapping them further by keeping them silent about those abuses. And though these workers had good reasons for keeping quiet, it would be hard to deny that such silence only made it more likely that ships like the *Oyang*s would continue operating irresponsibly and with impunity.

Before my investigator left the *Oyang 75,* one of the workers on board, a twenty-eight-year-old Indonesian man named Purwanto, pulled him aside. Purwanto seemed genuinely puzzled why anyone would take an interest in the conditions of his work, whether he was satisfied and paid. "No one has ever asked about us before," said Purwanto, who had been working on the ship for a year. "Why do you want to know about life on the ship?" he asked. The investigator and the union inspector responded that they were simply checking for labor violations. Purwanto said that even if there were violations, it didn't matter—he needed the job, so he would not say anything more. There was nothing else for him back in Indonesia, he said. "This is the best we can get."

# *ADELAIDE*'S VOYAGE

A rat in a maze is free to go anywhere, as long as it stays inside
the maze.

—Margaret Atwood, *The Handmaid's Tale*

It's an odd quirk of the modern world that we think every inch of land
is claimed and every country at least pretends to be ruled by law, that
by boating a mere thirteen miles from shore, we suddenly find ourselves on the "high seas," beyond the reach of governments.

And yet, like the sea itself, maritime law is opaque. Though it is not
entirely accurate to describe the ocean as a lawless place, it is certainly
a confounding knot of jurisdictions, treaties, and national laws litigated
over centuries of seafaring travel and commerce. Determining whether
activity at sea constitutes a crime often depends, in a sense, on where
in the water it happens. A provision in maritime law treats a ship in
international waters like a floating embassy, in effect a detached chunk
of the land whose flag it flies. That means the laws that apply on board
are only those from the country where the ship is registered.

Few people are as adept at capitalizing on such loopholes in maritime
law as Rebecca Gomperts. The Dutch doctor and founder of Women
on Waves traverses the globe in a converted medical ship carrying an
international team of volunteer doctors that provides abortions in
places where it has been criminalized. Running these often-clandestine
missions since the early years of the twenty-first century, Gomperts has
repeatedly visited the coasts of Guatemala, Ireland, Poland, Morocco,
and a half dozen other countries, dangerously skating the edge of federal and international law.

Where a country's federal law may forbid abortions, the jurisdiction of that law only reaches the limits of national waters or, twelve miles from shore. At the thirteen-mile mark, where international waters begin, abortion is legal on Gomperts's ship because it flies the flag of Austria, where the procedure is permitted.

The ocean, and the opportunistic quirk in maritime law, allowed Gomperts, in her words, to help women "give themselves the license" to induce a miscarriage. More broadly, Women on Waves aims to "demedicalize" an issue that, for Gomperts and many other women, is a matter of personal health. By taking her passengers offshore, Gomperts said she was trying to remove doctors (including herself) and the state as intermediaries between women and control over their own bodies. As one observer described it, Gomperts's approach is to use the oceans to move women "past land, past law, past permission."

In reporting on maritime mayhem, I'd found no shortage of bad actors who thought nothing of breaking the law. Mostly, their objective was to make more money, whatever the consequences might be for the workers and the health of the oceans. And yet, there was also a small handful of others that I encountered who held unwavering beliefs and who used the quirks of maritime law as a kind of secret weapon to advance their agendas. While not everyone would agree with their positions on an issue, there was no arguing that these advocates and activists were clear about their beliefs.

By April 2017, when I joined Gomperts's boat, which is called the *Adelaide,* most of my reporting had focused on the crimes and tragedies of the sea. Here, off the Mexican shore, was a group that took to the sea to circumvent misfortunes on land. Partly my motivation in covering this story was that I needed a break. I was emotionally worn out, having spent over a year on dozens of ships in the darker corners of the outlaw ocean. I craved a story with a different type of protagonist. In the *Adelaide*'s discreet comings and goings, there was also a vivid reminder of just how arbitrary, bordering on silly, some of the laws are, though with very real consequences for the lives of many. Masterful in taking advantage of such laws, Gomperts has caused no end of frustration to countries that impose them.

Built in 2002 in France, the *Adelaide* was a type of sailboat called a fractional sloop. The boat's interior was draped in bright blues, laden with cushions, and cozy. Fast when its sails were open, the boat was re-

The *Adelaide* carries Mexican women needing abortions into international waters, where they can legally have them.

lying only on its 29-horsepower diesel engine because the wind was blowing against us as we sought to leave Mexican waters.

For several months, I had pressed Gomperts to allow me to join her on one of her trips. She said that men were usually not permitted on board. "It makes women uncomfortable," she told me. Seth Bearden, the captain of Gomperts's ship in Mexico, was an exception because he had been vetted and had previously worked for the group onshore, helping survey boats. Eventually, Gomperts gave me permission to join her team in the port of Ixtapa, Mexico, on the condition that I protect the identities of the women on board.

Freckled and fair-skinned with striking green eyes framed by jet-black hair, Gomperts has the build of a long-distance runner. Seeming to never tire, she darted about, often typing on her phone while simultaneously talking to anyone nearby, usually about the logistics of a next mission or the fallout from a past one. Though spunky, she has the moody complexity and weathered aloofness of a lonely Cassandra. Always multitasking, she rarely gives the intimacy of undivided attention or, for that matter, anything but fleeting eye contact. She answered her cell phone gruffly like it was always 3:00 a.m. When I hemmed and hawed through branching and indecisive questions, she impatiently chopped them to their stumps: "So you're asking me whether much of this is a play for press?"

Gomperts usually alerted local media in advance that she was coming, because one of her goals was to spur debate. This trip from Ixtapa was initially clandestine, however, because Gomperts wanted to avoid a repeat of what had occurred two weeks earlier in Guatemala. Tipped off to the group's plans, the Guatemalan government sent police to the marina where Gomperts was docked. After preventing people from boarding the ship, the government expelled Women on Waves from the country, declaring the group a national security threat.

This was not unusual for the organization, which rarely received a warm welcome from the countries it visited. In Ireland, the ship faced bomb threats. In Poland, Gomperts was met in port by protesters throwing eggs and red paint. In Morocco, she was nearly accosted by an angry mob. In Spain, opponents tried to tow her boat. Gomperts stopped them by cutting their ropes.

Abortion critics accused Gomperts of operating a "ship of death." They said her organization undermined countries' sovereignty while orchestrating a macabre theater that preyed on women at emotionally vulnerable moments to make a political point.

Gomperts saw it differently. "We are simply and creatively" leveraging the law to provide "harm reduction" and control to women over their lives. "Banning abortions doesn't make them go away," she told me. "It makes them go underground."

. . .

I boarded the *Adelaide* in the port of Ixtapa, Mexico, and we were in a rush to get out to sea. The waves were getting worse and threatening to lock us inland. Gomperts's team also feared that Mexican authorities would soon hear that we were carrying pregnant women to sea and turn us back.

Our departure was not going smoothly. Eight-foot waves crashed across the bow of the *Adelaide* as captain Bearden struggled to keep control of the thirty-six-foot fiberglass boat. A storm was coming, and the pounding Mexican surf would only get worse. The *Adelaide* had already run aground twice; the second time we just barely avoided being slammed against the jagged boulders lining the shoals twenty feet on either side of us.

On the deck, I clung to the guylines for stability as the waves slammed into us and dashed our faces with salty spray. Beside me, two Mexican women cowered. They were both in their twenties. Both wanted abortions, which were illegal in most of Mexico. To administer the procedures, the crew planned to ferry the women thirteen miles out from Mexico's Pacific coast, just past the edge of Mexican criminal law.

The mouth of Ixtapa's harbor was narrow and waves were pounding inward, making our exit perilous. If we timed our departure poorly we would likely be toppled or slammed aground. So, Bearden sat perched at the mouth waiting for the right moment to make his mad dash.

"You have to go now," Gomperts finally ordered Bearden, a note of strained urgency in her voice. Time was running out, she added. The authorities policing the port in Ixtapa were already suspicious of why this boatful of foreigners seemed so determined to sail into dangerous sea conditions. "They're going to call us back in and then it's over," Gomperts said.

Bearden, a thirty-five-year-old South Carolinian with a thick drawl and a torso laced with tattoos, was an experienced captain—he taught himself to pilot boats while working the docks in Oakland—but he was rattled because he had bumped the pier on his way out of the slip in Ixtapa several hours earlier. In between the waves, stretches of calm water lasted for about two minutes and thirty-six seconds; I was timing the surge, watch in hand, calculating the window of opportunity as I stared at the surf. For our sluggish *Adelaide* to make it through that window and out of port would require a burst of speed and no small measure of luck. As Gomperts and Bearden debated the risks of trying to beat the waves, one of the volunteers sat with the Mexican women, sharing a bag of Doritos and trying to distract them with chitchat about the Mexican rock group Maná.

"Fuck it," Bearden finally said. Walking away from Gomperts, he grabbed the boat's wheel and gently throttled forward, idling within feet of the crash zone. After the next wave broke, he gunned the engine, fixing his stare on the horizon as we raced ahead trying to beat the next crest. "Everyone to the back!" Bearden yelled. Seconds later, the wave slammed our prow head-on, making metal and glass things below deck noisily fall from their shelves, with a terrible crashing sound and shoving the *Adelaide* back like a high school bully might pin the skinny kid against the lockers. The *Adelaide* stood still for a tense moment as though the wind had been knocked out of it. Then it slowly began inching forward again. One of the Mexican women had buried her face in her hands. As the *Adelaide* regained its footing, everyone began applauding, and the Mexican woman looked up with the relieved expression of a child just awoken from a bad dream.

Once the *Adelaide* finally cleared Ixtapa's harbor, our collective adrenaline subsided, and a silence fell over the deck as we motored on, the two-story yachts parked along the dock shrinking from view. The Mexican women had taken seasickness medicine, which makes some people drowsy. Their quiet seemed heavy, no doubt in part because of the weight of their decisions to end their pregnancies.

Seeing a chance to sit with one of the Mexican women, I moved next to her, and we began chatting in Spanish. "I don't have the money to raise a child," she said. "Mostly I'm not ready to be a mother." She explained that she had a steady boyfriend and they had used a condom, which broke. In most places in Mexico, it was dangerous for women like her if word got out that she had an abortion, or even tried to get one, she said.

Mexico has for centuries been a Roman Catholic stronghold. Since late in the first decade of the twenty-first century, dozens of Mexican women have been reported by family, hospital staff, or others for having an abortion and were later prosecuted for the crime. Abortion remains illegal, but an estimated one million women find clandestine ways to undergo the procedure each year. More than a third of those typically lead to complications, including infection, tearing of the uterus, hemorrhaging, or cervical perforation, according to research by the Guttmacher Institute, a reproductive health research center.

In some areas of the country, any pregnancy that did not bring a healthy baby into the world raised suspicions about the mother. Hundreds of women have been jailed after seeking medical care due to botched abortions. Hospitals were expected to report suspicious miscarriages to the police just as they would gunshot wounds. Some Mexican states, such as Veracruz, required unspecified "educational" measures for women who were suspected of having abortions.

In April 2007, Mexico City decriminalized abortion, allowing the termination of pregnancies without restriction during the first twelve weeks of gestation. That triggered a backlash across the country. At least half of the country's thirty-one states passed constitutional amendments declaring that life begins at conception.

Before boarding the *Adelaide,* I read about the case of one woman named Patricia Mendez, who miscarried in 2015 when she was twenty. Mendez later described how police and detectives were summoned to the hospital ward. She was forced to sign papers, and a nurse held the fetus to her face. "Kiss him," she recounted being told by the nurse. "You have killed him." Her boyfriend's family held a funeral for the fetus, and Mendez was required to attend.

. . .

Borders are bullshit," Bearden said a couple of hours after we made it out of Ixtapa. This bombast grabbed me. Bearden was the type of guy who seemed always to be thinking out loud thoughts that others would keep shuttered in their heads. He regularly punctuated his sentences with candid self-interrogations: "As if that makes any sense," or, "I'm not even sure I believe that point." His dismissiveness of borders seemed ironic, I said, given that he was risking life and limb to cross one. That's not because the lines drawn on the sea or anywhere else make sense, he replied. It was simple pragmatism; helping the women on board required recognizing, not ignoring, Mexico's rules and borders, he added.

Having sailed the waters of the Caribbean, Mexico, and California, Bearden was fluent in reading maps and nautical charts. And yet, his view was that these man-made constructs were only ever works in progress and almost always serving someone's interest. He lifted up his shirt to show a sprawling tattoo on one side of his stomach. It was a map with the outline of Mexico from 1848, before the Treaty of Guadalupe Hidalgo and before the lines were redrawn by those who conquered the region. On the other side of his stomach was a map of Africa, overlaid with the silhouette of the United States. Its point, he explained, was to show Africa's true size, in contrast to how it's typically misrepresented on most maps of the world. States draw borders based on their own interests, he said. And while they might have the power to do so when it comes to maps of land and sea, Bearden said, states should not be in the business of determining the borders on women's bodies. "Women should have full sovereignty over their bodies," he said, echoing a standard Women on Waves talking point.

Maritime borders may seem arbitrary, but their consequences can be stark. Consider the Death on the High Seas Act. Passed in 1920, this American law dictates that a lawsuit over the accidental death of a sailor on the high seas is limited to pecuniary loss, meaning his family can only seek repayment for monetary losses and not for pain, suffering, emotional distress, and other hard-to-estimate damages. If the same person were killed in an accident at a garment factory or on a cattle farm, relatives could sue the worker's employer for heftier sums that include damage and future earnings.

The law is a vestige of English common law that views death at sea as an act of God for which shipowners can't possibly be held liable. In the early days of shipping, that might have been true. Today, though, advances in safety—self-righting lifeboats, emergency locator beacons, and watertight holds, for example—mean that many fatal accidents on the high seas are not unavoidable or acts of God. Instead, they are often examples of gross negligence by ship captains and the companies that oversee them. This anachronistic law allows some of these companies to elude safety concerns and to hide behind an interpretation of the high seas as inevitably deadly. Indeed, companies take advantage of this line in the water that designates the high seas, not unlike Gomperts or other outlaw characters I'd covered, including Roy Bates and Paul Watson.

The work of the team on the *Adelaide* presented an unusual case study in the meaning of borders at sea, raising for me all sorts of interesting hypotheticals. For example, the women's decision to take the five pills to induce an abortion was legal because Gomperts was on an Austrian-flagged ship in international waters. But what if Gomperts and her patients had been on a Mexican-flagged ship, and when they reached international waters, they went swimming for just a few seconds to take the pills? Wouldn't the act of diving into the water still have put them outside the reach of Mexico's prohibition since they removed themselves from the Mexican flagged ship?

Before heading to Mexico, I chased some of these hypotheticals in historical and legal journal articles, and I found some partial answers in a grisly nineteenth-century story. Battered by a brutal storm in the South Atlantic in 1884, a British-flagged yacht called the *Mignonette* sank, but its captain and three other men escaped in a dinghy. About three weeks later, they were nearly dead from hunger and thirst. Facing certain death, the captain lunged at the seventeen-year-old cabin boy in the dinghy, slitting his throat with a penknife and killing him. The three men were rescued several days later by a passing German ship, having survived by eating much of the cabin boy, parts of whose body the Germans discovered in the boat.

Once onshore, the survivors were put on trial for murder and cannibalism. The lawyer for the accused argued two points in their defense. First, because the cabin boy was killed not on the British-flagged yacht but in a dinghy, which was floating on the high seas, neither English law nor any other applied. Second, the circumstances facing these men were so extreme that it was incongruous to think of laws applying at all. They were in "a state of nature, where there are no legal rights, duties, or crimes," wrote A. W. Brian Simpson in his book *Cannibalism and the Common Law*. Neither argument succeeded, and the men were convicted.

Simpson explained that while the sailors' lawyer was technically correct on the law, the verdict in the case had less to do with jurisprudence than with politics. The crown's magistrates hoped to send the public a message that their authority had to be maintained even in the distant arteries connecting the British Empire. The story left me convinced that whether the scenario was a group of hungry and desperate men eating a cabin boy, or my hypothetical notion involving women diving into international waters to take abortion pills, government tolerance of extralegal behavior had its limits.

·  ·  ·

Gomperts was well aware of the limits of Mexican tolerance for her mission, and so the offshore expedition I joined was launched largely under a cloak of secrecy. Cruising at a speed around ten knots, the *Adelaide* took three hours to reach the twelve-mile invisible border, with Bearden announcing the moment. As the engine slowed, Gomperts emerged on deck. She nodded gently and smiled comfortingly at one of the women, a sign for her to head below deck to a room that doubled as the boat's clinic.

In the downstairs cabin, Gomperts administered a sonogram on one of the Mexican women to see how far along she was (a month). After asking some questions about allergies and medical history, Gomperts held a fifteen-minute counseling session to advise her of factors to consider before the abortion. She offered information about contraceptives and explained the procedure, warning her that she could expect bleeding and pain. "Are you sure that you want to proceed?" Gomperts asked. The woman said yes, and Gomperts handed her five white pills: one mifepristone (what used to be called RU-486) and four misoprostol.

"Miso," as it is often called, has been used around the world in various ways, including to treat postpartum hemorrhages and to prevent ulcers. In many countries, it is stocked on pharmacy shelves primarily for these ailments. Women desperate to end a pregnancy often have no way of knowing that the right dosage of this readily accessible drug can also be used to trigger a miscarriage.

To get the pills to dissolve into their bloodstream faster, Gomperts instructed the women to place the drugs in their mouths under their tongues or between their cheeks and gums. After the first Mexican woman on the *Adelaide* returned from below deck, the second went downstairs. When the second emerged, they both sat breathlessly still toward the front of the boat, not saying a word.

Aside from several hushed interviews with a few of the women on board, most of my ride out to the edge of Mexico's sovereignty was spent in silence. Since my first experience as an observer at sea, I had internalized the advice about fitting in on ships by not taking up space, but I was more diligent to keep quiet on this trip because of the intensely private nature of the mission and because on this ship full of women, I was more of an outsider than usual.

I thought about the quiet I'd found on ships. Sitting sometimes for hours wordlessly staring at the sea opened space for voices in my head that I typically did not hear or ever allow myself to engage for very long. You get very good at talking to yourself at sea, one seafarer had told me. Another had described these voices as "soul whispers." Some are dark, others less so, but they all feel deeply personal. While valuable in its own right, this internal dialogue also seemed relevant to my understanding of the outlaw ocean. It hinted at why so many of the people I met around the world on this watery frontier seemed to share an independent mindedness that I rarely encountered on land.

. . .

After initially arriving in Mexico, I had rented an Airbnb apartment next to Gomperts, overlooking the marina. I wanted to avoid any chance of being left behind if she and her team decided to take the *Adelaide* out late at night. The evening before we launched on our first voyage, I woke up around 2:00 a.m. and went out onto the balcony. I could overhear Gomperts on the phone switching between Spanish, English, and Dutch in an intense discussion about how they could discreetly transport several women needing abortions to the port from a village over two hundred miles away. Several hours later, as dawn broke over the docks, Gomperts wouldn't tell me whether she had slept the night before. Instead, she pulled out nautical charts to study with Bearden.

I joined Rebecca Gomperts as she prepared to launch her boat, the *Adelaide,* off the coast of Mexico. She carried two young pregnant women to international waters, where she performed medical abortions, which are illegal in Mexico.

Born in Suriname (her father is from the former Dutch colony), Gomperts moved when she was three to the Netherlands, her mother's home country. Most of her formative years were spent in the port of Vlissingen, where she fell in love with boats while sailing with her family on the North Sea.

In the mid-1980s, she enrolled in medical school in Amsterdam while taking art classes on the side. She specialized in making art installations, using video to explore the female body and its relation to fertility. After completing her medical training, she worked for several years as a ship's doctor on a Greenpeace vessel called the *Rainbow Warrior II*. During that time, she met a woman who had been raped by a man who was supposed to help her get an abortion. Gomperts also met an eighteen-year-old girl in South America who was trying to raise her three younger siblings. Gomperts said that the girl had recently lost her mother to a back-alley abortion.

"Their stories personalized what before had just been statistics to me," she said, explaining why she began raising money to rent a ship and to build an abortion clinic on board, inside a converted shipping container. She contacted former art school friends, including Joep van Lieshout, a well-known Dutch artist, to design and help build the clinic.

Shortly before Gomperts was scheduled to leave for Ireland on her first trip in 2001, the Dutch Transport Ministry threatened to revoke her ship's authorization because of the clinic. Though abortion in Holland was legal, clinics had to meet certain specifications. Gomperts faxed Dutch authorities a certificate saying that the clinic was not a berth on the ship but a work of art, titled *A-Portable*. As such, she argued, it did not need to comply with certain maritime rules. The ship was allowed to sail, and van Lieshout later held an art showing at the Venice Biennale, featuring his design drawings and mock-ups of the clinic.

Gomperts had initially planned on performing surgical abortions on her ship, but the permitting and logistics became insurmountable. So the group sticks to medical abortions, which entail administering pills to induce miscarriage. Others have floated similar ideas, but none have left the drawing board. They include an Israeli entrepreneur named Na'ama Moran, who for years has tried to launch a company that would park a ship thirteen miles off the U.S. coast and provide medical services at cut-rate prices beyond the reach of U.S. criminal law or medical licensing rules. Though Moran has failed to raise the start-up capital, the demand is real. More than a million Americans travel abroad each year to places like Mexico, South Africa, and Thailand to save money on face-lifts, hip replacements, heart-valve repair, and liposuction.

As the *Adelaide* made its way back to port, I joined Gomperts below deck. While wealthier women seeking abortions can get on a plane and fly to a country where such procedures are legal, she observed, this is not an option for most women. "We can't bring them to Austria," a volunteer from Ireland named Eimear Sparks chimed in. "But we can bring a bit of Austria to them."

Gomperts recounted some of the distressed emails and phone calls she had received in recent years. A woman in Morocco wrote to say that she was considering drinking bleach to end her pregnancy. An American soldier serving in Afghanistan who had been raped explained that she was unable to get an abortion on or near the base. A British woman in an abusive relationship said that her boyfriend would beat her if he found out she was pregnant or that she was trying to get an abortion.

I asked Gomperts whether she saw herself as an outlaw. I fully expected her to answer with a qualified yes. I assumed her explanation would be a version of the porch scene toward the end of *To Kill a Mockingbird*, where we see two systems of justice intersect and we get a compelling argument that doing what's lawful is not always the same as doing what's just. This was not Gomperts's answer. "We don't break the law; we use it to our advantage," she said, adding that she thinks of herself more as an artist. There was an art to finding legal loopholes, she added, and an art to provoking a public debate while protecting patients' privacy. One thing was for sure: there was undeniably a theatrical quality to the work that Women on Waves did. And Gomperts was comfortable and adept onstage.

One of the organization's most successful provocations happened during Gomperts's visit to Portugal in 2004. The group tried to visit the country's coast but was rebuffed by the government, which sent two warships to create a blockade. In the ensuing media firestorm, Gomperts was invited on Portuguese television to defend Women on Waves. Instead, she used the airtime to explain how to end a pregnancy using miso pills. Though abortions were illegal in Portugal, miso was available in local pharmacies, she boldly pointed out to the country's hundreds of thousands of television viewers. Gomperts's interview was widely seen as a catalyst for a national referendum that led to the legalization of abortion in Portugal in 2007.

"In many places, women don't even know that the pills exist and are affordable," Gomperts said when I asked about her bold move on Portuguese television. Globally, more than twenty million women annually have "unsafe" abortions, and about forty-seven thousand of them die each year as a result, according to the World Health Organization.

After our first and clandestine journey offshore, Gomperts began stirring the pot on the second day of our stay in Ixtapa, using much the same flair for publicity as in Portugal. A scenic town, Ixtapa, which now has a population of about forty-five thousand residents, emerged as a popular tourist destination in the late 1970s. Lined with extravagant self-contained resorts, the city is located on the Pacific coast of Guerrero, one of Mexico's most dangerous states, notorious for gang- and drug-related murders and abductions. The town was crawling with plainclothes and uniformed police officers sent by the Mexican government hoping to counter the epidemic of kidnappings.

Gomperts convened a press conference at a hotel not far from the marina to announce that Women on Waves had taken a trip the day before carrying women out to international waters for abortions and that it would be doing so again the next day. "This is a matter of social justice," Gomperts said to the crowd of about fifty reporters and women's advocates.

After the press conference, I telephoned a health official in the state government for his views on Women on Waves. "We do not believe they are acting lawfully," the official said. "But we are still getting details."

An hour later, Mexican authorities called Gomperts. First, port officials cited bad weather as a reason that her boat would not be permitted to leave port. Gomperts pointed to other smaller ships that were allowed to launch. The officials backed down. Next, immigration authorities alleged that Gomperts's staff had entered the country under a false pretext by claiming to be tourists rather than maritime workers. Gomperts produced their visas, indicating that in fact they had properly identified themselves. After that, the government questioned whether the boat had proper permits to carry passengers. Gomperts showed its classification as a yacht, exempting it from those rules. Finally, it looked as if Gomperts might be expelled from Mexico. Her lawyers sought and received a ruling from a Mexican judge protecting her right to stay.

Clearly, when it came to what happens at sea, some laws were enforced more aggressively than others. In my reporting, I'd seen far less effort from governments in policing minimum wage rules, limits on working hours, or catch quotas. And unlike the captains I'd watched elsewhere take fish from protected marine zones or the companies that condoned slave labor, Gomperts was not breaking the law but taking advantage of a loophole. That she was doing so publicly, that she was a woman, and that she was a foreigner were all likely contributing factors to the government's reaction. And as with the *Mignonette,* that reaction had far more to do with politics than with law.

After clearing what seemed like the last bureaucratic hurdle that day, Gomperts called her crew. "Hurry up," she told them. "We need to go before the government finds another obstacle to put up." With two more women in tow, the group hustled to the *Adelaide* for its second venture out to international waters. At the helm, Bearden checked several nautical charts on his phone. Then he pushed the throttle forward and carefully avoided the pier this time.

# JAIL WITHOUT BARS

For I say there is no other thing that is worse than the sea is for breaking a man, even though he may a very strong one.

—Homer, *The Odyssey*

Life on the ocean has long been romanticized as the ultimate expression of freedom—an escape from landlocked life, a chance to explore, to reinvent. This narrative has been locked deep within our DNA for centuries, starting with stories of daring adventurers setting off to discover new lands. It has also given rise to the puzzling contradiction of the modern-day cruise industry, peddling the notion that a massive floating hotel that chugs between choreographed stops to buy local trinkets will provide relief from the predictability of daily life. Even the simple phrase "at sea" seems to carry an implicit soundtrack of possibility and power.

It was against this backdrop that I kept discovering stories that seemed to directly contradict this narrative. These stories demonstrated that while the sea was an escape for some people, it was a prison for others. So, I set out to explore the diversity of ways that people end up captive at sea. Who are the captors, and when is it tough to distinguish them from their captives? How does the sea lend itself to various forms of bondage, and in what ways does the sea itself entrap people? I also wanted to understand the way this confinement punishes not just the body but also the mind. Throughout this exploration offshore, I became keenly aware that I had options. I always knew that I would be returning to land soon. For the captive and the stranded, on the other hand, the ocean was a vast jail without bars.

Among the most haunting of the stories I found involved a new verb that I learned during my travels: "rafted." For as long as ships have crossed the sea, people—usually desperate, occasionally dangerous—have tried to sneak aboard, and these stowaways have had a term for what can happen to them if they were found on a ship. "Rafted" refers to a particularly ominous fate whereby a crew, discovering such uninvited guests, sets them adrift in the middle of the ocean and leaves them to die.

Over the centuries, countless stowaways, mutineers, and pirates have walked the plank. Late in the first decade of the twenty-first century, European and American immigration laws tightened amid terrorism fears, and heavier penalties were imposed on ships arriving with people not listed on their official crew or passenger manifests. Nations shifted the responsibility of handling stowaways from government immigration agencies to shipping companies and their insurers. This put new pressure on shipowners who, in turn, put it on captains and their crews. If stowaways were discovered on board while a ship was at sea, crews were sometimes ordered to "make the problem go away." Rafting was one solution.

In May 2011, David George Mndolwa and his friend Jocktan Francis Kobelo snuck aboard a 370-foot cargo ship in Cape Town called the *Dona Liberta,* a Greek-owned refrigeration ship. They had overheard a deckhand in port mention that the red-bottomed ship waiting dockside without a night watchman was leaving soon for England. Like dozens of other Tanzanians living in the shanties alongside the port of Cape Town, they viewed stowing away as a shot at a better life. They hoped to escape Africa and go anyplace else.

Carrying their passports, a loaf of bread, and a plastic bag filled with orange juice, the men shinnied across the ship's mooring rope that night, crept down to the engine room, and climbed underneath the floor grating, where they stayed, whisperingly still. Fighting sleep, they crouched in chest-deep water oily with engine runoff. But their hiding spot grew unbearable. When the turbines came to life and the ship departed Cape Town, the endless clamor of the engine made their ears ring, and they grew light-headed from the fumes. The heat "stole our breath," Mndolwa said. Within two days, their food ran out. They emerged from under the floor and crept through the maze of lower levels up to the deck, where they found crackers and bottled water in an enclosed lifeboat. For several more days, they hid in the lifeboat.

After nine days, the hungry, defeated men crawled out of hiding again, but this time they presented themselves to the ship's crew. The infuriated captain locked Mndolwa and Kobelo in a room. On some ships, the crew would have just kept the stowaways detained in a cabin until they reached the next port. Not so on the *Dona Liberta*. The crew built a rickety raft made of empty oil drums and a wooden tabletop. Wielding a knife, one of the crewmen fetched the stowaways and marched them up to the deck, where a rope stretched down to the raft bobbing on the waves. The crewman then ordered Mndolwa and Kobelo over the railing. "Go down!" the man with the knife yelled. "Go!"

As they climbed onto the slick raft, the Tanzanians, neither of whom knew how to swim, nearly slid into the ocean. The waves were about six feet tall. The crew cut the rope, releasing the raft, which quickly drifted away. The *Dona Liberta* steadily shrank in the distance before dipping below the horizon.

As Mndolwa and Kobelo drifted on the raft, they watched dark clouds gathering on the horizon. The stowaways tied themselves together and to the raft with a rope and waited for the approaching storm. Soon, twenty-foot swells seesawed the seven-by-eight-foot raft. To help balance the raft and to avoid flipping over, the men splayed flat on their backs. Their hands chafed from grasping a piece of rebar poking up from one of the rusty blue drums. "This is the end," Mndolwa said to himself.

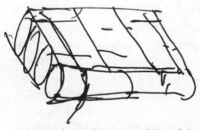

A drawing by David George Mndolwa of the makeshift raft that he and another stowaway were put on and abandoned at sea

Kobelo and Mndolwa's experience was unusual, but increasingly port authorities were refusing to allow ships to off-load stowaways on their shores, often citing security concerns and the cost of detaining them. In some cases, stowaways got stuck on board ships for years.

In 2014, two Guinean stowaways were pushed or leaped overboard off the French coast after several African countries would not let them disembark, according to media accounts and human rights advocates. One of the men drowned. Two years earlier, a crew threw four African stowaways into the Mediterranean (all survived by swimming to shore). Fines for the captain or insurers can run up to $50,000 per stowaway for arriving in port with them. Such costs typically doubled if cargo delays were involved.

Over a thousand stowaways are caught each year hiding on ships. Hundreds of thousands more are sea migrants, like those desperately fleeing North Africa and the Middle East on boats crossing the Mediterranean. For the people making these crossings, few routes are as perilous. In interviews, half a dozen stowaways compared their experience to hiding in the trunk of a car for days, weeks, or months traveling to an unknown place across the most brutal of terrains. Temperatures are extreme. It is impossible to bring enough food or water. And if you try to flee en route by jumping off the ship, as one former stowaway in Durban, South Africa, told me, "the ground swallows you whole."

To get on board, some stowaways posed as stevedores or deck cleaners. Others swam under the stern and squeezed through a space where the rudder meets the ship. Many brought "stowaway poles"—long bamboo sticks with toeholds and a hook—that they used to scale the sides of ships. Supply boats bringing fuel or food to anchored vessels also sometimes carried uninvited passengers. After sneaking on board, they would hide in hulls or shipping containers, crane cabs or tool trunks.

They might have believed they had won a free ticket to a new life, but concealed corners that might at first look safe often turned deadly once ships set sail. Refrigerated fishing holds became uninhabitable, exhaust pipes heated up, shipping containers were sealed and fumigated. Maritime newsletters and shipping insurance reports offered a macabre accounting of the victims: "crushed in the chain locker," "asphyxiated by bunker fumes," "found under a retracted anchor." Most often, though, death came more slowly. Vomiting from seasickness led to dehydration. People passed out from exhaustion or starvation.

When the storm finally hit, Mndolwa and Kobelo barely survived the night. For eight pitch-black hours, the men stared upward in a driving rain, keeping their mouths closed because of the waves that kept washing over them. They squinted because shutting their eyes intensified the seasickness. Storms are more punishing on the open water because they pummel from above and below. Mndolwa compared it to experiencing an earthquake and a hurricane at the same time.

The next morning brought a radiant blue sky. They untied themselves and began passing the time talking about soccer and their families. Holding on to the raft was a constant struggle. Lack of food and water, and the frigid ocean spray, had sapped them. It was a gusty spring day. By sunset panic had set in because the temperature began falling. "Words dried up," Mndolwa said. He began reciting the Lord's Prayer, first in his head, then aloud. Kobelo joined in until he began coughing and vomiting blood.

In an extraordinary stroke of luck for the men, hope soon appeared as a speck on the horizon. Before long, a ten-foot wooden boat with a loud outboard motor pulled alongside the Tanzanians. "Why are you there?" a fisherman yelled at them in English as he tossed a rope to the raft. "I don't know," Mndolwa replied.

Half a day later, the fishing boat deposited the rafted stowaways at a pier several miles outside the port city of Buchanan, Liberia, where Liberian immigration officials detained them for being undocumented. "Why do you put us in jail and let the crew go?" Mndolwa recalled asking one official, referring to the crew of the *Dona Liberta*. "We deal with crimes on land," the official responded. "Not on the water." Kobelo's bloody cough had grown worse, and he died six days after reaching shore. He was twenty-six.

The *Dona Liberta* arrived in the port of Truro, near the southwestern tip of England, in June 2011, about a month after Mndolwa and Kobelo were set adrift. The British police, apparently alerted by Liberian officials, boarded the ship and interviewed the captain. They later closed the investigation for lack of evidence, according to port officials.

I called Captain Mark Killingback, the harbormaster for the port of Truro, to ask him about the stowaways. He said it was clear from its weatherworn appearance that the *Dona Liberta* had fallen on hard times. Without irony, he added that his office had received several requests to detain the ship, but the request had nothing to do with the cruel treatment of the stowaways cast off at sea. The requests came from the ship's foreign creditors, who were afraid of losing money on their floating investment.

·   ·   ·

Twenty years ago, this likely would not have been possible. A reporter sitting in Washington, D.C., probably could not have tracked down a person of unknown name or whereabouts, living in a shanty encampment in South Africa. And it took me three months and no small amount of luck, but thanks to the global interconnectivity of smart phones, digital records, and social media tools like WhatsApp and Facebook, I found and made contact with Mndolwa.

I had first heard about his story from a UN official who was unsure of the names of the stowaways but knew that one of them had died in Liberia from the ordeal. I called in a favor from a Liberian friend of mine, who put me in email touch with his cousin living in the Liberian capital of Monrovia, who was dating a police officer there. That police officer discreetly introduced me by Facebook Messenger to a former port official who had access to useful records.

No money exchanged hands, just lots of phone calls, text messaging, and genuine pleading. "You have no reason to help me and I'm not allowed to pay for this information," I said at each juncture. "But I've been told you were a friend and this is a story the public should know."

My big break came when the port official agreed to pull an incident report that described what happened to two stowaways who washed ashore. Though sparse, the report had Kobelo's full name, and with that I hired a local reporter in Monrovia to survey local media, most of which was not online, and to check with human rights groups to help me find Kobelo's family.

Within a week, we had located Kobelo's thirty-seven-year-old brother, Michael, who was living in Tanzania. I spoke to him by phone, and eventually I hired another local reporter to visit him in person and to facilitate a phone call between us. Sitting in a one-room house in Dar es Salaam, Michael conceded that his brother had broken the law by stowing away. But he should not have died because of it, Michael said. "Even here in Tanzania we are told if you catch a thief, you don't beat him," he added. "You don't throw him into the sea." I asked Michael if he could help me find Mndolwa, and he agreed.

Though Mndolwa was living hand to mouth, homeless on the streets near the port of Cape Town, he had a pay-as-you-go smart phone. He also knew the spots in the city where he could access free internet service, and several times a day he went online. Kobelo's brother connected us by Facebook Messenger. For the next several months, I spoke

David George Mndolwa

or texted with Mndolwa almost daily. He was not fully literate in English, having grown up speaking Swahili. So, he usually spelled words phonetically, which meant I often had to read his texts aloud to figure out what he was trying to say.

After Mndolwa's experience on the *Dona Liberta* in 2011, the immigration officials in Liberia jailed him for five months as an undocumented immigrant. He was then flown to Tanzania and eventually made his way back to the encampment near the Cape Town port.

Asked why he had stowed away aboard the *Dona Liberta,* Mndolwa simply said, "I wanted a new life." He told me that Kobelo had stowed away on ships three times before—bound for Singapore, Angola, and Senegal. In Singapore, he had spent a year as a night watchman and a firefighter in a small dry dock. In each country, immigration authorities eventually found him and sent him back to Tanzania.

Mndolwa described a meager existence in Cape Town, roaming the sidewalks near South Africa's Table Bay selling knockoff watches and soccer jerseys during the day and sleeping in a makeshift lean-to under a bridge at night. To Mndolwa, who was barely literate and had never before left Africa, Kobelo's descriptions of his time in Singapore—free hospital visits, restaurant meals, beaches where the police never shooed him away—sounded far better than life in Cape Town.

I talked and texted with Mndolwa for a couple of months before he agreed to let me send two videographers to Cape Town. My goal was for the videographers, Ed Ou and Ben Solomon, to spend some time with Mndolwa and the other stowaways who lived together in an encampment near the port. In December 2014, Ou and Solomon went to Cape Town and for several weeks shadowed the stowaways, including during the Christmas and New Year's holidays, filming and photographing their daily lives.

At the time, Mndolwa was living on a port-side slope of dirt and gravel, strewn with trash and excrement. On the ground inside his thatch-and-stick lean-to was a soiled blanket, where he slept. Suspended from the ceiling were dozens of losing lottery tickets, dangling like a mobile.

To make ends meet, Mndolwa sold packs of gum and hair ties to drivers waiting at a nearby stoplight. His tenuous existence helped explain the risks he was willing to take to stow away, which he told me he planned to do again and as soon as possible. "I just believe the ship is going to change my life," he said. "I believe that."

The area where Mndolwa lived was dangerous. One afternoon, Ou went alone to meet some of these stowaways, and he was mugged on the way. After his assailants punched and kicked him—giving him a black eye and bruised ribs—they made off with thousands of dollars' worth of video equipment. It was unclear whether Mndolwa or the other stowaways were involved or if the culprits were simply delinquents from the area.

I stayed in touch with Mndolwa by Facebook. In the two years after my *New York Times* story about him was published in 2015, he stowed away from Cape Town three more times, ending up twice in Senegal and once in Madagascar. He told me that each time captains discovered him on board, the shipowners paid him $1,000 to get off their vessels. This sum was enough to keep him afloat for half a year, he added. Each time, Mndolwa then made his way back to his destitute life in the shantytown alongside the Cape Town port, hoping to launch anew.

I found it mind-boggling that he kept doing something that so nearly killed him the first time. And yet he pointed out to me that while he might end up dead stowing away, he might also arrive some place better or get paid $1,000 to be delivered back home. To him, the odds were worth it.

·　·　·

Stowaways like Mndolwa have for centuries been a nightmare for ship operators, turning the tables on the roles of captor and captured. Since the early years of the twenty-first century, Peter Rabitz has run a firm called Unicon, based in Bremen, Germany, that handles the logistics of repatriating stowaways on behalf of shipping companies and their insurers. Rabitz recounted a case from 2015 of a sixteen-year-old Guinean stowaway who was found aboard a Danish tanker.

The stowaway refused to disembark or provide his name or country of origin. The shipping company declined to have him forcefully removed in part because it could not figure out where to send him. In a case like this, the roles of captor and captive get confusing, Rabitz said. The stowaway is trapped while also holding the ship hostage.

Incredibly, the Guinean stowaway stayed on board for a year and a half, locked most of the time in his cabin, as the ship traveled the globe to half a dozen ports. One day, having grown tired of life at sea, the stowaway asked to see the captain. A crewman escorted him to the bridge. He told the captain his name and that he was ready to go home. He also said that his passport had been hidden under the mattress all the while.

It was a bizarre story but one I was inclined to believe. Maybe owing to that independent mindedness among seafarers that I was coming to understand, or perhaps because life at sea is so divorced from that on land, it did not seem far-fetched that a stowaway and a captain might end up in some stubborn face-off lasting years. Seasoned seamen are masters of waiting, partly because time and distance get stretched when traveling by ship.

I contacted Edward Carlson, a maritime and trade lawyer based in New York, who worked on many cases involving stowaways. He added that stowaways are often savvy and skilled adversaries to captains or the shipping companies left with figuring out how to handle them. Many stowaways know, for example, that if they allege that they were assaulted by the crew, they can tie up a ship with a long investigation in port, leading to delays costing millions of dollars, Carlson said. "You have a tanker carrying $200 million worth of crude for Exxon or Mobil, tugs, supply boats, dock agents, an entire port refinery scene waiting to unload it in an extremely tight window of time before that ship needs to clear the berth," Carlson said. "Then you have a fifteen-year-old kid who could delay the entire thing."

Some stowaways are "frequent fliers," who are caught multiple times, Rabitz explained. To pin down their nationality, Rabitz's staff consists of speakers of nearly a dozen languages, including an array of Arabic and African dialects. The stowaway's accent, word choice, and facial features usually give away his home country, he said.

When a shipping company hires Rabitz's firm, his staff flies to the country where the ship is docked. They board the vessel and gently (he emphasized that intimidation never works) try to convince the stowaways that they are not going to receive asylum and that life in a detention center is not an attractive option for them. Once the stowaway acquiesces in leaving, he is usually escorted on the flight home. A guard or two are also often sent on the flight. Sometimes, the stowaways stage a final dramatic protest by threatening to disrobe publicly or cause some other type of scene unless they are paid. Rabitz said his colleagues always keep cash on hand for such occasions. He said his firm once paid $10,000 to a single stowaway to persuade him to board a plane. It still ended up being cheaper for the client than keeping the stowaway under guard at a hotel for weeks as he attempted to renegotiate his repatriation, Rabitz explained.

The lesson here seemed to be that stowing away might start out as a mix of desperation and romanticism: a kind of hitchhiking, grabbing a ride without any cost or pain to anyone because the ships are traveling to their destinations one way or the other. But the reality was far bleaker: stowing away quite often turned into a showdown, where somebody won or lost, paying with either money or his life.

. . .

As I traveled and collected stories about maritime captivity, I came to realize that people end up at sea one of two ways: the lure of the ocean draws them, or they're taken there involuntarily. Like Mndolwa, the drawn typically leave dry land pulled by the prospect of profit and opportunity.

Ahmed Abu Khattala, on the other hand, was among the taken. The aftermath of the September 11, 2001, terror attacks created an entirely new realm of jurisprudence over questions of detention and interrogation not just on land but also on the high seas. Abu Khattala's was one of those national security cases: he was not shanghaied by human traffickers like the migrant deckhands I met in Thailand and Borneo. Abu Khattala was abducted and whisked away to sea by American soldiers. Why? Because he was the alleged ringleader of the September 11, 2012, terrorist attacks in Benghazi, Libya, that killed the U.S. ambassador J. Christopher Stevens and three other Americans.

On June 14, 2014, a small group of U.S. Navy SEALs and at least two FBI agents approached the Libyan coast on rubber speedboats hoping to nab Abu Khattala. U.S. Army Delta Force commandos were already nearby on land. Tension surrounding the mission was high. The U.S. military had made plans to capture Abu Khattala more than a year earlier, but that operation was aborted at the last moment when plans of another, nearly simultaneous terrorist-capture raid in a populated area of Tripoli were revealed on Twitter, making Abu Khattala's arrest too risky.

This time American forces had lured Abu Khattala to a seaside villa south of Benghazi, and when they encountered him, he was alone. Abu Khattala, a burly man at six feet three and 230 pounds, tried to fight off the Americans and suffered minor injuries before he was wrestled to the ground. The commandos then whisked him off to the USS *New York,* a 684-foot-long amphibious transport vessel parked in international waters.

For the next five days, a specialized U.S. military unit made up of intelligence and law enforcement officials questioned Abu Khattala. Called the High-Value Detainee Interrogation Group, the unit grilled Abu Khattala about what he knew of planned or past attacks. At that point, a second group of FBI agents told Abu Khattala that he was under arrest and read him his *Miranda* rights. Abu Khattala immediately requested a lawyer. Because they were at sea, no lawyer was available. The FBI agents interrogated Abu Khattala for seven more days.

The detention and interrogation of Abu Khattala in international waters aboard the USS *New York* raised new questions about how the United States was handling terrorism suspects. For much of the decade after the September 11 attacks, detainees were sent to secret prisons, known as black sites, in foreign countries such as Romania, Poland, and Egypt under a program called extraordinary rendition. The CIA questioned them over long periods, sometimes using torture methods like waterboarding, without giving them access to lawyers. Detainees were also sent to the U.S. detention facility at Guantánamo Bay, Cuba. These practices were supposed to stop with the election of President Barack Obama, who had vowed during his campaign to end the use of torture and rendition and to close the black sites and the Guantánamo Bay facility.

It was a principled stand but one that created a challenge for the intelligence community, which needed to know where to send terrorism suspects. If the CIA or the military relocated detainees to the

United States, the criminal process would likely begin as soon as they arrived on American soil, which meant reading them their rights and providing access to lawyers. For a time, U.S.-run prisons in Afghanistan were used, but these detention facilities were soon handed over to the Afghan government, which did not want to handle the legal and political fallout of hosting foreign suspects.

International conventions dictate that prisoners of war are to be held on land at fixed addresses that outside monitors can locate and inspect. When detainees were moved by airplane, there was a good-faith expectation that they would be delivered quickly to their destination. A ship, on the other hand, could take weeks or months for the trip.

On the high seas, the legality of detention and interrogation is murky. American military ships fly the U.S. flag, of course, and as such they are under the jurisdiction of American law. This would seem to require that detainees on these vessels be read their *Miranda* rights. It is not clear, however, to what extent *Miranda* rights apply on the high seas, even to American detainees.

Under federal rules, a suspect taken into custody—even one arrested overseas—must be presented to a magistrate judge for an initial hearing in a timely fashion. That generally means within forty-eight hours. While the federal courts had ruled that the penalty for a violation of this requirement would be limited, they had also provided several examples of what constituted an unreasonable delay in transferring detainees. One judge summed up the unreasonable durations as "delays for the purpose of gathering additional evidence to justify the arrest, a delay motivated by ill will against the arrested individual, or delay for delay's sake." In a separate case, one not specifically about detention at sea, the Supreme Court reiterated this perspective in a narrow 5–4 decision in 2009. In *Corley v. United States,* Justice Souter wrote, "Delay for the purpose of interrogation is the epitome of 'unnecessary delay.'"

The circumstances surrounding Abu Khattala's interrogation would seem to fit within these descriptions of unreasonable. Still, the Obama administration defended its practice of transporting detainees by sea. Department of Justice lawyers argued that it was more practical and a security imperative to bring them through international waters than to transport them to an airport in a European or North African country, which would require the permission of the host government.

In pleadings before the U.S. District Court, Abu Khattala's attorneys argued that interrogating him in such contexts made a mockery of the law. The government's use of the high seas, they said, was little more than "well-planned lawlessness." Testimony given by Abu Khattala at sea while tortured should be withheld, they said. In August 2017, a federal judge dismissed the request and ruled that Abu Khattala's statements made during his detention at sea would be admissible in court.

Abu Khattala was not the first terrorism suspect to be questioned at sea. In 2013, Abu Anas al-Libi, the alleged mastermind of the 1998 terrorist attacks on American embassies in Kenya and Tanzania, was held aboard the USS *San Antonio*. In 2011, Ahmed Abdulkadir Warsame, a military commander for the Somali terrorist group al-Shabaab, was captured on a fishing boat in the Gulf of Aden and detained for two months by the navy on the high seas. The so-called American Taliban, John Walker Lindh, was kept aboard the amphibious assault ship the USS *Peleliu* in 2001 and the USS *Bataan* until January 22, 2002, while the Bush administration decided what to do with the twenty-year-old California native.

Of course, none of these specific terrorism suspects were available for me to interview. So, instead, I got in touch with Mansoor Adayfi, a former terrorism suspect and detainee from the Guantánamo Bay prison. He knew and had written about many of the other people held there, and I wanted his opinion about the use of the high seas for interrogation.

He explained that many of the Afghans held at Guantánamo Bay had no knowledge of the ocean. To them, the sea was a fearsome beast, he said. "All that the Afghans knew was that it was a lot of water that killed and ate people," he told me, adding that American interrogators took advantage of this. " 'When we finish with you here, you will be taken to the sea and you all will be thrown there,' " he recounted them saying. I believed the anecdote if only because it was, after all, the job of these interrogators to instill fear in their detainees so as to leverage them for information.

The ocean was not just a convenient location for holding suspects, Adayfi said. "It was also a powerful psychological tool for getting information from these same suspects." Most of the detainees at Guantánamo were held in outdoor cells, which happened to be only a couple hundred yards from the water's edge, but none of the detainees could see the ocean fully because the surrounding fences were covered in tarps. They stole glimpses, though, through the slivers of openings at the bottom of the tarps. Whenever the detainees wanted a look, they asked the other men to watch for approaching guards, then lay on their stomachs to peak.

The tarps came down for a few days in 2014 in preparation for an approaching hurricane. The sea had frightened the detainees when they were only able to smell it and hear it. Once they were able to see it, the water became a source of wonder, a type of escape, Adayfi said, and some of the men even tried to paint it. Much as it had been for the stowaways in South Africa, the reality and symbolism of the sea was for these terrorism suspects something contradictory: at once outlaw and beyond the reach of normal rules, signifying the ultimate freedom and the scariest captivity.

. . .

Sometimes in reporting, one finds that the most urgent stories hide in plain view. The truest examples of men being detained at sea were all around me, but only after I stopped looking for them did I take notice. Time and again, I had stumbled across men on broken ships anchored far from shore. These men were abandoned but unable to leave their ships.

The backstory was usually the same: Having stretched their resources to the limit, cash-strapped shipowners declared bankruptcy. Cutting their losses, they disavowed their ships, stranding crew members who were usually still on board the ship far off at sea or anchored in a foreign port. Like the Flying Dutchman, these men were left to roam or sit and wait, sometimes for years. Usually, they lacked the immigration papers to come ashore and the resources to get home. Annually, there were thousands of these men globally languishing at sea, slowly falling apart, physically and mentally. Some of these men died, typically while trying to swim to shore.

I kept running into these battered souls while reporting other topics. In Athens, Greece, while exploring how ships are stolen by maritime repo men and corrupt port officials, I came across the crew of the *Sofia*—ten desperate Filipinos, marooned on an asphalt tanker, anchored half a dozen miles from shore, and unpaid for over five months. While in the Gulf of Oman on a floating arms depot called the *Seapol One,* where private maritime security guards wait in international waters between deployments on ships, I heard from half a dozen guards whose employer had stopped taking their calls. Their ship had grown rancid and overrun with vermin. At one point, they lifted their shirts, revealing bright red rashes of infected bedbug bites.

But it was George Cristof, a Romanian with a pockmarked face and ice-blue eyes, who taught me the most about seafarer abandonment. A veteran sailor, Cristof knew something was wrong from the moment he stepped on board the 370-foot *Dona Liberta* in June 2011 in the port of Truro, England. Cristof boarded the month after the *Dona Liberta* had rafted the two stowaways. When the ship arrived in the port of Truro, the operator had quickly sent its crew home and looked to hire an entirely new batch of sailors who had no role in the cruel banishment of Mndolwa and Kobelo.

Hired by a manning agency, Cristof had been instructed in a brief call with a Greek shipping company to fly immediately to England because a full crew was waiting, ready to launch. When he arrived, however, he discovered that the provisions were gone, the cargo hold was empty, and most of the crew had departed. The *Dona Liberta* had barely enough fuel to power the wheel room's overhead lamp, much less to run the ship's 5,600-horsepower engine. Anchored in British waters,

George Cristof (right) and Florin Raducan (left) were hired as seafarers on a ship, the *Dona Liberta,* in 2011. They were abandoned in port in the U.K., where they were stranded in terrible conditions.

a couple miles from land near the port of Truro, the *Dona Liberta* was not going anywhere. Cristof said he stayed put because he had no plane ticket home and hoped the job might eventually pan out.

Cristof was soon joined by another Romanian, Florin Raducan. For the next several months, the two men survived by fishing over the side and pleading for canned goods and bottled water from passing ships. Some days they did not eat. Worse than the hunger was the "shame of having to beg," Cristof said. They had no heat, running water, or electricity. Their cell phones died. The toilet paper ran out. So, too, did the cigarettes. Nerves frayed. They collected rainwater for drinking and bathing. "It wasn't enough," Cristof recounted. He soon developed a severe skin infection on his chest, his medical records show. Each day the men waited for orders that never came. "Jail with a salary," Cristof said, reciting a common expression about work at sea. "Except the salary isn't guaranteed."

I had heard about Cristof's experience because I was investigating the *Dona Liberta* and its involvement in the abuse of stowaways. When I contacted him in Galati, Romania, Cristof said that getting stranded was commonplace in the industry, especially on poorer ships like the *Dona Liberta*.

In whispered phone calls or surreptitious notes, past crew members from the *Dona Liberta* regularly contacted the international seafarers' union, ITF, pleading for help. They described safety violations, harsh conditions, wage theft, and abandonment, union records show.

By 2012, the reported mistreatment led the union to warn mariners not to work for the *Dona Liberta* and other ships operated by the same owner, Commercial SA. "Lack of winter jackets, hard hats and safety shoes," one union inspector wrote, describing crew members working outside in Norway in November, where the average temperature was below freezing. In Spain and South Africa, the crew complained that the captain routinely doctored the log to show wages that were never paid and ship repairs that were never made.

"When your contract is over, they send you home, saying they've transferred the money," Yuriy Cheng, a Ukrainian, wrote in Russian in an undated post on an online mariners' forum about the *Dona Liberta*'s owner. "You get home, and there is nothing there." Cheng described a standoff on his ship between management and the mostly Filipino crew members, who stopped work after a year of not being paid despite threats of jail time if they failed to deliver the ship's cargo. "These guys are 40 or 50 years old," he wrote, "and they were crying like babies out of frustration."

Cristof and Raducan were stranded on the *Dona Liberta* for five months off the coast of England before they were rescued by an aid organization called the Mission to Seafarers. They had survived on canned goods and by burning wood from the ship to boil water for rice and ramen.

The *Dona Liberta* in 2014

"They did not want to stay but they refused to leave," Ben Bailey, project manager of the organization, said as he explained how he tried to orchestrate a plan to remove Cristof and Raducan from the ship. In situations like these, a tangle of financial ties knot the men in place. Each of the Romanians had paid more than $1,000 to the manning agency to get their jobs on the *Dona Liberta*. Leaving the ship would mean forfeiting any chance of recouping that deposit or collecting the wages promised to them. Acting without the owner's consent risked being blacklisted from future work.

After five months, Cristof decided he could take no more. The breaking point came when he learned that his children had been pulled from school because there was no money for its costs. For Raducan, it was finding out that his wife had resorted to begging in public. Both were flown home to Romania on plane tickets purchased by the Mission to Seafarers.

The fate of these men raised a larger question. How can such a pervasive problem get so little public attention? One answer is that wage theft and seafarer abandonment are crimes of neglect. And no matter how intentional and cruelly calculated, this abuse represents a passive form of harm that, on its face, seems less violent. Stories of neglect usually whisper rather than scream, and where an audience looks for a clear villain, they find ghostly indifference instead. The consequences of such neglect typically unfold in slow motion and at a distance. Unfortunately, the old reporter's adage "If it bleeds, it leads" is true—and so too is its inverse. The more pervasive and less dramatic a tragedy, the less it seems a tragedy, or even a story worth telling.

This uncomfortable fact was apparent in my own reporting. I dedicated the majority of my time to investigating acute abuses—murder caught on camera, workers shackled on ships, rapes at sea—and not the chronic crimes that affected more men, like the abandonments I had found on the *Sofia,* the *Seapol One,* and the *Dona Liberta.* After all, a Somali pirate with a rocket-propelled grenade launcher slung over his shoulder is more gripping than a faceless, nameless bureaucrat in some far-flung office who one day stops answering emails and turns off his cell phone. In both instances, though, the men left on the ship are hostages.

I traveled to the U.A.E. to spend several days with Paul Burt, the regional director of the Mission to Seafarers and a clergyman in the Anglican Church. Along the hundred-mile stretch of coastline between Dubai and the northern tip of the Arabian Peninsula, there are roughly a dozen ports, ranging from the largest ones like Jebel Ali, which primarily handled large container ships, to smaller ports, like Port Rashid, that were frequented mostly by tugs and supply vessels. In the middle were several ports that have big berths but low prices, ideally suited for operators down on their luck or looking to skirt oversight. Ajman and Sharjah Hamriyah were such ports where Father Burt spent most of this time.

These ports offered variations of the same basic story over and over. Left in this liquid desert, the men were typically stuck on a ship that was officially in port, but in fact was only visible to but not reachable to shore, a couple miles from land. On the *Falcon,* for example, five men—from Sudan, Eritrea, and the Philippines—who were waiting to take diesel to Yemen were marooned when their ship was sold to a new owner who refused to pay them nine months of back wages. Their professional certificates and qualifications had expired while they were incarcerated at sea, setting them back even further. Their phone cards ran out of credit, cutting off communication with their families. "We just want to go home," the captain kept saying to me. Mostly, these men were devoutly religious. They referenced divine fate often when I talked to them. The afterlife was not a concept to them but a destination, and hell (or whatever their term for that might be) was the here and now.

Dubai saw a lot of seafarer abandonment cases because the price of oil had fallen from a peak of $130 a barrel in 2008 to $47 a barrel in July 2017, idling much of the oil industry's marine traffic in the region. Labor unions were forbidden in most of the Gulf states in the Middle East, including in the U.A.E., making the mission's work even more vital. At any given moment, there were more than 250 seafarers stranded in ports near Dubai. Burt's staff of five received an average of three urgent calls per day. With no legal leverage, the mission relied mostly on shame to pressure owners to take responsibility for their crews.

About six miles off the coast of Dubai, Burt's colleague Nelson Fernandez, also a clergyman in the Anglican Church, took a boat to visit a diesel tanker called *The Admiral.* Passing seafarers had phoned Burt to report that the men on *The Admiral* were pleading for bottled water. The men were also cooking food on an open fire on a highly flammable deck. When Fernandez boarded *The Admiral,* the captain, a Filipino man in his sixties, appeared on deck, cell phone in hand. "This happens every day," the captain kept saying, showing him photographs on his phone of a toilet filled with blood.

The ship's engine had broken down, and the captain and his crew of six other Filipinos had been stuck there for nine months without clean water. The desalinator was not working, and drinking salt water was causing his stomach to ulcerate, the captain theorized about his hemorrhaging. "So much terrible," he kept muttering under his breath as he frantically scrolled through 144 text messages he had sent to the owner of the ship, pleading for a reply.

Fernandez listened patiently to the captain for half an hour and when it came time to depart, the clergyman made his way to the ladder to climb back into his transport boat. In the art of leave-taking, Fernandez was Picasso. He put his hand on the captain's shoulder, his stare converting his words into a promise. "I will return within three days with clean water and food," he said. The captain replied in a painfully quiet voice: "Please take us with you." Fernandez said nothing more as he slowly but decisively exited, his calm demeanor somehow bolstering his promise. Still, if eyes were arms, the captain's stare would have reached out and clutched Fernandez as he started his engine.

I never found out why the men were stuck on *The Admiral*. Some shipowners refused to pay salaries because they believed (sometimes rightly) that the crew had siphoned off fuel from their own ship and sold it on the black market. More often, though, the shipowners said they could not pay because, quite simply, they didn't have the money.

The scope and intensity of the problems I witnessed during this reporting felt like a scandal. If the public discovered that an industry had a de facto policy of looking the other way as workers in factories around the world were routinely locked behind chained doors for weeks or sometimes months, with no freshwater or food, unpaid and given no sense of when they might be permitted to go home, wouldn't there be immediate outrage, criminal investigations, and consumer boycotts? Not so at sea.

Whether we cite the industry as fishing or merchant shipping, the fact remains. There is a tacitly accepted practice to ignore a clear pattern that screams at anyone willing to look at it and that ranges from debt bondage to systematic abandonment. In the rare instance that such cases get covered in the press, they are dismissed by industry spokespeople as aberrations, or they get watered down by discussions of the inevitable bureaucratic challenges that are distinct to transnational and offshore commerce. Those workers are independent contractors and not our responsibility. Those ships are flagged to another country. A manning agency should be handling their repatriation and pay. The shipowner, not the industry, should be held accountable. And so on. The self-serving talking points are well-worn tools in an increasingly globalized economy, but nowhere are they more effective than on the ocean.

Over the years, I'd spoken to dozens of industry consultants, lawyers, insurers, and ship operators, and they often contended that the industry was not unified enough to solve problems like debt bondage, human trafficking, wage theft, or seafarer abandonment. In fact, they often told me, there was no industry to speak of, certainly not one that could act efficiently or with consensus to tackle such thorny problems. There was, instead, just lots of independent ships and fleets, flying a plethora of different flags, they said. What was striking to me, however, was that when it came to issues like countering Somali piracy, resisting unions, standardizing port protocol, countering terrorism threats, or resisting measures that might put large fisheries off-limits or impose stricter pollution or wage rules, these industries were surprisingly efficient and united.

The unfortunate truth was that in much of the maritime world the law protects a ship's cargo better than its crew. In 2017, partly motivated by bad press and union pressure, the shipping industry came together in an unprecedented fashion and tried to confront their tendency to abandon seafarers. The industry imposed a new rule requiring ship-owners to carry insurance to cover the costs of sailors marooned in port. But as Burt pointed out, the smaller vessels that were most likely to strand mariners were not, under this new rule, the ones required to carry such insurance.

I had seen this problem often in the maritime world. What few worker protections existed at sea usually applied to the ships that needed them least. For example, the international agreement that safeguards many basic rights among seamen, called the Maritime Labour Convention, exempted fishing boats, where abuses were most severe. Many of the new rules introduced by the Thai government to combat sea slavery on boats in the South China Sea focused on bigger ships because new rules would be too financially burdensome to the midsized ones, even though the midsized ships were far more numerous and more prone to trafficking.

In fact, this tendency toward solutions that just ever so barely missed their target was so common that it became tough not to wonder whether it was intentional. While some people might dismiss this speculation as conspiracy theory, I see it more as pattern recognition. I also wondered whether this slick practice was just the sort of sleight of hand that industries pay high-priced consultants to provide. Either way, the near misses and almost fixes were only allowed to continue thanks to lawmakers with short attention spans and a general public prone to the sort of dissipated outrage I'd found in New Zealand.

.  .  .

Whether a person has been abandoned by a negligent shipowner, kidnapped by a foreign government, or sent overboard by a disgruntled captain, the sea can be a cruel prison. David George Mndolwa, Ahmed Abu Khattala, and George Cristof had very different experiences of being trapped offshore, but in each case I wondered about the coping mechanisms they'd used to maintain their sanity.

As I read up on the topic, I came across the story of a Belgian research ship called the *Belgica,* which offered an instructive and early lesson about the mental strains of being stranded at sea. In 1898, the wooden, 118-foot ship became stuck in a pack of Antarctic ice in the Bellingshausen Sea. On board were nineteen men: nine sailors, two engineers, and an international team of eight officers and scientists, including a geologist, meteorologist, and anthropologist. As the sun disappeared for two months, the group hunkered down for a brutal winter. With no hope of being rescued, their true enemy was not the cold but madness. Within weeks, a crewman became paranoid and hid at night. Another announced plans to walk home to Belgium.

The *Belgica* broke free from the ice and made it back to the port of Antwerp nearly a year later. The remaining crew members were haggard and thin, but their faculties were largely intact because the captain had imposed a rigorous regimen meant to maintain their mental health. This regimen included a "baking treatment" in which the men were required to sit in front of a warming stove for half an hour and eat a diet of foul-tasting but vitamin-rich penguin meat. There was also mandatory participation in routine exercise outside on the ice and in social gatherings, including a beauty contest between images of women torn from the ship's magazines.

News of the *Belgica*'s survival tactics spread among ship captains. The lesson that many of them took from the incident was that it is sometimes as important to take psychological precautions as meteorological ones. Ship captains on subsequent Antarctic excursions began packing straitjackets. Later in the twentieth century, infirmaries on many ships destined for the North or South Pole or any other long journeys also began stocking antipsychotic drugs. In 1996, an anthropologist named Jack Stuster used the journals written on the *Belgica* to help design the space stations. If astronauts were to survive, Stuster suggested, they would need to prepare for the melancholy and disorientation from spending long periods in extreme isolation. There was a lot to be learned from the men who had made similarly grueling voyages at sea.

I was intrigued by the psychological challenges faced by the millions of other seafarers who go offshore willingly. Even under normal circumstances, the loneliness and boredom of long voyages at sea can be emotionally brutal. One study by the ITF found that over half of the six hundred mariners interviewed reported feeling depressed during their time at sea. Another study published in the journal *International Maritime Health* found the global percentage of suicides among seafarers while at sea was more than three times higher than that of land-based suicides in the U.K. or Australia.

Seafaring has always been an isolating profession. This intensified, though, after the September 11 attacks, when antiterrorism laws in the United States and much of Europe restricted crews' access to ports. Crews were required to park no closer than half a mile from shore as they waited for a call from ship operators informing them of their next destination. On board, a crewman can sit, sometimes for months, within sight but out of reach of sending his wife an email, eating a decent meal, having a doctor check the toothache that keeps him up at night, or hearing his daughter's voice on her birthday.

In many ports, dockside brothels adjusted their business models to these new norms. "Love boats," or floating bordellos, began shuttling women or girls, along with drugs and alcohol, out to the parked ships. But the longer the men were stuck, the less such boats came calling. Everyone knew that a stranded seafarer is soon a penniless seafarer.

And yet for all the homesickness involved in this work, most of the mariners I interviewed said they were reluctant to leave their ships, even in the face of abuse or abandonment. Often, there was shame in returning home unpaid. On land, these men were spouses, fathers, and sons. At sea, they had a rank that carried status. With this status came strict rules, and abandoning their post was a violation of the highest order. Seafarers were overwhelmingly male, and their ship, almost always called "she," had a distinct emotional hold over them. They loved her as much as they resented her. Having traveled together, grown annoyed with each other, protected each other, these men often said their ship was as much a wife as a workplace to them.

Virtually all of the stranded men said that once they found their way home, they hoped to go back to sea. This seemed puzzling in light of what they'd been through. Obviously, necessity was driving them: it's a decent-paying job where options are few. But there is also a pull to life offshore. For all the suffering I heard about from these men, this pull seemed closer to resignation than enchantment, though powerful nonetheless. Spend enough time away from land, I was told, and you rarely come out the other side the same. "It changes you," one of the stranded men said.

After stints at sea, I sensed in myself subtle changes in how I related to sleep, conversation, and food. On trips, I grew accustomed to extremely tight bunks, long and extreme silence, and eating whatever was put in front of me, most often half-cooked fish and barely boiled rice. When I got home, I noticed I ate faster, more dutifully than for enjoyment. I snuggled with my wife tighter in bed, uncomfortable with the extra space. I tired faster of talking, wanting more often to withdraw behind my headphones. A grumpier version of my former self returned to shore each time.

The biggest change, though, I felt in my stomach. During several years of reporting at sea, I grappled with a worsening case of what some mariners called sway. Others referred to it as dock rock, land sickness, reverse seasickness, or *mal de débarquement* (French for "disembarkation sickness"). As important as it was to get your sea legs when adjusting to life on a ship, it was equally essential to restore your land legs when you returned to shore. Sometimes, though, re-acclimating was difficult, and the result was as bizarre as it was nauseating. The minute I stepped back on land, I started feeling sick.

The experience was akin to drunken bed spins. My head felt like a bobbing buoy as my body's vestibular system, the internal gyroscope for balancing, created a persistent rocking sensation. In a spatial equivalent of jet lag, my body clung to the memory of a place it had already left. Usually people who are least susceptible to seasickness are most vulnerable to land sickness. I never once threw up on a ship due to seasickness, but I twice vomited after stepping on land. The longer the stay offshore and the rougher the waters, the more stubborn the sway was when I got home. Sometimes it lasted days.

Working at sea was not my lifelong profession, of course; I was a mere visitor, a land creature passing through. Unlike many of the men I interviewed, I always had the option to leave. Still, this strange disorder instilled in me a respect for the sea's grasp. It changed me—not just psychologically, but also physiologically. I had to imagine it also changed the many mariners I'd met.

# RAIDERS OF LOST ARKS

In a closed society where everybody's guilty, the only crime is getting caught. In a world of thieves, the only final sin is stupidity.

—Hunter S. Thompson, *Fear and Loathing in Las Vegas*

When people I encountered on my various reporting trips asked me what I was working on, I usually answered with something about offshore crime. Their response was almost always "Oh, so, Somali piracy, like *Captain Phillips*?" I tended to clumsily reply, "Yes, that, but other types of piracy too."

Larceny has been a part of maritime life since humans first took to the seas, and though snatching a ship the size of a skyscraper has a ring of absurdity, it happens with surprising frequency. Indeed, piracy does not just involve fast-boat attackers. Buccaneers often wear business suits, hijacking ships in port through opportunism rather than force. "In some ports in the world," I'd been told many times before, "possession isn't nine-tenths of the law. It is the law."

Over my months of reporting, I had seen stealing of every kind—illegal fishing, FAD raids, kidnapping of fishermen, wreck scavenging, and human trafficking. Making off with a ship, on the other hand, was a thievery of a different order, almost too preposterous to believe. So, I went to Greece in November 2016 to learn about this other type of piracy but with a specific eye toward the role played by corruption in port. For all the lawlessness at sea, I needed to study its roots on land.

My introduction to this topic came months earlier in a nine-by-twelve-inch manila envelope that had been mailed to my home. It arrived at my house with no indication of who sent it. Inside was a tattered, ten-page document titled "Port Scams" that consisted of a glossary of terms describing how to steal a ship, change its identity, surreptitiously siphon fuel, or pilfer cargo. The envelope had been mailed from Greece and probably came from a somewhat shady guy I had hired on a prior trip to Athens in 2014 to take me around the Piraeus port. He had mentioned that he started but never completed a manuscript about port crime. Perhaps he saw me as a way to bring some of these scams to life; I was happy to oblige.

The glossary was a reporter's gold mine. The stuff of *Ocean's Eleven,* the scams had names like "Unexpected Complications," which referred to a ruse for overbilling, where a shipyard did repairs on fictional problems. Or "Cappuccino Bunker," a scam where suppliers heated bunker (the fuel used by ships) or pumped in air to froth it, like a cappuccino, which inflated its volume and allowed the supplier to charge more for less.

If insurance fraud was the goal, the glossary offered a tried-and-true tactic. A corrupt operator hired a crew to take the ship to sea, where the ship would ostensibly break down. The operator then arranged for the vessel to hire a mechanic who was in on the scheme and deemed scuttling as the only affordable option. The mechanic and the ship operator then split the insurance money from the scuttling, and the operator re-flagged and renamed the ship before heading off with a new identity.

The glossary also provided some helpful guidance for changing a pilfered ship's identity. To sever ties between a ship and its past, the document suggested removing all tracking devices that might be built into the ship's console or hull. Get rid of anything on the vessel with its name written on it, including life jackets, bridge paperwork, buoys, stationery, and lifeboats, the glossary advised. "Replace the ship's first or build name," it said, which is usually welded onto both sides of the bow and on the stern in foot-high, raised steel letters. "Don't forget the serial plate on the ship's main engine," the document added, because it's a favorite way for investigators to trace a stolen ship's original identity.

If the glossary taught me anything, it was that maritime swindles take skill. Absconding with a ship—whether repossessing it on behalf of mortgage lenders or stealing it for personal gain—was far from easy but also far from uncommon. I hoped to get closer to the topic by embedding with someone engaged in this line of work. And by all accounts, a man named Max Hardberger was a master of the craft.

. . .

With the lights of Athens far in the distance, the stolen ship began to churn out into the Saronic Gulf off the coast of Greece under the cloak of night. Aboard the 261-foot freighter called the *Sofia,* all the signal lamps were doused. No cabin lights spilled from the portholes. Even the bridge was dark, the nervous captain peering out over the waves as he opened the ship's throttle and the port of Piraeus, six miles off the stern, fell farther away. It was a moonless night, leaving no way to tell where the water ended and the sky began. The ship was visible only as a darker shade of black, a smudge of shadow cutting through the waves.

The *Sofia* was a Greek-owned ship that Max Hardberger was hired to sneak out of the port of Piraeus near Athens. His client was a group of New York mortgage lenders who were owed money tied to the ship.

The purloined ship resembled a darkened twenty-six-story building that had been turned on its side and made to glide through the water. Its prow split the cold night air with the force of a 1,774-horsepower engine. Running at eight knots, the *Sofia*'s massive screw spun furiously underwater, churning a foamy white wake. The Panama-flagged tanker sat high in the water because it was empty of cargo and light on fuel, having left port in a hurry. The ship was moving fast enough to create a low humming sound in the sea, but slow enough that the Greek Coast Guard could catch it in no time if the government decided to try.

On the *Sofia*'s bridge, tension ran high. The captain of the ship was taking orders by phone from two opposing groups of disgruntled creditors, and it was unclear who was in charge. On one side was a management company named NewLead, which ran the ship's day-to-day operations, including looking after the crew, who were owed tens of thousands of dollars in back wages. These were the operators. On the other side was the ship's mortgage lender, a New York venture capital firm called TCA Fund Management Group, which was owed $4.2 million by the shipowner. These were the bankers.

Both the operators and the bankers wanted to get the *Sofia* as far from port as fast as possible because there was a feeding frenzy under way for assets of the ship's owner, a widely feared Greek man named Michalis Zolotas. He had been arrested and extradited to Cyprus a couple of weeks earlier on bribery and corruption charges. Zolotas owed a lot of people money, but until his arrest no one was brave enough to demand repayment. Now it was open season on everything he owned, and his creditors were hoping to snatch his ships. The contours of maritime law roughly follow the contours of an imaginary line that runs twelve miles from a country's shores. But for the right amount of money, that line is easily bent.

On the *Sofia*'s bridge, the short but stern Filipino captain, Bernardo del Rosario, was at the helm. The furtive dash out of Greek waters was only his second voyage as a captain, after rising through the ranks for over a decade. Though he had extensive training in maritime school in Manila, nothing had prepared him for a trip like this. As a heated argument intensified around him, del Rosario's main concern was that he might end his career as a captain after it had just begun. Defying a shipowner's orders can jeopardize a captain's license. Del Rosario's problem was that it was unclear who, in fact, was the owner. "Not good," he kept muttering. "Not good."

The week prior to the *Sofia*'s sprint from Piraeus had involved a high-stakes game of chess. Hired by the bankers, Max Hardberger, widely considered the best maritime repo man in the business, had flown from Mississippi to Athens, where he managed to persuade the crew of the *Sofia* to let him on board. The next challenge, though, was getting the ship out of Piraeus, the port of Athens, because word was already spreading fast among creditors that the ship was a ready foothold into Zolotas's estate. Every time Hardberger had tried to clear the ship of its liens and arrest warrants, a new one walked in the door. A pack of angry creditors, some making fake claims and others real, was scrambling to the courthouse in Athens. Everyone was showing up with bills in hand that Zolotas had not paid: the food service company that fed the *Sofia*'s crew, the fuel provider that filled the ship's tanks, the travel agency that bought plane tickets for the deckhands.

If the bankers didn't make a bold move, Hardberger had argued, the *Sofia* would hemorrhage all its value. The bankers employing Hardberger were owed the most amount of money, but there were dozens of other creditors as well. How these creditors would be handled and who should get first dibs varied depending on the country where the claims were filed. To level the playing field in their race with other creditors, they needed to get the *Sofia* to a jurisdiction where debt disputes were treated under British common law, which was far more favorable to mortgage lenders and foreign litigants. Two decent options: Malta, about five hundred nautical miles away, or Gibraltar, roughly three times that distance. The courts there did not favor shipowners like those in Greece. Plus, Gibraltar also had a reputation for being especially fast at the business of buying, selling, and auctioning ships.

"This is partly a game of timing," Hardberger told me one afternoon at a restaurant in Athens, as he waited for the right moment to make his move. I had flown to Athens to shadow him during this extraction and to see a maritime repossession in person. Over a plate of jumbo shrimp, Hardberger explained that a quirk in maritime law dictated that once a ship is sold, prior debt and arrests are cleared. If he could get the *Sofia* to one of these two countries, he could "scrub her bottom," maritime jargon for cleaning it of prior liens and arrests. That way, the bankers could resell the ship and quickly recoup its losses. The challenge was to get the ship there.

The right moment came soon enough. Lingering for hours around the Athens courthouse, Hardberger and a Greek lawyer hired by the bankers saw their opportunity near closing time on a Friday. They watched as half a dozen new debt claims were filed, most of them for mere thousands of dollars. Ten minutes before the court closed, they swiftly settled all the claims, removed the arrest warrants, and sped to port to catch a fast boat out to the anchored *Sofia*.

The plan was to hustle the *Sofia* past the twelve-mile mark, beyond the reach of Greek authorities, before someone at the courthouse tipped off Zolotas's other debtors. Clearing the debts before the Athens court closed for the week would buy Hardberger enough time to run to the high seas. Then engineering an auction in a foreign jurisdiction would allow him and the bankers to shake any remaining debt entirely by scrubbing the ship's bottom. The stakes were perilously high and the plan made sense, if only the captain of the ship played along. That's not what happened.

. . .

When the phone rang in Hardberger's dilapidated double-wide trailer deep in the woods of Lumberton, Mississippi, it usually meant that someone, somewhere was in an especially tight bind. Hardberger was a person whom nobody liked to call. The most seasoned maritime repo man in the business, he took only the toughest jobs. His company was called Vessel Extractions, and its specialty was sneaking—some might call it stealing—ships out of foreign harbors, usually under the cover of

Max Hardberger in front of his trailer in Lumberton, Mississippi, with his dog, Morgan le Fay

night, and moving them to jurisdictions where his clients might have a fighting chance of taking legal ownership of them. Ships like the *Sofia*.

Hired by the bankers to get this ship out of Greek waters as fast as possible, Hardberger humored my pleas to join him in Athens for the job. I was on a plane two days later. The backstory behind the *Sofia* was complicated, and en route I wondered which side of the law I would be on if I shadowed Hardberger. On the flight, I plowed through reams of court records, news clips, and police documents to get my bearings.

Most of Zolotas's fleet of half a dozen ships, including the *Sofia,* were tankers carrying bitumen, or liquefied asphalt. Bitumen, which looks like thick black paint, is used primarily to build roads, so the market for this product is global. But the ships that carry it are expensive to maintain, because the bitumen has to be kept heated at all times or else it solidifies. Because of his fleet's unusually valuable cargo, Zolotas had powerful friends in far-flung governments.

Zolotas had many enemies, too. The collapse of the Cypriot banking system in 2013 started opening a crack for them. As the Greek and Cypriot governments began investigating the banking collapse, Zolotas was arrested and charged in 2016 with using one of his companies to pay a bribe to the former governor of the Central Bank of Cyprus.

With Zolotas's arrest, the bankers in New York sprang into action. They might not have another shot at getting their money back unless they quickly seized the *Sofia,* which had been put up as collateral. That was when the bankers picked up the phone and called Hardberger.

TCA was not the only one to pounce on Zolotas's assets. In Savannah, Georgia, U.S. marshals stormed one of his sugar freighters called the *Castellano,* ordering it to stay put due to unpaid debt. In Baltimore, the U.S. Coast Guard detained one of his asphalt tankers called the *Granadino,* ostensibly because it had stranded a dozen of its crew. Another Zolotas tanker called the *Iola* sat in the port of Drammen in Norway as creditors argued over it. The crew on the *Katarina,* also a bitumen carrier, had taken matters into their own hands, seizing control of the ship to demand back wages.

The net around Zolotas's properties was tightening fast, and if the *Sofia* was arrested in Greek waters, neither the bankers nor the unpaid Filipino crew on the ship could expect to see their money anytime soon. The Greek legal system was not known for its efficiency or for being sympathetic to foreign lenders or crews.

In the maritime world, Greece was a superpower, and roughly half the country's prominent shipping families came from Chios, a minuscule, mountainous Greek island five miles off the coast of Turkey. Always more a merchant-marine outpost than a fully integrated part of the empires and nations that had claimed it over the centuries, this sparsely populated flyspeck had historically served as a gateway between east and west. The people from this island were known as much for their outlier spirit as for their business acumen in navigating the lawless seas.

Zolotas was from Chios. A third-generation shipowner, he also had his tentacles in banking and politics. In Athens, he was as respected as he was feared. In Chios, which I visited soon after arriving in Greece, people described Zolotas with the same awe as the fictional Keyser Söze, the mythical character in the 1990s film *The Usual Suspects*—the guy behind the guy behind the guy, hiding in plain sight. "Yes, he's from here, but if you plan to write about him, you probably shouldn't be on the island," a former associate of his warned me. "It's not safe."

. . .

Athens was not my first meeting with Hardberger. A friend of mine who is an investigator for the U.S. Coast Guard had once mentioned in passing that ships get stolen all the time. Often it's not pirates, my friend explained to me, but banks and repo men who do the stealing. I'd known of illegal acts of piracy, but this quasi-legal (or at least not expressly illegal) commandeering of ships was new to me. As I asked more sources about it, I kept hearing Hardberger's name. I learned that over the prior two decades Hardberger had seized more than two dozen ships and he had a reputation for taking on the toughest of grab-and-dash jobs, usually on behalf of banks, insurers, or shipowners. So, I tracked Hardberger down and sent him an email. I told him that I wanted to understand his techniques and outlook, and he agreed to let me write about his work.

In 2016, I met up with Hardberger in Haiti. I had gone to the island to embed with its Coast Guard, which was struggling to deal with rampant maritime crime. Hardberger was there to help a Pakistani shipowner wrest his freighter from a corrupt charterer who was alleging a breach of contract. The repo job was called off when the courts ruled

On a patrol, I posed with a group of Haitian marine police officers who were gifted a fish by a small fishing boat they had just boarded for inspection.

in favor of the shipowner, so Hardberger had time to kill, and he joined me as I traveled the island.

While waiting for a call from the Haitian Coast Guard, I met Hardberger to interview him where I was staying at Port-au-Prince's Oloffson Hotel. The hotel was a crumbling nineteenth-century Gothic mansion with gingerbread trim where Graham Greene stayed while he wrote *The Comedians,* his novel about the Papa Doc Duvalier years in Haiti. For me, the hotel was a welcome respite from the grimy ships I had been calling home for long stretches. Swapping sea stories, Hardberger and I ate club sandwiches and drank beer on the veranda, looking out over tropical fruit trees, sculptures of voodoo gods, and bats flitting under the hotel floodlights.

A walking encyclopedia of underworld activity, Hardberger was able to recite, country by country, the ports that had yet to go digital. Useful information, he explained, because the ports still relying on paper records are far less likely to flag your name or passport number. I asked him to describe the ruses he had used over the years for boarding ships. "Let's see here," he responded, his face lighting up as if I'd asked a grandfather to show me photographs of his grandchildren. Most often, he explained, he posed as an interested buyer, a port official, or a charterer. He plied guards with booze and distracted them with prostitutes; spooked port police with witch doctors; and duped night watchmen into leaving their posts by lying to them about a relative being hospitalized.

Despite his muscle-bound name, Hardberger lacked the casting-call looks one might expect for someone in his bruising line of work. At five feet eight and 150 pounds, he had the build of a marathoner and the beard of a homesteader. He wore glasses with durable frames and recounted his stories in a fast, high-pitched voice, as if a record player had been sped up. Traces of his Cajun upbringing remained in his accent, which turned "well" to "wull" and "because" to "becawse." Upping his twang at will, he could play the naïve provincial for effect despite usually being the best traveled person in the room. His bookish air contrasted sharply with his decades-old blue jeans. At one point, he recited lines from *The Rubáiyát,* an eleventh-century Persian poem written by a scholar named Omar Khayyám.

Irrepressibly curious, Hardberger always kept a small black spiral notebook close at hand to jot down thoughts and observations. He was raised Methodist but is now an avowed atheist, and as he recounted past adventures and described future schemes, he usually wore the impish grin of a man continually on the verge of stealing third base. None of the repo men I'd met suffered from a lack of self-regard. All of them to varying degrees were self-mythologizing showmen. An impatient raconteur, Hardberger listened as if he was eager for you to finish your story so he could start telling his (which was invariably better).

Both of Hardberger's parents were teachers. As a hobby, Hardberger's dad regularly captured and froze snakes so he could preserve their skeletons to use in classes. He would put their carcasses on top of a fire-ant pile he had built years earlier in the backyard. Over the next several weeks, the ants would pick the skeleton clean, which he would then spray with adhesive and transfer to a mounting board.

Standing up as he ordered his fifth beer, Hardberger told me of his family's pet alligator and demonstrated how, at feeding time, his father would thrust a store-bought whole chicken into its pen on the end of a stick. Like many rural southerners, Hardberger grew up around guns. He excitedly described how his father taught him and his brother, Karl, to make black powder, which they would use to blow up cypress stumps in controlled explosions behind their house. When laws were about to be passed in the mid-1960s restricting mail-order gun sales, Max senior allowed his sons to order one rifle and one pistol each to be delivered by the postal service, which enabled the youngsters to skirt age requirements. The boys regularly went target shooting in the nearby swamps but never hunted actual game. "Just seemed like an unfair fight," Hardberger said about hunting animals.

As a teenager, Hardberger was fond of reading nautical adventure books like the C. S. Forester Hornblower series. He dreamed about running away to sea, or flying planes. In 1966, he headed to college at Nicholls State University, where his father worked. The school was known as Berkeley on the Bayou because of its liberal reputation.

Hardberger fell in with an international circle of friends through one of his roommates, Bernie Somoza, son of Anastasio Somoza, the Nicaraguan dictator. He also joined groups opposed to the Vietnam War. One afternoon in 1968, in what university officials later called the "Conspiracy Under the Oak," Hardberger sat by a tree on campus and explained to some of his antiwar friends the simplicity of building a reliable explosive device. Several days later, a crude bomb exploded in a trash can on campus. It might have been Fourth of July fireworks (perfectly legal in patriotic Louisiana), but word spread about Hardberger's impromptu bomb-making seminar. "All involved thought it best that I transfer," Hardberger said curtly about his switch to the University of New Orleans.

During his college summers, Hardberger worked as a deckhand on a boat that delivered drilling fluid to offshore oil rigs and worked his way up to eventually earn his captain's license, which allowed him to skipper his own cargo ship in the Caribbean before the age of twenty-eight. He also earned his airplane pilot's license and supplemented his income flying crop duster planes and airlifting corpses to mortuaries that were too far away to transport the bodies by road. A true polymath, he also taught English and history at a high school in Vicksburg, Mississippi, and later at a parochial school in Slidell, Louisiana, before enrolling in a master's degree program at the University of Iowa Writers' Workshop, where he focused on fiction and poetry.

In 1990, Hardberger was working odd jobs on ships when a shipowner friend called and asked him for an unusual favor. A corrupt port manager was holding his ship in Puerto Cabello, Venezuela, waiting for a hefty bribe. The shipowner, who happened to know Hardberger as an adventurous and slick guy, asked him to fly down there and sneak the ship out of port. Hardberger took the job with glee, and his escapade was eventually covered in the maritime press, after which his phone started ringing with similar requests.

Hardberger said he liked the work and that by 1998, after a four-year correspondence course through Northwestern California University, he passed the California bar exam on his first try, without sitting a single day in law school. Four years later, he founded Vessel Extractions with Michael Bono, one of his former high school history students. The firm's jobs occasionally involved mega-yachts. More often, they were called to retrieve small- to medium-sized "tramp steamers" that trade on the spot market, where ships have no fixed schedule or ports of call, carrying goods between developing countries with poor or unstable governments. Hardberger charged clients in two stages: an initial investigation fee to research the case, and a payment if they managed to successfully repossess the vessel. According to Hardberger, extracting a $5 million ship might earn them a quarter million in fees.

But sometimes, the risks were so high that Hardberger regretted taking the job. He always pulled them off, but the danger was more than he enjoyed, he said. And yes, he had a story to make his point, which he shared as we ordered another round of beers.

It was 2004. Haiti had erupted in an armed rebellion. The ship, Hardberger's target, was the ten-thousand-ton, ten-story-tall *Maya Express*. After hiring the vessel to haul 235 used cars from the northeastern United States to Haiti, an American businessman refused to pay for the trip. This caused the owner of the ship to default on his mortgage, leading Haitian authorities to detain the ship in port. In league with corrupt local officials, the American businessman set up a rigged auction in which he planned to buy the ship. It's not a common move, but it's far from unheard of. Maritime auctions allow for anonymous purchases, and only the corrupt Haitian officials, who expected hefty kickbacks if the scheme succeeded, would know that the actual buyer of the ship was the same person who had caused the mortgage default in the first place.

The shipowner hired Hardberger and sent him to Miragoane to steal the ship from port before his adversaries stole it at auction. Shortly after arriving, Hardberger discovered that watchmen stationed on the *Maya Express* were selling fuel from the vessel on the black market. He also discovered a small but important fact: port authorities could only use their cell phone at the harbor's soccer field—the lone spot in the area with reliable service. Thinking fast, Hardberger paid 6,000 Haitian gourdes, roughly $100, to a *houngan,* a local witch doctor, to publicly put a curse on the soccer field to keep guards away. He then tricked the ship's crew into leaving the ship by inviting them to a meeting at a local bar to discuss buying some of their stolen fuel.

With the crew off the ship, Hardberger boarded the *Maya Express* with his three-man team and went to work. The glare of their blowtorch to cut through the ship's anchor chains almost gave them away, but they successfully freed the ship from its berth in Miragoane and sailed it to the Bahamas, where a judge upheld the repossession. To justify his decision, the judge wrote that the ship's ownership could not have been properly handled in Haiti because the country's port and judicial system were rotten. "Cronyism and corruption are the order of the day," he concluded. I scoured the court papers and could find no mention from the judge about the (arguably extralegal) way the ship had ended up in his jurisdiction.

After passing time with Hardberger in Port-au-Prince, I asked him to join me on a trip to Miragoane for my embed with the Haitian Coast Guard. He agreed. "A chance to visit with old friends," he said. During our drive, we talked about what motivated him to do repo work. He was less scared of dying than of not living fully, he said at one point.

He struck me as an older Tintin. He was a man with a master's degree in poetry and fiction whose grand opus he envisioned being lived by him but written by someone else. Once, without a hint of regret, he recounted to me how just two hours after his daughter was born, he boarded a 6:00 a.m. flight headed to Guatemala for a twenty-eight-day hitch on an oil rig in the jungle. No wonder he now lives alone, I thought. After showing me pictures of the ramshackle mobile home where he stays in Lumberton, Mississippi, he added that he had always measured his life not by the money in his pocket but by the wealth of his experiences. After too many beers, Hardberger and I toasted our final swigs to mistakes yet made and parted company for the night.

The next day, I made some due-diligence calls to the U.S. Coast Guard Office of Investigations, Interpol, and the bar association in California, where Hardberger was licensed as a lawyer. I wanted to check for records of complaints, disciplinary actions, or arrest warrants for him. There were none.

I contacted Charles N. Dragonette, who monitored maritime crime for the U.S. Office of Naval Intelligence until 2012, and asked for his perspective on the maritime extraction business. Dragonette cautioned me. There's no denying that Hardberger and his ilk are vigilantes, he said. They erode the rule of law in places that are already struggling to establish it. "I do worry about how these guys undercut local authorities, embarrassing them by stealing ships from under their noses," Dragonette said, "and worsening the overall corruption problem by paying bribes to local helpers to pull off these heists." After a long pause, Dragonette added, "But Max is the real deal, and to the extent that there are any rules in these situations, I think he follows them."

.   .   .

Though the drive from Port-au-Prince to Miragoane is only about forty miles, the trip took us four bone-jarring, dusty, and sweltering hours. At one point on our way out of the capital, as we swerved through lines of brightly painted tap-tap buses, traffic abruptly stopped. When we finally crept forward ten minutes later, we came across a pack of uniformed police officers, some with machine guns, crowded around an intersection. The officers were standing over the dead body of a man who had been shot while riding his motorcycle. I asked one of the officers what happened. The man had been a robbery suspect, he explained. Hardberger glanced at me with a knowing look because only the night before he had made the point that Haitian authorities have their way of dealing with people who steal things.

We arrived in Miragoane just after dark, and the city was starting to bustle as the heat subsided. Hardberger explained that this port town's heyday was in the late 1960s, when it served as a processing hub for Reynolds, the aluminum foil company. The region's red soil was rich in bauxite, an ore and the main ingredient in aluminum. But Reynolds abandoned its Miragoane plant in the 1980s after a dispute with Jean-Claude "Baby Doc" Duvalier, the Haitian dictator at the time. Control of the port and nearby plant reverted to local authorities. "They run it now like an independent fiefdom," Hardberger said.

People often took ships to Miragoane to give them new identities. The port was remote and relatively unpatrolled, its waters deep and ideal for bigger vessels. Someone who wanted a fast makeover and new paperwork for a stolen boat could have it done in under two days— removing all names, prying loose the serial plate from the engine, and welding off the original metal name. As we wound our way down Miragoane's narrow boulevards choked with motorbike traffic and lined with food stalls selling *griyo* (fried pork) and *lambi an sòs kreyol* (conch in creole sauce), Hardberger explained the simple math of giving a ship a new identity. "All you need is about $300, four welders, and a fax machine," he said. "But especially the $300."

Bribery is ubiquitous in many developing-world countries, but nowhere is it more pervasive than at their ports. Harbormasters wield unusual power. Inspectors can detain a ship for any number of reasons, including the condition of the hull, the size of the sleeping quarters, and the legibility of the logbooks. In poorer countries, keeping a ship in port as long as possible is an easy way to boost the local economy. Even if an inspector does not directly profit by detaining a ship, his relatives and friends will, selling fuel, food, repairs, and booze to the crew stranded in port.

Some ports are more notorious than others for widespread bribery. The Panama Canal is often called the Marlboro Canal because of its preferred black-market boodle. The port of Lagos in Nigeria has one of the worst reputations for bribery, perhaps because for many years a ship required more than 130 signatures from inspectors before it could off-load any international cargo. Everyone in commercial shipping suffers from bribes, but no one wants to fight the problem publicly because virtually all of them are complicit to some degree in the illegal behavior.

Miragoane is among the Caribbean's largest ports for used clothing and other secondhand goods. The city is also a popular spot for stolen ships and for smugglers waiting to move their drugs to Miami. As we arrived port side, we wended our way through the bustle, alongside ships that were stacked impossibly high with used mattresses, cast-off shoes, discarded bicycles, and old cars. The scene overwhelmed the senses—louder, smellier, hotter, more crowded, colorful, confusing, and thoroughly foreign to me—and was one of those not-rare moments when I felt embarrassingly lucky for the job I have.

Hardberger was soon joined by his longtime local assistant, Oge

Cadet, whom he had contacted while we were en route to Miragoane. The three of us immediately boarded a fifteen-foot wooden rowboat for an offshore view of a tucked-away section of beach. The two men had previously discussed a plan to build a new private dock, so the reunion was a chance for them to prospect potential real estate. Their hope was to start a business in ship breaking, which involves chopping up old vessels. "The beautiful thing about scrap metal," Hardberger said about the allure of this type of demolition work, "is it doesn't have serial numbers."

The oars dipping and splashing in the azure water, Cadet rowed Hardberger and me out in the surf toward six rusty freighters parked near shore. From the rowboat, they pretended to be potential ship buyers and shouted up questions to the crews. On two of the ships, the crews yelled down that they had been detained by local officials. One ship was being repaired after a suspicious fire. The crew said openly that they believed the fire to have been set intentionally for the sake of insurance fraud. The crew on the second ship told us, again with surprising candor, that their vessel was being detained because local police suspected it of drug smuggling.

As I looked down over the side of the rowboat into the water, I could easily make out several sunken ships below us. Like ghosts, we glided over these ferrous cadavers, their towers just several feet from scraping our bottom. Pausing over one of the wrecks, I joked that it represented a lost opportunity for the ship-breaking business. "No one will be chopping it up any time soon," I observed. The boat driver reminded me that just because it was sunk didn't mean someone couldn't still steal it. After all, this is why there are "sea scrappers," he said.

Of course he was quite right, I admitted. I'd learned about these underworld characters when I was reporting in Indonesia. In that country, sea scrappers came mostly from the Madurese ethnic group and were renowned for their efficiency in stripping sunken ships of their valuable metals. They paddled their wooden boats out a couple miles from shore, equipped with crowbars, hammers, hatchets, and a diesel-powered air compressor tethered to what looked like a garden hose for breathing. Diving sometimes deeper than fifty feet, the men chopped away huge chunks of metal from the wreck, attaching them to cables for hoisting. In boom times, the metal and parts from a bigger ship, though rusty and barnacled, could sell for $1 million.

In Haiti, on the other hand, the ship breakers stayed mostly above the waterline. Miragoane's beach was thick with acrid fumes, hissing compressors, and thudding sledgehammers. Sinewy, shirtless men used blowtorches and dull axes to pick apart the vessel in sections, like ants on an elephant carcass. Yelling in Creole, they warned the men below about falling debris. Engine parts pulled from the ships were fixed and cleaned in flimsy beachside shanties. Metal hunks torn from the ships were melted down into reinforcing rods, or rebars, used in the construction of concrete walls.

After tooling around the port in Miragoane, we went out the next day with the Haitian Coast Guard, which had been alerted by its U.S. counterpart that a suspicious and potentially stolen vessel was entering Haitian waters. Several hours passed as we headed across choppy waters toward the western tip of the island. Louhandy Brizard, one of seven Coast Guard officers on board, described the two most recent boat heists that had kept him and his fellow officers busy. The first had occurred several months earlier, he said, and involved the theft and subsequent recovery of a private ship hired by the Haitian government to search for gold in its national waters. The second case, he said, involved a small ship that had still not been found and belonged to a wealthy former Haitian government official. "We usually don't catch them, and they know that," he said.

In light of the scrapping efficiency we had seen in Miragoane, it seemed possible that the Coast Guard might be looking for something that was no longer the sum of its parts. I asked Brizard whether foreign repo men might help them find elusive ships before they ended up in pieces. "They deserve to be arrested," he responded flatly, having no idea of Hardberger's line of work. Standing nearby, Hardberger shot me a look that I was playing with fire. I quickly moved on to other lines of questioning.

The hardships and perils in places like Haiti didn't seem to trouble Hardberger. He clearly relished his work at the edges of life and the law. With some distance after my adventures with him, I came to appreciate this gray area where Hardberger operates. I also saw how it breeds the scheming debtors, dishonest port mechanics, testy guards, disgruntled crews, and extortionist port authorities that such maritime repo men are hired to outsmart. Before Hardberger headed home, I asked him what he liked so much about this gray area and places like Haiti. For much the same reason that he liked living in Mississippi, he said, "Few laws."

. . .

Hardberger gave me one perspective on maritime repossession. But he wasn't the only player in this murky field. To learn a few more tricks of the trade, I called Douglas Lindsay, another maritime repo man and the lead partner with a recovery firm based in England called Maritime Resolve. He explained that although stealing a ship is sometimes the goal of maritime scams, most port corruption consists of "squeeze and release" bilking schemes. Corrupt local authorities typically used this tactic to detain a ship just long enough to extort fees. And their pretexts varied: from inflated repair bills and fake docking charges to bogus liens, or trumped-up environmental violations.

"But squeeze long enough and you strangle," Lindsay added. Even an idle cargo ship can cost up to $10,000 per day to support. Shipping businesses go bankrupt as waiting cargo spoils, delivery deadlines pass, and owed wages accumulate. Sometimes these detentions are part of a broader plot to take ownership of the vessel through a hastily convened public auction or judicial sale.

Lindsay described one job he handled in 2011. An insurer hired him to win the release of a Greek-operated cargo ship carrying sugar from Brazil, which, upon arriving in the West African country of Guinea, accidentally damaged a pier. The captain was arrested, as was his ship. He was detained pending a $50 million fine based on what the insurer estimated was less than $10,000 worth of damages. "They fly you in; you find the right official and negotiate him back to planet Earth," Lindsay said, adding that the ship and its captain were ultimately released for under $200,000.

I wasn't sure whether to be impressed or scandalized by Lindsay's story. Granted, $200,000 was a lot less than the $50 million originally sought but far more than the meager $10,000 actually owed. In the end, though, I realized that the number that truly mattered was the cost of the ship: $3 million. That's how much was actually at stake. That's roughly how much the repo man had saved the shipowner.

For all the expense imposed by this sort of port corruption, shipping is still highly lucrative because most seasoned operators know whom to pay off and how to pass to consumers these hidden and inevitable costs of doing business. More than 90 percent of the world's goods, from fuel to food to merchandise, is carried to market by sea, and bribery in ports adds hundreds of millions of dollars each year in unofficial import taxes and added costs of cargo and ship fuel, which in turn raise transport costs, insurance rates, and sticker prices by more than 10 percent.

There are also geopolitical costs to the world's vast "phantom fleet" of purloined ships, which are virtually impossible to track as they are used to carry out a broad array of crimes. In Somalia, Yemen, and Pakistan, for example, phantom vessels are used to transport fighters tied to Islamic militant groups, and they were used in 2012 by the terrorists who attacked Mumbai. In Iran and Iraq, phantom ships have been popular for circumventing international oil or weapons embargoes. Elsewhere they are typically used for other purposes: in Southeast Asia, human trafficking, piracy, and illegal fishing; in the Caribbean, smuggling guns and drugs; and off the coast of West Africa, transporting illegal bunker.

Maritime scams (or for that matter, shipping generally) typically involve four main actors: the charterer, the shipper, the receiver, and the ship's owner. The charterer leases the vessel from the ship's owner to carry cargo. The charterer's job is to find shippers who want their cargo carried. The receiver buys the cargo from the shipper. Other supporting roles include the management company, which oversees the crew and day-to-day logistics of the ship, and the insurer or Protection and Indemnity Club, more commonly called the P&I Club, which covers the risks of environmental damage like spills or damage to the ship or cargo.

Some peculiarities of maritime law play into crooks' hands. A captain's logbook carries unusual legal weight in a courtroom, for example. If a corrupt charterer pays a captain to write that the cargo was damaged during the trip, that ship is probably not leaving port until someone pays up. Ship sales are also more anonymous and final than sales of other types of property. This is one reason why ship purchases are a popular method for laundering money and dumping assets that corrupt individuals or corporations don't want governments to find and tax. Because a ship may be bought in one country, flagged to another, and parked in a third, it becomes difficult for countries to trace the origins of the money invested in a ship.

The anonymity of ship trading also makes stealing easier. If the rightful owner can catch up with a stolen painting, car, or artifact at an auction, he can make a claim and, in many cases, repossess his property. Such redress is far more difficult under international maritime law. A vessel sold at a judicial auction is deemed in industry parlance to have had its "face washed" clean of liens and other previous debts, including mortgages.

Police struggle to chase stolen ships. In most cases, marine authorities can pursue, intercept, board, and seize a foreign-flagged ship on the high seas only if the pursuit started in the authorities' territorial waters and they kept the fleeing vessel in visual contact the entire time. In many courts of law, visual contact means neither satellite nor radar observation but actual line of sight with the human eye. From the bridge of a ship, that's usually about seven miles in clear weather.

If a chase starts on the high seas, it's even more fraught. Except under special circumstances, a ship may only be stopped in international waters by a warship of its own flag or with permission granted from the fleeing ship's flag state. Liberia, the country with the most vessels sailing under its flag—more than forty-one hundred—has no warships. The country with the second most, Panama, does not routinely operate warships beyond its own coast. Therein lies the beauty of international ship thievery: crooks only have to run if someone's chasing them, and that's rarely the case. This truism explained a lot about Hardberger's world.

. . .

Some ships are wider than the Empire State Building and longer than it is tall. As I pondered the art of stealing such a craft, it seemed inconceivable that such an enormous vessel could be snatched and hidden from authorities. But the reality is that tens of thousands of vessels, from minuscule to massive, are stolen around the world each year. Finding them is far more difficult than it might seem.

Once it's on the move, a stolen ship can travel thousands of miles in under a week. Investigators post reward notices, comb sale listings, and contact port officials. Seeking clues, they publish fake job advertisements and call on the relatives, ex-wives, or jilted girlfriends of the ship's former crew. Sometimes, they send up planes, hire speedboats, and alert shipping companies to keep watch. These tactics rarely work.

Unlike pilfered cars, which tend to stay in the country where they're taken, and planes, which are tracked more closely because of terrorism fears, stolen ships are among the toughest types of property to recover. Even domestic recoveries of boats in the United States are difficult because the relevant databases are not well connected across states and they have less information than the ones dedicated to automobiles.

The best chance to catch a stolen ship is to grab it before it sets sail. Often, that requires savvy negotiation. Charlie Meacham, a maritime repo man based in Florida, described a job from several years earlier in which he was hired to retrieve a ship that was trapped in a West African port (he would not disclose which one). The ship and its crew were under arrest and facing a $60 million fine for allegedly spilling about fifty gallons of oil into the water near port. After a case of Jack Daniel's was delivered to the port master's office and $55,000 was discreetly wired to his bank account, the men and ship were quietly set free. "Bribing is illegal," Meacham emphasized to me. "Negotiating a fine is not."

Usually such negotiations are ho-hum affairs, involving paperwork and banks, but they can become waterborne jailbreaks when local authorities are uncooperative. This is when a repo becomes an "extraction." Common cases involve ships being taken to "unfriendly jurisdictions"—ports in countries like Venezuela, Cuba, Mexico, Brazil, or Haiti—where local governments are less sympathetic to foreign shipowners. In such instances, options for recovery range from bad to worse.

Meacham described being sent to Havana several years earlier to take back a stolen American-owned mega-yacht being used by a prominent Cuban hotel for fishing tours. After renting the boat privately for the day and taking it into international waters, Meacham and his team informed its Cuban captain that he had a choice: return with them to the United States or take a lifeboat back to shore. The captain chose the latter. Meacham said that several times a year he travels to foreign countries to secure the release of a stolen boat or a fraudulently seized ship. Many of the boats stolen from the United States are taken by criminal cartels involved in the smuggling of people, guns, or drugs.

John Dalby, a maritime repo man and the chief executive at Marine Risk Management, a British firm, said he tried to avoid recovering stolen vessels while they were in "unfriendly" ports because the criminals who took them tended to have friends in the local government. As an alternative, he cited an example where his men posed as drug enforcement agents to board a suspect ship on the high seas. Dalby's team secretly placed a tracker on the vessel and, after disembarking, waited for it to enter Indonesian waters, where he had friends in law enforcement who were willing to arrest it.

Devising a plan for sneaking a ship out of port typically starts with surveillance, several repo men told me. Watch long enough and there is almost always a thirty-minute block each day, typically during the guards' shift change, when the vessel is unmanned. Most extraction teams need less than fifteen minutes to board a vessel, the repo men said. But getting it out of port takes longer because larger ships have engines that need half an hour or more to warm up. For surreptitious boarding, repo men said that they need little more than a headlamp and a knotted rope attached to a grappling hook. It's helpful to wrap this metal hook with a cloth to muffle the clank when it lands on the ship's metal railing, one of the repo men added.

Whenever possible, Hardberger preferred to talk his way on board, using the collection of fake uniforms and official-sounding business cards he maintains. Among them: "Port Inspector," "Proctor in Admiralty," "Marine Surveyor," "Internal Auditor," and "Buyer's Representative." If he could win himself a formal tour from the ship's crew, Hardberger wears glasses with a built-in video camera. He also leaves a tape recorder on the bridge in some corner where it will go unnoticed so he can capture what officers say when he is not in the room, and then he picks it up at the end of his tour. To verify the identity of the ship, he checks the engine serial number, which thieves often forget to remove. If he can get private access to the engine room, Hardberger carries a glass vial of magnetic powder to sprinkle on the hull where the ship's original or "build" name has often been pried off. The shadow of the name still shows up because welding it off changes the metal's valence, which makes the magnetic powder adhere differently.

Sometimes getting a ship out of port requires a clever diversion. Repo men hire local politicians to close nearby roads, street youth to set alley fires, or bar owners to host grand parties on the opposite side of town. Hardberger said the worst thing he had ever done to get a guard off a ship was to pay someone to lie to him, saying the guard's mother had just been hospitalized. More often, he said, he preferred to hire prostitutes. "They're the best actors because they have a lifetime of practice," he observed.

None of the half a dozen repo men I interviewed said that they had ever been caught removing a vessel, though they'd found themselves in a fair share of tight binds. Lindsay described a former business partner who snuck out of Russia in the trunk of a car after a deal went south with a port master in Vladivostok. Dalby said that one of his men was taken hostage during a repo and later rescued with help from government troops. Meacham added that a drug cartel still has a bounty on him in Mexico after he took dozens of their boats.

In the end, though, my impression was that for all their crafty diversions, well-placed allies, fake uniforms, and handy gizmos, the skill that seemed most essential to this work was a flexible outlook on the law. A bribe, a fine, a tax, a fee—how you label the money required to solve a problem often depends on who's paying. And what some people might call theft, others would call an extraction, a jurisdictional relocation, or a maritime repo. Regardless of what it was called, Hardberger was about to pull it off with the *Sofia,* and I wanted to be there to see it.

.   .   .

By Hardberger's standards, extracting the *Sofia* from Greece was supposed to be an easy job. He hadn't needed to sneak on board the ship. There were no fake uniforms or smooth talk needed to dupe the crew, no grappling hooks or prostitutes, no voodoo curses. His client, the New York bankers at TCA, had reassured him the crew was on their side. Though he wouldn't tell me an exact number, Hardberger's firm was charging an unusually low day rate because he was so confident of the outcome.

NewLead, the ship's operators, agreed on the need to get away from port authorities in Athens. But they were starting to worry about what would happen after that and where Hardberger would take the ship. They wondered whether it might be a place where they would have less control over the ship's fate.

Soon after Hardberger arrived in Athens, it became clear to him that this job was going to be far tougher than he expected, not because of the logistics of snatching the ship, but because the two major creditors—the bankers in New York and the operators of the ship—didn't see eye to eye. He sensed hesitation from the ship's operators, but he remained coy about the ship's destination. "Let's just get it out of Greek waters first," he kept saying. "Then we can worry about where to go after that." His point was that the *Sofia* could keep making money by moving bitumen, but only if they could get it away from these smaller and potentially fake creditors who were tying it up in Greece.

What Hardberger didn't tell the *Sofia*'s operators was that his real plan was to get the ship into international waters, then instruct the captain on authority of the bank to sail to Malta or Gibraltar, five hundred and sixteen hundred nautical miles away, respectively, where the courts were far friendlier to mortgage lenders than to shipowners or operators. For the several days that Hardberger had been scrambling on land in Athens, shoring up small debts and clearing arrest warrants, he had gotten away with being evasive about the *Sofia*'s next port of call.

That changed the minute Hardberger put his plan into action. Before a ship leaves port, someone has to inform the port manager of its new destination. When the operators saw Malta listed, they knew something was afoot because there are no bitumen factories there. This meant the bankers likely intended to take full ownership of the ship once it got to Malta, potentially cutting the operators out of their stake.

After I joined Hardberger in Athens, the plan seemed to be veering far off course in the days leading up to our sprint from Piraeus. In angry phone calls from New York, the bankers had expressed their deep annoyance that the mission was not already completed. Hardberger and his business partner, Michael Bono, tried to calm them, explaining that the *Sofia* could not leave Piraeus until it received proper clearance from port authorities. "I hired you for a piracy action," Bono recounted a lawyer in New York working for the bankers yelling at him during one call. "And you keep telling me about clearance orders?" Bono replied that this was Greece, not Haiti. Absconding with a ship was a tougher proposition in this part of the world.

The sprawling geography of Greek islands meant the *Sofia* would have to travel for up to seventeen hours to reach international waters, where Hardberger would have a more credible legal argument for taking over the ship. The smallest error would have serious consequences,

Bono explained. If the ship's operators called the authorities and told them the *Sofia* was on the run, he said, "Max would be arrested in under an hour." Seventeen hours was plenty of time for the operators to call friends in the Greek government or to get word to someone in Piraeus that their last chance to collect on Zolotas's debt was quickly slipping away.

Several tense days passed while Hardberger worked the Greeks, Bono calmed the New Yorkers, and I sat at a hotel near port, waiting with a local reporter named Dimitris Bounias, whom I had hired to help me. I finally got a text on my phone from Bono: Hardberger was making a run for it. Bounias and I raced to a rented small speedboat for our hour-long trip into the Aegean Sea to coordinates where we were told to hide behind another tanker near the *Sofia*. Hardberger did not want the *Sofia*'s captain seeing us, worrying that we might spook him and the crew. For the same reason, Hardberger had instructed me to stay off the radio and not to call his cell.

Parked near the tanker, we waited for the next five hours as Hardberger and the *Sofia*'s crew readied the ship to leave after dark. The swells were high enough that cutting off our engines risked capsizing, so we made small circles. Our boat was a hard-bottomed ten-foot skiff with low sides—very fast but roofless and exposed to the splashing waves and the worsening weather. As night fell, the temperature dropped and the waters picked up, splashing us more. I struggled to stop shivering. Bounias, who is diabetic, checked his blood sugar level and saw that it had fallen dangerously low. We decided to dart to a nearby island to get some food and something warm to drink.

No sooner had we climbed onto the dock and ordered some food than my iPhone started beeping. Tracking software indicated that the *Sofia* was in motion. "Shit," I said. "We need to go right now." To defray the chill, Bounias had ordered shots of ouzo, an anise-flavored Greek liquor, which we threw back, before grabbing our take-out fries and racing back to our boat. Within half an hour, we were caught up. In the darkness, we trailed the *Sofia* as it trundled full throttle toward the high seas.

The argument on the bridge hadn't changed. The *Sofia*'s destination was still up in the air. The bankers and the operators were still in a standoff, and the captain was stuck in the middle. The operators did not like the idea of heading to Malta, but they weren't offering an alternative. Hardberger worried that they might try to redirect the *Sofia* to a port in Libya, Egypt, or Tunisia, where they were known to have powerful allies in government. These were countries where the *Sofia* had docked previously and were more likely to ignore the demands of a New York mortgage lender or its repo man on board. "I'm not try-ing to die in a Middle Eastern prison," Hardberger had said a couple nights earlier over dinner in Athens. It was a troubling reminder that wherever he took the ship, he also had to disembark. The destination had to be favorable not only to the shipowners but also to him.

At the time, the *Sofia* was crewed by thirteen Filipino men who had been recruited by a Greek manning agency. The crewmen had gone unpaid by the owner for the past several months. In a rare move for this industry, the agency was now stepping in to avert a crisis, send-ing money back to the Philippines to the crew's families. The agency's owner took pity but also had a reputation to uphold among Philippine seafarers because he would likely want to recruit more of them in the future. If Hardberger could figure out a plan to get the ship to a port where the crew could be flown home with at least some of their wages in their pockets, the manning agency—and the crew—supported it. With luck, Hardberger had persuaded the bankers to pay half the crew's back wages before leaving port and the other half once they helped deliver the ship to Malta.

The crew was happy with this plan, but Captain del Rosario was in a bind. Head to the high seas or stay in Greek waters? Should he listen to the bankers in New York or the ship operators in Athens?

As the *Sofia* raced out of Piraeus, a lawyer representing the operators phoned the captain to say that he was absolutely not to take orders from Hardberger. Because the ship was still in Greek waters, the operators remained rightfully in control, they said. "Under no circumstances are you to enter international waters," the lawyer said, warning the captain that he could be prosecuted if he followed Hardberger's orders. "Piracy is not an option!" the operators emailed Hardberger, adding that they were considering criminal legal action against him and Bono. "Leave Piraeus and go to a nearby island and drop anchor there," NewLead ordered del Rosario.

As Hardberger and del Rosario stood on the *Sofia*'s bridge, con-flicting orders flew at them by fax, email, text, and satellite phone. The bankers argued that as the mortgage lenders they had legal authority over the ship. "Head to Malta immediately," the bankers instructed the captain in a call. To bolster their claims, Bono went so far as to email the captain a letter from a maritime lawyer in Panama, the *Sofia*'s flag state. It explained that in a situation like this the mortgage lender had authority. "You are on the verge of committing barratry," Bono warned del Rosario during one call, referring to a criminal offense in which a ship's crew or master acts against the interests of a shipowner. If you do not head to Malta, Bono told the captain, the bankers will abandon the ship entirely. "And you can forget about ever getting paid," he warned.

The argument lasted nearly ten hours, during which the *Sofia* stayed in Greek waters but tried to get as far from Piraeus as possible. In our double-engine speedboat, I followed the *Sofia* for several hours, getting occasional updates from Hardberger and Bono, until we began hitting waves too big for us, and we returned to port.

On the bridge, del Rosario played his cards close, not revealing which side he believed. Finally, he slowed the ship near the Greek island of Agios Georgios. Dropping anchor, he gave a defiant order of his own, as if he were a mother sick of her bickering kids. "I will be staying right here," he told Hardberger. "You two figure out your differences."

For the next week, they sat there. Hardberger later told me how he played good cop to Bono's bad. The two men tried to convince the operators that the *Sofia* should leave national waters before the Greek Coast Guard arrived and took the ship permanently out of commission. The bored crew passed the hours watching and rewatching the Fast and the Furious series, some of the few movies they had on board. Hardberger spent time in his bunk in the ship's hospital, the only available berth, reading Forester's *Brown on Resolution,* about the sole survivor of a sunken British warship. I hunkered down in a hotel back in Athens, texting my family my whereabouts and revised travel itinerary. I wondered who was getting the upper hand on the *Sofia.* I also wondered if the dramatic squabble over the *Sofia* was just one match of a much larger type of game that, in ways hidden from consumers, inflated prices for much of what we ship globally.

Finally, the next day, the two sides reached a deal. The operators agreed to allow the *Sofia* to sail to Malta if the bankers paid $50,000. The bankers and Bono described the money as "extortion, pure and simple." The operators, on the other hand, had their own description

Standing with binoculars on the bridge balcony of the *Sofia*, Hardberger makes a run for it from the port of Piraeus toward the high seas and checks to see if the Greek Coast Guard will catch up with them.

of the proposed sum: "an act of generosity" on their part. They argued that in light of the expensive delays they had endured due to the bankers' "attempted piracy," this money was a pittance of what they were truly owed.

The trip to Malta took six days at a lethargic six knots, the best the ship could manage against heavy winds and seas. During that trip, the *Sofia* fell into severe disrepair. The toilets began overflowing with gray water because of a deep clog. Their contents sloshed around the bathroom floor in a three-inch-deep fetid pool that had to be bailed with buckets, carried upstairs, and tossed overboard by the crew. The radio system conked out, so the bridge had to rely on the satellite phone. Finally, after one of the ship's main generators died, the *Sofia* hobbled the last leg into Malta on a backup emergency generator. "So much arguing over a complete piece of junk," Hardberger told me during a call.

When they arrived in Malta, Hardberger filled his backpack, the only piece of luggage he brought, and made the rounds to say good-bye to the crew, with whom he'd grown close. Unpleasant conditions at sea have a way of creating a quick and deep bond—that is, if they don't pit crew members against each other. The crew had reason to be angry. The thirteen Filipinos hadn't been paid for nearly five months.

"We're going to have the *Sofia* sold or back in operation within weeks," the bankers told Bono. The crew was skeptical. So was I. Hardberger flew back to Mississippi, his role in the saga complete. Several months later, he checked tracking software on his phone to see where the *Sofia* had ended up. It was still sitting at anchor in Malta.

I lost track of the crew at that point and never found out if they ever made it home, or ever got the money promised them. Long after the bizarre heist, I wondered about those thirteen Filipino men and how or whether they kept their sanity trapped on that foul ship. In so many of the stories I found on the outlaw ocean, the protagonists set out to sea to make a claim: an ill-gotten bounty, like the *Thunder;* an elusive right on land, like the women aboard the *Adelaide;* a rusty bit of territory, as with Sealand; or a piece of property, as was the case of the filched *Sofia.* Almost as often, the crews on these ships merely sought livelihoods but were caught between bigger players.

Hardberger told me the *Sofia* had been sent to sea without a functioning rescue boat. He also said that the chief engineer had spent months asking the ship's owner for parts but never received them. The Filipino crew seemed genuinely stuck in a dangerous and awful bind. Their ship was not prepared for a calamity but seemed to be headed for one. If the crew were to ever get off the ship, it would only be with the permission of the owner or operators.

Hardberger moved on. There were other ships to repossess, a steady supply of business for him thanks to those gray areas of maritime law that he so cherished and thanks to the legions of bandits in business suits he was hired to outwit.

# THE MIDDLEMEN

In this world, shipmates, sin that pays its way can travel freely, and without a passport; whereas Virtue, if a pauper, is stopped at all frontiers.

—Herman Melville, *Moby-Dick*

When Eril Andrade left the small village of Linabuan Sur in the Philippines in September 2010, he was healthy, full of hope, and expecting to earn enough money working on a fishing boat to replace his mother's leaky roof. Seven months later, his body was sent home in a wooden coffin.

The corpse was jet-black from being kept in a fish freezer aboard his ship for more than a month. He was missing an eye and his pancreas. Cuts and bruises covered his body. An autopsy concluded the wounds had been inflicted before death. "Sick and resting," said a note taped to his body. Handwritten in Chinese by the ship's captain, it stated only that Andrade, who died in February 2011 at the age of thirty-one, had fallen ill in his sleep.

I heard of Andrade's story in 2015 from a human rights worker, and though I knew of plenty of people dying on fishing boats, this case interested me more because Andrade had landed his job through a manning agency. I had heard about these firms from labor unions, port officials, and seafarer advocates, and they had a reputation for bilking workers.

Though federal prosecutors in the Philippines had tried to figure out how Andrade died, they had failed to get to the ship operator. In fact, they failed even to get at the owners of the manning agency. I wanted to know why. So, I went to the Philippines as much to learn about the cause of

Eril Andrade died under suspicious circumstances on a Taiwanese tuna long-liner after having been recruited in 2010 for the job by an illegal manning agency in Singapore called Step Up Marine.

Andrade's death as to better understand how workers like him get recruited onto these ships and what role the manning agencies play when things go wrong.

Andrade's family told me that in the summer of 2010, Andrade was growing restless. He had studied criminology in college in hopes of becoming a police officer, not realizing that he was two inches shy of the five-foot-three minimum height requirement. He took a night watchman job at the local hospital instead, earning less than fifty cents an hour. When not working in his family's rice paddy, he spent much of his time watching cartoons on television, his older brother, Julius, told me.

When a cousin told him about possible work at sea, Andrade saw it as the chance to travel the world while earning enough money to help his family. He was introduced to Celia Robelo, a woman from his village who was serving as the local recruiter for a Singapore-based manning agency called Step Up Marine. Robelo told Andrade that each month he would earn $500 plus a $50 allowance.

Andrade leaped at the opportunity, handing over 10,000 Philippine pesos, or about $200, in "processing fees" and traveling to Manila, where he paid $318 more to fly to Singapore in September 2010. A company representative met him at the airport and took him to Step

Up Marine's office, in Singapore's crowded Chinatown district. The men that Step Up recruited bunked in a filthy two-bedroom apartment on the sixteenth floor above its office, where they waited before and after stints at sea.

Andrade stayed in the apartment for about a week, according to family members who spoke to him briefly by phone. There was no television. Pots and pans were stacked in the corners, and the walls were greasy from the fried fish that the men said they were served for almost every meal. The floor was so dirty that some sections had grown moss. The windows were sealed, and the rooms smelled of urine and sweat, according to court records and interview transcripts that a Philippine police investigator provided me. The men were ordered to come and go in secrecy. The apartment manager who also controlled the work sometimes demanded sex from the men at night.

It was during his grimy stay in this apartment when Andrade's family lost track of him. "Bro, this is Eril," Andrade texted to his brother at 4:29 in the afternoon of September 15. "I am now here in Singapore I was not able to text earlier I ran out of phone credit." That was the final message the family would receive from Andrade before he boarded a Taiwanese-flagged fishing ship, the *Hung Yu 212*.

. . .

If the ocean serves as the vast space in the global economy that must be crossed to connect producers and consumers, then mariners are the go-betweens, living their ghostly lives afloat, invisible, and constantly in motion as they help move commodities from one port to another.

The seafaring industry is primarily divided between shipping and fishing. Though the merchant mariners in shipping face their own hardships, especially abandonment, these men tend to be better protected than the far more numerous and poorer workers on fishing boats. Fishing crews are rarely unionized, thus lacking political clout, which is part of why they are exempted from the Maritime Labour Convention, an international agreement signed by dozens of countries that is meant to safeguard seafarers and ensure they get paid properly.

Over 56 million people globally work at sea on fishing boats. Another 1.6 million people work in shipping on freighters, tankers, container ships, and other types of merchant vessels. For the most part, both kinds of workers get their jobs through employment firms called manning agencies. Thousands of these firms operate around the world, playing a vital role in supplying crew members from dozens of countries to ships that are almost always on the move.

Manning agencies like Step Up Marine handle everything from paychecks and plane tickets to port fees and passports. These agencies are also poorly regulated and frequently abusive. When mariners get trafficked—transported from job to job against their will, often driven by debt, coercion, or scams—manning agencies are often to blame. Taking that blame is part of their job, in fact. These firms provide ship operators plausible deniability and easy deflection of responsibility—an even more valuable role than the logistical support they offer. Indeed, manning agencies take the blame but are rarely held accountable because they tend to be in places far away from where the workers live and from where the abuses occur.

For the men they recruit, these firms promise an open doorway to another, more lucrative life. Andrade, like many of the other deckhands recruited by Step Up Marine, came from the village of Linabuan Sur, which has a population of roughly thirty-four hundred and is located on the northern coast of the Philippine island of Panay, about 224 miles southeast of Manila. Most men I spoke to there said that before they were recruited onto fishing boats, they had never before traveled abroad, worked on the high seas, heard of the term "trafficking," or dealt with a manning agency.

If Andrade's experience was like that of the other Filipino men from his village whom I interviewed, he was probably told when he arrived at the Step Up Marine office in Singapore that a mistake had been made and that his pay would be less than half of what he had been promised. Forget that original quote of $500 per month. The new salary was $200 per month, which would shrink even further when the company factored in "necessary deductions."

These deductions would have been loosely explained amid a flurry of paperwork, rapid-fire calculations, and unfamiliar terms: "passport forfeiture," "mandatory fees," "sideline earnings." Half a dozen other men from Andrade's village—who prosecutors said were also recruited by Step Up Marine—described how they were required to sign a new contract, which typically stipulated a three-year binding commitment. The contract also specified that there would be no overtime, no sick leave, eighteen- to twenty-hour workdays, six-day workweeks, and a $50 monthly food deduction and that captains were granted full discretion over reassigning crew members to alternate ships. Wages were to be paid not monthly to families but in full only after completion of the contract, a practice that is illegal in most countries.

Next, some of the men signed a prepaid bill for food supplies (a onetime fee of $250, which, like most of the deductions, was kept by the agency). Then came the "promissory note," confirming that the mariner would be hit with a "desertion penalty" if he left the ship (usually that penalty was more than $1,800). The document noted that to collect their wages, crew members had to fly back to Singapore at their own expense.

I went to Linabuan Sur to talk to half a dozen of these men who had known Andrade and who had similarly been recruited by Step Up Marine. The village was a tidy crossroads with one main avenue studded with palm trees, a quaint roadside chapel with flags snapping over its front terrace, and a convenience store advertising internet games and Pall Mall cigarettes. I met the men one by one in their small cinderblock homes, which were typically deep in the woods with chickens and pigs meandering nearby. The men were almost all shirtless, wearing flip-flops, and they always needed virtually no introduction before they agreed to sit down with me.

When I asked them about their contracts, it became clear that none had received a copy of the signed documents, which would have helped the workers ensure that they were at least entering into an agreement binding for both sides. These men also did not know why it was troubling for a boss in a foreign country to confiscate their passports, which rendered them powerless to leave.

By the time these men reached Singapore, most of them were deeply in debt—some by more than $2,000, or more than six months of wages for the average Filipino. To raise this money, the men had usually borrowed from relatives, mortgaged their homes, and pawned family possessions. The list of what they sacrificed included "the family fishing boat," "my brother's home," and "a carabao," a type of ox farmers use to work their land, the documents showed.

Even though Andrade and the other Filipino men traveled to Singapore at different times over a several-year period, virtually all of them described in nearly identical terms the apartment above Step

Up Marine's office. Jolovan Wham, executive director of the Humanitarian Organization for Migration Economics, an advocacy group in Singapore, visited this apartment in 2014 while trying to help a seafarer trapped there. He told me the men in the apartment were "packed like sardines."

A short Filipino man in his forties named Bong managed the apartment for the company, along with a Chinese woman, Lina, several of the men told me. New recruits were instructed to keep their voices down and to avoid moving around. Some of the men were required to leave the apartment before 7:00 a.m. and to return after dark. Others were sequestered in the apartment, the front door of which Bong always kept locked.

At night, twenty or more men lay on flattened cardboard on the floor, inches apart from each other. If Bong pointed at you, three of the seafarers recounted, it meant you were to sleep in his room, where, they said, he demanded sex. " 'No' was not an option," one of the seafarers said, because Bong controlled who got what jobs.

I knew the answer, but it was still hard at times not to wonder how these men could have walked into what was so obviously a trap. Desperate for a new life, they were easily duped, and once they were caught in the agency's clutches, it became much tougher for them to do a U-turn.

. . .

Over the past decade, no country has exported more seafarers annually than the Philippines, which provided roughly a quarter of the crews on merchant ships globally, despite comprising less than 2 percent of the world's population. By 2017, the Philippines was sending roughly a million workers—about 10 percent of its population—abroad annually. These workers, who collectively sent more than $20 billion a year on average back home, were in high demand because many spoke English, they tended to be better educated than workers from Sri Lanka, Bangladesh, and India, and they had a reputation for being compliant. Philippine immigration authorities insisted that they did not promote the export of workers, but merely helped manage the process.

Academics and human rights advocates rejected this claim. They said the government drove the export of workers, which was turning the Philippines into a "nation of gypsies." These critics also faulted the government for failing to create enough domestic jobs to keep its citizens from leaving home and then failing to protect them once they were abroad.

In 2016, more than 400,000 Filipinos sought work as officers, deckhands, fishermen, cargo handlers, and cruise ship workers. If Andrade's death showed anything, it was that even governments with decades of experience in the maritime labor market struggled to safeguard their citizens at sea, though, as I would soon learn, their efforts often seemed halfhearted at best.

The federal agency that is supposed to protect people like Andrade is called the Philippine Overseas Employment Administration, which is headquartered in Manila. Located in a blistering-hot building downtown, the agency is a caricature of bureaucracy, worthy of a Graham Greene novel. In floor after floor of cavernous rooms, clerks sit in rows behind big wooden desks, pressing their ballpoint pens hard on triplicate forms, surrounded by stacks of manila folders to be filed in tall metal cabinets with squeaky, uncooperative drawers. This lumbering administrative dinosaur seemed particularly ill-suited for tracking—much less safeguarding—a million-strong workforce in constant motion around the world.

I spent almost a full day wandering through this building and leafing through the administration's case files on abused workers. These documents read as dryly as a hotel bill but included some hidden surprises. For example, one filing cabinet held a 2012 study showing that the Philippine embassy in Singapore had received more requests for assistance (about sixty-three between January 2010 and April 2011) related to trafficking from Filipino men coming off fishing vessels than from Filipina women involved in the sex and nightlife entertainment industry (work that is widely considered far more prone to trafficking abuses).

The documents also included fake forms created by recruiters to trick men into paying fees for jobs that didn't exist. Some had been stamped in the upper right corner to appear more official. Looking closer at the fine print inside one of the stamps, I noticed that it had been made using a children's stamp kit and included the face of Minnie Mouse.

During a lunch break, I ventured across the city to a packed, two-block stretch of sidewalk on T. M. Kalaw Street near Manila's bay. Hundreds of seafarers were looking for work. Recruiters from manning agencies—some legal, many not—carried signs around their necks listing job openings or pointed to brochures arrayed on tables.

A popular Tagalog rap song, "Seaman lolo ko" (My grandpa is a seaman), boomed in the background. "These days," rapped the singer, Yongas, "it's the seaman getting duped." Mariners, he warned in the song, used to be the cheaters—by being unfaithful to their spouses—but they were now the ones being cheated by everyone else. As the men worked their way through the crowd, many of them seemed to know the lyrics by heart and sang along. I wasn't sure who was playing the music, but the irony of it blaring at a recruitment fair seemed lost on the crowd.

When I returned to the government's overseas employment agency, Celso J. Hernandez Jr., the head of the Operations and Surveillance Division, was at his desk and agreed to answer my questions. He explained that if a Filipino housekeeper in Kuwait was raped by her employer, she could go to the Philippine embassy for help. "At sea, on the other hand," he said, "there are no embassies." Of the seventy or so cases of worker abuse that Hernandez handled each week, ten to fifteen involve mariners, he said.

He explained that for a while the government tried to stem the flow of men recruited by agencies with reputations for abusing workers. Immigration authorities at the Manila airport stopped Filipino men bound for abroad who fit a certain profile. In this effort, the government focused on men between the ages of twenty and forty who gave off signals that they might be from rural areas: darker skin, cheaper clothes, less savvy about traveling. The strategy had minimal effect, Hernandez said, because the manning agencies simply began instructing the men on how to answer questions that would otherwise get them flagged. The recruiters also paid off certain immigration authorities so that their crews would get waved through, no questions asked.

I told Hernandez about Andrade and showed him the evidence I had collected. He checked his computer as I spoke. Looking up blankfaced, he said he had no records of Andrade's death or of Step Up Marine. "Are you sure?" I asked, unable to hide my incredulity. Hernandez nervously explained that many manning agencies like Step Up Marine were completely invisible to the government. I told him I'd look into it further on my own. Hernandez shook his head and invited me to let him know what I found.

. . .

Despite the absence of records in Hernandez's office, Step Up Marine was well known in the industry. Established in 1988, the company initially recruited household staff, or domestics, such as live-in maids, who were sent to Singapore from the Philippines to cook, clean, and provide child care.

For several weeks, I contacted seafarer advocacy and human rights groups around the world and asked them to check their files for any mention of this company and to share with me whatever documents they could. It was quickly apparent that Step Up Marine was notorious for misconduct. The documents I received indicated that in the decade before Andrade died, the company was involved in half a dozen cases of trafficking, severe physical abuse, neglect, deceptive recruitment, and failure to pay wages to hundreds of seafarers in Indonesia, India, Tanzania, the Philippines, and Mauritius. None of this made it easier for me to understand why the Philippine government's overseas employment agency hadn't heard of the company.

With a fishing crew in the Sibuyan Sea. They told their stories about having been trafficked by a manning agency called Step Up Marine.

Step Up Marine was not the only negligent manning agency I came across during my reporting. Others had recruited the Indonesians who were raped and beaten on the Oyang ships. Manning agencies also played a central role in the abandonment of the sailors I met in Dubai.

All these firms shared a playbook. They used debt, trickery, fear, violence, shame, and family ties to recruit, entrap, and leave men at sea, sometimes for years, under harsh conditions. These firms also showed that trafficking of mariners was more routine than rogue and usually orchestrated not by shady underworld crime bosses but by incorporated businesses allowed to operate with impunity by government agencies willing to look the other way. In reporting about ship repos, I'd seen how corruption often reaches from land out to sea. In studying manning agencies, I found that law enforcement's interest in crimes within its borders often stopped at the coastline, even though its jurisdiction and responsibility extended far beyond that.

But I was also coming to understand that there was a larger role that manning agencies play in the global fishing industry. These firms were not just there to provide a buffer of responsibility and culpability between the crew and their employers. Their purpose was also to help bolster a certain illusion about globalization. The manning agencies— especially the shady ones prone to undercutting wages and tricking workers—provide the efficiencies that fishing companies need to hold up a fantasy that consumers around the world desperately want to believe.

This fantasy is that it is possible to fish sustainably, legally, and using workers with contracts, making a livable wage, and still deliver a five-ounce can of skipjack tuna for $2.50 that ends up on the grocery shelf only days after the fish was pulled from the water thousands of miles away. Prices that low and efficiencies that tight come with hidden costs, and it is the manning agencies that help in the hiding.

Hidden costs are by no means distinct to fishing. Since the Industrial Revolution, other industries have been allowed to dump carbon into the air for free, for example, and that hidden cost to the public has accumulated into what we now call climate change. There is, however, far less awareness of the hidden costs that exist in fishing because the oceans are such a removed realm.

Fishing companies would most likely struggle to stay financially afloat if they had to recruit and handle the logistics for the men who work such dangerous jobs at impossibly low wages. Lawlessness at sea and the willingness of consumers and governments to ignore these hidden costs were a kind of subsidy helping keep many of these fishing fleets financially afloat.

Such is the inconvenient truth of globalization: it is based more on market sleight of hand than on Adam Smith's invisible hand. By outsourcing this task to manning agencies, the people who work in the corporate responsibility and human resources offices of the grocery store chains and fish wholesalers further down the supply chain need not try to understand or explain how it is possible that the captains on these boats found workers willing to work for so little. They need not question the hidden costs and whether or not the real price of fish is what appears on the menu. They need not explain how it's possible to affordably move fish so fast across the globe or what happens to the families of the crew who die or are injured on their boats. Manning agencies make these questions unanswerable. That is, if consumers or anyone else even asks them in the first place.

.   .   .

In Singapore, I hired a local reporter to discreetly visit the Step Up Marine's main office. He took pictures on his cell phone and emailed them to me. Located in a second-floor shopping mall, across from a sex-toy shop and a massage parlor, the office was small and cramped. For weeks, I tried to interview Victor and Bryan Lim, the owners of Step Up Marine. They declined repeated requests for comment. But a lawsuit heard by the Philippine Supreme Court in 2001 offered a window into their thinking. "Total strangers," Victor Lim said when asked about his ties to a seafarer who sued for unpaid wages. The firm had no responsibility for these men once they got to their ships, he added.

There were illustrative parallels between the way the Lims distanced themselves from their recruited workers and the way the Philippine government did the same with their exported workers. Neither would take responsibility for placing workers in dangerous and abusive settings because that would mean they were accountable for fixing the problem.

The court eventually rejected Lim's claim. The only thing worse than having sent "unlettered countrymen to a foreign land and letting them suffer inhumane treatment in the hands of an abusive employer," the court decision said, was that the company had conspired to deny workers their pay. For all my criticisms of the Philippine government, this court verdict was a refreshingly blunt and forceful condemnation of abuse.

Unfortunately, this court decision was also a turning point. It was roughly when Victor Lim and Step Up Marine shifted away from using registered manning agencies in the Philippines and instead started relying, illegally, on Filipino domestic workers in Singapore to recruit their relatives from small villages. Celia Robelo, for example, was hired as a recruiter by her sister-in-law, Roselyn Robelo, who previously worked as a domestic helper for Lim.

After Andrade died, officials from Step Up Marine and the owner of the Taiwanese fishing ship where Andrade worked offered to pay his family about $5,000, according to a 2012 letter from the Philippine embassy in Singapore. It was a woeful offer considering that a seafarer's death benefit provided by a legal manning agency in the Philippines is typically at least $50,000. The family declined and instead filed a formal complaint against Step Up Marine in November 2011 with Singapore's Ministry of Manpower.

I hoped to follow up on their complaint, but virtually everyone I contacted about Andrade's case redirected me to Step Up Marine. In Singapore, labor department officials struggled to explain to me why they had not prosecuted the firm for trafficking and other violations. They said they had investigated and concluded that Step Up Marine's role was purely administrative. It was a mere middleman, the bureaucrats contended, providing introductions between fishing companies and workers and offering logistical support to facilitate their deployment onto vessels by helping with accommodations, airfare, and maritime paperwork.

The Singaporean labor officials conceded that because their department lacked overseas jurisdiction, it had not interviewed any of the Filipino workers who alleged debt bondage, physical abuse, or trafficking. Asked why Step Up Marine had required up-front fees, deceived the men about true wages, and refused to assist them in getting home after being abused, Singapore officials said those questions needed to be taken directly to the firm.

In Taiwan, I hired an investigator to question police, fishery authorities, and the owner of the ship where Andrade died. I had tried to persuade my editors to put me on a plane to Taiwan so I could do it myself, but time was tight, and we also figured that as a foreigner who doesn't speak Chinese, I'd get better information using a local. Taiwanese police and fishery officials said they had no record of having ever questioned Shao Chin Chung, the captain of Andrade's Taiwanese-flagged ship, the *Hung Yu 212*. A secretary at Hung Fei Fishery said the company's owner was abroad fixing another vessel and unavailable to talk. Questions about the crew would need to be taken up with the manning agency, the secretary suggested.

Meanwhile, Step Up Marine remained unavailable. After leaving half a dozen unanswered messages at its office, I hired a courier to hand deliver a letter detailing my findings and describing the accusations made by Filipino law enforcement and others. No reply ever came. "They're answerable to no one," said Shelley Thio, a board member of Transient Workers Count Too, a migrant advocacy group in Singapore. "That's exactly how this business is designed."

. . .

On April 6, 2011, Andrade's body arrived at port in Singapore on the *Hung Yu 212*. Dr. Wee Keng Poh, a forensic pathologist with Singapore's Health Sciences Authority, conducted an autopsy six days later. He concluded that the cause of death was "acute myocarditis," an inflammatory disease of the heart muscle. His report offered little more.

The body was then flown to the Philippines, where Dr. Noel Martinez, the provincial pathologist in Kalibo, performed a second autopsy, which contradicted the first. There was no evidence of a longer-term heart condition, he said. Instead, he cited "myocardial infarction," a heart attack, as the cause of death. This autopsy report noted extensive bruises and cuts, inflicted before death, on Andrade's brow, upper and lower lips, nose, upper right chest, and right armpit.

I spent nearly a week trying to get in touch with the two pathologists—emailing government officials and former employers and getting help looking for phone numbers from *Times* reporters based with the foreign desk. I got nowhere. The only utility in reaching this dead end was that it made an important point: If a full-time investigative reporter, with all the resources of *The New York Times* behind him, couldn't even find these pathologists, how did Andrade's family expect to ever get answers?

I finally got some help from a provincial police investigator who reviewed the autopsy reports and suggested to me that Andrade's missing pancreas and eye could have been removed or mistakenly destroyed by the coroner during the autopsy. The police investigator added, however, that he doubted this is what happened. The more likely explanation, he said, was that these organs were irreparably damaged during a serious accident.

In September 2015, I traveled to Linabuan Sur, Andrade's home village, and interviewed half a dozen men who had been recruited by Step Up Marine. Like Andrade, all of these men had worked in the South Atlantic Ocean between South Africa and Uruguay. They all had also worked on Taiwanese tuna long-liners, which, in the fishing industry, have among the worst reputations for labor abuses.

Several of the men said they believed that lower-level Philippine government employees were complicit in the trafficking. They recounted being directed to specific people at certain windows in the Manila airport who would wave the workers through, even though they lacked the required overseas work permits. A spokesman for the government denied these allegations, citing new anti-trafficking laws and examples of enforcement efforts as proof of the Philippine government's commitment to worker protection.

I hoped to interview a close friend of Andrade's named Condrad Bonihit y Vicente, but when I found him, he was heading offshore to work on a fishing boat. So, I got permission from his boss, a boat captain, to travel with their ten-man crew on an overnight fishing expedition about forty miles from shore. For the first seven hours of the trip, the crew on the boat said little and kept their distance from me. But at one point, I needed to use the bathroom, and I asked one of them where I could go. Urinating on these sorts of fishing boats tends to be relatively easy. Defecating, on the other hand, takes a gymnast's balance.

At the back of the boat, just over the motor, there were two parallel but foot-apart planks, which is where you were supposed to squat and aim for the space between. The wood was extremely slippery and grotesquely filthy because users routinely missed their target and hit the planks. The men on these boats had incredible sure-footedness, but for visitors like me falling into the water was a real possibility—even scarier because the boat's propellers churned directly below. I did not fall into the water that night, but slipped with my pants down and came very close to doing so, which spurred uproarious laughter from the crew. When I regained my footing, I pulled my pants up and took a bow, to which the men promptly clapped with gusto. It was embarrassing and horrifyingly scary, but the incident successfully broke the ice.

An hour later, I approached Bonihit y Vicente while he hoisted a fifty-foot net filled with anchovies. I asked him to speculate on Andrade's reasons for taking his chances with an illegal manning agency like Step Up Marine. "You need money to make money," he said. "That's something most of us don't have."

Bonihit y Vicente explained that he had also worked for Step Up Marine, though he tried to avoid it at first. After borrowing more than $2,100 over several years from relatives for seafaring coursework, Bonihit y Vicente wound up $9 short of the bribe that professors charged students to take final exams. He'd run out of time and people to ask for a loan, Bonihit y Vicente said, and without certification, he had no choice but to use an illegal manning agency.

In 2010, Bonihit y Vicente took a job that he landed through Step Up Marine, working for $5.30 a day with thirty other men on a Taiwanese tuna long-liner called the *Jihorn 101*. He decided to flee the ship ten months later when it docked in Cape Town, he said, because he witnessed the captain and the bosun beat crew members weekly, once leaving a deckhand unconscious. With help from a local priest, Bonihit y Vicente flew back to Singapore, where Step Up Marine required him to sign a form allowing the company to use all his owed wages to pay for a plane ticket for the final leg home. Bonihit y Vicente said he never returned to the high seas after that. When I interviewed him several dozen miles off the Philippine coast, he was earning $1.20 per day.

After we returned to shore, I tracked down another of Andrade's friends who was working at a fast-food restaurant in a nearby town. His name was Emmanuel Concepcion, and recounting his own experiences, he dismissed the possibility that Andrade had died in his sleep.

Recruited by Step Up Marine, Concepcion worked in the South Atlantic on a Taiwanese tuna ship, called the *Fuh Sheng 11*, for about nine months starting in October 2010. Every few weeks, he said, the captain beat the crew (typically with his fists or feet but oftentimes jabbing the men with a long wooden baton) for minor infractions like working too slowly or dropping a fish.

One evening after a particularly savage attack by the captain on the cook, the crew spotted blood on the floor of the wheelhouse, and they soon discovered that the captain was missing. For the next week, the crew was paralyzed about what to do, and the ship drifted until the engineer took command and piloted the vessel to Cape Town. Police immediately arrested the cook, who later confessed to stabbing the captain and throwing his body overboard. Concepcion, who said he was never paid, flew home immediately after the incident. Returning to my original question, Concepcion said, "Do I think Andrade died in his sleep? No, it doesn't happen that way."

A lot of time and effort went into finding and interviewing these villagers—a process that felt both worthwhile and pointless. Hear enough of these stories of abuse, and you become numb to them. Worse still, they begin echoing each other because they are so uniform. None of what I was doing would bring Andrade back, nor did I believe at this point that I would be able to bring to light anything that would force the fishing industry or the Philippine or Taiwanese governments to act.

The process began feeling like explanation for its own sake. That single abiding certainty at the core of journalism, that there was merit in bearing witness and giving voice to those who lacked it, felt much less than certain. Still, I clung to the hope that by my putting the information out there, other people might use it somehow to change things. Deep down inside, though, I wondered if these were legitimate motivations or professional delusions.

．　．　．

In 2014, police in the Philippines charged ten persons tied to Step Up Marine with trafficking and illegal recruitment of Andrade and others from his village. In the end, only one person was prosecuted: Celia Robelo. She was arguably the lowest-ranking and least culpable person involved with the abuse of these workers.

At forty-six years old, Robelo faced a potential life sentence for what prosecutors said was her first recruiting effort, earning at most a $20 commission, combined, for all the men she handled. The other people tied to Step Up Marine were charged in absentia by Philippine authorities and were believed to be in Singapore, which meant they would likely never be brought to justice because there was no extradition treaty between the countries.

Celia Robelo, the woman who told Eril Andrade about the job on the Taiwanese tuna long-liner ship, where he died under suspicious circumstances, sits in a rural prison called the Aklan Rehabilitation Center in the Philippines. Her nine-year-old son, Xavier, stands in the background.

The failure to prosecute anyone other than Robelo was a powerful reminder of the so-called tragedy of the commons, the idea that we neglect what we don't own individually. Because the high seas belong to everyone and no one, governments fail to cooperate in protecting marine workers or investigating abuses. International waters are a margin for error, a frontier to pass through at your own peril. This place lends itself to a bystander's syndrome: a pathological and unshakable assumption that someone else will police those crimes or fix those wrongdoings. And to companies like Step Up Marine, this void is not a tragedy but an opportunity.

Several days after returning to shore from having fished with Andrade's friend, I went to visit Robelo in jail. I drove down a dirt road in a remote area surrounded by rice paddies to reach the five-acre Aklan Rehabilitation Center, where she was incarcerated. Ten-foot-high cinder-block walls held about 223 prisoners, 24 of them women. The prison had the feel of a bustling shantytown. Chickens and visiting children scurried underfoot. Prisoners squatted on a sheet-metal roof overlooking the courtyard. The thick cloying smell of feces wafted from a sewage gulley that ran alongside one of the buildings.

Jailed since May 2013, Robelo cried while explaining what led to her arrest. "When I got a name," she said, "I called it to Singapore." She never met or spoke directly to any of the Lims, she said, communicating instead only with her sister-in-law in Singapore, Roselyn Robelo, who had asked her for assistance. The Lims promised but never paid $2 for each person that she referred; the money was to help offset her commuting costs to drive many times back and forth to the young men's houses to help them fill out and send their paperwork, she said. Before Andrade's death, she said, she never heard from the ten recruited men about what happened in Singapore or at sea. Some of the men that prosecutors say she recruited were her relatives.

"If no one has work, a job is something you share," said Robelo, who went to college to be a teacher but never taught. She described her role in the village not as a labor recruiter but as someone who tried to help others by spreading the word about employment opportunities abroad.

The day I visited Robelo in jail, her husband, Mitchell, was also there visiting. So were her two children—nine-year-old Xavier and seven-year-old Gazrelle. Mitchell had been unemployed since he sold his auto-rickshaw to raise the $2,800 to pay for his wife's first lawyer, who then disappeared without doing any work on her case, the couple said.

Before visiting the jail, I spent a day in the provincial capital, Kalibo, at the office of the prosecutor Reynaldo B. Peralta Jr., who had spearheaded the trafficking case related to Step Up Marine. I waited several hours for a scheduled interview; Peralta never showed up and did not answer subsequent emails. He did, however, eventually talk to an investigator I hired. He said that local police had not interviewed other crew members from Andrade's ship to determine how he died because they were elsewhere in the country, beyond his jurisdiction.

Asked whether Robelo was merely a low-level player, perhaps minimally culpable, Peralta said that "were it not for her recruitment, these victims would not have left the country." She knew she was recruiting illegally, he claimed, because some villagers gave her money to send to Singapore and she did not have a license to be lining up jobs.

On my last day in the Philippines, I returned to Andrade's village, hoping to visit his mother's house for a final glimpse back into his life. The villagers I tried to interview were shy, and when I mentioned

Andrade's case to them, they clammed up even more. I sensed that their hesitation was less fear of consequences for speaking publicly about the topic than shame that both the victims and the culprits were locals.

The one man I got to open up I met on a muddy back road next to a lonely fruit cart. The man said he knew of the case and would likely have fallen into the same trap himself had the job been offered. I asked why. He said nothing in response, but he simply gestured toward his meager selection of half-rotting mangoes, santols, and bananas. I took him to mean "If this is all you had, wouldn't you leap at an opportunity that came your way?"

I finally found Andrade's mother's house, and it was abandoned and surrounded by an overgrown thicket of banana trees. Walking around the house, I found half a dozen unpaid electric bills wedged into cracks in the front door, addressed to his mother, Molina, who died in 2014 of cancer. The front door was unlocked, so I went inside. Water dripped through the ceiling not far from a dusty stack of family photo albums and college yearbooks. Alongside the house sat the coffin that had been used to send Andrade's body back to the Philippines.

Before I went to the airport, I went to visit with Andrade's brother, Julius, at his house. He told me that his family was still waiting for someone to be prosecuted for the death. I pointed out that Celia Robelo was already in jail. He dismissed this as a miscarriage of justice. The real culprits—"the ones to blame," he said—were still free, working in Singapore and at sea. "They stay far away," he said. Not by accident, I thought.

# THE NEXT FRONTIER

*I asked the darkened sea
Down where the fishers go—
It answered me with silence,
Silence below.*

—Sara Teasdale, "Night Song at Amalfi"

About 150 miles off the coast of Brazil, I climbed into a tiny two-person submarine and wondered if I had made a terrible mistake. Under the punishing equatorial sun, I could feel the sweat trickling down my chest and neck. In the cramped compartment of the fire-engine-red submarine, the knobs, buttons, and scenes surrounded me.

The crew of the Greenpeace ship that brought us here pulled a thick glass dome down over my head. My compartment sealed with a loud suction sound and a pressurizing hiss, and the crew did the same with the sub's pilot, John Hocevar, to my left. Our heads bobbing in the twin turrets as if in side-by-side fishbowls, he gave me a thumbs-up, and I gave him a sickly smile back.

A crane then lifted the submarine thirty feet into the air, swiveling us over the side of the ship before lowering us alongside the ship's dark green hull to the waterline. The crane dunked us into the waves, and a cascade of bubbles surged over the dome as we began our dive toward the seafloor, more than 350 feet beneath us.

I had come to Brazil to watch a fight. On one side was a trio of energy companies; on the other, a team of Brazilian scientists. The prize? Control over a stretch of seafloor. The energy companies paid top dollar for the right to drill for oil in the area. The Brazilian researchers hoped to stop them, claiming that the drilling would jeopardize a 621-mile-long coral reef nearby.

In the Atlantic Ocean off the coast of Brazil, a crane lifts a submarine from a helipad and swings it over the side. Hoping to document a coral reef that stretches more than six hundred miles along the ocean floor, a team of Brazilian scientists were in a race in January 2017 to block oil-drilling plans in the area.

Odds favored the drilling companies. They had the resources to hire teams of lawyers to argue for the right to access to these waters and to dispatch underwater drones and ships using sonic devices to hunt for the wealth hidden below. The Brazilian government was also on their side. In 2013, it had granted the companies permission to drill. To help even these odds, Greenpeace had sent one of its biggest ships, the *Esperanza* (Spanish for "hope"), and a rented submarine to transport the Brazilian scientists to the contested patch of ocean floor, where these researchers hoped to video the natural riches that needed to be protected.

I quietly suspected the oil companies would win. They usually did in such fights, and not just because of their much deeper pockets. The rules, after all, were written in their favor. Brazilian authorities, like those in most countries, required an environmental impact assessment before they would allow companies to drill or mine in their national waters. Such documents provide hollow protection, however, especially in this part of the world, because few people or organizations could afford to verify the accuracy of the documents. Independently assessing the ocean depths where the drilling or mining occurred tended to be too expensive. As a result, the public had little option but to take the environmental assessments at face value.

This showdown in Brazil was a stark reminder that the seafloor is earth's final frontier, a lawless and enigmatic domain of vast mineral wealth and undiscovered biological diversity. Arguably the least policed realm on the planet, the sea bottom is also a world over which scientists, conservationists, industry, and governments routinely tussle for access and control. And yet we have mapped more of the night sky than we have charted the ocean's depths. Lawlessness on the high seas may be rampant, but deep underwater there are immense voids—literal and legal. I wanted to explore those voids firsthand, and this battle over the reef in the Atlantic Ocean was just the chance.

Partly, the undersea void is created by how little we know about what happens there. This fact is not distinct to Brazil. In 2010, during BP's Deepwater Horizon oil spill in the Gulf of Mexico, U.S. federal authorities struggled not just to cap it but also to discern who had authority in this type of offshore disaster. Marine authorities later told me that the U.S. government had never done a comprehensive study nor even fully mapped the vast ecosystems in the 4.5 million square miles of ocean that fall under its jurisdiction.

There is a long history to this intellectual blind spot, and some mesmerizing misconceptions have arisen over the centuries from our lack of knowledge about the ocean. By far, my favorite is the Victorian-era belief that seawater became denser at lower depths, so much so that layers of more viscous deep water prevented some objects from descending below a certain point. As such, people believed that a sinking ship could only fall to a fixed level in the sea, hovering there, never reaching the bottom. A dead person only dropped to a depth dependent upon the size of his midriff, the weight of his clothing, and, according to some, the density of accumulated and unrepented sins. In this mélange of superstition, religion, and science, the sea became, for all intents and purposes, a terrestrial purgatory: the most evil sank to the bottom, while the morally ambiguous drifted for eternity.

Science and modernity have since corrected many of these quaint misconceptions, of course, but most countries still know very little about the waters under their jurisdictions. When Barack Obama took office in 2009, he issued an executive order creating what was meant to be a unified ocean policy, part of which involved mapping American waters, including large swaths of the ocean floor.

Most people tend to think of countries' territory ending at their shorelines. But under international law, a nation's jurisdiction usually stretches two hundred miles from its coasts (although various parts of its sovereignty peter out along the way, which is why Gomperts and her ships had to sail only twelve miles off the coast of Mexico, and Sealand had to be only three miles from Britain's shores). As a result, the area under U.S. control is actually more sea (roughly 4.5 million square miles) than land (about 3.5 million square miles). American territories like Guam, Samoa, Puerto Rico, the American Virgin Islands, and the Northern Marianas may be tiny islands, but they add huge swaths of ocean to U.S. jurisdiction. As a result, no country has a bigger maritime domain than the United States.

And yet the Obama administration realized that the U.S. government had no central governing body to make decisions about how to chart and manage this offshore territory. Altering this reality posed a threat to the drilling and fishing industries, which lobbied aggressively against the federal efforts to exert more control over this region, as they had in the past. These industries viewed mapping the oceans as a precursor to zoning them, which would likely lead to greater limits on the industries' reach. In April 2017, President Trump revoked Obama's executive order.

·   ·   ·

In Brazil, environmental policy had always been less restrictive than in the United States. A multinational consortium of three oil companies—the U.K.'s BP, France's Total, and Brazil's Queiroz Galvão Exploração e Produção—had collectively paid the Brazilian government more than $110 million in 2013 to drill for oil in the Atlantic Ocean near the mouth of the Amazon. But in the paperwork they submitted to the government applying for the right to drill, these companies made virtually no mention of the reef, despite knowing of its existence.

Though no scientist had seen the reef up close, fishermen had passed along stories of its existence, like some lost but living Atlantis. It was not until 2016 that a team of Brazilian scientists published a groundbreaking academic paper in *Science Advances* pinning down key details about what came to be called the Amazon Reef, including its size and location. Published three years after the oil companies filed their paperwork and won permission to drill, their research was based on shells, fish, and other evidence pulled from the ocean floor in the scientists' nets. Still, no one had laid eyes on the reef itself. Or so the researchers initially thought.

Rumor circulated among Brazilian scientists that video footage of the reef existed. Several of the Brazilian scientists, including the ones I joined on board the *Esperanza,* started sleuthing and discreetly talking to researchers working for the oil companies. They soon discovered that long before receiving the permit to drill, these companies had sent ROVs—remotely operated vehicles—to the seafloor in the Amazon Reef area and had collected footage of the sprawling and vibrant structure. The company had declined to release the footage to the public, however. "They pretended like the reef didn't exist when they applied to drill," said Ronaldo Bastos Francini-Filho, one of the scientists on the *Esperanza.*

This is when, and why, Greenpeace stepped in to help in 2017. The scientists set out to see the reef for themselves, document its existence, and publicize the footage. If they found new or endangered species at the reef, the Brazilian government would likely force the drilling companies to apply anew for drilling rights, resulting in costly delays and possibly a cancellation of their plans.

Before I left the United States, Greenpeace officials set strict terms for me. For their safety, I would not be allowed to photograph several of the Brazilians on their staff. As I traveled to the ship, especially once I flew into Brazil, I was to avoid discussing details of the work with other people. Some of the ship's crew were told not to wear Greenpeace logos until they were safely on board the *Esperanza,* which was docked on the Amazon River in Macapá.

The group had good reason for caution: Forty-nine environmentalists were killed in Brazil in 2016, more than in any other country. By July 2017, another forty-five had been killed in Brazil. Rarely was anyone prosecuted for such crimes, which were often brutal and brazen. One environmentalist had his ears severed and sent to his family. A nun who had been protesting logging in the Amazon rain forest was shot in broad daylight. Over the past decade, roughly half the murders of environmentalists worldwide took place in Brazil.

Of the three ships in Greenpeace's global fleet, the *Esperanza* was the biggest, at 236 feet long. Built in 1984 in Gdansk, Poland, as a firefighting vessel with berths for forty crew members, it had a maximum speed of sixteen knots and flew a Dutch flag. Chosen for the mission because it was stable in rough currents, the *Esperanza* also had the strongest crane and the biggest helicopter pad, which were used for launching and storing the submarine.

I arrived in Brazil with time to spare, and before I set out on the *Esperanza,* I was invited to go with a Greenpeace pilot on the organization's pontoon plane to get a bird's-eye view of the mouth of the Amazon River. The Greenpeace advocates explained that their fight over the ocean was the same as that over the rain forest. Each was an attempt to get the government to resist the temptation to make money allowing lucrative industries—oil drillers offshore and loggers in the forest—to despoil public resources.

We boarded the pontoon plane early in the morning and crossed Amapá, one of Brazil's least populated and most densely foliated states. The Amazon rain forest generated roughly 20 percent of the planet's oxygen, and as we headed toward the coast, we flew over a patchy quilt of greens that was punctuated by squares of clear-cut brown.

Deforestation leveled seventy-five hundred square miles of rain forest a year, the equivalent of six soccer fields a minute. The speed of this devastation created a vicious cycle. Normally, half the moisture above the forest was released by its trees, but the clear-cutting accelerated drought. As trees were chopped down, the cuttings decayed or were burned off, spewing carbon into the atmosphere. Typically trees function as sponges for carbon, absorbing it while emitting oxygen. So, aside from destroying the Amazon, the deforestation was transforming localized areas from carbon sinks into carbon emitters.

The missing patches of forest were conspicuous proof that Brazil's struggle to protect its habitat was as much an onshore fight as an off-shore one. For all the stories I'd heard about deforestation, none prepared me for seeing these jagged, burned patches carved into the rain forest. It left me with a deep foreboding feeling of inevitability, like you get when you watch an injured prey being chased down by a healthy predator. This is not going to end well, I thought.

As we arrived at the coast, we flew over the largest continuous mangrove forest in the world, stretching roughly 124 miles. Mangrove swamps protected coastal areas from erosion, storm surges (especially during hurricanes), and tsunamis. Barely explored and with little of its vast biodiversity cataloged, the mangrove swamps are lush and otherworldly places. The trees seem to teeter over the water on delicate, spidery roots. Neither fully terrestrial nor marine, the swamps are brackish habitats teeming with fish, crabs, shrimps, turtles, and mollusk species below the water, and bird and mammals above. If an oil spill occurred in the new drilling fields near the Amazon, these mangroves, which were far older than the world's obsession with oil, would likely pay the price.

The next day, after I settled into my cabin on the *Esperanza,* Randolfe Rodrigues, a senator from Amapá and a member of Brazil's Network of Sustainability Party, visited the ship for several hours along with two dozen journalists and advocates from local environmental groups. It was a chance for them to tour the *Esperanza* before it left port and to hear from the scientists who explained the risks of a spill. The oil companies had claimed that damage from a spill would be limited because the outflow of the Amazon River pushed currents away from shore and away from the reef. But the currents off the coast of Brazil flow in different directions at varying depths, the scientists explained. "You have to remember that the sea is not a two-dimensional flat surface," one of them added. "It is a three-dimensional, multidirectional space."

After the presentation on board, the guests left the *Esperanza,* and I asked Francini-Filho if he worried whether a spill could kill off entire seafloor species before the public even knew they existed. This wasn't about individual species, he told me. "It's about habitats that are home to hundreds or thousands of species," he said. "We're trying to protect an entire solar system, not just a planet."

.   .   .

On the final day before our launch, I woke up early to write and slipped quietly from my bunk on the *Esperanza,* trying not to wake my roommate. Ships are twenty-four-hour workplaces, even in port, but at this hour only the engine room and the galley were active. The decks were dark and quiet. Breakfast was not until 7:00 a.m., the morning meeting was at 8:00, and chores started at 8:30 a.m.

I'd been warned that journalistic projects like this one were prone to overreporting, gathering more information than could possibly be conveyed. So much time is spent traveling that little is left for writing.

At the outset, I resolved to avoid this mistake by forcing myself to write at least a little every day, even while I was at sea. My routine was to wake up at 4:30 a.m. and write until 7:00 or 8:00 a.m. During this block of time, sleepiness became an ally. Later in the day, my head usually filled with several voices that argued and second-guessed each other, sending me off on random tangents. In those predawn hours, though, only one of the voices seemed able to drag itself out of bed with me, and we could have quiet, calm, and clear conversations while the other voices slept in. The result was an Adderall-like focus, even amid the stifled yawns.

I headed outside toward a chair on the port side, where a stronger wind would be more soothing in the heat. Rounding the corner, I nearly spilled my coffee. Crawling near my ankles was what appeared to be a giant cockroach as large as my palm. Another was on the ground several feet in front of me. One was climbing the railing. A fourth sat in the center of my path, ten feet ahead. The night before had been my first on board the ship, so I hadn't yet encountered these morning creatures.

I learned later that they were giant water bugs or Belostomatidae, locally called *barata d'agua*. When found in the United States, typically in the Deep South, they were called "toe-biters" or "alligator ticks." Aggressive predators, they primarily feed on aquatic invertebrates, though they are known to attack and eat water snakes and baby turtles. To kill their prey, they use a beak-like needle to inject powerful digestive saliva, which dissolves their prey's innards in minutes; then they stay attached, sucking out the liquefied remains. Though not fatal to humans, Belostomatidae bites are considered among the most painful bites inflicted by any insect.

I inched my way around the giant bugs, and as I passed, one took flight. In the soft light of dawn, its silhouette looked like a sparrow. Reaching my chair, I sat down to gather myself and take stock of the place. The steamy air made my laptop screen bead with condensation. Above the ship, morning rush hour bustled: Birds chirped, shrieked, clacked. On a pipe running up the side of the ship, army ants marched single-file down one floor and across the rope tethering us to the pier. In the water, what appeared to be a floating stick, about six feet long, started slithering when a bird dove at it. Sitting there, watching this exotic place pulsate around me, I felt a humbling sense of marvel, a wide-eyed quiet, as if I were an alien secretly visiting someone else's domain.

The *Esperanza* launched later that day, and the mood immediately shifted to serious, almost tense. Several weeks earlier, the ship had received written permission from Brazil's local and federal environmental authorities to dive to the reef using the submarine. Such permission was not needed in Brazil's exclusive economic zone, or EEZ, the offshore region where a coastal nation has sole control under the UN Convention on the Law of the Sea. But Greenpeace had asked (and received) permission anyway as an extra precaution to protect the Brazilian staff and scientists on board who might face dire consequences if the government felt antagonized. After a day of sailing, though, the captain of our ship received a blunt message from the Brazilian Navy: if we put the submarine in the water, we would be arrested, even though no permission was required.

The navy's intrusion into a perfectly legal scientific exploration demonstrated how, in the outlaw ocean, countries and virtually everyone else make up rules as often as they ignore them. Clearly, this fight I had come to see had high stakes not just for the oil companies but also for the Brazilian government. The oil reserves underneath the mouth of the Amazon were estimated at between fifteen billion and twenty billion barrels. This was about double the amount of untapped oil in the famously massive reserve located in Alaska's coastal plain. The three oil companies had purchased from the Brazilian government the right to drill exploratory wells off the coast, but these licenses were to expire in about two years. A new environmental impact assessment could likely prove fatal to any hope for tapping these reserves because it would give environmentalists more time to stoke public opposition or to delay the projects in the courts.

The Brazilian public was especially apprehensive about the safety of offshore drilling because the country had recently seen several severe accidents elsewhere along the coast. An accident on a Petrobras rig in 2015 killed nine workers. In 2011, an oil well drilled by Chevron in Campo do Frade leaked more than three thousand barrels of oil, creating an eleven-mile slick off the coast of Rio de Janeiro.

As the *Esperanza* sailed toward the Amazon Reef, we were broadcasting AIS, a locational signal, so that the authorities knew where to find us. We didn't know whether the Brazilians would dispatch any law enforcement vessels to intercept us; more likely, the navy would detain us when we returned to any Brazilian port, if only to check that we had not violated its orders.

Discussions on board moved behind closed doors in the captain's quarters, probably because the senior officers did not want me witnessing the tensions. I paced nervously outside the room as if a surgery were happening inside. As people left the meeting, they told me the Greenpeace staff wanted the mission to go forward. They argued we should dive on the site despite the navy's orders, because permission was not required to do so. While we were still in Brazil's EEZ, the Greenpeacers in the meeting argued, the law allowed us to explore the water as long as we just observed and did not remove specimens.

"You don't understand how the Brazilian Navy operates," one of the scientists who wanted to proceed with the dive said during a particularly heated discussion. "They're not going to arrest anyone," he said, adding that they were just trying to exert authority.

But Nuytco Research Limited, the owner of the submarine that Greenpeace was renting, was wary when it learned that the navy had interceded. The company's CEO called by satellite phone to say he did not want to risk having the Brazilian authorities confiscate his $1.8 million submarine.

After a day of arguing, the group decided on a new plan. We would make a run for the French Guianan sea border, more than two hundred miles to the northwest, and drop the submarine in the water there at the opposite end of the reef wall, just outside Brazil's EEZ and the reach of the Brazilian Navy. The Guianans had little reason to oppose the dive. Because they had not authorized drilling in their waters, they did not stand to gain or lose the hundreds of millions of dollars in revenue from oil companies. Plus, Guiana viewed Brazil's drilling plan with skepticism since were there to be a spill, currents would probably push some of the oil to Guiana's coasts. The lack of law enforcement at sea also played to the *Esperanza*'s advantage: the Guianans had an even smaller navy than the Brazilians to deploy if they decided to stop the submarine.

But this new plan to head to Guianan waters put us in a race against the clock. It would take us two days to reach the new dive site, and we had only ten days before the submarine had to be shipped back to North Vancouver for its next job. The ship was running so low on freshwater that the captain had locked the laundry room. It was summer and the ninety-five-degree Fahrenheit days were sweaty. On deck, the women wore cutoff overalls and sports bras, and the men went shirtless. Some of the crew members, myself included, were beginning to smell. To avoid stinking up the cabins, shoes were left outside the rooms. Soon, though, shirts, jeans, and socks were hung there too, giving the halls the look and unfortunate odor of a high school locker room.

A strong storm was now fast approaching that would make it extremely risky to deploy the sixty-eight-hundred-pound submarine. Onshore, Greenpeace lawyers were scrambling. A team in French Guiana was talking to authorities to get permission for us to visit the Guianan seafloor. In Brazil, allies of the scientists on the *Esperanza* called in political favors and contacted Randolfe Rodrigues, the Brazilian senator who had toured the ship before its launch, hoping to win his help persuading the Brazilian government to reverse its stance.

The mood on the *Esperanza* was turning gloomy. The nightly game of darts over beers in the second-floor lounge was called off. To fill the grumpy silence, someone put on *Edge of Tomorrow,* the sci-fi thriller with Tom Cruise as a soldier doomed (not unlike Greenpeace) to fight the same battle over and over again. But halfway through the film, the door to the lounge swung open. One of the scientists stood in the backlit entryway, grinning ear to ear. "We got it!" he said with a toothy smile. The Brazilian government had reversed course and granted permission to us to dive. I asked everyone I could but never got a straight answer for why the decision had been reversed. My best speculation was that the government realized that blocking the submarine might look incriminating.

. . .

This was not Greenpeace's first or only fight over the seafloor. For years, the organization battled bottom trawlers. Often referred to as strip-mining of the sea, bottom trawling involves dragging large weighted nets across the ocean floor to catch the fish that live at those depths.

It is highly destructive in two ways. Though efficient, trawling is also undiscriminating. In minutes, the nets wipe out coral reefs that might have taken thousands of years to grow, leaving a flattened lifeless field in their wake. The indiscriminate carnage it causes is not unlike, as one writer put it, hunting for squirrels by stringing a net a mile wide between immense all-terrain vehicles and dragging it at speed across the plains of Africa. The main difference is that in the case of the African plains, the public would be outraged to learn that the vast majority of what gets caught is needlessly killed and tossed aside to rot. Further destruction awaits the bycatch in trawling. Fishing crews discard much of what they net because there's no market for the fish or because the fish are simply too small or too squashed.

In 2008, Greenpeace set up its sites on the North Sea. To stop a fleet of German trawlers, Greenpeace spent months strategically placing more than a hundred stone boulders on the ocean floor near Germany around the perimeter of the Sylt Outer Reef, which the fishermen were rapidly leveling. In port, everyone knew what Greenpeace was up to (it's tough to hide objects that huge), but as is often the case with maritime matters, it wasn't clear whether its actions were illegal. So, no one knew whether and how to intervene and stop it.

Weighing a little over three tons each, the boulders were roughly the size of a two-door refrigerator—big enough to destroy trawlers' nets if they were dragged over the boulders. Using cranes, Greenpeace lifted each, one by one, and dropped them to the seafloor in designated spots. Hoping to stop the trawling, not to destroy the fishermen's expensive nets, Greenpeace provided local authorities and fishing boat captains with updated charts, showing where it was placing the boulders. By 2011, Greenpeace was using the same tactic in the North Sea off the coast of Sweden.

Government officials from several countries were livid about the boulders, which ground trawling to a halt. To local fishermen, the boulders were like bombs dropped on their livelihoods. The Dutch minister of fisheries, Gerda Verburg, announced plans to arrest the *Noortland,* the ship that Greenpeace had used to deposit some of the massive rocks. In protest, Dutch fishermen began mailing thousands of packages, many of them with bricks and dead fish carefully sealed in plastic, to Greenpeace's headquarters. Fishermen also sued Greenpeace in several countries, alleging that the boulders were a type of dumping that posed a danger to the lives of fishing crew members. Courts in Germany, Sweden, and the Netherlands rejected these claims.

In the fight for control over the ocean floor, however, Greenpeace's biggest adversary has for many years been the oil and gas industry. In 2010, Greenpeace took on BP, the owner of the Deepwater Horizon drilling rig that exploded in the Gulf of Mexico and caused the largest oil spill in American history. For months after the explosion, BP struggled to cap the well, and oil spewed from a pipe near the seabed. The company said it was cleaning up the spill by using a chemical dispersant to break up the surface slick. Skeptical of these claims, Greenpeace and researchers from half a dozen universities launched several submarines in the Gulf to check on the health of the ocean. A team from Penn State University returned with shocking footage that showed the seafloor looking more like an asphalt parking lot than the colorful kaleidoscope it had been just months earlier. Rather than dissipating the oil, the dispersant had in fact been sinking it to the ocean's bottom, coating virtually everything on its way down. I covered the BP spill for the *Times,* and I remember reading the internal documents and court records where BP scientists discussed this problem. The concerns about the dispersant seemed so academic and inconsequential until I watched the before-and-after footage that came from the affected seafloor.

This sort of spill was just one reason why many environmentalists were concerned about energy companies venturing into another untapped region: the Arctic, where cleanup would be especially difficult if the oil spread across the seafloor and in the water under the thick ice.

Advances in drilling technology have made previously untouchable Arctic reserves accessible, and countries are fighting over rights to tap these resources. Drilling occurs now so far offshore that rigs can no longer be anchored to the seabed because it is too deep to be practical. Instead, they are held in place by propellers, each as big as a school bus. Their locations far from shore mean these drilling rigs are no longer fully subject to the territorial laws of the countries for which they're drilling.

In 2017, I traveled on a Greenpeace ship called the *Arctic Sunrise* to the Barents Sea, off the north coast of Russia and Finland. Statoil, the partly state-run Norwegian oil company, had parked a drilling rig called the Songa Enabler in the Korpfjell oil field there. Like the drilling planned off the coast of Brazil at the mouth of the Amazon River, the

Located in the Barents Sea off the north coast of Russia and Finland, an oil-drilling rig called the Songa Enabler sits in international waters, the farthest north incursion into Arctic waters by a drilling company.

project near Norway represented a new level of risk-taking by the oil industry. No company had ever tried to drill this far north into the Arctic. Statoil's well was even more controversial because it was located in international waters, over 258 miles north of mainland Norway.

The laws covering drilling and other activities in international waters were even more tangled than the ones governing national waters. That gave Statoil greater latitude to drill—and Greenpeace to protest. Complicating matters even more, the drilling rig was beyond Norway's exclusive economic zone, but it was still within the nation's extended continental shelf zone. Under international law, coastal states were given full rights to explore and exploit natural resources in their exclusive economic zones, like the reef area off the coast of Brazil. Farther out in the continental shelf, however, these rights were not to "infringe" or "unjustifiably interfere" with "navigation and other rights and freedoms," including the right to protest. Courts had ruled that drilling companies were allowed to create a security zone of half a kilometer in radius from the outer edge of the ring around their rigs. These companies were also required to tolerate some level of "nuisance" as long as it did not amount to an "interference with the exercise of its sovereign rights." In other words, the rules left a lot of room for interpretation.

Initially, Greenpeace intended to outrun the rig, get to Statoil's drilling site in the Arctic first, park there, and refuse to leave. Its goal was to impede work on the well and hopefully instigate a long and costly court battle with the oil company over rights to the location. But logistical issues delayed the launch of the *Sunrise*, and Statoil's rig reached the drilling site first. So Greenpeace resorted to its fallback plan. After arriving at the oil field, the advocates would breach the security zone to get near enough to capture footage for a publicity campaign about the perils of expanded drilling. For the Norwegian government and Statoil, a lot was riding on Korpfjell field; seismic testing had shown it was likely home to millions of barrels of oil. Despite its reputation for having especially protective environmental policies, Norway depended on oil and gas production for roughly 40 percent of its export revenue, and it wasn't about to give up a significant portion of that to placate some pesky environmental group.

When the *Sunrise* arrived on-site, a Norwegian Coast Guard cutter, the 344-foot KV *Nordkapp*, was waiting to intervene if Greenpeace broke the law. Three days later, Greenpeace did just that. A team paddled into the security zone in four kayaks carrying protest signs. Another team driving a speedboat dragged a buoy topped by a giant metal globe to represent the planet at risk. Eight hours after the breach, the Norwegian Coast Guard boarded the *Sunrise,* arresting everyone on board. Attaching a cable to the ship, the Coast Guard towed the *Sunrise* and its crew for two days back to Tromsö, Norway, where five crew members were fined a total of nearly $20,000 and released. In the subsequent months, the Norwegian government held on to several of Greenpeace's boats, and a long court fight ensued over them and the legality of the arrests.

The Statoil project proceeded with barely a delay while Greenpeace spent months and tens of thousands of dollars in court fighting to get

Greenpeace's *Arctic Sunrise* in July 2017. Several advocates prepare to engage in direct action against the Songa Enabler, part of an effort to block Norway's plan for drilling.

its confiscated equipment back. Being on board this mission in the Arctic, I found myself torn between two important lessons. The first was that the odds were definitely stacked against the advocates. The second was that the advocates knew this and sometimes they were engaged more in choreographed theater than in true bouts.

. . .

Whether the fight at sea near Brazil was real or choreographed and whether the Brazilian scientists had any chance of blocking this drilling project remained to be seen. But first Greenpeace needed to build its case to protect these waters and the mysterious reef that stretched this span of ocean floor.

Coral was at the heart of the Brazil expedition, and the *Esperanza*'s small library was stacked with books and journals about it. The scientists on the expedition were dead serious about coral, which is why the Greenpeace submarine driver, John Hocevar, decided to needle me. One afternoon, he entered the ship's lounge, where I sat among scientists and crew working quietly on our laptops, and cleared his throat to make an announcement. Everyone in the lounge looked up expectantly, including me. "So," he said, as if announcing a papal encyclical, "Ian thinks corals are boring." People turned to me with looks of skepticism bordering on contempt. I shot Hocevar my best go-to-hell look. "Just thought people should know," he said, smiling faux innocently back at me.

He wasn't entirely wrong. There was a time when I saw corals as little more than glamorized rocks. I'd known Hocevar for five years, and over that time he and I had kept up a friendly banter about coral reefs. He talked about them with the excitement of someone making a case for the best action film of all time, and periodically he'd pitch story ideas about them that he wanted me to write. I always turned him down. We all have our intellectual blind spots, and when it came to the ocean, coral reefs were one of mine. Yes, I knew they were colorful homes to lots of species, and a boon to the diving industry the world over, but my curiosity never quite latched onto them.

To listen to Hocevar talk about corals and marine biology was to be reminded of the Mark Twain line about how the two most important days of your life are the day you're born and the day you found out why.

Hocevar was born to advocate for the oceans. At six feet three and 190 pounds, he was lanky but athletic. Growing up in Connecticut, he had dreamed of working for the U.S. Forest Service, parachuting into forest fires. But he later fell in love with marine biology, earning his master's degree in 1993 from Nova Southeastern University in Florida, near Fort Lauderdale.

Tattoos covered much of his body. Down his right arm was a colorful mosaic of Bering Sea canyons with sponges, skates, and a giant Pacific octopus pulling down a pollack factory trawler. On his right shoulder blade was Picasso's *Don Quixote*—an idealistic character that some might see as a fitting symbol for Greenpeace and its mission.

Hocevar's infectious enthusiasm eventually overcame my skepticism. Before joining this trip, I had resolved to wrap my brain around the significance of coral reefs. My goal was to understand why so many smart people found them fascinating, important, exciting even. That the reefs were habitats didn't move me much. I needed to know the residents to care about their home. So, as we sailed toward our dive spot, I passed the time pulling books and magazine articles from the ship's small but specialized library and reading up on the topic. I also quizzed the scientists on board, receiving extempore lectures from the enthusiastic coral advocates.

I quickly learned how misguided I had been about reefs. Corals are expert builders, arguably the best on the planet, though they are slow. The result of 200 to 300 million years of evolution, they grow at a snail's pace—most expanding less than an inch a year. For example, Australia's Great Barrier Reef, big and bright enough to be visible from space, had grown to 133,000 square miles, over double the size of Pennsylvania, and is still relatively young at about 600,000 years old.

I learned that corals are masterful hunters. They use minute poisonous barbs to spear tiny planktonic prey or deploy nets made of mucus to nab their victims. I learned that corals are also densely populated microcosms with more marine species living in a two-acre area than there are different species of birds in all of North America. And that these microcosms were unusually efficient, producing virtually zero waste, because the by-product of every organism was the resource of another. If most of the ocean is a liquid desert—barren and nutrient poor—reefs are so teeming with vibrancy and biodiversity that they are the equivalent of the Amazon rain forest in the middle of the Sahara.

I looked up at the clock one afternoon to realize I'd had my head in a book for four hours and had almost missed dinner.

What made the specific reef we were exploring so intriguing was that its existence seemed to defy many beliefs about coral reefs. Although corals were not plants, sunlight was usually essential to their survival. They needed it to power the zooxanthellae, the microscopic algae that live inside them and make up most of their food. This is why most corals grow in shallow, clearer water. The Amazon Reef, on the other hand, was located in deep, turbid waters that were a mix of fresh and salt water. During part of the year, the Amazon River's ghostly plume turned out the lights entirely on the seafloor. Rather than photosynthesis, the scientists believed that the Amazon Reef relied largely on chemosynthesis, which uses bacteria to produce organic matter and energy from carbon dioxide, water, and other inorganic substances (like ammonia, iron, nitrate, and sulfur) without the presence of light. Scientists hypothesize that life began on earth with chemosynthesis and that such organisms today are distant descendants of the planet's first living organisms.

"Okay, now for the bad news," Francini-Filho, the scientist, said at one point, interrupting my sanguine thoughts on reefs. Global warming was imperiling the world's corals because the rising temperatures were changing the ocean's chemistry, he explained. Corals thrive in alkaline waters, but fossil-fuel emissions were making the seas more acidic. As climate change overheated the air, it curdled the water. Roughly a quarter of the carbon dioxide released into the atmosphere was being absorbed by the world's oceans, measurably lowering their pH levels and making it harder for coral skeletons to calcify.

As temperatures rose, the zooxanthellae, which gave reefs their dazzling colors, began producing too much oxygen, and the polyps expelled them. The corals began turning white and dying—a process called bleaching. The planet is in the midst of one of the most severe instances of coral bleaching in human history. Just a few more decades of emissions would lead all coral reefs to "stop growing and begin dissolving," wrote a team of scientists in a science journal called *Geophysical Research Letters*. That would mean the loss of millions of species.

No wonder so many people in the ship's lounge seemed aghast when Hocevar revealed my dirty secret. The more I learned, the more I realized what was at stake in the Brazilian scientists' eagerness to visit this patch of ocean floor. Drilling represented more than the threat of a ruinous spill. The oil drawn from below the seafloor would ultimately contribute to the forces of climate change that were wiping out coral reefs around the world. The fight over the Amazon Reef was but one battle in that larger war, and I was about to dive into the middle of the skirmish.

Viewed from an even higher altitude, the campaign to protect the Amazon Reef sought to drive a paradigm shift in how the global public views the ocean. To the Brazilian scientists and Greenpeace conservationists, the ocean was not meant to be a thing we use or a place where we extract resources or dump waste. It was a vast habitat that we should leave alone or, better still, protect and help to flourish. Less meant to fill our wallets or stomachs, the ocean was an opportunity to expand our humanity, foster biodiversity, and prove our ability to live in balance with the rest of the planet's occupants.

. . . .

After four days of sailing, the *Esperanza* slowed to a halt. The scientists told the captain that based on old nautical records and fishing logs, we were in a promising place to hunt for the reef. Since our departure, the bright red Dual DeepWorker 2000 had been lashed tightly to the deck. Now the crew prepared the sub to dive. Though the sky was hazy and overcast, the stifling heat pressed down on us, even with the ocean winds that tugged at our hair.

Built in 2004, the submarine, which was as compact as a Mini Cooper and Pixar cute, had room enough for just the pilot and one passenger. Because we sat in separate, sealed compartments, we had to communicate by radio, which also kept us in touch with the ship. I wore shorts and a T-shirt to stay cool. The sub was temperature controlled to keep us comfortably warm in the cold depths of the ocean. Powered by six 1-horsepower thrusters that looked like small fans, the submarine's maximum speed was 2 knots (about 2.3 miles per hour or a leisurely walking pace), and its maximum depth was two thousand feet, or about a third of a mile. Along one side of the submarine were deep gashes from a job a couple years earlier when strong currents pinned the submarine against the side of an oil platform in the Santa Barbara Channel.

The submarine technicians trained me the day before on how to pressurize my cabin, how to communicate with the *Esperanza* once we reached the ocean floor, and what to do if there was an emergency like a fire, loss of engine power, or a drift net that trapped the submarine. Despite the training, I managed to delay the dive with a rookie mistake. Shortly after sealing my capsule, I bumped something with my elbow and heard a small pop at my side and a hissing noise. I asked about it over my headset. A technician jogged across the helipad to peer at a gauge through the glass hatch of my capsule. The look on his face was not reassuring.

"We need to open him up," he said to one of his colleagues. "Like, right now!" I had not twisted a knob fully as instructed and pure oxygen, which can be deadly to breathe and highly explosive if sparked, was flooding my compartment. Thirty seconds later, Hocevar and I climbed out to wait for the technicians to fix the settings. It was another reminder that I was a foreigner in these realms. Not particularly clumsy on land, I had spilled coffee on a captain's laptop, nearly electrocuted myself on a fishing boat, and now come perilously close to sparking a deadly explosion in my personal submarine.

After I regained my composure, I asked the scientists why drilling efforts in this area had failed so often. I had read that over the past several decades, oil and gas companies had attempted—at least ninety-five times—to drill in the area but had never successfully tapped oil. Nearly a third of the attempts ended with companies pulling out. "Mechanical error" was the cryptic explanation usually given in Brazilian government records that I had studied. The drilling industry had become more sophisticated technologically with fracking and with more offshore practice, which might have partly explained their willingness to try yet again in these waters. I had assumed my question of the scientists to be an innocuous one. I was wrong.

The scientists shot each other glances that were almost gleeful, as if they were relishing the opportunity to share a ghost story around the campfire. These were notoriously difficult waters, they told me. At its mouth, the muddy river was the color of chocolate milk and the currents were strong. Of all the freshwater that flowed into the world's oceans, about 20 percent of it came from the Amazon. Because of their differing densities, the mix of freshwater and salt water made the underwater world here look like a layer cake. The seafloor was mud in some areas, sand in others. This further complicated the way the water moved.

As the Amazon River poured sediment into the Atlantic Ocean, a plume formed in some places that turned crystal clear waters opaque. Like an underwater sandstorm, the plume traveled unpredictably with the currents and could reach several hundred miles from the mouth of the Amazon. One of the scientists on board, Eduardo Siegle, an oceanographer from the University of São Paulo, explained that the sediment delivered by the plume had settled over hundreds of thousands of years, creating a steep shelf. The front edge of this shelf formed a cliff that plunged the ocean floor from 492 feet deep to more than 9,840 feet.

Another scientist, Nils Asp, an oceanographer from the Federal University of Pará in Brazil, told me that one of the biggest challenges for drillers was simply piercing their way through thousands more feet of thick and unstable silt than was typically found elsewhere. The plume was a marauding threat, the scientists explained. It could swallow a driller's ROV in a matter of minutes. And the front edge of the sea shelf, where most of the oil was thought to reside, routinely experienced massive underwater landslides that could topple rigs.

The lecture on the deck would probably have continued but for the interruption by the submarine technician, who told me to climb back into my capsule so I could pressurize my cabin again and start my descent to this daunting place the scientists had described. As the technician began to close the hatch, Francini-Filho shot me a sly smile. "Good luck," he said.

. . .

The submarine began to sink, and the rushing waves closing in over my dome triggered a claustrophobic panic. I'd spent the past several years traveling on ships all across the globe, but I'd never boarded a submarine until now. Was there really enough air in my compartment? What would I do if that seal popped again and I was flooded with pure oxygen far from the ship?

Hocevar turned on the thrusters, propelling the submarine downward. Suddenly the underwater space seemed vast, neck snapping my claustrophobia to agoraphobia. I felt naked and small in a huge, murky, and foreign world. Slowly, my fears gave way to awe. As I looked up through the glass bubble, the sea surface glistened in the sun, a shimmering of glassy blues. It was louder than I expected in the compartment, with the growl of the engine and the sound of the air scrubbers removing carbon dioxide from the cabins. I checked my watch: about two minutes had passed. The sweat on my neck began to dry, and the compartment felt cool and comfortable. The prehensile arm of the rover extended out in front of us, outfitted with a high-definition underwater camera. Lamps on either side of the rover stabbed into the gloom as we slowly descended.

John Hocevar, the oceans campaign director at Greenpeace, drives a submarine to the seafloor in the Atlantic Ocean.

It took about fifteen minutes for the sub to dive 315 feet to the ocean floor. Along the way, a skate with a four-foot wingspan glided by and neon-colored fish darted to and fro. We passed over arrow crabs, giant lobster, and brittle starfish. Though we were not in the Amazon plume, visibility varied drastically, not unlike passing through clouds in an airplane. One second, we could see nothing; the next moment, there was sparkling clarity.

A school of long gray suckerfish, or remoras, charged the submarine, trying to latch onto us as they do whales and sharks. A six-inch-long white fish moved in and out of a hole in the seafloor. Over the radio, Hocevar noted the fish was called a slippery dick, after its reputation for escaping nets and fishermen's hands. We approached what from afar looked simply like a pile of craggy rocks, but as we neared, I found myself leaning into a Lilliputian metropolis, bustling and vibrant with electric blues, oranges, and yellows.

Hocevar got my attention and pointed to a mound of round jagged-edged rocklike nodules called rhodoliths. Made of a kind of red algae that can form a variety of different shapes, the rhodolith pile was a busy place that looked like the inside of an anthill, a high-rise apartment complex for tiny wormlike creatures. One area served as a "cleaning station" where fish would visit to rid themselves of parasites. Cleaners tend to be colorful and boldly patterned to attract potential customers. For more aggressive advertising, the cleaners sometimes wave antennae or undulate their bodies.

"Even the most voracious predators are welcome," Hocevar explained over the intercom. The cleaners would swim or crawl into their mouths and feed on the parasites and dead skin. We watched a team of delicate peppermint shrimps and long-nosed arrow crabs standing ready to decontaminate their next visitor. Hocevar said some species at feeding stations pretended to be cleaners, only to take bites out of the soft tissue of the trusting fish that invited them in. Predators could be just as deceitful, he added. Occasionally they gulp down the hardworking cleaners. "It's a jungle down here," he said, smiling at me through the glass.

Hocevar soon spotted species of butterfly fish and shimmering fish called wrasse darting around the reef. After later consulting the scientists and comparing photographs of the fish with research books, we learned that some of the fish we saw had never before been documented. In subsequent dives over the next several days, the scientists also filmed several southern red snappers and snowy groupers, both listed by the Brazilian government as endangered. These documented sightings were the ammunition that the Brazilian scientists needed.

The Amazon Reef spread all around us. As the rhodoliths fuse together, they form larger structures that create the skeleton of the reef itself. Over the course of several dives, Greenpeace would map the undersea reef, discovering its contours and filming much of its six hundred miles from the mouth of the Amazon to French Guiana. In every direction, the lamps illuminated some new, strange evidence of biodiversity as the sub circled and rose, following the contours of the seafloor. Sometimes the light from above would reach us and glimmer across the ocean floor. As I looked out at the teeming world around us, I knew I would never again dismiss corals as merely "glamorized rocks."

For an hour, Hocevar and I puttered along the ocean floor before the radio interrupted us.

"DeepWorker, Topside," said a voice.

Hocevar pretended not to hear them so we could keep exploring.

Three minutes later: "DeepWorker pilot, come in."

"Go ahead," Hocevar replied.

"We're going to need you guys to return to the surface."

"Copy that," Hocevar said.

We began our ascent. Through the glass dome, I looked up as we approached the stained-glass window of the surface. I felt a certain euphoria from having visited this vulnerable and foreign world, populated by creatures that didn't fit neatly into our usual animal-mineral-plant categories. I was also reminded that it's tough to make people want to protect what they have never seen. We know more about the dark side of the moon than we do about the bottom of the sea, Hocevar said. That helps some companies because it makes public scrutiny that much less likely and makes it tougher for the likes of Greenpeace to get in the way. "Unfortunately," Hocevar added, "what we don't know actually can hurt us."

When we reached the surface, Hocevar and I sat bobbing silently in the water, like a fishing lure waiting to be reeled in by the *Esperanza*'s crane. My trip in the pontoon plane over the Amazon forest had given me a big-picture sense of what was at stake in climate change, but the submarine had provided a front-row perspective on the threat. I thought back to another time I'd seen the ocean floor up close: the footage from the BP spill in the Gulf. The black lifeless scene in that video stood in stark contrast to the color bursts and bustle of the rhodolith mound and cleaning station.

Six months after we returned to shore, I received an email from one of the scientists who had been on board the *Esperanza*. He said that in response to the research they had gathered during our dive, Brazil's federal environmental agency requested more information from the oil companies, who declined to provide it. As a result, the government revoked, at least temporarily, their licenses to drill near the Amazon Reef.

It was a rare instance of a country exerting control over activity in waters that it could have just as readily opened for business. The Brazilian scientists and Greenpeace had won this battle. Still, I remained pessimistic or at least sober about the larger war because I knew the hunt for oil by deep-pocketed companies would continue in no small measure with the tacit support of average consumers like me.

# SEA SLAVERY

What would an ocean be without a monster lurking in the dark?
It would be like sleep without dreams.

—Werner Herzog, *A Guide for the Perplexed:*
*Conversations with Paul Cronin*

While forced labor exists throughout the world, nowhere is the problem more rampant than in the South China Sea, and especially in the Thai fishing fleet. Partly this is because in a typical year, this country's fishing industry is short about fifty thousand mariners, according to the UN in 2014. As a result, tens of thousands of migrants from Cambodia and Myanmar are whispered into Thailand each year to make up this chronic shortfall. Then, unscrupulous captains buy and sell the men and boys like chattel.

With rising fuel prices and fewer fish close to shore, maritime labor researchers predict that more boats will resort to venturing farther out to sea, making the mistreatment of migrants more likely. The work is brutal. And in this bloated, inefficient, and barely profitable national fleet, captains require crew members to simply do what they were told, when they were told. No complaints, no matter how long the hours, how little the food, or how paltry the pay. In short, these captains rely on sea slaves.

"Life at sea is cheap," said Phil Robertson, deputy director of Human Rights Watch's Asia division. Conditions are worsening, he said, because of lax maritime labor laws and an insatiable global demand for seafood, even as overfishing depletes fish stocks.

Thanks to excellent reporting that preceded me, I had an inkling of the problem of sea slavery. But the level of depravation that I encountered—the abject cruelty that I witnessed directly and the lasting effects on men I interviewed—has haunted me ever since I finished reporting. In the outlaw ocean, the victims are many—above and below the waves—but the abuse of the men who help put food on our plates was a shock to me. As consumers, there is a growing sense that cell phones have become a kind of police force to counter such abuses in almost all aspects of life. If something bad is happening, it will likely be captured and posted on YouTube. But that rarely happens at sea, where indentured servitude remains a standard business practice.

. . .

I wish I had never seen it," said the security guard Som Nang, describing what he had witnessed hundreds of miles from shore. In late 2013, Som Nang embarked on his maiden voyage on a boat that resupplied fishing vessels in the South China Sea. After four days on the water, Som Nang's ship pulled up alongside a dilapidated Thai-flagged trawler.

A Thai fishing ship in the South China Sea

At the front of the trawler, a shirtless, emaciated man huddled with a rusty metal shackle around his bruised neck and a three-foot chain anchoring the collar to a post on the deck. The man had tried to escape the boat, the captain of the fishing vessel later explained, so he locked the metal collar on the man and chained him up every time another ship drew near.

The name of the shackled man was Lang Long, and like thousands of other men and boys in the Thai fishing fleet he was trafficked across the border from Cambodia into Thailand. Long had never intended to go to sea. Near his village outside Phnom Penh, Cambodia's capital city, he met a man at a Buddhist festival who offered him a construction job in Thailand and help getting into the country.

Long, who was thirty, saw it as his chance to start over; he was tired of watching his younger siblings go hungry because their family's rice paddy back home could not provide for everyone. So, Long traveled by night to a port city on the gulf coast of Thailand over bumpy dirt roads in the back of a flatbed truck. When he arrived, he waited for days in a room guarded by armed men near the port at Samut Prakan, more than a dozen miles southeast of Bangkok. The trafficker then sold Long to a boat captain for about $530, less than the going price for a water buffalo. He was then herded with six other migrants up a gangway onto a shoddy wooden ship. It was the start of three brutal years of captivity at sea, during which Long was resold twice between fishing boats.

I met Long in Songkhla, on Thailand's southeast coast in September 2014 while I was reporting on forced labor. Long had been rescued seven months earlier by a Catholic charity called the Stella Maris International Seafarers' Center, which paid a captain for his release. With offices in over two hundred ports in more than thirty countries, Stella Maris offers social services to seafarers and their families. I was in Songkhla because the social workers at Stella Maris said they would help me meet victims of trafficking and introduce me to the officials charged with investigating those abuses.

As I waited to meet Long, I spent hours at the Stella Maris office poring through a binder full of case files. It was a horrifying catalog of cruel abuses, torture, and murder at sea. In page after page, in photographs and scribbled notes, the documents described the sick being cast overboard, the defiant beheaded, and the insubordinate sealed for days below deck in a dark, fetid fishing hold. "We get a new case every week," said Suchat Junthalukkhana, the center's director.

Surviving these ordeals often depended upon chance encounters with altruistic strangers who contacted Stella Maris or other groups involved in the clandestine rescue of sea slaves, part of a mariners' underground railroad stretching through Malaysia, Indonesia, Cambodia, and Thailand. Som Nang was one of those rescuers. A forty-one-year-old Cambodian man, he said his name meant "good luck" in Khmer. Introduced to me by Stella Maris, Som Nang was squat and stern, and he was quick to show off the retractable metal rod he kept tucked in his belt for protection. Having worked dockside for several years, Som Nang had heard the tales of brutality. None of it prepared him, however, for what he saw on the supply ship, he added.

Som Nang had worked on a type of boat known as a mother ship. Carrying everything from fuel and extra food to spare nets and replacement labor, these lumbering vessels, often over a hundred feet long, functioned as the Walmarts of the ocean—floating, all-purpose resupply stores. The same kind of boat delivered Long to captivity and subsequently rescued him as well.

Mother ships were the reason slow-moving trawlers could fish more than fifteen hundred miles from land. They allowed fishermen to stay out at sea for months or years and still get their catch cleaned, canned, and shipped to American shelves less than a week after netting.

Once a load of fish was transferred to a mother ship, it was combined with other catch below deck in cavernous refrigerators, and there was almost no way for port authorities to determine its provenance. It became virtually impossible to know whether it was caught legally by paid fishermen or poached illegally by shackled migrants.

After a four-day trip from shore, Som Nang's mother ship pulled alongside Long's battered Thai-flagged trawler, whose eight-man crew had just finished two weeks of illegal fishing in Indonesian waters. Long was shackled at the time. The captain typically put the collar on him once a week, whenever other boats approached. The only Cambodian among the Burmese deckhands and Thai senior crew, Long stared unblinking at anyone willing to make eye contact. "Please help me," Som Nang recounted Long whispering in Khmer. Som Nang added that image, seared into his memory, was the reason he did not work at sea anymore.

After Long was rescued, a police report later described his captivity and the way he had been traded at sea between boats several times. "Three fishing boats surrounded the supply boat and began fighting for Long," the report said. This far from shore there was always a short-

During his several years of captivity in the Thai fishing fleet, Lang Long was shackled by the neck and sold between fishing boats.

age of workers. Similar arguments broke out a year later when Long was sold again in the middle of the night between trawlers.

After I read Stella Maris's case files about the rescued deckhands, a social worker brought me to meet Long in a seating area one floor down from a room full of cots where he and other former crew slept. He had been staying there for several months while waiting to be transferred to a government shelter, where he would live until federal authorities could investigate his case.

Thin and tall, Long had pockmarked skin the color of creamed coffee. He sat unnaturally still, like an upright cadaver, and breathed only through his nose as though he was afraid to open his mouth. A shell of a man, he wore a perpetually vacant gaze.

I knew this would likely be one of the tougher conversations I would have. And so that he did not trip things up, I warned my translator about some of my tactics: I will likely sit for fifteen to twenty minutes in silence at the outset after you introduce me to Long, I told him. I will want you simply to concisely and politely tell Long who I am and that my goal is to capture the story of what happened to him. Then I will shake Long's hand, and you will say that I need to collect my thoughts several minutes before we start. Then we will sit in silence. It will be awkward, I warned, but please let the quiet do its work. The point will be to build up pressure so that hopefully Long becomes as eager to talk as I already am. The translator nodded that he understood my request.

At some point, I will pull out a pack of chewing gum, I continued. I will put a piece in my mouth, and I will also hand you a piece that I need you to chew. This will show Long that it is okay to partake. I will place a piece of gum on the table in front of Long and gently gesture that it's for him if he wants it. I may just stare aimlessly. I may scribble notes in my notebook. Later, I will get up from the table and leave to get several bottles of water. When I return and hand you a bottle, I will need you to open yours and drink, and I will do the same. Yes, this is all very choreographed and premeditated, manipulative even, I conceded. But it's also effective in breaking the ice, I've found. The translator seemed to understand and agreed to play his part.

After sitting for nearly half an hour—water bottles drunk, gum being chewed—I gently began asking Long about his experiences. He said that at first he had tried to keep track of the passing days and months at sea by using a rusty fishing hook to etch notches in the wooden railing. Eventually, he stopped. "I never thought I would see land again," he said, his voice trailing off. Long then added that he never wanted to eat fish again. When talking became too much, he looked past me. At one point, I discreetly and slowly turned around to see where he was choosing to rest his eyes. It was nothing, just a stark white patch of wall.

The longer he worked on the boats, the lighter Long's debt should have become for the money he owed to the captain who had paid the cost for his illegal travel across the border. Instead, time only tightened Long's bondage. His captivity began looking like a life sentence. The more experience he gained at sea, the higher the price other short-handed captains were willing to pay to buy him for their boats.

At first, he made rookie mistakes. Having no fishing experience and having never seen the sea before his captivity, Long seemed to tangle his portion of the nets more than other deckhands did, he said. All the fish looked the same to him—small and silver—making sorting difficult. Slowed at first by intense seasickness, Long said he sped up after witnessing a captain whip a man for working too slowly.

Despite his efforts, Long faced severe punishments. "He was beat with a pole made of wood or metal," his case report from the Thai government's Office of the National Human Rights Commission said. "Some days he had rest of only one hour." When drinking water ran low, deckhands stole foul-tasting ice from the barrels of fish. If one of the seamen put gear away incorrectly, the crew master docked the day's meal for the offender.

Long said he often considered jumping overboard to escape. He told a doctor who later treated him that he never once saw land during his three years at sea. At night, there were times when no one was guarding the ship's radio, but Long said that he had no idea whom to call for help, or how. His sense of captivity and isolation worsened because others on the ship did not speak his language.

As much as he feared the captains, Long said, the ocean scared him more. Waves, some of them several stories high, battered the deck in rough seas. When Som Nang's boat showed up, Long had been wearing the shackle on and off for about nine months.

The only thing more shocking than seeing the man shackled, Som Nang said, was the fact that no one else around him on the mother ship seemed surprised by it. After returning to port, Som Nang contacted Stella Maris, which began raising the 25,000 baht, roughly $750, needed to buy Long's freedom. I remember being sickened when I heard this number: the price of Long's life was less than my plane fare from D.C. to Bangkok.

It was not the last time Som Nang would see Long. Over the next several months, Som Nang resupplied the fishing boat twice. Each time the mother ship drew alongside, Long was shackled. "I'm trying to get you free," Som Nang whispered to him on one of the supply runs.

In April 2014, Long's captivity ended in the most anticlimactic of ways. On his supply ship's next rendezvous with Long's captors, Som Nang carried a brown paper bag full of Thai currency from Stella Maris to a meeting point in the middle of the South China Sea, roughly a week's travel from shore. What the rescuers saw as a ransom, the captain viewed as a "debt payment"—an amount still owed in work from Long. With few words, Som Nang handed the bag of money to Long's captain. Long then stepped onto Som Nang's boat and began his journey back to solid ground.

During his six-day voyage back to shore on the mother ship, Long cried and slept most of the time. The crew hid him to avoid word getting out to other fishing boats about their role in the rescue because they feared that other ship captains might resent that a supply company was playing a role in what they viewed as a labor dispute. Som Nang stopped working at sea shortly after his rescue trip. He took a new job as a factory security guard. I visited with him in his cinderblock home just outside Songkhla, and Som Nang said he still had nightmares about what he saw offshore. "I don't like what is out there," he said.

· · ·

My story about Long ran as part of the Outlaw Ocean series on the front page of *The New York Times* on July 27, 2015. Thai anti-trafficking officials contacted me afterward to say they found the story credible and that a special unit of federal police hoped to arrest and charge the boat captain, who at the time was at sea on another boat. Over the next two years, Long also became something of an icon: the then U.S. secretary of state, John Kerry, recounted his story half a dozen times at news conferences and diplomatic events to emphasize the need to end labor trafficking.

One afternoon, Pisan Manawapat, the ambassador to the United States from the Thai military junta government, requested a meeting with me to discuss my reporting. Joined by two persons from his staff, we met for lunch at a restaurant in Georgetown, a ritzy neighborhood in Washington, D.C. Initially, we stuck to bromides: the impressive punctuality of Bangkok urban transit, the ever-growing numbers of tourists visiting Phuket, the promising job prospects awaiting his daughter as she finished law school.

Then we got down to business. "We're taking these things very seriously, you know," Manawapat said, referring to sea slavery, before explaining for the next half hour the various steps his government was taking. He cited an increase in the number of investigations and prosecutions of cases involving labor abuse. He described the creation of several shelters around the country for trafficking victims. He explained how immigration authorities were conducting a registration drive to count undocumented workers and provide them with identity cards.

At the end of the lunch, Ambassador Manawapat handed me his personal cell phone number. "All I ask," he said, "is to keep an open line of communication." I held my tongue rather than say what crossed my mind. Before my story ran in the *Times,* the Thai government had mostly stonewalled me, not acknowledged my emails, and refused to take my phone calls. I was happy that it seemed as if this would no longer be a problem for me.

Several weeks later, as I finished giving a presentation to the U.S. Agency for International Development, a State Department official approached the lectern. She asked whether I had heard from Long in recent weeks. I said no. "He's disappeared," she said. "The government seems to have picked him up." She added that her colleagues in the anti-trafficking section of the Bangkok consulate were very concerned about his safety. I thanked her for letting me know and immediately contacted Ambassador Manawapat. Politely but firmly, I told him that in light of what we had discussed over lunch in Georgetown, I fully expected his colleagues in Bangkok to find Long immediately and to provide me with verification that he was not being detained. My view was that because my reporting had possibly been the cause of Long being picked up, it was journalistically my responsibility to figure out where he was and, to the extent possible, ensure his safety.

Long was located the next day at a government facility where immigration officials were assessing his mental health and discussing with him whether he preferred to return home to Koh Sotin, his native village in Cambodia, or to stay in Thailand. It was never clear to me whether Long had already been at that facility or he had been moved there after my phone call. But Long said that if he went home to Cambodia, he hoped to go back to his old job cleaning a local Buddhist temple.

Roughly two years later, I returned to Thailand to check on Long, who was still living in the government shelter near Songkhla. Thai police had pinned down the name of the last boat, *N. Poo-ngern 8*, where Long had been shackled. Thai authorities had also identified the boat captain who was Long's captor. He was a Thai man named Suwan Sookmak. Long and Som Nang identified Sookmak when they were shown a lineup of photographs of suspects. After staking out Sookmak's mistress's house in Songkhla for over a month, police arrested him when he finally came back to shore. The owners of the *N. Poo-ngern 8*, Manas Phukham and Srisuda Phukham, were also arrested because the captain said they were the ones who had sold Long into captivity, but they were released for lack of further evidence.

I spent a day at the Songkhla shelter watching Long. His mental and emotional wiring seemed frayed, perhaps beyond repair. I had intended to interview him again—to ask him about his future plans and thoughts on the government's handling of the case—but after seeing how fragile and withdrawn he seemed, I opted just to observe. He struggled to follow along during a therapy session in which he and four other trafficked men were instructed to use crayons to draw a story. Theirs showed stick-figure people in fields with trees or next to thatch houses. Long's drawing was just lines and blobs. The shelter's social workers told me that he often spoke of wanting to go home, but they doubted he was ready to live on his own, hold down a job, and stay on his medicine.

In August 2017, roughly six years after Long's nightmare began, the Thai court sentenced Sookmak to four years in prison on a human-trafficking charge and required him to pay Long over 450,000 baht, roughly $13,500, in damages. On December 28, 2017, Long left the Songkhla shelter and returned to Cambodia.

Every couple months I still text with a senior anti-trafficking official in the Thai government, a woman who over the years became one of my best sources. Even after Long returned to Cambodia, she kept tabs on him. She struggles to get information about his well-being now that he's so far away. We both are pessimistic about his long-term prospects; he remains easy prey; neither of us quite knows what we could do if we found out that he was sucked into another trafficking pipeline.

. . .

Long's case was extreme. Most fishing captains don't resort to shackling their crew. Typically, debt and distance from shore are enough to keep workers captive. The ships in the Thai fleet that were known to have the worst conditions were the long-haul boats that stayed away from shore for months or years on end and relied most on migrant workers.

It felt journalistically important to try to see this deprivation and exploitation in person. Human rights advocates and journalists had described these boats before. But their reporting was usually based on testimony taken on land from escaped deckhands. Joined by a British photographer, Adam Dean, and a young female Thai translator, I hoped to see for myself the conditions on these long-haul ships. I soon discovered this was an ambitious goal.

While UN pacts and various human rights protections officially prohibited debt bondage, Thai military and law enforcement authorities did little in practice to police misconduct on the high seas. Complicating the enforcement problem further, some of these officials were complicit in the fishing industry's human trafficking, taking bribes to allow safe passage across the border. Many migrants had reported to

UN officials and human rights groups of being rescued by police from one smuggler, only to be resold by police to another smuggler.

Over the years, readers of the *Times* have often emailed me to ask how I get people to talk so candidly about things that might not reflect on them well. I rarely have a good answer for this question except to say that I am perpetually surprised in this line of work by how much people want to tell their own story. As a reporter, I've found that if a person sizes you up and decides that you seem trustworthy, he typically will talk.

Sometimes it paid to be coy, others times nakedly transparent. I'm not especially good at the former; I've been told that my eyes project information like a ticker tape. When I was in edgy settings like ports, crowded markets, or sketchy neighborhoods where I didn't want my curiosity, confusion, or fear projected so publicly by my face, I wore sunglasses. Mostly, though, I tried to win people over by being bluntly candid and by having done my homework beforehand so that I could impress the person from the outset that I understood at least a little about his perspective. These tactics served me especially well with fishing captains who tended to be astute judges of character and to have zero patience for obfuscation.

Still, it wasn't easy to get long-haul captains to agree to take us on board. Dean and I set up camp in Songkhla, one of Thailand's biggest fishing ports. Night after night, we went out for dinner and drinks with long-haul boat captains, hoping to persuade them to let us join their crews. Virtually all of them turned down our requests. No one wanted to be seen shuttling foreigners out to sea, they explained. The industry's reputation was bad enough already.

*The Guardian* and a nongovernmental organization called Environmental Justice Foundation, known as EJF, had done extensive reporting a year earlier, exposing brutality and trafficking in the industry. In response to this reporting, Thailand was already the focus of the U.S. State Department's anti-trafficking office, and seafood buyers and sellers had also hired investigators to assess how much their supply chains were tainted by sea slavery.

As Dean and I courted them, captains seemed baffled as to why we would want to spend time on ships that everyone knew to be dangerous and dirty places. I said we simply wanted to witness the work and chronicle the lives of these men. When we finally found a captain willing to transport us partway out to sea, he refused to allow us to board at port. We instead had to hire a skiff to carry us seven miles offshore and climb on board his ship there, where no one would see us.

As instructed, we took a skiff out, traveled for almost ten hours on another boat, then transferred to a third vessel for almost as long before we spotted the Thai purse seiner that would ultimately become the focus of my reporting. This ship had a crew of forty Cambodians, some of whom were boys who appeared no older than fifteen. Worse for the wear, the ship was crowded and rusty, looking as if it had been at sea for years. I desperately wanted to get on board.

Communicating in these moments was a lot like playing charades. Few of the captains or their crew spoke English, and at this point in our trip our Thai interpreter had fallen severely seasick. She was vomiting whenever she stood up, which meant her translations were garbled, apologetic, and abbreviated.

I had worried about bringing a female translator on this reporting trip, not because she might be more susceptible to seasickness, but because I was unsure how the men who had been at sea for months with no women aboard would respond to her presence. But this translator was famously tough and fearless, having reported in equally dangerous settings, including in Rohingya refugee camps in the mountains along the Thai-Burmese border. I was not disappointed. Even sick, she stayed engaged and refused to turn back.

As we tried to negotiate our way onto the fishing boat, I wondered whether I would look back on the decision to board this rust bucket as a glaring and reckless miscalculation. In reporting, times like these are flooded with adrenaline and dread. There is little choice but to assess risk in milliseconds, based on the scarcest of information. How are these guys looking at the woman with us? Are the captains shooting loaded glances at one another? Does this ship even look seaworthy?

So much of the context is foreign that reading the cues becomes pure guesswork. You bank a lot on your instincts, which, at this point, are usually deeply hampered by exhaustion. It is what the *New York Times* Delhi bureau chief, Jeffrey Gettleman, once described as the "transitive property of trust." Reporters invest their lives in it all the time, he said. People you trust put you with people they trust who pass you to others they trust. The longer it gets, the more you hope the chain will hold.

While the captain of our ship pitched our proposal, the purse seiner captain looked me over skeptically, which, for some reason, I took to be a good sign, as if he were more worried of me than perhaps I should be of him. After several minutes, he agreed to bring us on board his vessel for a couple days, under two conditions. We were not permitted to name him or his ship. And we were required to stay out of the way of his workers at all times. The captain explained that we were roughly 120 miles from port and that his ship was heading back to shore soon, after more than nine months of fishing. We would stay on his ship for a final stint of fishing, and then we would ride with him back to shore.

We quickly climbed aboard the purse seiner, and I gestured for our first captain to hurry up and leave, fearing that our new host might change his mind while he still had a chance. For the next several minutes, the Cambodian crew stared at us in deep puzzlement until the captain barked at them in Thai over the loudspeaker to get back to work. Night was setting in, and it was time to lift the ship's net. The dipping sun shifted light on the water from shimmering tinfoil to swampy emerald to tar black.

Thailand's fishing fleet consists mostly of bottom trawlers, which drag a wall of mesh behind them. Purse seiners use more rudimentary circular nets that are dropped to target fish closer to the water's surface, hauled upward, then constrained at the top like a drawstring coin purse. To ensure the fifty-foot mouth of the nets closed properly, the boys dove into the inky-black sea. If one of them was to get tangled in the mesh and yanked into the fathoms below, it was likely that no one would notice right away over the frenzy, darkness, and noise.

For the crews, injury was a constant danger. Throughout my reporting, deckhands on these ships routinely turned to me as though I had medical expertise. Because they saw me take vitamins in the mornings, they figured that meant I knew how to administer medicine. On one boat in the Philippines, a man showed me his scalp wound that he said was crawling with worms (I couldn't see them). Off the coast of Somalia, I met a deckhand who coughed up blood and spat it in the water as though it were normal. It had been that way for months, he told me through a translator. Rashes were the most common ailment. In Indonesia, a deckhand worked without pants or underwear, just a towel around his waist because, he told me, the itchy sores on his crotch were otherwise too uncomfortable. In many of these cases the men asked me for help and I gave them what medicines or ointments that I thought might at least ease their symptoms. When I got back home after each trip, I described to my physician what I'd seen. She and I refined and expanded the range of antibiotic powders and other pills that I packed for the crew I might encounter on my next voyage.

The hygienic conditions on the Thai purse seiner with the Cambodian crew that I boarded were among the worst I'd seen. This was apparent in the sheer number of roaches of all sizes and colors crawling on virtually every surface. This filth is part of what gave me pause when several of the boys, after working through the night, gestured for me to eat with them. Meals consisted of a once-daily bowl of rice, flecked with boiled squid or other God-knows-what. An intestinal gamble for me, their invitation was a rare chance to bond. I was also really hungry, because my rations of peanut butter and dried fruit had already run out.

Hunger was a constant companion for me during these trips offshore. I usually dropped ten pounds by the time I returned home. I'd become adept at tricking my body: filling my stomach with water, fooling my mouth with gum, propping up my stamina with coffee. I also squelched any instinct to complain by reminding myself that as hungry, thirsty, or tired as I might be, the people around me were likely far more so.

When there was food to be had during my reporting for this book, it was often an adventure. At home, I'm a vegetarian. When I travel, I eat what's put in front of me. To say no to an offer of food would have been as socially appropriate as spitting indoors. "Sea bug soup," raw squid on rice, the aggressively pungent durian—some of what was served took fast chewing, closed eyes, and ample chasers.

At a roadside restaurant near the Burmese-Thai border, my translator ordered me a mound of giant prawns. As big as my forearms, they were steamed but fully intact, eyes, antennae, and all, looking like postapocalyptic cockroaches. One time, when I was on a ship in Indonesian waters, my hosts proudly served me a giant clam they'd netted. Still in its shell, the creature stood fifteen inches tall when set on the galley counter. Before being boiled, the clam kept closing its shell each time the cook forced it open. I emailed my fourteen-year-old son a video—subject line: "Tonight's dinner"—showing the chef and the clam in battle. My son, Aidan, texted back, "Stop!"

Some of the Cambodian boys on the Thai fishing boat looked

younger than Aidan, which really got to me when I thought about how different their lives were. Handing me a steaming bowl of speckled rice, the boys watched me closely. I made sure I didn't hesitate. Using my fingers, I shoveled squid rice into my mouth. The boys broke into laughter, mocking me for how fast I ate. "Like us," one of the boys said, pointing at me. His name was Pier and he was seventeen years old. After a couple of minutes, I took the laughter as an opportunity to ask him about life on the boat.

"You just have to work hard," he said. Having worked on the boat for nearly a year, Pier said he liked it better than home. "Nothing to do there," he said, flexing his sinewy bicep to show the return on his labor.

Pier added that he still owed the captain in part for the cost of getting from the border to port with the help of a smuggler. The rest of his debt, he said, was from a large cash advance he sent back to his family. Eventually, Pier and I found that we were sitting alone. I took the chance to gently ask about more sensitive topics, but got little from him. Though he seemed open to answering most of my questions, Pier silently looked down when asked whether he had ever been beaten or whether he might consider leaving the boat, even before paying off his debt.

Common in the developing world, especially in construction, agriculture, manufacturing, and the sex industries, debt bondage is particularly pervasive and abusive at sea because these workers are so isolated. In Thailand, boat captains historically paid large up-front sums in advance to deckhands so that these workers could sustain their families during their long absences. However, because more of the deckhands were migrant workers, captains no longer paid the up-front money to the men themselves. Instead, these captains paid this money to the smugglers who snuck the deckhands into the country.

I asked some of the deckhands on my ship about their experiences. They said that once they left shore, their debt became difficult to repay fully. The stubbornness of that debt can be traced back to global economic and historical forces. Typhoon Gay in 1989 was a turning point for Thailand's seafood industry. Because it sank hundreds of Thai vessels and killed over eight hundred men, the storm instantly created a reputation for the fishing industry as an extraordinarily dangerous line of work. For generations, fishing boats had offered relatively lucrative employment for young Thai men, especially from villages in the country's northeast. The seasonal trek was a rite of passage memorialized in a popular Thai song called "Seagoing Trawler" (Tang-ke).

Thailand's sea slavery problem is also connected to the emergence of the country's middle class. Among Asia's "tiger economies," Thailand's gross domestic product grew in the late 1980s by an average rate of 9 percent annually, peaking at 13 percent in 1988. Its exports also expanded by an average of 14 percent each year. Wages on land rose, making Thai nationals even less inclined to take jobs offshore. As of 2016, Thailand had one of the lowest unemployment rates in the world—generally less than 1 percent. The fishing industry became dependent on cheap foreign labor, particularly from Myanmar, Cambodia, and Laos. Still, the Thai fishing fleet was chronically shorthanded. The shortage was worse because the industry resisted investing in laborsaving technologies, relying instead on gear like purse seines that require large crews.

Thailand's labor and human rights abuses are also connected to its environmental problems. As the number of Thai boats grew, so did the size of their hauls, causing fish stocks to plummet. In fisheries and conservation biology, the catch per unit effort, or CPUE, is an indirect measure of the abundance or scarcity of a target species. In both the Gulf of Thailand and the Andaman Sea, on Thailand's western side, the CPUE on fishing boats fell by more than 86 percent between the mid-1960s and the early years of the twenty-first century, making Thai waters among the most overfished on the planet. Even though there were fewer fish to catch, Thai boats were catching more, partly by traveling to more distant waters. All of these grander economic and environmental forces conspired to make debt bondage that much more tightly woven into the fabric of fishing on the South China Sea.

.  .  .

In the early morning after my quick meal with the crew, a lull settled over the purse seiner. Virtually the entire crew disappeared into an intensely hot crawl space toward the back of the ship. Its four-foot-high ceiling was tight for even the small Cambodians. Deafening but almost soothing, the engine turbines throbbed incessantly. The ship's wooden deck shuddered every so often as the engine coughed a black cloud of bunker fumes into the sleeping quarters. The smoke was almost a welcome change from the wet stench of body odor that filled the room.

I stank too. My pants were smudged with fish guts, my shoes caked in ripe chum. But as much as I wanted to wash away the accumulated filth during some of these trips, bathing was less inviting because it entailed standing fully exposed on the back deck and pouring a bucket of seawater over myself. The most intensive fishing happened at night, filling the back deck with tackle and busy men. That meant broad daylight was usually the only option for using the deck to bathe.

By this point, my body odor had convinced me that I'd need to buy new clothes after this trip. No amount of washing could salvage this wardrobe. Embarrassment had taught me that before boarding long flights, it was best to just throw away any shoes that I'd worn on the fishing boats because ridding them of their smell was virtually impossible. Wearing the shoes on a flight, even carrying them sealed in a plastic bag, resulted in passenger complaints. ("Excuse me, I think there may be something rotting in the overhead.") Returning home after my clothes were infested with bedbugs during a stint in Haitian waters, I was instructed by my wife to enter the house through the garage. What clothes I did not throw away were washed, then put in the freezer for a week, then washed again, to kill anything they carried.

The Cambodian boys on the purse seiner slept in two-hour shifts in cocoon-like hammocks made from torn fishing nets and suspended from above. I didn't understand why the boys bothered sleeping in tight hammocks rather than on the floor. We had not slept for forty-eight hours, so we decided we should try to get a little rest. The quarters were so cramped that we could only fit by tucking on the floor under the crew's hammocks, lying on our backs, like corpses in coffins. Most of the crew had stripped down to their underwear. My nose nearly brushed the swinging hindquarters of the boy above me. Being that close to a complete stranger and breathing in his funk felt like an invasion of his privacy and a self-inflicted assault on mine. I was practiced at tolerating pungent odors, but this room was unusually challenging. Squeeze the fluids out of some old football pads, add urine and pureed fish to the liquid, and boil it: such was the steamy aroma in that nook.

As strong as that odor was, my fatigue was stronger, and I fell fast asleep immediately. But that lasted just ten minutes before a jolt of

In cramped sleeping quarters on a Thai purse seiner, the hammocks are typically made of converted fishing nets, and deckhands avoid sleeping on the ground partly because the floor is overrun with rats, a lesson I learned the hard way.

Compared with the crew's cramped, rat-infested quarters, the captain's sleeping area on a Thai fishing ship was more hospitable.

adrenaline woke me. Something scampered across my legs. Trying to sit up, I slammed into the boy just inches above me, knocking my headlamp off. Putting it back on, I turned on the light. The floor was teeming with dozens of rats. Some were cleaning the crew's half-empty dinner bowls; others looked like rioters looting stores, darting in and out of the boys' duffel bags.

I woke up the translator and Dean. Both were lying by my side. We moved to the roof of the captain's quarters. I now understood why the boys opted for cramped hammocks just barely off the floor. Lesson learned, I vowed to myself that the first thing I'd buy once we got to a big city was a travel hammock.

. . .

Between reporting trips, I returned to the United States, and universities often invited me to give talks to students and faculty about the journalism. During the question-and-answer session, someone invariably asked about the danger involved in the work, and I usually felt torn in responding. My ego enjoyed the idea of me as some globe-trotting action hero. And yes, I faced some very real moments of risk. But they always paled in comparison to the risks faced by the people I was writing about, by the sources and in-country staff (translators, photographers, fixers) who stayed behind when I left, and by the local reporters who covered these issues long before I parachuted into their world.

The real danger to me on these ships in Thailand and elsewhere tended to be the conditions: falling from a slippery ledge, getting sick from the food, walking in front of a swinging piece of machinery. I managed to develop a healthy—some might argue unhealthy—relationship with fear. The more intense or risky the predicament I found myself in, the more sanguine I grew, assuming I'd make it through just fine. After all, I figured, if I didn't survive the danger, who else would recount what happened? The stories I was reporting needed to be told, and I was lucky enough to be doing the job.

This deeply nonsensical outlook is why I also assumed that if calamity was to befall me on these reporting trips, it was far more likely to occur on the back of a taxi moped weaving at rocket speed through Accra traffic or bouncing around in the back of a pickup truck on a dirt, cliff-shouldered road in the mountains of Borneo, because one's guard is down during such banal activities. I'm not defending this convoluted logic, but it was helpful to me in its own way as I reported this book.

Truth be told, the few times I faced real bodily harm during my many reporting expeditions were usually my fault. In Mogadishu, climbing a rope ladder to get from a police boat onto a gigantic cattle carrier whose sides were four stories tall, I nearly fell about thirty feet because I had tried to carry too much gear. In the port of U.A.E., I was stuck with five maritime security guards for twenty-four hours while I waited for the next boat to pick me up. For most of the time, we sat in a port bar and worked our way through three bottles of Oban single-malt whiskey. By the third bottle, one of the guards was getting raucous— loud high fives, spilling drinks, hollering at the soccer match on the TV, falling out of his chair. A pack of other guards, seated a couple of tables over and twice our number, grew tired of the noise, and they made some comments essentially telling us to quiet down. This nearly led to a brawl until the saner few among our group ushered our friend outside.

In Hargeisa, Somaliland—an autonomous region in Somalia—my photographer, Fabio Nascimento, and I were nearly lynched by a dozen men who did not take kindly to our photographing them using khat, a mildly addictive, amphetamine-like leaf that many men chew. I had told Nascimento it was okay to photograph the men; our driver sped us off from the scene in the nick of time.

I had recruited Nascimento after meeting him on a ship in the South Atlantic Ocean where he was filming a team of scientists. A young Brazilian man, he had reported for years in the Amazon rain forest, and he had impressed me with his ability to work in uncomfortable settings—to say nothing of his talent for shooting still photographs and video, especially using drones. I hired him for a year to join me on a dozen trips, one of my wisest decisions. An all-weather companion, Nascimento more than once steered me away from harm. During one trip in Mexico, I made a comment in Spanish meant partially as a joke to a taxi driver. He had charged us triple what we'd been charged the same route inbound, and I said something about the fare being a form of robbery. It escalated and the taxi driver and I nearly came to blows. Nascimento talked me down.

My biggest fear on fishing ships, in Thailand and elsewhere, was falling overboard. If it happened at night, there was a good chance no one would notice for hours. What I knew about surviving such an incident, I had learned during a weeklong embed with the U.S. Coast Guard search-and-rescue team in Clearwater, Florida. Most of the time during that embed I spent on board their Sikorsky Jayhawk helicopters watching officers practice scooping people out of the sea in specialized rescue baskets. When I described to these officers my reporting at sea and polled them for ways I might heighten my chances of survival if I ended up in the water (I'm a decent swimmer), they looked at me as if I'd asked how to patch my wrist if I decided to cut off my hand. "Best plan is to avoid it," deadpanned one pilot.

Other officers offered more helpful tips: Wear a headlamp and bright colors when on deck. If the water is cold when you fall in, clench your jaw and resist taking that first panicked gasp because it's usually the one that drowns you. Limit heat loss by keeping your knees to your chest, they told me. Never swim against the current. Kick off heavy boots or shoes. If it's not too cold, remove and tie off the ends of your pants or shirt to capture air in them and to use them as floatation devices. Learn "drownproofing" techniques, which are low-energy swimming methods that focus on holding air in your lungs, keeping your body vertical, relaxed, and with the minimum required effort, your head just above water.

Most of the fishing boats I boarded lacked life jackets, so in the beginning I brought my own. I stopped traveling with it, however, after security guards in Indonesia detained me at the airport in Jakarta because they believed the aerosol canister for inflating the jacket was a bomb. Initially, I carried a satellite phone in a waterproof bag strapped to my belt, but the per-minute rate for calls soon became too expensive. I resorted instead to traveling with Garmin inReach, which provided GPS coordinates and text (though not voice) messaging capabilities. Strapped to my belt at all times, the device had a button that, when pressed, alerted a designated list of people, informing them that I was in trouble, though I never quite figured out what those people were actually supposed to do if they got such an alert.

During the day, I used a portable solar panel to charge an all-purpose battery, which at night enabled me to recharge the trackers and other gizmos. Aside from serving as my only hope if I went over the rail, the trackers told me (and others who logged in to a certain website) where I was on the planet at any given moment. They also provided me with a crucial communication line to my family. Typing on them was awkward and data slow to transfer, but I sent fairly regular updates to my wife, Sherry. ("All fine. Weather delays. Back in 5 days.") These brusque haikus always ended with "TQ," for *"Te quiero,"* or "I love you" in Spanish. We also had a secret code in case of emergency. If ever in a call or text I mentioned the name "Yorel" (a high school classmate of mine whose name was Leroy backward), it meant I was in trouble but couldn't say so openly, like in a hostage or piracy situation. Sherry had a list of phone numbers of people at the *Times,* in law enforcement, and at the U.S. State Department that she could alert in such an emergency. Thankfully, I never had to invoke Yorel's name.

And yet, the fear I most suffered in writing this book was not the kind that audiences at the talks I gave seemed to expect. The more I witnessed riveting and urgent moments in this reporting, the more I worried that I would not be able to live up to them in my writing. How would I find the narrative arc, make the tough decisions about what to leave in and what to leave out, and protect sources? Was I pulling out of my reporting trips too early and missing once-in-a-lifetime opportunities, or was I lingering too long and wasting valuable time that I could spend elsewhere?

.  .  .

To be sure, I did encounter a couple of intimidating characters on these reporting trips. And one of them was the bosun on the Thai purse seiner with the Cambodian boys in the South China Sea. His name was Tang. After the rats woke me up that night, I was too wired to go back to sleep. So I eventually made my way up to the wheelhouse, where Tang was on the late shift, from 1:00 a.m. to 5:00 a.m. Tang was Thai, but he spoke Khmer. Stoop shouldered and missing three front teeth, he was a paunchy and short man whose primary job was to keep the crew in line.

In choppy English, Tang told me that deep-sea captains are under intense pressures. Caught fish don't keep for long, he explained. Melting ice in a fishing boat hold is a race against the clock. As fish thaw, their protein content falls, taking their sale price with it.

Globally, fishing boats had to venture farther just to break even. Fuel costs typically eat up at least 60 percent of a long-haul vessel's earnings, double what it did two decades ago. Thai-flagged boats, for instance, used to fish mostly within two days' travel from shore. By 2005, they were venturing as far as Bangladesh and Somalia, staying at sea sometimes for years. Despite its dependency on bonded migrants and outdated boats, the Thai fishing fleet grew into a global player.

Most deep-sea fishing ships around the world work on commission. "Crews only get paid if we catch enough," Tang explained. This means tensions run high on the boats, and captains fear their crews as intensely as they drive them. Language and cultural barriers add further divisions; most boats have three Thai officers (the captain, the engineer, and the first mate), while the rest are foreign migrants.

I asked Tang why discipline tends to be so heavy-handed on board. With visible annoyance at the question, he recounted a story of a gruesome mutiny by a crew of Burmese and Cambodian men who, wielding a dull machete, butchered their ship's three Thai officers. He cocked his chin in the direction of a handgun lying on the dash near the wheel. "You have to show them," he said about teaching the crew a lesson. The nonchalance on his face reminded me of a saying that truly dangerous men are not of a certain size but of a certain look.

From what research I could find, it seemed that mutinies are not common on Thai fishing boats, but over the past decade and a half two out of every five pirate attacks worldwide took place in the South China Sea. My suspicion when I read that statistic was that it was another case of skewed data and in fact what Thai authorities categorized as piracy was actually more likely mutiny. Pointing through the front window, Tang said, "Very dangerous." It was unclear whether he meant the men, the work, or the region. Whatever his meaning, he also seemed to be warning me not to cross him.

I still wasn't ready to go back to bed, so I climbed the stairs to the captain's quarters and knocked on his door. He invited me in. We were moving from one fishing ground to another, and he was staring at several monitors. One showed the weather; the other, the schools of fish in the waters below. Chain-smoking, he occasionally poked a button or adjusted a knob. We sat silently as I waited to ask him questions, a show of respect for the quiet he needed to do his work. After about twenty minutes, he looked at me and smiled slightly, a sign I took as a gentle invitation to talk. So, I recounted to him some of what Tang had said.

Tales of forced labor were not always what they seemed, the captain told me. Some migrants signed up willingly, only to change their minds once at sea because the work was so hard or they did not realize they would be away from home for so long. Other migrants made up stories of mistreatment in hopes of getting a ticket off the boat to go back to their families, he added.

In the weeks before boarding the purse seiner, I had spoken to half a dozen other captains in Songkhla. All of them agreed that forced labor was common and unavoidable—an unfortunate consequence of the country's rapid economic growth over the past two decades. Every time a boat docked, they fretted that their willing workers would bolt to better-paying ships. This was also when captive migrants often made a run for it back across the border, trying to get home.

Shorthanded at the eleventh hour, captains sometimes took desperate measures. "That's when they just snatch people," one captain explained to me with remarkable candor, referring to cases where workers were drugged or kidnapped and forcefully put on boats. In these cases, brokers charged double, he said.

. . .

After two days aboard the purse seiner, Dean, the translator, and I returned to shore. We had accomplished what we had set out to do—witness firsthand life at sea on a long-distance ship—but the reticence of the crew and the evasiveness of the captains didn't bring into clearer focus the abuses I had heard about. Still, as I waited to climb off the ship, one of the Cambodians mentioned in passing that his debt was bigger, his bondage more difficult to escape, because he had been held for several weeks by his trafficker at a karaoke bar before being sold to a fishing captain.

This was new—I hadn't heard before that karaoke bars played a role as a staging ground in the human-trafficking pipeline. Intrigued by this tip, I headed next to Ranong, a town along the Thai-Myanmar border, hoping to see how these watering holes double as brothels and debt traps. Infamous for corruption, Ranong was a notorious place where traffickers operated with impunity and immigration officers were more predators than protectors.

The karaoke bars we planned to visit catered primarily to locals. Dean is white and British. I am American and of mixed race: black Latino father, white Irish mother. Needless to say, we stuck out in

Ranong. The *Times*'s rules dictated that reporters answered accurately if ever asked whether they were journalists. Reporters did not, however, have to volunteer that information unsolicited. Once I started talking in any depth to a potential source, I was usually transparent about my purpose, but I generally tried to be discreet and avoided announcing my employer to the general public unless it was necessary. So, as we sat for drinks at these bars, Dean and I carried ourselves as though we were two somewhat clueless travelers out for a good time.

The bars generally looked the same: multicolored lights strung near the door, and a dark front room with a big, boxy karaoke machine topped by a screen blaring pop songs in Thai, Burmese, or Khmer. Toward the back was a hanging, beaded partition in the doorway, leading to a hallway of rooms where the men went for sex.

At a karaoke bar that doubles as a brothel in Songkhla, Thailand, trafficked women and girls are sometimes used to ensnare trafficked Burmese men and boys.

At one tavern, a man whose forearms were the size of my thighs sat out front, holding a black wooden baton, looking like Cyclops guarding his cave. A group of scruffy men who seemed one six-pack of beer away from trouble stared at us from nearby. We went inside and the tavern owner, who was named Rui, sat down to make his pitch. Smiling, he gestured to two prepubescent girls sitting in the corner, wearing caked-on makeup and tight, glittery miniskirts. He then proudly spread across the table a stack of Polaroids of the girls, each looking scared and clutching a stuffed animal. The pictures were taken a year earlier, Rui told me, pointing at the girls now and seeming to want to show off how much he had improved them. "Popular," he said. "Very popular now." I tried to hide my revulsion that he was peddling children for sex. It was one of many moments during this reporting when, though I was a journalist and my job was to bear witness, I felt guilty for not doing something more to stop what was happening before me.

In port towns like Ranong, there was a hand-in-glove relationship between labor brokers and karaoke bar owners. Often they were the same person. Usually in the very back or upstairs at the bars, there were spare rooms where the girls lived and where men being trafficked onto fishing boats also waited during the final leg of their trip from the border to the port. In some cases, the men were shanghaied at the brothels or drugged, only to wake up later far from shore. More often, though, kidnapping wasn't necessary—debt was enough to entrap the men.

Beer at Rui's tavern cost the equivalent of $1. Sex with a "popular" girl: $12. After a couple of days, these tabs added up to kingly sums for the tattered Burmese and Cambodian men, many of whom trekked hundreds of miles by foot, not a cent on them, hoping for work. Meals, drugs, and lodging offered at first as free favors showed up later as unpaid fees. To clear these bills, migrants were then sold to the sea. When the men came back to shore between fishing trips, ship captains also often paid them not in cash but in credits at the karaoke bar.

Of all the evil things I saw while reporting for this book, the karaoke bars in Ranong were perhaps the most sinister. Not only did these brokers and bar owners use one type of trafficked migrant to entrap another type of trafficked migrant, but the sex workers and their indebted clients were both, quite often, children. When I finally left Ranong, I hoped never to return.

·  ·  ·

And yet sometimes the darkest places create the truest heroes. When deckhands fled their captains, their best hope to escape could be found in an underground railroad of anti-trafficking advocates who operate safe houses near ports. These advocates hide sea slaves and often orchestrate their clandestine passage back home across the border. Once they decided to flee, captive workers typically jumped from their boats and swam to shore, or they stowed away on mother ships that visited their captains with supplies. Having paid hefty up-front fees for the men, captains viewed such escapes as a type of theft. So they usually kept their crews under guard and in locked rooms while in port.

To better understand how these men escape, I traveled to Borneo in November 2014. The world's third-largest island (after Greenland and New Guinea), Borneo's roughly 287,000 square miles are divided between three countries: Indonesia, Malaysia, and Brunei. I chose Borneo simply because I had a source in Kota Kinabalu, the capital of the Malaysian section of the island, who was part of this underground railroad. Like most people who do this risky work, my source asked to remain anonymous.

In Kota Kinabalu, I met a thirty-eight-year-old Cambodian deckhand named Pak who said that during his year of captivity on a fishing boat he had been temporarily dropped off for several weeks on what he and other migrants called a "prison island." One of thousands of mostly uninhabited atolls in the South China Sea, it was a place where fishing captains routinely disembarked captive workers, sometimes for weeks, while their vessels were taken to port for repair. Typically, the captain would leave the crew with a guard who was equipped with water, canned goods, and means to fish. The guard ensured that the men were fed and that none of them tried to leave with another boat. Pak did not know the name of the atoll where he was left, but he said there were other crews there, being sold between boats or waiting for their next deployment.

"You belong to the captain," Pak told me about his time at sea after he was held on the prison island. "He can sell you if he wants." He recounted having watched a man, racked by desperation, jump overboard and drown. Pak eventually escaped his captain by also leaping over the side of his Thai trawler and swimming what he thought was nearly a kilometer to one of the remote Kei Islands, in Indonesia's eastern Banda Sea between East Timor and New Guinea.

The UN estimates there are over a thousand migrants who over the past decade have escaped fishing boats on the sparse but livable Kei Islands. I was surprised by the daring and desperation of Pak's decision to jump overboard not long after having watched another man drown doing the same thing. I made a remark to this effect, and he replied that he did not know if he would survive swimming but he did know that he would die staying on the ship.

Several days after I interviewed Pak, my primary source in Borneo called me at my hotel at 6:00 a.m. He said a recently escaped deckhand was hiding a hundred miles outside the city. "I will be there to pick you up in twenty minutes," he said. For the next three hours, we rode in the back of a flatbed truck deep into a wooded area. When we arrived at the house where the runaway was supposed to be hiding, a weeping and panicked woman emerged. She was a relative of the runaway's and said that two armed men had visited her house the night before and taken the deckhand away.

"What do I do?" she kept asking. My source sat with her for a while and gave her phone numbers of some other rescue workers to contact. We climbed back into our truck and left. "He's either back on a boat or locked down somewhere," my source said. "Either way, it's really bad." Captains paid good money for the crews they enslaved, and they did not often allow escape to go unpunished. A painfully heavy silence rode with us during what seemed like a much longer drive back to Kota Kinabalu.

Before traveling to Borneo, I had interviewed other rescuers in the Thai port cities of Samut Sakhon, Songkhla, and Kantang. Their work consisted of a life-or-death version of hide-and-seek. Several times a week they received a panicked and whispered call from a runaway, who rarely knew his location but urgently needed help getting away from a ship. Typically, the runaway had slipped out of port and was hiding in a nondescript field or was locked somewhere in a bathroom, under a porch, or in an abandoned building. The lucky ones had been equipped by other deckhands with cell phone numbers for advocacy groups like Stella Maris.

Once they found the runaway, the advocates' first step was to get him off the streets and keep him out of sight. Local motorcycle taxis often doubled as informants for the traffickers, they explained. If they could sneak away from the port, many of the runaways tried to survive in the woods until they felt as if enough time had passed that they could safely emerge. Patima Tungpuchayakul, a rescuer from a Thai organization called the Labour Rights Promotion Network, described the case of a Thai man whom she helped return home from an Indonesian island called Ambon. He had fled a ship and survived in the woods for nearly a year by eating dogs and cats that he captured at night from villages.

The day before I was due to leave Borneo, my cell phone rang again. My source picked me up and we drove for several hours, this time into the mountains to an area of sprawling rubber plantations. On either side of the dirt road were straight and narrow rows of tall, skinny, speckled trees, stretching for miles. The trees were striped diagonally with bark incisions deep enough to reach the latex without cutting into the sap vessels. These cuts slowly bled a viscous milky goo into small "tapping" buckets strapped to the lower trunks. This goo was then coagulated with chemicals and rolled into two-by-three-foot rectangular mats that were hung on clotheslines to dry before shipping.

The farms were orderly and sparse, though their huts seemed rudimentary and barely livable. The few tappers we drove past looked dirty, tired, and poor as they stared back at us, puzzled to see an unfamiliar truck in these remote parts. When we finally arrived at our destination and climbed out of the truck, I was immediately met by thick, acrid air—a smell that came from the putrefaction of bacteria in the tapped latex. Those mats were then cleaned and sold to rubber wholesalers.

We were waved into a nearby forty-square-foot hut. Topped by a corrugated-metal roof, it was dark inside and filled with mosquitoes. We sat on a dirt floor with a Cambodian deckhand in his mid-thirties. Missing several front teeth, he had deep bags under his eyes, and his skin bore an unhealthy yellowish tint. He swallowed often, perhaps out of nervousness.

"Did you run away from a boat?" my source asked him in Khmer. "I am running now," the man replied before telling a story that echoed what I had heard so many times before from other escaped deckhands. He had been promised a construction job by a man in Myanmar, only to wind up on a Thai fishing boat. "Screaming, hitting, punching, kicking, no food some days, no water if he's angry," the man said, recounting the captain's treatment of his crew. Finally, two weeks earlier, the deckhand saw his chance and he leaped at night into the sea, swimming to a nearby island to escape his captivity. He hid in the woods for a week until he found a local fisherman who seemed kind and gave him a ride to Borneo.

We never quite got to the issue of why he was staying at this rubber plantation. Half an hour into our conversation, two men knocked on the hut door. Clad in blue jeans and with sunglasses perched on their heads, they were better fed and dressed than the local tappers that I'd seen on the drive in. But these men were also too young and casual to be plantation owners. I caught a glimpse of holstered guns on their belts beneath their untucked T-shirts, before they waved for the worker to step outside with them.

I asked my source what was going on, and he gestured to me, finger to his lips, to be quiet as he tried to eavesdrop through the door. After a couple of minutes, our menacing visitors came back into the hut, and the taller one, who seemed to have rank over his partner, stared at me. "This interview is over," he said in perfect but accented English. "Excuse me," I said, standing up and staring back at the taller man. As my mind raced to figure out how to argue my case, the smirk on his face suggested that he almost hoped I'd push back or escalate things.

Mostly, I worried about leaving the deckhand. I turned to my source and quietly told him that we could leave but not without the deckhand. The armed man intervened as we gestured to the deckhand to quickly follow us to the truck. "No, this conversation is over," the armed man said to me, adding that the deckhand would stay back. "We can't let this be," I said to my source. After a few more tense words with the visitors, my source turned back to me and said that we didn't have a choice. "We need to leave immediately," he said.

On the drive back to the city, my source said that those men were most likely serving as bounty hunters on behalf of the fishing boat captains. I couldn't help but wonder whether I might be the one inadvertently tipping off the traffickers. Had I just killed that man? Through my actions, did I just sentence him to a return to slavery? These were deeply troubling questions. I trusted my source's discretion and thought we were taking all the necessary precautions to ensure the safety of the people we interviewed. We had used different and vetted drivers each time. On the second trip, I was picked up away from my hotel and in a vehicle with tinted windows and local license plates.

My source, who had been doing rescue work for over a decade, said he did not think we were the problem. It was likely that the traffickers already knew about the deckhand's location and they were waiting for an opportune moment to take him back to the boat. "These are small places," he said. "News travels fast." I suggested that we contact the police. My source looked at me with surprise, or maybe disdain. "Ian," he said, "those were the police."

. . .

In the summer of 2017, I returned to South Asia for more reporting on maritime slavery. In preparation for the trip, I had asked the Thai government if I could watch how it conducted spot checks on fishing boats at sea. The government said I was welcome to join it on patrols and that it would board and inspect whichever ships I chose, so long as the vessels were not too far from shore.

It was an unusually accommodating response. Thailand's sea slavery problems had garnered international attention. Thai news outlets and nonprofit groups, followed by *The Guardian,* National Public Radio, and international organizations like EJF, did some of the earliest and best reporting on these labor abuses. In 2015, in addition to the coverage of the issue in *The New York Times,* an intrepid team of Associated Press reporters did groundbreaking work exposing the stories of dozens of men on the Indonesian island of Benjina who had fled, been abandoned, or in some cases been imprisoned by fishing companies. Their work, which won two of the highest awards in American journalism, a Pulitzer and a Polk, led to thousands of such men being repatriated to their homes in Indonesia, Myanmar, and elsewhere.

In returning to Thailand, I knew that much of what I would see during an at-sea embed with Thai authorities would be purely for show. Still, it seemed worthwhile because any mistakes the government made when it was trying its best would be especially instructive. "You will need to supply us with the list of ships," the government kept reiterating as the visit approached. I knew which ships were at sea because most were publicly broadcasting their positions. I hoped to board any of the ships that had reputations or prior records of abuse. I told the government that I would put forward some names of ships that I considered, based on my own reporting, worthy of boarding. But I added that I also expected the government to come up with its own, longer list. As we got closer to the date when we were supposed to leave port, however, the government still had not produced its own target list.

I had mistakenly assumed that based on its interviews with workers, as well as records of port inspections, prior violations, and ongoing police investigations, the Thai government would be able to prioritize the fishing companies or ships that it should be inspecting. It was not. This type of intelligence was either not being collected or not organized in a way that would allow the government to focus its attention on the highest-risk vessels. "We will be relying on your list," one navy official told me days before we were due to launch. I quickly turned to local anti-trafficking groups to help me cobble together additional options of ships to board. Drawing mostly from interviews they had done with recently escaped deckhands and by tapping local police whom they trusted, these advocates produced in forty-eight hours the list that federal authorities had not been able to compile in three weeks.

This lapse spoke to a broader shortcoming in Thai policing efforts. Corruption eroded trust between agencies, curbing their willingness to hand over sensitive information for fear of leaks. Thai authorities relied far too much on human rights advocates for information about how men were being trafficked, who the main culprits were, and what tactics were being employed to circumvent new protections. To gather its own intelligence, the government would need to interview workers, which it was still not doing effectively.

This was especially apparent during the week I spent at sea on two Thai navy ships. A team of inspectors from the fisheries and labor departments conducted half a dozen spot checks on fishing ships that typically had crews of about thirty men and boys, mostly Cambodian and some Thai and Burmese. Most of the ships were large purse seiners—lumbering beasts as sturdy as bulldogs, stacked impossibly high with dozens of royal blue barrels for storing the caught fish on ice below deck. Before inspectors could board the ships, a heavily armed, flak-jacketed security team spent twenty minutes patting all the fishing crew down, checking for weapons, barking at them to sit in a tightly packed group, facing away from us. This step made sense from a security perspective, but it also put the crew on edge and gave them the impression that they were the ones under suspicion rather than the fishing ships' officers.

At one point, I stood alongside a captain in the wheelhouse of a purse seiner as inspectors conducted their sweep. The captain's clothes reeked of cigarette smoke, his breath was stale, and empty cans of Red Bull littered the floor around his feet. In front of the wheel were five human skulls, which the captain said he kept for good luck, having pulled them up in nets. The story seemed dubious to me. Quietly, I surmised that the skulls were more likely meant as a reminder of the consequences of insubordination.

On deck, the thirty Cambodians were a haggard crew. Some of the men seemed unusually determined to avoid eye contact. Each inspector carried a small binder and ran through a questionnaire. Contract? Check. Recent payment? Check. Crew manifest? Check. Nets the right size? Check. At one point, I asked a captain if he thought any of the workers on his ship might be unhappy and want to go home. "They cannot," he told me. "My papers are all in order." His remark inadvertently summed up for me why these inspections seemed to miss their mark.

Thai police board a Thai fishing ship, and the mostly Cambodian crew are instructed to wait in a corner.

One of the differences between a paperwork exercise and a proper inspection was how the questions were asked. For example, when two workers gave different answers about wages and neither answer matched the contract, did the inspector dig further or coach the workers to the "right" response? When workers were asked whether they were being beaten, were they told first that they would be removed from the ship and taken to safety if they answered yes?

The labor department inspector was an older man, with a warm demeanor, who went to great lengths to reassure the crew that he was there to help them. He sat on the floor, smiled often, and made self-deprecating jokes. In a fatherly tone, he lectured the crew on the importance of getting enough sleep and keeping track of their hours—well-meaning but pointless suggestions for the crew, because they had no control over either. I stood with a translator off to the side and listened.

The inspector carried out his work gently and genuinely, but the process felt more perfunctory than investigative. His leading questions demanded facile yes or no answers: "You worked just twelve hours on and then twelve hours off, correct?" and "Everybody's happy on your boat, right?" If a worker had a government-issued identity card, the inspector seemed to take it to mean he was not trafficked. Such cards only indicated that the workers were documented, and not, for example, whether they were debt bonded or sold by a trafficker to a captain. Questions that should have been broad were often narrow. They asked, "Are you injured? Is anyone on the ship hurt?" A more effective line of questioning might have been this: "I know the work can be difficult and dangerous out there. When was the last time a worker on your boat was hurt? What happened?"

Terms that should have been red flags went unnoticed. Thai law required employers to pay workers monthly. Captains were not allowed to withhold wages, which they often did to keep crew from leaving before their contracts ended. In interviews, when workers mentioned their accounts having been "cut" or "cleared" after long fishing trips, a telltale sign of withheld earnings, the inspector did not stop them and dig deeper. As I watched hours after hours of these at-sea inspections, I wrote notes furiously fast, trying to keep track of the problems I saw. I remained deeply impressed that the Thai authorities were being so open but disappointed by the execution of many of their reforms.

The inspection team did not include a Cambodian or Burmese interpreter, which meant they typically relied on the ship's bosun—guys like Tang, whom I'd met previously on the ship with Cambodian boys—to translate what deckhands were saying. On Thai fishing ships, the bosun is often the same ethnicity as the crew and is bilingual in Thai and his native tongue. He is also often closely allied with the officers and in charge of administering discipline. To get honest answers about beatings, withheld wages, hours worked, disappearances, or injuries, the bosun was precisely the wrong person to use as a translator. Instead, he should have been separated from the rest of the workers during the interviews.

To interview every crew member on the ships we visited would have taken hours. The inspector had only enough time to talk to a select few. Several of the crew looked especially nervous. Two seemed quite young, maybe fourteen or fifteen years old. Three of the deckhands looked dangerously exhausted or drugged out, barely able to sit up, their eyes drifting shut. Many of the men clearly did not speak Thai and seemed to be hiding in the back row behind their peers. Instead of selecting any of these workers for interviews, the inspector chose the ones who made eye contact, spoke more, sat up front, and appeared ready and eager to engage. This struck me as backward. Wasn't the goal to find the crew members who were in the worst shape, not the best?

Back on shore, I contacted Jason Judd to discuss what I had seen. Judd was a program manager based in Bangkok who worked for the International Labor Organization, or ILO, a branch of the UN. Part of his job was to push Thailand to reform its labor laws and improve its inspections. We discussed two major legal hurdles. The first was Thailand's prohibition on migrant workers joining unions. The second was the fact that while the country had a law against trafficking, it lacked one on forced labor. So if workers took jobs willingly but were then abused or held captive, the government had little recourse to prosecute.

Judd also described how far Thailand had come in just two years. He pointed out that the government had imposed a thirty-day limit on how long a ship could stay at sea and banned transshipment—transferring goods at sea between ships—for its overseas fleet. The government was trying to register all commercial fishing ships with unique numbers, like license plates, and requiring them to have VMS, which is an electronic tracking system for onshore monitoring.

Aside from inspecting hundreds of vessels at sea each year, the government was conducting similar worker interviews on land. An interagency collaboration overseen by the Royal Thai Navy, Thailand's PIPO, or "Port-In, Port-Out," checkpoints reportedly inspected every fishing vessel weighing thirty or more gross tons each time it entered and left port. PIPO officials checked fifteen different aspects of each boat, from the vessel registration and engineer's certificate to the crew manifest and safety equipment.

These were genuine accomplishments. For all the critical attention focused on Thailand, most other countries in the region, including Indonesia, which had been widely praised by the environmental community for its fisheries management, lacked any of the labor protections or spot checks that Thailand had implemented.

But I also described to Judd some of the problems I saw during the Thai inspections. He followed up by sending me statistics that pointed to a stark disparity in perspectives on the sea slavery problem in Thailand. When the Thai Ministry of Labor conducted over fifty thousand inspections of fishing crews in 2016, it found not a single instance of laws being broken on matters such as conditions and hours of work, wages, and treatment on board. On the other hand, when the ILO interviewed the same types of workers from the same period, it revealed a very different picture. Nearly half of the workers had illegal deductions being taken from their wages, less than half the workers could recall having signed a contract, and about 16 percent had their identification documents taken away by employers to ensure they stayed on the boats. The contrast in these two sets of statistics said a lot.

The Thai government was getting a different impression during its worker interviews because it was asking superficial questions. And this was affecting the ability of Thai authorities to decide which ships to target, which fishing companies to prosecute, and which migrants to rescue. Judd suggested that it would help to hire more interpreters who spoke the languages of the boat workers and who were independent from the government so that workers might trust them enough to answer questions honestly. Inspectors needed better training on how to spot warning signs. They also needed to learn how to push workers hard enough to break them from their rehearsed scripts, without causing the conversations to descend into frustrating games of wits.

But it also mattered how interviewers envisioned their mission, Judd added. Did inspectors think they had permission, the duty even, to find abuses? Were they looking for wrongdoing, or were they marching workers through questionnaires? Did success mean finding more legal violations or fewer?

Part of my challenge in answering these questions was their framing. There was, in fact, no unified Thai government approach to combating sea slavery. Different agencies were committed to differing degrees. The Foreign Ministry and the prime minister seemed genuinely dedicated to reform; the department of labor, not so much; the fisheries agency and much of the police force were somewhere in between. This problem was by no means distinct to Thailand, but the stakes were far higher.

. . .

On November 7, 2015, the Thai government arrested eight persons for human trafficking tied to a company called Boonlarp in Kantang, a port city along Thailand's southwest coast. Among Thailand's most high-profile trafficking cases, the arrest attracted international attention to the problem of sea slavery. The case represented the first time the Thai government had targeted high-level company officials on trafficking charges rather than just low-level labor brokers. Six persons were convicted, including the former owner of Boonlarp, Sompon Jirotemontree. Three captains and one security guard were acquitted.

I went to Yangon, Myanmar, in May 2017 to talk to half a dozen of the men who had previously been trafficked to Kantang, most of whom worked at Boka Pier, which was owned by Boonlarp. All of the Burmese men I interviewed complimented the Thai government for trying to prosecute their former employer. However, several were critical of the fact that the charges filed were for trafficking rather than murder. This meant that some of the worst culprits got away without jail time.

The workers cited one name in particular: Liam. Notoriously brutal and short-tempered, Liam, who also went by Beh Gyan Gyi—Burmese for "wicked man"—was the senior security guard at Boka Pier. Though he had been acquitted on trafficking charges, Liam allegedly committed over a dozen murders, dating back to the 1990s, typically shooting, stabbing, or beating migrant workers to death, occasionally in front of multiple eyewitnesses, before throwing their bodies into the Trang River, according to EJF and Thai police records. And yet, while the allegations against Liam were clear and well documented, Thai authorities had never prosecuted him. Getting witnesses to testify was a difficult challenge, these authorities told me.

Some of the eyewitnesses to these murders were among the men I went to Myanmar to interview. The most gruesome murder they described happened in 2013 and involved a Burmese worker who had allegedly pulled a knife on a boat captain. Near Boka Pier, Liam chained the man, who was in his twenties, to a large fruit tree called a *thit-to* in Burmese or "santol" in English. His hands were tied behind his back around the trunk, several of the men told me. As dozens of workers watched, Liam beat the man to death with an iron rod. "It took a half hour," said Tun Nge, one of the Burmese deckhands I interviewed.

"How tough are you now?" Nge recounted Liam yelling as he hit the man. After the beating, the man's body was left, tied upright, for over an hour for people to see. Shirtless and clad in green shorts, the dead man had gashes on his chest and blood pouring from his head, Nge said.

I had come to know and trust a man named Jaruvat Vaisaya, a lieutenant general and the commissioner of the Office of Legal Affairs and Litigation for the Royal Thai Police. Vaisaya had previously led the federal investigation of the Kantang case. I called him from my hotel in Yangon and asked him why murder charges had not been filed in the Thai government's prosecution of trafficking and other abuses related to the Boonlarp fishing company. After all, the murders were a key part of the forced labor and the trafficking crimes because the violence kept workers fearful and compliant.

Vaisaya told me his team had dug up areas near the port looking for bodies and found none. Workers were reluctant to testify, and the information they did provide was often contradictory, he said. If workers were willing to testify now, Vaisaya added, he would certainly consider reopening the case.

Though Vaisaya, who was based in Bangkok, did not want to say so on record, I knew for a fact that part of the reason murder charges had never been filed was that local police had been tacitly involved. For years, local Kantang police turned a blind eye to the dozens of bodies that washed up on the banks downriver from Boka Pier, many of them showing signs of torture and execution-style killings. Photographs of some of these bodies showed that most of them were buried not at the port but in unmarked graves at a widely known graveyard off the main road to Kantang from Trang city.

Before leaving Myanmar, I asked the workers what they would tell Liam, the guard, or any of the acquitted captains if they ever had the chance. "Everyone knows what you did," one of the workers replied immediately. "You will pay," another said. I was skeptical that anyone would ever pay. Still, I figured the least I could do was deliver the message. So I flew next to Kantang, Thailand. As always, I carried with me the assumption—possibly foolhardy but essential to do this work—that being a journalist and a foreign one would give me whatever protection I might need when I confronted these people.

. . .

By now, many of these Thai port towns looked the same to me, but Kantang was different. Situated at the mouth of the Trang River, the city had an aristocratic grandeur, having been the capital of the district between 1893 and 1916, until frequent floods forced the provincial government to relocate farther inland. Tourists were drawn to the city's old rail station, which was still in operation. Stately but neglected, building facades downtown hinted at old wealth, mostly in the hands of several enterprising Chinese families who still controlled local commerce.

In the world of Thai sea slavery, Kantang was in a category all its own, the biggest snake pit of criminality of all the ports I had previously investigated. In Kantang, the trafficking syndicates were better funded and the corruption wider spread. Part of the reason was that Kantang was a deepwater port that had always been the primary base for Thailand's distant-water fishing fleet. These ships went farther, stayed out longer, and relied far more on trafficked workers.

Kantang's fishing industry was dominated primarily by three Sino-Thai companies, which together operated a mix of fishing vessels, carriers, piers, ice factories, cold storage, processing facilities, and fish-meal plants. These three companies—Boonlarp Fishing LP, Jor Monchai LP, and Wor Wattana Sohpon LP—owned three nearby premises known, respectively, as Boonlarp, Chon Sin, and Wor Suphaporn piers.

"It's a place with lots of temples, not much religion," I'd been told about the city. Along the Trang River was a string of unusually gaudy Buddhist temples, some of them half-built. As much a show of wealth as of piety, these temples were commissioned mostly by the same fishing families accused of using forced labor and engaging in illegal fishing.

Sompon Jirotemontree, the former owner of Boonlarp Fishing, operated one of the many fishing piers lining the Trang River in Kantang, as well as a fleet of more than sixty fishing vessels. A member of one of the most powerful families in Kantang, Jirotemontree served two terms as the municipal mayor, a position his brother Soranont held before him. At the time of the 2013 Kantang trafficking case, Jirotemontree was listed as a "consultant" on the Kantang municipal website. Jirotemontree was also the president of the Trang Fishing Association, and he headed the Council for the Monitoring and Inspection of the Kantang Police.

Much of the trafficking case against Boonlarp was based on investigative work done by EJF, which had provided authorities with a detailed portfolio of worker testimonies and other evidence relating to trafficking, forced labor, and murder. In several reports released between 2013 and 2015, EJF chronicled, in careful and stark detail, crimes committed by Boonlarp, including ones that involved local corrupt officials.

Before heading to Kantang, I hired a very capable Thai interpreter, a young Thai woman who doubled as a fixer, a jack-of-all-trades job that involved handling logistics like drivers, hotels, and government permits. After I emphasized to the fixer the need for heightened discretion, she hired us a driver in Kantang whose regular job was as an undercover narcotics officer. He worked elsewhere in the region and seemed like a good fit because he was armed and less likely to be bribed by locals since he was not from Kantang.

The first order of business was to look for a man named Thaworn Jantarak, one of the acquitted Boonlarp captains, who was reputed to

have been the company's most violent employee. The fishing community was fairly close-knit, and my fixer knew whom to ask at the port for Jantarak's whereabouts. He was not home in the morning but answered the door later that day. Saying he wanted to change clothes before sitting down with us, he emerged a couple minutes later wearing a spotless white short-sleeve shirt with the image and logo of the company that makes Glock handguns. In his mid-fifties, he looked as if he had aged and thinned a lot compared with the photographs of

After gathering witness testimony in Myanmar from a dozen Burmese deckhands who said they had witnessed murder on ships and in port, I sat down with one of the alleged culprits, a notoriously violent captain named Thaworn Jantarak, to get his response to the accusations.

him before he was in jail. He had been incarcerated for nearly a year during the trial that ended with his acquittal.

Jantarak unequivocally denied ever beating his crew, adding that he "always paid them in the end." He had cleaned up his life, no longer drinking or gambling, which was why he said he did not want to discuss the past. When I told him that I interviewed workers in Myanmar who specifically identified him as the most abusive captain in the Boonlarp fleet, he pressed me for the names of the workers. Whenever he claimed that he never used violence, he always followed with "What happens in port is not my responsibility" or "I can't say what others did."

At one point about fifteen minutes into the conversation, Jantarak became very aggressive, accusing me of being from the government and not a journalist. Standing up abruptly from the table and gesturing for me to leave, he darted looks at men standing nearby—presumably relatives, employees, or friends of his—as if to signal them in some way. I quietly motioned for my photographer, Fabio Nascimento, to pull back and get behind these guys in case the meeting turned violent. The conversation ended soon thereafter. For what it was worth, I had laid my cards on the table and passed along the message from the Burmese workers. Jantarak had never broken his poker face.

The next day, after figuring out Liam's home address, we called the undercover cop and asked him to pick us up at the hotel. As we drove, I told him our intended destination, and he promptly pulled the car over in a parking lot. "I can't do that," he said, explaining that Liam was far too dangerous to visit. I reassured him he would not need to knock on the door with us and that he could stay in the car. He still declined. I said that I understood, and we drove back to the hotel, where I paid him the wages I owed him.

I called Vaisaya, my source in the federal police force, to see if he might know another police officer who could drive us to visit Liam. I emphasized that it needed to be someone trustworthy. The goal was to avoid using local police officers for fear they would tip Liam off. Going in a taxi on our own also did not seem safe.

Vaisaya made some calls, and several hours later two uniformed police officers arrived in a tinted van. I had brought a British researcher with me who spoke Thai and knew Kantang especially well. Over coffee in the hotel lobby, the researcher and I explained our plan to the officers, who seemed friendly but quizzical. Before leaving, one of the officers excused himself to visit the bathroom.

"They've just arrived," the officer said in a whispered call from his bathroom stall. What he did not realize was that my researcher, who was fluent in Thai, happened to have headed to the same bathroom moments earlier and was within earshot in the adjacent stall. "We will be there in about thirty more minutes," the officer said. While I worried that we might be walking into an ambush, I figured the more likely possibility was that the officer was simply warning Liam.

Not surprisingly, Liam never came out of his house when we knocked on his door. His wife answered, and we stood with her for forty-five minutes as her story shifted. First, she said Liam was never at that address. While I interviewed her, the researcher spoke to neighbors who said Liam was there every afternoon. Then the wife said that Liam sometimes visited the house but he did not live there. We showed her the photos on an iPhone that we had of Liam from a year earlier at the house. In the photos, Liam wore a checkered shirt and sat on a red scooter. The exact same shirt was hanging on her clothesline, near an identical red scooter parked by the porch. Pointing this out, I tried again: "Are you sure Liam doesn't live here?"

Confident that Liam was likely within earshot, hiding just inside the doorway, we made a point of recounting to the wife the alleged incident involving him beating to death the man chained to a tree. "Everyone knows," I said, telling Liam's wife what the worker had told me. She said nothing. I then asked her if she would allow the two police officers to look inside. "You'll need a warrant," she replied, before ordering us to leave. In the end, nothing Jantarak or Liam's wife said seemed surprising or especially informative. That Liam never came out of his house annoyed me more than I can describe.

By all appearances, the trip to Kantang had been a wash. I still trusted Vaisaya as a source and got reliable help and information from him later in my reporting. But the whispered call from that local police officer in the bathroom stall was nonetheless instructive. That tip-off hinted at one reason why prosecutions by the Thai government were difficult and why it sometimes tackled easier targets, like prosecuting trafficking rather than murder cases. If nothing else, the trip served as a reminder that playing poker is tough when the other side knows your hand.

Governments and legal systems the world over show the value of a human life by handing down penalties to those who abuse it. The relentless gut-punch reality for me, though, was how completely the framework of a civilized society was abandoned at sea, especially on fishing boats on the South China Sea. Thailand, it seemed to me, was genuinely trying to face these realities. But tall obstacles remained, including corruption and ineffective inspections.

Slavery is a harsh reality that our better angels would like to think ended two centuries ago, when many countries passed laws against such bondage within their borders. But this sort of bondage is a global blind spot, because governments, companies, and consumers either don't know it occurs or, when they do, prefer to look the other way.

# WASTE AWAY

You wouldn't think you could kill an ocean, would you? But we'll
do it one day. That's how negligent we are.

—Ian Rankin, *Blood Hunt*

For centuries, humanity has viewed the ocean as a metaphor for infinity. The assumption was—and frankly still is for many people—that the enormity of the sea came with a limitless ability to absorb and metabolize all. This vastness is what lends the ocean deity-like potential. And more narrowly, it is also what has provided us over the years with the license to dump virtually anything offshore. Oil, sewage, corpses, chemical effluvium, garbage, military ordnance, and even at-sea superstructures like oil rigs could disappear into the ocean, as if swallowed up by a black hole, never to be seen again.

I began my explorations of the sea with investigations of the exploitation of men and how life and work at sea damaged them. Over time, I realized the abused fishermen I talked to and the illegal fishing vessels they worked on were just one tiny part of a vast ecosystem. Looking at exploitation of the ocean required looking at the ocean itself—not as a passive backdrop, a canvas for bad behavior, but as a living organism in its own right, a creature that men and women skate across the surface of, like the sea lice that cling to the skin of a whale. It wasn't enough for me to study the lice; I needed to understand the whale as well and how its parasitic passengers were making it sick.

A newly hired engineer on an American cruise ship, the *Caribbean Princess,* Chris Keays was also trying to understand how things work offshore. But on August 23, 2013, he knew immediately that something was amiss in the ship's engine room. The twenty-eight-year-old Scotsman was a low-level engineer who had just graduated from nautical school when he had signed up for what he believed was his dream job aboard the 952-foot-long ocean liner, one of the largest passenger ships on the planet. The famed ship was a floating village, with a mini golf course, a casino, an outdoor movie theater, and nineteen decks, with room for more than three thousand passengers and roughly a thousand crew members.

Keays was on his second stint on the ship, which was twenty-three miles from its destination in Southampton, England, when he went exploring in the engine room. A cavernous three-story maze of tangled metal with massive shiny pipes big enough that a small child could crawl through them, the engine room was located in the bowels of the ship and staffed by four dozen men who were surrounded by dozens of pulsing machines and glowing monitors. Venturing into an unfamiliar section where he did not typically work, Keays saw something that swiftly soured his exuberance over his new job: an illegal device known in the industry as a magic pipe.

From his marine studies in Glasgow, Keays knew exactly what he was looking at. Several feet long, the pipe stretched from a nozzle on a carbon filter pump to a water tank. Its magic trick? Making the ship's used oil and other nasty liquids disappear. Rather than storing the highly toxic effluent and unloading it at port, as the ship was legally required to do, the pipe was secretly flushing the waste into the ocean, saving the ship's owner, Carnival Corporation, millions of dollars in disposal fees and port delays.

"This is fucking ridiculous," Keays said to a co-worker when he saw the pipe. Returning to the scene later when no one else was around, he used his cell phone to take shaky video and pictures of the pipe, as well as photographs of the engine-room computer screen that showed how discharges were being manipulated. To an untrained eye, the pictures, which I later saw in court documents, looked banal: snaking pipes, dials, and holding tanks dotted the image. Keays knew better.

The cruise ship industry is one of the more bizarre creations of modern society, a floating jumble of contradictions. It peddles freedom and exploration, but the actual experience is designed to be predictable, choreographed, and familiar—like a Vegas hotel with an amusement park. It advertises the great outdoors, but mostly keeps people

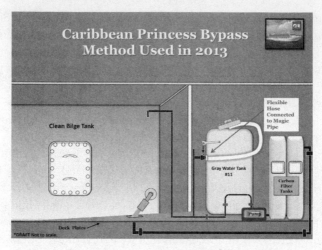

This diagram, drawn by the federal prosecutors involved in the case against Carnival Corporation, the company that owned the *Caribbean Princess,* shows how the magic pipe redirects waste so that it is illegally discharged into the ocean.

distracted from it with ice-cream Sunday bars, waterslides, and go-kart tracks (yes, go-kart tracks). The ships have grown so large that they have become floating cities—holding as many as five thousand passengers—and as with all cities there are parts of them that people would rather not know about, or see. And what happens below the waterline, much like what happens below deck, is out of sight and therefore out of mind.

Passengers may dream of frolicking with sea turtles at ports of call, but many would cringe at what their ships dump into the very same waters these tourists have come to see. The cruise industry represents a kind of gentrification of the ocean; with enough money and steel and aluminum and all-you-can-eat buffets, anyone can enjoy the very best the oceans have to offer without the unsavory parts. The ships are supposed to be self-contained vessels, like campers who have to carry their garbage with them to leave no waste behind. However, the ships often resort to dumping their waste into the ocean when nobody's looking.

Despite their image as safe and squeaky-clean, family-friendly getaways on the high seas, these cruise liners are often massive polluters, and as Keays found out, even the most prestigious are willing to foul the waters illegally. Cruise liners, like most large ships, burn massive amounts of the dirtiest fuel on the market. Known as bunker, this viscous tar is more a solid than a liquid at room temperature and has to be heated for it to flow. Before it is used, the fuel is filtered and spun to remove water, debris, and chemical impurities, a process that produces what is called engine sludge. Disposing of this especially toxic waste is costly.

Cruise liners also produce millions of gallons of oily water. This is the runoff of lubricants and leaks that drip from the ship's many diesel generators, air compressors, main propulsion engines, and other machines and that drain into the ship's bilge tanks. Other liquid wastes accumulate, too. "Black water" refers to sewage from hundreds of toilets flushing day in and day out. "Gray water" comes from washing dishes and clothing for the thousands of passengers aboard, or from the slimy food scraps and grease from the ship galleys and restaurants. Some of these liquids can be released into the ocean after light treatment, but ship engineers are responsible for ensuring that none of the nastiest fluids get discharged. Sometimes, though, these engineers and their companies resort to magic pipes to make those fluids disappear.

After the *Caribbean Princess* arrived in the port of Southampton, Keays alerted British authorities of the crimes, provided them with his photographs and video, and promptly resigned from Carnival, scared for his life if more senior engineers found out he had photographed their handiwork. Because Carnival was an American-owned company, British authorities contacted the U.S. Coast Guard, which opened an investigation.

In subsequent court papers, Carnival called the *Caribbean Princess* an isolated case. But oil logs from the company's other ships, also disclosed in court records, indicated that oil dumping was a widespread practice and that on occasion engineers on other Carnival ships tricked the monitoring equipment by pulling in the same volume of salt water to replace the liquids they dumped.

On the *Caribbean Princess,* the company had installed three separate machines to monitor and collect waste oil, well beyond what was required by law. Carnival often pointed to the additional machines as proof of its commitment to environmental stewardship. Meanwhile, onboard engineers had devised systems to bypass each of the three monitors. After discovering these ruses, federal prosecutors wrote that Carnival, whose income in 2016 was roughly $2.7 billion, had a "high consciousness of guilt." In 2016, a federal judge levied a $40 million fine against the company, the largest penalty of its type in nautical history.

Keays, who is slim and fair with a wide smile and deep crow's-feet around his eyes, was long gone by the time the case was brought against Carnival. He had no illusions about working for Carnival again; in the rough brotherhood of the sea, he was a turncoat. Keays had worried about the safety of his fiancée at the time, who also worked on the ship, and asked her to disembark with him in Southampton when he alerted police. "That might sound overly dramatic," Keays said. "But if you know anything about the culture on some of these ships, you'd realize it's not."

·   ·   ·

A hundred years ago, what happened on the *Caribbean Princess* would have been a nonissue, and the idea of fines might have been laughable. The practice of ships dumping oil and other waste at sea was perfectly legal for most of maritime history. And dump we did. After World War II, Russia, the U.K., and the United States loaded about a million tons of unexploded mustard gas bombs and other chemical munitions onto ships, which were dispatched offshore to scuttle the matériel overboard. Those munitions continue to haunt fishing boats the world over. In 1965, a trawler near Virginia landed a bomb that detonated on board, killing eight crewmen. In 1997, a mustard gas bomb pulled up in a fishing net sent four fishermen off the Polish coast to the hospital. In 2016, the same unlucky catch of a mustard gas bomb off the Delaware coast left a clam fisherman with second-degree burns.

Well into the twentieth century, the rhyming mantra among scientists was "dilution is the solution for pollution." As a result, the more toxic the waste, the more likely the ocean would be its final resting place. More than a dozen countries, including the United States, the U.K., and the Soviet Union, dumped nuclear sludge and unwanted reactors, several still containing their radioactive fuel, into the Arctic, the North Atlantic, and the Pacific Oceans. The practice was only banned in 1993, at which point the remaining business shifted to an underworld of global waste traders operating in the Mediterranean, Southeast Asia, and off the coast of Africa. The most infamous of these syndicates was the 'Ndrangheta, a criminal organization from Calabria,

Across three oceans and two seas, the cat-and-mouse pursuit of the *Thunder* would take
Sea Shepherd's crew on an epic journey through a perilous obstacle course of icebergs,
a violent storm, and a near collision.

The *Adelaide* leaves the port in Ixtapa, Mexico.

Palauan marine authorities approach the Taiwanese tuna long-liner called the *Sheng Chi Huei 12* in Palauan waters.

A crew of Cambodian boys and men, most of them trafficked, work on a Thai fishing ship a couple of hundred miles off the coast of Thailand in the South China Sea.

Working conditions in factories below decks on fishing ships are among the most dangerous of any industry in the world. This undated picture comes from New Zealand authorities who boarded a South Korean ship at sea.

David George Mndolwa in his lean-to near the port of Cape Town, South Africa. In 2011, a couple of hundred miles off the coast of West Africa, Mndolwa and another stowaway were discovered hidden on a ship at sea, put out onto a raft, and left to die.

Before I embarked on some of the more perilous offshore reporting overseas, I did a weeklong embed with the U.S. Coast Guard airborne search-and-rescue team based in Clearwater, Florida, where officers tutored me on what to do if I fell overboard.

The *Bob Barker* hits heavy seas.

In Somalia, some of our guards looked younger than sixteen.

The port of Bosaso in Puntland, Somalia

A port-side karaoke bar in Songkhla, Thailand, that doubles as a brothel. Many of the traffickers who find migrant workers for fishing boats also run these bars. The debt bondage used to trap workers for both industries is similar. Mostly trafficked, the migrant women who are sex workers are used to service and entrap the migrant men, who are also trafficked and eventually dispatched onto fishing boats.

An Indonesian patrol vessel called the *Macan* is parked next to a Vietnamese blue boat that it detained in contested waters. Before they leaped overboard to escape, dozens of arrested crew waited at the back of the *Macan*.

Port workers sort fish in Kantang, Thailand.

In Thailand, many of the worst ship operators famous for illegal fishing and sea slavery are in the distant-water fleet, which is overwhelmingly based in Kantang. Some of these large ships can be seen heading toward port down the Nha Trang River.

Indonesian officers remove deckhands from a Vietnamese fishing boat seized in contested waters.

Men pull anchovy nets in the Sibuyan Sea, off the coast of Kalibo in the Philippines.

On a fishing ship anchored in Songkhla, Thailand, the blue barrels are filled with ice and used to store caught fish in the holds below decks.

Dozens of Vietnamese detainees escape by leaping from the back of an Indonesian patrol ship and swimming toward a Vietnamese Coast Guard ship. Some of the men nearly drown. In the background is a ship that the Vietnamese authorities rammed and sank while an Indonesian marine officer was on board. The officer was captured by the Vietnamese and taken hostage.

Italy, which sank hundreds of drums of radioactive waste in the Mediterranean and off the coast of Somalia, according to criminal prosecutors and journalists who investigated the matter.

And yet, for all the detritus pitched overboard, the worst ocean pollution gets there by air and directly from land. Trash blown from streets and landfills ends up first in inland waterways before making its way downstream to the sea. Much of that rubbish is made of plastic— particularly bags, water bottles, and tiny balls called microbeads found in body washes and facial scrubs—that does not readily biodegrade. Global currents grab, swirl, and accumulate this floating debris, channeling some of it into a Texas-sized gyre, the giant clockwise circuit of currents that revolves between East Asia and North America. The growing awareness of this problem is what has driven companies to move away from plastic, cities to ban plastic bags at stores, and the #StopSucking movement to get restaurants to cease automatically putting a straw in every drink you order. Of course, these initiatives are a mere drop in an ocean-sized bucket.

Airborne pollution is a less visible but even more destructive form of ocean dumping. Over the past two centuries, the concentration of mercury in the top three hundred feet of the oceans has tripled because of human activity, especially the burning of coal. Likewise, carbon dioxide levels in the air have risen about 25 percent since 1958. A great deal of this extra carbon dioxide has dissolved in the oceans, thereby dangerously spiking carbon levels. Carbon dioxide dissolves in water to create carbonic acid and perilously high acidity levels across the world's oceans. Despite the vastness of the sea, these pollutants are affecting marine life and ocean ecosystems, dissolving the shells of many creatures, and leading to hazardous mercury levels in some types of fish.

The real crime of ocean dumping, though, is that it is barely even seen as a crime. Accidents like spills evoke much greater outrage. For all the attention paid to oil spills, for example, the truth is that far more oil is dumped in the water on purpose. Ships illegally discharge more than eighty million gallons of oily bilgewater and engine sludge into the oceans each year, often using magic pipes like the one found by Keays, according to research done at the University of Delaware. In the span of three years, that's more than the amount spilled in the BP and *Exxon Valdez* accidents combined.

Many governments give big industries permission to use the ocean for waste disposal on a grand scale. Off the southwest coast of Indonesia's West Nusa Tenggara province near Bali, for example, a four-foot-diameter pipe runs from the Batu Hijau copper and gold mine into the Indian Ocean. The pipe spews 160,000 tons a day of a toxic sludge, consisting of heavy metals and pulverized mine cuttings, called tailings, into the ocean. At least sixteen mines in eight countries, including Papua New Guinea and Norway, also get rid of mine waste by dumping it offshore.

Much of the dumping from ships is accepted as standard industry practice. To avoid capsizing at sea, for example, cruise ships, cargo carriers, and large tankers have weighed themselves down with ballast since time immemorial. These days, this ballast consists of millions of gallons of seawater that ships suck into their tanks on their way out of one port. Later, they pump it out halfway around the world as they approach the next port. Scientists now know, however, the ruinous effect of this practice on local habitats. This purged water carries invasive species like the zebra mussels that hitched a ride to the Great Lakes from Europe. These mussels have caused over $5 billion in annual damage, clogged water intake pipes, and caused a salmon collapse in Lake Huron that spurred a botulism outbreak that killed thousands of birds.

Ships also dump inordinate amounts of human sewage. In small quantities, dilution does indeed work. But some modern cruise ships now carry thousands of people and flush more untreated waste into the sea than is handled by small-town sewage plants. In addition to this nitrogen-rich sludge from ships, urban sewers spew even larger amounts of toxic runoff into the sea, and farms produce still more in the form of animal manure and chemical fertilizers. Together, this fecund waste spawns red tides and other harmful algal blooms, some larger than California, which rob oxygen from the water, kill sea life, and sicken seafood consumers.

Hardly anything is more toxic than oil, which only became illegal to dump at sea in the early 1970s. At least that's when the international community imposed rules with any specificity. The action came in response to a disaster involving a 974-foot tanker called the *Torrey Canyon* that ran aground off the coast of England in 1967, spilling oil into the English Channel. In a wildly foolhardy gambit to contain the spill, the British government had sent fighter planes to the scene to bomb the ship, intending to set the spewing oil on fire to burn it up and limit its impact on the shoreline. But the bombing campaign instead only worsened the spill, which despoiled more than 50 miles of French and 120 miles of Cornish coast. In 1973, more than a hundred nations reacted to the *Torrey Canyon* disaster by signing a maritime pollution pact called the International Convention for the Prevention of Pollution from Ships, widely known by the shorthand version MARPOL, which governed how oil and other waste on ships should be handled.

Announced with great fanfare, these new rules were supposed to do many things to protect the sea, including stopping ships from heedlessly dumping oil. While MARPOL was a landmark agreement, it governs only the narrow slice of pollution that results from ocean dumping. Ocean contamination comes in myriad forms, and many types of ocean pollution have no rules or regulations. Indeed, part of the difficulty with stopping waste being jettisoned into the sea is defining it; one man's dumping is another man's recycling. Consider the fate of offshore oil platforms once they reach retirement age. By 2020, thousands of these platforms, many of them constructed during a global building boom in the 1980s, will have to be decommissioned. Countries will have to decide whether to sink, remove, or repurpose them.

Few proposals have been put into practice, but there's no shortage of ideas for how to use these aging behemoths. They include high-security super-max prisons accessible only by boat, private luxury homes with 360-degree ocean views, deepwater scuba schools, fish farms, and windmill stations. The option that oil and gas companies generally prefer, because it's cheapest, is to sink the platforms. Many scientists back this approach, too, arguing that it creates underwater marine habitats where fish can hide and mate and provides a foundation for the growth of coral reefs. Scientists also argue this solution is less expensive and carbon intensive than removing the platforms. Just renting the tugboat to tow a rig to shore for scrapping can cost more than $500,000 a day.

. . .

In early 2015, I became interested in these aging platforms. They intrigued me because, according to some conservationists, their disposal represented another type of dumping—beyond that of oil, sewage, mine waste, and ballast—that was occurring offshore and at the edges of the law, sometimes with government approval. At the time,

As part of a broader debate of how to avoid sinking drilling platforms when they become too old, an international architectural group called [AC-CA] held a competition in 2013 to design a new prison on a converted offshore oil platform.

the most vigorous debate about how to get rid of these platforms was playing out in Malaysia, where more than six hundred offshore oil rigs and other structures were due for immediate removal. The Malaysian government said it wanted to avoid sinking them but was unsure of realistic alternatives.

One idea floated by the government was to convert at least some of them into hotels. The only working example of this idea that I could find was called Seaventures, which billed itself as a haven for scuba divers and snorkelers. I decided to visit the platform to see if the approach could be replicated elsewhere. And yes, I confess I was looking forward to spending time at a hotel on the ocean, even if the accommodations were basic, because it would be a nice break from some of the rat-infested ships I had visited.

The closest Malay island to Seaventures is called Sipadan, a speck of an island known as a scuba-diving paradise. It's also known for another reason: in 2000, Islamic militants abducted twenty-one tourists there, holding them in the Philippines. The region has for more than a decade been home to various militant factions, and before heading there, I checked with a friend at the U.S. State Department for an update on security in the area. The friend advised me not to go there because a group of Philippine rebels had recently killed a Malaysian police officer in the area and kidnapped another, who was still missing. I went anyway, figuring I could get in and out quickly and discreetly enough to avoid trouble.

Like a lot of industrial facilities, drilling rigs tend to be located in remote places, where regulations are fewer (or less enforced) and the fees for drilling rights are lower. Seaventures was located off the coast of Malaysian Borneo near the state of Sabah. Getting there took some effort: First, a flight to Kuala Lumpur, the capital of Malaysia. Then a propeller plane to Tawau. Next, an hour's drive to the tiny port city Semporna. Finally, a two-hour boat ride into the Celebes Sea. This was certainly not a hotel you stumble across in your travels.

Reporting the outlaw ocean was nothing if not a lot of travel. It was not unusual for me to wake up feeling as if I were experiencing early dementia as I struggled to recall what country I was in and why I was there. Because I was often bound for ships where quarters would be tight, the trips also presented me with countless hard choices, seeing as how sometimes I needed to fit everything into one big backpack. Better to bring the drone or a wool sweater? Sardines, gum, and cigarettes to break the ice with crew or peanuts, M&M's, and dried apricots to content myself? Fortunately, I didn't need to worry about lugging around water. Most of the smaller boats carried ample bottled water, and larger ships had desalinators or onboard tanks.

A year into the project, I ran out of virgin pages in my passport, having filled them up with stamps from nearly two dozen countries. I ordered a new passport and a duplicate so I could keep one in hand while leaving the other with whatever embassy needed to keep it for two weeks to provide me with a visa for my next stop.

I developed a personal relationship with the security staff at my credit card company. At one point, they froze my Visa card while I was in Somalia due to suspicious activity (mine). This caused me no small amount of heartburn because I urgently needed to use the card to buy plane tickets online and to top up my Skype account to make phone calls. "Your card showed charges coming from the Maldives, Somalia, U.A.E., and Mexico," the Visa fraud alert office said to me at one point during a call. "Can you explain how that's possible?"

As I made my way to Malaysia and then to Seaventures, I contacted several engineers from Malaysian universities who had researched creative ways to deal with the aging platforms. They told me that the best plan was to convert them into aquatic hatcheries, with fish cages that would hang down into the water from the rig. To power any small equipment, like lights or electricity for scientists based on board, the platforms could be equipped with solar panels or wind turbines. The flow of the ocean currents would wash away the fish feces that tended to accumulate in onshore fish farming and create severe health hazards, they explained.

The argument against repurposing the platforms—for scuba hotels, fish farms, solar platforms, or anything else—was that the metal on these structures, some as long and wide as a football field, corrodes and leaches dangerous pollution over time. "Oceans shouldn't be junk yards," said Richard Charter, a senior fellow at the Ocean Foundation, a marine research and advocacy organization. Sinking the rigs so that they could become scaffolding for reefs was an equally bad idea, he contended. Collapsing the rigs onto the seafloor does not actually promote aquatic life; it just attracts fish, which makes them easier cap-

Located off the coast of Malaysian Borneo near the state of Sabah in the Celebes Sea, Seaventures is a former oil-drilling platform that has been converted into a dive resort—one of the many creative answers to how to dispose of these structures when they reach retirement age.

ture, he said. While the rules surrounding maritime dumping have come a long way in recent decades, he added, energy companies and other industries are still permitted to jettison things at sea like mining waste, sewage, and old equipment that they would never be allowed to abandon on land.

The other critique of sinking platforms at sea was that the practice encourages more drilling. By sinking the platforms or converting them into hotels, companies (and consumers) save money on disposal that makes it more profitable to extract more fossil fuels. The repurposing of platforms also shifts the burden of long-term maintenance and liability from energy companies to the public.

When I left Semporna by boat, I could see the rig far in the distance, a spidery fleck on the horizon. As happened when I visited Sealand off the coast of England, the rig slowly took shape as my water taxi drew closer, but unlike Sealand, Seaventures was set in a tropical heaven, the sun beaming down on me, the ocean a sparkling aqua bath, as tempting for a swim as the dark, turbid waters of the North Sea were uninviting.

The platform resembled a ship on stilts, with a former helipad jutting from the front and angled joists beneath creating the illusion of a boat's prow. The platform had been converted into a combination observation deck and lounge, with a tropical, open-air cabana strung with hammocks in the middle, deck chairs facing out over the water, and potted palms. My boat puttered up directly beneath the rig to a landing platform with old tires for bumpers. After I disembarked from the boat, winches raised the platform up to a lower deck. There were half a dozen Chinese scuba tourists on board. The view from the platform was as breathtaking as the accommodations were spare. Rooms were converted forty-foot steel shipping containers. Gym lockers served as closets. On one of the decks where roughnecks had in years past wrestled with drill bits, guests could now order drinks at a half-moon-shaped bar and listen to reggae.

"No mosquitoes, no flies, no sand to get in your gear, and no tiring yourself out by lugging around equipment before or after the dive," said Suzette Harris, managing director of the Seaventures Dive Rig, listing the hotel's distinct attributes. Room rates were 3,050 Malaysian ringgit (roughly $700) for three nights.

Over dinner, the platform's crew explained that Seaventures' remoteness created logistical challenges. They described a war of attrition against weather and rust. The seawater quickly corroded the platform's metal frame, they said, requiring them to repaint it every several months. The elevator to get from the waterline up three stories to the platform had only recently been repaired after being out of service for several weeks, as Seaventures' crew waited for replacement parts.

That night, after several hours of the best sleep I'd gotten in years, I awoke in my spartan bedroom and went upstairs to wander the upper deck and to see the stars. Instead, I was startled to meet half a dozen men, clad in head-to-toe black military outfits, carrying semiautomatic weapons. For a moment I thought the militants that the State Department had warned me about had crept on board under cover of darkness, but they were Malaysian special forces. One of them told me that the government had sent them to stay on the platform at night to guard against ransom-seeking guerrillas.

It was another surreal scene that I would never have predicted: shooting the breeze with heavily armed soldiers on the deck of a playground for wealthy tourists. I asked a soldier whether he thought other decommissioned platforms like this one might be turned into hotels. He laughed. It would be too costly to deploy that many troops to protect additional offshore hotels, he said. Far easier, he suggested, to sink them.

. . .

After returning from this trip to Malaysia, I recounted to several ocean conservationists what I had learned about the disposal of oil platforms at sea. They were quick to point out that oil companies and governments weren't the only culprits dumping offshore. Researchers and entrepreneurs did it as well, they said, typically under the guise of science. I asked for examples. All of them cited an entrepreneur and marine researcher named Russ George.

In July 2012, George, who had formerly worked managing fisheries, chartered a large boat, loaded it with more than a hundred tons of iron dust, and ferried it to international waters in the Pacific Ocean, hundreds of miles off the coast of British Columbia. He then poured the iron ore into the sea. The experiment's stated goals were to help counter the effects of climate change and to speed recovery of the local salmon fishery for the Haida, the native population of the Haida Gwaii archipelago off the coast of northern British Columbia. The Haida paid George $2.5 million to conduct the experiment. Because he was outside national waters, George said that he did not need, nor did he seek, scientific oversight or government permission for what he described as cutting-edge research. Others criticized it as egregious polluting.

In George's telling, the experiment is a creative and enterprising approach to solving the intractable problem of global warming, and he talks about it with an evangelist's exuberance. By providing missing nutrients to the ocean, he claims, the iron ore was supposed to stimulate a plankton bloom, which, as it grew, would suck up carbon dioxide, much like plants on land. The bloom would serve as a kind of at-sea "pasture" to feed herbivorous species that in turn would feed the salmon, restoring their historic abundance. The plan had an economic aspect to it as well. The Haida had hoped that by capturing carbon in the bloom, they could also sell so-called carbon offset credits to companies and make money for the tribe. Under cap-and-trade programs in various countries, polluters offset their emissions of greenhouse gases by buying credits from projects that store carbon or otherwise mitigate global warming.

Many scientists do not share George's enthusiasm for the experiment, assailing it as unscientific, irresponsible, and a violation of international agreements meant to protect the oceans. Among George's critics were fellow researchers in the geo-engineering field, who in the past had conducted smaller and sanctioned experiments with iron ore dumping, or "iron fertilization."

George's experiments and those of more circumspect, cautious geo-engineers have the same scientific roots. Iron is a trace element necessary for photosynthesis in all plants. It is highly insoluble in seawater and an essential nutrient for phytoplankton growth. Little research had been done on the idea of ocean fertilization until the 1980s, when the oceanographer John Martin published his findings, arguing that a scarcity of iron micronutrients was limiting phytoplankton growth and overall productivity in the ocean's most "desolate" regions. Researchers in this niche scientific field of ocean fertilization posited that this depletion of iron-hungry phytoplankton was worsening climate change. Martin thought he could easily restimulate phytoplankton and slow global warming, quipping, "Give me a half a tanker of iron and I will give you another ice age."

Many scientists feared, however, that George was taking things too far and too fast. They warned that conducting ocean fertilization on such a grand scale could trigger dead zones, toxic tides, and other unintended consequences. Because George did not use a methodology that had been vetted beforehand by the broader scientific community, his findings would not be publishable by a reputable peer-reviewed journal. The absence of oversight and review threw a credible theory into scientific limbo: Was this legitimate science or reckless dumping? Skeptics also questioned the long-term environmental benefits of George's experiment. If the bloom was eaten by the salmon and other fish, they would reemit the captured carbon dioxide as waste, sending it back into the atmosphere and canceling out the climate-change benefits, they said.

Before and since, there was not much that anyone could do to stop George or others like him. He operated mostly in secret, and for what it was worth he had been granted permission by the local Native governing councils nearest to the dumping grounds. The international agreements relating to geo-engineering were nonbinding and unenforceable.

After news of his experiment became public, government responses were mixed. The Spanish and Ecuadoran governments barred George's vessels from their ports. The U.S. Environmental Protection Agency warned him that flying a U.S. flag on vessels used in such experiments would violate U.S. laws. Canada's environment ministry executed search warrants of George's office as part of a still-pending investigation of the experiment. The bad publicity around George apparently soured his sponsors on him and his work. In May 2013, the Haida Salmon Restoration Corporation, the Native company that hired George and permitted his ocean fertilization plan to proceed, cut all ties with him, including removing him as a director.

George subsequently vowed to continue with his work, which he claimed had already provided a wealth of valuable data. Within months of his 2012 ore dump, satellites captured images from space of a plankton bloom spanning an area of nearly four thousand square miles. Alaska reported a record salmon harvest for 2013, which George attributed to his work.

If nothing else, George's experiments represent an aggressive, perhaps quixotic measure in the face of a looming global crisis. As the oceans face catastrophic effects of global warming, should such wild experiments be encouraged, rather than discouraged, to respond to a catastrophe that is taking shape in our lifetimes? Did the ends justify the means? I found it difficult to know whether George's experiment achieved its goals because there was no external oversight or standardized scientific method. It is unclear who, if anyone, could hold George accountable if his experiment caused dead zones or other harm.

What is clear is that as worries about climate change increase, there will likely be more controversial technological experiments at sea beyond the reach of most governments. Renewable-energy firms have started planning wind farms, wave-energy converters, and floating solar panels in international waters. Who will be responsible for cleaning up the contraptions if they do not work, if their companies go bankrupt, or when they become obsolete, like the oil platforms in Malaysia? Who will decide whether these experiments constitute legitimate research or illicit dumping? My hunch was the answer was no one. If individual governments and the international community are unable to address, or even fully investigate, sea slavery, it seemed unlikely they would find a cohesive, effective approach to science experiments in international waters.

Some researchers did contend that the machinery we plant in the ocean to create energy—fossil or renewable—wasn't really dumping per se. My view was that if mankind puts something in the ocean that causes pollution of one kind or another, this is arguably a form of dumping. Maybe it is justified because a greater good comes from the action. But it should be called what it is. The ocean may be vast, blue, and deep, but it's still being used as a junkyard.

. . .

George's iron fertilization fell into a legal gray zone—not permissible, but not quite forbidden either. Other types of ocean dumping are unequivocally against the law. When I met Richard Udell, the federal prosecutor who handled the *Caribbean Princess* magic-pipe case, he was quick to point out that unlike iron fertilization or rigs-to-reefs programs, dumping oil at sea is clearly illegal.

That legal delineation is what makes it possible to catch polluters who use magic pipes. Authorities rarely see the dumping itself because it typically happens far out at sea, perhaps under cover of night, and cloaked in a veil of secrecy and intimidation. In those cases, it's usually the cover-up, not the crime itself, that snags companies, Udell explained. Sometimes a whistle-blower will produce photographs or video of pipes, as Keays did, but often fudged oil record logs produce damning evidence as well. It's the alteration of those logs, which are required under MARPOL, that usually brings hefty fines and sometimes jail time. The logbooks are often so heavily falsified, Udell said, that engineers on a Norwegian cruise liner began calling them *Eventyrbok,* the Norse word for "fairy-tale book."

Law-abiding ships have several options for properly handling the millions of gallons of oily water that they produce. They can run it through a separator, pulling the oil from the water and incinerating the remains on board. Or they can unload the waste for a fee at a port-side waste depot, if one exists. For larger cruise ships, the cost of properly disposing waste onshore can be more than $150,000 per year. Some companies offer their engineers personal bonuses if they stay under budget—creating an incentive to skirt the law with magic pipes and massage the ship's logs to cover it up.

Akin to forensic accountants, magic-pipe investigators employed by the U.S. Coast Guard or maritime insurers comb these records, searching for odd inconsistencies and unlikely consistencies. If the oil record shows a discharge at one latitude and longitude, but the captain's log for the same time says the ship was two hundred miles away from that location, investigators start asking tough questions. Investigators also look for clues of what's called "pencil whipping" or "gun decking," which they describe as lazy bookkeeping with telltale repetitions, like discharges that occur at the same time of day, week after week. Some speculate the origin of the term "gun decking" dates to the practice of painting fake cannon ports on the side of a ship to make it appear to have more guns, in hopes of intimidating any adversaries who might see the images.

Investigators also inspect the ship itself. They hunt for pipes that should show wear but look freshly painted. They check for oil residue on the inside of pipes that shouldn't have it. On the outside of the ship, they watch for "comet streaks" of incriminating oil lining the hull near the overboard valve. They check for scratched and chipped paint on piping and flanges, which might indicate that a bypass pipe was dismantled shortly before inspection. Investigators can often take these measures only when a ship is in port or in national waters. On the high seas, they are not allowed to board vessels without the permission of the captain, and even if they did find evidence of wrongdoing, if it happens outside any country's borders there's no reliable way to prosecute. Sometimes investigators just get lucky, added Steve Frith, a special agent for the Coast Guard Investigative Service in New York who worked the *Caribbean Princess* case. "You get on board and you get a guy just smiling at you," he said. "And then he head-nods you toward evidence."

When Coast Guard officials find enough evidence to seize a ship, they immediately detain and separate crew members from each other. Prodding them to tell the truth is much easier when the crew has less time to coordinate their stories. Investigators test the crew to see if they even know how to operate the oil separator. They also take advantage of the fact that engineers hate statistical anomalies. When ship engineers pretend not to have known about the existence of a magic pipe on

board their vessel, Frith said he plays dumb and tries to gently antago-
nize them into breaking script. "Something just doesn't make sense
here," Frith said, reenacting what he says over and over to engineers
as he confronts them with anomalies in their oil logbooks. "Either this
data is sloppy, you made a mistake, or I'm not understanding something here. Help me out."

In recent decades, the U.S. government has prosecuted over a dozen
magic-pipe cases. All told, these prosecutions have led to more than
$200 million in fines and a total of seventeen years in prison for ship
officers and executives. Part of the success of these cases stems from a
"bounty" provision within U.S. law that permits courts to share up to
half of the money collected in fines with any whistle-blower responsible
for reporting an incident that results in a successful prosecution.

George M. Chalos, a maritime attorney who frequently defends
cruise and shipping companies in magic-pipe cases, said that offering
bounties actually creates more pollution because it provides an incentive for disgruntled crew members to "break the rules, pollute the sea,
and blame the misconduct on others in the hopes of receiving a dis-
proportionately huge reward." There are very few companies that do
not have a strong commitment to protecting the marine environment,
he added. The cost and delays for shipping companies are worsened,
he explained, by a lack of shoreside disposal facilities where ships can
legally and efficiently get rid of their waste.

Chalos's claim that bounties create pollution seemed far-fetched. I
found it unlikely that a crew member at the mercy of his mates at sea
would take such a risk. More to the point, his critiques did not help
me understand the transgressions in the *Caribbean Princess* case. Disposal capacity is not an issue in British ports. It's also difficult to question Keays's motives for blowing the whistle. He reported the crime in
England, which does not offer bounties, rather than waiting a month
longer for the ship to dock in the United States, where he would have
been virtually guaranteed a reward. When I asked Keays if he considered waiting until he was in U.S. jurisdiction, he laughed and said
absolutely not. "You don't get mugged and tell the police a month later,"
he said.

.   .   .

The cruise industry is a lucrative business. With more than 450 large ships globally, the international cruise line industry generates roughly $117 billion of revenue annually. It employs more than a million workers, who cater to nearly twenty-five million customers a year. With any enterprise on that scale, lawbreaking is inevitable. Dumping oil is by no means the only crime that occurs on these ships.

Sexual assaults of passengers and staff on cruise liners, for example, have been especially difficult to investigate and prosecute. Cruise ships are often registered in foreign countries, the incidents occur in international waters, and the alleged perpetrators can be foreign nationals. When Congress held hearings on this problem, lawmakers discovered that nearly a third of the reported sexual assaults on these ships were against minors. When the *Costa Concordia,* another cruise ship owned by Carnival, infamously capsized off the coast of Italy in 2012, investigators uncovered reports of prostitution and Mafia-stashed drugs on board.

For the hundreds of thousands of people who work on them, cruise ships are a world of extremes. These floating resorts are designed for luxury, for leisure, and to make passengers happy. But the crew, which on some ships is more than fifteen hundred people, typically live in a parallel and sometimes bleak universe, kept apart by an elaborate system of hidden stairways and floors that passengers don't know exist. While much of my reporting took me to derelict vessels with decrepit conditions, investigating the cruise industry reminded me that crime— whether at sea or otherwise—can be found behind even the most polished and expensive of facades.

I interviewed a former firefighter who used to work on large cruise liners. He recounted how eastern European women, hired to be servers in the ship's restaurants, were often expected to double as prostitutes for passengers and staff. If these women wanted to switch shifts or bump up to a restaurant with better tips, they had to have sex with certain managers or officers, he said. The ships had strict dress codes for staff, and the in-house laundering services functioned like an extortion racket, he explained. If you didn't pay dues to a certain someone, parts of your uniform went missing or came back with mysterious stains on them, which would get you docked or reprimanded. Such black-market services and payoffs are standard fare in prisons, of course, and not quite what I had expected in floating laps of luxury.

At one point, several Indonesian kitchen staff, who were not allowed to disembark during port calls, asked the firefighter to change money for them, swapping smaller, crumpled bills with crisper ones in larger denominations that got them better exchange rates from banks back home. The firefighter did the favor, because it cost him nothing. Late one night he got a knock on his door. "Do you give them new bills?" the ship's onboard money changer, a muscular, no-nonsense Russian, said in broken English. The firefighter said yes. "No, you don't," the Russian responded. The firefighter got the message.

The engine room on a cruise liner tends to be isolated from the rest of the ship. For safety reasons, it is a "no-go zone" for anyone but the engineers. Loud and unwelcoming, engine rooms are almost always staffed by males of a certain type. These machinery mechanics are older (the work takes more schooling than many other posts). They tend to have longer-term relationships with the vessel (engine quirks take a while to learn, and staff turnover in an engine room can be risky because its machinery is so essential). Their work is dirty (everything is greased, and the place is hot and sweaty) and antisocial (the engines are so loud that ear protection is required).

In the engine-room hierarchy, officers are usually one nationality. In the case of the *Caribbean Princess,* they were Italian. The lower-level workers, like the wipers, boilers, and fitters, tend to be another nationality; on the *Princess,* they were Filipino. More so than deckhands or cooks or even than the senior officers on the bridge, engineers speak a language of their own because the work and the machinery are so technical. The culture of engine rooms makes them close-knit, making it harder for investigators to crack.

In the case of the *Caribbean Princess,* Keays, who blew the whistle about the oil dumping, was a relative outsider. As a young Scotsman with little experience, he was a different nationality and junior to his peers in the engine room. A third assistant engineer, he had only once before worked on the *Caribbean Princess* for several months.

By the time investigators from the U.S. Coast Guard began questioning the crew on the *Caribbean Princess,* it was several months after the crime. The chief engineer and senior first engineer had already ordered the crew to get rid of the magic pipe. The senior engineers had also, one by one, pulled engine-room staff into the hall, to avoid being recorded by microphones in the engine-room office, and told them to lie if asked by investigators about the magic pipe, according to workers who later recounted the incident to prosecutors.

On the *Caribbean Princess,* the chief engineer had two nicknames. The first, his colleagues gave him: *braccino corto,* or "short arm," an Italian expression for a cheap person who can't reach his wallet. The second, the chief engineer gave himself. With new hires to the ship, he warned them that he was known as "El Diablo," due to his short temper and strict expectations.

El Diablo knew what was at stake in the magic-pipe case. At one point, he convened a meeting with his staff in the engine-room office. As he talked about the ongoing investigation of the *Caribbean Princess,* he surreptitiously held up a sign warning them of hidden microphones and to speak carefully, ship workers later told prosecutors. The sign said, "LA is listening," a reference to Los Angeles County, where the company's headquarters were located.

El Diablo's efforts to silence his *Caribbean Princess* crew didn't work. Prosecutors won the case. In the final stages of the case in 2016, Udell wrote to the judge with a special request. Keays had done the right thing, Udell said, and he had done it at considerable risk to himself, for the right reasons, and with no expectation of financial gain. Might it be appropriate to bend the rules, Udell asked, and allow a bounty in this case, even though Keays did not originally report the crime directly to American authorities? The judge agreed, and Keays received roughly $1 million from the penalties paid by Carnival. Keays continued working in the maritime industry but in a shipyard in Spain. "It didn't seem wise to go back to sea," he told me.

Will such penalties deter cruise ships from illegal dumping in the future? Ultimately, it will likely come down to a matter of conscience for cruise ship operators and their employees. Otherwise, the rewards of dumping may indeed be worth the risks. There is money to be saved and made by flushing all manner of waste into the ocean. Generally, it's a crime without witnesses outside the engine room. And what of the victims? Who are they? Hard to tell. Unlike with men trafficked by manning agencies or fishermen killed at sea, the waste spewed into the waves will eventually affect us all. At some point, though, dilution reaches its limits, and it is no longer the solution.

# FLUID BORDERS

Ask no questions, and you'll be told no lies.
—Charles Dickens, *Great Expectations*

I met Susi Pudjiastuti, the minister of Indonesia's fisheries agency, in September 2016 at the Our Ocean Conference in Washington, D.C., an annual event hosted by the U.S. State Department that brings together global leaders, dignitaries, and a few celebrities involved with ocean policy. The two of us were on an afternoon panel, sitting side by side on a stage at the front of a conference hall. Pudjiastuti gave a speech about Indonesia's conservation efforts and how illegal fishing was a transnational organized crime with ties to fuel theft, money laundering, and the drug trade. The audience reacted with enthusiastic applause.

Following her presentation, it was my turn to address the gathering. In my talk, I raised the question of whether the definition of illegal fishing should be broadened to include crimes not just against fish but also against the people doing the fishing. After all, beating crews, not paying them, and depriving them of the right to leave are practices that allow for the artificially reduced cost and competitive advantage that illicit operators have in poaching, I contended. The audience, which consisted largely of people focused on environmental issues and not human rights, reacted to the idea with polite clapping.

After I sat down, Pudjiastuti tapped me on the shoulder. "You need to come to Indonesia," she said. "I want you to see what we're facing." I'd like that, I replied. Eight months later, in May 2017, I was on a plane headed to Indonesia.

Four days after that, I was standing on the back of a patrol ship anchored near the city of Pontianak as the stout captain of the ship paced the deck and roared at his heavily armed crew in the early morning darkness. "We catch the people who steal from us," bellowed the captain, Samson, facing his seventeen men in fatigues, who stood rigidly at attention on the rear deck of the vessel. "Let's catch them on this mission."

Samson, the captain of the *Macan,* points at the much larger Vietnamese Coast Guard ship that is rapidly approaching his vessel.

It was 4:00 a.m., and a weighty heat lay like wet wool over the port on the west side of Borneo, Indonesia's largest island. Samson had decided his ship would leave while it was still dark to avoid tipping off the culprits. Gesturing for his men to gather around him, he put his open hand in the center, and the other men stacked theirs on top, as if in a football huddle. "Guys, this is what we do," he said, lowering his voice. "So, let's just do this as usual." With a loud cheer, the group broke the huddle and prepared the patrol boat to leave.

The patrol boat churned out across the turbid harbor waters, the night-lit gantry cranes along the inner harbor shrinking in our wake, for what should have been a routine patrol looking for foreign ships fishing illegally in Indonesian waters. I was back in Indonesia and had come on board at the invitation of the Indonesian government because

I was curious about the country's rare no-tolerance policy that banned all foreign boats from fishing in its waters. Other countries like New Zealand banned foreign boats from fishing in their national waters, but Indonesia was taking the extra step of sinking or blowing up the ones that it caught breaking this law. I brought my photographer, Fabio Nascimento, and an Indonesian translator with me, a young woman who could help me speak with detained fishermen.

After the patrol headed out to sea, an officer brought me below deck to a nook where he pointed to a spot on the floor. The cramped corner would be my sleeping quarters. Indonesians are not usually tall people; the officers' bunks were too small to fit me, he explained apologetically. The floor suited Nascimento and me just fine, I told him. My translator got a more comfortable, private lodging in the officer's quarters.

It would be hours before the patrol would reach fishing waters and the foreign poachers that trolled there. Dropping my backpack in the spot the officer indicated, I headed back up to the bridge to spend time with Samson, who, like many Indonesians, went by only one name. Having arrested and sunk dozens of illegal ships since he started working with the ministry in 2000, Samson was a legend among the several hundred marine officers who worked on the thirty ships in Indonesia's fisheries fleet. Samson patrolled the most crime-ridden outer edge of Indonesian waters, an area with bigger and more violent poacher ships than those encountered nearer to the Indonesian coast.

Samson's ship was called *Hiu Macan 1,* which means "Tiger Shark" in Indonesian. The crew mostly called it just the *Macan.* Illegal fishermen referred to it as "the Ghost" because it appeared with virtually no warning. Built in 2005, the *Macan* was 117 feet long and relatively fast for its size, with a maximum speed of twenty-five knots. Most of the fishing boats Samson chased had a top speed of about eighteen knots. The Chinese boats were the exception. Not only could the bigger ones reach thirty knots, but their captains were more aggressive and known to ram their adversaries, including foreign military or police ships. This was especially worrisome for Samson because the *Macan* was fiberglass, rather than having a steel hull, and therefore easier to sink. The *Macan* tried to make up for this Achilles' heel by being better armed than most other Indonesian fishery boats. Its forward deck had a mount for a formidable 12.7 mm deck gun, and its crew carried submachine guns.

Samson was forty-seven and the father of two boys; one was a second-year medical student, and the other was in high school. His wife and sister also worked for the fisheries agency. In addition to speaking Indonesian, Samson was fluent in Chinese, having grown up on Kalimantan, the Indonesian area of the island of Borneo and home to many ethnic Chinese. A squat man, his forearms and hands were so thick they looked like machine tools. He had big, expressive eyes, amplifying the impish look that made it seem as if he were perpetually about to crack a joke. He rarely wore his military uniform, preferring loose blue jeans and a black biker shirt that said "Bloody Rangers" and "Flying into the Darkness." His men usually wore flip-flops and shorts.

Samson seemed like an uncle to his crew. Six of the men were his former students. For nearly a decade, Samson taught maritime courses—sailing, chart reading, boat driving—at various Indonesian vocational schools. His men described him as fair, and in a job where respect was a hard-earned currency, Samson was wealthy. The men cited his bravery, levelheadedness, and cooking skills as the foundation of their loyalty to him. Even though he was among the most experienced captains in the country, Samson had repeatedly declined promotions to bigger boats in the fleet, because he felt wedded to this ship and what he called his "family of men." Tracing his hands along its ledges, railings, and walls, Samson knew the *Macan* as much by feel as by sight, and I struggled to keep up when he hustled around. On board, the men worked in four-hour shifts, twenty days on, ten off. Their patrols lasted from several days to a couple of weeks. This crew, most of them in their mid-thirties, had been together since about 2012, but nothing in their experience could have prepared them for what would happen on this trip.

Samson explained that while radar allowed him to see boats in a forty-mile radius, years of practice told him, based on movement patterns, which boats were foreign and actively fishing. A devout Muslim, he got help from other sources, too. On his left hand, a chunky gold ring with the Chinese character *Fu* consistently brought him good luck, he said. Hanging from his belt was a wooden pipe carved from *sentigi* wood that carried magical powers. His bracelet was made from Hercules stone, which he said gave him strength. Around his neck hung a string of bear teeth, a talisman that he said made him fierce.

Earlier in his career, he had been a fishing boat captain for more than a decade, working these same waters for Filipino, Korean, and

Indonesian fishing companies. He joked that he was especially good at finding outlaws because he used to be one himself. "You don't teach a crocodile to swim," he said, to make his point. "They already know how."

.  .  .

Every nation dealt with the problem of illegal fishing in its own way, but none had as draconian a policy as Indonesia. The reason is that the country had an extreme problem. A sprawling nation of seventeen thousand islands, Indonesia is the world's largest archipelago, and for decades its waters were a playground for illegal fishing boats. That changed in 2014, when Indonesia appointed Minister Pudjiastuti, Samson's boss, to head the national fisheries agency. A former seafood and airline industry executive, Pudjiastuti initiated an aggressive crackdown, drastically expanding the number and range of patrols by the fisheries ministry. She banned foreign vessels from fishing in Indonesia altogether and then took a further step to demonstrate the country's seriousness about its new policy. Rather than just arresting ships and sending them home, Pudjiastuti's ministry began burning or blowing them up after removing their crews, broadcasting the events on television and online for the world to see.

Especially by the standards of a conservative Muslim country like Indonesia, Pudjiastuti was an iconoclastic firebrand. She had been kicked out of her preparatory school due to political activism when she was a teenager and had never gone back to school. When we met, she was fifty-one years old and a divorced mother of three. An expert scuba diver and a chain-smoker, she had a raspy voice, a throaty laugh, and a colorful tattoo of a phoenix down her right shin. (It represented "strength and beauty," she told me.) No-nonsense and disdainful of pomp, she had banned her staff from using confusing jargon or what she called "words with wings." The recipient of countless ocean conservation awards, she had become the darling of environmental groups like WWF and Oceana that had struggled for a long time to get governments to take illegal fishing seriously. One of Japan's most reputed comic books, *Golgo 13,* had modeled a character after her. In the comic book, Pudjiastuti wore a beret and sunglasses while she commanded men to blow up a fleet of fishing boats.

Pudjiastuti's assault on illegal fishing did not please everyone, least of all China. A major investor in Indonesia, China had become an increasingly aggressive maritime player—not only globally, but especially in the South China Sea, where overfishing had exhausted catches close to shore. Economic growth in China pushed it to look to the sea for new oil and gas reserves. Both of these pressures had led China to claim sovereignty over rocks, shoals, and reefs throughout the South China Sea.

Generally, China had tried to avoid armed clashes, relying instead on its civilian maritime force—in other words, its million-boat fishing fleet—to establish its foothold in the region. One Asian scholar explained it this way: China is "putting both hands behind its back and using its big belly to push you out, to dare you to hit first." Ultimately, China's goal has been to establish national outposts across an expanded region and to assert renewed ownership over valuable fishing grounds and subsea reserves. And while it's easy to portray China as the villain in this jockeying for control, the truth is that other countries, including Vietnam, Indonesia, and the Philippines, are engaged in the same geopolitical scramble to expand their territorial claims in the South China Sea.

China was different primarily because it was far stronger militarily and economically than these other countries. Aside from having the largest fishing fleet, China had the largest Coast Guard protecting it, including two ten-thousand-ton ships, each more than five hundred feet long. Known in naval circles as the "monsters," these two Chinese patrol ships were enormous, bigger than any non-icebreaker ship in the U.S. Coast Guard. Despite this military might, Indonesia was taking an increasingly firm stand toward China. In her first two years in office, Pudjiastuti sank more than two hundred illegal fishing boats, dozens of them from China.

Tensions between China and Indonesia came to a head in March 2016. Indonesian fisheries police arrested a Chinese boat in what Indonesia claimed were its waters. While the Indonesians towed the Chinese boat back to Indonesia, a much larger Chinese Coast Guard warship intervened and cut the cable that officers had tied to the fishing boat. After the clash, the Indonesian government said it planned to relocate several of its F-16 fighter jets to the Natuna Islands in the middle of the South China Sea to respond if there was another such incident. Confrontations have never escalated to the point where Indonesia needed to scramble its jets to respond to Chinese fishing incursions. Not yet, at least.

I had done a similar journalistic embed in Palau, an archipelago nation with many of the same marine challenges that Indonesia faced. Hundreds of foreign fishing boats raided the waters of both countries each year. Both had taken a hard line on the problem but had impossibly large areas to patrol. The one big difference was that Palau's fisheries force had one patrol boat; Indonesia had thirty. The size of Indonesia's enforcement effort meant that Pudjiastuti's forces were making a lot of arrests—several hundred boats per year, which was creating logistical difficulties, like how to handle the thousands of men being removed from these boats.

Among the hundreds of "sea refugees" held in Indonesian detention centers, like this one in Pontianak, was a boy who could not have been older than thirteen.

Before starting my stint aboard the *Macan*, I spent the day at the Pontianak Shelter, one of the country's five detention centers where these crews were held while the Indonesian government determined their fate. Human rights groups had begun referring to these men as "sea refugees." Because most were deckhands and had no say over where their ships fished, they were not criminally charged with illegal fishing, and they were supposed to be efficiently repatriated as undocumented immigrants. Instead, they were lingering in detention, sometimes for years, forgotten in bureaucratic limbo. Having willfully signed on to the ships, these men were also not trafficking victims, which meant they did not usually get help in the repatriation process from organizations like the UN International Organization for Migration. They weren't criminals, weren't immigrants, and certainly weren't Indonesians. I was curious to see what Indonesia was doing with them.

Pudjiastuti was as frustrated by these sea refugees as the human rights groups were. Their numbers had grown sharply under her crackdown, and handling them was expensive for the Indonesian government. A major reason that it took so long to process and repatriate these men was that the governments from their home countries, particularly Vietnam and Cambodia, did virtually nothing to help in the effort.

Built to house sixty men, the Pontianak detention center was crammed with over twice that number. Muddy and mosquito-ridden, the fenced-in area looked like a POW camp and smelled like a sewage treatment plant. Mangy dogs scurried between piled engine parts. Men in tattered, dirty clothing squatted in tight packs under a tarp to avoid the blistering sun. Opposite them was a narrow and musty building with a wall of bunk beds, stacked three levels high, where the men slept and ate.

I had assumed that some of the men would be Chinese, Indonesian, Burmese, or Thai. I was wrong. Virtually all were Vietnamese, which I later learned was also the case at most of the other detention centers in the country. Next to the detention area was a port run by the fisheries agency. It looked like a waterlogged junkyard, with nearly three dozen rusting, half-sunken boats parked almost on top of each other. Most of them were Vietnamese "blue boats," named for their brightly colored hulls. The boats were being "adjudicated," I was told, which meant they were being kept on-site as Indonesian authorities determined whether to prosecute these crews.

Adjudication seemed to me to be a misnomer for this ruinous and drawn-out process. While the authorities determined whether to charge these men, their boats rotted beyond repair, their accreditations as fishermen lapsed, and their families back home suffered acutely from the lost income. Just being arrested amounted to being convicted, whether they were guilty or not.

Roughly two-thirds of the detainees were said to be deckhands and the other third officers. The average amount of time that the men had been held in the detention center was a year and a half, though some of them said they had been there since before 2015. I asked them about violence, and they said there were occasional fights between detainees. Once in a while, the guards hit them, they said, if they failed to follow orders precisely or quickly enough. All detainees were required to do daily chores like cleaning their quarters, tending the small plot of vegetables behind the volleyball court, or fixing the gutters or roof of the building where they slept. None of the guards or fishery officials running the facility spoke Vietnamese. Instructions were conveyed largely through hand gestures, they said.

Mostly the detainees complained about the food, the mosquitoes, and the fact that they were being held in the first place. None had ever talked to a lawyer, they said. All were unsure how long they would be there or how and whether they would ever get home. Among the detainees was a boy named Le Trucing An. He must have been about thirteen, possibly younger. (He hesitated when I asked his age, then said he was sixteen.) He seemed deeply shy or afraid, unable to keep eye contact, and answered my Vietnamese translator mostly in one-word utterances. He was from the Tien Giang province in the Mekong delta region of southern Vietnam and said he had been working for two months at sea with his uncle before his boat was arrested by the Indonesians. He had been in detention for two weeks.

After interviewing the boy, I stepped out to call Pudjiastuti's cell phone. "You realize that you have a small child locked up at this detention center with 120 grown men, right?" I asked her. Defensive, she rejected the premise of the question, saying it was not a "detention center" but a "shelter"—the distinction being that there are no barred cells. "If the boy is there with his uncle," she added, "then his family should not have let him get on the fishing boat in the first place."

Once we got back to the *Macan*, I asked Samson about something I had heard from dozens of detainees in Pontianak. Almost all of them said that when they were arrested, they thought they were still in Vietnamese waters. "I know some of them were bluffing," I said. "But is there a chance that it might be true for at least some of them that they thought they were in their own waters?" Samson waved his hand as if to swat away the stupid question. "Absolutely not," he said. "The lines are clear."

.  .  .

The *Macan*'s mission was to patrol what the Indonesian officers called the "rough neighborhood." Because all foreign ships were banned from fishing in Indonesian waters, anyone we spotted was fair game. Samson showed me on a map where we were headed, which was a couple hundred miles northeast of the Natuna Islands. Déjà vu set in. In 2015, I had flown with a photographer to the region with a similar goal. On that trip, we had paid a local fisherman to take us to the same place in hopes of talking with some foreign captains who were fishing illegally. No fisherman had wanted to take us because, they said, it was too dangerous. A local captain named Rio finally agreed after we raised our offer to $400, double what he could earn in a month of fishing.

In the dead of night, he ferried us in a creaky, forty-foot wooden fishing boat that struggled to cut through the eight-foot swells. Rio hunched over a regional map I had brought that was color coded to indicate the ocean borders of different countries' national waters. Rio seemed fit but old—how old I couldn't tell, sixty-five perhaps—with leathery skin and crow's-feet framing his eyes. Tapping his finger on the map, he touched several dots that I had marked to indicate where several countries' waters converged. Shaking his head, Rio widened his eyes in fear. Then he silently reached over and opened a dashboard compartment revealing a Glock handgun.

Not unlike frontiers on land, border zones at sea were notoriously dodgy places. The ones with three-way intersections were especially attractive to fish poachers, human smugglers, gunrunners, and sellers of illegal bunker fuel because they knew that if they were chased by authorities from one country, they could flee in two other directions—a pickpocket's hideout with easy exits.

The trip with Rio proved unsuccessful. We did not find any illegal fishermen, because Rio's radar broke down, which meant we could only spot vessels around us with our own eyes. Our chances were a lot better on the trip with Samson, and we were much better armed.

Despite the seriousness of Samson's mission, the *Macan* lacked the formality of most military-grade patrol ships. Malay-pop music was usually playing on the bridge. The television in the mess hall looped reruns of *The Fast and the Furious*. On the Xbox in the downstairs lounge, the men challenged each other in raucous, trash-talking games of *Pro Evolution Soccer*.

For me, being at sea meant fighting with boredom and lots of downtime. Most ships, including the *Macan,* did not have internet, and while being off-line was painful, it forced me to pay closer attention to my surroundings because there was less escape from them. Before each expedition, I digitally stockpiled my devices with sanity-saving staples (new pictures and videos from home, episodes of SundanceTV's *Rectify* and HBO's *Leftovers*). As I ran out of reading material, I grew to resent *The New Yorker* for not letting me load onto my Kindle a full archive of past issues. Hours into one fourteen-day tour, my Spotify app crashed, taking its off-line library down with it. For two long weeks, I was stuck with the dozen painfully grating jingles by Parry Gripp that my son denies having snuck onto my phone as a prank.

But on the *Macan,* I found plenty to do. If I was not on the bridge watching the guys interact, I passed the time reading or writing while seated on the ship's back deck, an unusually tranquil area lined with wooden shelves holding dozens of bonsai trees. Samson had started collecting them in 2007, when his ship was on a mission along the eastern coast of Indonesia, near the country's Nusa Tenggara Timur province. Bungee cords tightly strapped the plants to shelves that had been built on top of the ship's life rafts. How these trees survived at sea was a mystery to me.

When the Indonesian officers had detainees that they were carrying back to shore, they usually kept them on this back deck. Alongside the bonsais was a cage where Pesut, the ship's six-year-old parrot, lived. When she was a baby, Pesut was given to Samson, who had kept her on board ever since. In Indonesian, *pesut* means "river dolphin," creatures that are famously fast and agile. The name was ironic because the bird couldn't fly and was clumsy on its feet, having once even fallen off the ship's railing into the water, rescued later with a net. When detainees were on board, Pesut was let out of her cage for the men to play with her. "It distracts them," Samson said, adding that when there were only five officers on board and a hundred detainees, it was important that the arrested men, who were usually not handcuffed, didn't decide to fight back. If these men did decide to rise up, Samson observed, they'd likely win.

Samson's casual observation about rebellious detainees would soon be tested. More than six hours after leaving Pontianak, Samson announced he had spotted his mark. A cluster of seven Vietnamese ships appeared on his radar, fishing roughly sixty miles within Indonesian waters. "We've got targets," Samson instructed his men, who hurriedly shed their flip-flops and shorts and suited up in SWAT-type gear: all black, visored helmets, shin guards, bulletproof vests.

The Vietnamese boats were spread out, a quarter mile between them. Approaching the first one, the Indonesians radioed the captain and ordered him to stop. Then, when we got close enough, Samson gave the command over the loudspeaker. The Vietnamese fishing boat captain sped up instead. After several minutes of chase, the Indonesians gave the same order again. No luck. An Indonesian officer then fired his submachine gun across the bow of the Vietnamese boat. Several minutes later, he fired another warning round. The third time he fired on the lower hull of the ship, and the Vietnamese captain immediately turned off his engine.

The Indonesians clambered onto the fishing boat and ordered the

A Vietnamese "blue boat," caught illegally fishing, flees Indonesian authorities, who try to signal for it to stop, eventually opening fire on the boat and arresting its crew.

entire Vietnamese crew to climb onto the *Macan*. The crew of eleven on the fishing boat looked utterly confused. One of the men trembled with fear. An Indonesian officer instructed the detainees to remove their shirts. I was told later that this made them less likely to jump overboard and try to swim back to their boat because they did not want to leave without an article of clothing. This explanation didn't entirely make sense to me, even though several guards mentioned it. I theorized that the real reason might be it made the detainees easier to smack and made them feel more vulnerable and thus more compliant.

Over the next two hours, the *Macan* chased and arrested four more Vietnamese boats. In each case, the officers fired on the fishing boats to get them to stop, their quick shots sounding like rapid beats on a kid's tin drum. On one of the Vietnamese boats, the captain, in an act of defiance, threw the engine keys into the sea as the Indonesian officers boarded. When this captain was sent to the back of the *Macan*, he began yelling at the other detainees to fight back as a group. In response, one of the Indonesian officers stepped forward and slapped the captain squarely across the face. The blow was hard enough that I could hear it from ten feet away over the roar of the waves and moan of the engine. "Sit down!" the officer yelled. The captain did as he was told.

The crew from an arrested Vietnamese fishing ship is detained on the back of an Indonesian patrol ship called the *Macan*. Within the hour, a large Vietnamese Coast Guard ship confronted the Indonesians, ramming and sinking one of the boats with an Indonesian marine officer on board.

After each arrest and before we headed to the next, I climbed on board each Vietnamese blue boat and scurried around to see what was there. All of the Vietnamese crew had been removed, so there was no one that I might encounter. But I wanted to check the living conditions. The Indonesian officers kept their distance, wondering why I would set foot on such a filthy ship. They were decrepit vessels. Their engines groaned when turned on or off, like an old man bending down to pick up a dropped cane. Samson allowed me five minutes to explore each boat, and I found myself drawn to the Vietnamese deckhands' sleeping quarters. I wanted to see what they brought with them.

The men slept in a room toward the back of the boats, open to the rear with walls on the other three sides. The ceiling was low enough that the space required even short men to crawl on all fours. There was no privacy and no way to secure belongings, which tended to be crammed into torn plastic grocery bags: eight-ounce cans of Red Bull, packs of Vietnamese cigarettes (some torn in half), an occasional prayer book, muscle ointments that smelled like Tiger Balm or Bengay. Several had shiny royal blue soccer jerseys with "Fly Emirates" written on them. One man had a small water-damaged photograph of a young girl, maybe six years old, his daughter perhaps, shoeless and in a white dress. There were no great epiphanies to be had in riffling through their stuff, except for a humbling recognition of how few possessions they brought with them for months at sea.

After the officers finished boarding and arresting the fifth Vietnamese vessel, Samson told his men they were going to have to let the remaining two ships escape. With about eleven crew on each of the arrested boats, there were fifty-five detainees now on the *Macan* and not enough officers to guard them all, Samson explained.

The *Macan* began heading toward the Indonesian island of Batam to unload the captured men. Samson had left an officer at the helm of each of the arrested Vietnamese boats, which convoyed behind us about half a mile apart.

As the seized fleet drove toward shore, I sat silently for nearly an hour with the fifty-five detainees on the *Macan* until they seemed accustomed to my being there. The Indonesians gave them cigarettes, bottled water, and bowls of rice mixed with fish. Many of the Vietnamese from different boats seemed to know each other. As I watched them, it became clear they were suffering from many ailments: crotch itch and chronic cough, confusion and longing, bad teeth and a smoking habit, hunger and anger, and a lot of worry etched onto their faces. One of the Indonesian officers spoke a little Vietnamese and, with help from my interpreter, translated as best he could for me when I started to ask questions. Several of the captains told me that they were not, in fact, fishing illegally. They ignored or did not understand my questions about being in Indonesian waters.

Fish do not obey national borders, several of the captains noted, so why should fishermen? "Fish are from God," one of them added. "We only borrow them from Indonesia." Another of the men made the same point but more tongue-in-cheek. "We only catch the fish that swim to Indonesia from Vietnam," he said.

As we headed toward Batam, there was a celebratory mood on the *Macan*. Samson poured a round of shots of arak, a traditional Indonesian liquor, for me and him. I downed mine, and it felt like battery acid in my throat. Samson showed off the strength of the alcohol by pouring some on the table and setting it on fire. The young officer whose job had been to shoot his submachine gun at the Vietnamese fishing boats seemed especially pumped up, giving high fives to anyone willing to reciprocate.

.  .  .

An hour into the trip to Batam, the celebration abruptly ended. Two officers came running into the mess hall. "Captain, come now," one said, a look of panic on his face. "Mas Gun is in trouble." The youngest and newest officer on the ship, Mas Gun had been driving one of the seized Vietnamese fishing boats several miles back in the convoy, the last in line following the *Macan*. Samson stood up so fast that he spilled his cup of arak. The men ran to the bridge, where Mas Gun could be heard on the radio. "Help!" he yelled. "Where are you guys?"

In choppy, breathless radio transmissions, Mas Gun said that as we were heading back to Batam, a Vietnamese Coast Guard cutter had suddenly appeared, presumably called by one of the arrested fishermen. Cutting in front of Mas Gun, the Vietnamese ship had split him off from the convoy. Unsuccessfully trying to outrun the cutter, Mas Gun said the Vietnamese ship was now ramming him. "*Macan*, my boat is sinking!" he screamed on the radio. "Help! *Macan*. Please. Help!"

Panic gripped the bridge. "Where are you?" the officers kept yelling into the radio to Mas Gun. "What are your coordinates?" Mas Gun seemed not to know. In all likelihood, his GPS was off. He was also driving someone else's fishing boat and likely did not know how to read some of its instruments. The *Macan* made a U-turn to head back to where they thought Mas Gun might be. The radio then fell silent. "Mas Gun?" Samson said in a stern voice. "Mas Gun, respond." Samson turned to the officers who were hunched over the radar. "Figure out where he is!"

They did not have to look for long. Within a few minutes, a Vietnamese Coast Guard cutter appeared on the horizon. At 262 feet long and nearly three thousand tons, the ship was over twice the size of our vessel. Samson immediately ordered his men to get the 12.7 mm machine gun from storage and set it on its mount on the forward deck. As we raced toward the Vietnamese cutter, Samson radioed his officers piloting the four other seized blue boats. "Turn off your AIS now," he said, referring to the device that transmits their location publicly, a step he hoped would help avoid the Vietnamese taking more of his men captive.

On the satellite phone, Samson tried calling his commanding officers in Jakarta. No answer. On his third attempt, someone picked

In a rapidly escalating situation, an Indonesian marine officer calls for more ammunition as a large Vietnamese Coast Guard ship approaches in contested waters in the South China Sea.

up. Samson quickly grew irritated with the person on the other end, because he did not seem to understand the urgency. "Our crew is in the sinking ship," Samson yelled at one point. "We will be face-to-face with the Vietnamese Coast Guard in a matter of minutes. I'm waiting for your direction." The connection dropped out, and Samson slammed down the receiver.

What had begun as a routine enforcement action was quickly turning into a tense and dangerous confrontation. We arrived at the Vietnamese Coast Guard ship, which towered over the *Macan* in much the same way we had towered over the blue boats only hours earlier. When the fifty-five Vietnamese detainees saw the government's ship, they began to scream and cheer. We could not see if Mas Gun was in the water because the cutter was blocking us from getting close to the sinking blue boat.

Samson's radio crackled as the Vietnamese called the *Macan,* and Samson handed me the receiver. The Vietnamese officer was speaking English, which neither Samson nor the other officers on his bridge spoke. I quickly handed the radio to my translator, hoping to maintain some journalistic remove. The Indonesians said something to my translator, who promptly tried to hand the radio back to me. "They want you to talk, not me," the translator said, explaining that they did not want a female as the intermediary in this situation. I paused and considered refusing the radio again. If this situation took a turn for the worse, might the translator get in trouble with her own government? Was it fair of me to force her into this potential bind? I took the radio.

At this point, we didn't know whether Mas Gun had been taken on board the Vietnamese ship or whether he might still be inside the sinking blue boat and possibly drowning. Samson told me to ask them if they had his officer. "Vietnam, this is Indonesia," I said into the radio. I explained that I was an American journalist on board the *Macan.* I said I would be temporarily acting as a translator for the captain of our vessel, which was an Indonesian fisheries ship. There may be an Indonesian officer on board the sinking ship you just rammed, I said. "Please explain what's going on."

The Vietnamese man on the radio told me that he was a Coast Guard officer. "You are in Vietnamese waters in violation of United Nations Convention, Law of the Sea," he said. His words stunned me. I turned to Samson: "Are you sure we're in Indonesian waters?" He said yes. "Absolutely sure?" I asked. "You're positive that we're not in some contested region that I don't know about?" Samson said yes again, this time more emphatically. "We're at least forty miles into Indonesian territory," he added.

It seemed best not to engage the Vietnamese on this issue, so I shifted to Mas Gun's safety and whereabouts. "The captain here needs to know whether his officer is safe," I said. The Vietnamese officer radioed back: "We want our boats. Where are our boats?" I repeated several times that the Indonesians first needed reassurance that their man had been rescued. "After you confirm that, you and the Indonesians can discuss an exchange." The Vietnamese yelled back at me: "Boats. Boats. We want our boats!"

Samson tried to get closer to the sinking blue boat, which brought him nearer to the Coast Guard ship. The Vietnamese cutter revved its engines, and the booming growl sent a clear message. The Vietnamese officer then radioed to make it explicit. "Move away from our ship," he said. I conveyed the order to Samson, who backed off.

The blue boat began sinking faster. The *Macan*'s crew speculated that Mas Gun might have passed out. "He may be in there, drowning," one officer said, staring at the disappearing fishing boat. Having boarded that very vessel during its arrest a couple of hours earlier, I could think of several things in the wheelhouse that might have knocked Mas Gun out: intense heat, thick diesel fumes, and a tangle of exposed wires I had seen spark while the Indonesians were removing the Vietnamese crew. After another arrest I had boarded the Vietnamese boat to investigate and when a wave suddenly tipped us I grabbed what I thought was a railing but instead was a scalding-hot pipe, severely burning my palm. The pain was so intense I thought I was going to pass out. Might Mas Gun have made the same mistake or worse and be lying on the floor of his wheelroom?

"Vietnam, this is the translator," I said over the radio. "You need to know that if the Indonesian officer is on that sinking ship and you prevent us from rescuing him, his death will be your fault and that's a clear violation of international law." Since the Vietnamese had trained their guns on our ship, my top priorities were to try to de-escalate the tensions that might just get us killed and try to ensure that Mas Gun was not drowning as we stood by. The Vietnamese officer did not reply. We waited for what felt like an eternity, though it was probably only about twenty minutes. We were waiting for instructions from Jakarta. I hoped those instructions would be for us to leave or that backup was on the way. I also knew those instructions could just as easily be for us to fire on the Vietnamese.

Troubled by the idea that we might actually be the ones in the wrong, I asked the Indonesian officers to give me our coordinates from their radar. I took a picture of the radar screen so that I could study it closely later. One of the Indonesians jabbed his finger again at a map to show me where we were in Indonesian waters, roughly fifty miles from the border of Vietnamese waters. I also checked the GPS tracking device that I kept strapped to my belt during these trips. Though I trusted the Indonesian officers not to lie to me, I had no way to independently verify what they were telling me because the maps I had brought with me did not delineate these sea borders specifically enough.

As Samson talked with his men about their next move, bedlam broke loose on the *Macan*'s aft deck. The screaming from the Vietnamese escalated into what sounded like a mob preparing to rampage. The detainees, none of whom were handcuffed, outnumbered us roughly four to one. As the crisis escalated, most of the biggest officers had joined us on the bridge, which meant they were not helping guard the detainees. I stepped outside onto a balcony of the bridge. Samson, who was inside, could not hear the ruckus. I warned him that things might be getting out of control. I heard a splashing sound and leaned over the side of the ship to see what was happening. One by one, the detainees were leaping into the ocean.

Many of the Vietnamese barely knew how to swim. As I looked down at the men thrashing in the water, my mind raced, weighing the different outcomes of the chaos unfolding in front of me. I wondered what I should do if I witnessed some of them starting to go under. Should I jump in the water and try to grab one of them? Or was it better for me to stay on deck and throw life rings at them? Were there even any life rings on this boat? I knew I couldn't just stand and bear witness if I saw men start drowning. What I didn't know was how best to help the situation.

The weakest swimmers soon turned back and returned to our boat, where the Indonesian officers hoisted them back on board. The rest of the detainees in the water swam toward the Vietnamese cutter, but its sides were two stories tall, and there was no easy way for them to climb on board. They switched direction and headed toward the doomed blue boat instead, which was sinking fast, with more than two-thirds of it already submerged.

Some of the Vietnamese detainees cling to a sinking ship because they do not want to return to the Indonesian police vessel where they had been under arrest, but they also cannot climb aboard the Vietnamese ship, because its sides are too high.

The Vietnamese Coast Guard cutter launched two small skiffs, which began picking up the fishermen in the water. Samson moved his ship back to give them a wide berth. The Vietnamese officer radioed to say that he wanted to talk to one of the dozen detainees who had stayed on our boat. He said he wanted to check on their well-being. I conveyed the request to Samson, who had one of his officers fetch one of the detainees and put him on the radio.

When that conversation ended, Samson told me to inform the Vietnamese that he wanted to see his officer, Mas Gun, on the deck of their ship. The Vietnamese confirmed that they rescued Mas Gun from the sinking blue boat. But for the next fifteen minutes, the Vietnamese officer told me that before proving Mas Gun was alive, he first needed him to sign some papers. Samson asked what I thought was happening. I said I imagined the Vietnamese were likely requiring Mas Gun to sign a "confession statement" or something saying that he was in Vietnamese waters. Samson replied to me that he didn't care because he had the radar and GPS records indicating exactly where everything happened. Saving face and keeping the Vietnamese detainees did not matter, Samson said. All that mattered was getting Mas Gun back.

Finally, the radio cut in. "We are showing you the officer now," the

Vietnamese officers said. Samson, reaching for his binoculars, could see Mas Gun standing near the window of the cutter's bridge. The Indonesians let out a collective sigh. The mood was yanked down again when the *Macan*'s satellite phone rang. The military attaché in Jakarta informed the crew that the nearest navy was hundreds of miles away in Natuna. Backup could not reach us for fifteen hours.

Then things got even worse. An officer interrupted Samson's call with the military attaché. "The radar," he said, pointing to the screen. Two dots were heading in our direction. It was unclear whose ships they were. What was clear, however, was that they were big, moving fast, and only eighteen nautical miles away from us. The Indonesian officers assumed they were Vietnamese Coast Guard or Navy.

Samson ordered his officers on the other four arrested blue boats to pull alongside us so they could climb back onto the *Macan*. He did not want any more of his men captured, he said. The Vietnamese radioed us again to insist that we put their fishermen in a boat and send them to the cutter. I told them that we could not fulfill this request because we did not have a skiff. I asked the Vietnamese to put their skiff in the water to make the exchange of Mas Gun for their fishermen. "The captain here wants to give you your fishermen back," I reassured them. "We just need help figuring out how to make the handoff."

I was trying to speak slowly, using short sentences and simple words, because the Vietnamese officer's English was weak. I could tell he was getting annoyed. He didn't understand me and seemed to think that the Indonesians were being intransigent.

My translator then pulled me aside to tell me that ten minutes earlier she overheard a phone conversation between Samson and someone in Jakarta who instructed him to leave the scene immediately before things turned more violent. She said that Samson had been told that diplomatic authorities would handle the negotiation of Mas Gun's release—an order that he seemed to be ignoring.

Samson was also getting angrier, and I saw him say something to two officers who, hustling to the front deck, began pulling on the loaded, mounted machine gun. Taking its safety off, the guard leveled the gun in the direction of the Vietnamese Coast Guard officers, who, I could see through my binoculars, had already done the same thing in our direction with their mounted gun. This standoff was spiraling out of control, and it looked as if it would be suicide for the Indonesians to fire even a warning shot near the Vietnamese cutter.

I kept trying to apply pressure on the Vietnamese. Every five minutes for the next fifteen minutes, I asked my counterpart on the radio whether he was sending Mas Gun back. "Yes, but you need to wait," he scolded me. "Tell the Vietnamese to stop stalling," Samson yelled at me at one point. "Send Mas Gun in a boat now, and we will send back all the fishermen." I relayed the message. The Vietnamese again barked at me to wait.

Samson got another call from Jakarta, but this time he did not put it on speakerphone. It was brief, and he looked sick when he hung up. "We must leave now," he said. The two large vessels were indeed Vietnamese military and they were now just a few miles from us. Jakarta said we could not risk waiting longer. Samson ordered his first mate to turn the *Macan* around and head full throttle toward Sedanau, a nearby Indonesian island, roughly fifteen hours away. As we left the area, the Vietnamese officer continued to radio. "Where are you going?" he asked. "We want our fishermen." Samson instructed me not to respond.

As we fled the standoff, the bridge was humid with worry. Everyone nervously watched the radar to see if the Vietnamese Coast Guard cutter or the two military ships, which were much faster than we were, planned to give chase. The rest of the ship filled with silent stoicism: lots of jaw clenching, avoided eye contact, and long stares out the window. My guess was that everyone also felt embarrassed to have backed down and guilty to have left Mas Gun behind.

Two hours later, one of the officers said we were safely out of reach of the Vietnamese. Samson did not slow down. Most of the men left the bridge, retreating to their own nooks to stand alone and smoke cigarettes. I noticed that more of them than usual went to the *musholla,* the ship's tiny mosque, to pray.

We arrived in Sedanau around 5:00 a.m. the next day and stayed for five hours. The military then ordered us to refuel nearby on the island of Pulau Tiga and then to take the detainees to Batam, an eighteen-hour trip.

As if Samson and his men hadn't already been through enough, on our way to Batam we slammed into a vicious storm. I had felt it coming; my left ear throbs when there are drastic changes in pressure, a consequence of a burst eardrum during my high school years. Stepping outside, I saw the ceiling of clouds lower and darken and felt the winds grow into a gale. I asked Samson if we were headed into a front. He motioned with his arms and eyes that it was a big one.

. . .

As a ship moves through water, a wave forms at the bow and another at the stern. Between them a trough is created. The faster the ship goes, the deeper it sinks into the trough, a phenomenon called squat. Samson was driving the *Macan* at twenty-three knots—fast for this ship—so we were squatting deep, making it easier for the twenty-five-foot waves to slam across the aft deck where the Vietnamese detainees were being held. Fearing that the detainees might wash overboard, the Indonesians brought them inside. Pesut remained in her cage outside. No one risked trying to rescue her. The cage was bolted to the deck, and she probably wouldn't cooperate anyway, the men told me.

After seeing one of the bonsai pots torn from its straps and go flying off the side of the ship, I cracked open the door to the back deck and stuck my head out for a minute to feel the air. The spray blowgunned tiny darts at my face. The sea gusts were kelpy, cold, and salty. When I encountered this flavor of air again in subsequent months, it had a Pavlovian effect: a full-body memory of excitement, fear, and wonder.

The *Macan* thrashed violently for most of the night. Anything that was not properly secured was now on the floor. A pile of plastic cups, seat cushions, chairs, napkin dispensers, and loose papers slid from one side of the galley to the other with the rocking. At one point, the ship listed so far that the refrigerator broke from its bungee-cord lashing, falling on its side and smashing across the room. Several men leaped up and refastened it. I joined them in trying to clean up the cooking oil that spilled on the floor, but their efforts just spread the slippery sheen, creating a black-ice hazard for anyone who tried to cross it.

After the Indonesians brought them inside from the back deck, the Vietnamese detainees lay on their backs, tightly packed on the floor. Downstairs, the scene was the same: the crew had left their rooms—I never understood why—and were lying on the floor in hallways and in the lower lounge, reminding me of the schematic drawings of a slave ship from high school history class.

At night, the sea is more a place of sounds than sights, and walking around the lower decks, I felt like a blind man in a haunted house. Metal whined. Hallways rattled as if someone had poured a bucket of loose screws into the walls. Waves slamming our sides sounded like the relentless crashes of a demolition derby. The only reassuring sound, deep in the background, was the engine thrumming with a determined murmur. It was as though we were inside a lumbering beast that was being attacked, and we slowly rolled, twisted, and groaned our way forward.

Among the ocean's many moods, this type of violent and devouring rage was something I had always hoped to experience, having only read or heard about it. I was more electrified than afraid, but I did think about cast-off stowaways who face storms with nothing more than a makeshift raft and capsized fishers who drown in these conditions. Mostly, I marveled that passing through forces this strong was something some people did routinely.

Sleep was not an option. So I passed the time in the wheelhouse. As the ship heaved over the waves, it felt like a playground swing. At the top, there was a hovering, zero-gravity euphoria that tickles your stomach. Sometimes, we hung airborne for durations that seemed to defy the laws of physics. When we fell down the front of the waves, we landed with a violent and clanging crash that made me wonder whether the ship could handle the pounding. I learned to keep my jaw clenched after I nearly chipped a tooth. After a while I was ready for the storm to be over, and I noticed how time felt stretched. It's 3:00 a.m., I remember thinking, and in another hour it will be 3:05 a.m.

Samson kept a wide stance at the helm, counter-swaying to the wild rocking of the ship, with his legs serving as shock absorbers as he gripped the wheel as if he were holding up a cinder block. At one point, he turned to me and confessed that he kept hearing Mas Gun's voice in his head. My translator was asleep, so Samson explained to me in broken English, pantomime, and help from other officers on the bridge. Mas Gun joined his crew only five months earlier from another fisheries patrol boat, he said. "Like sons," Samson said of his officers, before adding that Mas Gun was special because he had also been one of his former students.

Mas Gun was forty-two years old and originally from Klaten, Yogyakarta—a municipality 270 miles east of Jakarta on the island of

Java. He had three kids, the oldest around six, Samson said. He watched television news incessantly during longer voyages at sea. Samson recounted Mas Gun's biographical details as if we were drafting his obituary. Feigning optimism, I reassured Samson that the diplomats would get Mas Gun back. "I've seen this type of situation before," I lied. The truth was that I'd never actually seen one country's Coast Guard venture so far into the territorial waters of another, or seen two armed ships come so close to opening fire on each other.

As Samson stared out the window, I just sat quietly with him. Our intense confrontation with the Vietnamese was taking its toll on the man who blinked first. By this time, my translator had woken up and joined us. "We've arrested so many of their fishermen," Samson said after a while, still baffled by how uncharacteristically aggressive the Vietnamese had been. Perhaps they'd built up a grudge, he speculated. "Even ants eventually fight back if you step on them," he added.

. . .

The last time an Indonesian fisheries officer was taken captive was in 2010. The Indonesians arrested five Malaysian boats that were fishing illegally in Indonesian waters near Bintan Island (Indonesia) and Johor Island (Malaysia). As they escorted the arrested fishing boats back to port, several larger Malaysian marine police boats appeared and removed three of the Indonesian officers from the boats. "They had bigger guns," said Seivo Greud Wewengkang, one of the captured officers, whom I visited when we got to Batam. "We did what they told us to do." The Malaysians put the three officers in a Malaysian jail for three days until a diplomatic deal was reached for their return.

Samson said most incidents get resolved on-site. He recounted a clash with the Chinese in 2005 in which three Chinese military ships surrounded his patrol boat and removed three of his officers from several seized Chinese fishing boats. "The Chinese are much more efficient," Samson said. They gave his officers back within fifteen minutes of having arrived at the scene, as soon as the Indonesians agreed to release the detained fishermen and their boats.

The fisheries port in Batam looked much like that in Pontianak: packed with dozens upon dozens of half-sunken fishing ships, almost all of them from Vietnam. I met with the fisheries station chief, a man named Slamet, who seemed as surprised as Samson by the behavior of the Vietnamese.

Slamet told me that before 2013 his officers were mostly arresting Thai boats, which were heavily armed and occasionally confrontational. Since then, the Indonesians had primarily been encountering Vietnamese fishermen, who tended not to be aggressive and had never before called for backup from their Coast Guard. When asked what he thought drove this shift, Slamet speculated that in 2013, Thailand started receiving greater attention from Thai and foreign media for its illegal fishing habits.

In subsequent years, the EU also began threatening to give Thailand a maritime version of a yellow card, a warning that it needed to clean up its poorly regulated seafood industry, due to these marine crimes and its sea slavery problems. In response, the Thai government slowly started cracking down on its fishing industry, Slamet said. Vietnam, on the other hand, had received virtually no attention from foreign media, the EU, or the United States for illegal fishing or other abuses on ships, he said. I asked Slamet about Mas Gun, and he declined to discuss the topic. "That is a diplomatic negotiation now," he said curtly.

In the days after the confrontation, I emailed James Kraska, an international law professor at the U.S. Naval War College in Rhode Island and an expert on the South China Sea. I sent him the coordinates of where the clash occurred and asked him whose waters those were. "Impossible to say," he replied. Countries have to agree on where to draw these lines, he said. In the South China Sea, Indonesia and Vietnam have never come to such an agreement, he explained.

That the borders were such a gray area was a surprise. During the confrontation, Samson had been so confident about the *Macan*'s location. By the same token, the guards at the Pontianak detention center had been so dismissive of their detainees' claims that they thought they were fishing in their own waters. The Vietnamese officer I negotiated with over the radio had also been certain about jurisdiction.

For all the solidity of lines on a map, offshore jurisdiction and sea borders are determined most by military might. Whoever has the biggest guns in a confrontation is automatically in friendly waters. On the other hand, the detainees had made a compelling point about the fish they caught. We like to think there are five major oceans and dozens of seas. Yet there is in fact but one big, interconnected, circulating body of water, without borders or self-evident laws. The fish know this, and so do the fishermen, even if the politicians and marine officers like to think otherwise.

As I sat down to sift through my notes and piece together what happened on my reporting trip in Indonesia, I started by trying to pin down the simplest and most neutral way to describe the events. Each side took the other's men. Who was justified in doing so? In whose waters was the incident? What did the law say was permissible? Who nearly killed Mas Gun? These were difficult questions to answer because the facts were shifty. Soon, these facts got even more shifty.

After holding him for six days, Vietnam sent Mas Gun back to Indonesia. "This was not a hostage situation but a rescue effort," said Rifky Effendi Hardijanto, Indonesia's secretary-general of the Ministry of Marine Affairs and Fisheries, during a subsequent press conference in which he cast the Vietnamese Coast Guard more as savior than as aggressor. In later interviews, the Indonesian government told reporters that Mas Gun had been driving one of several arrested Vietnamese fishing boats back to shore when his boat began sinking and the Vietnamese Coast Guard saved him.

This narrative was a fantasy at odds with actual events, of course. What the Indonesian government failed to tell reporters was that the Vietnamese boats were more than fifty miles into what Indonesia claimed as its territorial waters. The Indonesians also omitted the fact that the "rescue" was only necessary because the Vietnamese had rammed Mas Gun's boat. Also unmentioned were the hours of heated negotiations, during which the Indonesians repeatedly offered to hand back all of the Vietnamese fishermen but the Vietnamese Coast Guard refused to turn over Mas Gun.

I called Minister Pudjiastuti and asked her bluntly why her government was whitewashing the incident. "We conveyed our dismay; the Vietnamese apologized," she said. "And our diplomats did not want a big clash." She added that she was still livid about the conflict. Only a week before my telephone call, she said, her officers had arrested yet another batch of Vietnamese blue boats in Indonesian waters.

Pudjiastuti added that unlike the Chinese, who stopped the incursions after Indonesia blew up several of their boats, the Vietnamese government either could not or did not want to rein in its fishing fleet. I told her that perhaps the Vietnamese did not see those fishing trips as incursions because they believed they were in their own waters. Pudjiastuti laughed. "They can say that," she said. "But I can show you on a map where the lines are."

# ARMED AND DANGEROUS

The sea, in fact, is that state of barbaric vagueness and disorder out of which civilisation has emerged and into which, unless saved by the effort of gods and men, it is liable to relapse.

—W. H. Auden, *The Enchafèd Flood*

The daytime sky was clear and bright, the sea dark and choppy, as the man bobbing in the waves flailed his arms at the men in the ships circling him. He had no life jacket, and neither did the other men floating in the ocean near him, some clinging to what looked like the wreckage of an overturned wooden boat. Several large white tuna long-liners surrounded them. None of the men aboard the long-liners made a move to help the swimming men. This wasn't a rescue. One of the men in the water raised his arms over his head, palms open and forward, in what looked like a gesture indicating surrender. A bullet drilled into the back of his skull, knocking him face down. A cloud of glowing red blood slowly mushroomed around him in blue water.

And so began a slow-motion slaughter. It unfolded over more than ten minutes; as the tuna boats' engines idled loudly, men aboard fired at least forty rounds, methodically executing those in the water. "I've shot five!" someone standing on one of the tuna boats shouted in Mandarin. Soon after, a group of crew members laughed while posing for selfies.

In late 2014, a source at Interpol emailed a cell phone video of the incident to me with the subject line "Brace yourself." When I opened the email and watched the shaky footage, I sat back in my chair, stunned at what I was seeing. In my reporting on sea slaves, like the captive Cambodian man Lang Long, I had seen the worst types of violence inflicted on fishermen, and I had certainly heard many times of

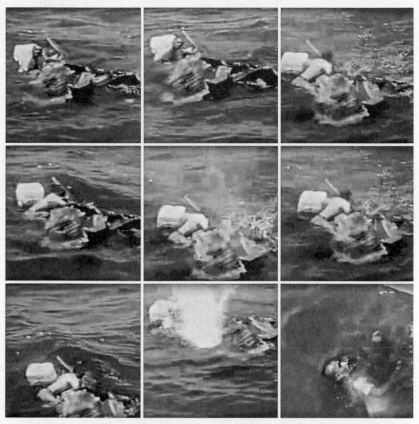

A man clings to the wreckage of a small boat moments before he is gunned down in footage that was found on a cell phone left in a taxi in Fiji showing the murder of at least four unarmed men by gunmen on at least one Taiwanese tuna long-liner.

cold-blooded killings at sea. But the scene playing on my laptop was a naked abomination, the killers exhibiting the glee of big-game hunters bagging their prey. Compounding the horror was that my Interpol source said that virtually nothing was known about these killings. In this era of drones and GPS, of big data and crowdsourcing, it seemed unthinkable that law enforcement would not have tracked down the perpetrators or the victims, or at least figured out the location, timing, or motives of this atrocity.

In contrast to life on land, crimes at sea are very rarely caught on video. In many countries, most fishing boat deckhands have their phones confiscated while on board. This is one reason why the conditions I witnessed time and again at sea persist today. Unless something is brought to life on YouTube, it might as well not have happened. And so here was rare video footage of a gruesome crime at sea, yet the broader outrage it should have triggered seemed muted.

Given all the evidence in the video, I hoped to piece together what had happened. With enough effort, you sometimes make your own luck, and this case would need a bunch of breaks to solve.

On so many levels, the story didn't make sense. Despite dozens of witnesses on at least four ships, the circumstances surrounding these killings had remained a mystery. No one even reported the incident; there was no requirement to do so under maritime law, nor any clear procedures for mariners to volunteer what they knew as they traveled from port to port. Law enforcement officials only learned of the deaths after the video capturing the incident was found on a cell phone left in a taxi in 2014 in Fiji and posted on the internet.

Absent the carelessness of the cell phone's owner, no one would have known that a crime even took place, beyond the witnesses and perpetrators aboard the tuna boats. Without evidence, bodies, or suspected culprits, it was unclear which, if any, government would take responsibility for leading an investigation. Taiwanese fishing authorities, who identified one of the boats at the scene, told me that they believed the dead men were part of a failed pirate attack. But maritime security experts, warning that piracy had become a convenient cover for sometimes fatal score settling, said it was just as likely that the men were local fishermen in disputed waters, crew that had mutinied, cast-off stowaways, or thieves caught stealing fish or bait.

"Summary execution, vigilantism, overzealous defense, call it what you will," said Klaus Luhta, a lawyer with the International Organization of Masters, Mates & Pilots, a seafarers' union. "This boils down just the same to a case of murder at sea and a question of why it's allowed to happen."

The oceans, plied by more ships than ever before, are also more armed and dangerous. Most merchant vessels hired private security starting in 2008 as pirates began operating across larger swaths of the ocean, outstripping governments' policing abilities. The arms race at sea has escalated to the point that guns and guards at sea are so ubiquitous that a niche industry of floating armories has emerged. Part storage depot and part bunkhouse, these vessels, positioned in high-risk areas of international waters, housed hundreds of assault rifles, small arms, and ammunition, along with guards who waited sometimes for months in decrepit conditions for their next deployment.

Though pirate attacks on large container ships had dropped sharply since 2011 because most ships had started carrying armed guards, other forms of violence remained commonplace. Maritime security officials and insurers estimate that thousands of seamen are robbed or assaulted annually and hundreds are killed and kidnapped in the Indian Ocean, along the West African coast, and elsewhere.

The ocean is not the place to go hunting for good-guy-versus-bad-guy narratives. In some parts of the world, the line between pirates and guards is blurry. Armed gangs in the Bay of Bengal near Bangladesh run protection rackets requiring ship captains to pay for safe passage. Near Nigeria, marine police routinely work in concert with fuel thieves, according to maritime insurance investigators. Off the coast of Somalia, pirates who used to target bigger ships have transitioned into "security" work on board foreign and local fishing vessels, finding an aura of legitimacy in fending off armed attacks while also firing on rivals to scare them away. But these are more like pitched battles with known belligerents than summary executions by rival fishing groups.

Unprovoked attacks are frequent. Countries are racing one another to map and lay claim to untapped oil, gas, and other mineral resources deep in the ocean, and as the stakes grow, so does the aggression. Tankers transporting valuable cargo carried armed guards for transits through waters they expected to be dangerous. From the Mediterranean to offshore Australia to the Black Sea, human traffickers hauling refugees and migrants routinely ram and sink competitors' boats.

Violence between fishing boats is especially widespread and getting worse. Heavily subsidized Chinese and Taiwanese fishing boats outnumber all others in much of the world's tuna-fishing grounds, said Graham Southwick, the president of Fiji's Tuna Boat Owners Association. Radar advancements and more widespread use of fish-aggregating devices—floating objects that attract schools of fish—have heightened tensions because fishermen are more prone to crowd the same spots. "Catches shrink, tempers fray, fighting starts," said Southwick. "Murder on these boats is relatively common."

. . .

Crime is countered only as much as it is counted, and at sea that isn't much. Charles N. Dragonette, who tracked seafaring attacks globally for the U.S. Office of Naval Intelligence, estimated that the violent-crime rate on fishing boats was easily twenty times that on tankers, cargo ships, or passenger ships. But no international agency, not even the U.S. military, comprehensively tracks maritime violence, he said. "So long as the victims were Indonesian, Malay, Vietnamese, Filipino, just not European or American," he said, "the story never resonated."

I'd built plenty of databases before—on coal-mining violations, on sex-trafficking prosecutions, on truck driver deaths—and it usually takes a couple days to clean the data and make it uniform and readable. To get a sense of scope on the problem of violent crime at sea, I tried to do the same, and three weeks into the process I realized I was dealing with a bigger undertaking.

The tough part wasn't scrubbing the data; it was getting it in the first place. I met with Coast Guard investigators, navy intelligence officers, Interpol authorities, academics, and human rights advocacy groups, and most of what anyone had was partial. The private investigative firms—those typically hired by maritime insurance companies to research accident claims—had some of the best information, but because it was proprietary, they were the least willing to share it. To get the information, I usually had to agree not to share any of it publicly except in aggregate form.

Eventually, I finished building a database that consisted of six thousand crime reports from around the world, drawing largely from information provided by the U.S. Office of Naval Intelligence, two maritime security firms (OCEANUSLive and Risk Intelligence), and a research group called Oceans Beyond Piracy. Far from comprehensive, the database offered a cursory snapshot of lawlessness at sea. Typically, the death tolls captured in the records were murky because follow-up investigations were rare and reports often lacked details. On land, police can dig up graves to investigate murders. Offshore, "the dead stay gone," as one investigator said.

The database showed, however, that in 2014, the latest year for which data was available, more than fifty-two hundred seafarers were attacked by pirates and robbers, and more than five hundred were taken hostage in three regions alone—the western Indian Ocean, the Gulf of Guinea, and Southeast Asia. The culprits were a diverse cast of characters: rubber-skiff pirates armed with rocket-propelled grenades, night-stalking fuel thieves, and slash-and-dash bandits wielding machetes. Others used deception. Hijackers masqueraded as marine police, human traffickers posed as fishermen, and security guards moonlighted as arms dealers. I could wrap my head around most of these accounts, but some were more difficult to parse.

Victims one minute, people could become perpetrators the next. In 2012, for example, ten refugees, including women and children, were smuggled by a crew member onto a fishing boat in Sri Lanka. When their demands to set a new course for Australia were refused, the refugees attacked the crew, killing four men by throwing them overboard.

There was also an incident in 2009: three captive Burmese workers escaped their Thai trawler in the South China Sea by leaping overboard. They swam to a nearby yacht, killed its owner, and stole his lifeboat.

The waters near Bangladesh provide a stark case study of how and why maritime violence frequently gets overlooked by the international community and why countries are eager to downplay crime and violence in their waters. In the five years after 2009, nearly a hundred sailors and fishermen were killed each year in Bangladeshi waters, and at least as many taken hostage, in a string of attacks by armed gangs, according to local media and police reports.

Armed assaults had been an ongoing problem in these waters at least since 2000, when early reports of the violence emerged. In 2013, the Bangladeshi press recounted the abductions of more than 700 fishermen throughout that year, 150 of which were in September alone. Forty of the captives were allegedly killed in a single incident, many with their feet and hands bound as they were thrown overboard.

These attacks were usually conducted by the half a dozen armed gangs that operate protection rackets in the Bay of Bengal and the swampy inland waters called the Sundarbans. In 2014, these groups engaged in gun battles with the Bangladesh Air Force and Coast Guard during government raids on coastal camps and hostage ships.

Bangladesh's foreign minister, Dipu Moni, took umbrage at the bad publicity and reprimanded both the international shipping industry and the media for referring to the waters around her country as a "high risk" zone for piracy. Such a characterization, she said, was defamatory.

"There has not been a single incident of piracy in years," she said with a straight face during a December 2011 news conference. Most of the violence off her nation's coast involved petty theft and robberies, most often committed by *dacoits* (a term derived from the Hindu word for "bandits"), she added.

Moni's claims pivoted on a legal distinction between piracy, which under international law only occurred on the high seas or in waters farther than twelve miles from shore, and at-sea robbery, which involved attacks closer to land, never mind that the outcome of the attacks can be equally gruesome. Based on this distinction, Bangladeshi officials sent a protest letter in 2011 to the International Maritime Bureau (IMB), an organization that runs the Piracy Reporting Centre. Located in downtown Kuala Lumpur, the center was founded in 1992 and is primarily funded by shipping companies and insurers. It is the principal way that governments, militaries, and the public get statistical information about piracy attacks.

In their letter to the IMB, Bangladeshi officials argued that their country should not be stigmatized as a high-piracy zone. They also complained that insurers who previously charged $500 for each trip to the ports located near Bangladesh had raised their rates to $150,000, after the region became known for violence. Shortly thereafter, the IMB responded: though records indicated that the region was subject to attacks, the IMB would amend its website, swapping references to "pirates" with "robbers."

Defending the website edit, Pottengal Mukundan, director of the IMB, told me that his organization had not caved to pressure from the Bangladeshi government. "Whether they are called pirates or robbers is a legal distinction based on the location of the incident," he said. "It does not change the nature of their act or the danger to the ship or crew when armed strangers get on board their ship." The IMB did not attempt to determine the exact location of attacks or whether they were in national or international waters, he said, in part because these details were often contested by countries. His point seemed like the kind of bureaucratic whitewashing that drains urgency and severity from problems. Plus, as I'd learned in Indonesia, territorial claims offshore are often murky.

I asked Jon Huggins, the director of Oceans Beyond Piracy at the time, why there was no comprehensive, centralized, or public tracking of violent crime at sea. He explained that shipping companies, maritime insurers, private security firms, embassies, and flag registries tracked violence to varying degrees. For nearly a year, Oceans Beyond Piracy tried but failed to persuade these groups to share information. Risk management companies asked why they should share data that they could sell instead. Coastal states worried that such information might show their waters to be dangerous and scare away business. Flag registries were reluctant because this information might obligate them to act on such crimes, which they had little ability or motivation to do, Huggins said.

Dragonette, the former navy intelligence official, added that tracking the violence was difficult enough and that cracking down on such crimes was even tougher. Prosecutions were rare—one former American Coast Guard official put it at "less than 1 percent"—because many ships lacked insurance and captains of attacked ships were averse to the delays and prying that came with police investigations. The few military and law enforcement ships that patrolled international waters were usually forbidden to board ships flying another country's flag unless given permission. Witnesses willing to speak up were scarce; so was physical evidence.

Violence at sea has always been handled differently from crimes on land. "Ashore, no matter how brutal the repression or how corrupt the local government, someone will know who the victims are, where they were, that they did not return," Dragonette said. "At sea, anonymity is the rule."

·   ·   ·

As violence at sea has grown so too has the market for private security forces offshore. Indeed, the oceans are becoming militarized, awash in guns like never before. Over the past decade, Somali piracy led many governments to encourage merchant vessels to arm themselves or hire maritime mercenaries, a break from the long-standing practice of nations claiming a near monopoly on the use of force at sea.

At the same time, growing terrorism concerns motivated port officials globally to tightly restrict the number and kinds of weapons that were carried into their national waters. That created a paradox: security-conscious countries want greater law and order on the seas, but they don't want arms coming into their countries from offshore. Everyone should arm themselves, the logic went, but no one was allowed to bring those arms into their territory.

For the shipping industry, floating armories emerged as a way around this bind. Essentially waterborne dormitories for guards, these armories double as depots for their weapons, and they allow maritime security companies to avoid moving their guards on and off shore with every new assignment. Private security firms pay the armories as little as $25 per night for room and board for each guard, who tends to deploy for six to nine months or longer at sea. Generally owned by British, American, and Sri Lankan companies, the armories also charge the security companies to carry the men to and from client ships—typically several thousand dollars for each trip. When the men arrive at the armories, they check their weapons into a locked storage container. Then they wait, sometimes for weeks, for their next deployment on a merchant vessel.

In the winter of 2015, I traveled to the Gulf of Oman with Ben Solomon, a *Times* staff photographer, to visit some of these armories. We spent several days on the *MNG Resolution,* a St. Kitts and Nevis–

Floating arms depots like the *Resolution,* a St. Kitts and Nevis—flagged floating armory anchored in the Gulf of Oman, are positioned in high-risk areas of international waters.

flagged floating armory with a couple dozen guards. I sat one evening with half a dozen guards on the upper deck of the *Resolution,* which was anchored in the gulf about twenty-five miles from the United Arab Emirates. After we traded war stories about past encounters with pirates, the conversation turned to a shared concern: the growing influx of untrained hires into the booming maritime security business, now worth $13 billion a year.

"It's like handing a bachelor a newborn," one guard complained, describing how some of the new recruits reacted when given an automatic weapon. Many of the rookies lacked combat experience, spoke virtually no English (despite the requirement that they speak the language fluently), and did not know how to clean or fix their weapons, the guards said. Some of the new hires arrived for their first day on the job carrying their personal ammunition in ziplock bags or shoe boxes. Still, they get hired because these security companies do minimal vetting.

Like soldiers everywhere, they were a motley group. The men were a mix of brash and reticent, muscular and slim, gruff and friendly. The younger guards, some of them in their twenties, clearly felt overtrained and underused, hungry to see action, test their skills, prove their merit. The older men, typically in their mid-forties to fifties, were more jaded and withdrawn. They complained less about the boredom than about the distance from home. Generally, everyone stuck with his own countrymen—from Greece, the United States, India, Estonia, the U.K., and South Africa. Almost all of them had done tours in Iraq, Afghanistan, or conflict zones in Africa. They were macho in that distinctly but subtle mariner way: avoiding touching the hallway walls or railings even when we rocked heavily or filling their coffee mugs to the brim to show how no amount of wobbliness could cause them to spill even a drop. Virtually all of the guards on the armories spoke to me on the condition that I not name them, out of fear they would be blacklisted for future jobs.

With a steel hull and 141 feet long, the *Resolution* was among dozens of converted cargo ships, tugboats, and barges that were anchored at the time in high-risk areas of the Red Sea, the Persian Gulf, and the Indian Ocean. At the height of the piracy attacks in 2008, the guards who bunked aboard ships like the *Resolution* typically made $500 per day, whether deployed or waiting on an armory. Overall, pay has steadily fallen in recent years, with typical payouts of only $250 while

Private maritime security guards eat in the mess hall on the *Resolution*.

waiting at the armories and $550 per day while deployed as protection on shipping vessels. As the threat level fell, pay levels dropped further, and the nationalities of the guards shifted. By 2011, western Europeans and Americans were largely being replaced by eastern Europeans and South Asians, who in some cases were paid as little as $650 per month.

The guards said that the maritime security industry included fewer fly-by-night companies than it had in prior years. Though the men described the *Resolution* as the best in the business, the younger men had plenty of complaints nonetheless—about the bad food, the filthy conditions, the lack of Wi-Fi, and, above all, the boredom. But their biggest concern generally was the potential for mishandling attacks—with possibly deadly consequences—because of cost-cutting measures, they said. To save money, the shipping industry moved from four-man security teams to teams of two or three less experienced men.

The "team leaders" on the *Resolution*—most of them American, British, or South African military veterans—explained to me why more seasoned guards were important and what made gun battles at sea so different from those on land. Maritime fighting was tactically different from land combat and experience was crucial. "Between fight or flight, out here there's just fight," said Cameron Mouat, a guard working aboard the *Resolution*. There was no place to hide, no falling back, no air support, no ammunition drops. Targets were almost always fast moving. Aim was shifty because of waves. Some ships were the length of several football fields—too big, these guards contended, for a two- or three-man security detail to handle, especially when attackers arrived in multiple boats and from different directions.

It had also become extremely difficult to discern what was a threat and what was not. Automatic weapons—formerly a pirates' telltale sign—were now commonplace at sea, found on virtually all boats traversing dangerous waters, they said. Smugglers, with no intention of attacking, routinely nestled close to larger merchant ships to hide in their radar shadow and avoid being detected by coastal authorities. Innocent fishing boats also sometimes tucked behind larger ships because they churned up sea-bottom sediment that attracted fish.

"The concern isn't just whether a new guard will misjudge or panic and fire too soon," explained a South African guard. "It's also whether he will shoot soon enough." If guards hesitate too long, he said, they miss the chance to fire warning shots, flares, or water cannons or incapacitate an approaching boat's engine. By the time you shoot in such cases, he said, the only option left is "kill shots."

The armories were controversial because many countries didn't like having foreign-operated arms depots so close to their shores. If armed guards did not have the option of disembarking in international waters, they would need to come all the way into port, but weapons were forbidden in most harbors. Sometimes, though, these guards traveled to national waters and simply hid their guns on board or dumped them over the side if inspectors approached.

One night around 11:00, a ship that was transporting Solomon, me, and a dozen private guards to an armory slowed to a crawl after losing power from one of its two engines. The ship's captain seemed nervous. I asked why. "See that?" he said, pointing to the mountainous coast visible from our port side. "That's Iran." The current was pushing us toward its shores, he explained. If the second engine dies, our ship will drift into Iranian waters, less than half a mile away, he said, adding, "Not a welcome place for a ship full of armed British and American private security guards." I didn't have to ask whether my status as a journalist would spare me the Iranian government's ire.

His fear was not unwarranted. On October 12, 2013, a floating armory called the *Seaman Guard Ohio* entered India's national waters because the men aboard were seeking food, water, and fuel. The crew of the *Ohio*, which was owned by AdvanFort, a U.S.-based private maritime security company, later said that they alerted Indian Navy authorities that they were carrying weapons but that their ship was "in distress" and they were given permission to proceed. The Indian government doubted that the men on the *Ohio* needed rescuing, and police eventually arrested the ship's twenty-five guards and ten crewmen, charging them with various weapons violations. The men were convicted and, after multiple appeals, received five-year sentences at the Puzhal Central Prison in Chennai, in southeast India.

"Don't you think the U.S. government would react if thousands of machine guns and other heavy weaponry was flowing unregulated thirteen nautical miles off the coast of New York City?" an Indian military official said to me when I called and asked him about the *Ohio*.

India had other reasons to worry about the presence of mercenaries near its shores. In the 2008 Mumbai terror attack on two luxury hotels and other targets, the attackers came by sea, and the Indian government feared it could happen again. And in 2012, roughly a year before the arrest of the *Seaman Guard Ohio*, two Italian marines working as guards on board an Italian oil tanker, the *Enrica Lexie,* shot and killed two Indian fishermen, mistaking them for pirates. The incident occurred about twenty nautical miles off the coast of the southern Indian state of Kerala.

The *Enrica Lexie* killings escalated into a diplomatic dispute between Italy and India, culminating in the Italian foreign minister quitting his position in March 2013. The Italian minister said he was resigning to protest his government sending the Italian marines to India for trial, which he called an offense to the "honor of the country and of the armed forces." If border disputes on land are diplomatically fraught, this was a reminder that those disputes at sea are often deadly.

While on board the *Resolution,* I asked the men about the *Ohio*. One of the guards told me he had gotten off the ship several months before it was detained. The arrests were unjustified, he contended. "Guests shouldn't be arrested if their hotel breaks zoning laws," he said. Because six of the men arrested from the *Ohio* were former members of the British armed forces, the British prime minister, Theresa May, pressed Indian officials for a speedy release of the men during the 2017 G20

Summit. Joanne Thomlinson, the sister of John Armstrong, one of the incarcerated men, later emailed me to say that what frustrated her most was that so much evidence had been presented during the trial that should have exonerated her brother and the other guards. "And then the result is a maximum sentence?" she said, adding that she thought the case had been decided more by politics than by law.

Tensions can also flare up aboard the armories themselves among the security guards who bunk there. The conditions on some armories were abysmal, which made them potential crucibles for conflict. For example, while I was on a transport ship back to shore, I got an earful from a group of security guards who had been garrisoned aboard another armory in the Gulf of Oman. An hour after we left the *Resolution,* the transport pulled up to another floating armory, the *Seapol One,* to pick up some guards who were also headed back to land. A Sri Lankan firm called Avant Garde Maritime Services (AGMS) ran *Seapol One,* which they said was a far different world from the relatively orderly, clean *Resolution.*

Pulling out their smart phones, the guards vacating *Seapol One* showed me pictures of cockroaches that infested the ship. Other photos showed cramped cabins bunking eight men and strewn with trash because the ship had run out of places to keep the waste. Several guards lifted their shirts to show inflamed patches of red dots on their backs and arms from bedbugs.

Because the guards locked away their weapons when they boarded, the armories made attractive targets for pirates who might want to commandeer the arsenal. Like most floating armories, the *Seapol One* had no armed security of its own to police its guests or protect against external threats. Many coastal nations opposed the armories, though there was little they could do to stop them because they operated in international waters. There was no international registry of the location or number of arms depots, nor any international regulatory agency with jurisdiction over them.

None of the guards I interviewed knew of any fatal clashes on the armories, but there was no shortage of flash points. They told me about a Latvian guard who, at more than three hundred pounds and over six feet four inches tall, was too big to fit in the *Seapol One*'s tight bathroom stalls. So he used the shower to defecate, they said. Told to clean it up, he refused, daring anyone to try to force him.

They also recounted an incident from two days earlier, when several guards had to intervene to calm a heated argument that had erupted between two South African guards and their team leader. The dispute started because the men had not been paid for thirty days since their security company abandoned them on the *Seapol,* with no way to get back to port.

Mostly, the guards complained of boredom. Though intangible, this boredom had weight, and the longer it sat on the men, the more it crushed them. Nowhere was it heavier than on these armories. Partly that was because these ships were anchored. Having a destination and being in motion lightens the pressure of time and waiting. There was also less social cohesion among armory guards compared with most ship crews. The guards came from different security teams, countries, and cultures, which heightened their skepticism of each other and led to testosterone-steeped displays of macho gruffness.

Boredom turned these armories into "psychological pressure cookers," Kevin Thompson, a guard I met on one of them, told me. And to understand the volatility of these men, he added, you first have to reckon with the stress created by this boredom.

Mostly, the men coped by lifting weights (usually helped by "juicing" with steroids) or drinking alcohol (when they could sneak it on board). They also cut the tedium by inventing juvenile—and at times dangerous—games. "Bow Riding" entailed working your way to the front of the ship during a storm where you try to stay on your feet as waves crash across the deck. "Rodeo" was a game of balance and endurance, also played when seas were rough. It involved getting on a treadmill, turning up its speed, and seeing how long you could stay on. I enjoy distance running and fancied myself an above-average rodeo player. But I learned the hard way that if you were decent at the game, they upped the ante and turned out the lights ("night rodeo!"), which tended to end the round painfully fast.

In a more restrained moment one afternoon, I sat with three of the guards on the upper deck of the *Resolution,* and I pulled out my iPhone to show them the video of the killings on the Taiwanese tuna longliners. Huddled together, the men watched all ten minutes and twenty-six seconds of the footage. No one spoke as the video scrolled and we listened to the sound of gunshots and the men's screams through the phone's tinny speaker. In the men's loaded silence, I could feel the gulf

Private maritime security guards spar while living on a floating arms depot in the Gulf of Oman as they await their next deployment.

between us. Shooting the breeze over conditions on armories and the threat of violence at sea came easily, but this was something different. I was no longer one of the guys. I was a reporter asking about something they did not want to discuss. These men lived by a dangerous and sometimes brutal code of the sea, and they were clearly uncertain whether I understood that.

Finally, one of the men leaned back and broke the awkward silence. "Not how I would've handled it," he said. "But that's how it sometimes gets handled."

. . .

The experience aboard the *Resolution* gave me powerful insight into the gunslinging culture at sea, but it got me no closer to understanding what happened to the men whose deaths had been captured on video, especially given the crew's reticence on the topic. After returning to shore from the Gulf of Oman, I began to pursue the details of the case in earnest, starting with police in Fiji, where the phone with the shooting video was found. The police there gave me little useful information; in fact, they had already closed their investigation, having concluded that the incident did not involve their vessels and did not occur in their national waters.

Glen Forbes, director of the maritime investigations firm OCEANUSLive, seemed unsurprised by the conversation I had with the Fijians. When governments investigated cases like this, he observed, their goal was typically not to find the culprit but to distance themselves from the incidents to avoid any role or responsibility.

The nature of the video made it hard to assign blame. There was no obvious single nationality that the men shared; the video included people speaking in Chinese, Indonesian, and Vietnamese. There was little to be gleaned from the images of the three large vessels circling the floating men, other than a banner that read in Mandarin, "Safety is number one," hanging in the background on one of the ship's decks. But a fourth vessel seen passing in the background provided a crucial clue: numbers on its hull indicated that it was a 725-ton Taiwanese-owned tuna long-liner called the *Chun I 217.*

With one of the world's largest tuna fleets, Taiwan's fishing industry was among the nation's biggest and most politically powerful employers. In Taiwan, I tracked down the owner of the *Chun I 217,* a man named Lin Yu-chih, who was also a board member of the Taiwan Tuna Association. He owned more than a dozen ships and confirmed that the *Chun I 217* was present during the shooting but said he did not know whether any of his other ships were there when the men in the video were shot. "Our captain left as soon as possible," Lin said, referring to the scene of the shooting.

I pressed him. Lin refused to tell me any details about the crew of the *Chun I 217.* He also would not share the report that he asked the captain to write about the incident after the Taiwanese police contacted his company. The private security guards on his ships were provided by a Sri Lankan company, he said, but he would not name the company.

I also contacted the Taiwan prosecutor's office, which was looking into the matter. They declined to comment on the case. But two Taiwanese fishing officials later said that the company authorized to put private security guards on Taiwanese ships was AGMS. This was the same company that ran the *Seapol One,* the armory in the Gulf of Oman where the guards had complained about horrid conditions and were covered in infected rashes. AGMS refused to answer questions about its guards or its floating armories.

During an interview, Tzu-yaw Tsay, director of the Taiwanese fisheries agency, declined to provide the *Chun I 217*'s crew list, captain's name, or information about its routes. He suggested, though, that the men in the water were likely pirates. "We don't know what happened," Tsay emphasized. "So there's no way for us to say whether it's legal." Because the *Chun I 217* was in the Indian Ocean and fishing for tuna, I contacted the Indian Ocean Tuna Commission (IOTC), which oversees the granting of fishing licenses in the region, and the government of the Seychelles, which is also involved in permitting. Neither responded.

To describe this stonewalling as frustrating would be an understatement. Getting the runaround is an occupational hazard in journalism, but I have found in my years of investigative reporting that there is usually someone in a position of authority who is willing to help twist arms to get the kind of information I was seeking. Concerns about reputational damage can also motivate companies or governments to make at least a minimal effort to respond to a reporter. Not so in the maritime world, where all the actors seem to set their own ethical and moral compasses in different directions.

After weeks of spinning my wheels, I griped about it to a shipping-industry lawyer, who told me there was a term for what I was experiencing. On the "maritime merry-go-round," no one answers for wrongdoings at sea, the lawyer explained. If they do, it's only to send you and your questions to someone else. It's an insular world, and people in it work to keep it that way. It was another reminder that I was an outsider in this environment. I got on board ships at the pleasure of the captain, and I would speak to shipowners at the pleasure of just about no one.

In a last-ditch effort, I gathered maritime and corporate records related to the *Chun I 217* and other suspect ships. They offered a small but useful detail: three ships—the *Chun I 217,* the *Ping Shin 101,* and the *Chun I 236*—shared the same business address. Digging further, I found that there were seven vessels in the Chun I group. All were more or less of the same size, roughly between 170 and 190 feet long. Five were flagged to the Seychelles (the *Chun I 307, 316, 318, 326,* and *628*) and two to Taiwan (the *Chun I 217* and *236*).

This was noteworthy because most maritime experts that I interviewed speculated that the ships at the murder scene were likely connected to each other, perhaps even as "sister ships" that were jointly owned. "You don't rob a bank in mixed company," a former U.S. Coast Guard official said. "Look for your shooters on a ship connected to the *Chun I 217*." It was a good suggestion, but it didn't get me very far. I needed a bigger break.

.    .    .

My article about the shooting incident ran in *The New York Times* in July 2015. Not long after, Jon Huggins from Oceans Beyond Piracy got back in touch with me. Like me, he was troubled by the inaction after the shooting and doubted the official claim by the Taiwanese fishing company that the men in the water were pirates. He had reviewed the video closely and found hints that suggested otherwise. "None of it adds up," he said.

The pieces of wreckage floating in the water, for example, were likely too large to be from a skiff or a motorboat, which are often used by pirates. The boat was more likely a dhow, a fishing boat with one or more masts and lateen sails, commonly used in the Red Sea and the Indian Ocean.

Pirates don't typically use dhows, because they are not fast enough to catch powerful fishing boats or cargo ships. One exception is when pirates work in pairs. They stretch a rope across a sea-lane, usually at night, and when a cargo or fishing ship comes through, it catches the rope at the bow, pulling the two boats alongside. The pirates then heave up grappling hooks and climb aboard. This tactic didn't seem likely to apply to the murder video, because it was filmed during the day and there was no rope in the water.

The sinking boat was flying a flag, Huggins said, which was unusual for pirates. The flag's colors were green, red, and white, making it likely that the boat came from Somaliland, an autonomous state in Somalia, or Iran. Neither location was a popular launching spot for pirates. Based on the complexion and facial features of the men in the water, they looked more likely to be Indian, Sri Lankan, Pakistani, or Iranian, Huggins added.

As I pursued new leads after the publication of the article, a source pressed me at one point. He asked, "Why are you so determined to understand what the men were doing before they were shot?" Pirates, mutineers, fishing competitors, thieves, he said, they're all just dead men.

The question did not make sense to me, like a picture that would not come into focus. Figuring out what the men were doing just before they were shot was the entire point. The adjectives around this violent incident mattered. Were the men best described as fleeing, unwitting, attacking, or robbed before they ended up in the water? Were the shooters rejoicing, reluctant, or fearful? These adjectives would distinguish a fatal incident from a vendetta, a murder from an act of self-defense. They would indicate more precisely what kind of lawlessness was at play. Was it a vengeful pursuit of justice? A quest for righteous retribution? An orgiastic expression of capitalist violence? A hunting-humans-as-sport episode, à la "The Most Dangerous Game"? An assertion of territorial sovereignty? I was light-years from pinning down these descriptors of the attacked or the motives of the attackers, but I felt certain of the value of the pursuit.

I soon got a call from a source at a Norway-based maritime investigations firm called Trygg Mat Tracking (TMT). The firm had determined that the ship carrying some of the shooters during the incident was most likely called the *Ping Shin 101*. TMT had reached this conclusion, I was told, by comparing imagery from the original video with a database it created of more than three thousand archival photographs of over three hundred fishing vessels. The firm's top two analysts, Duncan Copeland and Stig Fjellberg, focused on distinct features of the ship where the video was filmed and the shots were fired, including the color of the trim, unique rust marks on the hull, the placement of fishing and safety gear, the number of portholes, and the shape of the railings. The *Ping Shin 101* matched many of the features of one of the ships that appeared in the video.

In a report provided to Interpol, TMT revealed that this was not an isolated case. A nine-minute video that TMT found on the internet, titled "Somalia," showed three tuna long-liners harassing and ramming a smaller fishing vessel somewhere in the Indian Ocean before July 2014. The three long-liners on the attack included the *Ping Shin 101*, the *Fortune 58*, and the *Fortune 78*, both flagged to the Seychelles.

The TMT report also offered a small clue to explain my experience on the maritime merry-go-round. I had repeatedly contacted authorities in the Seychelles and at the Indian Ocean Tuna Commission, which licenses fishing boats in the region, but they had been unwilling to talk to me. TMT's report identified a man named Rondolph Payet who held an interesting combination of roles: he was a director of a Seychelles-based company that was tied to the *Chun I 217* and the executive secretary of the IOTC, which granted a fishing license to the *Chun I 217*.

This was not just a conflict of interest. It also showed that powerful political figures had close connections to at least one of the suspect ships. "This will require a politically sensitive approach," the TMT report said about the discovery of Payet's ties to the suspect ships. Payet resigned from his position at the IOTC in November 2015, for reasons never made public. I suspected his resignation had to do with sensitive ties unveiled by TMT.

I had been pursuing this story and trying to solve the mystery for months. My editor at the *Times* rightly wanted me to move on and begin reporting the next story. But I had trouble letting the case go. How can a murder this well documented be allowed to stand? In an effort to keep the case alive, I compiled an online summary of my new findings about the case and published it on Facebook, hoping someone might use it.

Roughly a year later, National Geographic aired a television program called *Lawless Oceans*. The program followed a private investigator named Karsten von Hoesslin who—venturing to Taiwan, Thailand, India, Iran, Somalia, the Seychelles, and elsewhere—pushed tirelessly to figure out what happened in this deadly incident. Hiring local journalists and fishermen to provide him with information and locate sources, von Hoesslin interviewed witnesses to the shooting, families of the potential victims, jailed Somali pirates, anonymous government officials, and others. It was an impressive advance in the investigation, the break that I had sought but had been unable to find.

A Toronto native based in London, von Hoesslin previously worked as a senior analyst with Risk Intelligence, a firm that specialized in advising companies on security matters. He also headed his own company called the Remote Operations Agency, whose website described itself as "a niche investigations agency that specialises in solving cold cases & crisis response operations particularly in remote environments." On camera, von Hoesslin came across as driven and macho. One episode ended with slow-motion shots of him running on the beach. On his Instagram account, he taunted a man he said was the lead suspect in the murder. "You will find out who I really am," von Hoesslin wrote. "I will break you!"

His aggressive approach began getting results. Von Hoesslin identified three witnesses to the crime. Two were Filipino deckhands, named Aldrin and Maximo, who served on the *Ping Shin 101*. Maximo could be seen in the video smiling and posing for selfies after the shooting. He was wearing an oversized navy-blue T-shirt that said "Hang 10" on the front. A third deckhand from Indonesia named Anwar was on the *Chun I 628*, which was also at the scene. The three witnesses appeared on camera for the National Geographic filming crew, who shared only their first names.

The day that they shot the men in the water started like any other, the witnesses said. Sometime in August 2012, they were fishing in the Indian Ocean, somewhere between Somalia and the Seychelles. Work stopped abruptly after they received a radio alert that a nearby ship was under attack by pirates. It remained unclear which ship was being attacked, but the *Ping Shin 101*, the *Chun I 217*, and the *Chun I 268* headed to the location of the reported clash.

When they arrived, the fishing ships surrounded the smaller boat. There was yelling back and forth, and the men in the smaller boat seemed to be unarmed, the witnesses said. When shooting started, the men in the smaller boat leaped into the water. Some of them began yelling that they were not a threat. "No Somali!" Maximo recounted hearing them saying. "No pirates!"

At the time, the captain of the *Ping Shin 101* was a Chinese man named Wang Feng Yu, whom the deckhands called "Captain Hoodlum." "He was a rough guy," a deckhand named Art said. "He hits people." Aldrin added that Captain Wang—who had a dragon tattoo on his left arm and was in his late thirties, which is young for a captain—had a ferocious temper: "He punched, then kicked, if you did a mistake."

Built in 1989, the *Ping Shin 101* was a little over 165 feet long and owned by a Shanghai businessman named Lee Chao Ping. "It's more of a prison than a vessel," recounted Duncan Kawino, who in interviews with National Geographic said he worked on the vessel when it docked in Mombasa in 2013. "Very tiny beds, very thin mattresses, no pillows. It's totally filthy, lice and bedbugs everywhere." Kawino added that safety was not a concern on the *Ping Shin 101*. "It's pathetic," Kawino said. "There were no life rafts, no floaters, the fire extinguishers were not up to date."

Though it fished illegally most of the time in Somali waters, the *Ping Shin 101* falsely reported that its catch came from Seychelles waters, where it had a license, Kawino said. The *Ping Shin 101* and the *Chun I 628* had three armed guards each, all Pakistani, on board, the witnesses said. Though the video footage showed at least four men in the water being killed, Aldrin and Maximo said there were likely more people shot, possibly between ten and fifteen men.

The witnesses offered more revelations. The men who were shot were not likely pirates, they said. "They didn't have any guns, only fishing equipment on their boat," Maximo explained, without elaborating on the reason the men were murdered. "It was wrong, people getting shot. But there was nothing I could do about it." This killing was also not an isolated event, Aldrin added offhandedly. A similar murder happened at around 3:00 a.m. a week prior to the incident captured on video, he said, his attitude conveying that these attacks were not unusual and he was not particularly surprised by them. The circumstances were virtually the same: alleged pirates, rammed, shot, killed, their bodies left floating in the water. My suspicion was that this violence, like the incident I had investigated, was probably the result of tension over turf or because one ship had perhaps run over and damaged the other's fishing gear.

The captains on two ships—the *Ping Shin 101* and the *Chun I 628*—didn't just order the killings, the witnesses said. They fired the weapons at certain points, taking them from the guards. "I think my ship shot the most," Anwar said about the *Chun I 628*. Maximo said he spoke to one of the guards on the *Ping Shin 101* shortly before that guard began shooting. "I don't want to shoot them," Maximo recounted the guard saying before he was ordered to fire his weapon. "These people have families," the guard said. "I think it's wrong."

At one point, a man in the water climbed back onto the boat that was under fire. He started the engine, in what looked to be an escape attempt, witnesses said. Two of the long-liners immediately rammed the boat, breaking it to bits. "We were following it, chasing it, and then hitting it," Maximo recounted.

Meanwhile, the crews on the *Ping Shin 101* and the *Chun I 628* continued shooting and killing the other men who were still in the water. "After we finished, it was like a normal day," Aldrin continued. Everyone was ordered back to work. Anwar's captain collected all of the cell phones aboard the *Chun I 628* and deleted footage from them. But at least one person on board didn't follow the captain's instruction, and that crewman's footage ended up in the backseat of a taxicab in Fiji.

. . .

As often happens with crimes at sea, this story—or at least the essential evidence needed to solve this murder—ended up on the ocean floor. The *Ping Shin 101* sank on July 7, 2014. As it went down and its crew climbed into lifeboats, the captain broadcast a distress signal, citing an unspecified mechanical failure on board. Two crew members who were on the ship at the time later described the incident as highly suspicious. The captain and the engineer were unusually calm throughout the ship's sinking, the crewmen said. The sinking might have been the climax of a plot to dispose of evidence of a crime while also, perhaps, collecting insurance on what was supposed to look like an accident.

"Something exploded," said one of the crewmen named Aljon. "There was water coming in." Several hours later, the crew was rescued by a nearby cargo ship named the MV *Sam Tiger* and taken to Sri Lanka. Before the crew was sent home, each man was handed $100 cash. "'If police ask,'" Art recounted Captain Hoodlum telling them, "'don't say anything.'"

Meanwhile, von Hoesslin had also managed to pin down the names of some of the shooting victims from the video, three of whom were brothers from Pakistan. Their mother, a woman named Khadija, said the murders left her with no sons, and now she was raising her grandchildren. "My sons were my life," she said. "When will my heart heal?"

In subsequent months, von Hoesslin tried to present his findings to law enforcement in Taiwan, Somalia, and the Seychelles. None of the countries were willing to pursue the case. Wang, the Taiwanese captain and likely ringleader in the murder video, had since moved on to work on another fishing ship. As of 2017, he had not been charged, and the maritime merry-go-round continued to turn.

# THE SOMALI 7

The world, that understandable and lawful world, was slipping
away.

——William Golding, *Lord of the Flies*

When the engine stalled for the third time, we were clearly in trouble. The fishing boat I shared with several AK-47-toting guards was about a mile off Somalia's coast. We were near an area where the militant Islamic group al-Shabaab routinely attacked villages. A few weeks earlier, two persons had been shot there and several others kidnapped. The Islamic State, or ISIS, was also active in the region. Retreating to shore was not an option, particularly because we did not look so friendly ourselves.

With me, I had a team of fifteen men, seven of them hired armed guards, part of a security squad that cost me $3,000 for two weeks of protection. The three thirty-foot-long wooden fishing boats with outboard motors traveling in a convoy strained under the weight of so many men. Dusk was approaching, and the engine was sputtering.

We were on our way to meet up with a military-grade, private police ship run by a company called the Somali Security Service. More commonly known as SSS, the company patrolled Somali waters on behalf of the local government of a semiautonomous region called Puntland, looking for foreign ships that were fishing illegally in its waters. After years of grim publicity over Somali piracy, Puntland's aggressive moves against illegal fishing seemed like a good news story; the government had even set up its own maritime police fleet, called the Puntland Maritime Police Force (PMPF), to enforce fishing laws alongside the private

SSS. Puntland officials had offered me a chance to join an SSS patrol if I could find someone willing to take me out to its ship. At the time, the SSS ship was anchored a couple miles from the village of Habo, located at the very tip of the Horn of Africa, directly south of Yemen. We had to travel there by sea because over land was too dangerous.

The day did not start well. When we embarked, two of us made the mistake of stepping to the same side of the boat. Each boat was equipped with a large steel drum full of petrol, and when the boat shifted under our weight, the fuel sloshed, nearly capsizing us. After an hour's journey along the shore, one of the guards ordered me to sit on the floor to avoid being seen by anyone who might consider me a profitable kidnapping opportunity. Roughly half a mile from shore, we were easy-to-spot targets. We were traveling parallel to a beach that backed up to flat, orange-tinted scrubland stretching inland as far as the eye could see.

As we travel down a dangerous section of the Puntland shoreline in Somalia, guards tell me to sit on the floor to be less visible from shore.

Every fifteen minutes, our boat pilot, Mohamud, took a hose and stuck one end in his mouth and the other into the fuel drum to siphon more gas into the boat's tank. Inevitably, he spilled some in the boat, which mixed with water puddling near me and soaked my clothes and backpack. Before long, I reeked of gas and felt high from the fumes. At one point, Fabio Nascimento, who was lying on his back in the puddled gas, closed his eyes to avoid the glare. A couple minutes later, he opened his eyes again to discover that one of the guards sitting on the side of the boat had moved nearby and the muzzle of his loaded AK was now inadvertently two inches from Nascimento's head.

The Somali sun overhead cooked us with a mean, dry heat—the headache-inducing type that makes thoughts evaporate and tempers shorten. As I sat in the boat, I could see Mohamud chain-smoking in the stern, and I kept my distance for obvious reasons having to do with the flammability of my clothes. About three hours in, I offered him a piece of gum, partly to break the ice, partly to get him to stop smoking long enough so I could get near and we could chat. Lanky and stern-faced, he declined my gum but stubbed out his half-smoked cigarette and saved it for later. Reaching into a plastic bag, he pulled out a hand-ful of khat, a plant commonly chewed in Somalia with amphetamine-like effects. The owner of two fishing boats, he had plenty of complaints about corruption within the Puntland government. He also dismissed the media and government claims to have cracked down on foreign fishing boats. Outsiders were still being given free rein on local waters, he said.

The trip to the SSS ship was supposed to take five hours. The engine failed at about four and a half. "Mr. Ian, we have a problem," Mohamud said, glancing furtively at the guards. Seeing his facial expression was like sniffing spoiled milk. I didn't need more information to know it was bad. "I see that," I replied, nodding toward the engine. "No, bigger," he said. A text on his phone had informed him of new coordinates of the SSS ship. It would now take another nine hours to reach our desti-nation, he told me. It seemed, for security reasons perhaps, that the SSS ship had moved farther away from us since we had launched.

The expedition was deteriorating rapidly into a dangerous situation. If we stayed the course—assuming we could even get the engine going again—we would be traveling after dark, when pirate and al-Shabaab attacks were more common. The bigger risk, though, was the water. At night, the winds picked up, turning five-foot swells into twenty-foot waves that would easily capsize us. Our boats were low-sided and prone to taking on water. Each had a 25-horsepower motor, barely stronger than an engine in a riding lawn mower. These vessels were not meant for carrying five men, much less the weight of heavy weapons and steel drums full of petrol, traversing coastal waters with night swells.

Not a hard call: I told Mohamud that we needed to turn back. He looked at me, nodded, and continued tinkering with his outboard motor as though he had more important concerns on his mind. One of the armed guards seemed especially nervous, his eyes darting, his fingers fidgeting with his gun. I asked him if he was worried about al-Shabaab or ISIS. "PMPF," he replied, much to my surprise. It wasn't the terrorists that most worried him, he said. It was the police.

. . .

Some of the trips I took while reporting on the outlaw ocean turned out to be more perilous than I expected. But in preparing to go to Somalia, I knew that I was taking risks. For all the talk of improving conditions in this part of the world, Somalia was a place where the authorities and criminals were shape-shifting characters, which made danger unpredictable but ever present.

Racked by drought, civil war, starvation, piracy, and terrorism, the country had been a poster child of national dysfunction for years. In 2009, Somali piracy burst into the world's consciousness with the saga of the *Maersk Alabama* and the hardscrabble pirates who seized that ship. After the raiders attempted to ransom the crew, the U.S. Navy's storied SEAL Team Six rescued the men. And the nail-biting story turned into the big-screen action thriller *Captain Phillips*.

My wife had become relatively numb to concerns about my traveling. Or at least she gave that impression. My mother, on the other hand, was a different matter. She was a consummate worrier, and when I was home, she always questioned me where I planned to go next. Then she would suggest that I make the next trip my last one. So, in the lead-up to Somalia, I kept my plans vague in my conversations with her. "Somewhere in East Africa," I would say. "I'm starting in Kenya, then I'll go around the region from there." It wasn't a lie, just not the full truth. The fact of the matter was that there was no way to write a book about lawlessness at sea and not go to Somalia. To bypass the country would be akin to skipping the Galápagos while reporting on the diversity of animal species.

But the real reason I went to this most dangerous of places was to tell a good-news story about the country's recent successes in offshore policing. Somali piracy was on the decline. There had not been an attack on a commercial foreign vessel since 2012. Merchant traffic was picking up again through the Gulf of Aden between Somalia and

Yemen, a welcome development for shipping companies moving fuel and other cargo between Asia and Europe, given that circling the Cape of Good Hope added three weeks to a typical journey. Some shipping companies and their insurers were softening their security requirements and manning their ships with fewer armed guards. A NATO naval force had pulled out several months earlier, though an EU contingent remained.

The Puntland Maritime Police Force was the only true government presence in these waters, the supposed white hats fighting off poachers and pirates. In the PMPF and the SSS, Somalia had created new models for patrolling its waters. It had even scored a recent victory in an unusual collaboration with the Kenyan government, resulting in the arrest of two persistent poaching ships called the *Greko 1* and the *Greko 2*, which had been operating using fake fishing licenses. The detention of the ships caught my attention because I knew it to be rare that the Somali government arrested illegal fishing boats raiding its waters. "Things are definitely looking up," one D.C.-based security specialist said before I headed to the region. As part of my pre-trip research, I compiled a list of fishing boats plying Somali waters. If I was to go offshore, I wanted to know what ships I might encounter. On that list were seven Thai ships owned by a company that had a bad reputation for labor abuses.

Within several days of arriving in Mogadishu, I discovered a far more complicated and troubling story about maritime malfeasance off Somalia's coast. It was a story largely ignored by the Western press because it didn't fit neatly in the black-and-white narrative rendered in movies like *Captain Phillips*.

What became starkly clear was that illegal fishing and piracy in Somalia are closely intertwined. A weak federal government based in Mogadishu and rebellious local governments in autonomous states like Puntland compound the problem by blurring the lines between what is legitimate fishing and what is not. The real story in Puntland, I would soon find out, was that the government there was protecting illegal ships, including those seven Thai-owned trawlers on the list that I compiled.

My education about the volatility and complexity of this place had started before I climbed into Mohamud's boat. In the days prior to launching offshore, I spoke to Puntland fishermen who predicted that piracy would return soon. Their argument, which turned out to be right, was that locals were fed up with the Puntland government for focusing more on protecting foreign fishing boats than local ones. The logic was that if the government was going to protect foreign boats, which often bullied Somali fishermen, then clan leaders, who had their own local power, would sanction pirates to start attacking foreign boats again to redistribute the wealth—leveling the playing field, as it were. Those rumblings should have warned me that all was not as it appeared with PMPF and SSS.

As our three-boat convoy bobbed in the waves while Mohamud struggled with the engine for the long return to shore, the men in my boat began telling me stories that further complicated my vision of Puntland and its offshore policing efforts. A second guard said that he too worried about the PMPF, which might mistake us for militants and open fire on our boat. Could we blame them for making such an error? I wondered. After all, our boat was full of heavily armed men not wearing government uniforms. None of our boats had a radio, so there was no way to properly identify ourselves.

A third guard piled on. Adding to our list of worries, he pointed out that these waters were a popular hunting ground for pirates. The Western media might have claimed that piracy in Somalia was dead, he said, but it had simply shifted to non-Western targets.

Mohamud, my chain-smoking boat pilot, added that Puntland's government worsened the potential for danger by empowering private security firms to target boats like the ones we were in. Foreign boats already had the upper hand, he said, because they were larger and more efficient than those belonging to local fishermen. Then the local government gave these foreign boats licenses and allowed them to put armed security on board, a significant advantage in such dangerous waters.

"At night, they cut our nets, fire on us, ram our boats," he said about the foreign boats. Such clashes sometimes stranded Somalis in the water, miles from shore, where they were often left to drown. Foreign fishing boats usually didn't help the local economy either. Instead of entering ports in Somalia, they preferred to off-load their catch in Yemen, Oman, Iran, or Kenya.

As we discussed the list of reasons why it was not good to be stranded in these waters, my translator chimed in, too. He said that the real threat to us was the SSS, the group we had set out hoping to visit offshore. The company acted as a state-sanctioned bounty hunter, the translator said. When it caught illegal fishing vessels, the SSS was allowed to keep half of any fines that the Puntland government was able to levy. "I don't trust them," the translator said. He speculated that the SSS had intentionally misled us about how long it would take to reach them, leaving us open to being kidnapped and lucratively ransomed.

I didn't know whom to believe. So many reasons to worry. Each of the armed groups supposedly prowling these waters had at one time or another claimed to be a security force. And, just as often, each group had also been characterized by outside experts as rogue operators.

There were early signs that this trip offshore might have been a very bad idea. Before arriving in Puntland, I had hired a fixer to help me navigate this volatile place and arrange logistics. The fixer was a well-educated young Somali man who lived in another Somali state but traveled often to Puntland and knew it well. I had found him through a friend at the UN. He had good credentials and he seemed reliable over email and during our occasional call. He also had been vetted by several trusted sources.

He and I had agreed that I would pay him $2,500 to travel with me while I was in Puntland, where he would also serve as my primary fixer. The Puntland government insisted on providing me with its own translator, whose main role was to serve as my minder. But I occasionally wanted someone else around who could also translate for me to make sure I was getting accurate information. My fixer could serve this purpose.

But after arriving in Somalia, I discovered several things about my fixer that had not been apparent during our brief phone calls. First off, he answered virtually every question with an exuberant "Absolutely, 100 percent," even when that answer was patently incorrect. Are we sure that we will have internet at the hotel, I asked him at one point. "Absolutely, 100 percent." (We barely had electricity.) Are we certain that we can get to the port and out on the water without government interference? "Absolutely, 100 percent." (The local government put us under house arrest soon after we got back to our hotel.)

The second issue was that the fixer also had a severe stutter that worsened significantly under the kind of stressful conditions that were not uncommon in Puntland. Never was that stutter worse than when we were climbing into the fishing boats for our fateful voyage out to the SSS ship. At the last minute, my fixer turned to me and painfully forced out his confession: he was too scared to go, he said, and he planned to stay onshore. "If you aren't coming with us," I asked shortly before launching, "are you sure it's safe for us to go solo?" Without missing a beat, he replied, "Absolutely, 100 percent."

Hours later, as we sat stalled in those boats, I thought about these warning signs and worried that I'd made a horrible mistake. I had dragged Fabio Nascimento, my young photographer, with me, and I winced at the idea that my misjudgment might have been driven by naïveté and ambition, with potentially dire consequences.

To my relief, our pilot, Mohamud, got us moving again after about twenty minutes of tinkering with the engine. Our small convoy hobbled its way back to Bosaso port in Puntland. I never made it to my embed on the SSS ship, and in retrospect I questioned whether the invitation was sincere in the first place. But my impression was that things were hardly "looking up" in Somalia, as others had previously told me. In fact, far more remained broken than fixed, it seemed to me. And along with the locals, I was straining to tell the bureaucrats from the bandits, and the police from the outlaws.

.   .   .

I'd been told that to understand Somalia, it was best not to think of it as a functioning nation, because it's not. To outsiders, Somalia was a construct created by movies and news reports, a land awash in weapons and racked by famine. In UN parlance, it was a "failed state." To insiders, Somalia was a loose collection of highly autonomous enclaves. This had been especially true since the civil war in 1991. Mogadishu was the seat of the feeble federal government, which controlled only a small portion of that city, to say nothing of its oversight of the rest of the country.

Politics in Somalia was largely clan based. Puntland, for example, was home to six major clans: the Harti, Majerteen, Warsangali, Dhulbahante, Dishiishe, and Lailkase. When one clan or subclan dominated government, money and favors circulated among its members. This was not considered graft or favoritism; it was, by and large, the accepted norm of balance-of-power governance.

This lack of a central authority on land was even more pronounced offshore. Though Somalia had more coastline than any nation in continental Africa, the country ranked lowest in terms of per capita fish consumption. Fishing had never been a popular livelihood in Somalia. Its people settled more inland and were largely farmers. In the late 1970s and early 1980s, the country's dictator, Mohamed Siad Barre, tried, especially after several droughts and famines, to force a shift in cultural perceptions and habits around fishing. His government resettled inland nomadic communities along the coast and broadcast radio ads about the health benefits and potential profits of fishing. The campaign had little lasting impact, however.

Puntland was home to roughly 40 percent of Somalia's two-thousand-mile coastline. The best fishing was close to shore, partly because the continental shelf near Puntland created a shallow plateau, making fish easier to catch. Foreign vessels, most of them illegal, were bigger, more efficient, and in some areas more numerous. On average, the foreign boats landed three times more fish from these waters than did the Somali boats.

Piracy, which grew into an acute problem in 2008, was concentrated primarily in the Gulf of Aden, a stretch of water that is roughly 550 miles long and 200 miles wide between Yemen and Somalia. For Somalia, this piracy resulted from decades of onshore corruption and statelessness. In the absence of any central authority in the country, semi-organized groups of bandits that previously targeted rival clans onshore moved their attention offshore toward deeper-pocketed targets, sometimes invoking, with varying levels of legitimacy, illegal fishing and other grievances as a justification for their attacks.

Part of the difficulty in policing these waters has always been financial. Authorities in Mogadishu and in the semiautonomous Somali states along the coast have little money to pay for their own marine force. So they have in recent years funded the work by making private companies stakeholders in the business of granting fishing licenses. This model proved financially unstable and prone to corruption. Through these licensing fees, foreign fishing companies were paying the salaries of armed police forces on Somali waters. The consequence was that armed guards working for companies like the SSS were more concerned about protecting foreigners from Somalis than the other way around—or at least that became the perception locally.

Aside from the SSS, the second force patrolling the coast of Somalia was the PMPF, which had roughly a thousand men, three inflatables with rigid hulls, a transport aircraft, and a helicopter. The PMPF was funded not by fishing licenses but almost entirely by the government of the United Arab Emirates. Located less than nine hundred miles northeast of Bosaso, the U.A.E. had an interest in protecting the shipping routes through the Gulf of Aden. Further complicating the regional geopolitics, the U.A.E. also hoped to establish a military base in Puntland to conduct military operations in Yemen, which was in the midst of a brutal civil conflict.

There have been other concerns about these groups. UN officials and human rights groups have pointed out that both the PMPF and the SSS were answerable to virtually no one and that there was little ability to monitor where the money went from the fines tied to arrests they made. It was also nearly impossible to check whether these forces were justified when they opened fire on boats.

The third group patrolling Somali waters was a coalition of UN member nations. For the first time since World War II, all five permanent members of the Security Council deployed forces on the same side of a conflict, sending navy vessels and aircraft to the region, starting in 2009. This military presence allowed for more efficient deployments of sniper teams, coordination of ransom payoffs, and safe evacuations during hostage situations.

Complicating matters further, the shipping industry reacted in its own way, and the economics of that response was at times perverse. For example, freight companies and their insurers began imposing piracy fees—upwards of $23 per standard shipping container—to cover additional security costs, which on bigger ships could mean a quarter of a million dollars per trip. Even factoring in the cost of private guards and the occasional multimillion-dollar ransom payouts exacted by pirates, shipping companies and crews were sometimes profiting from the threat of Somali piracy.

Some security analysts have pointed out that the international naval patrols likely worsened Somalia's illegal fishing problem. Legitimate and local fishing boats piloted by Somalis were routinely sent back to shore by coalition forces because they often looked like possible pirates. Meanwhile, illegal foreign vessels, especially from China, Taiwan, and South Korea, were allowed to fish in Somali waters unharmed because coalition forces had a narrowly circumscribed antipiracy mission that did not authorize them to police the crime of at-sea poaching.

Still, it's hard to deny that the security response generally worked. Most naval experts attribute the decline of Somali pirate attacks by 2013 to the combination of the allied patrols and, in particular, the increased presence of armed guards on commercial vessels. Needless to say, as I headed to Somalia, I knew it to be a complex place, but piracy seemed to be in remission, the government in Puntland seemed to be earnest about its commitment to countering illegal fishing, and the private security forces were said to have cleaned up their acts. Overall, things appeared to be "looking up."

. . .

Puntland, always on edge, was especially chaotic when I got there. In the weeks beforehand, a dozen local soldiers had staged a brief mutiny in Puntland's capital, Garowe, and seized a section of Parliament because the soldiers had not been paid in months. Al-Shabaab fighters had stormed the International Village Hotel in Bosaso, killing several guards in the attack. A state lawmaker had been killed by a car bomb. Puntland's population of four million was in the throes of a severe drought, which had already led to the deaths of several hundred people.

Prior to my arrival, Puntland officials repeatedly assured me that I would have full access to the PMPF, the SSS, and the state president. They also provided me with a monthlong visa to the state. By the time I got to Africa, however, the posture of these officials had changed, and I was informed of a different arrangement. I would no longer be guaranteed access to the PMPF, and while an interview with the president and an embed with the SSS were possible, I would need to wait at my hotel and see. "No guarantees," the Puntland president's chief of staff told me by phone a couple of hours after I landed on Bosaso.

The reason for the shift, I later found out, was that my request to visit Puntland had set off a panic in the state's Ministry of Fisheries. The Puntland president's chief of staff and other members of his inner circle said that the main critic of my trip was the state minister of fisheries, Abdirahman Jama Kulmiye. They explained that he was worried I would write about how Puntland and his ministry were granting fishing licenses, because some might question whether the process was corrupt and why so little of the revenue was being used for public purposes. I did my best to placate them, assuring them that my focus was Somalia's recent successes, including the arrests of the *Greko*s.

Eventually, I called Kulmiye directly to give him more context and to hear from him his concerns. I explained that I intended to look at the PMPF and the SSS and how they policed Puntland waters. "I have no problem with you coming to Puntland," Kulmiye said. "I will help your reporting. You have my full support." I hung up feeling worried by his tone.

Heated debate ensued within the Ministry of Fisheries over how to handle my now-unwelcome visit. One side had argued that they should block my visa. The other side, which won the debate, wanted to allow me into the state but to limit my access. So they granted a visa but assigned me the translator who was to serve more as my minder. His primary job was to stay by my side for all conversations, even, or especially, for those where everyone spoke English and no translator was needed.

I soon learned the reason for Kulmiye's opposition to my visit. The seven notorious Thai fishing boats that I'd noticed on my list before I arrived in Somalia were anchored in Bosaso when I began my journey to the region. The Puntland government didn't want me asking questions about that fleet. Nicknamed the Somali 7, the Thai ships consisted of the *Chotpattana 55*, *Chotchainavee 35*, *Chotpattana 51*, *Chainavee 54*, *Chainavee 55*, *Supphermnavee 21*, and *Chaichanachoke 8*. These trawlers, each with light blue or aqua hulls and the capacity to hold more than two hundred tons of fish, were owned by a prominent and very wealthy Thai family whose last name is Sangsukiam. Ships within the Sangsukiam fleet were alleged to have been involved in forced labor and human trafficking and were being investigated by Thai and Indonesian authorities for related crimes. All seven ships held Puntland fishing licenses of questionable validity.

The sketchiness surrounding the Sangsukiam fleet dates back to 2015, after the Thai government began imposing tougher rules and closer inspections on overseas ships flying the Thai flag. In response to the new restrictions, the Sangsukiam family removed the seven ships destined for Somalia from the Thai registry, re-flagging them in 2016 to Djibouti, Somalia's northern neighbor. I knew very little about these

One of the Somali 7 fleet unloads fish in the port of Bosaso.

Thai vessels as I headed to Puntland, but the more the local government panicked about them, the more interested I became.

In Puntland, the Somali 7 carried extra political baggage. Puntland deemed the vessels legal because it had given them permission to fish in its waters for three months. But federal officials in Mogadishu considered the ships illegal because they had not given them fishing licenses, a power reserved to them under federal law. Worse still, the Thai ships were trawling, which was banned under federal law, and they were foreign-flagged vessels fishing within twenty-four nautical miles of the coast, which at the time was also prohibited.

The backdrop of this dispute was an ongoing tug-of-war between Puntland, which coveted its autonomy, and Mogadishu, which argued that for Somalia to become a fully functioning nation, states like Puntland had to comply with federal law. Since 2011, Puntland routinely asserted its independence from Mogadishu by engaging directly in bilateral negotiations with Yemen, for example, over illegal fishing and human trafficking and by signing contracts with international security companies.

In Mogadishu, where I stopped before Puntland, I learned just how much of a flash point the Somali 7 ships had become. During my visit to the capital, I stayed near the airport in a fortified, privately run compound. It resembled a military base more than a hotel. Fifteen-foot blast walls surrounded a graveled patch lined with two dozen steel shipping containers, which included makeshift living quarters where I resided. Each corner of the compound had its own watchtower, with two Somali soldiers who manned large, mounted machine guns. Not the most hospitable retreat I'd stayed in.

Headed to an Egyptian cattle carrier that was anchored several miles off the coast of Mogadishu, we are carried by Somali guards in a small cutter.

My reporting interviews in Mogadishu were at the port. Though it was less than three miles from the compound, it took two hours to get there. In an armored vehicle trailed by a heavily armed convoy of private security guards, we crawled our way around gutted husks of cars and buses, passing leveled buildings. At practically every third block, soldiers manning heavily armed checkpoints stopped us. The devastation was apocalyptic. If the government needed to exert this level of control simply to hang on to a section of its capital, I wondered, how could it hope to impose its authority over the hinterland and vast stretches of coastline?

At the port, I visited an anchored cattle carrier to talk with its crew about security in Somali waters, after which I sat down onshore with government officials first from Mogadishu, then from Puntland. I stuck initially to my plan to focus on recent Somali successes. I asked the men about the crackdown on the *Greko* ships, but in each interview the men wanted to talk about something else: the Thai ships anchored near Bosaso. On the one hand, federal officials said they were considering various ways to punish Puntland for having issued the licenses, including the possibility of withholding teachers' salaries, which largely came from international donor funds and were channeled through the federal government. On the other hand, the Puntland officials were equally incensed that Mogadishu was once again meddling in their

In the port of Mogadishu, Fabio Nascimento and I talk to Captain Mohamud H. Moghe, a senior Coast Guard officer, hoping to arrange a boat to take us up the coast.

affairs. Both sides warned me that Puntland believed I was being dispatched to their state to investigate the Thai ships.

I told them, as I had repeatedly told the others, that the seven Thai ships were not my focus. But I was beginning to believe that perhaps they should be, as they seemed to offer an unusual window into the problem of licensing corruption. Despite my desire to maintain some journalistic distance from the story, I was also finding myself increasingly pulled into the center of a power struggle between two would-be governments, neither of which had full control over the territory it claimed. The trip was reminding me that in journalism you don't always get to pick your story. Sometimes it picks you. And sometimes it pulls you into the middle.

. . .

I took a flight from Mogadishu to Hargeisa, Somaliland, and a couple of days later I flew to Bosaso, Puntland, where I stayed at the Ga'ayte Hotel. A garishly painted inn, the hotel was near the port facing out over Bosaso's harbor across a wide, desolate plaza adorned with a few stunted shrubs and trees. I spent most of my time in the hotel courtyard, where local businessmen often convened small meetings over coffee. I made friends quickly because people were eager to introduce themselves to the visiting American. Though I doubted it, we were told that there were no other Westerners in Puntland at the time.

The consensus among these courtyard elites was that illegal fishing was at an all-time high—sometimes by outsiders simply raiding Somali waters, other times with Puntland authorities granting fake licenses and pocketing the payments. Some of these businessmen spoke with remarkable authority and candor about buying counterfeit licenses. Piracy would soon return, if only as a local and opportunistic reaction to these foreign boats, they predicted.

In the regional capital, news of my visit had spread quickly. Several of the people who lounged in the courtyard worked for the local fisheries ministry. Virtually all of them confided in me that Kulmiye was panicked about my stay in Puntland. He was convinced, they added, that I was not just conspiring with Mogadishu to promote a "Western agenda" shaped by the UN fisheries agency. Kulmiye and his deputy minister were also telling the local port authority, the CEO of the SSS, the director of the PMPF, and the president of Puntland that I was with the CIA. I had encountered (and simply ignored) this sort of allegation while reporting in other countries, but the stakes seemed higher in Somalia.

While we waited at the hotel to hear whether Puntland fisheries officials would allow me to pursue my fishing enforcement story, I heard new rumblings of the chaos that my visit was causing. Several Puntland officials described how the previous week the Puntland government had told the Thai vessels that they needed to vacate the port immediately, before the foreign reporter arrived. The Thai captains could not leave, however, until a wire payment cleared for the more than $650,000 cost of the three-month fishing license they had purchased for the seven vessels. The payment cleared forty-eight hours before I arrived in Bosaso, and the Thai boats bolted so quickly that they left behind the two Puntland observers they were required to bring along to document their catch. A couple of hours later, the ships were called back to port to pick them up.

Before they left again, an argument erupted. The Thai boat captains insisted that the observers hand over their cell phones, because the captains did not want them taking any video or pictures. The standoff did not last long. Even though the observers were on board to document what they saw, Puntland capitulated; the men turned over the phones, and the ships set off.

That the Puntland government had assigned a minder to keep tabs on me was not surprising, and I quickly grew to like him. His English was good, if bookish. He sometimes used fake words that were just barely but delightfully off, like "insinnuendo" and "comfirmative." His tendency to preface every disclosure with "literally," "candidly," or "honestly" suggested an earnest hunger for familiarity. He was a smart man in his twenties with a restless intellect. He had an endearing if exhausting habit of strafing me with rapid-fire questions when we had downtime. "Have you been to Cleveland?" "Who started terrorism?" "Are there Hindus in America?" He asked me not to use his name in what I wrote and I agreed.

Still, he and I shared a mutual distrust, and I was confident that he was back channeling information to the government about my reporting even when he assured me he wasn't. As we sat together one day between interviews and surveyed the courtyard, a rare silence between us expanded like a bubble. Soon, the translator leaned in to puncture it. "Level with me, Mr. Ina," he said. (Most Somalis could not pronounce my first name.) "Tell me, confidentially only, the real reason for your trip to Puntland." He added: "Are you looking into the Thai ships?"

This seemed like an opportune moment to test our relationship. I told him that I wasn't originally planning on investigating the Thai ships, but I was changing my mind. On my iPhone, I showed him AIS tracking information about their current movements. The Thai boats were moving in a zigzag pattern at about two knots, and I explained that it was a likely indication that they were trawling. I pointed out that trawling was illegal under Somali federal law. "Wow," he said several times as he watched my screen. "I will keep this between us," he added at the end of our discussion. I excused myself from the table, saying that I needed to make a phone call and check in with my wife. "Stay put," I said. "I'll be back in forty-five minutes."

I did not actually plan to call my wife. The truth was, I hadn't spoken with her or my son in weeks, and not because of poor cell reception, which is one of the few things that works well virtually everywhere in Somalia. I had avoided calling them because the faster the situation was deteriorating in Puntland, the more dangerous things were becoming and the less I wanted them to know about it.

The real reason I left the table was to test my new friend's trustworthiness. Shortly after arriving at the hotel, I had recruited someone to be a discreet and extra set of eyes and ears for me. The young man who spoke decent English agreed to my offer of $5 a day (the equivalent of his weekly salary at a nearby store) to sit in the hotel's outdoor courtyard where all meetings happened and listen to as many conversations as he could. When I sat with people, he knew to move quietly to the adjacent table and eavesdrop on the discussions after I left. The waiters knew that anything this young man wanted to eat or drink was to be put on my tab.

Later that afternoon, my young friend told me that right after I left to make my supposed call to my wife, my government minder had phoned someone. "He knows everything about the Thai trawlers," the minder said. "He even can see them on his iPhone. I don't know how he can do that, but he can."

·  ·  ·

In this kind of reporting, journalists routinely put their lives (and the lives of those traveling with them) in the hands of total strangers and people you have only split seconds to size up. My security in Bosaso, for example, was being provided by a local power broker named Mohamed Yusuf Tigey. Though I was introduced to Tigey through a contact at *The New York Times,* he was otherwise a complete unknown. I had no option other than to rely on an un-vetted cast of characters during this trip because the *Times*'s point man in Somalia had recently fled to Finland after receiving death threats, leaving me on my own to find trustworthy allies.

A former governor from the Somali administrative region of Mudug, Tigey came from a wealthy landowning family, part of the Majerteen clan. He was in his mid-fifties and prayed five times a day, like most of the men I met in Puntland. Preternaturally calm, he had the casual manner of someone with nothing to prove. He also had a fondness for Adidas tracksuits and pristine white tennis shoes. Widely viewed as incorruptible, Tigey was among Puntland's top coordinators for responding to drought emergencies, which added to his popularity and his ability to move more freely in a region where government officials were routinely the targets of assassination attempts.

Though he had assigned fifteen private soldiers to protect me and my team, usually only a dozen of these guards were on duty at any given time, except when we had to travel to riskier neighborhoods of Bosaso or surrounding regions. Despite pressure from the Puntland government not to help me, Tigey was unwavering. "He is my guest," I overheard Tigey tell Kulmiye during a call at one point. "You gave him a visa to visit. I gave him my word that I would take him wherever he needs to go and guarantee his safety." Tigey was, after all, earning top dollar for this sort of service. But so too were certain translators and guards, and I was much less certain of their commitment.

Tigey was good at his job, and even though the unsuccessful trip to visit the SSS patrol ship was a nail-biter, he kept me safe. At the same time, I recognized that his job was getting more difficult the longer I stayed in Puntland. The day after we returned to shore in Bosaso, the Ministry of Fisheries informed Tigey that I would not be allowed to leave the hotel, even with Tigey's soldiers.

I was not to visit the port again, nor would I be allowed to go to the fisheries office, where I had an appointment the next day. So much for

In Puntland, Somalia, a team of privately hired guards hustles to usher us offshore before local authorities who did not want us to investigate a Thai fleet fishing in nearby waters arrive at the Bosaso port to stop us.

having a Puntland visa, I thought. It was a reminder that whether it was the *Grekos*' (supposed) fishing licenses or the Thai trawlers' (questionable) fishing licenses, documents are only as good as the issuing country decides for them to be. Paper is just paper.

At my hotel, I met with another source to get more information about the situation unfolding around me. "You're officially under house arrest," he told me. The fisheries minister was now convinced I was out to get him and to destabilize Puntland. I had been promoted from a spy to a saboteur in the eyes of the Puntland government. My source said that Kulmiye and others in Puntland were trying to get me out of Puntland immediately. I responded casually that I was more than ready to leave Puntland except that there were no flights soon. The source must have sensed that I was being flippant. "No, Ian," he said. "They're considering all options," my source said with an ominous stare that seemed to be a warning. Whereas elsewhere in the world killing an American journalist (or a CIA officer) would have been highly improbable because of the harsh repercussions likely to follow, Somalia was a different sort of place.

I heeded his caution. I also noticed I had the opposite feeling I had experienced in places like Indonesia and the Philippines reporting on the Oyang fleet or Eril Andrade's death. In these places, authorities could not have cared less about my reporting. In this case, on the other hand, it seemed perhaps too many people cared.

The stakes soon began to escalate quickly. That afternoon, I felt a blast, and the walls of the hotel trembled. A bomb had exploded less than two blocks away. Al-Shabaab claimed responsibility. Five persons were injured. More attacks were likely, according to security officers in the city. My eyes-and-ears friend in the courtyard checked in. He told me that he had overheard Tigey say that he feared he may soon be assassinated, partly because he was protecting me and my team.

The message was the same from my sources in Mogadishu. "Puntland says you're PNG," one of them texted me, meaning "persona non grata." You should leave Bosaso immediately, another source from the British security company wrote. "Easier said than done," I replied. Virtually all the surrounding roads were impassable because al-Shabaab and ISIS were attacking convoys. There were no private planes to rent. The first commercial flight out was not for forty-eight hours.

The next day I asked Tigey and Nascimento to meet me in my room so I could update them on what I had been told and my plans for the next two days. I told them about the two distinct security threats that were apparently escalating. The first threat was coming from outside the hotel, I had been warned by a security company that tracks intelligence in Puntland. These security officers had told me that al-Shabaab and ISIS might try to enter the compound because it was weakly fortified and now it was widely known that Westerners were staying there. The second threat was coming from inside the hotel, I was told. Kulmiye's alarmist rhetoric was creating risks. Many soldiers from different groups were inside our compound, sources explained, making it virtually impossible for us to distinguish friend from foe.

At the hotel, many of these soldiers looked as if they could be younger than fifteen. Some of them lugged around heavy rocket-propelled grenade launchers. Others carried belt-loaded Kalashnikov PKMs, a hundred-round bullet bandolier strung around their necks and waists as if they were showing off their pet boa constrictors. The boys who mugged it up and made eye contact worried me less than the stern-faced ones who looked away when I caught them staring at us.

Tigey said he did not believe Kulmiye would harm us, because, even if they did not see eye to eye, he and Kulmiye shared a clan kinship. This was reassuring but only until Tigey added that he was uncertain whether Kulmiye would prevent others from doing harm to us. Tigey suggested we prepare for the worst. I was deeply worried—a dry mouth, mildly queasy, tense-neck-type worry—but I tried to hide it because I didn't want to lose face with the others around me.

The head of the hotel's security soon visited my room, asking me about our plans for staying safe until the flight out of Bosaso early the next morning. I told him that we would pack our belongings in case we needed to leave on short notice. We would remain in one of our rooms, avoiding the courtyard. Late in the evening, we would quietly vacate our rooms but leave the lights on and drapes pulled to give the impression that we were still there. We would move as a group up a side stairwell to the roof. I recognized that there was risk in telling all this to the hotel security chief, but there was no alternative. Other than him, only Tigey and two of his guards would know our whereabouts. We would spend the night on the roof until 5:00 a.m., when we would convoy to the airport. Tigey and the hotel security chief agreed that if there was an attack, we would be harder to reach on the roof, where we had better sight lines and more exit routes.

Shortly after our meeting, there was a furtive knock on my door. Standing there was the hotel manager, who asked me if he could step inside. He came in and closed the door before handing me a basketball-sized wad of cloth. "You need," he said, instructing me to open his wrapped offering. I unraveled the cloth to find a loaded Glock 9 mm. I removed the magazine and opened the chamber and saw that the gun was loaded. "Keep this with you," the manager said. I gently declined. My carrying a weapon would only add to suspicions that I was not a journalist.

Leaving our room lit and the shades pulled, we made our way up the back staircase to the roof after sundown. The night was breezy and cool. Over the low, concrete balustrade circling the roof, we looked out on Bosaso. The city was mostly dark and quiet, but every few hours we saw bursts of grenades and machine-gun fire. For obvious reasons, I didn't even try to sleep.

The hours dragged by, but dawn eventually arrived. As much for distraction as anything else, I passed the time texting with several government sources in Mogadishu and abroad who provided some insights on the bind I was in and possible reasons for Kulmiye's behavior. I learned that his antipathy toward my reporting might have been exacerbated by a political uproar: Puntland lawmakers were preparing to vote "no confidence" in the Puntland president Abdiweli Mohamed Gaas's cabinet, which would cripple his ability to govern. There was chatter that if the vote did not succeed in removing him, lawmakers might take "other steps," which sources said meant a coup.

Gaas's many critics believed that he and his administration were pocketing money from the sale of fishing licenses to foreign fishing boats. A fellow clansman, Kulmiye was the president's personal friend and he took the lead on all fishing-related matters. If the president fell due to allegations about fishing corruption, Kulmiye would fall even harder.

In light of this political unrest, the paranoia toward me made more sense. The timing of my arrival at Puntland corresponded to growing questions about local corruption and fishing license revenues. Suspicions about me were only worsened since my minder had reported to his bosses that I was mysteriously tracking the Thai vessels in real time from my iPhone. I was also suspect because I had headed out to visit the SSS without government permission. Add to that: I was traveling with a drone (for aerial photography).

Taken together, all these factors contributed to a picture of me as a CIA saboteur or some other type of implant sent by federal authorities in Mogadishu aiming to squelch local autonomy in Puntland. Of course, none of these variables changed the fact that the local government was indeed corrupt, issuing false licenses and likely pocketing the money that should have gone to public coffers. Still, the bubbling conspiracy theories about my reporting had come to a boil, and our departure could not come soon enough.

It was no secret in Bosaso which flight we were planning to take that morning, because there was only one flight out of Puntland. The hotel was only a short distance from the airport, and there was only one route to get there from our compound, much of it on streets that were narrow, easily blocked, and vulnerable to ambush. Tigey had called in a favor and recruited six extra soldiers, bringing our total to twenty-five, to reinforce our convoy to the airport.

But an hour before we were set to depart, my fixer came up to the roof. Breathless and sweating as if he had sprinted across town, he insisted through a stubborn stutter that we leave immediately. The airport had called and informed him that the flight would be departing earlier than had been publicly posted on its website. The problem with this plan was that most of our guards had not arrived at the compound yet. This left us with a tough decision: go without an armed convoy or risk missing our plane and waiting for two more days for the next flight out. In Mogadishu, we had only ever traveled in "hard shell" trucks, which had bulletproof windows and blast-proof encasement inside the vehicles' frames. In Bosaso, we only had access to "soft shell" trucks, meaning regular old Toyota Highlanders.

We made a run for it. Staying in Bosaso any longer seemed too risky. We dashed down from the roof, threw our bags into the truck, and careened out of the hotel compound. The sun not yet up, it was still dark outside. Nascimento looked pale with worry. No one said a word to each other. It felt like a clichéd scene in an action movie that rarely ends well. We raced out of the parking lot, but two blocks from the hotel were abruptly cut off by a truckful of soldiers that pulled in front of us, appearing from a blind side street. My stomach sank.

The soldiers in the truck were not wearing recognizable uniforms. This was the first and only time I ever saw Tigey look nervous. He got out of our truck, and some of the soldiers walked past him. They opened our doors and stared at me. I fully expected them to yank us from the car. In one pocket, I had my passport and a wad of cash. In the other pocket, I had my hand on the SOS button of my Garmin tracking device. I was thankful to have the Garmin but, truth be told, I was very doubtful its SOS service would offer anything more than a sense of panic to the people back home if I transmitted the alert.

This was a fear like none I'd before experienced, the sort that isn't just in your head and heart but on your skin. I bet it even came with some kind of primordial smell. My mouth turned into the Sahara. Blinking, much less breathing, did not feel like an option. These guys did not speak English, so words from me were useless. Any attempted gesture—"Please don't shoot," "I've got money!" "I'm a journalist"— seemed idiotic, trite, and dangerous. There was just paralysis.

Tigey talked for a while with the person who looked to be in charge. Then he abruptly returned to our truck. The men who had cut us off got back in their truck and pulled ahead. We began following them.

"Tigey," I said after a minute, "can you tell me what's going on?" Those were the added security he had hired, he replied. He had not realized who they were at first because these men were on loan to him from a military friend, and he did not know them personally. "We will get to the airport," he said. As joltingly as the incident started, it ended.

We arrived at the airport, safe and sound. Several hours later, after waiting nervously in the gate area of the long, low terminal, I shouldered my bags and walked across the dusty dirt tarmac to our plane. Finally, we staggered up the stairs into the rickety, half-empty Ocean Airlines 747. I fell into my seat, relieved and exhausted. As we took off, I'd never been so happy to leave a place.

. . .

A week later, I was on a ship near Dubai when a text buzzed my satellite phone. A source in Mogadishu said that for the first time since 2012 a large foreign merchant ship had been hijacked in Somali waters. The incident happened in Puntland waters near Habo, not far from where I had recently been stranded with my team in the little fishing boats. The merchant ship was a tanker flagged to Comoros and carrying diesel. The pirates said in an interview with Somali media that they were not seeking a ransom. Their motivation, they said, was to highlight the problem of foreign-flagged fishing vessels in their waters. This turn of events was exactly what those businessmen in the courtyard of the Ga'ayte Hotel had predicted would happen.

Over the next couple of months, the Puntland cabinet was ousted, and there were half a dozen more piracy incidents. In several stories, the local press reported that the "Coast Guard from Somalia's Galmudug state," just south of Puntland, had exacted fines before releasing boats accused of fishing illegally. Of course, there was no such thing as the Galmudug Coast Guard. This was just the name that the newest breed of pirates had given themselves. The chutzpah would have surprised me had I not grown accustomed to people—be it Roy Bates, Max Hardberger, Sea Shepherd, or Russ George—taking such liberties at sea.

This is probably where my Somalia story should have ended. As I left the Horn of Africa, I assumed that I would shift from reporting to writing. I would spend the next several weeks trying to make sense of my trip and, more specifically, figuring out who in Puntland among the private security forces, thieving local bureaucrats, and marauding offshore bandits were the real pirates. Then, best I could, I would write it all up in some straight-line explanatory narrative.

No such luck. Something kept itching at me, and I was unable to stop asking questions. I could have written a good-news-turned-bad piece about maritime policing in a failed state, but this felt partial, trivializing even. I needed to look not just at the problems within Somalia but also the way other countries suffered from, took advantage of, and often worsened those same problems.

This itch pestered me for the next nine months and it's the reason I found myself on flights to the Maldives, Djibouti, Texas, then back to Thailand and Cambodia. Mostly, I wanted to know about the Thai ships that Puntland authorities so desperately had hoped I'd ignore. For reasons I can't fully explain—guilt and stubbornness perhaps—I felt that I now had an obligation to figure out what was happening on those ships and most especially who were the men working on them. One of the worst parts of doing this work is the haunting feeling that you might be engaging in misery porn and that you are making theater of so much evil while doing so little to correct it. I refused to put this story down partly because I was running scared from that haunting feeling.

Several weeks after I left Puntland, the Thai fishing ships halted their trawling and anchored near Bosaso. Officials in Mogadishu were increasingly angered that Puntland had allowed the ships to fish in Somali waters without federal permission. The crew off-loaded some of their catch to a refrigerated cargo ship called the *Wisdom Sea Reefer,* which would eventually carry the fish out of Somali waters to land the load in Vietnam. Thai authorities had asked the Vietnamese to halt the ship and inspect the catch and crew of the vessel if it entered their waters, but the Vietnamese ignored the request.

After my departure from Somalia, I stayed in touch with a source there who knew the private security guards stationed on the Thai fishing boats. Through this source I was able to get one of those guards to sneak a cell phone on board one of the Thai ships that were parked at sea near each other. The guard began sending me pictures and reports showing the crew and working conditions. Another source in the Puntland government began providing me with essential documents, including catch reports, registration records, and a copy of the Puntland-issued fishing licenses for the boats.

The bigger journalistic break in this reporting, though, was getting the phone number for another cell phone that a dozen or so of the men on board the Somali 7 ships were using to surreptitiously communicate with their families. Having run out of credit, the men using this phone had gone silent. I introduced a human rights advocate to a friend of mine in Bosaso who knew how to anonymously and remotely top up the crew's account online. The advocate wired money to the cell phone account, which allowed the men to start texting their families again. With the fishermen's permission, I was eventually looped into their exchanges.

From this convoluted pipeline of information, I began building an initial picture of what was happening on the Somali 7 ships. Anchored together about two miles from Bosaso port, the seven ships had roughly 240 Cambodian and Thai men on them. A Puntland fishery official who visited several of the ships during this period told me that the men worked continuously (he estimated twenty-hour days). The men who worked in the freezers suffered from frostbite because of improper clothing, he said. One of the Cambodian deckhands had gone crazy, I was told. "He just sits in the corner and talks to himself," another Cambodian wrote. Mostly, the other men pleaded in texts to come home. "Is this someone from our side coming for rescue?" one of the crew wrote to his family after seeing a helicopter circling nearby.

The Thai ships were still intermittently broadcasting their whereabouts through AIS, and at one point I noticed one of the ships, the *Chotchainavee 35*, leaving Somali waters. I watched it for a couple of days, at which point it became clear that it was heading back to Thailand, over three thousand miles away. I alerted a source in the Thai government and informed him of the ship's possible illegal fishing and labor abuses. This person, an anti-trafficking adviser to the Thai prime minister, orchestrated a plan to board the *Chotchainavee 35* with eight Royal Thai Police officers and six naval officers. In exchange for having tipped them into my investigation, the Thai government agreed to allow me to send my own investigator to go on board the ship when their officers detained it so I could remotely and independently interview the crew.

Late in the night of May 4, the *Chotchainavee 35* entered Thai waters and set a course for the Thajeen Union Port in Samut Sakhon. By this time, the ship had turned off its AIS, so the Thai authorities dispatched a helicopter and a fixed-wing aircraft to search for the ship. Spotting it, they directed a navy ship to intercept it before it arrived in port. The fourteen officers and my investigator then boarded the boat several miles from shore.

The crew had clearly been coached. During interviews with my investigator, all of the crew answered with what seemed like rehearsed talking points. They had signed on willingly to work. They had been paid in full and on time. The food and conditions were fine, they said. Neither the government inspectors nor my investigator believed them, but poking a hole in their stories was a challenge. Everything was fine, the men kept saying. That is, until around 6:00 a.m. on May 5, when one of the Cambodians gestured to my investigator that he wanted to talk away from the others.

"It's all lies," the Cambodian, named Kea, said in a hushed tone as the other workers slept on deck nearby. He explained that several hours before entering Thai waters, the captain of the *Chotchainavee 35* received a call on his cell phone alerting him that his ship was about to be boarded by authorities. The captain called the crew into a room below deck and instructed them on how to answer any questions. Kea said he was breaking script because his brother was among the men still captive on one of the other Thai ships that had been left behind parked off the coast of Puntland. He explained that the others were likely not telling the truth for fear that they might not receive money still owed to them by their employer.

After Kea opened up, my investigator updated Thai authorities on what we had learned and Kea was immediately separated from the rest of the crew. The other deckhands were told that he had been sent during the night to the hospital because he was suffering from kidney stones and a bladder infection. In fact, the government moved Kea to a shelter in Pathum Thani, Thailand, where I visited him a month later.

Looking like a high school kid you might see at a shopping mall in downtown Phnom Penh, Kea had bleached streaks in his jet-black hair. Twenty-four years old, he was five feet four, sinewy, and covered in tattoos on his forearms and legs. He told me that the captains on the Somali 7 ships occasionally beat the crew. They withheld food and medicine if they thought men were lazy, he said. Some of the Cambodians on the fishing boats had been told when they were being recruited for the job that they would be fishing within Thai waters only. These men were shocked once they realized they were bound for Somalia, Kea added.

Over the next five months after my interview with Kea, the Thai government tried to find a way to rescue the men on the Somali 7 ships, but what should have been a clear-cut enforcement case fell into a morass of bickering and recalcitrance. This morass was profoundly galling to me, but it also shed light on the ways that Somalia's internal problems intersect with the outside world, and in particular the ways that the ocean becomes even more outlaw in places where chaos reigns onshore.

Officials in Mogadishu said they could not rescue the men on the Somali 7 trawlers because they did not have a ship capable of making the trip to Bosaso. I knew there were additional factors at work. Most important, the federal government had no desire to go up against Puntland, the country's most prickly autonomous region. To do so might trigger an armed confrontation with local forces like the PMPF and the SSS, which answered exclusively to the Puntland president, who was protecting and profiting from the Thai ships. Such a clash would not end well for Mogadishu. It was also unclear, even to authorities in Mogadishu, what rights Puntland actually had over water near its shores.

Initially, officials from the antipiracy coalition of European and Asian warships patrolling Somali waters said they could not rescue the crew because their mandate did not include illegal fishing, so they had no legal authority to get involved. But after being approached by the Thai government, EU officials said they might be able to dispatch a ship if federal authorities in Mogadishu put in writing that the Somali 7 ships had fished illegally.

This document request from coalition forces should have been a simple matter because the federal law clearly forbids trawling by foreign boats in a stretch of water where these Thai ships had done so and the Puntland licenses were also unauthorized. Officials in Mogadishu, however, were proving to be extremely shifty when it came to putting in writing their claims of illegality. One week, a federal official wrote to Thai officials and to me separately that the ships were illegal. The next week another Somali official would write the opposite. Meanwhile, the only thing that all these officials—be they in Puntland or Mogadishu—shared was a rhetoric of outrage about the thievery of foreign fishing boats raiding their national waters.

Other barriers were equally vexing. Because the men trapped on these ships were Cambodian, Thai authorities asked the government of Cambodia to help orchestrate a rescue, but those requests were largely ignored. While officials from the U.S. State Department asked the Thai government to update them regularly on the situation, they were unwilling to get more involved. Meanwhile, Thai authorities worked to gather enough evidence to pressure the owner of the ships. They also tried (and failed) to keep the UN Office on Drugs and Crime and its hostage negotiator from publicly releasing information about the trapped crew in an online bulletin describing the office's recent efforts. The leak tipped off the operator of the ships that he was under investigation not just for illegal fishing but also for human trafficking.

In July, fearing that the ships would permanently turn off their AIS transponders and disappear on the high seas with their captive crews, Thai authorities published a notice through Interpol asking all governments to alert them if any of the Somali 7 ships appeared in their ports. Two of the ships promptly left Somali waters, disappearing for weeks, only to reappear in Iranian waters, where officials from the ITF, the global seafarers' union, told me that the Thai owners were seeking to sell or re-flag the ships.

Because the ships were flagged to Djibouti, its registry could have solved the crisis by ordering the trawlers to return to port for inspection. Djibouti had the authority to do this based on concerns being raised about their crews and the legality of their fishing. Thai authorities formally asked Djibouti to issue such an order. Instead, the registry promptly washed its hands of the problem by de-flagging the vessels. I had seen this move before: it was exactly how Nigeria had handled a similar request when Sea Shepherd was chasing the *Thunder*, Interpol's most wanted poacher ship. This action was yet further proof that the notion of flags of convenience as oversight bodies is pure fiction.

. . .

The story behind how the Thai trawlers came to fly Djibouti's flag was also instructive. It demonstrated how ship operators shop around for the most lax registries with the lowest prices and fewest regulations. Long before I became aware of these ships, the owner of the Thai trawlers had removed their Thai flags in August 2016, largely to avoid complying with tough new rules that the government had imposed to prevent sea slavery and illegal fishing. The operator of these ships was not alone in wanting to shift away from Thai oversight. In the several years after Thailand imposed stricter rules on its overseas fleet, every one of the country's fifty-four long-haul fishing ships dropped its Thai flag, and most of them switched to Oman, Iran, Myanmar, or elsewhere.

To decide what new flag to fly on their ships, the operators of the Somali 7 fleet flew officials from the Djibouti registry to Bangkok for wining and dining and to discuss terms and prices. The Thai operators soon agreed to pay $80,000 for the right to operate the seven trawlers under the Djibouti flag. As part of the package, the Thai operator was also granted temporary fishing licenses in Puntland. The official with the Djibouti flag registry who recounted these details to me said he was unsure whether the Puntland fishing licenses were authentic. I responded that even if Djibouti somehow had the authority to offer such perks, I didn't understand anymore what "authentic" Puntland fishing licenses were, because, at least according to federal Somali authorities in Mogadishu, Puntland could not issue such licenses. It was all quite surreal—so much so that I felt as if I were back to reporting on Sealand, where I had strained to distinguish fictitious duplicates from dubious originals.

Of course, none of this backstory mattered to the stranded Cambodians anchored near Bosaso. As Somalia, Djibouti, Thailand, and authorities at the UN traded emails and struggled to figure out what to do, the men on those ships continued pleading for help through urgent texts. "Dad, please send news," one of the men wrote. "I am afraid they will hurt me." Describing what happened after the crew chief hit him, another Cambodian wrote, "They refuse to give us the medicine." He added, "It is like living in hell even though we are still alive."

Daily, I received increasingly urgent messages. One of the crew sent a video in which he whispered that the men representing the Thai operators had visited the ship and told the Cambodians that they would be killed if they did not sign documents stating that the ships were free from abuse. "Let's not talk about the past," the company representative who visited one of the ships can be seen telling the crew in a video sent to me. "Let's talk about the future."

Another text came one day with a shocking photograph of a Cambodian man in a village hut, dressed neatly in a white short-sleeved collared shirt with flower-patterned shorts in front of a silky red curtain. He was dead and hanging from a noose. The man was the father of one of the crew members who worked on the *Chotpattana 51*. Having grown so distraught by his son's captivity, he had killed himself, according to two of his relatives, who sent me the photo. The man's wife, also in despair about their captive son, had previously tried to hang herself but was saved by neighbors who intervened, the relatives said.

I passed along what I was learning to various police officials and anti-trafficking authorities in Thailand while also pressing UN, Somali, and Djibouti authorities about what they planned to do. Mostly my questions met with silence, except from the Thai government. It seemed unfathomable to me that these men could so clearly be in need of rescue but no one was able or willing to escort them off the ships. By early September 2017, only two of the original seven vessels were still anchored near Bosaso. The others had disappeared from radar, the fate of their crews unknown.

On the afternoon of September 10, Thai authorities were alerted by one of the Somali 7 crews that eighteen Cambodian deckhands had been taken off their ships, had been driven to the Bosaso airport, and were en route back to Cambodia. Thai police scrambled to Phnom Penh to interview the men when they landed. During the men's layover in Dubai, a company official offered each crew member 20,000 baht, about $625, to not speak negatively to Thai or Cambodian police about their experience. The company official was the same man who can be seen in the video I'd previously been sent from Somalia telling the crews not to talk about the past.

Some of the men took the money. One crew member, who the company official knew had communicated over Facebook with his wife about abuse on board, was offered 300,000 baht, roughly $9,380, to keep quiet. He turned down the money and corroborated to Thai police in subsequent interviews what Kea had previously told me. I later learned that one of the Cambodian deckhands from this group hanged himself when he returned home. Neighbors said that the deckhand had been despondent after learning that his wife had left him during his captivity.

Two months later, on November 13, another group, this time twenty-nine crew members, all Thai, were flown out of Bosaso to Bangkok. Again, most of the men told police they had no complaints about their time on the ships other than that the hours were brutally long and that the company stopped paying their salaries to their families shortly after they arrived in Somali waters.

Thai authorities continued aggressively chasing the Somali 7 fleet for what they believed were human rights abuses and fishing violations. The Thai government eventually confiscated the *Chotchainavee 35,* which was the ship the police had boarded with my investigator in May 2017. In the ship's hold were roughly five hundred tons of frozen fish worth about 14 million baht, or $440,000, including lucrative bigeye tuna, protected reef fish like parrotfish, triggerfish, snapper, grouper, and goatfish as well as redcoat squid, stingray, and mackerel.

By this point, I was surprised that Thai authorities were still on the case. The government was spending enormous sums of money and hundreds of man-hours pursuing these ships, and not because they had an obligation under maritime rules to do so. After all, the Somali 7 ships were operated by a company that was incorporated abroad. They were also flagged outside Thailand, fishing beyond Thai waters, and crewed largely by non-Thais.

Pinpointing the Thai government's motivations is difficult, but my hunch was that Thai authorities hoped to avoid more bad press about sea slavery. They also clearly wanted to send a message to the owners of their overseas fleet that they were serious about cracking down on labor and fishing abuses, even on Thai-owned ships flagged to other countries, as was the case with the Somali 7.

The motivation of the thieving bureaucrats and foreign poachers that I encountered in Somalia was easier to explain. As on land, what drives crime offshore is money, not depravity for its own sake. Cruise liners dump oil into the ocean not because they hate the planet or love pollution but because doing so is cheaper than disposing of it legally. Stowaways are rafted, seafarers abandoned, and migrant deckhands indentured because it costs more to do otherwise. In Somalia, it was neither sport nor patriotism but money that motivated pirates to board ships, police to hunt for poachers, or government officials to issue false licenses. Likewise, Djibouti hadn't allowed these seven Thai trawlers to fly its flag out of sympathy for their operators who wanted to evade Thailand's new rules. Djibouti had simply seized on a business opportunity.

My reporting in Somalia had not led to where I expected. Perhaps I should have known better. Really, who travels to a failed state looking for good news? From the moment I touched down in Mogadishu my journalistic compass had not stopped spinning. I strained to understand who could be trusted and which, if any, of the many armed groups patrolling the waters was in the right.

In some small way, justice began catching up with the Thai trawlers for poaching in Somalia. On January 23, the Thai prosecutor's office charged members of the Sangsukiam family with illegal fishing and confiscated the catch on board the *Chotchainavee 35*. Because this fish had been caught illegally, Thai authorities were forbidden to sell it, and they subsequently struggled to find any charity or other country willing to take it.

In the meantime, the Thai government was paying the equivalent of roughly $20,000 each month to keep the ship locked and guarded in port and its catch warehoused in cold storage. Thai federal lawyers and investigators struggled to get cooperation from Cambodia, Djibouti, and Somalia to build a case against the ship operator and human traffickers. It was patently obvious why governments prefer to look the other way in such cases of abuse.

My time working on the topic of ocean mayhem had instilled in me a healthy sense of the absurd, but the outcome of this seized fish was an unusually dense little piece of satire. Three years earlier, my reporting on the plight of a shackled Cambodian deckhand named Lang Long had spurred Thai officials to try to convince me that they were cracking down on sea slavery. Now, as the Somali 7 case slowly unspooled and Thai authorities aggressively tried to prosecute the ships' operators, the ill-gotten gains from these trawlers sat frozen and expensively under government lock and key, evidence that could be neither sold nor given away nor discarded.

Aside from making for a long chapter, my inability or unwillingness to put this story down also crystallized for me a core journalistic conundrum, even if it didn't give me an exit from that conundrum.

Three months after I forced myself to stop reporting on the Somali 7 fleet, I got a phone call from a source telling me that the ships had been re-flagged and renamed but were still essentially owned by the same Thai family. A new batch of trafficked Cambodian men were now trapped off the coast of Puntland, the source said. I began reporting anew and pushing out my findings through Twitter.

This cycle of abuse felt like an old story that in repeating itself became serially new. In this case, in every case, it felt so new because the story was always still in the middle of happening, and it unfolded, for me at least, with both an uncertainty of how it would end and a hope that maybe I could influence that ending. I was unsure how to escape this cycle, but I resigned myself to the idea that the only thing worse than telling a tale of abuse over and over again was not telling it all.

More simply, I asked myself what I'd learned about lawlessness at sea near the Horn of Africa, and I came up with competing answers. I'd seen how Somalia was the victim of illegal fishing, but I'd also experienced how the Somali and Puntland governments were deeply complicit in the crimes. The local antipiracy police and fishery authorities were as much a part of the problem as a solution to it. I'd also found yet more sea slavery and illegal fishing in the Thai fleet. But I'd meanwhile witnessed how the Thai government was the only one doggedly trying to solve this case, even though under maritime rules that responsibility belonged at least as much to several other nations—including Djibouti, Cambodia, and Somalia—that did virtually nothing to help.

# HUNTING HUNTERS

*The sea*
*isn't a place*
*but a fact, and*
*a mystery.*

—Mary Oliver, "The Waves"

On November 18, 2016, women with toddlers in their arms waved from the pier to the ships sailing out of the Japanese port city of Shimonoseki. The ships were joining a flotilla of vessels bound for Antarctica, and their flagship was a floating slaughterhouse called the *Nisshin Maru* that was leaving to hunt minke whales. More than four hundred feet long, the *Nisshin Maru* loomed over the smaller, faster harpooners with it. Known as a factory whaling ship, it was an abattoir on the waves, equipped with special steel slipways used for winching harpooned whales onto a wooden flensing deck, where the crew quickly sliced the animal into pieces that were sent down a conveyer belt below deck for the meat to be treated, frozen, and boxed for sale. In bold capital letters, the word "research" adorned the hull on both sides.

The *Nisshin Maru* hunted in a pack. The small fleet of supporting vessels trailing "the mother ship," as the floating factory was known, included three harpoon ships, a refueling tanker, a security ship, and a small krill spotter that looked for the tiny crustaceans that whales eat. In the 1950s, there were over fifty factory whaling ships prowling the Antarctic, mostly from Japan, the Soviet Union, and Norway. By 2017, the *Nisshin Maru* was the only one left. The ship did its grisly job with industrial efficiency: its crew of about eighty men could butcher a twenty-ton animal to skin and bones in less than thirty minutes, discarding almost half the animal overboard as unusable.

The *Nisshin Maru*

Shortly after the Japanese whalers left port, two ships belonging to Sea Shepherd, the same ocean conservation group I accompanied on its chase of the *Thunder* in 2015, set sail from Australia. They, too, marked a course for Antarctic waters. As in previous years, Sea Shepherd planned to sweep the Southern Ocean and find the Japanese fleet. Then these advocates intended to prevent the harpoon ships from transferring their catch onto the *Nisshin Maru*. They would use any means at their disposal to stop the hunt.

Over the prior decade, Sea Shepherd and the Japanese whalers had sparred with escalating violence each hunting season, making this no-holds-barred fight an annual ritual. The Japanese crew used flash-bang grenades, tear gas, and acoustic crowd control weapons to defend their ships. Sea Shepherd threw smoke bombs and explosive canisters of paint and foul-smelling chemicals. Both sides deployed prop foulers, which consisted of long steel cables or knotted coils of polypropylene meant to tangle ship propellers and rudders. Both sides also fired high-powered water cannons at each other's smokestacks, which reach down into the ships' engine rooms. Flooding the engine room could debilitate a ship, but it also risked electrocuting the people working inside.

One of Sea Shepherd's ships had a customized device called the "can opener." It was a sharpened-steel I beam jutting from the ship's starboard side, ideal for scraping or puncturing the hulls of adversaries. During attacks, Sea Shepherd's crew tried to pull small Zodiacs alongside the *Nisshin Maru*, and armed with nail guns, they quickly sealed shut the factory ship's scuppers, which were the outflow portals for discharging whale blood into the ocean. The Japanese responded with water cannon fire and by throwing grappling hooks attached to long ropes at Sea Shepherd's Zodiacs, aiming to yank the boats from the water or tear them in two. No one died in these clashes, but many people believed it was just a matter of time.

Each side was also armed with well-worn syllogisms to defend its behavior. Despite a global moratorium on whaling, the Japanese argued that their hunt was part of a scientific program to collect data that they said would prove that there were plenty of whales in the sea and that stocks were not being depleted. Sea Shepherd admitted it broke the law by ramming its adversaries and blocking their passage. But the organization argued that its actions were justified to focus attention on the failure of governments to enforce the laws meant to protect whales and other marine life.

Though these clashes between Sea Shepherd and the whalers had become routine, 2016 was different. An international court had ordered the Japanese to stop whaling in Antarctica but the world's last remaining factory ship was ignoring the order. The Institute for Cetacean Research, the Japanese outfit that operated the whaling vessels, simply relabeled the expedition and announced that it would kill 333 whales that winter in the name of science. After a party on land and a warm send-off from the crowd on the docks, the captain of the *Nisshin Maru* steered the mother ship south, switched off the locational transponder to make the ship invisible, and slipped through the waves toward the ends of the earth.

. . .

By 2016, the violence between Sea Shepherd and the Japanese had grown into more than a battle of nerves and a high-stakes ideological clash. The aggressive theatrics in Antarctica had raised larger questions about the fate of the ocean.

If no one policed antiwhaling or antiharassment laws in the Antarctic, what would happen when countries or companies began mining or dumping illegally there? If the perpetrators simply called these activities research, like the iron fertilization off the coast of Canada, would they be allowed? And what if enforcement was left to volunteers or vigilantes like Sea Shepherd and those groups fell short—would the earth's poles become lawless no-man's-lands, governed by no one yet claimed by all?

Sea Shepherd had mastered the art of framing arguments in its favor so that it often appeared on the side of right. I tried to see past its artful rhetoric and smart branding touches and remind myself that the organization had its critics, and their arguments had merit, especially in faulting Sea Shepherd for its sanctimony, self-promotion, and frequent lack of nuance about the issues it tackled. That said, I was not immune to its white-hat charms. And I will confess that my reporting on its round-the-world chases offered a kind of respite from the world of grays I had been living in as I reported out many of the chapters in this book.

The maritime laws that do exist are often baffling, contradictory, and muddled. And there are also stunning legal voids at sea—a lack of laws despite a clear and obvious need. It's why there are so many outlaws on the ocean, because it is so easy to operate outside the law, and even easier when no laws exist. But the Sea Shepherd chases were not so much about enforcement as they were about force. The "can opener" the organization used to cripple ships was also a symbol of its views of maritime law and of its unapologetic plan to take matters into its own hands. On the oceans, Sea Shepherd deputized itself as the sheriff, and right or wrong, it was at least transparent about its intentions. Most of my reporting work for this book involved people who routinely obfuscated their true goals. This was not the case with Sea Shepherd.

Whaling was also a natural way for me to conclude my explorations of the outlaw ocean. In 1975, Greenpeace launched its first antiwhaling campaign, and the slogan "Save the Whales" became a clarion call for maritime conservationism, an early bellwether that all was not right beyond the distant horizon. Yet despite successes in curbing the whaling industry, the practice still lingers on the high seas with the *Nisshin Maru*—albeit under the banner of "research"—a stubborn vestige of a time when the ocean was seen as an endless bounty, a divine abundance that could never be depleted.

Whaling is an ancient practice, but much about the *Nisshin Maru*'s modern methods for slaughtering whales is shrouded in mystery. What little is known came from a Briton named Mark Votier, the first and only foreign journalist allowed to travel aboard the ship. During the 1992–1993 whaling season, the Institute of Cetacean Research permitted him to spend five months aboard the ship and to film whatever he wanted, so long as his footage did not include any "unsightly" tasks on board.

To locate their prey, whalers use a variety of sources of information, including published research about migration routes, historical data from animals that have been tagged with satellite transponders, maps of krill feeding zones, websites with crowdsourced sightings, and onboard sonar. The spotter ships that travel with the *Nisshin Maru* also act as the advance team.

While on board, Votier witnessed thirty whale harpoonings, and his footage showed that after these harpoonings, the *Nisshin Maru*'s crew dragged the creature, while it was still alive, onto the deck and began, in industry parlance, the "secondary killing." A dozen men surrounded the massive animal, which was usually still thrashing, and one of them electrocuted it with a prod to kill it. The men then measured it and, wielding knives as long as swords, cut out key organs and bits of blubber and tossed them into buckets. What remained was sliced into chunks the size of human torsos. Half a dozen men mopped the blood, while others loaded the pieces onto a conveyor belt that carried them below deck for freezing and boxing. On a boom day, they could process up to two dozen whales.

Just over half the whales Votier watched being killed were electrocuted once they were hoisted on board. On average, it took eight minutes for the electricity to immobilize the whales, though one electrocution took twenty-three minutes. When he returned to shore, Votier said he was haunted by what looked to him like torture. He soon published almost all of his footage, including the especially "unsightly" material. The institute subsequently sued him for 3 million yen, or about $45,000 at the time, in damages for breach of contract. Votier refused to pay the penalties, vowing instead never to set foot again in Japan to avoid prosecution.

Since that embarrassing episode, the Japanese whaling industry has aggressively guarded its privacy. Among the few things that the ship's owner has said publicly about its methods is that it no longer uses electric prods, opting instead for shotguns during secondary killings. To avoid being tracked by media or advocacy groups like Sea Shepherd, the Japanese keep their transponder, or AIS, switched off. Still, Sea Shepherd knew roughly when to launch its ships because the *Nisshin Maru*'s owner threw a well-publicized party before initiating its hunt.

Dubbing the 2016 mission Operation Nemesis, after the Greek goddess of inescapable justice, Sea Shepherd dispatched its flagship, the *Steve Irwin,* from Melbourne on December 3. On its helipad, the Irwin carried the *Blue Hornet,* a Hughes 300 helicopter used for reconnaissance. With a range of 160 nautical miles round-trip, the helicopter could stay airborne for about four hours in decent weather. Built in 1975, the *Irwin* was 195 feet long and painted blue, black, and gray, overlaid with the Sea Shepherd logo—a skull, with a trident and shepherd's staff in the shape of crossbones beneath it. The ship was named in honor of the Australian conservationist and beloved television personality who died in 2006 after a stingray punctured his heart during a dive.

Joining the *Irwin* was another Sea Shepherd ship, the 175-foot *Ocean Warrior.* A new and unusually fast patrol vessel built with financial support from proceeds from the Dutch, British, and Swedish lotteries, the *Warrior* left Hobart, Tasmania, for its maiden mission on December 4. Capable of speeds over thirty knots, the *Warrior* was fast enough to

The *Ocean Warrior*

outrun the *Nisshin Maru,* which topped out at sixteen knots, and its harpoon ships, whose maximum was about twenty-three knots. The *Warrior* was also equipped with a bright red water cannon with "To keep poachers at bay" written on the side. Capable of shooting over five thousand gallons per minute, the cannon had roughly four times the power of a standard fire-truck hose, enough to reach over two hundred feet and still lacerate skin or knock a man off his feet.

For Sea Shepherd, the hardest part was simply finding the *Nisshin Maru,* because its hunting grounds were roughly the size of Australia. Before each campaign, Sea Shepherd tried to narrow its search, focusing on areas where its odds of finding the whalers were better. Members of Sea Shepherd studied the movement of ice floes and historical weather maps. They read academic research papers about the migration routes of the krill that whales eat and reports from the whaling company itself about where its ships caught whales the prior year.

At the helm of the *Warrior* was a fifty-three-year-old former auto mechanic and charter-boat captain from Nevada City, California, named Adam Meyerson. The captain of the *Irwin* was a six-foot-tall, no-nonsense former Dutch navy lieutenant named Wyanda Lublink. There were fifty crew members total on the two Sea Shepherd ships,

Sea Shepherd crew from the *Ocean Warrior,* including Captain Adam Meyerson, who is in the front, center, wearing black pants

equally divided between men and women, who hailed from Australia, Germany, France, England, Austria, Spain, Canada, and the United States. I knew Meyerson, Lublink, and much of the Operation Nemesis crew, having been to sea with them on the Operation Icefish mission in 2015, when I joined them during a chase of the notorious poacher ship called the *Thunder,* which at the time topped Interpol's most wanted list.

Where Operation Icefish had been an effort by Sea Shepherd to focus on new adversaries like toothfish poachers and try new tactics like collaborating with fishing companies and the police, Operation Nemesis was a return to the advocacy organization's antiwhaling roots. A grudge match, Operation Nemesis was Sea Shepherd's chance to settle old scores and to put an end, once and for all, to Japanese whaling. Things didn't go as planned.

. . .

In parts of the world where it was too cold to grow crops or raise livestock, early man hunted whales for sustenance and nutrition. The meat provided a ready source of vitamins A, C, and D, as well as niacin, iron, and protein. Later, whale blubber was used to make highly prized, long-lasting, and relatively clean-burning oil. A staple of international trade for nearly 250 years, this oil was especially important to colonial America, which operated a veritable armada of whaling ships. In the 1840s, when Herman Melville sailed from New Bedford on the voyage that would inspire *Moby-Dick,* whaling was earning $120 million per year for the American economy, or approximately $3 billion in today's dollars.

Whaling was dangerous but lucrative work. A single whale could fetch the 2017 equivalent of a quarter-million dollars. Little of that went to the crew, whose working conditions on these ships were brutal. According to the historian Briton Cooper Busch, a whaler could be put in irons for everything from attempted sodomy to "throwing porpoise meat overboard" rather than eating it. On average, two-thirds of a ship's crew deserted after each voyage, Busch wrote in *Whaling Will Never Do for Me.* Sailors were commonly punished by tying their hands behind their backs or above their heads for an extended period, in what U.S. military interrogators now refer to as a "stress position."

Flogging appeared in nearly 10 percent of the whale-ship logs Busch reviewed from the 1840s.

Two reasons were given as typical justification for flogging. First, sailors got the whip for mistakenly making noise that tipped off the whales to flee. Second, a captain would shackle and lash crew if he discovered that they had tried to get help, often from religious advocates, to get off the ship before their tour was completed. The descriptions of discipline on these ships reminded me of what I'd seen of forced labor in the Thai fishing fleet.

Rival industries drove the decline of whaling in America. The gold rush of 1849 caused hundreds of whaling boats to be abandoned in San Francisco as their crews sought better prospects in the goldfields. Ten years later, the discovery of crude petroleum in western Pennsylvania dealt a death blow. In a day, one decent well could more cheaply pump the amount of oil that a whaler might produce from a three-year voyage at sea.

Elsewhere, the whaling industry was more durable. From 1892 to 1910, it accounted for roughly 10 percent of Iceland's national economy. One of the biggest whaling fleets was from Norway, which in the late nineteenth century was dotted with dozens of whaling stations, outfitted with machinery for processing carcasses. The Norwegians also developed the *granatharpun,* a grenade-tipped harpoon that could explode inside the whale's body, killing the creatures more efficiently.

The Japanese have hunted whales for hundreds of years, most of that time staying near their own shores. But in the 1930s, Japan pushed into international waters in the Southern Ocean as advancing technology, including steamships and bigger harpoon guns, led to sharp improvements in range and productivity. After World War II, the country was struggling through postwar poverty, and whale meat became a crucial part of the Japanese diet, including as a staple in school lunch programs, because it was a cheap source of protein. By 1958, whaling supplied a third of all meat consumed in Japan.

Since then, the Japanese government has stressed that it is very selective about the whales it targets, avoiding endangered species like the blue whale and hunting only more abundant ones like the minke. However, the International Union for Conservation of Nature, the primary environmental consultant for the UN, says it doesn't have enough data to make a determination on whether the Antarctic minke whale is threatened. The whale's population declined by 60 percent between 1978 and 2004, the organization said. "The Japanese Government is strongly opposed to uncontrolled commercial whaling," a consulate official wrote to me in response to questions about the program.

The whaling tradition remains entrenched in Japan partly out of pride and bureaucratic inertia. The Japanese government oversees the hunts through a program that has its own research budget and extensive administration. The downsizing of this administration would be an embarrassment to the bureaucrats and politicians tied to it and the industry it supports, especially if such cuts were the result of foreign pressure. As of 2012, the government subsidized the whaling fleet with more than $9 million annually. By some estimates, the government had more than five thousand tons of the meat frozen and warehoused.

Japan's sensitivity about its whaling is best considered in the broader context of its dependence on seafood. The country's per capita seafood consumption is among the highest of any industrialized nation. To many Japanese, whales are just another type of meat, albeit one with distinct cultural importance. They ask why foreigners should have any say over what they eat. After all, other countries consume beef, even though cows are sacred in some religions. Australians eat kangaroo, the British cook rabbits, the Chinese eat dogs. Considering that Faroe Islanders and Inuits also still hunt whales, why are the Japanese singled out for international criticism?

I posed this question to Meyerson. I pointed out that Norway annually catches more whales than Iceland and Japan combined. "Why not focus on them?" I asked. Sea Shepherd does not interfere with other countries because they whale only in their national waters, Meyerson said. The Japanese are the only ones who still whale in distant, international waters. "And that's where no one is policing but us," he added.

.   .   .

The hunting grounds of the *Nisshin Maru* are one of the wildest and most inaccessible places on earth. Though inhospitable to humans, these Antarctic waters are also a site of marvel and home to a thriving ecosystem like nowhere else on the planet. They constitute a habitat for huge colonies of emperor and Adélie penguins, the incredible colossal squid with eyes the size of bowling balls that allow it to see in the ocean's depths, and the largest animal on the planet, the blue whale, which has arteries that are wider than a human head.

Antarctica is also a feeding ground where everyone seems to be chasing someone else's meal. While the Japanese hunt the whales and Sea Shepherd tries to block them, the whales track the ships hunting longline toothfish. In a phenomenon known as depredation, whales routinely shadow these boats, sometimes for hundreds of miles, waiting for their lines to fill with fish. When captains begin retrieving their catch, the churning of the winch motor that tugs the fishing line makes a distinctive sound. This sound serves as an underwater dinner bell for the whales. Before crews can pull the fish on board, the whales attack the lines, stripping them clean. On a clear day, when sound underwater travels farthest, whales can hear this dinner bell from more than fifteen miles away.

A depredation specialist named Paul Tixier at Deakin University in Melbourne, Australia, told me that toothfishing boats in Antarctica lose over $5 million annually from whale attacks. He described a logbook that some toothfish captains keep with whale "mug shots," identifying culprits by their distinct colors, gashes, or fin curves. In the Southern Ocean, fishing captains know repeat offenders by sight, giving them nicknames like "Zach the Ripper" and "Jack the Stripper."

Whales stalk long-liners elsewhere, too, including off the coasts of Alaska, Washington, Chile, Australia, and Hawaii. In the western Gulf of Alaska in 2011 and 2012, killer whale depredation cost each vessel $980 per day in terms of additional fuel, crew food, and the opportunity cost of lost time, according to a study of six longline boats. The problem got worse in Alaska in the 1990s, after fishery authorities lengthened the fishing season from two weeks to eight months. Rather than tightly limiting boats' time at sea or, for example, giving boats two weeks to land as much as they wanted, the authorities permitted captains to take however long they pleased, but only to land a set quantity of fish.

The authorities' goal in extending the fishing season had been to discourage boat captains from taking dangerous risks as they tried to beat the weather and race the clock. But an unintended consequence of the policy was that by having boats in the water for longer, the likelihood of overlap between the whales and these boats went up. It also gave whales the time to hone their skills and pin down exactly when and how to best hijack the long-liners. "So far," Tixier said, "we haven't found an effective way to outsmart the whales."

In early 2016, I traveled to Antarctica to learn more about the competition between fishermen and whales. I did some research on the way, stopping in Punta Arenas, Chile, a global toothfishing hub and the site of the Coalition of Legal Toothfish Operators' convention, which drew operators from as far as Alaska and France. With a mix of exasperation and grudging respect, Eduardo Infante, who operates a toothfishing company called Globalpesca SpA, described the devious tactics of his below-water adversaries.

His three long-liners, crewed with about forty men, typically fish the Southern Atlantic Ocean from January to May. A grown whale can scrape all the fish from a five-mile line in under an hour. To avoid snaring their own mouths, the whales bite off the fish just below the hooks. Sometimes all that's left behind, he said, are fish lips dangling from the lines. More experienced whales bite the line, shaking loose the fish so they can eat them whole.

When feeding, whales make a certain sound that researchers call "buzz." This sound becomes accelerated as whales depredate, cuing other nearby whales to hustle to the scene for the all-you-can-eat buffet. "It's like getting jumped in an alley by a pack of thugs," one toothfish captain in the Falkland Islands told me about the experience. He added that on an unlucky day, a single toothfish boat can be "assaulted" by a pack with as many as a dozen sperm whales and twenty killer whales.

There are no clear rules on how fishing boats are supposed to handle depredation. Some companies have used decoy boats to trick the whales. Others blast heavy metal music to annoy them. Some fishing captains have tried waiting the whales out, not pulling in their lines until the whales decide to leave. Other captains attach satellite devices to serial offenders to avoid them. Attempting to outrun the attackers tends to be futile because they're too fast. When pursued by whales, some fishermen deliberately go near other boats, hoping to divert their pursuers.

Orcas are by far the worst, Infante told me, explaining that they are smarter and more persistent. Also known as killer whales, orcas are the largest apex predators on earth, meaning they sit at the top of the food chain and are not prey to any animals, except humans. Famous for their hunting acumen, orcas routinely ram sperm whales to daze them before trying to eat them. Orcas have also been known to slow dolphins down by flipping them into the air, and they sometimes swim in unison to "wave wash" seals and penguins off ice floes.

Infante recounted how in 2013, when the Chilean government reduced by two-thirds the amount of toothfish that boats were allowed to catch, there was a drastic drop in the number of fishing boats for whales to target, which led to what he called "a starvation panic" among the whales. That season, with fewer free meals to depredate, the orcas became extremely aggressive because they were so hungry, he said. His boat captains were radioing back to shore that the orcas were leaping out of the water and grabbing hooked fish right at the mouth of the opening of the ship hatch where the deckhands unhook the catch on board. "My men had to keep their arms inside the boat," Infante said. "It was that dangerous."

Infante added that over the past several years he tried using several types of audio equipment to repel the whales. The noisemakers worked for a couple of weeks until the orcas began ignoring the sound. He still uses *cachaloteras,* which are small cone-shaped nets that fall over the caught toothfish as the line is pulled toward the boat and up into the shallower depths where the whales typically strike. He added that most whale researchers do not object and that such tactics or tools are effective in deterring most types of whales. "But not the orcas," Infante said.

Understanding depredation is important because Japanese and Norwegian whalers sometimes invoke it in defending their whaling industries. They claim that too many whales are stealing fishermen's livelihoods and depleting valuable fishing stocks. Culling whale numbers through harpoon hunting helps restore the appropriate balance, they say. Most whale researchers reject these claims.

After I left Punta Arenas, I headed to Carlos III, a lonely twenty-eight-square-mile island outpost, located in the Strait of Magellan, on the southernmost tip of Chile, to talk to one of these whale researchers. Part of a government-protected nature reserve, Carlos III overlooks a whale feeding ground. During the Southern Hemisphere's November-to-May summertime, over a hundred humpbacks and, in smaller numbers, orcas and minkes visit the feeding area.

I got a ride to the island on the *Tanu,* a thirty-six-foot whale research ship named after a whale spirit of the sky from the Selk'nam tribe, a largely extinct native group from Tierra del Fuego. Launching from Punta Carrera, the *Tanu* rounded Cape Froward, the southernmost tip of mainland South America, and passed Isla Dawson, the island where, because of its harsh remoteness, Augusto Pinochet banished four hundred functionaries from Salvador Allende's government in 1973. We then continued northwest for nine hours, after which the *Tanu* deposited me on Carlos III, with a promise to return for me in a week.

I passed the cold and rainy days in the island's base camp, huddled near a wood-burning stove in a twenty-by-ten-foot tent, talking to Frederick Toro-Cortés, the resident whale scientist. Toro-Cortés was one of the island's four inhabitants. The three other inhabitants were Chilean men in their twenties, who fixed meals, stocked wood, and replaced slats on the perpetually rotting wooden walkway that extended from the base camp a mile inland up the side of the mountain to a sparse cabin that doubles as a science station.

Toro-Cortés explained that in the past fishing boat captains repelled depredating whales using rifles, harpoons, and dynamite, as well as "cracker shells" and "seal bombs," which resemble M-80 firecrackers. One study estimated that lethal responses to the whales were so common in the mid-1990s near the Crozet Islands in the southern Indian Ocean that it led to a near 70 percent reduction in the size of the killer whale population there.

Before traveling to Chile, I had read about a case from 2011 involving the shooting of a whale near New Jersey. Dan Archibald, a crewman of the fishing vessel *Capt. Bob,* had posted on his Facebook page in September 2011 a photograph of a partially eaten tuna on a hook. "Thanks a lot pilot whales," Archibald wrote beneath the picture. Elsewhere on his page, Archibald posted other pictures of bullets he had apparently used to shoot and kill a whale that police found later washed up on a beach in Allenhurst, New Jersey. After being arrested, Archibald told the police that he had "sprayed" fire at several pilot whales. They're hunters, he told police, competitors for the fish, just like him.

Toro-Cortés said fishermen still used these violent methods, but much less often. Captains now mostly just argue that they should be allowed to at least shoot sea lions, which are more numerous and brazen, he said. Toro-Cortés considered the whales gentle, harmless giants, a sharp contrast to the portrait of the aggressive, crafty competitors that Infante and Archibald presented of these creatures.

One night I hiked up the mountain to sleep in the science station. On the island, the sun did not set until around 11:00 p.m., but even then the moon was so bright that the scene was more glowing than dark. Overlooking the bay, I watched and listened to the whales sleep— half a dozen humpbacks that looked about fifty feet long drifting to the surface, exhaling steamy geysers, then sinking again for several minutes. It felt as if I had snuck into a den of hibernating behemoths.

On the final day before I left the island, Toro-Cortés showed me a neon-green three-ring binder. Inside were the records of eighteen years' worth of cold days spent at the outpost (primarily by Toro-Cortés's predecessors) and on the *Tanu* documenting whales, mostly humpback. Each of the binder's laminated pages contained zoom-lens photographs of the dorsal fin and ventral fluke or tail of a whale—182 in all—with names like Primo (cousin), Mariposa (butterfly), and Raspadita (scratch card). If a scientist photographed a whale in different years visiting the area at least twice, thereby establishing part of its migration pattern, that scientist won the right to name the whale. Toro-Cortés had yet to accomplish this goal. "That's what I'm doing now," he told me. I wished him good luck.

After a week, I left Carlos III, and as I boarded the *Tanu* and we pulled away to return to Punta Arenas, I marveled at the isolation of this tiny outpost and the painstaking slowness of the work that Toro-Cortés was doing. The pace of this research, to say nothing of whether it would have any role in protecting these whales, seemed outmatched by the factory-efficient slaughter of the *Nisshin Maru*.

Once back in Punta Arenas, I caught my ride to Antarctica on the *Arctic Sunrise*, a Greenpeace ship that was carrying a team of four Australian, American, and German scientists to the Weddell Sea and the waters along the western side of the Antarctic Peninsula, the finger of land that juts up toward South America. Though it was a different section of Antarctic waters from where the Japanese were whaling, we were headed to a waypoint in the Antarctic migration route of blue, right, humpback, and minke whales.

To reach Antarctica, we spent the better part of a week crossing the famously perilous Drake Passage, a strip of water below the southern tip of South America, where ferocious waves and fierce winds have sunk hundreds of ships over the centuries. Our ship was tossed so violently that most of the crew were seasick or on the edge of it. In a first for me, I nearly got sick. I broke suddenly into a sweat that I could not turn off, but some Dramamine and time in my bunk helped make the feeling pass. At one point, a wave hit us broadside, and I watched a deckhand tossed clear across the mess hall, as if thrown by an angry Darth Vader. The deckhand stood up, burst into laughter, and went on his way.

The international team of scientists on board the *Arctic Sunrise* was preparing an application to the body that governs the Southern Ocean, called the Commission for the Conservation of Antarctic Marine Living Resources, or CCAMLR. The goal was to create a marine protected area around the Antarctic Peninsula that would halt commercial fishing in an area where it had drastically increased in recent years.

Most of that fishing is for krill, which are small swimming crustaceans that look like shrimp, typically the size of a human pinkie. Living in schools called swarms that are so large they can be seen from space, krill are the main dietary staple of seals, penguins, albatross, squid, and especially whales. The most abundant species on earth, the krill population is still robust. The concern, however, is less about the global krill stock on the whole and more about the specific krill populations living in areas where whales feed on them. Over the past decade, the krill-fishing industry has begun intensively targeting the exact locations where whales migrate to eat these animals—near the ice and continental shelves along the western side of the Antarctic Peninsula. Over the past forty years, populations of adult Antarctic krill have declined by 70 to 80 percent in those areas, studies have shown.

Climate change is shrinking the pack ice where krill hide from predators and feed on plankton. Demand for krill has increased over the past decade, with catches growing 40 percent between 2010 and 2016, as the creatures are ground into fish meal to provide protein for pigs and chickens. Oils squeezed from krill are also popular as nutritional supplements, though their health benefits are still in question.

Using the same two-person submarine that had carried me to the seafloor off the coast of Brazil, the scientists on board Greenpeace's *Arctic Sunrise* hoped to gather evidence that the Chilean and Argentinian governments needed to support their application to create a 172,000-square-mile protected area in these waters. In applying to the relevant international oversight organization, CCAMLR, the scientists needed to document the existence of certain corals, sponges, anemones, and other species that are on the organization's list of marine creatures requiring extra safeguards.

To create the Antarctic marine protected area, the team of scientists would have to sway the countries that fish most heavily for krill—especially Norway, China, Russia, and South Korea. In recent years, these krill ships have drastically improved their efficiency using a newly developed method called "continuous fishing," which uses long, cylindrical nets attached to underwater vacuums that suck the massive swarms on board.

The efficiency of these machines reminded me of what I had concluded as I left the whale research outpost on Carlos III. Through time, humanity's capacity, both legally and scientifically, for extracting life from the oceans has greatly surpassed our ability to protect it. These vacuum boats are concentrated in the Weddell Sea near the continental shelf of the Antarctic Peninsula, where whales also feed. In studying the impact of these boats, I felt as if I were witnessing another part of the Antarctic cycle of predation and depredation. The Japanese hunted the whales, while Sea Shepherd hunted the Japanese. The whales stole the toothfishermen's meals, while the vacuum boats stole food from the whales.

After nearly a week's travel through Drake Passage, the *Arctic Sunrise* arrived at a frigid patch of water crowded with towering glaciers. The scientists announced this was a promising location for a dive because it was rich in biodiversity. So they readied the submarine, and I suited up to join them. This time, I vowed not to get spooked by the claustrophobia, as I had in Brazil, and also not to elbow any of the gauges. An hour later, we were 750 feet underwater.

As we cruised ten feet above the seafloor, we witnessed yet another example of this fierce cycle of Antarctic competition where predators preyed on other predators. In the illuminated cones of light from the submarine's lamps, dozens of bizarre, translucent, gelatinous creatures called salps writhed around us. Looking like snakes made of bubble wrap, salps propel themselves by pumping water through their bodies. The surprising abundance of these animals, some of them over five feet long, was worrisome to the scientists because they eat phytoplankton, which is what krill need to survive. The salps were proliferating because of the warming sea, which meant that climate change was dangerously tipping the balance, upending the food chain in a way that could have potentially dire consequences for whales. "Looks like the vacuum boats aren't the only thing threatening what whales eat," said Kenneth Lowyck, the submarine driver.

. . .

Whales differ from other sea creatures in a variety of ways. A consequential one is that whales mate rarely and produce few offspring. It takes an average of twenty years for a female whale to replace itself with one mature female offspring. This is one reason scientists worry about the estimated 2.9 million whales killed over the past century, mostly by whaling ships.

These concerns prompted fifteen nations to sign a treaty in 1946 to slow the slaughter, creating the International Whaling Commission, an organization that was meant to regulate the industry. In the 1980s, this commission imposed a moratorium, suspending the commercial hunting of the animals. This moratorium included, however, a loophole: an exemption for whaling tied to scientific research. And for years, Japan, which is a signatory to the moratorium, has claimed that exemption to continue its hunts.

In 2010, after prodding from anti-whalers, Australia challenged this practice, taking the matter to the UN International Court of Justice. The Australians argued that Japan's so-called scientific whaling program was an unlawful ruse. Among the pieces of evidence the Australians presented supporting their allegation was that large amounts of the meat from the whales ended up in Japanese restaurants.

The court ruled 12–4 against Japan in 2014, ordering it to cease whaling in Antarctica. Japan promptly canceled its 2015 whaling season, but by 2016 the Japanese government announced it had renamed its whaling program, fittingly called NEWREP-A, a shorthand for New Scientific Whale Research Program in the Antarctic Ocean. Under the new program, Japan would reduce by two-thirds the number of minkes that its ships could kill. The government added that it had granted the *Nisshin Maru* a new scientific permit for the factory whaler and its supporting fleet so that it could return to Antarctica. To avoid more regulatory headaches, the Japanese government also informed the UN secretary-general, Ban Ki-moon, that it was removing its whaling program from the jurisdiction of the International Court of Justice.

It was a brazen move by the Japanese, and one that whaling critics cited as proof that governance on the high seas was broken. What was the point of oversight if countries could simply withdraw from governing bodies when they disliked their rulings? Critics also faulted the international court for failing to tackle the real issue. Everyone agreed that research was legally protected in international waters, but no one knew who determined how to define research at sea.

After all, most scientists and governments defined research on land as an activity that used widely accepted and transparent methodologies. Research was also supposed to produce data, papers, or journal articles, preferably in peer-reviewed publications, based on analyses of results and sharing of data with colleagues. By this definition, the secrecy enshrouding the so-called research aboard the Japanese whalers hardly qualified. This was not a new conundrum for me. I had seen it before with Russ George and the debate surrounding his dumping of iron ore in the ocean.

In the case of Japanese whaling, the Australians had specifically pressed the international court to clarify this matter of what constitutes true scientific research at sea. Instead, the court opted to rule only on whether the number of whales that the Japanese were killing was higher than what was justified for research. This left the Japanese government the option to simply lower the number of whales it intended to kill and to renew its whaling activities under the guise of science. That is exactly what the Japanese government did.

Other courts of law had also failed to rein in the outlaw behavior in Antarctica. In 2015, the Australian Federal Court found the Japanese whaling industry in contempt for killing protected whales in the Australian Whale Sanctuary. The court fined a Japanese whaling company, Kyodo Senpaku, $1 million. But the company never paid, nor did it ever attend a hearing in the case.

Equally ineffective was the court decision against Sea Shepherd. In 2015, the U.S. Court of Appeals for the Ninth Circuit slapped the organization with a $2.5 million fine for breaching a 2012 restraining order that forbade the advocates to get within fifteen hundred feet of the Japanese whaling fleet. After paying the penalty to the Institute for Cetacean Research, which oversees Japan's whaling, Sea Shepherd promptly returned to the Antarctic, where it intended to again break the restraining order if it had the chance in the 2016 whale hunt.

. . .

Ten days after the Sea Shepherd ships left port in Australia in December 2016, they reached the whale hunting grounds in Antarctica and began the search for the *Nisshin Maru*. Near round-the-clock daylight helped visibility, but thick fog and bad weather soon erased this advantage. On calm days, the seas pushed ten-foot waves. During an especially fierce storm, a thirty-five-foot wall of water slammed across the bow of the *Warrior*. The wave rammed the starboard pilot door off its hinges, lifted a Zodiac out of its cradle, and flooded the *Warrior*'s hospital.

Sea Shepherd radioed other boats in the area to check if any of them had spotted the Japanese. Historically, fishermen viewed Sea Shepherd with suspicion— an adversary more than an ally. This trip, more fishing captains answered the radio call. Meyerson speculated that the fishing industry had warmed up to Sea Shepherd, partly due to the positive publicity the organization had received during its previous mission to chase fish poachers. "They back us because the legal boats resent the illegal ones who have a competitive advantage by breaking the law," Meyerson posited.

I was not on board either Sea Shepherd ship during this mission, unable to make the voyage because I was reporting elsewhere at the time. But I spoke by phone and emailed with Lublink, Meyerson, and others on the mission almost daily so I could chronicle the experience. Several weeks into the trip, I asked Lublink what she thought of the Japanese whalers. She paused before acknowledging that she respected them as tacticians. "They know our ships, they know our speeds, they know our habits," she said. Part of the reason that the Japanese had recently lowered their catch quota from 1,035 minke, humpback, and fin whales to 333 minke whales was that this would undercut Sea Shepherd's ability to hammer them with bad publicity, Lublink theorized. The Japanese had also recently doubled the area where they hunted to nearly twice the size of Australia to make it tougher for Sea Shepherd to find them. "They're smart," she said.

The daughter of two butchers, Lublink was a vegetarian, like most people who work for Sea Shepherd. She had joined in 2013 after a three-year stint rescuing and rehabilitating injured kangaroos, wallabies, koalas, and other wildlife at a refuge deep in the Australian bush. Among Sea Shepherd's most experienced captains, she had previously spent about eight years working as a mine warfare officer in the Dutch navy and two and a half years working for the Royal Australian Navy.

On December 22, two ships appeared as pulsating red dots on the *Warrior*'s radar. The blips indicated that the ships were moving slower than sixteen knots, which meant one of them might be the *Nisshin Maru*. Over the previous couple of weeks, Sea Shepherd had already sighted a fuel tanker and a krill spotter, but not the mother ship, which was its main target.

Meyerson alerted his crew and the *Irwin* before pushing the *Warrior* to twenty-five knots in the direction of the blinking dot on his screen. The fog was dangerously thick, cutting visibility down to a couple hundred yards. This area of the Antarctic was crowded with towering glaciers, some more than ten stories tall, and smaller icebergs known as growlers that were the size of trucks and grand pianos. The *Warrior*'s speed was kicking up heavy spray, which meant Meyerson could see clearly through his windshield for only a fraction of a second after each wiper stroke. If he went any slower, he might not catch up; any faster and he might slam into a wall of ice.

After a five-hour chase, Meyerson caught up to the first red dot, only to discover that it was not the mother ship but a harpooner from its fleet. Meyerson immediately did a U-turn to head toward the second dot on his radar. It too was moving slower than sixteen knots on the radar, but Meyerson knew not to get his hopes up. The Japanese ship often used this ruse of driving slowly to trick Sea Shepherd and divert it away from the mother ship. "Like a wounded bird flying away from her nest to fool predators," he said. The second dot was also a harpoon ship, the *Yushin Maru 2*.

The good news in finding the harpoon ships was that it meant the mother ship was likely nearby. After killing the whales, the Japanese usually dragged them by the tail alongside the harpoon ships to transfer them onto the *Nisshin Maru*. But dragging them too far damaged the meat.

The bad news in catching up to the harpoon ships was that the Japanese could now shadow Sea Shepherd, reporting its location back to the mother ship to help it avoid being seen. This was part of the reason the *Warrior* was built for speed. Meyerson opened its engines, taking the *Warrior* to twenty-five knots, easily ditching the Japanese ships that tried following it. The *Irwin,* on the other hand, was much slower, with a top speed of fifteen knots. So, for the rest of the campaign, it was never able to get the Japanese ship off its tail.

At 10:37 in the morning on January 15, Lublink launched the *Blue Hornet,* Sea Shepherd's marine surveillance helicopter. It was roughly two hours earlier than Lublink normally dispatched the helicopter. "I just have this feeling," she told me that day about the decision. The weather was also unusually clear. Communication between the helicopter and the *Irwin* was limited to text messages sent between satellite phones. Radio calls were too easy to intercept. At 11:34, a text appeared on the *Irwin*'s satellite phone: "NM and harpoon confirmed." The radio operator on the *Irwin* immediately read it aloud to Lublink. Excited screams erupted on the bridge.

Sea Shepherd's helicopter, the *Blue Hornet,* returns to the *Steve Irwin* to refuel after searching for the Japanese whaling ships.

Lublink, who speaks perfect English, even though it is not her native language, asked the radio operator to read the text a second time. "Again please," she instructed. Several weeks earlier, Lublink had been heartbroken after mishearing the radio operator who she thought had announced spotting the *Nisshin Maru.* The radio operator had actu-

WWW.icrwhale.org

A dead minke whale on the flensing deck of the *Nisshin Maru* Japanese whaling ship

ally pronounced a similarly spelled harpoon ship in the fleet called the *Yushin Maru.* Lublink wanted to save herself the emotional torture of making this mistake again.

After delivering the good news a second time over the loudspeaker to the *Irwin*'s crew, Lublink used the satellite phone to call Meyerson, who at the time was searching another area of the Antarctic, roughly six hundred nautical miles away. Lublink then plotted her course to the *Nisshin Maru.* The ship was deep inside the Australian Exclusive Economic Zone, where it was forbidden to operate. It was also within the Southern Ocean Whale Sanctuary, a 19.3-million-square-mile area designated as protected by the International Whaling Commission.

The next text brought bad news: "1 dead minke whale confirmed on deck." The crew on the *Blue Hornet* had filmed the mature female whale that sat on the bow of the *Nisshin Maru* with two harpoon or gunshot holes on its underside, each a foot wide. Two harpoon ships that were part of the *Nisshin Maru* fleet were about a mile away, and Lublink instructed the *Blue Hornet* to go check on them to see if they were actively firing on whales at that moment. (They were not, because their harpoon guns were covered by a blue tarp.) By the time the *Blue Hornet* returned to the *Nisshin Maru,* the whale was tarped as well. The mother ship had also been enmeshed by protection nets to guard against smoke bombs and canisters of rancid-smelling butyric acid that Sea Shepherd sometimes threw onto the whalers' decks.

The *Irwin,* which was roughly seventy nautical miles away, raced to catch up so that the *Blue Hornet* would not have to fly so far. Meanwhile, the *Blue Hornet* flew back and forth, trying to keep track of the *Nisshin Maru.* Each trip, the *Blue Hornet* went out to the whalers' last known position, found the Japanese anew, reported the coordinates, then returned to the *Irwin's* helipad to refuel. But after eight hours of reconnaissance and on the *Blue Hornet's* fifth trip, strong winds and fog rolled in. The pilot was dangerously fatigued.

Though southern Antarctica is light most hours in January, the chase had taken the ships farther north, creeping them into night, making flying even more perilous. "It's simply not safe," said Lublink, informing the *Blue Hornet's* frustrated pilot that she would not let the helicopter fly a sixth trip. Lublink had partly closed the gap to twenty-six nautical miles. The simple and discouraging fact, though, was that the *Nisshin Maru's* maximum speed was one knot faster than the *Irwin's.*

That night, sitting on the bridge talking with me by phone, Lublink was clearly dejected but trying to strike a hopeful tone. Forcing the Japanese to tail the *Irwin* meant they had one less harpoon ship for hunting, she pointed out to me. Chasing the factory ship had also driven it hundreds of miles outside its normal hunting ground. "While they're running from us," Lublink said, "they can't be hunting the whales." The footage of the dead whale would be useful for international publicity, she said. The tarping of the dead whale and harpoon gun was a guilty admission that they wanted to keep the evidence out of sight. "These are successes for us," she said.

After losing the *Nisshin Maru,* the *Warrior* and the *Irwin* headed to an area on the west end of the Cooperation Sea in the Southern Ocean. Meyerson had nicknamed this area Bergville because it was so crowded with icebergs. Already a treacherous maze, the region was even more dangerous because Meyerson had decided to turn off his radar, which of course would have helped him see nearby icebergs or other ships. But Meyerson had become convinced that the Japanese were somehow using his radar or other transmissions from his ship to track him. Every time he had come upon the harpooners, it was as if they knew in advance he was approaching. "They'd be just sitting there," he said.

On February 20, after several days of searching Bergville, the *Warrior's* crew spotted a slick of dark red foam in the water. When whales are harpooned, it produces a watery contrail of blood and blubber. But this slick was much thicker and bloodier and could only have been produced, Meyerson thought, from the *Nisshin Maru*'s below deck slaughterhouse, which during busy times pumped thousands of gallons of butchering waste overboard. Not knowing which direction to head along the slick, Meyerson guessed—and guessed wrong. After an hour, he came upon one of the harpoon ships, idling as if it had been waiting for him.

Swinging the *Warrior* around, Meyerson sped in the opposite direction along the slick. Several of the *Warrior*'s crew were on deck with binoculars, and one of them spotted a puff of black smoke drifting behind a distant iceberg. If it was burned diesel from the mother ship, they were within a mile. The crew launched a drone to help search. From behind the wheel, Meyerson stared at the water with the focus of a cat watching a bird. For the next three hours, the *Warrior* slalomed up and down long iceberg alleyways. The *Ocean Warrior* never caught sight again of its mark. As night fell, hope waned. Meyerson, fearful that they were burning too much fuel, called off the search, once and for all.

Operation Nemesis ended in March 2017 as the *Irwin* and the *Warrior* returned to ports in Australia. Though they tried to put a positive spin on the trip, crew from both ships told me as they disembarked that it was one of their most frustrating missions. The real sense of defeat was yet to come.

Five months later, Sea Shepherd announced that it would not return to Antarctica in 2017 for its annual antiwhaling mission, focusing resources elsewhere. "The Japanese have too much of an advantage over us," Meyerson later explained to me. They have more advanced drones and radar and access to military-grade satellite technology, he added.

The other reason Sea Shepherd was calling off its hunt was that the legal climate had changed, making it more risky for the advocacy group to pursue the whalers. In June 2017, Japan passed a controversial antiterrorism law that criminalized the "plotting or committing" of 277 acts, including the organized and forceful obstruction of a business, an offense that could result in five years in prison. Many people viewed some of the language in the law to be directed at Sea Shepherd.

With so little consistency in how the law is applied at sea, Sea Shepherd activists risked arrest and imprisonment by Japan even if the acts for which they were charged took place in international waters. Their own home countries, not wanting to get embroiled in a diplomatic dispute or undermine their own ability to arrest people harassing their ships, might not work for their release.

Meyerson was still fuming about the 2012 U.S. Court of Appeals injunction that put a restraining order on Sea Shepherd, forbidding it to get within fifteen hundred feet of the Japanese whalers. He compared the court decision to protesting in front of a brothel in Cambodia that sells underage girls for sex and then returning home to be sued under U.S. law for hurting the brothel's bottom line. The passage of the Japanese antiterrorism law had upped the ante to a dangerous degree for Sea Shepherd, he added. "Destroying the world is now seen as just the cost of doing business," he said. "And defending the earth is seen as terrorism."

Terrorist or freedom fighter—it's a semantic dichotomy that has been fraught with politics and ideology at least since Spartacus took up arms against the Romans. This distinction is especially murky in the moral and legal vacuum offshore. Sea Shepherd has its supporters and detractors; for good reason, the organization is both hated and revered. While I harbored neither view, I certainly understood its confrontational approach in the face of inaction by those responsible to act.

Most comfortable on this frontier, Meyerson did not stay away from it for long. After returning to shore in Australia, he flew home to the foothills of the Sierra Nevada in California. He'd been at sea for more than eleven months. A stack of mail awaited him, including a letter from the American law firm that represented the Japanese whaling company. Sent after Meyerson had already headed to Antarctica, the letter warned that as the master of the *Ocean Warrior* he "should expect to be held personally accountable" for any damage or harassment of the Japanese whaling ships. Meyerson tore up the letter before taking several weeks to rest and recharge. Then he called his operations boss at Sea Shepherd to determine his next mission.

# A VOID

After Meyerson told me in a phone call about his plans to continue his mission, I thought about the whales he had hoped to protect. Many of them were older than he and I. For that matter, they were older than the Principality of Sealand and the nation of Palau. The size and longevity of these whales gave them the appearance of invincibility and strength in much the same way that the vastness of the ocean lent it a deceptive sort of durability. In reality, both were facing dire threats, often in ways that were too subtle, slow, and disparate for most people to notice or for most governments to care.

Here again was that central paradox: the ocean is as large as it is small. Look at a map of the planet and you see mostly blue; the immensity of the sea is what makes it so tough to police and protect. And yet, as those arrested Vietnamese fishermen had told me, there aren't many oceans; there's just one. The sea is in myriad ways more connected by forces like acidification, dumping, and overfishing than it is parceled or defined by concepts like private property, national boundaries, or government regulation.

While Meyerson launched anew, I did not. It was time for me to stay onshore and return to my job at the newspaper. Leaving a dozen amazing stories unreported, I swallowed that painful writer's truism that a book is never finished, just abandoned.

The roughly four years I spent reporting on the outlaw ocean put me in constant motion—an experience at once disorienting and sublime. Viewed as one, this voyage had taken me to places so foreign that to experience them felt like space travel. It also felt like time travel as I witnessed things—piracy, whaling, slavery, privateers—that I had previously assumed were fully locked in the past.

Impunity is the norm at sea, not just because of the lack of enforcement but also due to the cast of characters out there who, with questionable credentials and motives, are left to take up the slack. Bureaucrats rather than investigators conduct what rare inspections actually occur on vessels suspected of environmental or labor abuses (as I learned in Thailand). Vigilantes and private mercenaries, as much as police or navy officers, patrol the high seas and pursue scofflaws (as I discovered on the floating armories or in the chases of the *Thunder* and the *Nisshin Maru*). What rules apply in international waters have been crafted over the years more by diplomats and the fishing and shipping industries than by lawmakers or labor lawyers. This has made commercial secrecy a higher priority than crime prevention (as I saw investigating the Somali 7 ships, the death of Eril Andrade, and the murders of the men who were shot on camera).

Mostly, I had explored the dark underbelly of this offshore frontier, places where the worst instincts of our human species thrived and flourished. But I also witnessed unparalleled beauty and true marvel. I met bizarre, sometimes heroic actors in a setting that drowned the senses, a world with brighter sun, louder waves, and stronger wind than I previously knew to exist, as if I'd been parachuted into one of those fanciful maps the medieval cartographers dreamed up.

One particular afternoon comes to mind. I stood on the front deck of a ship in the South Atlantic Ocean. Under an apricot sunset, I watched a winged fish fly through the air for hundreds of feet. Moments later, several birds dove into the ocean and swam deep underwater equally as far. That night was cloudless, and with flatness all around me, not a visual obstruction anywhere, the sky was as big as it ever gets. At night, shooting stars left white slashes like chalk lines on a blackboard. The most dazzling streaks, though, were not in the sky but underwater. As fish darted through certain areas, the sea was slashed with glowing blue lines, the result of a mesmerizing defense mechanism of bioluminescent plankton that allows them to produce light.

What grabbed me that day was how much of this place is magically upside down: fish in the air, birds underwater, white streaks above us, blue below. Part of its beauty is its exotic unpredictability. The wonder of it all is magnetic, and each time I returned to land, I felt an intense longing for this place, homesick for a location not my home, despite the suffering I'd seen there.

But there was something else that stuck with me and that transcended both the darkness and the beauty offshore. I thought back on the black expanse that swallowed the Cessna in Palau and how that same sort of vastness had long provided an excuse for dumping waste into the world's oceans. I thought about the crushing boredom at sea and the distinct way it tortured seafarers on abandoned vessels and armed guards on the floating weapons depots. I thought about the silence that fed gruffness on so many ships and how it bred resignation among the raped, robbed, and drowned men of the Oyang fleet. While some of those Oyang men paid a heavy price for breaking this silence, I also recalled the reward reaped by the magic-pipe whistle-blower, who spoke up.

These snapshots seemed to demonstrate that the outlaw ocean and the ships that traverse it are defined not just by the people who work these waters but also by intangible forces like silence, boredom, and vastness. I'd go a step further: the ocean is outlaw not because it is inherently good or bad but because it is a void, like silence is to sound or boredom is to activity. While we have for centuries embraced and touted the life that springs from these waters, we have tended to ignore its role as a refuge of depravity. But the outlaw ocean is real, as it has been for centuries, and until we reckon with that fact, we can forget about ever taming or protecting this frontier.

# REINING IN THE OUTLAW OCEAN

What can we do to mitigate the mayhem offshore? Given the scope of the problems, this is a difficult question. Tackling the topic can seem as overwhelming as solving climate change. We all recognize that our individual actions will not, on their own, stop the planet from overheating. Still, many people want to know how they can make a difference. They want to feel like they are a part of the solution, not part of the problem.

Albeit small, there are clear benefits to, say, making sure your tires are properly inflated to improve gas mileage or buying carbon offsets to lessen the impact of emissions from an airline flight. But the little and personalized steps that average people might take to guard against the illegal, dangerous, and inhumane acts at sea are tougher to pinpoint.

And yet, there are ways to make a difference. Among them is to support, financially or otherwise, the organizations that are on the front lines and tackling some of the stubborn realities portrayed in these pages. Vet them for yourselves, but here is a brief tour of some of the organizations doing this work. I also offer broader context on steps that governments and companies are taking—or should be taking, according to advocates and researchers—to better police the high seas.

## PROTECTING MARINERS

Mission to Seafarers and Stella Maris are two highly effective groups that directly help crew members who have been abandoned, not paid, physically harmed, or trafficked. Historically, the largest of international transport unions, ITF, has focused primarily on protecting crews on freighters, tankers, and cargo ships, but in recent years the union has broadened its mission to also guard against abuse of workers on fishing boats as well.

Several groups, including the Environmental Justice Foundation, Human Rights Watch, Greenpeace, and the International Labor Rights Forum, publish invaluable investigative reports about labor abuses on fishing ships, especially in South Asia and the Far East. These groups, along with the International Labor Organization, play an important role behind the scenes, pushing for stronger laws and better enforcement to protect workers on these boats. Sea Shepherd, on the other hand, relies less on research to apply policy pressure on governments or companies. It uses direct confrontations with its adversaries to produce publicity and raise awareness.

Forced labor is more common on fishing ships that stay at sea longer. These ships avoid docking and spot checks by onshore inspectors sometimes for years by relying on transshipment, with supplies carried to the fishing boats and the catch transported back to shore. Transshipment enables unscrupulous fishing boat operators to keep crews captive and to lie about their catch on documents they give to customs authorities, making it seem as if it were caught legally when it was not. That is why many labor and environmental advocates argue that governments and fish buyers should require fishing ships to make more frequent visits to shore. They also contend that transshipment at sea should be banned or limited.

In 2017, the UN's International Labor Organization took steps to prevent the stranding of hundreds of seafarers each year on abandoned ships at sea or in port. Shipowners were required to show proof of funds to cover four months of crews' wages and the costs to repatriate them. Operators also have to prove they can cover costs that result from death or long-term disability of seafarers due to occupational injury. Labor advocates say this sort of insurance is essential but the requirement should be expanded to fishing boats, which are currently exempt from this mandate and most of the labor organization's other major protections.

Anti-trafficking groups have encouraged seafood and shipping companies to minimize their exposure to labor abuses by avoiding or at least carefully vetting any manning agencies used to recruit and manage crew members. Companies can also insist that they be provided copies of the contracts signed by workers, while prohibiting the use of up-front recruitment fees that are often used to trap workers in debt. The most diligent companies can hire consultants to conduct spot checks as well as exit interviews of a subset of former workers to check for common problems like hidden deductions withdrawn from workers' paychecks, promised wages that were never paid after workers returned home, or blacklisting of workers who speak up about environmental or labor violations.

## A MORE TRANSPARENT FOOD SUPPLY

Current fishing practices are unsustainable, and many marine scientists have called for creating more marine protected areas that are mostly or entirely off-limits to large-scale commercial fishing and other industrial activities. Researchers also argue for scaling back the size of the global fishing fleet, tightening the quotas that limit how many fish can be pulled from the water, and removing the government subsidies that make seafood artificially cheap. All of these goals require aggressive enforcement and commitment from governments to prosecute illegal fishing companies.

In recent years and with mixed results, various industries have reckoned with labor and environmental abuses within their supply chain. Consider, for instance, conflict-free diamonds, dolphin-free tuna, fair-trade coffee, and sweatshop-free garments. The global seafood industry is slowly beginning to confront these problems.

Technology exists to better track fish as it travels from bait to plate, and an emergent movement is pushing to make seafood more traceable. Governments and large seafood sellers are considering mandating the use of DNA field kits for identifying species to combat the problem of counterfeit fish. They are also considering tracking packages more aggressively with bar-coded labeling, and employing algorithms to flag high-risk imports like those coming from vessels that have past violations and those carrying shipments routed through border crossings commonly associated with organized crime.

Grocers and restaurateurs are turning to nonprofit groups like Fish-Wise or for-profit firms like SCS Global and Trace Register for consulting services and supply-chain audits. Greenpeace's annual "Carting Away the Oceans" report card ranks supermarkets based on ethical purchasing decisions, supply-chain transparency, and fishery-to-shelf traceability. In 2018, more than 90 percent of retailers received passing grades, but only four—Whole Foods, Hy-Vee, Aldi, and Target—received "green" sustainability scores. Most, like Walmart, Costco, and Kroger, fell somewhere in the middle of the scale.

Seafood companies are also considering requiring any vessels that catch or carry their fish to have a unique vessel identifier or International Maritime Organization (IMO) number, which remains constant throughout the vessel's lifetime, regardless of change of name, ownership, or flag. If a ship lacks this type of identifier, companies that get goods or fish from it have no way of knowing where it traveled, whether its workers had contracts, and whether it is on any of the black lists maintained by regional fishery management organizations. In 2017, the UN's Food and Agriculture Organization has taken a step toward consolidating this information by publishing an online, global, one-stop database of vessels.

Advocates have called for fish buyers to source only from countries that have ratified international agreements such as the Port State Measures Agreement, a UN treaty that outlines rules for how ships visiting a nation's port should be inspected. Another important requirement is for fishing ships to carry observers, who are answerable only to local fishery authorities. The job of these onboard observers is to monitor and document a vessel's compliance with quotas and check for other possible crimes like shark finning, excessive bycatch, or high-grading (the practice of throwing older fish overboard to replace it with newer catch). These observers should also be responsible and empowered to report on labor conditions and violations.

Consumers are also paying more attention to these issues, and a

growing number of them are opting to avoid seafood (and meat) altogether. For people who eat fish but hope to distance themselves from
possible environmental or labor abuses, there are ways to be better
informed about the companies supplying the fish.

Among the smartest writers on this topic is Paul Greenberg, who
notes that the most problematic fish are shrimp, tuna, and salmon because they are overwhelmingly imported and they involve especially
long and opaque supply chains that may include companies that engage
in environmentally illegal or unsustainable practices. "Eat American
seafood and a much broader variety than we currently do," Greenberg
suggests. Mollusks like clams, mussels, and oysters are often ecologi-
cally beneficial to grow and can be produced with much lower impact
to the environment. Other American seafood that he says is worth
putting on your plate are Alaskan sockeye salmon, which are very well
managed and high in omega-3s.

Greenberg further advises consumers to steer clear of seafood and
omega-3 dietary supplements that are connected to the "reduction
industry"—a massive industrial sector that boils down twenty-five
million tons of wild fish a year into fish oil for dietary supplements
and fish meal that gets fed for protein to chicken, pigs, and farmed fish.
These pills remain popular despite a growing body of medical research
undercutting the idea that the supplements provide any real health
benefits. A better option to fish-based omega-3 supplements are ones
made from algae.

For further guidance, consumers can consult the Monterey Bay
Aquarium, which produces seafood report cards that rank fish from
an environmental perspective as "red" (avoid), "yellow" (good alternative), and "green" (best choice). Over fifty-five million of the cards have
been downloaded or otherwise distributed by the aquarium, which
recommends, for instance, that if a consumer wants to buy crayfish,
choose that which is farmed in the United States. The cards warn
against buying bluefin tuna, but tilapia, which is almost exclusively
farmed, is generally a good option. Much depends on where the fish
was caught or farmed and what methods were used to harvest it. Atlantic salmon farmed in marine net pens in Norway's Skjerstad Fjord is
considered a "best choice," for instance, while the same species farmed
in Canada's Atlantic should be avoided.

Recently, the aquarium began incorporating human rights into its criteria, joining Liberty Asia and the Sustainable Fisheries Partnership, to produce the "Seafood Slavery Risk Tool," a public database that can be searched by species or region to determine whether certain seafood comes with a higher chance of being tainted by slave labor. Patagonia toothfish, for example, is considered "low risk" if it is caught in Argentina, Chile, or Australia but "high risk" if it comes from South Korea. Searching "tuna" reveals a dismal state of affairs in the South Pacific: almost all tuna from Taiwan, except tuna certified by the Marine Stewardship Council, is considered "critical risk." The tool is produced primarily for businesses in the seafood and financial industries, but the aquarium encourages nonprofit groups, consumers, and anyone else with an interest in ethical seafood to use it. WWF also publishes a useful country-by-country guide on sustainable seafood.

## MONITORING AND INVESTIGATING OFFSHORE CRIMES

There's a surprising lack of publicly available information about violence at sea. To avoid the abuse or disappearance of seafarers, governments will likely have to increase their spot checks on ships returning to port and levy heavier penalties for incomplete or falsified crew lists. Human rights researchers also suggest that shipowners and crews should be legally obligated to report crimes at sea. The resulting data should not be held privately by insurance companies or flag registries but be made available to the public. Maritime investigators and insurers have called for the creation of a public database for tracking missing mariners. Flag programs should also be required to contribute to it.

For a useful framework on how to increase the amount of usable information about crime at sea, labor advocates point to two existing measures: the federal Cruise Vessel Security and Safety Act, which mandates reporting of criminal activity on passenger ships to the FBI, and the Declaration Condemning Acts of Violence Against Seafarers (the Washington Declaration), in which major flag states commit to reporting to the International Maritime Bureau when seafarers face violence at sea. These measures could be expanded to apply globally but would need to be obligatory and come with heavy fines and potential prison time for those who fail to comply.

Union officials and labor rights researchers also say that countries should sign the Maritime Labour Convention, which is a global set of standards for protecting workers' rights at sea that applies to all ships entering the harbors of parties to the treaty as well as to all states flying the flag of state party. By ratifying this measure, governments could enforce higher standards of paid leave, wages, medical care, and safety rules on foreign-flagged vessels as part of Coast Guard inspections during visits to their ports. As of 2018, over eighty-five countries, not including the United States, had ratified the measure. Labor advocates also call for countries to ratify the International Labor Organization Convention 188, which aims specifically to improve conditions on fishing boats.

The vastness of the oceans makes it easy for poachers to thwart government quotas, enter forbidden areas, and pillage sanctuaries. As a result, pirate fishing boats are responsible for over 20 percent of the wild-caught seafood imported into the United States, and the percentage is likely higher abroad. Requiring all fishing ships to have VMS and AIS tracking devices would help allow the public and law enforcement to track activity at sea.

Flags of convenience often provide cover for scofflaw fleets. Many registries fail to exert oversight of member ships. More responsible companies will require that the ships that are part of their supply chain only fly the flags with strictest accountability and transparency standards. The ITF and Seafarers International Research Centre provide ranking of flag registries based on labor standards.

Several organizations focus on improving offshore monitoring. Global Fishing Watch, for example, tracks fishing ships and makes the information public. Trygg Mat Tracking, FISH-i Africa, C4ADS, and Windward investigate ships suspected of engaging in criminal behavior. Human Rights at Sea produces reports on abuses of seafarers. Earthworks tracks mining companies that dispose of hazardous waste in the ocean. The Pew Charitable Trusts produces a steady stream of invaluable research on the global problem of illegal fishing.

In terms of clarifying and strengthening the rules about what types of commercial activities can occur in international waters, the High Seas Alliance, a coalition of more than thirty-seven organizations, has been an important driving force. In particular, the alliance has spearheaded the negotiations around a UN marine biodiversity treaty that will create a formal process for setting aside protected marine areas in international waters. Unlike on land, there is no legal framework on the high seas for creating areas that are off-limits to commercial activity. The treaty will also create procedures for environmental impact assessments and establish a method for the public to be informed about large-scale projects in these waters, including fishing, seabed mining, shipping, research, and other activities.

# ACKNOWLEDGMENTS

Regardless of what it says on the front cover, hundreds of people—researchers, fixers, translators, photographers, drivers, editors, investigators, and scores of others—made this book possible.

The first thank-you goes to the countless mariners around the world who trusted me to be their understudy. Good journalists traffic in anecdotes and I'm indebted to the mariners who so generously loaned me their most precious and personal stories. I finished my voyages awed by the quiet resilience and scrappy ingenuity of these men and women. I also felt lucky about the ticket I won in the lottery of birth. At every turn in this reporting, I was reminded how much of the world's population starts with far less, then survives and even flourishes in often grim living and working conditions.

I owe a great gratitude to *The New York Times,* my professional home for the past decade and a half. A world-class teaching hospital, the *Times* took me in, despite my being a neophyte to the profession, and a staff of master doctors patiently taught me the practice. On the Outlaw Ocean and other projects, Executive Editor Dean Baquet gave me the time, freedom, and trust to untangle the most convoluted and unwieldy topics.

With a marathoner's endurance and an X-ray vision for story architecture, my editor at the *Times,* Rebecca Corbett, embraced the idea for this project from the outset. She masterfully steered me through a two-year reporting slog, helping me boil it all down into clear and compelling narratives. Behind the scenes, other editors—Hannah Fairfield, Nancy Donaldson Gauss, Beth Flynn, Alexandra Garcia, Matt Purdy, Steve Duenes, Luke Mitchell, and Jake Silverstein—took a giant leap of faith in dedicating untold resources to the project. The series in the newspaper and online could never have been as evocative were it not for the grueling work and rare talent of a small group of *Times* photographers and videographers, namely, Ben Solomon, Ed Ou, Adam Dean, Hannah Reyes, Selase Kove-Seyram, Josué Azor, Basil Childers, Cristian Movila, William Widmer, and Benjamin Lowy. Also utterly essential were a handful of graphic designers and social media editors: Jacky Myint, Derek Watkins, Ari Isaacman Bevacqua, and Aaron Byrd.

Baquet generously gave me a fifteen-month book leave to try to turn the newspaper series into something bigger and more lasting. Making this goal possible was Christy Fletcher, who for nearly two decades has been as much my oracle and intellectual bodyguard as my literary agent—always savvy, always fiercely on my side. I'm also indebted to the team surrounding Christy: Melissa Chinchillo, Grainne Fox, Alyssa Taylor, and Sarah Fuentes. Equally important is Howie Sanders, my film and television agent, who has, with incomparable persistence and diplomatic acumen, carefully guided stories of mine through their metamorphosis into other creative forms.

During my book leave, no one was more essential than Chynna Fry. Handling everything from line editing to logistics and so much in between, she guided me through the minutiae of setting up these many trips and the muddle of keeping track of all the documents and reporting details they produced. My fact-checker, document sweeper, and all-around muse, Mollie Simon, was invaluable. My photographer on the book project, Fabio Nascimento, doubled as my all-weather travel companion, helping me to stay safe and sane during these excursions while taking real risks and working impossibly long hours in often brutal conditions to produce breathtaking video and still photographs. Among many other jobs, Annelise Blackwood tirelessly and masterfully prepared the visual content from all this reporting.

I drew endless research help from dozens of people, but most especially from Susan Beachy, Kitty Bennett, Charlotte Norsworthy, and Alexis Bravo, all of whom seemed incapable of saying no to my constant and ever-zany journalistic requests. I'm also grateful to Keith

Herndon, Joe Starrs, Charles Davis, and Carolyn Curiel and a cohort of student journalists who taught me tons about video editing and social media as we played with the footage produced by this reporting. They include Zach Hoffman, Madeline McGee, Lize Geurts, Holly Speck, Brooke Cary, Rahimon Nasa, Clarissa Sosin, Michelle Baruchman, Sarah Douglass, Sam Donnenberg, Mateo Menchaca, Gerardo del Valle, Anthony Nicotera, and Eric Erli.

For guidance on matters literary, legal, journalistic, medical, and financial, I had a deep bench of conscripted counselors: Chuck Fox, Dick Schoenfeld, Dr. Louise Moody, Sharon Kelly, Peter Baker, Emily Heaslip, Donna Denizé, Marc Lacey, Michael Thomas, Jacqueline Smith, and Joe Sexton. Thanks to Chip Noble and his team at Garmin and Jordan Hassin from Iridium for keeping me safe and oriented.

For reasons I still don't fully comprehend, Jason Uechi volunteered inordinate amounts of his time writing software, building databases, and designing web content for the project. Also magnanimously fulfilling my endless pleas for reporting help, often in far-flung corners of the globe, were Tanya Laohathai, Daniel Murphy, Milko Mariano Schvartzman, Karen Sack, Charles Clover, Su-hyun Lee, Rebecca Pskowski, Shih-Han Huang, Tony Long, Paul Greenberg, John Amos, David Pearl, Dimitris Bounias, Nikolas Leontopoulos, Shannon Service, Duncan Copeland, Alistair Graham, Peter Sol Rogers, Apinya Tajit, Phil Robertson, Steve Trent, Chutima Sidasathian, Puchara Sandford, Rika Novayanti, Budi Cahyono, and Shelley Thio.

Assisting the journalism in a variety of other ways, including providing material support, hosting speaking engagements, granting me access to closed-door conferences, providing me with proprietary ocean or trafficking-related data and analyses, amplifying the project's social media, lending me equipment and office space, and, quite especially, granting me unfettered access to their ships, crews, and researchers were Thomson Reuters, Stephen Glass, the Mission to Seafarers, Oceans Beyond Piracy, the Pew Charitable Trusts, Oak Foundation, USAID, Adessium Foundation, Interpol, Humanity United in partnership with the Freedom Fund, Synchronicity Earth, Parley for the Oceans, Shari Sant Plummer, the Campbell Foundation, National Geographic, Carpenter, Zuckerman & Rowley, Greenpeace, Peter Hunter Perot, Sea Shepherd Conservation Society, the Safina Center, Cyrill Gutsch, Stefan Ashkenazy, Petit Ermitage Hotel, Stella Maris International Seafarers' Center, SkyTruth, Windward, Waitt Foundation, Rockefeller Philanthropy Advisors, Environmental Justice Foundation, the U.S. Department of State's Office to Monitor and Combat Trafficking in Persons, Ann Luskey, the Tiffany & Co. Foundation, Shannon O'Leary Joy, the International Transport Workers' Federation, the Schmidt Family Foundation, OCEANUSLive, FISH-i Africa, Monterey Bay Aquarium Foundation, Human Rights Watch, and Trygg Mat Tracking.

The title of my book is a nod to William Langewiesche's singularly insightful work, published in 2004, called *The Outlaw Sea,* about mayhem on the oceans involving merchant and passenger ships in particular. I share with Langewiesche the view that the maritime world exists largely outside the law, and his writing on the topic was for me an invaluable inspiration.

I am fortunate to have quite a few talented and insightful friends, many of them journalists, who at different stages of this book generously took the time to critique chapters: Louie Urbina, Kimberly Wethal, Brett Dahlberg, Kyle Mackie, Amanda Lein, Mary Holman, Kirsten Larrison, and Marcia Seiler. Theo Emery was uniquely helpful in this regard. Amanda Foushee, who is the most rigorous reader and truest writer I know, showed me what taking the craft seriously really means.

For Ricardo and Corey Urbina, who in their everyday lives demonstrate the importance of service—my love and gratitude. To Adrienne Urbina, the family's first journalist, thank you for being my steadfast ally.

My longtime friend and former editor, Adam Bryant, did yeoman's work on this book, diving deep into the chapters, helping me tweak, tighten, polish, and clarify. A master stonemason, Bryant helped me never lose sight of the cathedral. Aside from being one of the humblest and kindest people I know, he also has an explanatory wit and playful fluency with metaphor so vibrant and clever that they often made me laugh out loud while tickling awake otherwise sleepy parts of my brain.

There would be no book were it not for the willingness of my publisher, Alfred A. Knopf, to take a daring plunge. Thank you, Robin Desser, Sonny Mehta, and Zakiya Harris. Never rushed, always easygoing, Andrew Miller, my editor at Knopf, asked all the right questions to nudge the book in the right direction, and, scalpel in hand, he meticulously trimmed and shaped it to its final form. I'm also thrilled to have worked with Will Hammond at Bodley Head in the U.K.

Despite my constant comings and goings, my son, Aidan, supported me by unflappably staying his course. Before each of the many trips abroad, two guardian angels—my mother, Joanne McCarron, and my brother-in-law, Chris Clark—quietly took up the slack in my absence, no questions asked, no thanks required. I could not have done this work without them.

The biggest debt is owed my wife, Sherry Rusher, who has forever been solid ground for me. The owner of my heart, she is a consummate teacher, always leading by example, and I happily remain her student, trying to match her work ethic, intellectual hunger, and unwavering honesty. I can't thank her enough for never once flinching at the risks entailed in my taking on this project, and never once complaining about the Herculean load she had to bear at home so that I might head out, again and again, to sea.

# NOTES

## Sources, Readings, Digressions

This book is based on more than four years of reporting and thousands of hours of interviews, and most of what I learned came from those conversations. But before delving into a new topic or launching on a new trip, I usually compiled news clips, journal articles, and anything else I could read to get oriented. I'm sharing those abbreviated bibliographies here in case they are useful. Where it seemed potentially interesting, I've also offered additional notes on sources, context, and brief asides.

### CHAPTER 1 STORMING THE *THUNDER*

3  Captain Peter Hammarstedt peered: The reporting about the chase of the *Thunder* came from my time on the *Bob Barker* and the *Sam Simon* but also from subsequent phone and email interviews between 2014 and 2017 with Peter Hammarstedt, Siddharth Chakravarty, Wyanda Lublink, and other Sea Shepherd crew.

3  As he stood on the bridge: "The Sam Simon Departs for Operation Icefish," Sea Shepherd, Dec. 8, 2014; "Bob Barker Departs for Operation Icefish," Sea Shepherd, Dec. 3, 2014.

3  Hammarstedt leafed through: "Vessel Report for Typhoon 1," *Lloyd's List Intelligence*, April 16, 2015. The *Thunder* had many names over the years, including the *Typhoon 1, Kuko, Wuhan 4, Batu 1,* and *Ming 5*.

4  At the time, Interpol's Purple Notice: Interpol, which played an integral part in the chase of the Bandit 6, issues various alerts that it calls

"notices." They are color coded—purple, red, blue, yellow, green, orange, black—based on the type of information that is being requested. These notices are issued only if Interpol receives an official request from one of the 190-member states. My reporting on Interpol's role in the chase of the *Thunder* began with several days in October 2016 spent at its headquarters in Lyon, France, where I worked closely with its Environmental Crimes Division and especially Alistair McDonnell, who directs Project Scale, a program focused on illegal, unreported, and unregulated fishing (more commonly known by its acronym, IUU). Project Scale was mostly funded by Norway, the United States, and the Pew Charitable Trusts.

5 Over the radio, Hammarstedt: "Radio Conversations with Marine Vessel Thunder," Sea Shepherd, 2015.

6 "Bob Barker will maintain": Most of the reporting in this chapter was based on ten days spent at sea on the *Bob Barker* and the *Sam Simon* in April 2015. It also derives from interviews from late 2014 through 2018 with the crew and officers from both ships as well as Sea Shepherd staff on land.

7 Five of the ship's Spaniards: Paul Watson, "Another Impossible Mission Made Possible by Sea Shepherd," Sea Shepherd, April 17, 2015.

8 The *Thunder* was among: Jack Fengaughty, "From the Deep South—Fishing, Research, and Very Cold Fingers," Icescience.blogspot.com, Feb. 17, 2012.

8 the grisly gray-black: Paul Greenberg, "The Catch," *New York Times,* Oct. 23, 2005.

8 creature can prowl: Cassandra Brooks, "Antifreeze Fish: Studying Antarctic Toothfish and the Special Proteins in Their Bodies That Help Them Thrive in Subfreezing Waters," *Ice Stories: Dispatches from Polar Scientists,* Nov. 3, 2008.

8 There, it is sold under: "Chasing the Perfect Fish," *Wall Street Journal,* May 4, 2006, adapted from Bruce G. Knecht, *Hooked: Pirates, Poaching, and the Perfect Fish* (Emmaus, Pa.: Rodale, 2007). Popularly called "Chilean sea bass" in North America, this fish is neither distinctly Chilean nor a true sea bass. This name was but a shrewd marketing ploy by an American fish wholesaler named Lee Lantz, who in the late 1970s relabeled the fish to make it sound more palatable. In Spain and Japan, this fish is called *mero* and in Chile *bacalao de profundidad.*

8 Demand soared in the 1980s: Alex Mayyasi, "The Invention of the Chilean Sea Bass," *Priceonomics,* April 28, 2014.

8 The oily fish: Grant Jones, "Ugly Fish with Sweet Meat Proves a Treat: The Rise of the Deep Dwelling Patagonian Toothfish," News Corp Australia, July 12, 2013.

8 For most of the 1990s: "Combined IUU Vessel List," Trygg Mat Tracking (TMT).

8 And yet surveillance planes: Andrew Darby, "Epic Chase of Pirate Fisher Thunder Continues," *Sydney Morning Herald,* March 15, 2015.

9 The 2,200-horsepower trawler: "Vessel Report for Typhoon 1," *Lloyd's List Intelligence,* April 16, 2015.

9 During that time, it flew: Vessel Record Images for the Arctic Ranger, Commission for the Conservation of Antarctic Marine Living Resources.

9 After it was added to the EU's blacklist: IUU Blacklist Vessels, Greenpeace.

9 For a ship of this size: Max Hardberger, interview with author, Nov. 2017.

9 In 2014, Sea Shepherd launched: "Thunder Captain and Officers Face Justice in the Wake of Operation Icefish," Sea Shepherd, Feb. 26, 2018.

10 When the *Bob Barker* spotted: Fisheries and Resources Monitoring System, "Southern Ocean Antarctic Toothfish Fishery—Banzare Bank," Commission for the Conservation of Antarctic Marine Living Resources, 2015.

11 Falling overboard would: Avijit Datta and Michael Tipton, "Respiratory Responses to Cold Water Immersion: Neural Pathways, Interactions, and Clinical Consequences Awake and Asleep," *Journal of Applied Physiology,* June 1, 2006; "The Chilling Truth About Cold Water," *Pacific Yachting Magazine,* Feb. 2006.

11 Toothfish can weigh: Sea Shepherd, Analysis of Toothfish Catch; "Antarctic Toothfish Poaching Ships Shrug Off New Zealand Navy," Associated Press, Jan. 21, 2015.

13 The *Sam Simon* delivered: Tony Smart, "Mauritius: The Best Africa Destination You Know Almost Nothing About," CNN, April 11, 2017.

15 He promptly founded Sea Shepherd: "The History of Sea Shepherd," Sea Shepherd.

15 Nicknamed Neptune's Navy: For an excellent profile of Sea Shepherd and Paul Watson, see Raffi Khatchadourian, "Neptune's Navy," *New Yorker,* Nov. 5, 2007.

16 Watson had formally stepped down: Tim Hume, "110-Day Ocean Hunt Ends with Sea Shepherd Rescuing Alleged Poachers," CNN, April 7, 2015; Elizabeth Batt, "Captain Paul Watson Steps Down as Sea Shepherd President," *Digital Journal,* Jan. 8, 2013.

16 As of October 2017, Watson: "Sea Shepherd CEO and Founder Paul Watson Back in the U.S. After Two Year Absence," Sea Shepherd, Feb. 21, 2018; Interpol, "Wanted by the Judicial Authorities of Japan: Watson, Paul Franklin," International Criminal Police Organization, Aug. 7, 2012; Mike De Souza, "Anti-whaling Activist Paul Watson Gets

Back His Canadian Passport, Four Years After Harper Revoked It," *National Observer,* June 27, 2016.

16 The group had decided: "Sea Shepherd Departs for Operation Icefish," *Maritime Executive,* Dec. 3, 2014.

17 Like the *Thunder,* the *Viarsa:* "Fishermen Caught in Epic Chase Acquitted," *Age,* Nov. 6, 2005; "Toothfish Crew Found Not Guilty," BBC, Nov. 5, 2005.

19 I usually brought lots: Before becoming a reporter for *The New York Times,* I was in a doctoral program at the University of Chicago, and I worked as an anthropologist in Mexico and Cuba, which is where I learned how important it is never to arrive at a village or anywhere else without something that you can share. Another more seasoned anthropologist in Oaxaca whom I worked under always kept his pockets full of *dulces,* or small hard candies. He never just handed them over; he always took one out first, unwrapped it slowly and in plain view, then reached back in his pocket and extended an open hand to the others in the room for them to grab one.

20 Chakravarty asked me to tell: Kwasi Kpodo, "Ghana Opens Talks with Exxon on Deepwater Drilling Contract," Reuters, Nov. 13, 2017.

23 "Roaring Forties": Kelly Tyler, "The Roaring Forties," PBS, Oct. 23, 1999; Jason Samenow, "'Roaring Forties' Winds, Gyrating Ocean Currents Pose Malaysia Plane Search Nightmare," *Washington Post,* March 21, 2014.

23 Winds can top two hundred miles per hour: "Climate, Weather, and Tides at Mawson," Australian Government, Department of the Environment and Energy, Sept. 21, 2015; IceCube South Pole Neutrino Observatory, "Antarctic Weather," University of Wisconsin–Madison, 2014; National Hurricane Center, "Saffir-Simpson Hurricane Wind Scale," National Oceanic and Atmospheric Administration, 2012.

27 *"Bob Barker, Thunder"*: "Radio Conversations with Marine Vessel Thunder," Sea Shepherd, 2015.

29 More than three thousand miles away: Sea Shepherd Operation Icefish Campaign Map.

29 Spanish police and other authorities: Kate Willson and Mar Cabra, "Spain Doles Out Millions in Aid Despite Fishing Company's Record," Center for Public Integrity, Oct. 2, 2011.

30 Other maritime records: "Thunder," Commission for the Conservation of Antarctic Marine Living Resources, May 26, 2016.

30 An email from Carlos: Carlos Pérez-Bouzada, email interview with author, 2015.

30 Sifting through these documents: What is known about the *Thunder's* ownership comes largely from confidential documents provided by Interpol and the prosecutor's office in São Tomé and Príncipe. In interviews, Interpol officials said that from 2000 to 2003 the vessel seems to have been owned by several companies tied to Spain, including Southern Shipping Limited, Vistasur Holding, and Muñiz Castiñeira SL. Also essential in this investigation was Glen Salmon, an investigator with the Australian Fisheries Management Authority. A former federal police officer, Salmon for years tracked illegal fishing in the Southern Ocean, including that of the *Thunder*. Salmon's personal archives include at least fifty reports from Australian surveillance boats and planes documenting illegal, unreported, or unregulated fishing activity in the Indian and Southern Oceans, according to Eskil Engdal and Kjetil Sæter.

31 Some of this forensic work: Eskil Engdal and Kjetil Sæter, *Catching* Thunder: *The True Story of the World's Longest Sea Chase* (London: Zed, 2018).

31 The bottles also contained: Captain Peter Hammarstedt to *Thunder* Crew, 2015.

33 Since its founding in 1977: "The History of Sea Shepherd," Sea Shepherd.

34 "Your ship is one of those": "Transcript of Communications Between Sea Shepherd, the Thunder, and the Atlas Cove," provided by Sea Shepherd, Dec. 2016.

36 It simply off-loaded the problem: Benjamin Weiser, "Fast Boat, Tiny Flag: Government's High-Flying Rationale for a Drug Seizure," *New York Times,* Oct. 28, 2015.

36 It was the clearest example: In the mid-nineteenth century, the English economist William Forster Lloyd began to notice the stark difference between privately owned pastures and those that belonged to entire communities, or "the commons" as it was referred to colloquially. Cattle raised on private ground were healthier, larger, less starved than those raised in the public realm. In his 1832 lecture, "The Checks to Population," Lloyd asked, "Why are the cattle on a common so puny and stunted? Why is the common itself so bare-worn, and cropped so differently from the adjoining inclosures?" See William Forster Lloyd, *Two Lectures on the Checks to Population* (Oxford University, 1833). Lloyd concluded that the pasture in the commons was degraded because the herdsmen were acting in their own short-term self-interest. At the point that the pasture is no longer capable of supporting more cattle, a herdsman will continue to add to his herd because his personal gain from an additional calf is greater than his share of the collective loss of resources. Unlike a farmer tending to private grounds, a farmer working in a public space has little

long-term incentive to keep the pasture in good condition. Lloyd's lecture inspired the phrase "tragedy of the commons," which was popularized by the ecologist Garrett Hardin in 1968 and came to refer to the notion that when everyone owns something, no one does, resulting in misuse and neglect. International law identifies four global commons: the High Seas; the Atmosphere; Antarctica; and Outer Space. Historically, access to the resources found within the global commons has been difficult. The advancement of science and technology in recent decades, however, has changed that. See Garrett Hardin, "The Tragedy of the Commons," *Science,* Dec. 13, 1968.

37 But in practice, flags: There are thirty-five countries that the International Transport Workers' Federation deems "flags of convenience." A 2012 report from the Institute of Shipping Economics and Logistics (based in Germany) said that 70.8 percent of merchant fleet tonnage (not number of ships) was registered under flags of convenience in 2012, up from 51.3 percent in 2005. See Institute of Shipping Economics and Logistics, "World Merchant Fleet by Ownership Patterns," *Shipping Statistics and Market Review* (2012). A United Nations conference on trade and development found that more than three-quarters of the ships in the global fleet are registered in developing countries, including in many open registries. The tonnage registered under foreign flags (where the nationality of the owner is different from the flag flown by the vessel) is 71 percent of the world total. See "Structure, Ownership, and Registration of the World Fleet," *Review of Maritime Transport* (2015).

40 Underneath were photographs: "Interpol Purple Notice on Fishing Vessel Yongding," New Zealand, Jan. 21, 2015.

41 "Assistance required": "Radio Conversations with Marine Vessel Thunder," Sea Shepherd, 2015.

42 By late morning on April 6: "Thunder Issues Distress Signal. Sea Shepherd Launches Rescue Operation," Sea Shepherd, Feb. 28, 2018; "Poaching Vessel, Thunder, Sinks in Suspicious Circumstances," Sea Shepherd, Feb. 28, 2018.

44 Chakravarty, who was wearing: "Video of Conversation Between Cataldo and Chakravarty," provided by Sea Shepherd, 2015.

45 Over the next six months, the Indonesian: "Poaching Vessel, Thunder, Sinks in Suspicious Circumstances"; "Massive Victory in the Fight Against Illegal Fishing," Sea Shepherd.

45 Cataldo and the ship's chief engineer: "Massive Victory in the Fight Against Illegal Fishing"; "Thunder Captain and Officers Face Justice in the Wake of Operation Icefish."

45 They were collectively fined: Throughout 2015 and 2016, I stayed in constant contact by phone and email with the attorney general of São Tomé and Príncipe, Frederique Samba Viegas D'Abreu, who was immensely helpful to my reporting. I also received guidance and documents from other law enforcement officers who assisted in the investigation but asked to remain anonymous.

45 But a separate civil case: Jason Holland, "Spanish Tycoon Hit with USD 10 Million Fine for Illegal Fishing," *Seafood Source,* April 24, 2018.

45 After some time off, Chakravarty: "Bangalore 2016," Moving Waters Film Festival, 2016.

## CHAPTER 2 THE LONE PATROL

47 This is why one of every five: Amanda Nickson, "3 Misconceptions Jeopardizing the Recovery of Bigeye Tuna in the Pacific," Pew, Oct. 13, 2015. While there is little debate that many global fish stocks are in jeopardy, there is deep uncertainty about the extent. Testament to the uncertainty around how fish get counted is the research of Daniel Pauly, a marine ecologist at the University of British Columbia, who, among others, has challenged the accuracy of the UN Food and Agriculture Organization's estimates on the matter. For decades, the global authority on fishing statistics published reassuring reports indicating that the tonnage of wild fish caught every year was going up, proof that stocks were healthy. But Pauly found that global catches, which had risen ever since 1950, began to decline in the 1980s. China was reporting rising catches and an implausible total of eleven million tons per year. This was, according to Pauly, at least double what was biologically possible. One plausible explanation for the skewed statistics was this: Officials in the Chinese government were promoted only if production increased. And so, production, on the books at least, increased.

47 By 2050, some studies: Fisheries Environmental Performance Index, Yale, Aug. 19, 2014; Sarah Kaplan, "By 2050, There Will Be More Plastic than Fish in the World's Oceans, Study Says," *Washington Post,* Jan. 20, 2016; "Plastic in Ocean Outweighs Fish," *Business Insider,* Jan. 26, 2017. Recycling plastic packaging could also help businesses. Businesses are losing $80 billion a year because of the use of new plastics.

47 The oceans are despoiled: Shelton Harley et al., "Stock Assessment of Bigeye Tuna in the Western and Central Pacific Ocean," Western and Central Pacific Fisheries Commission, July 25, 2014.

48 As he pounded out: Bjorn Bergman (SkyTruth researcher) and John Amos (director of SkyTruth) in discussion with the author. Much of the

reporting and backstory tied to the *Remeliik* and the *Shin Jyi Chyuu 33* came from multiple interviews between 2015 and 2018.

48 Nearly nine thousand miles: "Shin Jyi Chyuu No.33," Ship Details Document, Western and Central Fisheries Commission.

50 the team radioed: Apart from my time with Allison Baiei (a Palauan marine police officer) while I was on board the *Remeliik*, I stayed in constant touch by phone and email with him between 2015 and 2017.

50 Palau had also emerged: For example, in 2013, Palau turned to an Australian mining magnate, Andrew Forrest, who funded a trial run for using drones to patrol Palauan waters. The Palauan government ultimately back-burnered the idea because the drones were too costly and hard to fly and their cameras provided only a drinking-straw-wide perspective on the waters below. Seth Horstmeyer from Pew was uniquely helpful in this reporting, and we spoke dozens of times by email and phone between 2015 and 2018. I learned a lot about Palau's experiment with drones and other technology from a report by Aerosonde Ltd. titled "Background Briefing: The Aerosonde UAS," AAI Corporation, Textron Systems, Aug. 2013. I also read more broadly about the ways that technology is being used to police the seas near Palau and elsewhere. Some of that reading included Brian Clark Howard, "For U.S., a New Challenge: Keeping Poachers Out of Newly Expanded Marine Reserve in Pacific," *National Geographic*, Sept. 25, 2014; Robert Vamosi, "Big Data Is Stopping Maritime Pirates . . . from Space," *Forbes*, Nov. 11, 2011; Erik Sofge, "The High-Tech Battle Against Pirates," *Popular Science*, April 23, 2015; Brian Clark Howard, "Can Drones Fight Illegal 'Pirate' Fishing?," *National Geographic*, July 18, 2014; "Combating Illegal Fishing: Dragnet," *Economist*, Jan. 22, 2015; Christopher Pala, "Tracking Fishy Behavior, from Space," *Atlantic*, Nov. 16, 2014; "Pew Unveils Pioneering Technology to Help End Illegal Fishing," Pew Charitable Trusts, press release, Jan. 21, 2015.

While in Palau in the fall of 2015, I spent time with a Christian missionary group called Pacific Mission Aviation. This organization has a couple of small planes that it uses to deliver food and medicine to some of Palau's most remote islands. The government had put high-tech radars on the bottom of the planes to survey the waters for illegal fishing. The pilots who flew these planes also reported sightings of suspicious fishing ships. I flew with these pilots for a day as they made their supply runs. I hoped to learn more about how such public-private collaborations pairing existing groups with new goals and technology might work. Palau lacks its own air force, so patrolling the waters requires boats, but fuel is pricey and traveling by sea is slow. The partnership between the missionaries and the government seemed promising as a cost-saving tactic.

Still, the necessary radar they used was extremely costly. In the case of most poor countries, this cost would be prohibitive and the equipment would have to be donated or lent by wealthier governments.

51 Situated in the western Pacific: "Monitoring, Control, and Surveillance," Republic of Palau Exclusive Economic Zone.

51 But Palau's islands: Part V Exclusive Economic Zone, UN Convention on the Law of the Sea.

51 This means that while Palau: Richard A. Lovett, "Huge Garbage Patch Found in Atlantic Too," *National Geographic*, March 2, 2010; "The World Factbook: Palau," Central Intelligence Agency Library, Oct. 17, 2018.

51 These are rich fishing grounds: "Palau Burns Shark Fins to Send Message to Poachers," Agence France-Presse, May 7, 2003; Christopher Pala, "No-Fishing Zones in Tropics Yield Fast Payoffs for Reefs," *New York Times*, April 17, 2007; John Heilprin, "Swimming Against the Tide: Palau Creates World's First Shark Sanctuary," *Courier Mail Australia*, Sept. 29, 2009; Renee Schoof, "Palau and Honduras: World Should Ban Shark Fishing," McClatchy DC Bureau, Sept. 22, 2010; Bernadette Carreon, "Sharks Find Sanctuary in Tiny Palau," Agence France-Presse, Jan. 3, 2011; "Sea Shepherd Welcomes Palau Surveillance Deal with Japan," Radio New Zealand News, May 20, 2011; Ilaitia Turagabeci, "Fine and Ban," *Fiji Times*, Feb. 20, 2012; "Chinese Fisherman Killed in Ocean Confrontation with Palau Police, Search On for 3 Missing," Associated Press, April 3, 2012; XiaoJun Zhang, "Compensation Demanded for Slain Chinese Fisherman in Palau," Xinhua News Agency, April 16, 2012; "Palau: China Spying on Us," *Papua New Guinea Post Courier*, April 25, 2012; "Japan to Help Fight Poaching in South Pacific," *Nikkei Report*, Dec. 30, 2012; "Pacific Island Nations Band Together as Overfishing Takes Toll on Global Tuna Supply," PACNEWS, Jan. 24, 2013; "Pacific's Palau Mulls Drone Patrols to Monitor Waters," Agence France-Presse, Oct. 4, 2013; Edith M. Lederer, "Palau to Ban Commercial Fishing, Promote Tourism," Associated Press, Feb. 5, 2014; Michelle Conerly, " 'We Are Trying to Preserve Our Lives,' " *Pacific Daily News*, Feb. 16, 2014; Kate Galbraith, "Amid Efforts to Expand Marine Preserves, a Warning to Focus on Quality," *New York Times*, Feb. 19, 2014; "Marine Protection in the Pacific: No Bul," *Economist*, June 7, 2014; Amy Weinfurter, "Small Nation Palau Makes Big Waves," Environmental Performance Index, Aug. 19, 2014; "Wave-Riding Robots Could Help Track Weather, Illegal Fishing in Pacific," PACNEWS, July 29, 2014; Christopher Joyce, "Gotcha: Satellites Help Strip Seafood Pirates of Their Booty," NPR, Feb. 5, 2015; Elaine Kurtenbach, "Palau Burns Vietnamese Boats Caught Fishing Illegally," Associated Press, June 12, 2015; Jose Rodriguez T. Senase,

"Palau Closely Monitoring Foreign Fishing Vessels in EEZ," *Island Times,* Jan. 26, 2016.

51 It is also home to various types of tuna: Sienna Hill, "The World's Most Expensive Seafood Dishes," *First We Eat,* June 27, 2015; Chris Loew, "Chinese Demand for Japanese Cucumber Heats Up," *SeafoodSource,* Aug. 31, 2018.

51 Palau's president, Tommy Remengesau Jr.: Between 2015 and 2018, I stayed in contact with President Remengesau. I also consulted "Biography of His Excellency Tommy E. Remengesau, Jr. President of the Republic of Palau," Palaugov.

52 More than half of its gross domestic product: Yimnang Golbuu et al., "The State of Coral Reef Ecosystems of Palau," in *The State of Coral Reef Ecosystems of the United States and Pacific Freely Associated States: 2005,* ed. J. E. Waddell (Silver Spring, Md.: NOAA, 2005), 488–507.

52 One of Palau's biggest draws: Jim Haw, "An Interconnected Environment and Economy—Shark Tourism in Palau," *Scientific American,* June 12, 2013.

52 To offset poverty wages: Natasha Stacey, *Boats to Burn: Bajo Fishing Activity in the Australian Fishing Zone* (Canberra: ANU E Press, 2007). Information here is also from interviews with John Hocevar (campaign director of Greenpeace) in discussion with the author.

53 Scientists estimate that: Boris Worm et al., "Global Catches, Exploitation Rates, and Rebuilding Options for Sharks," *Marine Policy* 40 (July 2013): 194–204.

53 By 2017, roughly a third: On the topic of shark finning, my reading list included Juliet Eilperin, "Sharkonomics," *Slate,* June 30, 2011; Stefania Vannuccini, *Shark Utilization, Marketing, and Trade* (Rome: FAO Fisheries Technical Paper. No. 389, 1999); Krista Mahr, "Shark-Fin Soup and the Conservation Challenge," *Time,* Aug. 9, 2010; Justin McCurry, "Shark Fishing in Japan—a Messy, Blood-Spattered Business," *Guardian,* Feb. 11, 2011; Michael Gardner, "Battle to Ban Trade in Shark Fins Heats Up," *San Diego Union-Tribune,* June 1, 2011; Justin McCurry, "Hong Kong at Centre of Storm in Soup Dish," *Guardian,* Nov. 11, 2011; "Fisherman's Gold: Shark Fin Hunt Empties West African Seas," Agence France-Presse, Jan. 8, 2012; Adrian Wan, "Case Builds Against Shark Fin," *South China Morning Post,* March 4, 2012; Louis Sahagun, "A Bit of Culinary Culture Is at an End," *Los Angeles Times,* June 29, 2013; Doug Shinkle, "SOS for Sharks," *State Legislatures Magazine,* July 2013; Chris Horton, "Is the Shark-Fin Trade Facing Extinction?," *Atlantic,* Aug. 12, 2013; "Fine Print Allows Shark Finning to Continue," *New Zealand Herald,* Nov. 23, 2013; John Vidal, "This Could Be the Year We Start to Save, Not Slaughter,

the Shark," *Observer,* Jan. 11, 2014; Shelley Clarke and Felix Dent, "State of the Global Market for Shark Commodities," Convention on International Trade in Endangered Species of Wild Fauna and Flora, May 3, 2014; Nina Wu, "Documentary Film Shines Light on Shark Finning," *Star Advertiser,* June 8, 2014; Oliver Ortega, "Massachusetts to Ban Shark Fin Trade," *Boston Globe,* July 24, 2014; Mark Magnier, "In China, Shark Fin Soup Is So 2010," *Wall Street Journal,* Aug. 6, 2014; Felicia Sonmez, "Tide Turns for Shark Fin in China," *Phys.org,* Aug. 20, 2014, 1; "All for a Bowl of Soup," transcript, *Dan Rather Reports,* AXS TV, Jan. 24, 2012; "Bycatch," SharkSavers, a Program of WildAid, accessed Nov. 21, 2018, www.sharksavers.org.

53 "Small land, big ocean": This stems from several interviews with President Remengesau as well as with his chief adviser, Keobel Sakuma, between 2015 and 2017.

53 In 2006, it was among: Tse-Lynn Loh and Zeehan Jaafar, "Turning the Tide on Bottom Trawling," *Aquatic Conservation: Marine and Freshwater Ecosystems* 25, no. 4 (2015): 581–83.

53 In 2009, Palau created: Carl Safina and Elizabeth Brown, "Fishermen in Palau Take On Role of Scientist to Save Their Fishery," *National Geographic,* Nov. 5, 2013; "Healthy Oceans and Seas: A Way Forward," President Remengesau Keynote UN Address, Feb. 4, 2014; Johnson Toribiong, "Statement by the Honorable Johnson Toribiong President of the Republic of Palau to the 64th Regular Session of the United Nations General Assembly," Sept. 25, 2009, palauun.files,wordpress.com.

53 Palau's most aggressive move: Jane J. Lee, "Tiny Island Nation's Enormous New Ocean Reserve Is Official," *National Geographic,* Oct. 28, 2015.

53 In 2012, Palau partnered: Sean Dorney, "Palau Ends Drone Patrol Tests to Deter Illegal Fishing," ABC Australia, Oct. 4, 2013; Haw, "Interconnected Environment and Economy."

53 Palau claims to be the first: Aaron Korman, "Stand with Palau Campaign," *Indiegogo,* Aug. 4, 2014.

53 Palau had even started talking: To grasp Palau's outlook and plans for managing its waters, I often drew from an invaluable report from the president's office that was drafted with input from the Pew Charitable Trusts: "The Monitoring, Control, and Surveillance Plan for 2015–2020."

55 Stuck between the lip: The bulk of the reporting in this chapter comes from ten days spent in Palau, much of which was at sea aboard the *Remeliik* and other smaller Palauan police boats. I also spent a couple of days at the police headquarters listening to the interactions between officers. Especially helpful in this process was Seth Horstmeyer from

the Pew Charitable Trusts, which did a lot of work with Palau; Ben Fennell, lieutenant commander for the Royal Australian Navy; and Jennifer Koskelin-Gibbons, Pew consultant and adviser who directs the Pew Bertarelli Ocean Legacy Project in Palau. All three people knew a lot about the history of Palau's efforts to protect its waters.

56 Typhoon Bopha: Jethro Mullen, "Typhoon Bopha Carves Across Philippines, Killing Scores of People," CNN, Dec. 5, 2012.

56 Eleven months later, Typhoon Haiyan: Jethro Mullen, "Super Typhoon Haiyan, One of Strongest Storms Ever, Hits Central Philippines," CNN, Nov. 8, 2013.

56 With winds over 170 miles per hour: M. Barange et al., "Impacts of Climate Change on Marine Ecosystem Production in Societies Dependent on Fisheries," *Nature Climate Change,* Feb. 23, 2014.

56 A 2014 study: Ibid.

56 Another study from 2014: A. M. Friedlander et al., "Marine Biodiversity and Protected Areas in Palau: Scientific Report to the Government of the Republic of Palau," National Geographic Pristine Seas and Palau International Coral Reef Center, 2014.

56 Baiei agreed and explained: "Palau President's Report on Lost Cessna," Republic of Palau, 2012.

57 Over a stretch of several days: "Republic of Palau vs. Ten Jin Len," Criminal Complaint, Supreme Court of the Republic of Palau, 12-026, April 3, 2012.

57 But several of their bullets: Victoria Roe, "Request for an Investigation Memo," Office of the Attorney General, Republic of Palau, April 11, 2012.

57 Several of the officers took a smaller: Nick Perry and Jennifer Kelleher, "Billionaire's Yacht Hunts for Lost Plane off Palau," Associated Press, April 4, 2012.

57 Two Palauan policemen: "Search for Plane That Ditched over Palau Waters Ended," *Kathryn's Report,* April 5, 2012.

57 As night fell, though: For additional context on this incident, I read Walt Williams, "Map to the Bizarre and Peculiar Odd Nuggets Around in the Golden State," *Modesto Bee,* June 29, 1997, H-1; "Typhoon While on the Hard," *Latitude 38,* March 2007; "Easier with Climate Change," *Latitude 38,* Nov. 2008; "A Xmas Story—with Gunfire," *Latitude 38,* April 2010; "Delivery with New Owner," *Latitude 38,* Dec. 2011; "Palau Arrests Chinese Fishermen, 1 Dies After Being Hit by Gunfire; 2 Officers and Pilot Missing in Effort to Film Their Burning Vessel," Pacific News Center, April 3, 2012; Kelleher and Perry, "Billionaire's Yacht Hunts for Lost Plane off Palau"; Brett Kelman, "One Dead in High-Sea Chase," *Pacific Daily*

*News* (Hagatna, Guam), April 4, 2012; "Lost in Aviation Accident," *Latitude 38,* May 2012, A1; "Hawaii: Remains of Plane Found in Palau Not Missing 2012 Police Flight," *US Official News,* May 6, 2014.

58 The stadium lights at Palau's Asahi: Jeff Barabe and Kassi Berg, "Candlelight Vigil Held for Pilot and Two Police Officers Who Vanished, Search Suspended," Oceania Television Network, April 11, 2012.

58 One of Allen's crew: John Gibbons to the President of Palau, April 16, 2012.

58 "It swallowed them": In researching the disappearance of the Cessna, I communicated by phone and email with two persons who asked to remain anonymous. One was a relative of one of the police officers who died. The other was a relative of the pilot of the plane.

59 Mostly uninhabited except for four: Andrew Wayne et al., *Helen Reef Management Plan,* The Hatohobei State Leadership and the Hatohobei Community, 2011; Architect's Virtual Capitol, "Architect of the Capitol."

59 In coming decades, the sea: Stephen Leahy, "The Nations Guaranteed to Be Swallowed by the Sea," *Motherboard,* May 27, 2014.

59 By 2015, about ninety-four million: Paul Greenberg and Boris Worm, "When Humans Declared War on Fish," *New York Times,* May 8, 2015.

60 These ships surround an entire school: "Fishing Gear: Purse Seines," NOAA Fisheries, Nov. 30, 2017.

60 A crane lifts the net: "How Seafood Is Caught: Purse Seining," YouTube, Seafood Watch, May 2013.

60 These technological advances: Paul Greenberg, "Tuna's End," *New York Times,* June 22, 2010; "Catches by Type in the Global Ocean—High Seas of the World," *Sea Around Us;* "World Deep-Sea Fisheries," Fisheries and Resources Monitoring System, 2009.

60 "Think of the word 'seafood' itself": Based on interviews in 2017 with Paul Greenberg. For more of Greenberg's perspective on the subject, see Paul Greenberg, *Four Fish: The Future of the Last Wild Food* (New York: Penguin Books, 2011); Paul Greenberg, "Ocean Blues," *New York Times Magazine,* May 13, 2007.

61 The nineteenth-century British: Carlos Espósito et al., *Ocean Law and Policy: Twenty Years of Development Under the UNCLOS Regime* (Leiden: Koninklijk Brill NV, 2017).

61 This belief carried into the twentieth century: Daniel Hawthorne and Minot Francis, *The Inexhaustible Sea* (New York: Dodd, Mead, 1954).

61 Since the 1990s, ships: "Automatic Identification System Overview," U.S. Coast Guard Navigation Center website, Oct. 23, 2018.

62 As the 2015 capture: David Manthos, "Avast! Pirate Fishing Vessel Caught in Palau with Illegal Tuna & Shark Fins," SkyTruth, March 4, 2015.

62 Seen from above, the world's largest: Nicki Ryan, "The World's Largest and Second Largest Supertrawlers Are in Irish Waters," *Journal* (Dublin), Jan. 17, 2015.

63 The buoys, which modern: "Pacific Tuna Stock on the Brink of Disaster," Greenpeace, press release, Sept. 3, 2014.

63 To attract species like tuna: "Fishing Gear: Fish Aggregating Devices," NOAA Fisheries.

63 Over the past three decades, FADs: Wesley A. Armstrong and Charles W. Oliver, *Recent Use of Fish Aggregating Devices in the Eastern Tropical Pacific Tuna Purse-Seine Fishery, 1990–1994*, Southwest Fisheries Science Center, March 1996; "The Tuna-Dolphin Issue," NOAA.

63 These fleets used to find tuna: Elisabeth Eaves, "Dolphin-Safe but Not Ocean-Safe," *Forbes,* July 24, 2008.

63 This approach led to hundreds of thousands: Avram Primack, *The Environment and Us* (St. Thomas, V.I.: ProphetPress, 2014).

63 They moved out of the tropical eastern Pacific: Michael D. Scott et al., "Pelagic Predator Associations: Tuna and Dolphins in the Eastern Tropical Pacific Ocean," *Marine Ecology Progress Series* 458 (July 2012): 297.

64 A 2014 study found that the population: "WCPFC Statement to the 45th Pacific Islands Forum Leaders Meeting," Western and Central Pacific Fisheries Commission.

65 Tuna, like many large ocean fish: The transoceanic migratory patterns of tuna are a topic of growing research. For Pacific migratory movements, see Jeffrey J. Polovina, "Decadal Variation in the Trans-Pacific Migration of Northern Bluefin Tuna (*Thunnus thynnus*) Coherent with Climate-Induced Change in Prey Abundance," *Fisheries Oceanography* 5, no. 2 (June 1996). For Atlantic migratory patterns, see Barbara A. Block et al., "Electronic Tagging and Population Structure of Atlantic Bluefin Tuna," *Nature,* April 2005.

65 They are being picked off beforehand: "PNA-FAD Tracking and Management Trial," Western and Central Pacific Fishing Commission, Dec. 4, 2015.

65 In its grand fight: "Palau to Sign National Marine Sanctuary into Law," Pew, press release, Oct. 22, 2015; Brian Clark Howard, "U.S. Creates Largest Protected Area in the World, 3X Larger than California," *National Geographic,* Sept. 26, 2014.

66 In 2015, the average number: Tourism and economic statistics provided by Palau's Office of the President.

66 It turned out, though, that many of these tourists: To read more about the double-edged sword that is tourism in Palau, see Bernadette H. Carreon,

"Palau's Environment Minister to Take Action on Illegal Trade of Napoleon Wrasse," Pacific News Agency Service, July 19, 2016; Jose Rodriguez T. Senase, "Palau Hotel Accused of Illegally Cooking Protected Fish," *Pacific Islands Report,* Oct. 13, 2015; Jennifer Pinkowski, "Growing Taste for Reef Fish Sends Their Numbers Sinking," *New York Times,* Jan. 20, 2009.

66 Not coincidentally, the variety: B. Russell (Grouper & Wrasse Specialist Group), "*Cheilinus undulatus:* The IUCN Red List of Threatened Species," 2004: e.T4592A11023949; T. Chan, Y. Sadovy, and T. J. Donaldson, "*Bolbometopon muricatum:* The IUCN Red List of Threatened Species," 2012: e.T63571A17894276; J. A. Mortimer and M. Donnelly (IUCN SSC Marine Turtle Specialist Group), "*Eretmochelys imbricata:* The IUCN Red List of Threatened Species," 2008: e.T8005A12881238.

66 As a Palauan guide explained: Jellyfish from this lake have allegedly turned up in fish markets in Hong Kong. Alex Hofford, "Jellyfish from Palau's 'Jellyfish Lake' on Sale in Hong Kong," YouTube, April 2013. There have been a series of steps spearheaded by First Lady Debbie Remengesau. Steps by Palau to limit the adverse impact of unregulated tourism have created some tensions with China. Farah Master, "Empty Hotels, Idle Boats: What Happens When a Pacific Island Upsets China," Reuters, Aug. 19, 2018.

69 Most of the men in the report: "Official Statement from Tan Bin," Bureau of Public Safety, Koror, Republic of Palau, April 1, 2012.

69 Most said that on the day the marine officers: "Republic of Palau vs. Ten Jin Len," Criminal Complaint, Supreme Court of the Republic of Palau, 12-026, April 3, 2012.

69 In a plea deal, the crew: "Palau President's Report on Lost Cessna," Republic of Palau, 2012.

69 "He should not have received the death penalty": Victoria Roe, "Request for an Investigation Memo," Office of the Attorney General, Republic of Palau, April 11, 2012.

70 They strap lead weights: David Epstein, "The Descent," *New York Times,* June 20, 2014.

## CHAPTER 3 A RUSTY KINGDOM

72 On Christmas Eve 1966: Jack Gould, "Radio: British Commercial Broadcasters Are at Sea," *New York Times,* March 25, 1966; Felix Kessler, "The Rusty Principality of Sealand Relishes Hard-Earned Freedom," *Wall Street Journal,* Sept. 15, 1969; John Markoff, "Rebel Outpost on the Fringes of Cyberspace," *New York Times,* June 4, 2000; Declan McCullagh, "A

Data Sanctuary Is Born," *Wired,* June 4, 2000; Steve Boggan, "Americans Turn a Tin-Pot State off the Essex Coast into World Capital of Computer Anarchy," *Independent,* June 5, 2000; Declan McCullagh, "Sealand: Come to Data," *Wired,* June 5, 2000; David Cohen, "Offshore Haven: Cold Water Poured on Sealand Security," *Guardian,* June 6, 2000; Carlos Grande, "Island Fortress's 'Data Haven' to Confront E-trade Regulation," *Financial Times,* June 6, 2000; "Man Starts Own Country off Coast of Britain," *World News Tonight,* ABC, June 6, 2000; Tom Mintier, "Sealand Evolves from Offshore Platform to High-Tech Haven," *Worldview,* CNN, June 12, 2000; Anne Cornelius, "Legal Issues Online Firms Set to Take Refuge in Offshore Fortress," *Scotsman,* June 15, 2000; David Canton, "Creating a Country to Avoid Jurisdiction," *London Free Press,* June 16, 2000; "Internet Exiles," *New Scientist,* June 17, 2000; Theo Mullen, "A Haven for Net Lawbreakers?," *Internetweek,* June 19, 2000; Peter Ford, "Banned on Land, but Free at Sea?," *Christian Science Monitor,* June 23, 2000; Mara D. Bellaby, "An Internet 'Mouse That Roars' Pops Up off Britain," *Houston Chronicle,* June 25, 2000; "Rebel Sea Fortress Dreams of Being 'Data Haven,'" *Wall Street Journal,* June 26, 2000; Simson Garfinkel, "Welcome to Sealand. Now Bugger Off," *Wired,* July 2000; Edward Sherwin, "A Distant Sense of Data Security," *Washington Post,* Sept. 20, 2000; Ann Harrison, "Data Haven Says It Offers Freedom from Observation," *Computerworld,* Nov. 13, 2000; Grant Hibberd, "The Sealand Affair—the Last Great Adventure of the Twentieth Century?," Foreign & Commonwealth Office U.K., Nov. 19, 2010; Grant Hibberd, "The Last Great Adventure of the Twentieth Century: The Sealand Affair in British Diplomacy," *Britain and the World* 269 (2011); James Grimmelmann, "Sealand, HavenCo, and the Rule of Law," *University of Illinois Law Review,* March 16, 2012; Prince Michael of Sealand, *Holding the Fort* (self-published, 2015).

72 He had snuck out of his house: William Yardley, "Roy Bates, Bigger-than-Life Founder of a Micronation, Dies at 91," *New York Times,* Oct. 13, 2012.

73 Built in the early 1940s: Cahal Milmo, "Sealand's Prince Michael on the Future of an Off-Shore 'Outpost of Liberty,'" *Independent,* March 19, 2016.

73 "Roughs," as the abandoned platform: Rose Eveleth, "'I Rule My Own Ocean Micronation,'" BBC, April 15, 2015. Sometimes this platform was cited in the singular as "Rough Tower" or "HMF [His Majesty's Fort] Rough." Its name derives from the sandbar on which it stands. In nearby waters, Britain also erected several other platforms often called the Maunsell Army Forts. These typically consist of seven separate towers,

standing on legs above the sea, and connected by walkways. Grimmelmann, "Sealand, HavenCo, and the Rule of Law."

73 In its wartime heyday: Thomas Hodgkinson, "Notes from a Small Island: Is Sealand an Independent 'Micronation' or an Illegal Fortress?," *Independent*, May 18, 2013.

73 Suddenly obsolete with Germany's defeat: Grimmelmann, "Sealand, HavenCo, and the Rule of Law."

73 The London native: Elaine Woo, " 'Prince' Roy Bates Dies at 91; Adventuring Monarch of Sealand," *Los Angeles Times*, Oct. 14, 2012.

73 During World War II: Grimmelmann, "Sealand, HavenCo, and the Rule of Law."

73 In a later incident: Woo, " 'Prince' Roy Bates Dies at 91." Roy also told a reporter for *The Independent* in 2004 that during World War II he had been captured by the Italians. He said he tried to escape so often that he was sentenced to death, but he won a reprieve only at the last moment, as the firing squad raised its rifles. See Mark Lucas, "Sealand Forever! The Bizarre Story of Europe's Smallest Self-Proclaimed State," *Independent*, Nov. 27, 2004, 33.

73 Initially, Roy used Roughs: To learn more about offshore pirate radios, I read Robert Chapman, *Selling the Sixties: The Pirates and Pop Music Radio* (New York: Routledge, 1992). Also worthwhile is Steve Conway, *Shiprocked: Life on the Waves with Radio Caroline* (Dublin: Liberties, 2009). On the later history of pirate radio in the U.K., see John Hind and Stephen Mosco, *Rebel Radio: The Full Story of British Pirate Radio* (London: Pluto Press, 1985). The U.S. version of this story is well told by Jesse Walker, *Rebels on the Air: An Alternative History of Radio in America* (New York: New York University Press, 2001). The best pop-culture treatment is the movie *Pump Up the Volume*, directed by Allan Moyle in 1990).

74 "Now you have your very own island": Hodgkinson, "Notes from a Small Island."

74 The motto of the country: "Principality of Sealand," Sealand.

74 Constituted as a principality: In an interview, James Bates explained the colors of the flag as red for Roy, white for purity, and black for Sealand's pirate radio days.

75 The British government learned: Another similar incident happened in 1990 when Sealanders opened fire on a British military ship that allegedly came too near the principality. See James Cusick, "Shots Fired in Sealand's Defence of a Small Freedom," *Independent*, Feb. 24, 1990.

75 The British government soon brought firearms: Grimmelmann, "Sealand, HavenCo, and the Rule of Law."

75 Recently declassified U.K. documents: Dan Bell, "Darkest Hour for 'Smallest State,'" BBC, Dec. 30, 2008.

76 More recently, WikiLeaks explored: Katrin Langhans, "Newer Sealand," *Süddeutsche Zeitung* and the Panama Papers, April 25, 2016.

78 They were often called seasteads: My full bibliography on seasteading is as follows: Jerome Fitzgerald, *Sea-Steading: A Life of Hope and Freedom on the Last Viable Frontier* (New York: iUniverse, 2006); "Homesteading the Ocean," *Spectrum,* May 1, 2008; Oliver Burkeman, "Fantasy Islands," *Guardian,* July 18, 2008; Patri Friedman and Wayne Gramlich, "Seasteading: A Practical Guide to Homesteading the High Seas," Gramlich.net, 2009; Declan McCullagh, "The Next Frontier: 'Seasteading' the Oceans," *CNET News,* Feb. 2, 2009; Alex Pell, "Welcome Aboard a Brand New Country," *Sunday Times,* March 15, 2009; Brian Doherty, "20,000 Nations Above the Sea," *Reason,* July 2009; Eamonn Fingleton, "The Great Escape," *Prospect,* March 25, 2010; Brad Taylor, "Governing Seasteads: An Outline of the Options," Seasteading Institute, Nov. 9, 2010; "Cities on the Ocean," *Economist,* Dec. 3, 2011; Jessica Bruder, "A Start-Up Incubator That Floats," *New York Times,* Dec. 14, 2011; Michael Posner, "Floating City Conceived as High-Tech Incubator," *Globe and Mail,* Feb. 24, 2012; Josh Harkinson, "My Sunset Cruise with the Clever, Nutty, Techno-libertarian Seasteading Gurus," *Mother Jones,* June 7, 2012; Stephen McGinty, "The Real Nowhere Men," *Scotsman,* Sept. 8, 2012; Michelle Price, "Is the Sea the Next Frontier for High-Frequency Trading? New Water-Based Locations for Trading Servers Could Enable Firms to Fully Optimise Their Trading Strategies," *Financial News,* Sept. 17, 2012; Adam Piore, "Start-Up Nations on the High Seas," *Discover,* Sept. 19, 2012; George Petrie and Jon White, "The Call of the Sea," *New Scientist,* Sept. 22, 2012; Paul Peachey, "A Tax Haven on the High Seas That Could Soon Be Reality," *Independent,* Dec. 27, 2013; Geoff Dembicki, "Worried About Earth? Hit the High Seas: What Seasteaders Reveal About Our Desire to Be Saved by Technology," *Tyee,* March 1, 2014; Kyle Denuccio, "Silicon Valley Is Letting Go of Its Techie Island Fantasies," *Wired,* May 16, 2015; Nicola Davison, "Life on the High Seas: How Ocean Cities Could Become Reality," *Financial Times,* Sept. 3, 2015.

79 In 1982, a group of Americans: Anthony Van Fossen, *Tax Havens and Sovereignty in the Pacific Islands* (St. Lucia: University of Queensland Press, 2012).

79 Another wealthy libertarian: Pell, "Welcome Aboard a Brand New Country."

79 In 2008, these visionaries: "Frequently Asked Questions," Seasteading Institute.

80 The institute's primary benefactor: Bruder, "Start-Up Incubator That Floats."

80 Never getting beyond the drawing-board phase: Rachel Riederer, "Libertarians Seek a Home on the High Seas," *New Republic*, May 29, 2017.

80 Invited to Austria in 1978: Grimmelmann, "Sealand, HavenCo, and the Rule of Law."

80 Around 11:00 a.m. on August 10: Bruce Sterling, "Dead Media Beat: Death of a Data Haven," *Wired*, March 28, 2012.

82 But Achenbach was a man: Grimmelmann, "Sealand, HavenCo, and the Rule of Law."

82 Though Achenbach was not present: For more on Achenbach as mentioned in the Panama Papers, see Langhans, "New Sealand."

82 After returning to England, he enlisted: Alexander Achenbach, Declaration of August 10, 1978 (UK-NA: FCO 33/3355); "Sealand Prepares to Repel Boarders," *Leader*, Sept. 7, 1979, 16 (UK-NA: HO 255/1244).

83 "The imprisonment of Pütz": Bell, "Darkest Hour for 'Smallest State.'" See also "My Four Days in Captivity at the Hands of Foreign Invaders," *Colchester Evening Gazette*, Aug. 30, 1978 (UK-NA: HO 255/1244); "Tiny Nation's Capture of German Investigated!," *Los Angeles Times*, Sept. 5, 1978.

84 The killer, Andrew Cunanan: Emma Dibdin, "A Complete Timeline of Andrew Cunanan's Murders," *Harper's Bazaar*, Feb. 28, 2018; Martin Langfield, "Infamous Houseboat Sinks," *Washington Post*, Dec. 23, 1997.

84 The FBI, in turn, pointed: Adela Gooch, "Storm Warning," *Guardian*, March 27, 2000.

85 Later that same year, the Civil Guard: "Principality Notice PN 019/04: Fraudulent Representation of Principality," Sealand, Feb. 15, 2004.

85 The police then raided three: "Sealand y el tráfico de armas [Sealand and arms trafficking]," *El Mercurio* (Santiago), June 17, 2000; José María Irujo, "Sealand, un falso principado en el mar [Sealand, a false principality at sea]," *El País* (Madrid), March 26, 2000; "Owner of Fort off Britain Issues His Own Passports," *New York Times*, March 30, 1969.

85 Nearly four thousand were sold in Hong Kong: Gooch, "Storm Warning."

85 The Panama Papers included evidence: Langhans, "Newer Sealand."

86 Each of Sealand's two legs: Garfinkel, "Welcome to Sealand. Now Bugger Off."

87 In 2010, a team of researchers: A. D. Wissner-Gross and C. E. Freer, "Relativistic Statistical Arbitrage," *Physical Review*, Nov. 5, 2010.

88 One of the companies that HavenCo: Ryan Lackey, "HavenCo: What Really Happened" (presentation at DEF CON 11, Aug. 3, 2003). Within the video, see 30:15.

88 "Almost all time was spent": Thomas Stackpole, "The World's Most Notorious Micronation Has the Secret to Protecting Your Data from the NSA," *Mother Jones,* Aug. 21, 2013.

89 After Lackey quit HavenCo: Ryan Lackey, "HavenCo: One Year Later" (presentation at DEF CON 9, n.d.).

89 Sealand was never a utopian: Grimmelmann, "Sealand, HavenCo, and the Rule of Law."

90 The mall's merchandise is priced: "Sealand Shop," Sealand.

## CHAPTER 4 THE SCOFFLAW FLEET

91 At about nine cents per pound: In making these calculations, I was helped in April 2017 by Drew Cherry, editorial director at IntraFish Media.

93 That order would be Shin's last: Details about the sinking of the *Oyang 70* come partly from government interviews with forty-four surviving officers and crew members from the ship. These interviews were submitted to the Coroner's Court at Wellington in New Zealand as part of a broader investigation into the deaths of several workers on the ship. Through New Zealand's Official Information Act, the government will provide these documents on a DVD upon request. I also drew from "Findings of Coroner R. G. McElrea, Inquiry into the Death of Yuniarto Heru, Samsuri, Taefur," Wellington, New Zealand, March 6, 2013. This document, which had been drafted for federal hearings in 2012, was provided to me by researchers tied to the government investigation. Excellent reporting on this incident can be found in Lee van der Voo, *The Fish Market: Inside the Big-Money Battle for the Ocean and Your Dinner Plate* (New York: St. Martin's Press, 2016).

97 Not so on the open ocean: Besides interviews, I relied on a wide variety of printed sources for this chapter. Easily the best resource was Michael Field, *The Catch: How Fishing Companies Reinvented Slavery and Plunder the Oceans* (Wellington, N.Z.: Awa Press, 2014). More broadly, though, I consulted a wealth of other reporting from the time mostly focused on the South Korean fishing fleet generally and the human rights or environmental concerns associated with this fleet. These articles include Giles Brown and Charlie Gates, "Ship Sinks in 10 Minutes," *Press* (Christchurch), Aug. 19, 2010; Charlie Gates, "Disaster 'Only Matter of Time,'" *Press* (Christchurch), Aug. 19, 2010; Keith Lynch and Giles Brown, "Captain Had Too Many Fish in Net, Email Says," *Press* (Christchurch), Aug. 24, 2010; Sophie Tedmanson, "Asian Fisherman 'Abused' on Slave Ships in New Zealand Waters," *Times* (London), Aug. 12, 2011; Ridwan Max Sijabat, "Stop Slavery at Sea: Seamen's Association," *Jakarta Post,* Sept. 3, 2011; Michael Field, "National Party President in Fishing

Row," *Sunday Star-Times,* Sept. 18, 2011; Michael Field, "'Model' Fishers Face Grim Charges," *Sunday Star-Times,* Oct. 16, 2011; Helen Murdoch, "Fishing 'Slave Labour' Slated," *Nelson Mail,* Oct. 20, 2011; Michael Field, "Probe Exposes Fishing Underbelly," *Sunday Star-Times,* Oct. 23, 2011; Deidre Mussen, "Danger and Death in the South's Cruel Seas," *Press* (Christchurch), Jan. 14, 2012; Michael Field, "Toothless Response to Korean Toothfish Catch," *Sunday Star-Times,* Feb. 5, 2012; E. Benjamin Skinner, "The Fishing Industry's Cruelest Catch," *Bloomberg,* Feb. 23, 2012; Michael Field, "Action on Fishing Abuse Escalates," *Sunday Star-Times,* March 4, 2012; "Sailing Sweatshops on NZ Waters," *Nelson Mail,* April 14, 2012; Michael Field, "NZ Steps Up for Widows After Trawler Tragedy," *Sunday Star-Times,* April 15, 2012; "Coroner to Probe Korean Fishing Boat Deaths," *Press* (Christchurch), April 16, 2012; Michael Field, "TAIC Faulted for Lack of Assistance," *Press* (Christchurch), April 17, 2012; "Oyang Sinking Was '100 Per Cent Avoidable'—Expert," *Waikato Times,* April 18, 2012; Sophie Rishworth, "'Terrible' Conditions Aboard Trawler Described," *Otago Daily News,* April 18, 2012; Duncan Graham, "Anomalies Dog NZ-Indonesia Ties," *New Zealand Herald,* April 25, 2012; Duncan Graham, "Indonesians 'Slaves' in New Zealand Seas," *Jakarta Post,* May 1, 2012; Michael Field, "Sanford to Pay Crew Directly," *Nelson Mail,* July 31, 2012; Danya Levy, "Korean Fishing Firm Gags Crew with 'Peace' Contract," *Sunday Star-Times,* Oct. 7, 2012; "Fishermen Left to Die as Ship Sank," *Press* (Christchurch), March 9, 2013; Duncan Graham, "Exposing High Seas Slavery," *Jakarta Post,* April 8, 2013; Michael Field, "Fishermen Claim $17M in Wages," *Sunday Star-Times,* March 23, 2014; "Blitz on Fishing Ships off South Island Coast," *New Zealand Herald,* Sept. 17, 2014; Kim Young-jin, "Sunken Trawler Shifts Focus to Sajo," *Korea Times,* updated Jan. 6, 2015; Sarah Lazarus, "Slavery at Sea: Human Trafficking in the Fishing Industry Exposed," *South China Morning Post,* June 13, 2015; Stacey Kirk, "Reflagging Law to Help Fishing Boat Slaves," *Dominion Post,* May 2, 2016; Olivia Carville, "Exposed: The Dark Underbelly of Human Trafficking in New Zealand," *New Zealand Herald,* Sept. 22, 2016; Ko Dong-hwan, "In the Hurt of the Sea: Gloom of Migrant Seafarers on Korean Vessels in the Spotlight," *Korea Times,* updated Oct. 31, 2016; Choi Song Min, "Over 300 North Korean Fishermen Feared Dead from Fisheries Campaign," *Daily NK,* Dec. 30, 2016.

97 By 2010, the group had made: The Sajo company exports everything from traditional Korean bean chili and soybean pastes, imitation crabmeat, and fish cake to pickled seafood products and canned and sashimi-grade tuna. The company's fishing fleet is diverse. Its tuna long-liners and purse seiners typically operate in the Pacific, Indian, Atlantic, and Southern

Indian Oceans near the equator, targeting bluefin, bigeye, yellowfin, albacore, and marlin. Its cod trawlers and long-liners prowl the Sea of Okhotsk, the Bering Sea, and the Kuril waters near the North Pacific. The company also fishes for coho salmon, pollack, squid, and southern whiting in a variety of places around the world.

97 Southern Storm contracted with another company: For perspective on the true role of Southern Storm, I used a collection of documents (again obtained using New Zealand's open-records law). Those included New Zealand Department of Labour, *Findings of the PricewaterhouseCoopers Investigation of the* Oyang 75 *Crewmen Wages Dispute* (Wellington: New Zealand Department of Labour, 2012); Oceanlaw New Zealand, *Southern Storm Fishing (2007) LTD Response to Preliminary Audit Findings: Summary of Key Points, Chronology of Events, and Index* (Nelson: Oceanlaw New Zealand, 2011); Oceanlaw New Zealand, *F.V.* Oyang 75 *and Southern Storm Fishing (2007) LTD: Four Affidavits and a Notarial Certificate* (Nelson: Oceanlaw New Zealand, 2011); Oceanlaw New Zealand, *F.V.* Oyang 75 *and Southern Storm Fishing (2007) LTD: Six Affidavits* (Nelson: Oceanlaw New Zealand, 2011); Oceanlaw New Zealand, *F.V.* Oyang 75 *and Southern Storm Fishing (2007) LTD: Eight Affidavits and a Comparative Analysis of Vessel Catch Against Hours Recorded as Worked by Crew* (Nelson: Oceanlaw New Zealand, 2011).

98 Famous for representing several other controversial: To learn about Glenn Inwood, I read Matthew Brocket, "Government Slammed over Consultants," *Press* (Christchurch), Aug. 18, 2000; "Press Secretary Quits over Whaling Forum," *Evening Post*, Sept. 29, 2000; "Resignation Not Related to Conference Ban, Says Press Sec," New Zealand Press Association, Sept. 29, 2000; Glenn Inwood, "Whale Refuge Not Needed," *Press* (Christchurch), July 20, 2001; Ainsley Thomson, "Sealord's Whaling Link 'Could Harm NZ Stand,'" *New Zealand Herald*, Jan. 16, 2006; Glenn Inwood, "'It Tastes Like Chicken. Doesn't Everything?,'" *Press* (Christchurch), June 24, 2006; Ben Cubby, "A Maori Voice for a Japanese Cause," *Sydney Morning Herald*, Jan. 19, 2008; Siobhain Ryan, "Australia Accused over Anti-whaling 'Crimes,'" *Australian*, Dec. 30, 2008; Sarah Collerton, "PR Guru 'Paid for Whalers' Spy Flights,'" Australian Broadcasting Corporation, updated Jan. 6, 2010; Andrew Darby, "Whaler Spy Planes Track Protest Ships," *Sydney Morning Herald*, Jan. 6, 2010; Kristen Gelineau, "Conservationists File Piracy Claim Against Japanese Whalers After Antarctic Clash," Associated Press, Jan. 9, 2010; Peter Millar, "Ady Gil Drowned by Japanese Whalers," *Sunday Times*, Jan. 10, 2010; Kristen Gelineau, "Australian, New Zealand Scientists Readying for Key Antarctic Whaling Research Expedition," Associated Press, Jan. 27, 2010;

John Drinnan, "Larger-than-Life Trio to Shake Up Nation," *New Zealand Herald,* July 23, 2010; Ray Lilley, "Sea Shepherd, Whaling Protester in NZ Public Spat," Associated Press, Oct. 7, 2010; Field, "'Model' Fishers Face Grim Charges"; "Lobby Group Claims Untrue," *Timaru Herald,* Jan. 13, 2012; Rick Wallace and Pia Akerman, "Government Protest Precious, Say Whalers," *Australian,* Feb. 2, 2013; Glenn Inwood, "Do Sea Shepherd's Actions Make Them 'Pirates'?," interview by Leigh Sales, *7.30 Report,* Australian Broadcasting Corporation, Feb. 27, 2013, transcript; "Warlord Saw Wealth in Whales," *Timaru Times,* Jan. 11, 2014; "Fish-Dumping Trawler Likely to Be Seized," *Timaru Herald,* March 7, 2014.

99 Over the next year, a New Zealand journalist: I pulled from the following studies in researching the issue of worker abuses in New Zealand waters: Glenn Simmons et al., "Reconstruction of Marine Fisheries Catches for New Zealand (1950–2010)," Sea Around Us, Global Fisheries Cluster, Institute for the Oceans and Fisheries, University of British Columbia, 2016; Christina Stringer et al., *Not in New Zealand's Waters, Surely? Linking Labour Issues to GPNs* (Auckland: New Zealand Asia Institute Working Paper Series, 11-01, 15, 2011); Christina Stringer and Glenn Simmons, "Samudra Report—Forced into Slavery and Editors Comment," International Collective in Support of Fishworkers, July 2013; Christina Stringer and Glenn Simmons, "New Zealand's Fisheries Management System: Forced Labour an Ignored or Overlooked Dimension?," Department of Management and International Business, University of Auckland, Private Bag 92019, Auckland, May 12, 2014; Christina Stringer, D. Hugh Whittaker, and Glenn Simmons, "New Zealand's Turbulent Waters: The Use of Forced Labour in the Fishing Industry," *Global Networks: A Journal of Transnational Affairs* 16, no. 1 (2016); Barry Torkington, "New Zealand's Quota Management System—Incoherent and Conflicted," *Marine Policy* 63 (Jan. 2016); Margo White, "The Dark Side of Our Fishing Industry," *Ingenio: Magazine of the University of Auckland* (Spring 2014); Christina Stringer, "Worker Exploitation in New Zealand: A Troubling Landscape," Human Trafficking Research Coalition, University of Auckland, Dec. 2016; Christina Stringer et al., "Labour Standards and Regulation in Global Value Chains: The Case of the New Zealand Fishing Industry," *Environment and Planning A: Economy and Space* 48, no. 10 (2016).

103 The U.S. State Department released: "Trafficking in Persons Report 2012," U.S. Department of State, June 2012.

103 Fishing companies had two years: The best way to understand this action is to read New Zealand's 2011 report for the Ministerial Inquiry into Foreign Charter Vessels (FCV). Some highlights of their rationale: "FCVs

operate within New Zealand's domestic economy, and yet they constitute something of a legal anomaly in the New Zealand maritime safety context"; "As a matter of law, New Zealand does not recognise a class of vessels known as FCVs. In fact, FCVs do not constitute a homogenous class of vessels. Rather, legally, they are a loose collection of ships, distinguishable by their country of origin, their flag status, and the nature of the charter party agreement under which they are operating." When FCVs operate from New Zealand ports, the search and rescue (SAR) burden falls on New Zealand. *Oyang 70* sinking was managed by the Rescue Coordination Centre of New Zealand, investigated by the New Zealand Transport Accident Investigation Commission, and "will be the subject of a New Zealand Coroner's inquiry to be held later this year." "Once a vessel operates in New Zealand for two years it has to adhere to the Safe Ship Management (SSM) rules, but there are some exceptions—so this creates a legal system in which different legal standards apply, depending on whether the vessel is 'a new Zealand ship, an FCV that has recently commenced operations in New Zealand waters, or an FCV after the expiration of the two year SSM entry requirement.'" Maritime New Zealand recommended that all ships operating in New Zealand waters be subject to the same laws.

105 Under a fisheries deal: For a small example of how decisions based on price can have global repercussions, consider the story of the Filet-O-Fish sandwich, which was invented by Lou Groen, a McDonald's franchise owner in the Cincinnati area who realized he was losing many of his Catholic customers on Fridays because his menu lacked a fish option. First, the sandwiches were made from halibut, which put the cost of the sandwich at around thirty cents in 1960s prices. After McDonald's executives instructed Groen that he needed to sell the sandwich for twenty-five cents for it to be distributed nationally, he switched to a cheaper Atlantic cod until even less expensive options like pollack were found. See Paul Clark, "No Fish Story: Sandwich Saved His McDonald's," *USA Today*, Feb. 20, 2007.

105 The men could hear: Many of the documents relating to this case were provided to me by David Surya, a lawyer in South Korea who represents some of the survivors of the *Oryong 501* sinking and some of the families of the deceased. I also drew from various news reports and government records, including Dylan Amirio, "20 Indonesian Sailors Still Missing in Bering Sea," *Jakarta Post*, Dec. 6, 2014; "Another Accident at Sea," *Korea Herald*, Dec. 10, 2014; Becky Bohrer, "S. Korea to Take Over Search After Fishing Disaster," Associated Press, Dec. 10, 2014; Becky Bohrer, "S. Korean Vessel Heads to Bering Sea Where 27 Died," Associ

ated Press, Dec. 11, 2014; Park Boram, "Survivors of Sunken S. Korean Trawler, Bodies Arrive in Busan," Yonhap News Agency, Dec. 26, 2014; "Captain, Crew of Sunken Trawler Found Under Qualified," KBS World News, Dec. 8, 2014; "Death Toll from Sunken S. Korean Ship Rises to 25," Yonhap News Agency, Dec. 5, 2014; "DOLE to Repatriate Remains of 5 Seafarers," *Manila Bulletin,* Jan. 21, 2015; "Dozens Missing as S. Korea Fishing Boat Sinks in Bering Sea," Agence France-Presse, Dec. 1, 2014; Michaela Del Callar, "Two More Filipinos Confirmed Dead in Bering Sea Mishap," Philippines News Agency, Dec. 5, 2014; "Eight More Bodies Found near Sunken S. Korea Trawler," Agence France-Presse, Dec. 4, 2015; "Four More Bodies Recovered from Sunken S. Korean Ship in Bering Sea, Seven Indonesians Died," *Bali Times,* Dec. 9, 2014; "Gov't Launches Investigation into Oryong Trawler Sinking," KBS World News, Dec. 3, 2014; "Gov't to Step Up Safety Management of Deep-Sea Fishing Vessels," KBS World News, Jan. 20, 2015; "Identities of Three S. Korean Victims of Trawler Sinking Confirmed," KBS World News, Dec. 3, 2014; JoongAng Ilbo, "Ensuring Safety at Sea," Joins.com, Dec. 4, 2014; "Indonesia Trying to Save Nationals Aboard Capsized S. Korean Fishing Boat," Xinhua News Agency, Dec. 2, 2014; Lee Ji-hye, "Oryong Sinking Remains Open Sore," *Korea Times,* Feb. 10, 2015; Sarah Kim, "Korea to Deploy Rescue Ships in Oryong Mission," Joins.com, Dec. 5, 2014; Yoon Min-sik, "After Sewol Tragedy, Doubts Remain on Safety Overhaul," *Korea Herald,* April 16, 2015; "PM Orders Swift Rescue, Search Efforts for Oryong 501," KBS World News, Dec. 2, 2014; "Notorious Fishing Vessel Spotted in Uruguayan Port," *Nelson Mail,* Dec. 20, 2014; "OWWA Vigilant on Status of 7 Missing OFWs from Sunken Korean Vessel," Philippines News Agency, Dec. 9, 2014; "President Aquino Offers Condolences to South Korea on Sinking of Fishing Vessel," Philippines News Agency, Dec. 12, 2014; Kim Rahn, "Fishermen Worked in Bad Weather," *Korea Times,* Dec. 2, 2014; "Rescue Unlikely for 52 Missing Crew of Trawler," Joins.com, Dec. 3, 2014; "Rescue of 3 Filipinos from Sunken SoKor Vessel Confirmed," *Manila Bulletin,* Dec. 3, 2014; "Russia Finds Empty Lifeboats from Sunken S. Korea Fishing Boat," Agence France-Presse, Dec. 2, 2014; "Sailors' Families Blast Trawler Operator," *Korea Herald,* Dec. 2, 2014; "Russia Transfers Three More Bodies, Two Trawler Wreck Survivors to S. Korea," Interfax: Russia & CIS General Newswire, Dec. 8, 2014; "Russian Fleet Hands Over Bodies of 14 Fishermen from Sunken South Korean Trawler," ITAR-TASS World Service, Dec. 6, 2014; Choe Sang-Hun, "Dozens Missing After South Korean Trawler Sinks in Bering Sea," *New York Times,* Dec. 1, 2014; Bagus B. T. Saragih, "3 out of 35 RI Seamen Rescued from Sunken Ship in Bering

Sea," *Jakarta Post,* Dec. 3, 2014; Natalia Santi, "Minister Urges Korean Company to Compensate Victims of Oryong 501," *Tempo,* Dec. 11, 2014; "Search of Survivors from Sunken South Korean Trawler Hampered by Heavy Storm," Sputnik News Service, Dec. 6, 2014; Yoo Seungki, "Death Toll Rises to Seven in Sunken S. Korean Fishing Ship," Xinhua News Agency, Dec. 3, 2014; "Six More Bodies of S. Korea Trawler Crew Found in Bering Sea," Agence France-Presse, Dec. 2, 2014; "Skipper of Sunken Trawler Refused to Evacuate," KBS World News, Dec. 3, 2014; "S. Korea Set to End Search for Missing Crew of Sunken Trawler," Yonhap News Agency, Dec. 29, 2014; "S. Korean Consular Officials Arrive in Chukotka Regarding Ship Sinking," Interfax: Russia & CIS General Newswire, Dec. 5, 2014; "S. Korea to Toughen Penalty for Ship Safety Violations," Yonhap News Agency, April 13, 2015; Park Sojung, "S. Korea Sends Rescuers to Join Search for Missing Sailors," Yonhap News Agency, Dec. 5, 2014; "S. Korean Patrol Wraps Up Search Operation of Oryong 501," KBS World News, Jan. 6, 2015; Park Sojung, "Rescue Efforts for Missing Crewmen to Resume Tuesday," Yonhap News Agency, Dec. 8, 2014; Park Sojung, "Bodies of 6 S. Koreans from Fishing Tragedy in Russia Arrive Home," Yonhap English News, Jan. 11, 2015; Kim Soo-yeon, "Survivors, Bodies from Sunken Trawler Set to Be Moved to S. Korea," Yonhap News Agency, Dec. 9, 2014; Kim Soo-yeon, "S. Korea May End Search for Missing Fishermen off Russia," Yonhap News Agency, Dec. 19, 2014; Kim Soo-yeon, "South Korea Set to End Search for Missing Crew of Sunken Trawler," Yonhap News Agency, Dec. 29, 2014; "Survivors of Sunken Oryong Trawler Come Home," KBS World News, Dec. 26, 2014; "Third Day of Storms Hamper Rescue Efforts for Sunken South Korean Trawler," Sputnik News Service, Dec. 8, 2014; Kim Tong-Hyung, "11 More Bodies Recovered near Sunken SKorean Ship," Associated Press, Dec. 3, 2014; "Three of 13 Filipino Seafarers in Korean Trawler Sinking Come Home," ForeignAffairs.co.nz, Jan. 8, 2015; "Trawler Wreck Worst Maritime Accident in Recent Years in Far East," Interfax: Russian & CIS General Newswire, April 2, 2015; "Two Seaborne Aircraft to Join Search for Oryong-501 Crew—Navy Commander," Interfax: Russia & CIS General Newswire, Dec. 10, 2014; "US Rescue Teams Join Search for Missing S. Korea Boat Crew," Agence France-Presse, Dec. 2, 2014; "U.S. Rescuers Leave South Korean Trawler Wreck Site After Unsuccessful Search," Sputnik News Service, Dec. 10, 2014; Pia Lee-Brago, "Pinoy in Korea Ship Sinking Identified," *Philippine Star,* Dec. 5, 2014; "Death Toll of Indonesians in Sunken S. Korean Fishing Ship Rises to 12," Xinhua News Agency, Dec. 5, 2014; Park Yuna, "Survivors, Dead from Sunken Ship Arrive in Busan," Joins.com, Dec. 27, 2014.

108 I was able to meet with: Most of the material from former *Oyang* workers came from in-person interviews I conducted while I was in Indonesia on multiple occasions between 2015 and 2018. Supplemental material came from testimony workers provided previously in court or government documents.

109 Harding planned to appeal: Harding was uniquely important in assisting my reporting for this chapter. She shared hundreds of pages of documents with worker interview transcripts and expert witness testimony, including the Affidavit of Christina Stringer and Glenn Simmons, Statement of Claim for Relief Against Forfeiture, Affidavit of Michael Field, Affidavit of Craig Tuck, Memorandum of Submissions of Counsel for the 26 Fishing Crew Applicants—Seeking Relief for Unpaid Wages, and List of Applicants' names seeking relief from forfeiture. She also introduced me for interviews that I conducted in Jakarta with half a dozen former *Oyang* workers, including Saridah Tarsidi, Carwadi Karso, and Madrais. I also combed through sworn testimony from Fajar Adi Nugroho, Nasrul Hidayah, Ahmad Tohir, Slamet Raharjo, and Andi Sukendar. Also immensely useful was "Report of the Ministerial Inquiry into the Use and Operation of Foreign Charter Vessels," Ministerial Inquiry into Foreign Charter Vessels, New Zealand, Feb. 2012.

109 The perpetrators of physical: I interviewed Jong Chul Kim by phone and email on several occasions between 2016 and 2018.

111 Argentina's Coast Guard had but eight: Argentina has never relinquished its claims to the Falklands, which it calls Malvinas. After the Falkland Wars came the Squid Wars, which burned slower but were fueled by allegations of overfishing and infringements on sovereignty. For nearly two decades, Argentina and the Falkland Islands cooperated in managing the *Illex* squid, but in 2005 Argentina withdrew from the collaboration. These ships pursue a species of squid that roams across the maritime boundary between Argentina and the British-controlled Falkland Islands. The region near the Falklands called the City of Lights is a magnet for known scofflaws, and many of the ships that were expelled from New Zealand's waters relocated there because it draws less oversight. Occasionally, regional governments try to exert their authority over the fishing in and near these waters, and it can turn violent quickly. In March 2016, for example, the Argentinian Coast Guard came upon a Chinese fishing boat illegally fishing near the City of Lights, allegedly within Argentinian waters. After the Chinese ignored radio orders to stop, the Argentinian Coast Guard fired warning shots toward the fishing ship, after which the ship turned off its lights and attempted to ram the Coast Guard cutter. The Coast Guard then sank the fishing ship and

rescued three crew members and the captain as the ship sank. A similar incident occurred two months earlier when several Argentinian Navy boats backed by a military helicopter chased the *Hua Li 8*, a known pirate ship that had entered Argentinian waters. The ship escaped but was later caught fishing in Indonesian waters.

112 The fishing ships that worked these waters: The waters near the Falkland or Malvinas Islands are distinctly lawless and geopolitically sensitive. To learn about concerns surrounding the squidder boats in this area, I worked extensively with Milko Schvartzman, an investigator based in Argentina who specializes in illegal fishing and human rights matters in South America. I also read "Ship Hit and Sunk off Falklands," Associated Press, May 29, 1986; "Argentina Angered by Falklands Move," Associated Press, Oct. 31, 1986; "Fisheries-Argentina: Fishy Business in the South Atlantic," Inter Press Service, May 19, 1995; "Foreign Fishing Threatens Argentine Squid Industry," Reuters, Feb. 16, 2001; Oliver Balch, "Argentina 'Arrests' British Squid Trawler," *Sunday Telegraph*, Feb. 26, 2006; Larry Rohter, "25 Years After War, Wealth Transforms Falklands," *New York Times*, April 1, 2007; "Falklands War Turned Distant Outpost into Flourishing Community," *Irish Times*, March 26, 2012; Chuin-Wei Yap and Sameer Mohindru, "China's Hunger for Fish Upsets Seas," *Wall Street Journal*, Dec. 27, 2012; Michael Warren and Paul Byrne, "Falkland Islanders and Argentines Agree: Unlicensed Fleet Is Scooping Up Too Much Squid," Associated Press, March 24, 2013; Ellie Zolfagharifard, "Something Fishy Is Going on in the South Atlantic: Nasa Claims Mysterious Lights Seen from Space Are in Fact Fishermen Boats," *Daily Mail*, Oct. 25, 2013; Dylan Amirio, "Foreign Ministry Criticizes 'Slow' Taiwanese Response," *Jakarta Post*, March 13, 2015; John Ficenec, "Questor Share Tip: Falkland Islands Reports Another Record Squid Catch," *Telegraph Online*, June 8, 2015; Sara Malm, "Argentinian Forces Shoot and Sink Chinese Boat Illegally Fishing in the South Atlantic After It Attempted to Ram Coast Guard Vessel," *Daily Mail*, March 16, 2016; Alice Yan, "Chinese Fishermen Held by Argentina Head Home," *South China Morning Post*, April 10, 2016; John McDermott, "On Business: South Carolina Firm Is Now a Heavy Hitter in the Falkland Islands," *Post and Courier*, June 4, 2017.

112 Most of them had paid $150: Shwe Aung, a former blacklisted seafarer who went on to work for the ITF, which is the global transport workers' union, was helpful in my understanding of how manning agencies work globally to apply pressure on workers who blow the whistle on abuses. My interviews with Aung were in 2016 by phone and email.

CHAPTER 5  *ADELAIDE*'S VOYAGE

116 For several months, I had pressed Gomperts: Much of what I learned about Women on Waves came from interviews by phone, email, and in person with Rebecca Gomperts from August 2016 through 2018. Prior to joining Gomperts in Mexico, I read as much as I could about her. Among those writings was Katarzyna Lyson, "Abortion at Sea," *Mother Jones,* June 20, 2000; Leslie Berger, "Doctor Plans Off-Shore Clinic for Abortions," *New York Times,* Nov. 21, 2000; Valerie Hanley, "Irish Civil Servant Is Abortion Ship Chief," *News of the World,* June 17, 2001; Sara Corbett, "The Pro-Choice Extremist," *New York Times Magazine,* Aug. 21, 2001; John Kelly, "Artful Dodger; Abortion Boat Allowed to Sail After Group Claimed Clinic Was a 'Work of Art,'" *Daily Mirror,* June 9, 2002; Sean O'Hara, "Abortion Ship Back," *Daily Mirror,* July 8, 2002; Julie Ferry, "The Abortion Ship's Doctor," *Guardian,* Nov. 14, 2007; Graham Keely Valencia, "Protestors Threaten to Blockade Port as Abortion Ship Sails In to Challenge Law," *Times,* Oct. 17, 2008; Rebecca Gomperts, "100 Women: Rebecca Gomperts and the Abortion Ship," *100 Women,* BBC, Oct. 23, 2013, video; Emily Bazelon, "The Dawn of the Post-clinic Abortion," *New York Times Magazine,* Aug. 28, 2014; Helen Rumbelow, "Rebecca Gomperts: 'If Men Could Get Pregnant There Wouldn't Be Abortion Laws,'" *Times,* Oct. 22, 2014; Rebecca Gomperts, "Interview: Dr. Rebecca Gomperts, Who Brought Women Abortion by the Sea," interview by Jia Tolentino, *Jezebel,* Dec. 31, 2014; Katie McDonough, "'The Political Landscape Is Not Ready': Meet the Woman Leading a D.I.Y. Abortion Revolution," *Salon,* Jan. 6, 2015; Nadia Khomami, "'Abortion Drone' to Fly Pills Across Border into Poland," *Guardian,* June 24, 2015; Ryan Parry, "Shame Ship Sails," *Daily Mirror,* June 12, 2001; Mayuri Phadnis, "Champions of Choice," *Pune Mirror,* June 28, 2015; Michael E. Miller, "With Abortion Banned in Zika Countries, Women Beg for Abortion Pills Online," *Washington Post,* Feb. 17, 2016; Noor Spanier, "We Spoke to the Women Performing Abortions on International Waters," *Vice,* March 30, 2016; Maya Oppenheimer, "Rebecca Gomperts: Meet the Woman Travelling the World Delivering Abortion Drugs by Drone," *Independent,* May 31, 2016.

119 More than a third of those typically lead: Mexico City was the first area in the country to decriminalize abortion. The country's thirty-one states have varying restrictions on abortion. While all states allow it in cases of rape, abortion is illegal in many states in most other circumstances. As of 2017, only thirteen states allowed the procedure if a woman's life

was in danger, according to GIRE, a women's health advocacy group. Since 2008, sixteen states have reformed their constitutions to protect life from the point of conception. In Guerrero, where Ixtapa is located, a bill to legalize abortion was proposed in 2014, but it was voted down in committee. As of 2018, it was still illegal in Guerrero to have an abortion unless the woman's life was in danger. To get a broader sense of context on the abortion debate in Mexico, I interviewed by phone advocates from the Guttmacher Institute and the local Catholic diocese in Mexico City. I also read broadly. Here is some of that reading list: James C. McKinley Jr., "Mexico City Legalizes Abortion Early in Term," *New York Times*, April 25, 2007; "Breaking a Taboo—Abortion Rights in Mexico," *Economist*, April 28, 2007; Hector Tobar, "In Mexico, Abortion Is Out from Shadows," *Los Angeles Times*, Nov. 3, 2007; Elisabeth Malkin and Nacha Cattan, "Mexico City Struggles with Law on Abortion," *New York Times*, Aug. 25, 2008; Olga R. Rodriguez, "Mexican Supreme Court Upholds Legal Abortion," Associated Press, Aug. 29, 2008; Diego Cevallos, "Mexico: Rise in Illegal Abortions Buoys Call for Legislation," Inter Press Service, Oct. 8, 2008; Diego Cevallos, "Mexico: Avalanche of Anti-abortion Laws," Inter Press Service, May 22, 2009; Emilio Godoy, "Mexico: States Tighten Already Restrictive Abortion Laws," Inter Press Service, Aug. 17, 2009; Ken Ellingwood, "Abortion Foes Sway Mexico States," *Los Angeles Times*, Dec. 27, 2009; Lauren Courcy Villagran, "Mexico's Brewing Battle over Abortion," *GlobalPost*, Jan. 27, 2010; Daniela Pastrana, "Mexico: Extending the Reach of Safe Abortion," Inter Press Service, June 10, 2010; Tracy Wilkinson and Cecilia Sanchez, "7 Mexican Women Freed in So-Called Infanticide Cases," *Los Angeles Times*, Sept. 9, 2010; Caroline Stauffer, "Mexico Abortion Sentences Reveal Social Collision," Reuters, Sept. 20, 2010; Elisabeth Malkin, "Many States in Mexico Crack Down on Abortion," *New York Times*, Sept. 23, 2010; José Luis Sierra, "Mexico Leans to the Right on Abortion," *La Prensa San Diego*, Oct. 7, 2011; Mary Cuddehe, "Mexico's Anti-abortion Backlash," *Nation*, Jan. 23, 2012; Deborah Bonello, "Pope Visits Mexico Town Where Ending Pregnancy Means Prison," *GlobalPost*, March 23, 2012; Thanh Tan, "Looking to Mexico for an Alternative to Abortion Clinics," *New York Times*, Aug. 12, 2012; Davida Becker and Claudio Díaz Olavarrieta, "Abortion Law Around the World—Decriminalization of Abortion in Mexico City: The Effects on Women's Reproductive Rights," *American Journal of Public Health*, published online Feb. 14, 2013; Erik Eckholm, "In Mexican Pill, a Texas Option for an Abortion," *New York Times*, July 14, 2013; "Mexican Woman Fights Jail Sentence for Having Abortion," Agencia EFE, July 19, 2013; Kathryn Joyce, "Mexican Abortion Wars: American-Style,"

*Nation,* Sept. 16, 2013; "Unintended Pregnancy and Induced Abortion in Mexico," Guttmacher Institute Fact Sheet, Nov. 2013; Emily Bazelon, "Dawn of the Post-clinic Abortion."; Allyn Gaestel and Allison Shelley, "Mexican Women Pay High Price for Country's Rigid Abortion Laws," *Guardian,* Oct. 1, 2014; Jennifer Paine, Regina Tamés Noriega, and Alma Luz Beltrán y Puga, "Using Litigation to Defend Women Prosecuted for Abortion in Mexico: Challenging State Laws and the Implications of Recent Court Judgments," *Reproductive Health Matters* 22, no. 44 (Nov. 2014): 61–69; Tracy Wilkinson, "Mexico Abortion Foes Hold U.S.-Style Protests Outside Clinic," *Los Angeles Times,* March 15, 2015; "Mexico High Court Rejects Legalizing Abortion," Agence France-Presse, June 29, 2016; Maria Verza, "Mexico Court Lets Re-education for Abortions Stand," Associated Press, Sept. 7, 2016; Sarah Faithful, "Mexico's Choice: Abortion Laws and Their Effects Throughout Latin America," Council on Hemispheric Affairs, Sept. 28, 2016; "Abortion Ship Sailed Outside Mexican Territorial Waters for Second Time," *Waves on Women,* April 22, 2017.

127 The town was crawling: Picture perfect, Ixtapa's coastline features elaborate resorts, multistory yachts, and every water sport imaginable. And yet the U.S. Department of State issued a travel advisory at the end of 2016 prohibiting all U.S. government personnel's nonessential travel to the state of Guerrero, with the exception of Ixtapa by air, following gang- and drug-related shooting incidents in the Ixtapa-Zihuatanejo area. "In Ixtapa/Zihuatanejo, U.S. government personnel must remain in tourist areas," the State Department's advisory warned, noting the presence of "self-defense" groups operating independently of the government.

## CHAPTER 6  JAIL WITHOUT BARS

130 Rafting was one solution: Rules on land often conflict with realities at sea. For example, ships are required to bring oil waste for disposal in port, but many ports, especially in the developing world, lack the capacity to take the waste. Captains are prohibited from jettisoning stowaways, but they are blocked or fined if they bring them to shore.

132 Fines for the captain or insurers: Paloma Maquet, an expert on stowaways based at the Université de Poitiers in France, explained that nations have generally shifted the responsibility of handling stowaways onto the shipping industry, putting pressure on shipowners, captains, and crew.

132 People passed out from exhaustion: There is limited academic research on stowaways or sustained journalistic coverage of them. They emerge typically as isolated incidents. To look for patterns and drivers in stowing away, I read a variety of sources. Among them were Mark Bixler

and staff, "Human Contraband: The Asian Connection," *Atlanta Journal-Constitution*, Aug. 31, 1999; V. Dion Haynes and Liz Sly, "Smugglers Risk Lives of 'Cargo' for Profit: Lure of U.S. Tempts Numerous Chinese to Endure Boxed Stowage," *Chicago Tribune*, Feb. 14, 2000; Cleo J. Kung, "Supporting the Snakeheads: Human Smuggling from China and the 1996 Amendment to the U.S. Statutory Definition of 'Refugee,'" *Journal of Criminal Law and Criminology*, June 22, 2000; Nicole Tsong, "High Prices for Broken Dreams—a World Away from Home, Smuggled Chinese Stowaways Deal with Imprisonment, Fear, and, for Most, Crushed Hopes," *Yakima Herald-Republic*, July 8, 2001; "Two-Hour Sailing into a Life of Emptiness," *Irish Times*, Dec. 7, 2002; Yang-Hong Chen, "Stowaways and Illegal Migrants by Sea to Taiwan," Jan. 2003; Yang-Hong Chen, Shu-Ling Chen, and Chien-Hsing Wu, "The Impact of Stowaways and Illegal Migrants by Sea—a Case Study in Taiwan," International Association of Maritime Universities, Oct. 2005; Paul Schukovsky, Brad Wong, and Kristen Millares Bolt, "22 Stowaways Nabbed at Port of Seattle: Chinese Found in Good Health After 2-Week Trip in Container," *Seattle Post-Intelligencer*, April 6, 2006; James Thayer, "The War on Snakeheads: The Mexican Border Isn't the Only Front in the Struggle with Illegal Immigration," *Daily Standard*, April 19, 2006; Semir T. Maksen, "Transportation of Stowaways, Drugs, and Contraband by Sea from the Maghreb Region: Legal and Policy Aspects," World Maritime Universities Dissertations, 2007; Sheldon Zhang, *Smuggling and Trafficking in Human Beings: All Roads Lead to America* (Westport, Conn.: Praeger, 2007); Alison Auld, "Stowaways Arrested in N.S. Say They Came to Canada Looking for Better Life," *Canadian Press*, March 26, 2008; Michael McNicholas, *Maritime Security: An Introduction* (Burlington, Mass.: Elsevier, 2008); Melissa Curley and Siu-lun Wong, *Security and Migration in Asia: The Dynamics of Securitisation* (New York: Routledge, 2008); William Walters, "Bordering the Sea: Shipping Industries and the Policing of Stowaways," Carleton University, 2008; Florencia Ortiz de Rozas, "Stowaways: The Legal Problem," University of Oslo, Jan. 9, 2009; "Increase in Stowaway Incidents," London P&I Club, July 2009; "P&I Club: Take Care That Stowaways Can't Hide in Rudder Stock Recess," *Professional Mariner*, Oct. 9, 2012; Li Hong, "A Chinese Stowaway with No Legal Status in US," *Sino-US*, June 14, 2013; "Stowaways," *Loss Prevention Bulletin*, West of England P&I Club, 2013; Steven Jones, "Maritime Security Handbook: Stowaways by Sea," Nautical Institute, Jan. 1, 2014; "South Africa—Stowaways in Durban," West of England P&I Club, March, 17, 2014; "Gard Guidance on Stowaways," Gard; "Stowaways and Snakeheads," China Central Television. We used the same annual document each year from 2000 to 2018 to compile estimates for the number of stowaways found each year: *Gard Guidance on Stowaways* (Arendal: Gard, 2000–2018); *Reports on Stowaway Incidents: Annual Statistics for the Year 2010* (London: International Maritime Organization, 2010); Janet Porter, "Box Cells," Jan. 10, 2011; Janet Porter, "Thinking Outside the Box," Nov. 8, 2010; Janet Porter, "ACL Converts Containers into Prisons," Aug. 20, 2010; Janet Porter, "ACL Installs Onboard Cells for Stowaways," Feb. 4, 2010; Janet Porter, "ACL Installs Cabins on Ships to Hold Stowaways," Feb. 3, 2010; "BIMCO Increases Charterers' Liability in Stowaway Claims," Jan. 15, 2010; Jerry Frank, "Stowaways on the Increase Again, Warns London Club," July 14, 2009; Jerry Frank, "Stowaway Numbers See Steady Rise," July 13, 2009; "P&I Club Says Stowaway Claims Cost $20M a Year," June 9, 2009; "UNHCR: Urgent European Action Needed to Stop Rising Refugee and Migrant Deaths at Sea," United Nations High Commissioner for Refugees, July 24, 2014; Severin Carrell, "Stowaways Found Dead on Cargo Ship in Ayr," *Guardian*, May 27, 2008; Andres Cala, "Three Dominican Stowaways, Charging They Were Beaten and Abandoned at Sea, Say Two Others Dead," Associated Press, April 17, 2003; *Stowaways: Repatriation Corridors from Asia and the Far East* (Singapore: Seasia P&I Services, 2005).

136 It was unclear whether Mndolwa: The attack on Ou was hard to interpret. Solomon, Ou, and I doubted that Mndolwa was directly involved, but after the attack there were suspicious social media posts by some of the young men in his group that left us wondering. I mentioned the mugging incident in a later story published in the *Times,* and a local researcher from South Africa wrote me to emphasize that he was confident no stowaways had been involved in the attack. Stowaways in the area abided by a code of ethics, the researcher said, and they would never have orchestrated an attack on a photographer who had been accepted into the community. I remained unsure. Solomon, who had returned to Cape Town to report further on the stowaways, told me that local police had cracked down on the encampment.

137 He added that stowaways are often savvy: In 2010, one shipping company converted shipping containers on five of its most vulnerable ships into floating jail cells. When stowaways were discovered on board, they were housed in the living quarters inside these locked containers until they could be turned over to authorities. The company, Atlantic Container Line (ACL), took this step after three stowaways, two Moroccans and a Gambian national, furtively boarded an ACL ship in Hamburg, Germany. ACL discovered the men and attempted to turn them in when the ship docked in Belgium, but the Belgian Immigration Service refused to

take custody of the stowaways. The German government next refused to take the men without proof they had boarded in Hamburg. The men were transferred to another ship, the *Atlantic Conveyor,* which intended to drop them off in Sweden. On their arrival, the stowaways threatened the *Conveyor*'s crew with homemade knives in a tense standoff that only ended when the Swedish Foreign Ministry intervened. Most of the experts I contacted said that it was in the mid-1980s that they started hearing stories of stowaways being thrown overboard, a period that coincides with the increased restriction on migration. In the 1970s, many European countries had policies that actively encouraged migration in the postwar economic period particularly.

139 The commandos then whisked: There was symbolism in Abu Khattala's detention aboard the USS *New York,* which had been sent to the Mediterranean specifically to be a part of the secret operation. The ship's motto is "Never Forget," and its eight-ton bow stem was forged from steel from the World Trade Center towers. The ship usually travels with two helicopters and four Osprey aircraft on board. An Osprey can take off like a helicopter and then fly like a regular plane for long distances. Once the *New York* approached American waters, one of the Ospreys flew Abu Khattala to Washington, where he would be held for criminal prosecution.

139 These practices were supposed to stop: In 2009, President Obama issued an executive order aimed at limiting the use of torture and mandating that interrogators follow the Army Field Manual, which was written to comply with the Geneva Conventions. The manual allowed a variety of "rapport building" techniques, including direct questioning and the "good cop, bad cop" routine. It permitted tricking a detainee into revealing more information, inducing him to brag about his exploits, appealing to his emotions, threatening him with severe legal consequences, and a certain amount of sleep deprivation. Threats of torture were not allowed.

140 This would seem to require that detainees: It is worth noting that the Geneva Conventions require prisoners of war to be held on land at a fixed address that outside monitors can locate and inspect. It's also worth noting that the U.S. courts have recognized a "public safety" exception to *Miranda.* This allowed the government to interrogate suspects in particular cases without advising them of their *Miranda* rights. It also permitted un-Mirandized statements against them to be used at trial. Such an exception could, in theory, give the American government cover, except that most if not all of the instances when the "public safety" exception has been invoked in post-9/11 civilian terrorism cases lasted a matter of hours, not days or weeks.

141 In August 2017, a federal judge: From a practical standpoint, the use of the high seas for interrogation by the U.S. government in its war on terror was effective, if legally and ethically fraught. The American use of at-sea detention clearly chips away at the raison d'être of *Miranda* rights, which only have meaning if they are not delayed. To understand the legal concerns surrounding this issue, I relied heavily on Stephen Vladeck, a professor at the University of Texas Law School and an expert on the topic. At sea, he said, "there's no meaningful way for the suspect to object until it's too late." Detainees were being coerced into talking, after which they were informed of their right not to talk. "Normally, someone in military detention could file a habeas petition with a court," Vladeck said, "but by the time someone like Abu Khattala is in a position to do that, he's likely been transferred to the criminal process and so any habeas petition will be dismissed as moot." A major part of the problem with how terrorism detainees are handled relates to so-called cross-ruffing, where the government moves detainees back and forth between the civilian criminal justice and military systems in a way that allows it to take advantage of both.

141 Abu Khattala was not the first: To get a wider view on the use of offshore interrogation—be it in national or international waters—I interviewed several experts, including Hina Shamsi, a lawyer with the ACLU. I also read Ruth Sinai, "Trial Set for Lebanese Man Suspected of Hijacking," Associated Press, Feb. 23, 1989; Andreas F. Lowenfeld, "U.S. Law Enforcement Abroad: The Constitution and International Law, Continued," *American Journal of International Law* 84, no. 2 (1990): 444–93; Steven Lee Myers and James Dao, "A Nation Challenged: Expected Captives; Marines Set Up Pens for Wave of Prisoners," *New York Times,* Dec. 15, 2001; Neil A. Lewis and Katharine Q. Seelye, "A Nation Challenged: The American Prisoner; U.S. Expatriate Is Seen Facing Capital Charge," *New York Times,* Dec. 22, 2001; Steve Vogel, "U.S. Takes Hooded, Shackled Detainees to Cuba," *Washington Post,* Jan. 11, 2002; John Mintz, "At Camp X-Ray, a Thawing Life in the Animosity and Fear; Detainees Get More Comfortable, Talkative in Interrogation," *Washington Post,* Feb. 3, 2002; Jane Mayer, "Outsourcing Torture: The Secret History of America's 'Extraordinary Rendition' Program," *New Yorker,* Feb. 14, 2005; Sangitha McKenzie Millar, "Extraordinary Rendition, Extraordinary Mistake," *Foreign Policy in Focus,* Aug. 29, 2008; Matt Apuzzo, "Somali Man Brought to US to Face Terror Trial," Associated Press, July 5, 2011; Brad Norington, "Interrogation at Sea Gets Obama off Hook," *Australian,* July 7, 2011; Schuyler Kropf, "Graham: Ships Not Jails for Terrorists Says

Suspects Should Be Held at Gitmo Bay," *Post and Courier,* Oct. 6, 2013; Charlie Savage and Benjamin Weiser, "How the U.S. Is Interrogating a Qaeda Suspect," *New York Times,* Oct. 8, 2013; Stephen Vladeck and Abu Anas al-Libi, "Legal Questions over Special Ops Raids," interview by Robin Young, *Here and Now,* NPR, Oct. 8, 2013; "Is U.S. Using Warships as the New 'Floating Black Sites' for Indefinite Detention? Terror Suspect Just Captured in Libya Is Being Interrogated at Sea Instead of Sent to Gitmo," *Daily Mail,* Oct. 9, 2013; Ernest Londono and Karen DeYoung, "Suspect in Bombings Brought to U.S.," *Washington Post,* Oct. 15, 2013; James C. Douglas, "The Capture and Interrogation of § 1651 Pirates: The Consequences of United States v. Dire," *North Carolina Law Review Addendum* 91, no. 119 (2013); David D. Kirkpatrick, "Brazen Figure May Hold Key to Mysteries," *New York Times,* June 17, 2014; Carol Rosenberg, "Interrogating Benghazi Suspect at Sea Isn't a New Tactic," *Miami Herald,* June 18, 2014; Michael S. Schmidt et al., "Trial Secondary as U.S. Questions a Libyan Suspect," *New York Times,* June 20, 2014; Michael S. Schmidt and Eric Schmitt, "Questions Raised over Trial for Ahmed Abu Khattala in Benghazi Case," *New York Times,* June 26, 2014; Marisa Porges, "America's Floating Prisons," *Atlantic,* June 27, 2014; Giada Zampano, "Syrian Chemical Weapons Moved to U.S. Ship for Destruction at Sea Operation Is One of Last Phases to Dismantle Syria's Chemical Arsenal," *Wall Street Journal,* July 2, 2014; "Transfer of Syrian Chemicals to Cape Ray Is Complete," U.S. Department of Defense, July 3, 2014; "U.S. Ship Begins Neutralizing Syrian Chemical Weapons," Reuters, July 7, 2014; "US Begins to Destroy Syria's Chemical Weapons," *Al Jazeera,* July 7, 2014; "US to Affirm that UN Torture Ban Applies Overseas," Associated Press, Nov. 12, 2014; Spencer S. Hsu, "Benghazi Terror Suspect Challenges U.S. Interrogation Policy, Prosecution," *Washington Post,* Aug. 4, 2015; Meghan Claire Hammond, "Without Unnecessary Delay: Using Army Regulation 190-8 to Curtail Extended Detention at Sea," *Northwestern University Law Review* 110, no. 5 (2016): 1303–32.

141 The so-called American Taliban: Among the other examples worth citing: David Hicks, an Australian "enemy combatant" who was brought to Guantánamo the day the prison opened as Detainee 002. Hicks was captured by the Northern Alliance in Afghanistan in December 2001 and "turned over to U.S. Forces and incarcerated on the USS Pettiloo." He was inaccessible to lawyers or consular assistance. Abdul Salam Zaeef, who was the former Taliban spokesman and ambassador to Pakistan, was held and interrogated on the amphibious assault ship USS *Bataan* on the Arabian Sea. To go back even further in history: The former CIA official Michael Scheuer ran rendition operations from 1995 until 1999 and takes

credit for creating the extraordinary rendition program in 1995. The first suspect sent to Egypt was Talaat Fouad Qassem, an Egyptian linked to the assassination of the Egyptian president Anwar Sadat. In late 1995, he was kidnapped in Croatia, interrogated by U.S. agents on a ship on the Adriatic Sea, and then handed over to Egypt. Human rights advocates say that he was tortured, then executed—no record of any trial exists.

142 Some of these men died: To see how broad the problem of seafarer abandonment was, I read a variety of news articles: Jerry Hames, "Stranded Seafarers: Chaplains Face New Challenge," *Episcopal Life,* n.d.; Rick Lyman, "Abandoned, Cargo Ship and Seamen Wait in Gulf," *New York Times,* Dec. 5, 1998; Robert D. McFadden, "Crew of Ukrainian Freighter Stranded in New York Harbor," *New York Times,* Aug. 3, 1999; Albert Salia, "ITF Rescues Sailors Abandoned in Bulgaria," *Modern Ghana,* May 7, 2001; Solomon Moore, "Ship's Woes Leave 13 Sailors Stranded," *Los Angeles Times,* Dec. 11, 2004; Catalina Gayà, "Trapped in the Port of Barcelona," Consell Nacional de la Cultura, Dec. 2010; Rose George, "Sea No Evil: The Life of a Modern Sailor," *Telegraph,* Jan. 25, 2011; "Vietnam Embassy Team Visits Stranded Sailors at Chennai Port," *Times of India,* Feb. 20, 2011; "Sailors Stranded in Portland Port Could Soon Head Home," *Dorset Echo,* May 9, 2012; Arun Janardhanan, "Sailors Starve on Board Another Stranded Ship," *Times of India,* Nov. 3, 2012; "Georgian Sailors Abandoned by Ship's Owner," *Democracy & Freedom Watch,* Nov. 19, 2012; Dan Arsenault, "Stranded Sailors Heading Home Give Thanks for Help," *Chronicle Herald,* Jan. 17, 2013; S. Anil, "21 Indian Sailors Stranded at Egyptian Port for Five Months," *New Indian Express,* June 28, 2013; Ted Mann, "Computer Problems Leave Goods Stranded at New York Port," *Wall Street Journal,* Aug. 4, 2013; Anand Vardhan Tiwary, "Abandoned Seafarer Cases Rising, Less than Past Recessions: ITF," *Seatrade Maritime News,* Sept. 5, 2013; Joshua Rhett Miller, "Abandoned Ship: Sailors Left Adrift by Transport Firms' Legal Battles," Fox News, Oct. 6, 2013; Anita Powell, "Abandoned Indonesian Sailors Face South African Deportation," Voice of America, Dec. 2, 2013; Isaac Arnsdorf, "Stranded Sailors Signal More Danger than Somali Pirates," *Bloomberg,* Jan. 14, 2014; "Stranded Crew Given Vital Aid," Sailors' Society, March 21, 2014; "ILO, Maritime Sector to Address Abandonment of Seafarers and Shipowners' Liability," International Labor Organization, April 4, 2014; Isaac Arnsdorf, "Ship Owners Have to Provide Insurance, Bond for Stranded Merchant Sailors: New UN Rule," *Bloomberg,* April 11, 2014; JOC Staff, "ILO Backs Protection for Abandoned Seafarers," *Journal of Commerce,* April 11, 2014; "Abandoned Filipino Sailors from MV B Ladybug Finally Home," *World Maritime News,* April 29,

2014; "16 Indian Seamen Stranded on Ship in Dubai for Almost a Year," *Asian News International,* June 24, 2014; Noorhan Barakat, "Stranded Dubai Ship Crew 'to Return Home Soon,'" *Gulf News,* June 24, 2014; Faisal Masudi, "Marine Officials Work to Help Indian Sailors Stranded off Dubai," *Gulf News,* July 7, 2014; "Abandonment of Seafarers," Seafarers' Rights International Project, Sept. 29, 2014.

144 When I contacted him in Galati: Between January and August 2015, I interviewed Florin Raducan and George Cristof, mostly by phone, but I also hired an investigator to visit them personally so as to collect documents from their homes. During the same time period, I also interviewed by phone and email Ben Bailey, who handled the case for the Mission to Seafarers.

145 "These guys are 40 or 50 years old": The ITF was distinctly helpful in my reporting on the *Dona Liberta,* granting me access to its case files and inspectors at several ports around the world. I soon headed to Greece to try to talk to officials from the companies associated with the *Dona Liberta.* Shipping is a competitive, low-margin business, especially for refrigeration ships like the *Dona Liberta* that have been squeezed by competition from big container ship companies. I wanted to hear from the *Dona Liberta*'s operators about these pressures and get explanations for the array of its alleged crimes, including its dumping of thousands of gallons of oil at sea, its millions of dollars in unpaid debt, and the stories of abuse of crew and stowaways. In early 2015, I took a small propeller plane to Chios, a flyspeck Greek island about five miles off the coast of Turkey that is home to a disproportionate number of the world's wealthiest shipowners. I met with several shipping businessmen who, usually because of unpaid bills, were also trying to find George Kalimassias, the man who had disappeared after years running one of the companies tied to the *Dona Liberta.* In Athens, two Greek reporters, Dimitris Bounias and Nikolas Leontopoulos, who served as translators and guides, joined me on a visit to Fairport Shipping, one of many companies connected to the *Dona Liberta,* to find Kalimassias. We had heard rumors that Kalimassias was in hiding, living in the apartment on the floor above the Fairport office. Crossing the street, we rang the intercom buzzer of a neighbor. "We're looking for Mr. Kalimassias," we said. The person on the other end replied, "Oh, he lives directly across the street in the apartment there above his company's office." Turning around, we looked up at the apartment in Fairport's two-story building to see a long, second-floor window, where a man stood watching us. When we pointed at him, he quickly backed away from sight. A week or so later, a lawyer for Fairport

emailed me that his company did not intend to answer any questions related to the company's business or Kalimassias.

146 These ports offered: As I encountered this same basic story again and again, I also found myself reminded of a quotation I'd once read written by Anacharsis, a Scythian philosopher: "There are three sorts of people, those who are alive, those who are dead, and those who are at sea."

147 Dubai saw a lot: Making matters worse, the global shipping industry was in crisis in 2017, partly because the Chinese economy had slowed and less cargo was moving by sea. During boom times, the shipping industry ordered up too many new ships to be built, which resulted in a glut. One shipping executive in Dubai said that in 2014 it cost about $2,500 to ship a container from Shanghai to Europe. By 2016, it cost roughly $25 per container. For the company to break even and not lose money, it needed to charge at minimum $360 per container. Dry-bulk carriers, sometimes called tramp steamers, faced particularly tough times. In contrast to other ships, whose itineraries were set months ahead to meet manufacturing schedules, these shipping owners were more entrepreneurial, fetching cargo wherever it was needed, moving from one port to another at a moment's notice. As more freight shifted toward container ships, tramp steamers were spending more time sitting idle, losing money. More of their crews found themselves stuck in this ghostly limbo.

150 In 1898, the wooden: To read a firsthand account of these events, I consulted Frederick A. Cook, *Through the First Antarctic Night, 1898–1899* (New York: Doubleday, Page, 1909); Marilyn J. Landis, *Antarctica: Exploring the Extreme* (Chicago: Chicago Review Press, 2001); Beau Riffenburgh, ed., *Encyclopedia of the Antarctic,* vol. 1 (New York: Routledge, 2007); Bruce Henderson, *Truth North: Peary, Cook, and the Race to the Pole* (New York: W. W. Norton, 2005).

151 Another study published in the journal: Detached from the rest of the world, seafarers face higher suicide rates than landlubbers. Of seafarer deaths worldwide in the last fifty years, 5.9 percent were suicides, about three or four times the percentage of deaths by suicide in 2012 for the U.K. or Australia, according to a study in the journal *International Maritime Health.* The true rates of suicide are likely higher. Mysterious disappearances at sea and accidental drownings may also be the result of suicides, which are hard to track when an Indonesian national could be working on a New Zealand–flagged vessel owned by a South Korean company in Argentinian waters. The problem has also been chronically under-studied, and where research exists, it has focused primarily on Western fleets, which do not necessarily represent the East Asian

industry. These fleets paint a grim picture, though. In the U.K., of the professions with the top-ten suicide rates during the 1980s, merchant seafarers were the only group to still make the list in the early years of the twenty-first century, coming in at number two. Those who do not commit suicide may be living on the brink with little assistance to help guide them back. A survey of over six hundred seafarers by the International Transport Workers' Federation found that 50 percent of respondents in all but one country were depressed "sometimes" or "often." In a profession where medical attention for open wounds is hard enough to come by, as Santoso's lost finger reminded me, care for invisible wounds is nonexistent. This is especially dangerous in a job where there is easy access to a means of suicide. Robert Iverson was especially generous with his time and insights in interviews and correspondence with me. For further reading on the topic, I turned to Stephen Roberts et al., "Suicides Among Seafarers in UK Merchant Shipping, 1919–2005," *Occupational Medicine* 60 (2009): 54–61; Marcus Oldenburg, Xavier Baur, and Clara Schlaich, "Occupational Risks and Challenges of Seafaring," *Journal of Occupational Health* 52 (2010): 249–56; Robert Iverson, "The Mental Health of Seafarers," *International Maritime Health* 63 (2012): 78–89; Stephen Roberts, Bogdan Jaremin, and Keith Lloyd, "High-Risk Occupations for Suicide," *Psychological Medicine* 43 (2013): 1233; Altaf Chowdhury et al., "HIV/AIDS, Health, and Wellbeing Study Among International Transport Workers' Federation (ITF) Seafarer Affiliates," *International Maritime Health* 67 (2016): 42–50; Robert Iverson and Ian McGilvray, "Using Trios of Seafarers to Help Identify Depressed Shipmates at Sea," *Lloyd's List Australia,* May 19, 2016.

## CHAPTER 7 RAIDERS OF LOST ARKS

154 So, I went to Greece: I was especially interested in the murky distinction between piracy (like that near Somalia), semiofficial piracy (as when a state or a company is involved), theft, and repo work. These were some of the sources I read to get oriented: Kissy Agyeman-Togobo, "Pirate Paradise—Piracy Increases in the Gulf of Guinea," *Jane's Intelligence Review* 23, no. 10 (2011); Paul Berrill, "Plan Is Hatched to Tackle Nigerian Ports Corruption," *TradeWinds,* July 4, 2014; Keith Bradsher, "Insurance Premiums Rise as Threats to Ships Grow," *New York Times,* Aug. 25, 2005; Marcus Hand, "Organised Crime, Hijackings, and Stolen Vessels—the Murky World of Phantom Ships," *Lloyd's List,* Oct. 13, 2005; Marcus Hand, "Belize Defends Registering Stolen Ship," *Lloyd's List,* Dec. 22, 2005; Terry Macalister, "Southern Drift of Piracy off West Africa Is a Big Worry on All Fronts," *TradeWinds,* Feb. 14, 2014.

156 Its prow split: Most of the *Sofia*'s details come from a report by *Lloyd's List:* "Vessel Report for Sofia," *Lloyd's List Intelligence,* Dec. 13, 2016.

157 On the other side was the ship's: "TCA Fund Closes 10 Million USD Loan to NewLead Holdings," Business Wire, March 11, 2015.

157 He had been arrested: As this book was published, the Zolotas trial had not concluded.

160 As the Greek and Cypriot: The purpose of the bribe was to protect Zolotas's friend, Andreas Vgenopoulos, from the threat of a central bank challenge to his acquisition of a controlling interest in Laiki Bank through his Marfin Investment Group. In Cyprus, Vgenopoulos was widely held responsible for the collapse of the country's banking system. It was unclear whether he used Zolotas or the other way around, but both men were eventually charged. Shortly before Zolotas's extradition, however, Vgenopoulos died of a heart attack. For coverage of Zolotas's legal problems, I read "Focus Trial Defendants Ask for More Time," *Cyprus Mail Online,* April 4, 2017; Mary Harris, "Greek Judges Extradite Businessman Michael Zolotas to Cyprus," *Greek Reporter,* Nov. 8, 2016; Elias Hazou, "Zolotas and Fole Both in Custody," *Cyprus Mail Online,* Oct. 20, 2016; George Psyllides, "Former CBC Governor, Four Others Referred to Criminal Court on Corruption Charges," *Cyprus Mail Online,* March 22, 2017; "Zolotas Free on Bail," *Cyprus Mail Online,* Dec. 23, 2016.

161 In 2016, I met up with Hardberger: In preparation for meeting Max Hardberger, I read Mark Kurlansky, "Smugglers Sell Haiti down the (Miami) River," *Chicago Tribune,* April 19, 1989; Serge F. Kovaleski, "Cartels 'Buying' Haiti; Corruption Is Widespread; Drug-Related Corruption Epidemic," *Washington Post,* Feb. 16, 1998; Nancy San Martin, "Neglected City Feels Sting of Poverty," *Miami Herald,* Sept. 17, 2002; Richard Newman, "Hackensack Lender Accused in Ship Repossession Intrigue," *Record* (Bergen County, N.J.), May 9, 2004; "Repo Man Snags Cargo Ship from Haiti," United Press International, March 1, 2007; Dan Weikel, "He's His Own Port Authority," *Los Angeles Times,* March 1, 2007; Carol J. Williams and Chris Kraul, "Traffickers Exploit Haiti's Weakness," *Los Angeles Times,* Dec. 23, 2007; Peggy Curran, "How Haiti Lost Its Way: A Tale of Racism, Religion, and Revenge," *Montreal Gazette,* Jan. 30, 2010; Owen Bowcott, "Poverty Opens Haiti to Cocaine Trade," *Guardian,* July 7, 2000; Bob Rust Stamford, "Haiti Port Offers Hope," *TradeWinds,* Jan. 22, 2010; William Lee Adams, "High-Seas Repo Man Max Hardberger," *Time,* July 2, 2010; Graeme Green, "Piracy: Raider of the Lost Arks," *Metro* (U.K.), July 7, 2010; Sarah Netter, "Extreme Repo: Meet the Men Who Take Off with Planes, Ships, and . . . Cattle?," ABC News, Sept. 22, 2010; John Crace, "Max Hardberger: Repo Man

of the Seas," *Guardian,* Nov. 14, 2010; " 'Repo Man of the Seas' Shivers Pirates' Timbers," interview by Guy Raz, *All Things Considered,* National Public Radio, Nov. 21, 2010; Marco Giannangeli, "I Am the Man the Killer Pirates Fear," *Sunday Express,* Nov. 28, 2010; Aidan Radnedge, "I'm Max and I Steal Ships from Pirates," *Metro* (U.K.), April 19, 2011; Richard Grant, "Vigilante of the High Seas," *Daily Telegraph,* July 23, 2011; Michael Hansen, "More on the Jones Act Controversy," *Hawaii Reporter,* Aug. 13, 2013; Jenny Staletovich, "The Last Voyage of El Faro," *Miami Herald,* Oct. 11, 2015.

166 I scoured the court papers: The details of the *Maya Express* come from interviews with Max Hardberger between 2017 and 2018 as well as court documents that he provided. Those court documents include *Application for Temporary Restraining Order: Blue Ocean Lines Dominicana, S.A. v. Kennedy Funding, Inc., Joseph Wolfer, and Jeffrey Wolfer,* U.S. District Court of New Jersey, April 26, 2004; *Verified Complaint: Blue Ocean Lines Dominicana, S.A. v. Kennedy Funding, Inc., Joseph Wolfer, and Jeffrey Wolfer,* U.S. District Court of New Jersey, April 26, 2004; *Opposition to Motion for Preliminary Injunction: Blue Ocean Lines Dominicana, S.A. v. Kennedy Funding, Inc., Joseph Wolfer, and Jeffrey Wolfer,* U.S. District Court of New Jersey, May 10, 2004; *Order to Deny Preliminary Injunction: Blue Ocean Lines Dominicana, S.A. v. Kennedy Funding, Inc., Joseph Wolfer, and Jeffrey Wolfer,* U.S. District Court of New Jersey, May 14, 2004; *Judgement of the "Maya Express": Kennedy Funding, Inc. v. Skylight Maritime Limited,* Supreme Court of the Commonwealth of the Bahamas, Aug. 31, 2004.

168 Everyone in commercial shipping suffers: For an overview of the issue of port corruption globally, I consulted the following sources: "Bribe Poll Reflects Deeper Problems," *TradeWinds,* March 29, 2013; Adam Corbett, "Bribes Blight Reputation of Port-State Inspections," *TradeWinds,* March 29, 2013; David Hughes, "Fighting Port State Control Corruption," *Shipping Times,* Feb. 11, 2004; "Survey Seafarers Seek Fairer Treatment at Sea," *Lloyd's List,* May 26, 2009; "Port State Control: Different Interpretations and Applications," *Financial Express* (Bangladesh), Jan. 15, 2012; Jonathan Bray, "Stuck in the Bottleneck: Corruption in African Ports," Control Risks; Hannah Lilley, "Corruption in European Ports," Control Risks; Tomaz Favaro and Niels Lindholm, "Stuck in the Bottleneck: Corruption in Latin American Ports," Control Risks.

169 Diving sometimes deeper: In May 2017, I went to the village of Kepuh in Indonesia to learn about these sea scrappers and to dive on the USS *Houston,* which sank in February 1942. Over 640 sailors are believed to be entombed on that ship. That scrappers are slowly picking away at the

vessel is a source of acute frustration to the U.S. Navy, which has repeatedly asked Indonesia to put a stop to it. My reading list on this topic consisted of Sam LaGrone, "New Survey: USS Houston Wreck 'Largely Intact,' HMAS Perth Status Inconclusive," *USNI News*, Feb. 13, 2017; Michael Ruane, "A Broken Trumpet from a Sunken Warship Holds Its Secrets from WWII," *Washington Post*, Feb. 2, 2016; "WW II Cruiser USS Houston (CA 30) Final Report Completed," Naval History and Heritage Command, Public Affairs, Nov. 14, 2014. The issue of scrappers picking away at these sunken "war tombs" is so sensitive to the U.S. Navy that they declined to give me the coordinates of the ship unless I first signed a waiver promising not to remove anything from it, which I did. Fabio and I were greatly helped in this reporting trip by an Indonesian dive instructor named Budi Cayhono.

169 In boom times, the metal: Sea scrappers and treasure hunters are really two sides of the same coin, but with differently priced bounties. The United Nations estimates that there are more than three million shipwrecks on the ocean floor. For decades, offshore treasure hunting was confined to wrecks in shallow water with the help of scuba divers. In the mid-1980s, however, this changed with the advent of remotely operated vehicles, or ROVs: robots equipped with lights, cameras, and mechanical arms that could lift objects from depths as great as a mile. In a smart piece in *The New Yorker*, "Secrets of the Deep," from April 7, 2008, on this niche of the outlaw ocean, John Colapinto wrote, "As more submerged artifacts become accessible, countries have begun to challenge the 'finders keepers' concept that has traditionally governed salvage operations. In 2001, the UNESCO General Conference adopted a Convention for the Protection of Underwater Cultural Heritage, which seeks to thwart the activities of treasure hunters by prohibiting them from selling artifacts that are more than a hundred years old. The convention has yet to take effect, but laws already exist that grant nations 'sovereign immunity' over, or ownership of, their sunken warships in international waters. Lately, countries have successfully invoked these laws in court." To learn more about thievery of this sort as it played out on the ocean floor, I read Dale Fuchs, "The Battle for the 'Mercedes' Millions," *Independent*, Feb. 8, 2011; "Finders Keepers?," *Canberra Times*, Feb. 10, 2011; Abigail Tucker, "Did Archaeologists Uncover Blackbeard's Treasure?," *Smithsonian*, March 2011; Kate Taylor, "Treasures Pose Ethics Issues for Smithsonian," *New York Times*, April 25, 2011; Matthew Sturdevant, "$10 Million Policy Leads to Glittering Lawsuit; Buckets of Emeralds, a Hartford Insurer, a Fraud Battle," *Hartford Courant*, June 12, 2011; Philip Sherwell, "The Wrecks That Promise to Unlock Mystery of Drake's Final Resting Place," *Sunday Tele-*

*graph,* Oct. 30, 2011; "Maine Treasure Hunter Sets Sights on $3 Billion Worth of Platinum," *Portland Press Herald,* Feb. 2, 2012; Vanessa Gera, "From Shipwreck in Italy, a Treasure Now Beckons," Associated Press Online, Feb. 3, 2012; Betty Nguyen, Seth Doane, and Susan McGinnis, "For February 15, 2012, CBS," *CBS Morning News,* Feb. 15, 2012; Jasper Copping, "Closing in on Treasure Island's Hoard: An English Explorer Believes Hi-Tech Wizardry Can Finally Locate a Fabled $160M Stash Buried on Cocos, off Costa Rica's Coast," *Sunday Telegraph,* Aug. 5, 2012; Jasper Copping, "British Expedition to Pacific 'Treasure Island' Where Pirates Buried Their Plunder," *Telegraph,* Aug. 9, 2012; Snejana Farberov, "Reclusive Treasure Hunter Who Found 'Ship of Gold' in 1988 Sought by U.S. Marshalls 'for Cheating Investors out of Millions of Dollars,'" *Mail Online,* Aug. 25, 2012; William Cole, "Maui Man Sets Sights on Sunken Riches," *Honolulu Star-Advertiser,* Sept. 17, 2012; Garret Ellison, "Cargo of Whiskey, Gold Fuels Legend; Famous Shipwreck Discovered by Diver from Grand Rapids," *Bay City Times,* Nov. 18, 2012; Drew Dixon, "Real-Life Treasure Hunter; He Says Long-Lost Spanish Galleon May Be Under Nassau Sound Waters," *Florida Times-Union,* April 14, 2013; Seth Koenig, "Portland Treasure Hunter Faces New Challenges, Makes Another Push to Salvage Record $3 Billion Shipwreck Bounty," *Bangor Daily News,* April 24, 2013; Eve Samples, "Selling the Search," *Stuart News/Port St. Lucie News,* June 16, 2013; Adam Linhardt, "No End in Sight in Emerald Treasure Row," *Key West Citizen,* July 21, 2013; Eric Russell, "Key Investors Lose Faith in Gorham Treasure Hunter's Big Claims," *Portland Press Herald,* Dec. 30, 2013; Chris White and David McCormack, "Could Newly Discovered Gold Coins Be the Haul Stolen by Disgraced San Francisco Mint Employee in 1901? Treasure Hunting Enthusiasts Weigh In on Origins of Couple's $10 Million Find," *Mail Online,* Feb. 27, 2014; David McCormack, "Couple Who Found $10 Million Haul of Gold Coins Can Expect to Give Half of Their New Found Fortune to the Taxman," *Mail Online,* Feb. 28, 2014; Maureen Milford, "A Tale of Lost Treasure," *News Journal,* March 16, 2014; Karla Zabludovsky, "Sunken Ship Laden with Gold Lures Treasure Hunters—Again," *Newsweek,* March 28, 2014; Kim Victoria Browne, "Trafficking in Pacific World War II Sunken Vessels: The 'Ghost Fleet' of Chuuk Lagoon, Micronesia," *GSTF Journal of Law and Social Sciences,* April 1, 2014; Eric Russell, "Treasure Hunter Attracts Scrutiny: The Maine Office of Securities Says It Is Seeking Information from Potential Investors About Greg Brooks of Gorham," *Portland Press Herald,* April 15, 2014; Eric Russell, "Testimony in Suit Calls into Question Salvager's 'Plan B'; Did a Treasure Hunter Mislead Investors? One Crewman Says Yes," *Portland Press Her-*

*ald,* April 27, 2014; Eric Russell, "Former Crew Member Claims Gorham Treasure Hunter Staged Retrieval of Fake Gold Bar," *Portland Press Herald,* April 27, 2014; Kathy Lynn Gray, "Going for the Gold: The Odyssey Explorer Has Returned to the Deep Atlantic in Search of Shipwrecked Treasure," *Columbus Dispatch,* April 28, 2014; "A Quarter-Century and a Legal Nightmare Later, Gold Bars Finally Hauled from Treasure-Heavy Shipwreck," *Postmedia Breaking News,* May 5, 2014; William J. Broad, "X Still Marks Sunken Spot; Gold Awaits," *New York Times,* May 5, 2014; Doug Fraser, "Treasure Hunter Clifford Says He's Found Columbus' Famed Ship," *Cape Cod Times,* May 14, 2014; Savannah Guthrie, "Family of Treasure Hunters Hits Jackpot," NBC News, July 31, 2014; "Treasure Hunter Tommy Thompson Who Discovered the 'Ship of 'Gold' in 1988 and Made Millions Remains on the Lam Two Years After He Vanished amid Lawsuits from Insurers, Investors, and His Own Crew," *Mail Online,* Sept. 13, 2014; Bill Meagher, "Investors in Treasure Hunter Take Seeking Alpha Battle to SEC," *Deal Pipeline,* Oct. 10, 2014; Doug Fraser, "U.N. Group Sinks Barry Clifford's Santa Maria Treasure Claim," *Cape Cod Times,* Oct. 24, 2014; Charlie Rose and Erin Moriarty, "This Is Such an Odd Story Because Thompson Is Said to Be a Brilliant Engineer but He's Been the Subject of an International Manhunt Ever Since He Vanished in 2012," *CBS This Morning,* Jan. 29, 2015; Amanda Lee Myers, "Feds Chase Treasure Hunter Turned Fugitive," Associated Press Online, Jan. 29, 2015; David Usborne, "End of the Adventure for a Pair of Golden Fugitives; It Reads Like a Movie Plot, but the Tale of Tommy Thompson Is All Too Real," *Independent,* Jan. 30, 2015; Jo Marchant, "Exploring the *Titanic* of the Ancient World," *Smithsonian,* Feb. 1, 2015; Joe Shute, "Tory Lord Defends the Treasure Hunt for HMS Victory," *Telegraph,* Feb. 16, 2015; Gavin Madeley, "The Pirate Prince and the Secrets of Treasure Island," *Scottish Daily Mail,* May 23, 2015; Brent Ashcroft, "Shipwreck Discovery May Lead to Great Lakes Treasure," *Lansing State Journal,* May 31, 2015; Sam Tonkin, "Archaeologists Discover 18th Century Wreck of Slave Ship That Sank off the South African Coast in Disaster That Killed More than 200," *Mail Online,* June 2, 2015; Milmo Cahal, "Lost at Sea: A £1.9Bn Atlantic Treasure Mystery," *Independent,* June 20, 2015; Robert Kurson, "The Last Lost Treasure," *Popular Mechanics,* July 1, 2015; John Wilkens, " 'Pirate Hunters' Author Sails into Sea of Mystery," *San Diego Union-Tribune,* July 12, 2015; Simon Tomlinson, "You Can't Kidd a Kidder! 'Silver Ingot' from Legendary Pirate Captain Kidd's Treasure Horde Discovered off Madagascar Is a FAKE, Say UN Experts, Who Reveal It Is 95% Lead," *Mail Online,* July 15, 2015; Abby Phillip, "Inside the Turbulent World of Barry Clifford, a Pirate-Ship Hunter Under

Attack," *Morning Mix* (blog), *Washington Post,* July 16, 2015; Charlie Rose and Clarissa Ward, "First on CBS THIS MORNING, We Have Breaking News of an Incredible Treasure Find," *CBS This Morning,* Aug. 19, 2015; William Bartlett, "Diver Gets Hands on Gold," *Florida Today,* Aug. 20, 2015; Ken Raymond, "Book Review: 'Pirate Hunters: Treasure, Obsession, and the Search for a Legendary Pirate Ship' by Robert Kurson," *Daily Oklahoman,* Aug. 23, 2015; Andrew Casler, "Shipwreck Hunters Seek Cayuga Lake's Treasure," *Elmira (N.Y.) Star-Gazette,* Aug. 29, 2015; Tony Doris, "Lawsuit Says Treasure Hunters Scammed Man out of $190,000; Treasure Hunter Denies Allegations of Fraud; Palm Beach Gardens Man Alleges Elaborate Venture Was Big Fraud," *Palm Beach Post,* Nov. 23, 2015; Jim Wyss, "Colombian Deep: The Fight over Billions in Sunken Treasure," *Miami Herald,* Dec. 25, 2015; Jenny Staletovich, "Searching for the Lost Wrecks of the Dry Tortugas," *Miami Herald,* Jan. 2, 2016; "How the 'Holy Grail' of Treasure Ships Was Finally Found," thespec.com, Jan. 4, 2016; Jenny Staletovich, "Park Service Surveys Dry Tortugas for Wrecks," *Sun-Sentinel,* Jan. 9, 2016; Jenny Staletovich, "Salvage of Shipwrecks Pits Hunters Against Historians," *Charleston Gazette-Mail,* Jan. 19, 2016; Jenny Staletovich, "Searching for the Lost Shipwrecks: The Government Will Survey the Waters of the Dry Tortugas," *Los Angeles Times,* Feb. 14, 2016; Ed Farrell, "The Voyage Begins: Locals Hoping to Find Treasure Chest of Gold at 'the Ship,'" *Sharon (Pa.) Herald,* May 26, 2016; Michael Bawaya, "Booty Patrol," *New Scientist,* June 11, 2016; Stephanie Linning, "US Salvage Firm Risk Battle at Sea over £12 Billion Treasure on Spanish Galleon Sunk by the Royal Navy More than 300 Years Ago," *Mail Online,* June 19, 2016.

172 There are also geopolitical costs: Useful papers that I consulted that are focused on the topic are Chris Parry, "Phantom Ships" (Thompson Reuters Accelus, 2012); Jayant Abhyankar, "Phantom Ships," in *Shipping at Risk: The Rising Tide of International Organised Crime,* ed. Eric Ellen (Essex, U.K.: International Maritime Bureau of the International Chamber of Commerce's Commercial Crime Services, 1997), 58–74.

172 Because a ship may be bought: To understand the way that maritime law is distinct when it comes to the finality of certain types of property sales, I interviewed several experts on the matter by email and phone in 2016 and 2017. Among those experts were Edward Keane, an attorney at Mahoney & Keane, LLP; and Jovi Tenev, an attorney and partner at Holland & Knight.

173 Therein lies the beauty: Though risky, these scams can be lucrative, and in some parts of the world black-market transactions in stolen ships can be highly efficient. A study by the International Maritime Bureau found

that for about $300,000, a person can set up an order to have a ship hijacked in the Philippines and delivered within three days. Such thefts typically involve collusion between the shipowners and the thieves aimed at defrauding insurers, said the report, which was published in 1997. See Abhyankar, "Phantom Ships."

175 Dalby's team secretly placed: Dalby was immensely helpful in my reporting. We spoke by phone about sea repo work on half a dozen occasions in 2016 and 2017. To capture his backstory, I read Geoff Garfield, "Row Flares After Escort Deal Sours," *TradeWinds,* Dec. 2, 2011; Jack Hitt, "Bandits in the Global Shipping Lanes," *New York Times,* Aug. 20, 2000; Helen O'Neill, "Modern Pirates Terrorize the Seas," Associated Press, Nov. 6, 1999; Mark Rowe, "New Age of the Pirate-Chasers," *Independent,* Nov. 21, 1999; "When a Circus of Trouble Finds the 'Troubleshooter,'" *TradeWinds,* Sept. 22, 2000.

176 None of the half a dozen repo men: Some of the repo men I interviewed (between 2016 and 2018) asked to remain anonymous. Among those who were willing to go on record and provide me with useful input were J. Patrick Altes, private investigator for Falcon International; Douglas Lindsay, partner with Maritime Resolve; Charlie Meacham, the president of ICL Investigations; John Lightbown, an officer with Sea Cargo; Steve Salem, the director of Bahamas Sailing Adventures; Dom Mee, the founder of Protection Vessels International; and John Dalby, the CEO of Marine Risk Management. Also helpful was Michael Berkow, the director of the U.S. Coast Guard Investigative Service, which handles many of the investigations into stolen boats and ships in coastal U.S. waters.

## CHAPTER 8 THE MIDDLEMEN

183 I had heard about these firms: I was interested in Andrade's case partly because it seemed to have the potential to dispel two common misconceptions. The first one was that labor abuses on fishing ships are a problem distinct to the South China Sea and the Thai fleet. The second misconception was that these abuses occur at the hands of rogue captains. Over the past several years, most of the international attention to the problem of sea slavery has focused on the waters near Thailand, but the reality of trafficked and forced labor in the maritime world is much larger and more entrenched, and the central role played by manning agencies has remained relatively unexplored.

185 Over 56 million people: To estimate the global number of seafarers and fishing boat workers, I drew from International Labour Conference, *Conditions of Work in the Fishing Sector: A Comprehensive Standard (a Convention Supplemented by a Recommendation) on Work in the Fishing*

*Sector* (Geneva: International Labour Office, 2003); Seafarers, "Global Supply and Demand for Seafarers," Safety4Sea, May 24, 2016; *The State of World Fisheries and Aquaculture: Contributing to Food Security and Nutrition for All* (Rome: Food and Agriculture Organization of the United Nations, 2016).

186 Most men I spoke to there said: For additional reporting on the Andrade case and more generally about the fine line between labor brokers and human traffickers, see Sebastian Mathew, "Another Filipino Story: The Experience of Seven Filipino Workers on Board Taiwanese Long Liners Is a Tale of Breach of Contract," International Collective in Support of Fishworkers, *SAMUDRA Report*, no. 26 (Aug. 2000): 36–40; Joshua Chiang, "No Country for Fishermen," *Online Citizen,* Jan. 9, 2012.

186 If Andrade's experience was like: My investigation into the case of Eril Andrade could not have happened were it not for Shelley Thio and Hamish Adams, who in 2015 and 2016 worked with an advocacy and research organization in Singapore called Transient Workers Count Too. Among the documents they provided me was a compilation of court records, titled Eril Andrade y Morales Case Records: "Complaint," "Affidavit of Julius M. Andrade," "Certification of Police Blotter Signed by PSINSP AILEEN A RONDARIO," May 15, 2013, "Response Letter to PO3 Willian N Aguirre from Ms. Vivian Ruiz-Solano, Manager of Aklan Public Employment Service Office (PESO) Dated April 29, 2011," "Request Letter Signed by PSINSP AILEEN A RONDARIO Dated April 17, 2011 Addressed to PSUPT GEORBY MANUEL re Conduct of Post Mortem Examination to the Cadaver of Eril M. Andrade," "Medico Legal Report No. M-005-2011 (AK) Conducted to the Cadaver of Eril M. Andrade," "Letter of PO3 Willian N Aguirre Dated April 20, 2013 Addressed to the Provincial Chief, CIDU, Aklan re Retrieval of Inbox Messages on the Cellular Phone of Eril M. Andrade," "Consular Mortuary Certificate Signed by Jed Martin A. Llona, Vice Consul of the Philippines Dated April 16, 2011," "Report of Death of Philippine Citizen Signed by Jed Martin A. Liana, Vice Consul of the Philippines Dated April 16, 2011," "Cause of Death of Eril M. Andrade Issued by Dr. Wee Keng Poh of Health Science Authority Dated April 12, 2011," "Permit to Land a Body No. 0861 Dated April 6, 2011," "Permission to Export a Coffin Containing a Corpse No. 0000007865 Signed by Kamarul M. Yahya, Port Health Officer Dated April 13, 2011," "Certificate of Sealing Coffin No. 0166 Dated April 13, 2011," "Embalming Certificate No. 0719 Dated April 13, 2011," "Seaman Report (Vessel Hung Yu No. 212)," "Fortuna No. 5 with Name of Eril Andrade and Other Persons," "Passport of Eril M. Andrade," "Acknowledgement Receipt Signed by P03 Wil-

lian N Aguirre Dated 181435 April 2011," "Tourism Infrastructure and Enterprise Zone Authority (TIEZA) in the Name of Eril Andrade." Other documents came from the Kalibo prosecutor's office and included Reden S. Romarate, "Affidavit," Republic of the Philippines, May 20, 2011, 1–3; Jeoffrey L. Ruzgal, "Police Blotter of the Aklan Police Provincial Office, No. 0594," Provincial Investigation and Detective Management Branch, Camp Pastor Maitelino, Kalibo, Aklan, Philippines, Feb. 8, 2012, 1–2; Tyrone J. Jardinico, "Affidavit," Republic of the Philippines, Feb. 20, 2012, 1–2; Tyrone J. Jardinico, "Certification of Extract of Police Blotter," Aklan Police Provincial Office, Philippine National Police, Feb. 20, 2012, 1–2.

189 I spent almost a full day wandering: Most of my reporting in the Philippines occurred in September 2015.

191 The documents I received indicated: Step Up Marine was also tied to "one of the largest and most complex cases of human trafficking in Cambodia in recent history: the case of Giant Ocean International Fishery Co. Ltd.," according to a September 2012 report on Giant Ocean: Andy Shen, *Report on the Situation of Cambodian Fishermen Trafficked Overseas by Giant Ocean International Fishery Co., Ltd.,* Cambodian Working Group for Migrant Fishers, Sept. 2012. That report and stories in the press indicate that over a thousand Cambodian men had been sent by Giant Ocean to work overseas. Cambodian fishermen in Cape Town, South Africa, a destination for victims often used by Giant Ocean, suggested there might have been roughly a thousand Cambodians working on fishing vessels at any given moment. Hundreds of men were reported missing. "All who have been repatriated back to Cambodia have been identified by UN agencies and Cambodian NGOs as Victims of Trafficking" in what the working group called a "heinous form of modern-day slavery." In August 2012, a trafficking victim of Giant Ocean provided key pieces of documentary evidence that for the first time linked Giant Ocean to "a notorious Singaporean Agency Step-Up Marine Enterprise." The September 2012 report included nine case studies involving Giant Ocean trafficking victims from between 2010 and 2012. As of September 2012, the working group had identified 171 cases of individuals identified as victims of trafficking with Giant Ocean.

193 But a lawsuit heard by: The most useful court record pertaining to this case is *Mario Hornales v. National Labor Relations Commission, Jose Cayanan, and JEAC International Management Contractor Services,* G.R. No. 118943, Sept. 10, 2001.

194 The family declined: Step Up Marine had a long history of abandoning crew it placed in dangerous conditions. In 2009, eight Filipino crew members were jailed in Tanzania for ten months on charges of illegal

fishing after their captain fled. Step Up Marine, which had recruited and hired the crew, refused to hire lawyers or post bail. In a separate case, also in April 2009, for example, the Somali pirates who stormed the U.S.-flagged, Danish-owned *Maersk Alabama* container ship—in an incident made famous by the movie *Captain Phillips*—staged their attack using as a "mother ship," or base of operations, a seven-hundred-ton Taiwanese tuna long-liner called the *Win Far 161* that they had hijacked several days earlier after allegedly fishing illegally near Somalia. Among the crew of thirty on the *Win Far 161* were seventeen Filipinos, most of whom had been recruited by Step Up Marine, according to seafarer advocates who were involved with the case. The crew was held hostage for ten months, during which two of them died from malnutrition and sickness.

197 His name was Emmanuel: Finding men in the villages with these experiences was not difficult. Getting them to open up, however, took some doing, because many were embarrassed at having been scammed. "You go with pride," one of them told me about his experience, "and come back with shame." Some topics were especially sensitive: sexual abuse, debt still owed to relatives, and the violence faced at sea. To get the men to open up, I tried to talk with them in private. Helping all the while was Hannah Reyes, the photographer on this story. Born in the Philippines, she is a native speaker of Tagalog with a gentle but effective ability at breaking the ice. In one of the more remote villages, she and I trekked through the woods to find the house of a trafficking victim whose police report I had read previously. Though his uncle was reluctant at first, he eventually gave us permission to interview the young man. Over the course of a week, Reyes and I spoke to nearly a dozen young men, all of whom had stories to tell about having been trafficked onto fishing boats.

198 She was arguably the lowest-ranking: With help from the local prosecutor's office in Kabilo and Shelley Thio, I collected many documents relevant to Celia Robelo's case. Among the most useful were Jed Martin A. Llona, "MIS—2700–2011," email, Dec. 8, 2011; *People of the Philippines v. Celia Robelo y Flores, Roselyn Robelo y Malihan,* Republic of the Philippines, Regional Trial Court Sixth Judicial Region, Criminal Case Nos. 10273, Sept. 13, 2013.

198 At forty-six years old: At the time of the publication of this book, Robelo remained in the provincial jail. Some of the charges against her had been dropped but the human trafficking charges, which carry a mandatory life sentence, remained.

200 He did, however, eventually: The prosecutor said that Celia Robelo was charged for human trafficking and illegal recruitment and faces a life sentence in prison if she is found guilty. Five witnesses were presented

against Robelo, including two complainants and their mothers. Several others were charged with the same crimes, but none were prosecuted because the police did not know their whereabouts. The prosecutor also said that the family of Andrade did not want Robelo to be jailed, probably because they believed she was genuinely trying to help men find work.

## CHAPTER 9  THE NEXT FRONTIER

204 Arguably the least policed: Oversight of the ocean subsurface is fractured, and rules vary by depth. Although the water column and the seabed below two hundred meters are interconnected, they are managed on a sector-by-sector basis. The 1982 United Nations Convention on the Law of the Sea (UNCLOS) is an umbrella framework for international ocean management. Multilateral regional fishery management organizations regulate commercial fisheries harvests; the International Maritime Organization manages shipping; and the International Seabed Authority regulates mining of the international seabed. But the management of other activities like dumping, laying submarine internet cables, bio-prospecting for new medicinal discoveries, and military weaponry testing that affect the ocean column or floor are regulated by a single-sector approach or virtually not at all. Rarely do the different categories of regulators work together to get a holistic view of the combined pressures on an area.

205 In April 2017, President: Executive order 13795 of April 28, 2017, Implementing an America-First Offshore Energy Strategy.

205 It was not until 2016: Rodrigo L. Moura et al., "An Extensive Reef System at the Amazon River Mouth," *American Association for the Advancement of Science,* April 22, 2016.

206 Before I left the United States: *The Guardian,* in collaboration with Global Witness, maintains a useful list of murders of environmentalists. I also consulted Simeon Tegel, "Latin America Most Dangerous Place for Environmentalists," Public Radio International, Sept. 2, 2013; Monica Ulmanu, Alan Evans, and Georgia Brown, "The Defenders," *Guardian;* June 13, 2017; Michael E. Miller, "Why Are Brazil's Environmentalists Being Murdered?," *Morning Mix* (blog), *Washington Post,* Aug. 27, 2015; Oliver Holmes, "Environmental Activist Murders Set Record as 2015 Became Deadliest Year," *Guardian,* June 20, 2016; Andrew O'Reilly, "Brazil Becomes Most Dangerous Country in World for Environmental Activists," Fox News, June 20, 2016; Márcio Astrini, "Brazil: The Most Dangerous Country for Environmental Activists in 2015," Greenpeace, June 27, 2016; "Olympics Host Brazil Is the Most Dangerous Country in the World for Environmental Activism," Global Witness, Aug. 4, 2016.

206 One environmentalist had his ears: Miller, "Why Are Brazil's Environmentalists Being Murdered?"

206 A nun who had been protesting: Myrna Domit, "Rancher to Be Charged in 2005 Killing of Nun in Amazon," *New York Times*, Dec. 28, 2008.

207 So, aside from destroying: My reading on the Amazon consisted of Isabel Allende, "Spirits of the Jungle," *Australian*, April 19, 1997; Simon Barnes, "Good News from the Forest; Reportage," *Times*, Oct. 18, 2007; David Quammen, "A Test of Endurance: A Scientist Studies Conservation and Destruction Deep in the Amazon," *San Francisco Chronicle*, April 17, 1988; Alex Shoumatoff, "The Gasping Forest," *Vanity Fair*, May 2007; Oliver Tickell, "In Peru's Lush Rain Forest," *New York Times*, June 11, 1989; Ken Wiwa, "Saints or Sinners?," *Globe and Mail*, June 29, 2002.

209 Though not fatal to humans: Jennifer Frazer, "The Attack of the Giant Water Bug," *Scientific American*, Aug. 27, 2013.

210 After a day of sailing: The crew on the *Esperanza* during my time on the ship were immensely open. Especially useful were Thiago Almeida, Julia Zanolli, and Travis Nichols.

213 The indiscriminate carnage it causes: That writer is Charles Clover, who summed up this destructive power best in his book *The End of the Line: How Overfishing Is Changing the World and What We Eat* (New York: New Press, 2006). He writes, "Imagine what people would say if a band of hunters strung a mile of net between two immense all-terrain vehicles and dragged it at speed across the plains of Africa. This fantastical assemblage, like something from a *Mad Max* movie, would scoop up everything in its way: predators such as lions and cheetahs, lumbering endangered herbivores such as rhinos and elephants, herds of impala and wildebeest, family groups of warthogs and wild dogs. Pregnant females would be swept up and carried along, with only the smallest juveniles able to wriggle through the mesh . . . The effect of dragging a huge iron bar across the savannah is to break off every outcrop and uproot every tree, bush, and flowering plant, stirring columns of birds into the air. Left behind is a strangely bedraggled landscape resembling a harrowed field. The industrial hunter-gatherers now stop to examine the tangled mess of writhing or dead creatures behind them. There are no markets for about a third of the animals they have caught because they don't taste good, or because they are simply too small or too squashed. This pile of corpses is dumped on the plain to be consumed by scavengers. This efficient but highly unselective way of killing animals is known as trawling."

213 By 2011, Greenpeace was using: Most of the details about Greenpeace's dumping of boulders comes from multiple interviews in 2017 with Thilo Maack, a Greenpeace researcher.

215 Statoil's well was even more: It was on this trip that I started to understand some of what made travels offshore alluring and addictive to me. When I traveled across the Arctic, there were long stretches of downtime, much of which I spent staring off into the distance. The sea lends itself to this activity because the sky is huge and the waves give you something to look at without demanding all your attention. It's a mesmerizing thing that reminded me how little opportunity there was in my life on land for daydreaming or mere quiet reflection. As I walked around the ship, I noticed lots of people doing the same thing. Silently, often right near each other. When I did this at home, there was one spot in the kitchen that I would always go to during the day for it. The view offered enough depth, and the trees there were big and captivating. At the right hour, the sun would shine into the house at eye level, and I could bask in it like a cat on a windowsill at least until the next email came in or I realized I was running out of time to get done what needed getting done. On a ship, without internet or cell connectivity or much to do, that tranquil 360-degree vista was on offer virtually anywhere on deck, day or night.

215 In other words, the rules: To understand some of Greenpeace's legal tactics, I leaned heavily on Sune Scheller, a lawyer for the organization.

215 But logistical issues delayed: Greenpeace had tried this tactic before, with mixed results. In 2014, the *Esperanza* beat a drilling rig to the spot where Statoil intended to drill in the Barents Sea. Statoil could only establish its exclusion zone, where protesters were forbidden to enter, if the rig could drop anchor or engage its dynamic positioning thrusters, which allow the rig to stay in one spot. Once the rig was relatively stationary, its legal status changed in category from being a vessel in transit to a fixed installation. By getting there first and parking in its spot, the *Esperanza* prevented the drilling rig from creating an exclusion zone. After the *Esperanza* occupied the location for half a day, the Norwegian Coast Guard attached a cable to the Greenpeace ship, forcefully towing it dozens of miles away, which afforded Statoil enough time to take over the site.

218 So, as we sailed toward: Some of the more evocative writing I read on the topic were Tony Bartelme, "Fade to White: From South Carolina to the Florida Keys, Coral Reefs Are the Ocean's Masterworks. Will They Soon Be Gone?," *Charleston (S.C.) Post and Courier,* Oct. 19, 2016; "Dusk and Dawn Are Rush Hours on the Coral Reef," *Smithsonian,* Oct. 1993; Elizabeth Kolbert, "Unnatural Selection," *New Yorker,* April 18, 2016; "Rejuvenating Reefs," *Economist,* Feb. 13, 2016; William K. Stevens, "Violent World of Corals Is Facing New Dangers," *New York Times,* Feb. 16, 1993; Peter Weber, "Coral Reefs Face the Threat of Extinction," *USA Today Magazine,* May 1993; Karen Weintraub, "Giant Coral Reef in Protected

Area Shows New Signs of Life," *New York Times,* Aug. 15, 2016; Julia Whitty, "Shoals of Time," *Harper's Magazine,* Jan. 2001.

## CHAPTER 10 SEA SLAVERY

227 Thanks to excellent reporting: Before launching on this topic, I read "Forced Labour on Thai Fishing Boats," *Al Jazeera,* YouTube, posted May 28, 2013; Beate Andrees, "Caught at Sea: Fighting Forced Labour and Trafficking in the Fishing Industry," International Labor Organization, May 31, 2013; *Caught at Sea: Forced Labour and Trafficking in Fisheries* (Geneva: International Labour Office, 2013); "Chance for NZ to Curb Slavery at Sea," *Press,* March 28, 2012; Robyn Dixon, "Africa's Brutal Cycle of Child Slavery," *Los Angeles Times,* July 12, 2009; Environmental Justice Foundation, "Sold to the Sea: Human Trafficking in Thailand's Fishing Industry," YouTube, posted Aug. 14, 2014; Ashley Herendeen, "Sea Slaves in Asia," *Global Post,* Nov. 29, 2009; Kate Hodal, Chris Kelly in Songkhla, and Felicity Lawrence, "Revealed: Asian Slave Labour Producing Prawns for Supermarkets in US, UK," *Guardian,* June 10, 2014; Kate Hodal and Chris Kelly, "Captured, Tortured, and Sometimes Killed—the Brutal Lives of Thailand's Fishing Workers, Exposed by Kate Hodal and Chris Kelly in Songhal," *Guardian,* June 11, 2014; Dean Irvine, "Slaves at Sea: Report into Thai Fishing Industry Finds Abuse of Migrant Workers," CNN, March 6, 2014; Sharon LaFraniere, "Africa's World of Forced Labor, in a 6-Year-Old's Eyes," *New York Times,* Oct. 29, 2006; Amy Sawitta Lefevre and Andrew R. C. Marshall, "Special Reporter: Traffickers Use Abductions, Prison Ships to Feed Asian Slave Trade," Reuters, Oct. 22, 2014; Sarah Marinos, "The Children's Champion," *Herald Sun,* Aug. 7, 2010; "Cambodia-Thailand: Men Trafficked into 'Slavery' at Sea," IRIN, Aug. 29, 2011; Sian Powell, "Prisoners of the Sea," *Australian Magazine,* Oct. 16, 2010; Shannon Service and Becky Palmstrom, "Confined to a Thai Fishing Boat, for Three Years," NPR, June 9, 2012; Benjamin E. Skinner, "The Fishing Industry's Cruelest Catch," *Bloomberg Businessweek,* Feb. 23, 2012; *Slavery at Sea: The Continued Plight of Trafficked Migrants in Thailand's Fishing Industry* (London: Environmental Justice Foundation, 2014); "Southern Police Inspect Fishing Boats in Search of Human Traffickers," *Khaosad English,* June 19, 2014; Cindy Sui, "Exploitation in Taiwan's $2Bn Fishing Industry," BBC, June 10, 2014; George Wehrfritz, Erika Kinetz, and Jonathan Kent, "Lured into Bondage," *Newsweek,* April 21, 2008; Patrick Winn, "Sea Slavery," *Global Post,* May 21, 2012; Tan Hui Yee, "Deadliest Catch: Slave Labour on the Seas," *Straits Times,* Sept. 1, 2013.

232 All the fish looked the same: One of the more disturbing things about this story was where this fish was destined to go. After returning to shore,

Long learned that most of the forage fish on the final boat where he was held in bondage was routed to a processing plant called the Songkhla Canning Public Company, which, I later discovered, is a subsidiary of Thai Union Frozen Products, the country's largest seafood company. While I was reporting in Thailand in 2015, I followed the trucks carrying fish from the port where Lang Long's mother ship docked to their destination, which was typically this same processing plant. Then, using U.S. Customs documents, I found that in 2015, Thai Union shipped more than twenty-eight million pounds of seafood-based cat and dog food for some of the top brands sold in America including Iams, Meow Mix, and Fancy Feast. This use of fish is part of the global "reduction industry"—a massive industrial sector that boils down twenty-five million tons of wild fish a year into fish meal and fish oil. Much of the fish meal derived from the reduction industry is used to feed farmed salmon and a growing portion of the fish oil is put into dietary supplements. The United States is the biggest customer of Thai fish, and pet food is among the fastest-growing exports from Thailand, more than doubling since 2009 and in 2017 totaling more than $190 million. The average pet cat in the United States eats thirty pounds of fish per year, about double that of a typical American human. Though there is growing pressure from Americans and other Western consumers for more accountability in seafood companies' supply chains to ensure against illegal fishing and contaminated or counterfeit fish, virtually no attention has focused on the labor that supplies the seafood that people eat, much less the fish that is fed to animals. "How fast do their pets eat what's put in front of them, and are there whole meat chunks in that meal?" asked Giovanni M. Turchini, an environmental professor at Deakin University in Australia who studies the global fish markets. "These are the factors that pet owners most focus on." Bar codes on pet food in some European countries enable far-flung consumers to track Thai-exported seafood to its onshore processing facilities, where it was canned or otherwise packaged. But the supply chain for the twenty-eight million tons of forage fish caught annually around the globe, about a third of all fish caught at sea and much of it used for pet and animal feed, is invisible before that. Sasinan Allmand, the head of corporate communications for Thai Union Frozen Products, said that her company does routine audits of its canneries and boats in port to ensure against forced and child labor. The audits involve checking crew members' contracts, passports, proof of payment, and working conditions. "We will not tolerate any human trafficking or any human rights violation of any kind," she said. Asked whether audits are conducted on the fishing boats that stay at sea, like the one where Mr. Long was captive, she declined to respond.

Human rights advocates have called for a variety of measures to provide greater oversight, including requiring all commercial fishing ships to have electronic transponders for onshore monitoring and banning the system of long stays at sea and the supply ships that make them possible. But their efforts have gotten little traction. The profits for seafood businesses still far exceed the risks for those who exploit workers, said Mark P. Lagon, who formerly served as the State Department's ambassador at large focused on human trafficking. Lisa K. Gibby, vice president of corporate communications for Nestlé, which makes pet food brands including Fancy Feast and Purina, said that the company is working hard to ensure that forced labor is not used to produce its pet food. "This is neither an easy nor a quick endeavor," she added, because the fish it purchases comes from multiple ports and fishing vessels operating in international waters. Some pet food companies are trying to move away from using fish. Mars Inc., for example, which sold more than $16 billion worth of pet food globally in 2012, roughly a quarter of the world's market, has already replaced fish meal in some of its pet food and will continue in that direction. By 2020, the company plans to use only non-threatened fish caught legally or raised on farms and certified by third-party auditors as not being linked to forced labor. Though Mars has been more proactive on these issues than many of its competitors, Allyson Park, a Mars spokeswoman, conceded that the fishing industry has "real traceability issues" and struggles to ensure proper working conditions. This is even more challenging, she said, because Mars purchases fish not directly from docks but further up the supply chain. In 2016, Mars received more than ninety thousand cartons of cat and dog food from the cannery supplied by one of the boats where Lang Long was held captive, according to the customs documents. To track U.S. imports from Thailand, I turned to Allison Eckhardt with the Foreign Agricultural Service in the U.S. Department of Agriculture. Molly McGrath from the AFL-CIO was essential in sifting through customs data. I relied heavily on Abby McGill, director of campaigns for the International Labor Rights Forum; Steve Trent, the director of the Environmental Justice Foundation; Jason Judd from the ILO; and Phil Robertson, the regional director for Human Rights Watch. No one was more essential, however, than Tanya Laohathai, from the Office of the Prime Minister of Thailand, and Daniel Murphy, a regional expert on the issues.

234 Over the next two years, Long: Several examples of when Secretary of State John Kerry referenced the *Times*'s coverage of this topic: In October 2015 at the "Our Oceans" conference in Chile, Kerry finished a five-minute recap of the *Times*'s sea slaves article by saying he planned to make the

topic a focus of the 2016 conference, "to bring many more nations to the table and create a global system where we are able to enforce and prevent the kind of slavery that is laid out in this *New York Times* article." During the same event, he referred to Sea Shepherd as he cited another *Times* article, and he observed the travesty that nonprofit groups are doing the enforcement work that governments should be doing. "What we're trying to do is translate that accountability into governments," he said. "That's our goal." In July 2015 at a news conference, he said, "We want to bring to the public's attention the full nature and scope of a $150 billion illicit trafficking industry, and it is an industry." He went on, "Pick up today's *New York Times,*" he said, "about a young Cambodian boy promised a construction job in Thailand, goes across the border, finds himself held by armed men, and ultimately is pressed into service on the seas, three years at sea shackled by his neck to the boat."

234 One afternoon, Pisan Manawapat: In 2015, I also interviewed Vijavat Isarabhakdi, who at the time was serving as Thailand's ambassador to the United States.

236 The shelter's social workers: During my time reporting in Thailand in the summer of 2017, I visited several other facilities where rescued or detained crew from fishing boats were held, including Baan Pathum, a shelter in Pathum Thani province, and Thanon Phet Kasem, another shelter in Songkhla. Both were well run, but many of the men seemed to be in a similar limbo as Lang Long. They spoke of wanting to return home but needing to wait, sometimes for months, for the government to investigate their cases.

236 On December 28, 2017, Long: For insight on the government's decision to send Lang Long home, a useful document is the "Report on Lang Long's Return to Cambodia," Pathumthani Welfare Protection Center for Victims of Trafficking in Persons.

242 As of 2016, Thailand had: For comparative unemployment rates, I consulted "Unemployment, Total (% of Total Labor Force) (Modeled ILO Estimate)," International Labor Organization, ILOSTAT database, Sept. 2018.

252 In some cases, the men were shanghaied: For a useful resource on the topic of how karaoke bars intersect with sea slavery and other forms of human trafficking, I consulted a detailed pamphlet on the topic titled "Summary Report on Karaoke Bars in Thailand," Stella Maris Seafarers Center Songkhla, Oct. 6–Dec. 2010.

254 The lucky ones had been equipped: Some advocates have traced the origins of this clandestine network to a "Missing Persons" hotline that was launched in 2002 by the Mirror Foundation, an anti-human-trafficking

organization based in Bangkok. "Our focus was kidnapped children," explained Ekkalak Lumchomkhae, one of the founders of the hotline, which instead began receiving dozens of calls from families reporting that their adult sons, husbands, and brothers had taken jobs on boats, never to be heard from again. By 2008, the foundation interviewed some of the men who eventually made it home, and they reported a much wider problem of forced labor and human trafficking on fishing boats.

254 Local motorcycle taxis: Taxi drivers in border towns played a variety of roles, I found. They tended to be savvy sorts who knew all the local characters. They also often knew how to spot which migrants and out-of-towners were the best potential marks, and for a finder's fee they delivered these young men to the labor brokers. In such cases, the taxi drivers would take the new recruits to a local bar to drink, sing, and enjoy the company of women. At dawn the next day, the bar owner, typically in cahoots with the recruiter or taxi driver, would present a bill with hugely inflated prices. This was usually followed by threats of violence if the bill was not paid as well as offers of a chance to clear the debt by signing on to work on a fishing boat.

257 In the summer of 2017: At this point, I did a new sweep of all that had been written on the topic since my original round of reporting. Here is some of what I read at this stage: Sarah Hucal, "Thai Junta Asked to Crack Down Harder on Rogue Seafood Industry," *Premium Official News,* Aug. 14, 2015; Peter Alford and Gita Athika, "Fishermen Trapped in Slavery," *Australian,* Aug. 7, 2015; Peter Alford, "Stench of Seafood Slavery," *Australian,* Dec. 30, 2015; Peter Alford and Gita Athika, "Crews Go Missing in Ambon Bay amid Slavery Probe," *Australian,* Sept. 12, 2015; "Are Slaves Peeling Your Shrimp? Here's What You Need to Know," Associated Press, Dec. 14, 2015; "A Story of Modern Slavery in Thailand," *Thai News Service,* Sept. 4, 2015; "Bad Smell Hangs over Thai-German Fish Deal; Slave Labor," *Handelsblatt Global Edition,* Feb. 23, 2016; "Burmese Fisherman Goes Home After 22 Years as a Slave," *Thai News Service,* July 6, 2015; "Cambodian Labor Trafficking Victims Sue U.S.-Based Seafood Suppliers," *Plus Media Solutions,* Aug. 19, 2016; "Cardin Delivers Remarks on Ending Modern Slavery, Highlights Maintaining Integrity of Trafficking in Persons Reports," U.S. Senate Committee on Foreign Relations, Feb. 24, 2016; Sophie Cocke, "Petition, Lawsuit Filed over Isle Fishing Fleet," *Honolulu Star-Advertiser,* Sept. 23, 2016; Audie Cornish and Ian Urbina, "Oceans Called a 'Wild West' Where Lawlessness and Impunity Rule," National Public Radio, July 31, 2015; "Costco Sued over Claims Shrimp Harvested with Slave Labor," *Daily Herald,* Aug. 20, 2015; Thanyarat Doksone and Martha Mendoza, "Thailand Remains Black-

listed by US for Human Trafficking," Associated Press, July 28, 2015; "E.U. Urged to Act on Thai Fishing Slavery," *Maritime Executive,* Feb. 21, 2016; "FAO and the Vatican Condemn Illegal Fishing and Forced Labor on the High Seas, Urge Collective Action," States News Service, Nov. 21, 2016; "Fighting Slavery, One Seafood Supplier at a Time," *Denver Post,* Dec. 22, 2015; "Fishermen Who Fled Slavery in San Francisco Sue Boat Owner," Associated Press, Sept. 23, 2016; Tara Fitzpatrick, "6 Things You Need to Know About the Seafood Supply," *Restaurant Hospitality,* Oct. 5, 2016; Fakhrurradzie Gade, Margie Mason, and Robin McDowell, "Captain Arrested on Boat Believed to Contain Slave-Caught Fish," *Asian Reporter,* Oct. 5, 2015; Fakhrurradzie Gade, Margie Mason, and Robin McDowell, "Thai Man Arrested on Boat Believed to Be Carrying Slave Fish," Associated Press, Sept. 26, 2015; Rose George, "Saltwater Slaves," *New Statesman,* Feb. 10, 2016; *Get It Right This Time: A Victims-Centered Trafficking in Persons Report: Testimony Before the Subcommittee on Africa, Global Health, Global Human Rights, and International Organizations, House of Representatives,* 114th Cong., 2nd Sess. (2016) (statement of Matthew Smith, executive director of Fortify Rights); Nirmal Ghosh, "Thais Claim Success in Cleaning Up Fishing Sector," *Strait Times,* Feb. 13, 2016; Amy Goodman, *The War and Peace Report,* Democracy Now!, April 18, 2016; "Greenpeace Shuts Pet Food Factory Connected to Slavery and Destructive Fishing," *New Zealand Herald,* May 19, 2016; Nick Grono, "Perpetrators of Modern Slavery Are Devastating Our Environment Too," *Guardian,* Nov. 17, 2015; Nick Grono, "Traumatized and Vulnerable, Slavery Survivors Live with Mental Health Issues," CNN, Nov. 5, 2015; Matt Hadro, "If You Buy Shrimp You Might Want to Know This," *Eurasia Review,* March 7, 2016; Matt Hadro, "You Should Know This if You Buy Shrimp," *Eurasia Review,* Nov. 9, 2016; "Hagens Berman: Class Action Filed Against Nestlé for Slave Labor, Human Trafficking Used to Produce Top-Selling Pet Food," Business Wire, Aug. 27, 2015; Ruth Halkon, "Fisherman 'Enslaved for Five Years on Thai Fishing Boat Because of an Unpaid Beer Tab,'" *Irish Mirror,* May 19, 2016; Esther Han, "Prawns Linked with Trafficking and Environmental Damage Revealed," *Age* (Melbourne, Australia), Dec. 9, 2015; Kate Hodal, "Slavery and Trafficking Continue in Thai Fishing Industry, Claim Activists," *Guardian,* Feb. 24, 2016; Michael Holtz, Stephanie Hanes, and Whitney Eulich, "How to Free Modern Slaves: Three Tech Solutions That Are Working," *Christian Science Monitor,* Nov. 23, 2015; Esther Htusan and Margie Mason, "More than 2,000 Enslaved Fishermen Rescued in 6 Months," Associated Press, Sept. 17, 2015; David Hughes, "Don't Forget the Seafarers and the Fishermen; For Those at Sea, Work, Together with Its Inherent Risks, Carries On as Usual over the Christmas and New Year Season," *Business Times Singapore,* Dec. 23, 2015; Ralph Jennings, "Taiwan Seeks to Improve Conditions in Fishing Fleet," Associated Press, Oct. 4, 2016; John Kerry, "John Kerry's Remarks at the Chicago Council on Global Affairs," Oct. 26, 2016, transcript; Susan Krashinsky, "Clover Leaf Website Will Let Consumers Track the Source of Their Fish," *Globe and Mail,* Oct. 3, 2016; William Langewiesche, "Slaves Without Chains," *Vanity Fair,* Jan. 2016; Erik Larson, "Lawsuit Aimed at Products Where Forced Labour Used; Lawyers Hope to Push Major Firms to Better Police Their Supply Chains," *National Post's Financial Post & FP Investing,* Dec. 14, 2015; Erik Larson, "Slavery Labels Sought for U.S. Goods," *Naples Daily News,* Jan. 2, 2016; Erik Larson, "Slavery on the Label? Lawsuits Aim to Expose Forced Labor in Supply Chain," *Providence Journal,* Dec. 20, 2015; Erik Larson, "Suing to Put Slavery Labels on Goods; Lawyers Want Accountability for Supply Chain," *Vancouver Sun,* Dec. 12, 2015; Felicity Lawrence, Ella McSweeney, and Annie Kelly, "Irish Taskforce to Investigate Treatment of Migrant Workers on Trawlers," *Guardian,* Nov. 4, 2015; Felicity Lawrence et al., "Revealed: Trafficked Migrant Workers Abused in Irish Fishing Industry," *Guardian,* Nov. 2, 2015; Tom Levitt, "Our Love of Cheap Seafood Is Tainted by Slavery: How Can It Be Fixed?," *Guardian,* Oct. 7, 2016; Fault Lines, "A Trafficked Fisherman's Tale: 'My Life Was Destroyed,'" *Al Jazeera,* March 5, 2016; Jenna Lyons, "Fishermen Say They Faced High-Seas Slavery: Indonesian Fishermen Tell of Being Trafficked Before SF Escape," *San Francisco Chronicle,* Sept. 23, 2016; Margie Mason and Martha Mendoza, "AP Investigation Prompts New Round of Slave Rescues," Associated Press, July 31, 2015; Margie Mason, "Indonesia Nabs Ship Believed to Carry Slave-Caught Fish," Associated Press, Aug. 14, 2015; Margie Mason et al., "AP: Global Grocer Supply Chains Tied to Slave-Peeled Shrimp," Associated Press, Dec. 14, 2015; Adam Minter, "How to Fight Asian Slavery, One Supplier at a Time," *Chicago Daily Herald,* Dec. 26, 2015; "Missing Slave Fishing Boats Tracked to Papua New Guinea," PACNEWS, July 28, 2015; Carol Morello, "Changes on Human-Trafficking List," *Washington Post,* July 28, 2015; Sarah Murray, "Casting a Tight Net," *Stanford Social Innovation Review* 13, no. 4 (Fall 2015); "Myanmar (Burma): Trafficking Survivors Struggle to Rebuild Their Lives Back Home," Thai News Service, Dec. 23, 2015; Wassana Nanuam, "CCCIF 'Going All Out' to Revamp Fishing Industry," *Bangkok Post,* Feb. 27, 2016; "Nestle SA: Supports Slave Labor to Produce Fancy Feast, Suit Says," *Class Action Reporter,* Oct. 20, 2015; "Nestle Vows to Fight Slave Labour in Thailand," Agence France-Presse, Nov. 24, 2015; Wassayos Ngamkham and Penchan Charoensuthipan, "Govt Boosts

Slave Labour Crackdown," *Bangkok Post,* Dec. 18, 2015; Katie Nguyen and Alisa Tang, "Thai Traffickers Exposed by Campaign Group Investigating Fishing Industry," Reuters, Nov. 30, 2015; "Pacific Tuna Fishermen Detail Deplorable Working Conditions, Widespread Abuse in Video Testimonials," Targeted News Service, July 28, 2015; David Pinsky, "There's Slavery in the Seafood Industry. Here's What We Can Do About It," *US Official News,* July 22, 2015; Alecia Quah, "Thai Seafood Products Face Increased Risk of Export Ban in the Next Year over Illegal Fishing Practices," IHS Global Insight, Nov. 27, 2015; "Remarks by Secretary of State John Kerry at the Launch Ceremony for the 2015 Trafficking in Persons Report," *Federal News Service,* July 28, 2015; Cazzie Reyes, "Freedom from Slave Fishing Ships," End Slavery Now, Jan. 4, 2016; Michael Sainsbury, "Thailand's Human Trafficking Industry Is Australia's Problem," *Crikey,* July 5, 2016; "Secretary of State John Kerry Remarks at Our Ocean Town Hall Event in Valparaiso, Chile, as Released by the State Department," Oct. 5, 2015; "Slavery Horror Deepens," *Mizzima Business Weekly,* Aug. 6, 2015; Emanuel Stoakes, Chris Kelly, and Annie Kelly, "Revealed: How the Thai Fishing Industry Trafficks, Imprisons, and Enslaves," *Guardian,* July 20, 2015; Emanuel Stoakes, Chris Kelly, and Annie Kelly, "Sold from a Jungle Camp to Thailand's Fishing Industry: 'I Saw 13 People Die,'" *Guardian,* July 20, 2015; Alisa Tang and Beh Lih Yi, "Thailand's Upgrade in Human Trafficking Report Slammed as 'Premature,'" *Metro* (U.K.), July 1, 2016; "Thai Captains Jailed and Ordered to Compensate Fishing Slaves They Tortured and Worked 24 Hours a Day," *Postmedia,* March 11, 2016; "Thailand: Thai Shrimp Peeled by Slaves Taints Global Markets," Thai News Service, Dec. 17, 2015; "Today's Slaves Often Work for Enterprises That Destroy the Environment," *Fresh Air,* NPR, Jan. 20, 2016; Simon Tomlinson, "Inside the Shrimp Slave Trade: Migrant Workers and Children Forced to Peel Seafood for 16 Hours a Day in Filthy Thai Factories That Supply Retailers and Restaurants in the U.S. and Europe," *Daily Mail,* Dec. 14, 2015; Jewel Topsfield, "Australia to Counter 'Terrible Trade in Human Beings,'" *Sydney Morning Herald,* March 21, 2016; "USAID Bureau for Asia Speaks on Human Trafficking in Seafood Sector," Targeted News Service, Sept. 14, 2016; U.S. Senate, "Blumenthal and Portman Urge Administration to Address Human Trafficking in Fishing Industry," Federal Information and News Dispatch, Inc., Nov. 18, 2015.

257 Thai news outlets and nonprofit groups: Among the strongest reporting on this topic came as early as 2012, several years before *The New York Times* or the Associated Press began covering the topic. See, for instance, the work of Service and Palmstrom, "Confined to a Thai Fishing Boat, for

Three Years." Also see "Employment Practices and Working Conditions in Thailand's Fishing Sector," International Labor Organization, 2014; "Exploitation of Cambodian Men at Sea," United Nations Inter-agency Project on Human Trafficking, April 22, 2009; "Trafficking of Fishermen in Thailand," International Organization for Migration, Jan. 14, 2011.

260 On Thai fishing ships, the bosun: To get a small sense of the extent of needed reforms, consider the problem of translators. While I was reporting in Thailand in 2017, I was informed that the government had only just changed a long-standing rule against hiring foreign nationals to interpret for them. For years, the Ministry of Labor had been doing labor inspections in factories and on farms and on fishing vessels, where the workforce was almost completely foreign migrants who spoke no Thai. Sometimes the government used Thai nationals to interpret, but there were few who had the language skills working for the labor or other departments. More often, inspectors simply chose a bosun or shop foreman to translate the best he could on the spot for other workers.

263 Three captains and one security guard: "Press Release: 14 Year Jail Sentences for Thai Human Traffickers," Environmental Justice Foundation, March 21, 2017.

263 However, several were critical: It seems worth providing more detail about some of the allegations that these Burmese workers made. Several of the workers requested anonymity. Among those who were willing to go on record was Tun Nge, thirty-four, who worked for over a decade, until around 2015, as a member of a Kantang fishing cartel run by a woman named Mae Saw. Aside from the murder committed by Liam, Tun Nge described other incidents, including one on board a ship called the *Juanit*. The captain of this boat, nicknamed Pyaung Jyi, or "bald captain," is sentenced to jail for thirteen years for trafficking. He is the only captain among the Kantang convictions that is serving jail time. Tun Nge described several killings, one of which involved an incident where during a meal on the *Juanit* a deckhand dropped his plate and broke it. The captain attacked the man, slashing him with a knife. The worker then ran away, jumped overboard, and drowned. A second incident, which occurred on a different boat, the name of which Tun Nge did not recall, involved a worker who tried to escape and swam away, but he couldn't make it, so he swam back to the boat, at which point the captain attacked him until another man stepped in and shot the worker. A second Burmese worker I interviewed was named Min Thu. He said he was an eyewitness to additional murders committed by Liam. Min Thu also worked for Mae Saw for a total of eight years, and he said that during that time he witnessed four men killed in or around August 2012. He witnessed

these slayings from a boat tied up port side, but the men were killed on land, at the dock in the Boka port. Liam shot a drunken worker from a ship called *Phokasathaporn 12* who was fighting with another man. The drunken worker, injured by a gunshot wound, jumped from Boonlarp pier into the Trang River to escape, as did the second man. "He just kept shooting," Min Thu, a Burmese eyewitness, told me, describing how Liam proceeded to shoot both men while they were in the water in addition to another two migrant workers who entered the water in order to assist them, killing all four individuals. These four murders were committed in public in broad daylight, with somewhere between ten and thirty eyewitnesses from Boonlarp pier. After interviewing these men, I found further evidence of these allegations in a report: "Thailand's Seafood Slaves: Human Trafficking, Slavery, and Murder in Kantang's Fishing Industry," Environmental Justice Foundation, 2015. Finally, I also interviewed a third Burmese worker named Min Min Zaw who recounted a killing in 2015 aboard the *Juanit*. He remained uncertain of the motives for the killing, but in this case the captain of the *Juanit* shot four Indonesians from a supply boat that often serviced the Thai boats when they visited Indonesian waters.

## CHAPTER 11 WASTE AWAY

271 The twenty-eight-year-old Scotsman: "Caribbean Princess Fact Sheet," Princess Cruises, 2018.

271 Venturing into an unfamiliar section: Most of the reporting for this chapter comes from interviews throughout 2017 with the whistle-blower, Chris Keays, and the lead prosecutor, Richard Udell. Carnival declined repeated requests for interviews, so I attempted to capture its perspective drawing from its court filings and talking to other defense lawyers who handle such cases. In terms of court papers that were most helpful, see *United States of America v. Princess Cruise Lines, Ltd.*, U.S. District Court Southern District of Florida, April 17, 2017; *United States of America v. Princess Cruise Lines, Ltd.*, U.S. District Court Southern District of Florida, Dec. 1, 2016. I also consulted "Princess Cruise Lines to Pay Largest-Ever Criminal Penalty for Deliberate Vessel Pollution," Department of Justice, Dec. 1, 2016.

273 Carnival often pointed: In the sentencing memo, prosecutors and former employees of Carnival talk about the job of the onboard environmental officers. It was essentially "window dressing," they said, because these officers were directed to socialize with passengers, provide tours of the ship, and deal with birds that landed on the ship instead of focusing on ensuring compliance with environmental standards. See *United States*

*of America v. Princess Cruise Lines, Ltd.,* U.S. District Court Southern District of Florida, April 17, 2017.

274 In 2016, the same unlucky catch: On the history of munitions dumping, I read Randall Chase and Josh Cornfield, "Clammer Is Injured Dredging Up Old Bomb, Chowder Tossed," Associated Press, Aug. 12, 2016; Andrew Curry, "Chemical Weapons Dumped in the Ocean After World War II Could Threaten Waters Worldwide," *Smithsonian,* Nov. 11, 2016; United Press International, "Boat Snags Torpedo: Delayed World War II Blast Kills 8 Fishermen," *Kingsport Times,* July 25, 1965.

274 The most infamous of these syndicates: To delve deeper into this matter, I turned to Tom Kington, "From Cocaine to Plutonium: Mafia Clan Accused of Trafficking Nuclear Waste," *Guardian,* Oct. 8, 2007; Chris Milton, "Somalia Used as Toxic Dumping Ground," *Ecologist,* March 1, 2009.

275 In the span of three years: The BP and the *Valdez* spills combined released roughly 182.8 million gallons (or about 10.8 million in the *Valdez* spill and about 172 million in the BP spill). To understand how much oil wastewater and fuel sludge is routinely and intentionally dumped at sea, check a 2003 OECD Report, "Cost Savings Stemming from Noncompliance with International Environmental Regulations in the Maritime Sector," Director for Science, Technology, and Industry Maritime Transport Committee, Jan. 30, 2003. That report says, "Put in another perspective, according to one recent study, the illegal discharge of oil into the sea through routine operations is equal to over eight times the Exxon Valdez oil spill or over 48 times the 1997 Nakhodka spill off the coast of Japan—every year." Using that statistic of 84.6 million gallons deliberately dumped per year and projecting over three years would amount to 253.8 million gallons. After making these calculations, I verified the methodology and conclusions with Professor James M. Corbett, an expert on maritime pollution who is based at the University of Delaware.

279 It's also known for another reason: Thomas Fuller and International Herald Tribune, "20 Kidnapped from Malaysian Resort Island," *New York Times,* April 25, 2000.

284 If the bloom was eaten: The experiment in 2012 was not George's first foray into geo-engineering. As chief executive of a company called Planktos, he had proposed in 2007 a similar iron-fertilization project in the equatorial Pacific west of the Galápagos Islands, with the hope of selling carbon offsets. The project was canceled in 2008 after what George's company called a "disinformation campaign" by environmentalists and others who made it impossible to attract investors.

287 "You get on board": I interviewed Frith by phone several times in 2017.

289 While much of my reporting took me to derelict: To learn about crime on cruise ships, I read Curt Anderson, "ICE Dive Unit in Miami Targets Smugglers Using Freighter, Cruise Ship Hulls to Ferry Drugs," Associated Press Newswires, Feb. 28, 2011; Robert Anglen, "Comprehensive Reports of Cruise-Ship Crime Made Public, Led by Phoenix Man," *Arizona Republic,* Oct. 13, 2016; Donna Balancia, "Crew Member Sues Carnival," *Florida Today,* Feb. 13, 2008; "Brazil 'Rescues' Cruise Workers from 'Slave-Like Conditions,' " BBC News, April 4, 2014; Jonathan Brown and Michael Day, "Cruise Ship Limps In—but Costa's Nightmare Goes On," *Independent,* March 2, 2012; Michael Day, "Costa Concordia: Shipment of Mob Drugs Was Hidden Aboard Cruise Liner When It Hit Rocks off Italian Coast, Investigators Say," *Independent Online,* March 30, 2015; Richard Foot, "Gangs Smuggle Passengers on Cruises," CanWest News Service, Nov. 23, 2005; John Honeywell, "The Truth About Crime on a Cruise Ship," *Telegraph Online,* June 5, 2017; Vincent Larouche and Daniel Renaud, "Three Quebecers Charged with Smuggling $30M in Cocaine on Cruise Ship in Australia," *Toronto Star,* Aug. 30, 2016; Jim Mustian, "Feds Arrest Cruise Ship Crewmen in Alleged Plot to Smuggle Cocaine into New Orleans," *New Orleans Advocate,* Jan. 10, 2016; Natalie Paris, "Cruise Lines Defend Treatment of Staff," *Telegraph Online,* April 7, 2014; "Ten Individuals Charged with Importing Hundreds of Pounds of Cocaine, Heroin into United States Aboard Cruise Ships," *Hindustan Times,* June 10, 2005; U.S. Attorney's Office, Eastern District of Louisiana, "Georgia Man Sentenced in Honduran Cocaine Importation Scheme," Department of Justice, July 20, 2017. It's noteworthy that a report from the U.S. Senate (*Cruise Ship Crime: Consumers Have Incomplete Access to Cruise Crime Data,* U.S. Congress, Senate Committee on Commerce, Science, and Transportation, 2013) found that in 2012 a third of the assaults reported on these ships were against minors.

## CHAPTER 12 FLUID BORDERS

297 And while it's easy to portray: China also claimed the sea's gas-rich Natuna Islands, and most of the offshore scuffles involving Chinese fishing boats occurred in an area that security analysts call the nine-dash line, which covers more than 80 percent of the South China Sea. Though the designation is not recognized under international law, China declared this region in the 1940s part of its "traditional fishing grounds."

300 "If the boy is there": I later also visited another detention center or "shelter" in Batam, and conditions were similar. It held about 240 detainees, most of whom were Vietnamese. Some of the detainees had been there for over a year and a half. About 10 percent of them were charged with

illegal fishing because they were officers, according to Indonesian immigration officers whom I interviewed on-site. The rest of the detainees were crew who were being held as undocumented immigrants, though not charged with a crime.

308 I took the radio: Throughout the reporting for this book, there were half a dozen occasions like this one where language barriers between ships on the high seas escalated stressful situations into dangerous ones. So, I was not surprised to learn later that even in emergencies on the open ocean, there was, for a long time, very little international cooperation between ships in terms of an agreed-upon language or rescue protocol. When SOS was adopted by the International Radiotelegraphic Convention in 1906 to be broadcast by ships in distress, many countries and shipping companies refused to use it, preferring their own codes. As the *Titanic* sank in 1912, the operators on board, reluctant to rely on the new international code, intermixed the SOS code with another distress signal called CQD. The backstory behind SOS was symbolic not just of the sometimes chaotic nature of the high seas but also of how landlubbers often ascribe meaning, order, and intentionality onto offshore behavior where they do not exist. Shortly after SOS was created, people onshore began speculating what it meant, creating a so-called backronym or false etymology for it. The popular (and mistaken) interpretation was that it stood for "Save Our Souls" and "Save Our Ship." In fact, the distress signal that the convention embraced was in International Morse Code and consisted of a continuous sequence of three dots, three dashes, and three dots, with no spaces between the letters, repeated indefinitely. One way to decrypt that code in letters reads "SOS," though that, of course, was by no means the only or intended abbreviation. In Morse code, VTB, IJS, VGI, SMB, and VZE (among others) all also correctly translate three dots and three dashes, but these were tougher for people to remember.

313 to have left Mas Gun behind: One of the challenges in this reporting was trying to visually and emotionally capture certain experiences and then keep those captures alive in my head (with help from my notebook) during the long gap of time between reporting and writing. Normally in my work, the time between taking notes and producing the story is days or weeks, at most. During this project months passed. So that I could capture more notes, I created an elaborate system of acronyms for people and place and ship names. I used my iPhone often to film a room if I wanted to be able to describe it later. But emotions were the hardest thing to capture and maintain because finding the right descriptives typically required rumination. In moments like this one—sitting on the bridge as we fled the Vietnamese clash—I strained to take effective notes about

the mood. I soon tried to make a habit of matching sound to feeling, mentally scrolling through songs in my head that might fit the moment. I'd listen to the songs again later when it came time to write that scene. This note-taking tactic was a mnemonic device of sorts that helped me characterize in a nonverbal way and remember later the feeling of an experience. Thankfully, I have a sizable and handy library of songs stuck in my head because I listen to a lot of movie soundtracks when I write to help me focus. In the margin of the notes that I wrote as we all sat tensely on the bridge that day it says: "Wales" (by Marco Beltrami) and "The Night Of" (by Jeff Russo).

317 In the South China Sea, Indonesia: This sort of territorial fighting that uses foreign fishermen as pawns in larger geopolitical games is not distinct to the South China Sea. Since 2011, for example, over 1,200 Indian and 450 Sri Lankan fishermen have been arrested as the two countries assert their claim over a narrow strip of sea in the Palk Strait. For a smart piece about this, see Joshua Keating, "Fishermen on the Frontlines," *Slate,* June 10, 2014.

318 In later interviews, the Indonesian government: The subsequent news coverage of this incident that I found included Argianto, "Begini Detik-detik petugas patroli KKP diculik Cost Guard Vietnam," *Tribun Batam,* May 23, 2017; Muhammad Firman, "Penyergapan 5 kapal pencuri ikan Vietnam picu masalah diplomatik," *Katadata,* May 23, 2017; Pada Rabu, "Pemerintah selesaikan insiden Natuna Lewat jalur diplomatik," *Media Indonesia,* May 24, 2017; Muhammad Razi Rahman, "Indonesia-Vietnam selesaikan insiden Natuna secara diplomatik," *Antara News,* May 23, 2017; Sarma Haratua Siregar, "Vietnam lepaskan petugas PSDKP," *Sindo Batam,* May 24, 2017; Zulfi Suhendra, "Disergap KKP, kapal asal Vietnam tenggelam de Perairan Natuna," *Liputan 6,* May 24, 2017; Tiara Sutari, "Bentrok dengan Vietnam, Indonesia pilih solusi diplomatik," CNN Indonesia, May 24, 2017; Afut Syafril, "Luhut minta Indonesia tak emosional tanggapi insiden Natuna," *Antara News,* May 23, 2017.

## CHAPTER 13 ARMED AND DANGEROUS

323 From the Mediterranean to offshore Australia: My biggest regret with this book is the list of stories that I never found time to cover. Topping that list is the crisis involving human rights abuses tied to the sea migrants moving mostly from the Middle East and North Africa across the Mediterranean Sea. "Count sea migrants as a single demographic and this is the worst genocide in decades," one UN refugee official said in 2014, estimating that more than 4,272 persons were killed that year crossing seas and oceans, mostly the Mediterranean. The other figure he cited: at

least 40,000 persons have died between 2000 and 2014. On this topic, I read Tara Brian and Frank Laczko, *Fatal Journeys: Tracking Lives Lost During Migration* (Geneva: International Organization for Migration, 2014); Alice Ritchie, "UN Rights Chief Slams Indifference over Migrant Deaths at Sea," *Business Insider,* Dec. 10, 2014. For more about crimes tied to boats carrying Mediterranean sea migrants, see Suranga Algewatte et al., *Smuggling of Migrants by Sea* (Vienna: United Nations Office on Drugs and Crime, 2011).

324 Far from comprehensive: To build this database and for broader insights, I relied heavily on Charles N. Dragonette, who tracked seafaring attacks globally for the U.S. Office of Naval Intelligence; Claude Berube, who is the director of the U.S. Naval Academy Museum; Jon Huggins, a former U.S. Navy mission commander and the director of Oceans Beyond Piracy; Klaus Luhta, a lawyer with the International Organization of Masters, Mates & Pilots, a seafarers' union; David Pearl, a foreign affairs specialist with NOAA; Duncan Copeland and Stig Fjellberg from TMT; Dom Mee, the founder of Protection Vessels International; and Michael Berkow, the director of U.S. Coast Guard Investigative Service. I received data and documents from OCEANUSLive (in particular, Glen Forbes), Risk Intelligence, and the Office of Naval Intelligence. I also consulted the Office of Naval Intelligence's Worldwide Threats to Shipping Report, the Worldwide Navigational Warnings Service Broadcast Warning messages disseminated by the Global Maritime Distress and Safety System, and the IMB Piracy Reporting Centre.

324 On land, police can dig: Ocean crime scenes are difficult for so many reasons, including the distance to get there and the challenge of figuring out who has responsibility and jurisdiction. "There are no skid marks on the ocean" is how the maritime writer Rose George put it. When an accident does occur, it can be difficult to seek even meager justice. "There is no police force or union official to assist," she wrote. "Who do you complain to, when you are employed by a Manila manning agency on a ship owned by an American, flagged by Panama, managed by a Cypriot, in international waters?"

325 Victims one minute: See Gemma Jones, "Asylum Seekers 'Pirate' Story Disguises Possible Mutiny," *Daily Telegraph,* Oct. 19, 2012; MarEx, "Asylum Seekers or Pirates?," *Maritime Executive,* Nov. 19, 2011.

325 Forty of the captives: I read the following materials to get a sense of the offshore crime near Bangladesh: Agence France-Presse, "Bangladesh Launches Operation Against Pirates," DefenceTalk.com, Aug. 15, 2012; "Bangladesh out of Piracy-Prone Nations' List," bdnews24.com, Jan. 1, 2012; Bangladesh Sangbad Sangstha, "Four Abducted Fishermen Res-

cued," *Bangladesh Government News,* Sept. 10, 2013; Bangladesh Sangbad Sangstha, "2 Pirates Held, 4 Fishermen Rescued at Saronkhola," *Bangladesh Government News,* Sept. 10, 2013; Bangladesh Sangbad Sangstha, "8 Fishermen Abducted, 7 Others Received Bullet Injuries by Pirates," *Bangladesh Government News,* Aug. 26, 2014; "Beefing Up Bay Security," *Financial Express,* Feb. 20, 2015; "Coast Guards Conduct Abortive Drives to Rescue 50 Fishermen," United News of Bangladesh, Aug. 16, 2013; "Dhaka Trying to Get Safe Return of 7 Sailors," *New Nation,* July 14, 2013; "Fishermen Demand Steps to Stop Piracy," *New Nation,* Sept. 26, 2014; "Fisherman Killed by Pirates in Bhola," United News of Bangladesh, Oct. 9, 2013; "Foreign Minister Dr. Dipu Moni Chaired an Inter-ministerial Meeting on 11 December 2011 at the Ministry to Discuss About the Reports of the International Maritime Bureau (IMB) and ReCAAP and Other International Organizations as well as Media Depicting Bangladesh as a 'Piracy-Prone' Country and a 'High Risk' Zone for the Shipping Industry," People's Republic of Bangladesh, Ministry of Foreign Affairs, 2011; "Forest Robber Arrested in Satkhira," United News of Bangladesh, Feb. 7, 2015; "From Cowboy to Criminal," *Daily Star,* Oct. 2, 2004; "Give Protection to Coastal Fishermen," *New Nation,* Feb. 24, 2014; "Gov't Protests 'False' Piracy Reports," bdnews24.com, Dec. 26, 2011; "Gunfight with Police," *New Nation,* Dec. 15, 2011; "Hon'ble Foreign Minister Dr. Dipu Moni Called Upon the Relevant Institutions Including Government Agencies, Shipping Industries, and the Media to Work Together to Reduce/Eliminate the Incidence of Robbery at Sea in and Around Bangladeshi Waters," People's Republic of Bangladesh, Ministry of Foreign Affairs, 2011; Iqbal Mahmud, "Drugging Gangs Target Cattle Traders, Markets," *New Age,* Oct. 4, 2014; Krishnendu Mukherjee, "Pirates Loot Sunderbans Fishermen for 10 Hours," *Times of India,* Sept. 20, 2013; "Over 100 Fishermen Kidnapped in Bay," United News of Bangladesh, Sept. 5, 2014; "Pirates Kidnap 14 Fishermen in Patuakhali," United News of Bangladesh, Nov. 4, 2014; "Pirates Kidnap 40 Fishermen," *Financial Express,* July 7, 2014; "RAB-Ten Killed," United News of Bangladesh, Sept. 30, 2004; "Seven Abducted Sailors 'Alive,'" *Bangladesh Business News,* July 13, 2013; "Three Killed in Bagerhat 'Shootout' with Rab," *Financial Express,* Feb. 26, 2015; WorldSources Online Inc., "BNP Activist Slaughtered," *Independent,* Nov. 19, 2003; "4 Kidnapped Fishermen Rescued in Sundarbans," United News of Bangladesh, Feb. 4, 2014; "4 Pirates Held in Laxmipur," United News of Bangladesh, Aug. 31, 2013; "5 Kidnapped Fishermen Rescued in Sundarbans," *Financial Express,* July 7, 2014; "8 Fishermen Injured by Bullets in Bay," *Financial Express,* Feb. 17, 2015; "10 Suspected Terrorists Killed in Bangladesh Gun Battle,"

Japan Economic Newswire, Sept. 30, 2004; "25 Fishermen Kidnapped in Sundarbans," United News of Bangladesh, May 24, 2014; "40 Fishermen Kidnapped in Sundarbans; 15 Hurt," United News of Bangladesh, Feb. 17, 2014; "50 Fishermen Kidnapped," *Dhaka Herald*, Nov. 3, 2013; "68 Fishermen Kidnapped in Sundarbans, Sea," *Bangladesh Chronicle*, Sept. 15, 2013; "70 Abducted Fishermen Rescued, 26 Boats Seized," *New Nation*, Oct. 4, 2013; "100 Fishermen Abducted," *New Nation*, Aug. 18, 2013.

326 Moni's claims pivoted: It's worth fleshing out the fuller list of terminology. Under UNCLOS, Article 101, for an act to be considered piracy, it must meet all the following criteria: That the attack (1) involved either (a) illegal acts of violence or detention, (b) voluntary participation in the operation of a ship or of an aircraft with knowledge of facts making it a pirate ship or aircraft, or (c) the act of inciting or of intentionally facilitating an illegal act of violence or detention, or voluntary participation in the operation of a ship used for piracy; (2) was committed for private ends; (3) was committed by the crew or passengers of a private ship; and (4) occurred on the high seas or outside the jurisdiction of any State (meaning more than twelve nautical miles from a country's shoreline). On the other hand, an act is defined by the International Maritime Organization's Resolution A.1025(26)6 as an armed robbery against ships if it involves the following: any act which (1) includes any illegal act of violence or detention or any act of depredation, or threat thereof, as well as an act inciting or intentionally facilitating such illegal acts; (2) was not an act of piracy as defined under UNCLOS; (3) was committed for private ends; and (4) occurred within a State's internal waters, archipelagic waters, or territorial sea (twelve nautical miles). See Matthew R. Walje et al., "The State of Maritime Piracy 2014: Assessing the Economic and Human Cost," Oceans Beyond Piracy, 2014.

326 They also complained that insurers: Swadesh M. Rana, "A Template for Those at Risk: India's Response to Maritime Piracy, 2010–2011," UN Department of Disarmament Affairs, Aug. 14, 2014.

329 After we traded war stories: In researching the size of the private maritime security market, I read "Maritime Security Market by Technology and Systems, Category, Service, and Regions—Trends and Forecast to 2020," Research and Markets, Aug. 2015; "Research and Markets: Global Maritime Security Market Outlook 2019—Key Analysis of the $13 Billion Industry," Business Wire, Oct. 14, 2014. Much of the maritime security budget is spent not just protecting ships against Somali pirates but also safeguarding oil platforms elsewhere in the world. The armed guards on ships are reducing, PMSCs are cutting down on operators, and some

are struggling to maintain their level of business. Although numbers have reduced due to decrease of piracy attacks, some shipping companies may demand teams of four to relieve the stress on the ships' crews to provide additional lookouts. Insurers may change their requirements as part of the product, but a charterer may have its own demands on the level of protection. But also note that Oceans Beyond Piracy said in 2014 that $1.2 billion of the global expense is for the Indian Ocean region plus $300 million for the Gulf of Guinea. That would mean that the two regions most affected by piracy only account for roughly 10 percent of the global costs.

330 Though the men described the *Resolution:* Several private maritime guards were especially helpful to me in understanding this world. I interviewed them in person and by email and phone between 2016 and 2018. Those included Erich Mueller, a Canadian guard; Miguel Damas, a Portuguese guard; and Kevin Thompson, a British guard.

331 By the time you shoot: To capture the view that it was better to fire first and survive than to wait too long and die, many of the guards used the same expression. "Rather be judged by twelve than carried by six," they said. Twelve refers to a jury if the soldiers were to be prosecuted for unlawful killing. Six refers to pallbearers carrying a coffin if they were to be killed.

331 On October 12, 2013, a floating: To learn about the case involving the *Seaman Guard Ohio,* I interviewed and corresponded between September 2016 and August 2017 with Joanne Thomlinson, who is the sister of John Armstrong, one of the guards arrested on the *Ohio.* I also read "AdvanFort Thanks Indian Officials for Providing Safe Harbor for Its Vessel," AdvanFort International Inc., Oct. 14, 2013; Stephen Askins, "Seaman Guard Ohio—Indian Decision Shocks PMSCs," Tatham Macinnes, Jan. 19, 2016; "Indian Court Rejects Seaman Guard Ohio Appeal," *Seatrade Maritime News,* March 1, 2016; "MV Seaman Guard Ohio Guards & Crew in Chennai Prison for Christmas," *Human Rights at Sea,* Dec. 12, 2016; Petition for British Foreign Secretary, "Free the 6 British Veterans from Indian Jail #CHENNAI6," change.org; Krishnadas Rajagopal, "SC Demands Truth About Mystery Ship," *Hindu,* Aug. 31, 2016; Sandhya Ravishankar, "India Sentences 'Seaman Guard Ohio' Crew to Five Years in Prison in Arms Case," *GCaptain,* Jan. 11, 2016; Kathryn Snowdon, "British Ex-soldiers, the 'Chennai Six,' Spending Another Christmas in 'Hell Hole' Indian Jail," *Huffington Post,* Dec. 25, 2016; World Maritime News Staff, "Seaman Guard Ohio Crew Sentenced to Five Years," *World Maritime News,* Jan. 11, 2016; "Court Revokes Bail for Seaman Guard Ohio 35," Marine Log, Jan. 8, 2014; "British Anti-piracy Guards Held in

India Granted Bail," BBC, March 26, 2014; "Family's Relief as Soldier Is Released from Indian Jail," ITV News, April 7, 2014; *Mariya Anton Vijay v. The State,* Madras High Court, July 10, 2014; A. Subramani, "Madras High Court Quashes Criminal Case Against Crew of US Ship," *Times of India,* July 10, 2014; "India Drops Arms Charges Against British Crew of MV Seaman Guard Ohio," BBC, July 11, 2014; "British Crew of MV Seaman Guard Ohio Face New Setback," BBC, Oct. 3, 2014; "MV Seaman Guard Ohio Crew 'Must Be Allowed Home,'" BBC, March 11, 2015; "Support Groups Call For Cumbrian Man Held in India to Be Allowed Home," ITV News, March 11, 2015; "Unpaid and Unsupported, Seaman Guard Ohio Crew Still Stranded in India," *Maritime First,* March 11, 2015; "SC Sets Aside Madras HC Judgment Quashing Trial of 35 Crew Members of US Ships, Orders Trial to Be Completed Within 6 Months," Live Law, July 4, 2015; Jason Burke, "Britons Offering Protection Against Pirates Facing Five Years in Indian Jail," *Guardian,* Jan. 11, 2016; Reuters, "Seaman Guard Ohio Crew Sentenced to Five Years in Jail," *Maritime Executive,* Jan. 11, 2016; "Seafarers' Mission 'Horrified' at Anti-piracy Convictions," Anglican Communion News Service, Jan. 14, 2016; Stephen Askins, "Seaman Guard Ohio—Indian Decision Shocks PMSCs," Tatham Macinnes, Jan. 19, 2016; "Seaman Guard Ohio: A Travesty of Justice?," Isenberg Institute of Strategic Satire, March 5, 2016; Philipho Yuan, "Seaman Guard Ohio: Who Is Paying?," *Maritime Executive,* March 10, 2016; "HC Reserves Order in Appeal by US Anti-piracy Ship Crew," *Times of India,* Dec. 2, 2016; "Judge Reserves Order on Seaman Guard Ohio Appeal," *Maritime Executive,* Dec. 6, 2016; "MV Seaman Guard Ohio Crew to Stand Trial in India After 625 Days in Detention," *Marine Insight,* Jan. 23, 2017.

332 "Don't you think the U.S. government": For a useful overview of the need for increased regulation of private maritime security, I read Yvonne M. Dutton, "Gunslingers on the High Seas: A Call for Regulation," *Duke Journal of Comparative and International Law* 24, no. 1 (2013). She makes the point that, until recently, commercial vessels traveling through waters that pose the greatest risk of pirate attacks typically relied on the world's navies to protect them. Indeed, the world community has spent more than $1 billion in each of the last several years to support naval fleets that patrol pirate-infested waters, with the goal of repressing piracy. The vastness of the area in which pirates now operate, however, has meant that those navies simply cannot keep every ship safe. As threats have grown, and the range of pirates has increased as they strike farther from shore, navies have shrunk, and much of the burden of security has been shifted to companies seeking to traverse these areas. When it comes to under-

standing what efforts have been made to impose more rules on private maritime security forces, it is worth reading about the set of privately developed international standards, the 100 Series Rules on the Use of Force, and the work of the British maritime attorney David Hammond. The rules were endorsed by many members of the shipping and private security industries.

333 "And then the result is a maximum": For all the problems created by the lack of government oversight of private maritime security forces, it is also worth being aware of the risks in the opposite direction: when governments do get involved, they can make matters worse, depending on how they exert their authority. The *Seaman Guard Ohio* is certainly a case that might fit this point. For another example, consider the role the Nigerian government is playing in crime-infested waters off its coast. Due to the presence of so many factions in the region, it can be especially difficult for companies and captains to distinguish between government actors and armed extortionists. In Nigerian waters, foreign guards cannot be armed, and they are usually hired to "advise" the captain during hostile situations. Nigerian military and police are the only armed presence allowed on the vessels, but some guards and industry experts said these personnel were thought to be in cahoots with the hijackers. The captains and foreign guards that I spoke to about Nigeria said that if they were in Nigerian waters and hostile parties approached their vessel, the quietly agreed-upon plan was to merely take the weapons from the Nigerian authorities before the hijackers board. See David Osler, "Nigeria 'Ban' on Armed Ship Guards Throws Industry into Confusion," *Lloyd's List*, July 7, 2014.

338 Like me, he was troubled: Especially in the 2012–2014 time frame, there was a growing chaos in the security situation near Somalia's coast, according to the Somalia and Eritrea Monitoring Group, which pointed to an increasing use of unregulated and untrained Somali security guards to provide armed protection aboard vessels involved in regional trade and/or fishing activities. The organization said that the arming of these guards was in all likelihood in violation of the arms embargo that was at the time imposed on Somalia. In 2013, for example, Puntland authorities detained five Iranian vessels fishing illegally off the coast of Somalia, arresting approximately eighty Iranian crew members and twelve armed Somali security guards in the process. It is not at all clear whether this detention was conducted by rogue actors or legitimate state players and what that distinction even means in Somalia, where the federal state does not actually exert authority over most of the country, especially in Puntland.

339 As I pursued new leads: The exchange with this source reminded me of two unusually insightful passages about language and the meaning and purpose of explanation. The first passage is from Michael Ondaajte's novel *The English Patient*, between the two main characters, Katharine Clifton and Count Laszlo Almasy:

Katherine: I wanted to meet a man who could write such a long paper with so few adjectives.

Count Almasy: A thing is still a thing no matter what you place in front of it. Big car, slow car, chauffeur-driven car, still a car.

Katherine: Love? Romantic love, platonic love, filial love? Quite different things surely.

The second passage is from Clifford Geertz's essay "Thick Description: Toward an Interpretive Theory of Culture." In this essay, Geertz discusses the work of another anthropologist named Gilbert Ryle, who cites two boys and the rapid contractions of each of their right eyes. "In one, this is an involuntary twitch; in the other, a conspiratorial signal to a friend. The two movements are, as movements, identical; from an I-am-a-camera, 'phenominalistic' observation of them alone, one could not tell which was a twitch and which was a wink." Adding a third boy to the mix, one engaged in a parody of the other boys, who is winking but "laboriously, overlaboriously perhaps adding a grimace." The challenge that an anthropologist (or I might add, a journalist) faces is discerning between and explaining the twitch, the wink, the parodist. "The thing to ask about a burlesqued wink or a mock sheep raid is not what their ontological status is. It is the same as that of rocks on the one hand and dreams on the other—they are things of this world. The thing to ask is what their import is: what it is, ridicule or challenge, irony or anger, snobbery or pride, that, in their occurrence and through their agency is getting said."

340 Payet resigned from: Rondolph Payet's wife, Maureen Payet, was the main shareholder in the IOTC when Rondolph Payet was the executive secretary of the IOTC, creating a conflict of interest because he was both a director of a company that was a license holder of a vessel subject to regulation by the IOTC and executive secretary of that organization. Both Maureen and Rondolph were once directors of the Seychelles-registered company International Fishing Agency and Shipping, the company that licensed the *Chun I 217*. See Jason Smith, "Newspaper: IOTC Head 'Forced to Resign' amid Links to Videotaped Executions," *Undercurrent News,* Dec. 9, 2015.

343 Their mother, a woman named Khadija: To pin down the identities of the shooting victims, Nat Geo also turned to local fishermen in Iran, who described the fishing boat in the video as a dhow. Markings on the dhow

led the fishermen to speculate that it might have been built in Konark, India. A local journalist there subsequently found a boatbuilder named Rahim Bibak, who said that two boats he had built went missing a little over two weeks after going out to sea in August 2012. Shown the video, Bibak confirmed that he had built the boat being attacked, and he named some of the victims.

344 As of 2017: Stories like this one are difficult to put down because they lack any true sense of arrival. The crime in this instance was so egregious, the evidence so compelling, that it seemed like an especially acute travesty that so little came from the reporting around it. After the *Times* published our investigation, I continued to work on the topic and compiled information into pamphlets that I published on my own website and through Twitter. These pamphlets make for dry reading, but they have additional material that I hoped would help law enforcement or other journalists who subsequently followed up on the topic. An example of such a report can be found at ianurbina.com titled "A Document Reader: Murder at Sea."

## CHAPTER 14  THE SOMALI 7

349 It had even scored a recent victory: One of the main reasons I was drawn to Somalia was that success stories about combating illegal fishing are hard to find. I had heard from sources at the UN's fisheries agency about the arrest of two notorious poacher ships, the *Greko 1* and the *Greko 2*, which seemed to be a rare example of one such story. These two Greek-owned trawlers had operated in Somali waters near Puntland with impunity for years. They had fished in an area reserved for Somali-owned ships, using a prohibited type of net and refusing to report the size and species of their catch to Somali authorities. The *Grekos'* strategy had been to avoid Somali port authorities by off-loading their catch in Mombasa, Kenya. Hoping to check on the validity of the *Grekos'* licenses, Kenyan authorities told me they had tried to contact Somalia in 2015 but never received a reply. As I was finding is quite the norm on the outlaw ocean, a nongovernmental organization stepped in with the assist. Founded in 2012 to encourage communication among poorer African coastal countries and cooperation to improve offshore law enforcement, FISH-i Africa took up the case of the *Grekos*, putting the right officials in Nairobi and Mogadishu in touch with each other, then pressing them to collaborate. Kenya soon prohibited the *Grekos* from entering port, forcing the ships back to Mogadishu, Somalia's capital, where they were detained. The *Grekos* didn't stay put for long. Within days, the 190-ton vessels made a run for it, slipping out of port when authorities weren't

watching. Eventually, they had to dock in Kenya because a crewman fell ill, and the *Greko*s were detained again. Somali authorities settled outside court with the registered owner, Stavros Mandalios, whose company had to pay a $65,000 fine. This fine was a pittance, considering that the *Greko*s were still allowed to sell their illicit catch, estimated to be worth $300,000. Even so, it was rare for poachers to ever pay fines. This is when the *Greko* story took a complicated turn. Though he paid the fines, Mandalios claimed that he had in fact purchased legitimate licenses to fish in Puntland's waters. Puntland fishery authorities soon reviewed these fishing licenses and determined that the documents were real but contained unauthorized signatures. Adding that they were not certain who within their agency would have had access to such documents, Puntland officials confirmed that whatever had been paid for them had not gone to the ministry. In other words, someone had likely pocketed money that should have benefited the public. The director of FISH-i Africa, Per Erik Bergh, agreed to meet me in Nairobi to talk about the case. As he dug more into the *Greko*s' paperwork, he had discovered that Mandalios had received €1.4 million, the equivalent of about $1.6 million, from the EU in 2013 in exchange for promising to scrap the two *Greko* ships. Such subsidies were meant to prevent overfishing by putting older ships out of business and shrinking the world's bloated fleet. "So the *Greko*s were not just prohibited from fishing in Somalia," Bergh said. "These ships were not even supposed to exist." When contacted later by Greek prosecutors, Mandalios rejected these allegations, saying that the whole matter was a case of mistaken identity. The vessels detained in Kenya, he said, looked similar but were not actually the same ones that had been condemned by the EU. I was skeptical of his explanation, and the case generally reminded me of the mysterious manual of maritime swindles that had been mailed anonymously to my home when I was reporting about offshore repo work. I was also struck by the role FISH-i Africa had played in investigating this apparent crime. As I had witnessed in Thailand with that navy's reliance on human rights groups to select human-trafficking suspects, or on the Atlantic Ocean with Sea Shepherd as it chased the *Thunder,* here again with FISH-i Africa was an example of a nonprofit organization doing law enforcement work that should be done by governments. No wonder the oceans are outlaw; there are few actual police to apply what scarce laws exist. See Ian Urbina, "The Grekos: A Success Story in the Crackdown on Illegal Fishing," *National Geographic,* March 24, 2017. Here my reporting on the case of the *Greko*s was greatly helped by Nikolas Evangelides with Pew Charitable Trusts and Per Erik Bergh from FISH-i Africa.

352 Mogadishu was the seat: Before arriving in Somalia, I read the following: Mohamed Ibrahim and Jeffrey Gettleman, "Militant Alliance Adds to Somalia's Turmoil," *New York Times*, July 29, 2010; "A Knowledge, Attitudes, and Practices Study on Fish Consumption in Somalia," Food Security and Nutrition Analysis Unit, Nov. 2011; Mohamed Beerdhige, "Roots of Insecurity in Puntland," *Somalia Report*, May 1, 2012; Mark Mazzetti and Eric Schmitt, "Murky Legacy of Army Hired to Fight Piracy," *New York Times*, Oct. 5, 2012; Robert Young Pelton, "Puntland Marine Force in Disarray," *Somalia Report*, Oct. 31, 2012; Yara Bayoumy, "Somalia's Al Shabaab, Squeezed in South, Move to Puntland," Reuters, Nov. 9, 2012; "Somalia Fisheries," Food and Agriculture Organization of the United Nations, Jan. 2013; James Bridger and Jay Bahadur, "The Wild West in East Africa," *Foreign Policy*, May 30, 2013; "Vying with Somali Government for Autonomy," *Deutsche Welle*, July 10, 2013; "Somalia: Puntland Marine Police Forces Mark 3rd Anniversary," *Garowe Online*, Oct. 6, 2013; Martha C. Johnson, "State Building in De Facto States: Somaliland and Puntland Compared," *Africa Today* 60, no. 4 (June 2014): 3–23; Anthony Morland, "The State of State-Building in Somalia," *All Africa*, Oct. 23, 2014; "Somalia: Private Company Granted License to Patrol Puntland Waters," *Garowe Online*, April 23, 2015; "Somalia's Puntland Region Marks 17 Years of Autonomy," BBC, Aug. 3, 2015; "Somalia's Puntland Breaks Off Relations with Central Government," Reuters, Aug. 5, 2013; "Somalia: UN Report Blasts Puntland Leader for Security Failures, Corruption," *Garowe Online*, Oct. 21, 2015; Abdi Sheikh, "Small Group of Somali Al Shabaab Swear Allegiance to Islamic State," Reuters, Oct. 23, 2015; Abdi Sheikh, "At Least 17 Somali Soldiers Killed in Inter-regional Fighting—Officials," Reuters, Sept. 28, 2016; "Puntland President Gaas in Trouble as MPs Set for a Vote of No Confidence Motion," *All Africa*, March 1, 2017; "Puntland President Blames Officials of the Mutiny," *All Africa*, March 14, 2017; "Islamist Gunmen Kill Four Guards in Hotel Attack in Somalia," Reuters, Feb. 8, 2017; "Additional Reports of Recent Violence," *Garowe Online*, March 19, 2017; "Somali Security Forces That Freed Pirated Ship Say NATO Must Do More," Reuters, March 19, 2017; "Action in Countries," *International Rice Commission Newsletter*, vol. 48, accessed Nov. 18, 2018.

353 Piracy, which grew into an acute problem: By 2010, Somali pirates had taken more than a thousand hostages, according to the UN, and earned at least $100 million. In many cases, ships were captured, ransomed, and released within weeks. The efficiency of these transactions depended on the competency of the pirates and the willingness and ability of the shipping companies to raise the ransoms.

354 It was also nearly impossible to check: Among the private security companies that sought to work in Somalia was Blackwater. See Sharon Weinberger, "Blackwater Hits the High Seas," *Wired,* Oct. 9, 2007; Mark Mazzetti and Eric Schmitt, "Blackwater Founder Said to Back Mercenaries," *New York Times,* Jan. 20, 2011; Katharine Houreld, "Blackwater Founder Trains Somali Troops," Associated Press, Jan. 20, 2011; Giles Whittell, "Billionaire Mercenary 'Training Anti-piracy Forces,'" *Times* (London), Jan. 22, 2011; Mark Mazzetti and Eric Schmitt, "Private Army Formed to Fight Somali Pirates Leaves Troubled Legacy," *New York Times,* Oct. 4, 2012; Ivor Powell, "On the Slippery Trail of Military Deals," *Sunday Independent* (South Africa), Feb. 26, 2012; Ivor Powell, "Sterling Loses Anti-piracy Deal," *Independent on Saturday* (South Africa), Sept. 29, 2012; Eli Lake, "In 'the Project,' the Stormy Battle to Take on Somali Pirates," *Daily Beast,* April, 22, 2013; Armin Rosen, "Erik Prince Is Right: Private Contractors Will Probably Join the Fight Against ISIS," *Business Insider,* Oct. 10, 2014; Ian Shapira, "Was the U.N. Targeting Blackwater Founder Erik Prince on Somalia?," *Washington Post,* Jan. 2, 2015.

354 Complicating matters further: For useful reports on Somali waters and the intersection between illegal fishing and private security, see Peter Bauman, "Strategic Review of the Trust Fund to Support Initiatives of States Countering Piracy off the Coast of Somalia," *Bauman Global* (2016); "First Hijacking of a Merchant Vessel by Somali Pirates in Five Years," Oceans Beyond Piracy, 2017; Sarah M. Glaser et al., "Securing Somali Fisheries," Secure Fisheries, 2015; Saciid Jamac Maxamed, "Maraakiibta Thailand ee sita calanka Jamhuuriyadda Djabuuti," Federal Republic of Somalia, Ministry of Fisheries and Marine Resources, Office of the Deputy Minister, 2017; Said Jama Mohamed, "Thailand Fishing Vessels Carrying Djibouti Flag," Federal Government of Somali Republic, Ministry of Fisheries and Marine Resources, 2017; "The Somali Fisheries Sector: An Export and Domestic Market Assessment," US Aid from the American People: Somalia Growth, Enterprise, Employment & Livelihoods Project, 2016; "Sustainable Seafood and Responsible Investment," Sustainable Fisheries Partnership, Avista Investors, and Principles for Responsible Investment.

356 In response to the new restrictions: To learn more about the Sangsukiam family's fishing fleet, it is worth reading "Turn the Tide: Human Rights Abuses and Illegal Fishing in Thailand's Overseas Fishing Industry," Greenpeace Southeast Asia, Dec. 15, 2016. One of the challenges in maritime crime investigations stems from the variations in translated spellings of ship or family names. For example, in the case of the Sangsukiam

family, FISH-i used "Sangsukiam," as do several shipping registry sites I consulted. But Greenpeace used "Saengsukiam," and Interpol and Thai documents I obtained had a couple variations as well. There are three Sangsukiam brothers: Wichai, Wanchai, and Suwanchai. The family had two important fishing companies (Seavic and Chainavee), the control of which shifted between brothers. This spelling problem is distinctly acute when it comes to global efforts to track Chinese, Taiwanese, and Thai vessels because the translation of names into English introduces problematic variations. This is part of the reason that many researchers and advocates call for the requirement that every ship have a permanent and unique identification number that stays with it for the duration of its existence.

375 The official with the Djibouti: Some of the backstory behind how these Thai vessels came to be flagged by Djibouti was drawn from a tape-recorded conversation between a source of mine and Chris Warren, an American in his late fifties who worked with the Djibouti flag registry. Warren was disgruntled because he said he was supposed to have exclusive rights as the foreign agent brokering deals for ships to fly the Djibouti flag but he was cut out of the deal involving the Somali 7 ships. The audio recording of the meeting in June 2017 at Pappadeaux Seafood Kitchen in Austin was provided to me by a source who attended the dinner. Warren, who had hoped during that meeting to persuade my source to sign up additional Thai fishing boats, emphasized that he did not approve of mistreating crews and that he had no role in crewing the Somali 7 ships. However, in trying to persuade my source to put his ships under the Djibouti flag, Warren said that the registry would not meddle in the owners' affairs when it came to matters like working conditions. I took the information I received from the audio recording and subsequently interviewed another source from the Djibouti registry to corroborate details.

377 They were also flagged outside: This fleet and its alleged ongoing involvement with human trafficking, illegal fishing, and other labor abuses became a fixation for me. By 2018, I had moved on to new reporting projects for the *Times*, but I kept trying to put information out by publishing "Questions & Leads Alerts" using my own website and Twitter. Eventually, the Somali 7 fleet, minus two ships that were detained in the Maldives and the one that was arrested in Thai waters, were renamed variations of the "Al Wesam" ships. They were re-flagged to Somalia, and their operators recruited new crews, again most of them from Cambodia. Soon thereafter, in late 2017, I began getting new pleas for help from advocates in Somalia, Thailand, and Cambodia tied to these same

ships. Same basic story: some of the men who had been trafficked onto the boats had not been told they would be fishing outside Thai waters. Several of the men were asking to be rescued and sent home. The best compilations of this reporting are to be found in my "Questions & Leads Alerts" documents, but there is additional material in Ian Urbina, "The Somali 7: Fisheries Crimes Exposed by Open-Source Reporting," Safina Center, Aug. 30, 2018.

## CHAPTER 15  HUNTING HUNTERS

382 No one died in these clashes: In 2007, the *Nisshin Maru* rammed Sea Shepherd's ship the *Sam Simon*, which was blocking a Japanese fuel vessel. Though the *Simon* did not sink, the collision opened a hole in its engine-room wall, fractured its stern, and toppled its radio antenna. In 2010, a Sea Shepherd ship called the *Ady Gil* did sink, however, after colliding with a Japanese whaling ship. The *Ady Gil*'s captain spent five months in a Japanese jail, even though Maritime New Zealand, a national agency for the security of New Zealand waterways, later concluded that both vessels were at fault for the crash.

382 But the organization argued: In interviews, Sea Shepherd members routinely asked me, if Japanese whaling was scientific and not commercial, why did much of the whale meat get sold in restaurants? Sea Shepherd critics rebutted with their own question: If countries like Australia have concluded that Sea Shepherd was committing a crime by attacking whaling ships, why didn't the government arrest its ships when they visited their ports?

382 An international court had ordered: "Japan Ordered to Immediately Stop Whaling in Antarctic as International Court of Justice Rules Program Was Not Carried Out for Scientific Purposes," Australian Broadcasting Corporation, March 31, 2014.

384 During the 1992–1993 whaling season: For more on Votier, see Steve Boggan, "Japanese Sue over Whale-Killing Pictures," *Independent*, Dec. 12, 1995; Andrew Darby, *Harpoon: Into the Heart of Whaling* (Cambridge, Mass.: Da Capo Press, 2008); Alexander Gillespie, *Whaling Diplomacy: Defining Issues in International Environmental Law* (Gloucestershire, U.K.: Edward Elgar, 2005); "Japan: Electrocution of Whales Exposed by Journalist," Associated Press Archive; "Japan to Phase Out Lance," *Irish Times*, Oct. 24, 1997; Mark Votier, "One World: An Environmental Awareness Program for the Pacific," interview by Carolyn Court and Lisa Harris, Whales.org, April 1996.

388 The Norwegians also developed: For a broader understanding of whaling history, I read "A Brief History of Norwegian Whaling," *Norwegian*

*American,* June 15, 2015; Agence France-Presse in Tokyo, "Whale Meat on the Menu at Japanese Food Festival," *Guardian,* Oct. 9, 2015; Sandra Altherr et al., "Frozen in Time: How Modern Norway Clings to Its Whaling Past," Animal Welfare Institute, OceanCare, and Pro Wildlife, 2016; Australian Antarctic Division, "25 Years of Whale Protection in Australia," Australian Government, Department of the Environment and Heritage, 2006; James Brooke, "Yuk! No More Stomach for Whales," *New York Times,* May 29, 2002; Jóan Pauli Joensen, *Pilot Whaling in the Faroe Islands: History, Ethnography, Symbol* (Tórshavn: Faroe University Press, 2009); Keith D. Suter, "Australia's New Whaling Policy: Formulation and Implementation," *Marine Policy* 6, no. 4 (1982); Johan Nicolay Tønnessen and Arne Odd Johnsen, *The History of Modern Whaling* (Berkeley: University of California Press, 1982); "Whales and Hunting," New Bedford Whaling Museum.

390 On a clear day, when sound underwater: To learn about whale and seal depredation, I read Jason Allardyce, "Pretenders Singer Joins Seal Shooting Protest," *Sunday Times,* Aug. 9, 2009; John Arlidge, "Townies' Friend, Fishermen's Foe," *Independent,* Nov. 3, 1995; "ATF Cracks Down on Bombs Used to Scare Seals," Homeland Security Newswire, May 11, 2011; Margaret Bauman, "Changes Coming for Salmon Bycatch, GOA Sablefish Fishery," *Cordova Times,* April 17, 2015; Hal Bernton, "Whales Find Alaska Fishers' Catch Is Easy Pickings," *Seattle Times,* April 9, 2015; Erin Biba, "Alaskan Sperm Whales Have Learned How to Skim Fishers' Daily Catch," *Newsweek,* Nov. 22, 2015; "BIM to Survey Seals After Kerry Fishermen Demand a Cull," *Kerryman,* March 30, 2011; Lise Broadley, "Island Fisherman Makes Seal Repellant; Device Uses Sound of Killer Whales to Chase Mammals Away," *Nanaimo Daily News,* Feb. 25, 2012; Nelson Bryant, "Group Is Seeking Total Protection for Atlantic Salmon," *New York Times,* May 21, 1998; Ronan Cosgrove et al., "Seal Depredation and Bycatch in Set Net Fisheries in Irish Waters," Irish Sea Fisheries Board, Fisheries Resource Series, vol. 10 (2013); Andrew Darby, "Protected, but Pesky: Tasmania to Kill Its 'Bolshie' Fur Seals," *Sydney Morning Herald,* Oct. 19, 2000; "Evaluating and Assessing the Relative Effectiveness of Acoustic Deterrent Devices and Other Non-lethal Measures on Marine Mammals," Scottish Government, Oct. 28, 2014; "Fisherman Accused of Shooting Pilot Whales with WWII-Era Rifle," Associated Press, Feb. 20, 2015; Par Marie-Sophie Giroux, "Sperm Whales Robbing Fishermen of Their Catch," *Whales Online,* Nov. 12, 2015; Ben Goldfarb, "Sea Lions Feast on Columbia Salmon," *High Country News,* Aug. 17, 2015; Jason G. Goldman, "Killer Whales Are Stealing Fishermen's Catch to Make Extra Calves," *Guardian,* April 24, 2015; Zoe Gough, "Sperm Whales Target

Fishing Boats for an Easy Meal," BBC, Feb. 4, 2015; R. N. Harris et al., "The Effectiveness of a Seal Scarer at a Wild Salmon Net Fishery," *ICES Journal of Marine Science* 71, no. 7 (2014): 1913–20; Thomas A. Jefferson and Barbara E. Curry, "Acoustic Methods of Reducing or Eliminating Marine Mammal-Fishery Interactions: Do They Work?," *Ocean and Coastal Management* 31, no. 1 (1996): 41–70; Dan Joling, "Researchers Try Beads to Thwart Thieving Whales," Associated Press, May 15, 2011; Deborah Jones, "Technology May Help Seals, Fishermen Share Same Ocean," *Globe and Mail,* Dec. 30, 1986; Chris Klint, "Seal Bomb Fishing at Southeast Alaska Hatchery, Caught on Video, Nets Fine for Skipper," *Anchorage Daily News,* Jan. 16, 2016; Scott Learn, "Sea Lions' Lives Hang on Disputed Catch Counts," *Oregonian,* May 15, 2012; Jay Lindsay, "Fishermen: Seal Numbers out of Control," Associated Press, Sept. 29, 2006; "Marine Fisheries Research," Center for Coastal Studies; Lindsay McGarvie, "Terror on the Rock as Divers Are Trapped in Seal Killers' Firing Line," *Sunday Mail,* July 18, 1999; Bill Monroe, "Sea Lions' Fishing Prowess Catches Attention," *Oregonian,* Jan. 16, 2006; Doug O'Harra, "As Longlines Rise with Sablefish, Sperm Whales Take a Bite," *Anchorage Daily News,* Feb. 1, 2004; David Perry, "Callaghan Halted Cull," *Aberdeen Press and Journal,* Dec. 30, 2008; Tim Radford, "Wildlife: The Seal of Disapproval," *Guardian,* July 20, 1995; Andrew J. Read, "The Looming Crisis: Interactions Between Marine Mammals and Fisheries," *Journal of Mammalogy* 89, no. 3 (June 5, 2008): 541–48; Paul Rogers, "Change in Rules Protects Sea Lions from Fishing Crews," *San Jose Mercury News,* Dec. 20, 1994; Paul Rogers, "U.S. Biologists and Fishermen Agree the Animals' Population Is out of Hand Kill Sea Lions to Save Salon, Experts Urge," *San Jose Mercury News,* March 29, 1997; Zachary A. Schakner and Daniel T. Blumstein, "Behavioral Biology of Marine Mammal Deterrents: A Review and Prospectus," *Biological Conservation* 167 (2013): 380–89; Julia Scott, "Feds Begin Enforcement of Restrictions on Bombs Used to Scare Birds, Seals," *Contra Costa Times,* May 9, 2011; Lorna Siggins, "BIM Defends Decision to Shoot up to 45 Grey Seals Annually for Research," *Irish Times,* March 6, 1998; Scott Steepleson, "Seals' Fate May Be Sealed," *Los Angeles Times,* May 5, 1997; DJ Summers, "Black Cod Pots Approved, Buildup for Halibut Action in June," *Alaska Journal of Commerce,* April 16, 2015; "URI Grad Student: Minke Whales Are Predominant Prey of Killer Whales in Northwest Atlantic," University of Rhode Island, Feb. 22, 2016; Cecile Vincent et al., "Foraging Behaviour and Prey Consumption by Grey Seals (*Halichoerus grypus*)—Spatial and Trophic Overlaps with Fisheries in a Marine Protected Area," *ICES Journal of Marine Science* 73, no. 10 (2016): 2653–65; Laine Welch, "Looking at

Alaska Fishing in 2011," *Seward Phoenix,* Jan. 5, 2012; Natalie Whitling, "Seals Wreak Havoc on SA Fishing Industry, as Trials of Underwater Firecrackers Struggle," ABC News, March 31, 2016; Anna Wietelmann, "Fishermen, Scientists Seek Whale Avoidance," *Daily Sitka Sentinel,* July 26, 2016; "Woman Arrested for Explosives Scare at WA Hospital," Associated Press, Nov. 15, 2013.

390 A depredation specialist named Paul: For Tixier's research, see Paul Tixier et al., "Interactions of Patagonian Toothfish Fisheries with Killer and Sperm Whales in the Crozet Islands Exclusive Economic Zone: An Assessment of Depredation Levels and Insights on Possible Mitigation Strategies," *CCAMLR Science* 17 (Sept. 2010): 179–95; Paul Tixier et al., "Habituation to an Acoustic Harassment Device (AHD) by Killer Whales Depredating Demersal Longlines," *ICES Journal of Marine Science* 72, no. 5 (2015): 1673–81; Paul Tixier et al., "Mitigating Killer Whale Depredation on Demersal Longline Fisheries by Changing Fishing Practices," *ICES Journal of Marine Science* 72, no. 5 (2015): 1610–20; Christophe Guinet et al., "Long-Term Studies of Crozet Island Killer Whales Are Fundamental to Understanding the Economic and Demographic Consequences of Their Depredation Behaviour on the Patagonian Toothfish Fishery," *ICES Journal of Marine Science* 72, no. 5 (2015): 1587–97; Nicolas Gasco et al., "Comparison of Two Methods to Assess Fish Losses due to Depredation by Killer Whales and Sperm Whales on Demersal Longlines," *CCAMLR Science* 22 (2015): 1–14; Paul Tixier et al., "Influence of Artificial Food Provisioning from Fisheries on Killer Whale Reproductive Output," *Animal Conservation* 18, no. 2 (2015): 207–18; Paul Tixier et al., "Demographic Consequences of Behavioral Heterogeneity and Interactions with Fisheries Within a Killer Whale (*Orcinus orca*) Population," National Center for Scientific Research, Aug. 21, 2015; Paul Tixier et al., "Depredation of Patagonian Toothfish (*Dissostichus eleginoides*) by Two Sympatrically Occurring Killer Whale (*Orcinus orca*) Ecotypes: Insights on the Behavior of the Rarely Observed Type D Killer Whales," *Marine Mammal Science* 32, no. 3 (2016).

395 Over the past forty years: Andrea Thompson, "Krill Are Disappearing from Antarctic Waters," *Scientific American,* Aug. 29, 2016.

397 It takes an average of twenty years: Whales do not reproduce quickly. A female sperm whale can produce a calf only once every five years, and mortality is high when the animals are young. Anywhere from 5 to 20 percent of whales die in the first years of life. Further, "scientists believe that it takes around 20 years on average for a female whale to replace itself with one mature female offspring." "The Conservation of Whales in the 21st Century," New Zealand Government, 2004. In 2003,

Harvard and Stanford scientists shifted the approach for estimating historic populations of whales from sketchy records to genetics. They found that estimates for original population sizes should have been ten times higher. See Joe Roman and Stephen R. Palumbi, "Whales Before Whaling in the North Atlantic," *Science,* July 25, 2003; Roger Highfield, "Whale Numbers in Decline," *Telegraph,* July 31, 2003. There are not great numbers for total decline, but there are estimates by species. For example, you could say that humpback whales today represent only 10 percent of their all-time population high. Or the population of minke whales in the Southern Hemisphere alone has dropped by over 200,000 in the last twenty years. See "Whale Population Estimates," International Whaling Commission. Every year, Norway, Iceland, and Japan kill approximately fifteen hundred whales: "Stop Whaling," Whale and Dolphin Conservation, us.whales.org. An estimated three million whales were killed in the twentieth century alone. The gray whale was nearly wiped out in the mid- to late nineteenth century, and there are now only approximately 22,000 in existence. This is why efforts such as those by the Japanese now look to minke whales, which as of 2012 had an estimated population of 515,000 but has taken a hit of nearly 100,000 to whale hunting in the Southern Hemisphere.

397 This is one reason scientists: To learn about the decline in whale numbers, I read Ian Ith, "Threatened by the Throngs? Tourist Boats Bring Attention (and Maybe Trauma) to Orcas," *Seattle Times,* Sept. 5, 2004; Michael McCarthy, "20 Years On and Whales Are Under Threat Again," *Independent,* Jan. 2, 2006; Philip Hoare, "North Atlantic Right Whales: Hunted to the Edge of Extinction," *Independent,* July 1, 2006; Lynda V. Mapes, "No Easy Fix for Orcas' Recovery," *Seattle Times,* July 23, 2006; Rich Cookson, "The Whale's Tale," *Independent,* July 24, 2006; R. G. Edmonson, "Whale Watching: Ocean Carriers, Fisheries Service Clash over Proposed Rules to Protect an Endangered Species," *Journal of Commerce,* Sept. 18, 2006; Warren Cornwall, "Recovery Plan for Orcas: $50M, 30 Years," *Seattle Times,* Nov. 29, 2006; Norimitsu Onishi, "Whaling: A Japanese Obsession, with American Roots," *New York Times,* March 14, 2007; Scott LaFee, "A Hole in the Water," *San Diego Union-Tribune,* March 22, 2007; Matt Weiser and Bobby Caina Calvan, "Whale Worries Grow," *Sacramento Bee,* May 23, 2007; Kenneth R. Weiss, "A Giant of the Sea Finds Slimmer Pickings," *Los Angeles Times,* July 6, 2007; Caleb Crain, "There She Blew: The History of American Whaling," *New Yorker,* July 23, 2007; Bruce Barcott, "In the Shadow of Moby-Dick," *New York Times,* July 29, 2007; Kenneth R. Weiss and Karen Kaplan, "Gray Whale Recovery Called Incorrect," *Los Angeles Times,* Sept. 11, 2007; Pat Bren-

nan, "Whales Singing the Blues?," *Orange County Register,* Sept. 24, 2007; Justin Norrie, "Japan Defends Its Whale Slaughter," *Age,* Nov. 24, 2007; Matt Weiser, "Draft Federal Report: Delta System Hazard to Fish; Species' Threat of Extinction May Hurt Orcas," *Sacramento Bee,* Jan. 9, 2009; Juliet Eilperin, "A Crossroads for Whales," *Washington Post,* March 29, 2010; John M. Broder, "U.S. Leads Bid to Phase Out Whale Hunting," *New York Times,* April 15, 2010; Reese Halter, "What Whales Are Telling Us About the Earth," *San Jose Mercury News,* Dec. 3, 2010; Brita Belli, "Defender of the Seas," *E: The Environmental Magazine,* Jan.–Feb. 2012; William J. Broad, "Learning to Cope with Underwater Din," *New York Times,* July 17, 2012; Felicity Barringer, "Opposition as Aquarium Seeks Import of Whales," *New York Times,* Oct. 10, 2012; Kate Galbraith, "Campaigns on Multiple Fronts Against Whale Hunting," *New York Times,* April 4, 2013; Kate Allen, "Why Are These Humpback Whale Conservationists Applauding the Harper Government?," *Toronto Star,* April 26, 2014; Doug Struck, "The Whale Savers," *Christian Science Monitor,* Oct. 12, 2014; Darryl Fears, "Navy War Games Face Suit over Impact on Whales, Dolphins," *Washington Post,* Nov. 10, 2014; Craig Welch, "Ten Years After ESA Listing, Killer Whale Numbers Falling," *Seattle Times,* Dec. 21, 2014; Anthony King, "Are Grey Whales Climate Change's Big Winners?," *Irish Times,* Aug. 20, 2015; Matthew Berger, "The Story of the Arctic Is Written in Whale Earwax," *Newsweek,* July 1, 2016.

398 After paying the penalty: To read about these court battles, see "Environmental News: Japan Caught with Dead Whale in Australia," *Sun Bay Paper,* Jan. 19–25, 2017; Paul Farrell, "Australian Court Fines Japanese Whaling Company $1M for 'Intentional' Breaches," *Guardian,* Nov. 17, 2015; "Institute of Cetacean Research and Kyodo Senpaku to Receive $2.55 Million from Sea Shepherd for Unlawful Attack," June 9, 2015; Justin McCurry, "Campaigners Try to Halt Japan Whale Hunt in Last-Ditch Legal Fight," *Guardian,* Nov. 17, 2015; "Settlement Agreed in Legal Action Against Sea Shepherd," Institute of Cetacean Research. Aug. 23, 2016.

404 In June 2017, Japan passed: Ben Doherty, "Sea Shepherd Says It Will Abandon Pursuit of Japanese Whalers," *Guardian,* Aug. 28, 2017; "Japan Passes Controversial Anti-terror Conspiracy Law," BBC News, June 15, 2017; "Japan Anti-terrorism Law—Tourists May Be Unknowingly Arrested—Complete List of 277 Crimes," *Tokyo Zebra,* June 2017; "Japanese Protest over Passes Controversial Anti-terror Law," *National,* June 15, 2017.

405 Meyerson was still fuming: Associated Press, "Anti-whaling Group Must Keep 500 Yards from Japanese Ships, Court Rules," *Oregonian,* Dec. 18, 2012.

# ADDITIONAL READING

Afrika, Mzilikazi Wa. "SA Teen's Horror of the High Seas." *Sunday Times,*
    July 18, 2010.

Agnew, David J., John Pearce, Ganapathiraju Pramod, Tom Peatman, Reg
    Watson, John R. Beddington, and Tony J. Pitcher. "Estimating the World-
    wide Extent of Illegal Fishing." *PLOS ONE* 4, no. 2 (2009): e4570.

Albrecht, Gerhard, ed. *Weyer's Flottentaschenbuch 1979/81* [Warships of the
    world, 1979/81]. Munich: Bernard und Graefe, 1979. For data on the
    world's marine police and naval forces.

*Atlas of the Oceans.* London: Chancellor Press, 1996.

Auden, W. H. *The Enchafèd Flood; or, The Romantic Iconography of the Sea.*
    London: Faber & Faber, 1951.

Baboulene, David. *Jumping Ships: The Global Misadventures of a Cargo Ship
    Apprentice.* Chichester, U.K.: Summersdale, 2009.

Bahadur, Jay. *Deadly Waters: Inside the Hidden World of Somalis' Pirates.* Lon-
    don: Profile Books, 2011.

Barker, Ralph. *Goodnight, Sorry for Sinking You: The Story of the* S.S. City of
    Cairo. Glasgow: William Collins & Sons, 1984.

Bates, Quentin. "The Modern Face of Slavery." *IntraFish,* Nov. 2011.

BBC. "South Korea Trawler: Hopes Fade for 52 Missing Sailors." BBC, Dec. 2,
    2014.

Beavis, Bill, and Richard McCloskey. *Salty Dog Talk: The Nautical Origins of
    Everyday Expressions.* London: Adlard Coles Nautical, 1991.

BIMCO and ISF. *The World Wide Demand for and Supply of Seafarers.* London:
    BIMCO/ISF, 1995.

Bondaroff, Teale N. Phelps, Wietse van der Werf, and Tuesday Reitano. *The Illegal Fishing and Organized Crime Nexus: Illegal Fishing as Transnational Organized Crime*. Geneva: Global Initiative Against Transnational Organized Crime; Amsterdam: Black Fish, 2015.

Borisova, Yevgeria. "Abandoned Crew Starves in City Port." *St. Petersburg Press*, Dec. 5–11, 1995. For comparisons with pre–World War II conditions, see Ronald Hope, *A New History of British Shipping* (London: John Murray, 1990).

Bowditch, Nathaniel. *The Complete Nautical Dictionary*. Nautical Publications, 2017.

Bowermaster, J. "Slaves on the Seas: Global Fishing Fleets and Human Bondage." *Takepart*, Jan. 10, 2011.

Brennan, M. "Out of Sight, out of Mind: Human Trafficking and Exploitation of Migrant Fishing Boat Workers in Thailand." Washington, D.C.: American Center for International Labor Solidarity, 2009.

Breverton, Terry. *Breverton's Nautical Curiosities: A Book of the Sea*. New York: Quercus, 2010.

Brody, Michael. "Boom in Piracy—There's a Rising Tide of Marine Fraud." *Barron's*, Nov. 29, 1982.

Browne, David. "Murder at Sea: David Browne Reports on the Shocking Abuses Faced by Burmese Fishers." Transport International online, 2009.

Buckley, Christopher. *Steaming to Bamboola*. London: Flamingo, 1983.

Buglass, Leslie. *Marine Insurance Claims: American Law and Practice*. 2nd ed. Cambridge, Md.: Cornell Maritime Press, 1972. Readers interested in the technical aspects of marine insurance law underlying the discussion of marine insurance fraud are well advised to consult, for American practice, William D. Winter, *Marine Insurance: Its Principles and Practice*, 3rd ed. (New York: McGraw-Hill, 1952), and for English practice, J. Kenneth Goodacre, *Marine Insurance Claims*, 2nd ed. (London: Witherby, 1981).

Bullen, Frank Thomas. *The Men of the Merchant Service, Being the Polity of the Mercantile Marine for Longshore Readers*. London: John Murray, 1900.

Canadahistory.com. "Cod Collapse."

Center for Public Integrity and International Consortium of Investigative Journalists. *Looting the Seas II*. Washington, D.C.: Center for Public Integrity, 2011.

Ciceri, Bruno. "Fishermen, the Forgotten Seamen." *People on the Move*, no. 85 (April 2001).

———. "In Search of New Standards and Foreign Fishers on Board Taiwanese Fishing Vessels." Paper for FarEast ICMA Regional Conference, March 7–11, 2005.

Clare, Horatio. *Down to the Sea in Ships: Of Ageless Oceans and Modern Men.* London: Vintage, 2014.

Clark, Andrew. "Fraserburgh Trawler Skipper Death Confirmed." *Press and Journal,* Nov. 3, 2014.

Clydesdale, Simon. "Pole and Line Fishing—Catching Tuna One by One." Greenpeace, Nov. 2, 2012.

Commission for the Conservation of Antarctic Marine Living Resources (CCAMLR), ccamlr.org.

Commission of the European Communities. "Community Action Plan to Eradicate Illegal, Unreported, and Unregulated Fishing. Brussels: European Commission, 2012.

Couper, A. D. *Voyages of Abuse: Seafarers, Human Rights, and International Shipping.* London: Pluto, 1999.

Couper, A. D., Hance D. Smith, and Bruno Ciceri. *Fishers and Plunderers: Theft, Slavery, and Violence at Sea.* London: Pluto Press, 2015.

Cousteau, Jacques-Yves. *Silent World.* New York: Ballantine, 1977.

Crane, Stephen. *The Open Boat.* E-book, Electronic Text Centre, University of Virginia Library, 1995.

Cremer, Peter. *U333: The Story of a U-Boat.* London: Triad Grafton, 1986.

Darnton, John. "Pirates Plying Nigerian Seas." *New York Times,* Jan. 9, 1977.

De Botton, Alain. *The Pleasures and Sorrows of Work.* London: Hamish Hamilton, 2009.

de Coning, Eve. *Transnational Organized Crime in the Fishing Industry.* Vienna: United Nations Office on Drugs and Crime, 2011.

Dickens, Charles. *On Travel.* Edited by Pete Orford. London: Hesperus Press, 2009.

Dillon, Dana Robert. "Piracy in Asia: A Growing Barrier to Maritime Trade." Heritage Foundation, June 22, 2000.

Earle, Sylvia. *A Sea Change: A Message of the Oceans.* New York: Fawcett, 1995.

Ebbesmeyer, Curtis, and Eric Scigliano. *Flotsametrics and the Floating World: How One Man's Obsession with Runaway Sneakers and Rubber Ducks Revolutionized Ocean Science.* New York: Harper Collins, 2009.

*Economist.* "Brassed Off: How the War on Terrorism Could Change the Shape of Shipping." May 16, 2002.

Ekin, Des. *The Stolen Village: Baltimore and the Barbary Pirates.* Dublin: O'Brien Press, 2008.

Ellen, Eric F., and Donald Campbell. *International Maritime Fraud.* London: Sweet & Maxwell, 1981.

Environmental Justice Foundation. *All at Sea: The Abuse of Human Rights Aboard Illegal Fishing Vessels.* London: EJF, 2010.

———. *Dirty Fish: How the EU Hygiene Standards Facilitate Illegal Fishing in West Africa*. London: EJF, 2009.

Evans, Bob. *A Dog Collar in the Docks*. Birkenhead, U.K.: Countyvise, 2002.

———. *Mersey Mariners*. Birkenhead, U.K.: Countyvise, 2002.

"Everyday Phrases and Their Nautical Origins." Nautical Know How, 2001.

FAO. International Plan of Action for the Conservation and Management of Sharks. Rome: FAO, 1999.

———. International Plan of Action for the Management of Fishing Capacity. Rome: FAO, 1999.

———. International Plan of Action for Reducing Incidental Catch of Seabirds in Longline Fisheries. Rome: FAO, 1999.

Field, Michael. Evidence reported at Coroners Court Wellington, April 16–20, 2012.

———. "Families of Fishing Crew Face Backlash." Fairfax Media, Aug. 10, 2011. Quoting Glenn Inwood.

———. "Slavery at Sea Exposed." *Sunday Star-Times,* April 3, 2011.

———. "$10,500 Fine for Fishing Boat's Secret Dumping." Fairfax Media, Feb. 22, 2013. Quoting Glenn Inwood.

Fitzgibbon, Theodora. *A Taste of the Sea in Food and Pictures*. Vancouver: David & Charles, 1977.

Foulke, Judith E. *Is Something Fishy Going On?* Rockville, Md.: Food and Drug Administration, 1993.

George, Bill. *On the Bridge: A Story of King Billy and the Derby Grange*. Thame: Seaman Publications, 2008.

George, Rose. *Deep Sea and Foreign Going: Inside Shipping, the Invisible Industry That Brings You 90% of Everything*. London: Portobello Books, 2014.

George, Will. "Saving the Whales Helps Humanity, Too." *Miami News,* Jan. 26, 1983.

Gettleman, Jeffrey, and Nicholas Kulish. "Somali Militants Mixing Business and Terror." *New York Times,* Oct. 1, 2013.

Gianni, Matthew, and Walt Simpson. "The Changing Nature of High Seas Fishing: How Flags of Convenience Provide Cover for Illegal, Unreported, and Unregulated Fishing." Canberra: Australian Department of Agriculture, Fisheries, and Forestry, International Transport Workers Federation (ITF), and WWF International, 2005.

Gilje, Paul. *To Swear Like a Sailor: Maritime Culture in America, 1750–1850*. New York: Cambridge University Press, 2016.

Global Witness/IFT. *Taylor-Made: The Pivotal Role of Liberia's Forests and Flag of Convenience in Regional Conflict*. Sept. 2001.

Golden, Frank, and Michael Tipton. *Essentials of Sea Survival*. Champaign, Ill.: Human Kinetics, 2002.

Graham, Stuart. "Indonesian Fishermen Stranded in S. Africa After Horror Voyage." *Modern Ghana,* Dec. 1, 2013.

Grotius, Hugo. *The Free Sea.* Indianapolis: Liberty Fund, 2004.

Hamburger, Tom, and Kim Geiger. "Foreign Flagging of Offshore Rigs Skirts U.S. Safety Rules." *Los Angeles Times,* June 14, 2010.

Hanson, Neil. *The Custom of the Sea: The Shocking True Tale of Shipwreck and Cannibalism on the High Seas.* London: Corgi Books, 1999.

Hardberger, Max. *Seized: A Sea Captain's Adventure Battling Pirates and Recovering Stolen Ships in the World's Most Troubled Waters.* London: Nicholas Brealey, 2010.

Harlaftis, Gelina. *A History of Greek-Owned Shipping.* London: Routledge, 1996.

Heaton Vorse, Mary. *Time and the Town: A Provincetown Chronicle.* New Brunswick, N.J.: Rutgers University Press, 1991.

"High Seas—Strange Cargo—a Curious Trove of Soviet Arms." *Time,* July 4, 1983.

High Seas Task Force. *Closing the Net: Stopping Illegal Fishing on the High Seas.* London: Governments of Australia, Canada, Chile, Namibia, New Zealand, and the United Kingdom, WWF, IUCN, and Earth Institute at Columbia University, 2006.

Hilborn, Ray, and Ulrike Hilborn. *Overfishing: What Everyone Needs to Know.* Oxford: Oxford University Press, 2012.

Hohn, Donovan. *Moby-Duck: The True Story of 28,800 Bath Toys Lost at Sea and of the Beachcombers, Oceanographers, Environmentalists, and Fools, Including the Author, Who Went in Search of Them.* New York: Farrar, Straus and Giroux, 1990.

Hudson, Rex A., ed. *Peru: A Country Study.* Washington, D.C.: GPO for the Library of Congress, 1992.

Hurst, Peter. "Occupational Health and Safety in the Fishing Sector and Labour Inspection of Fishing Vessels." Final Report: Global Dialogue for Promotion of the Work in Fishing Convention 2007(188). Geneva: International Labour Office, 2013.

ICS/ISF. Code of Good Management Practice in Safe Ship Operation. London: International Chamber of Shipping and International Shipping Federation, 1981.

Imarato, Tetsuo. "The Safety of Maritime Traffic and Investigation on Traffic Rules Violations." Resource Material Series 16:244. Fuchu: UNAFEI, 1979.

International Chamber of Commerce. Guide to Prevention of Maritime Fraud. International Chamber of Commerce, 1980.

———. Piracy and Armed Robbery Against Ships Annual Report.

International Court of Justice. "Whaling in the Antarctic (Australia v. Japan: New Zealand Intervening)." 2014.

International Labor Organization. Abandonment of Seafarers Database. 2013.

International Maritime Organization. *International Shipping Facts and Figures: Information Resources on Trade, Safety, Security, Environment.* March 2012.

Interpol distributes purple notices "to provide information on modus operandi, procedures, objects, devices and concealment methods used by criminals."

Isil, Olivia. *When a Loose Cannon Flogs a Dead Horse There's the Devil to Pay: Seafaring Words in Everyday Speech.* Camden, Maine: International Marine, 1996.

ITF. *Migrant Workers in the Scottish and Irish Fishing Industry.* Irish Congress of Trade Unions Northern Ireland Committee, 2008.

———. *Out of Sight, Out of Mind: Seafarers, Fishers, and Human Rights.* London: ITF, 2006.

———. *The Top Twenty Worst Shipping Companies in the World.* London: ITF, 1998.

Iversen, Robert T. B. "The Mental Health of Seafarers." *International Maritime Health* 63, no. 2 (2012).

Jaynes, Gregory. "Pirates of Lagos: Once an Annoyance, Now a Major Threat." *New York Times,* March 14, 1981.

Johnson, Charles. *A General History of the Robberies & Murders of the Most Notorious Pirates.* London: Conway Maritime Press, 1998.

Johnson, Charles, and Christopher Lloyd. *Lives of the Most Notorious Pirates.* London: Folio Society, 1962.

Joint Nature Conservation Committee. "The UK Biodiversity Action Plan, 1992–2012." Joint Nature Conservation Committee, 1994.

Junger, Sebastian. *The Perfect Storm: A True Story of Men Against the Sea.* New York: W. W. Norton, 2009.

Kadfak, Alin, Nathan Bennett, and Raphaella Prugsamatz. *Scoping Study on Migrant Fishers and Transboundary Fishing in the Bay of Bengal.* Phuket, Thailand: BOBLME, 2012.

Katz, Alan. "Fighting Pirates Goes Awry with the Killings of Fishermen." *Bloomberg,* Sept. 16, 2012.

Kemp, Peter, ed. *The Oxford Companion to Ships and the Sea.* Oxford: Oxford University Press, 1988.

Kington, Tom. "Priest Appeals for Justice for African Migrants 'Left to Die' on Boat." *Guardian,* Sept. 7, 2011.

Koeppel, Dan. *Banana: The Fate of the Fruit That Changed the World.* London: Plume, 2009.

Kraus, Scott D., and Rosalind M. Rolland. *The Urban Whale: North Atlantic Right Whales at the Crossroads.* Cambridge, Mass.: Harvard University Press, 2007.

Laist, David W., Amy R. Knowlton, James G. Mead, Anne S. Collet, and Michael Podesta. "Collisions Between Ships and Whales." *Marine Mammal Science* 17, no. 1 (2006): 35–75.

Lamvik, Gunnar M. "The Filipino Seafarer: A Life Between Sacrifice and Shopping." PhD diss., Norwegian University of Science and Technology, 2002.

Langewiesche, William. *The Outlaw Sea: Chaos and Crime on the World's Oceans.* London: Granta Books, 2005.

Lanier, Frank. *Jack Tar and the Baboon Watch: A Guide to Curious Nautical Knowledge for Landlubbers and Sea Lawyers Alike.* New York: McGraw-Hill Education, 2015.

Laskier, Frank. *Log Book.* Aberdeen: Aberdeen University Press, 1949.

———. *A Merchant Seaman Talks: My Name Is Frank.* London: G. Allen & Unwin, 1941.

Law of the Sea Negotiations. Washington, D.C.: U.S. Government Printing Office, 1983. For relevant congressional debates on the issue, see *Hearing Before the Subcommittee of Arms Control, Oceans, International Operations, and Environment of the Committee on Foreign Relations.* U.S. Senate, 97th Congress, 2nd Sess., Sept. 15, 1982. Of scholarly interested is Gerald J. Mangone, *Law for the World Ocean* (London: Stevens & Sons, 1981).

Levinson, Marc. *The Box: How the Shipping Container Made the World Smaller and the World Economy Bigger.* Princeton, N.J.: Princeton University Press, 2006.

Lewis, Val. *Ships' Cats in War and Peace.* Shepperton, U.K.: Nauticalia, 2001.

Linskey, Bill. *No Longer Required: My War in the Merchant Marine.* London: Pisces Press, 1999.

Lloyd's Register. *The World Casualty Statistics.* London: Lloyd's Register, 1996.

Looper, Kenneth J. "Divers Comb Ocean Floor in Search of Ship's Booty." *Boston Globe,* Aug. 7, 1983.

Lyford, George J. "Boat Theft: A High-Profit/Low-Risk Business." *FBI Law Enforcement Bulletin* 51, no. 5 (1982): 2.

MacBain, M. "Will Terrorism Go to Sea?" *Security Management* 24, no. 8 (1980): 76–77.

MacDonald, Kenneth. *Three Dark Days.* Stornoway, Scotland: Acair, 1999.

MacKenzie, Mike. *SeaTalk Nautical Dictionary,* 2005–2012.

Magudia, Rosie. "How Pole and Line Fishing Enables Sustainability in the Tuna Market." *Guardian,* Aug. 30, 2013.

*Marine Terms Dictionary.* 2014.

Maritime and Coastguard Agency. *The Human Element: A Guide to Human Behavior in the Shipping Industry.* April 2010.

Maritime Transport Committee of the Organisation for Economic Co-operation and Development. *Competitive Advantages Obtained by Some Shipowners as a Result of Non-observance of Applicable International Rules and Standards.* Paris: OECD, 1996.

McGrath, Molly. *The True Cost of Shrimp.* Washington, D.C.: Solidarity Center, 2008.

McKenna, Robert. *The Dictionary of Nautical Literacy.* Camden, Maine: International Marine/McGraw-Hill, 2001.

Melville, Herman. *Moby-Dick; or, The White Whale.* 1851. Kindle edition.

*Miami Herald.* "The People Smugglers." Dec. 8, 1982.

Missions to Seamen. *Convoy X.K.234 Arrives: The War-Time Story of the "Flying Angel."* London: Missions to Seamen, 1947.

Moore, John, ed. *Jane's Fighting Ships, 1980–81.* London: Jane's, 1980. For data on the world's marine police and naval forces.

*New York Times.* "Aide Says Gulf Burning of Wastes May Go Ahead." Dec. 8, 1983.

———. "Five Nations Insist Nigeria Act to Curb Port Pirates." Nov. 23, 1977.

———. "Flotilla of Japanese Whalers Leaves on Antarctic Voyage." Oct. 23, 1983.

———. "Foes of Whaling Says Colleagues Will Be Freed." July 22, 1983.

———. "4 Arrested on a Boat in Raid on Gambling." Oct. 17, 1983.

———. "Judge Refuses to Bar Ocean Burning of PCB's." Nov. 20, 1983.

———. "Philippine Navy Forces Rebels to Yield Ship and 29 Hostages." Sept. 30, 1975.

———. "Pirate Vessel Sets Off a Hunt for Booty." Dec. 12, 1982.

———. "Plan to Burn PCB's in the Gulf Protested at Hearing in Texas." Nov. 22, 1983.

———. "Senators Warned of Damage Facing Historic Shipwrecks." Nov. 6, 1983.

———. "Sweden Improves Defenses Against Submarine Intruders." Sept. 18, 1983.

———. "Thai Pirates Kill 70 'Boat People.'" Jan. 11, 1980.

———. "Underwater Wreck Called Treasure Ship." Dec. 5, 1982.

Nielsen, Detlef, and Steven Roberts. "Fatalities Among the World's Merchant Seafarers (1990–1994)." *Marine Policy* 23, no. 1 (Jan. 1999): 71–80.

Oceans Beyond Piracy. "The Human Cost of Maritime Piracy." Working paper, 2012. For details of fatalities and human shields.

*Panama Star and Herald.* "Hundreds of Taiwanese, Cubans Enter U.S. Using Bogus Costa Rican Passports." Feb. 8, 1984.

Parker, Matthew. *Hell's Gorge: The Battle to Build the Panama Canal.* London: Arrow Books, 2008.

Parker, Tony. *Lighthouse.* London: Eland, 2006.

Pauly, Daniel, Villy Christensen, Johanne Dalsgaard, Rainer Froese, and Francisco Torres. "Fishing Down Marine Food Webs." *Science* 279, no. 5352 (1998): 860–63.

Pew Charitable Trusts, Environmental Initiatives. "Fish Aggregating Devices (FADS) Position Paper." June 28, 2011.

Phillips, Richard. *A Captain's Duty: Somali Pirates, Navy SEALs, and Dangerous Days at Sea.* New York: Hyperion, 2010.

Raban, Jonathan, ed. *The Oxford Book of the Sea.* Oxford: Oxford University Press, 2001.

Raymond, Catherine Z. "Piracy and Armed Robbery in the Malacca Strait: A Problem Solved." *Naval War College Review* 62, no. 3 (Summer 2009): 31–42.

Rediker, Marcus. *Villains of All Nations: Atlantic Pirates in the Golden Age.* Boston: Beacon Press, 2004.

Roberts, Callum M. *Ocean of Life: How Our Seas Are Changing.* London: Allen Lane, 2012.

———. *The Unnatural History of the Sea.* Washington, D.C.: Island Press/Shearwater Books, 2008.

Roberts, Stephen. *Mortality Among Seafarers.* Cardiff: SIRC, 1998.

Roberts, Stephen, and Judy C. Williams. "Update of Mortality for Workers in the UK Merchant Shipping and Fishing Sectors." *Risk* 1976 (2005): 58.

Robertson, Phillip. *Trafficking of Fishermen in Thailand.* Geneva: IOM, 2011.

Roland, Alex, W. Jeffrey Bolster, and Alexander Keyssar. *The Way of the Ship: America's Maritime History Reenvisioned, 1600–2000.* Hoboken, N.J.: John Wiley & Sons, 2008.

Rousmaniere, Leah Robinson. *Anchored Within the Vail: A Pictorial History of the Seamen's Church Institute.* New York: Seamen's Church Institute of New York and New Jersey, 1995.

Safina, Carl. *Beyond Words: What Animals Think and Feel.* New York: Picador, 2016.

———. *Song for the Blue Ocean: Encounters Along the World's Coasts and Beneath the Seas.* New York: Henry Holt, 1999.

Sampson, Helen. *International Seafarers and Transnationalism in the Twenty-First Century.* Manchester: Manchester University Press, 2014.

Sekula, Allan. *Fish Story.* Düsseldorf: Richter, 1995.

Sekulich, Daniel. *Ocean Titans: Journeys in Search of the Soul of a Ship*. Guilford, Conn.: Lyons Press, 2007.

———. *Terror on the Seas: True Tales of Modern Day Pirates*. New York: Thomas Dunne Books, 2009.

Sharpsteen, Bill. *The Docks*. Berkeley: University of California Press, 2011.

Sheppard, Charles R. C. *Natural History of the Coral Reef*. Dorset, U.K.: Blandford Press, 1983.

SIRC. *Proceedings of a Research Workshop on Fatigue in the Maritime Industry*. Cardiff: SIRC, 1996.

Smith, Angela. *Gender and Warfare in the Twentieth Century: Textual Representations*. Manchester: Manchester University Press, 2004.

Smith, David. "Scourge of the Seas: Pirate Fishermen Plunder the World's Fish Supply." *Economy Watch*, May 9, 2013.

Stopford, Martin. *Maritime Economics*. 3rd ed. London: Routledge, 2009.

Stringer, Christina, and Glenn Simmons. "Stepping Through the Looking Glass: Researching Slavery in New Zealand's Fishing Industry." *Journal of Management Inquiry* 24, no. 3 (July 2015): 253–63.

Surtees, Rebecca. "Trafficked at Sea: The Exploitation of Ukrainian Seafarers and Fishers." International Organization for Migration (2012).

Szymańska, Kinga, Bogdan Jaremin, and Elzbieta Rosik. "Suicides Among Polish Seamen and Fishermen During Work at Sea." *International Maritime Health* 57 (2006).

Todd, Paul. *Maritime Fraud and Piracy*. 2nd ed. London: Informa, 2010.

Trotter, Henry. *Sugar Girls & Seamen: A Journey into the World of Dockside Prostitution in South Africa*. Athens: Ohio University Press, 2011.

Tuck, Craig. "Slave Free Seas Condemns Employers Manning Agents Intimidating Fishing Crews." Slave Free Seas, press release, April 2014.

United Nations Convention of the Law of the Sea, Art. 230.

United Nations Office on Drugs and Crime. *Transnational Organized Crime in the Fishing Industry*. Vienna: United Nations Office on Drugs and Crime, 2011.

Verité. *Research on Indicators of Forced Labor in the Supply Chain of Tuna in the Philippines*. Amherst, Mass.: Verité, n.d.

Vidal, John. "Health Risks of Shipping Pollution Have Been 'Underestimated.'" *Guardian*, April 9, 2009.

Wada, Yoshio. "Criminal Investigations at Sea." Research Material Series 20:157. Fuchu: UNAFEI, 1980. It is noteworthy that in a single year (1978) the Japanese Maritime Safety Agency had to investigate 1,964 significant incidents of pollution. See Tatsuo Narikone, "Maritime Offenses," Research Material Series 18:130 (Fuchu: UNAFEI, 1979).

Warner, Kimberly, Walker Timme, Beth Lowell, and Michael Hirschfield. "Oceana Study Reveals Seafood Fraud Nationwide." *Oceana,* Feb. 2013.

Weber, Peter. "Abandoned Seas: Reversing the Decline of the Oceans." Worldwatch Paper 116. Washington, D.C.: Worldwatch Institute, Nov. 1993.

Whitfield, Martin. "Out of Sight, Out of Mind: Seafarers, Fishers, and Human Rights." International Transport Workers' Federation, 2006.

Whitlow, Jon. "The Social Dimension of IUU Fishing." In *Fish Piracy: Combating Illegal, Unreported, and Unregulated Fishing.* Paris: OECD, 2004.

Wilson, Jack (former assistant commissioner, Scotland Yard). Speech at a meeting of the Association of the Bar of the City of New York, program titled "Crime in the Maritime Industry." New York, Dec. 6, 1983.

Winchester, Simon. *Atlantic: A Vast Ocean of a Million Stories.* London: Harper Press, 2010.

Winn, Patrick. "Desperate Life at Sea." Public Radio International, May 21, 2012.

Woodard, Colin. *Ocean's End: Travels Through Endangered Seas.* New York: Basic Books, 2000.

Woodman, Richard. *The Real Cruel Sea: The Merchant Navy in the Battle of the Atlantic, 1939–1943.* London: John Murray, 2005.

Yea, Sallie, and Shelley Thio. *Troubled Waters: Trafficking of Filipino Men into the Long Haul Fishing Industry Through Singapore.* Singapore: TCW2, 2012.

Zach, F. "Why Fishing Boats Contribute to Drug Smuggling." 2009.

# INDEX

(Page references in *italics* refer to illustrations.)

Solomon, *The New York Times;* Page 156: Ian Urbina, *The Outlaw Ocean;* Page 159: William Widmer, *The New York Times;* Page 162: Josué Azor, *The New York Times;* Page 181: Max Hardberger, *The Outlaw Ocean;* Page 184: Hannah Reyes, *The New York Times;* Page 191: Hannah Reyes, *The New York Times;* Page 199: Hannah Reyes, *The New York Times;* Page 203: Fabio Nascimento, *The Outlaw Ocean;* Page 215: Fabio Nascimento, *The Outlaw Ocean;* Page 216: Fabio Nascimento, *The Outlaw Ocean;* Page 223: Fabio Nascimento, *The Outlaw Ocean;* Page 228: Fabio Nascimento, *The Outlaw Ocean;* Page 231: Adam Dean, *The New York Times;* Page 244 (top): Adam Dean, *The New York Times;* (bottom): Fabio Nascimento, *The Outlaw Ocean;* Page 251: Adam Dean, *The New York Times;* Page 259: Fabio Nascimento, *The Outlaw Ocean;* Page 266: Fabio Nascimento, *The Outlaw Ocean;* Page 272: U.S. Department of Justice; Page 278: AC-CA Architectural Competition; Page 281: Adam Dean, *The New York Times;* Page 293: Fabio Nascimento, *The Outlaw Ocean;* Page 298: Fabio Nascimento, *The Outlaw Ocean;* Page 303: Fabio Nascimento, *The Outlaw Ocean;* Page 304: Fabio Nascimento, *The Outlaw Ocean;* Page 307: Fabio Nascimento, *The Outlaw Ocean;* Page 311: Fabio Nascimento, *The Outlaw Ocean;* Page 321: Photographer unknown; Page 328: Ben Solomon, *The New York Times;* Page 330: Ben Solomon, *The New York Times;* Page 335: Ben Solomon, *The New York Times;* Page 346: Fabio Nascimento, *The Outlaw Ocean;* Page 357: *The Outlaw Ocean;* Page 358: Fabio Nascimento, *The Outlaw Ocean;* Page 359: *The Outlaw Ocean;* Page 364: Fabio Nascimento, *The Outlaw Ocean;* Page 381: Sea Shepherd; Page 385: Sea Shepherd; Page 386: Sea Shepherd; Page 401: Sea Shepherd; Page 402: Sea Shepherd

# ILLUSTRATION CREDITS

## PHOTO SECTION